# Play, Development, and Early Education



**James E. Johnson**
*The Pennsylvania State University*

**James F. Christie**
*Arizona State University*

**Francis Wardle**
*Red Rocks Community College, Colorado*

*Photographs by Francis Wardle*

PEARSON

A and B

*Boston ▪ New York ▪ San Francisco*
*Mexico City ▪ Montreal ▪ Toronto ▪ London ▪ Madrid ▪ Munich ▪ Paris*
*Hong Kong ▪ Singapore ▪ Tokyo ▪ Cape Town ▪ Sydney*

Series Editor: Traci Mueller
Series Editorial Assistant: Janice Hackenberg
Senior Editorial-Production Administrator: Beth Houston
Editorial-Production Service: Kathy Smith
Marketing Manager: Krista Groshong
Composition and Prepress Buyer: Linda Cox
Manufacturing Buyer: Andrew Turso
Cover Administrator: Linda Knowles
Electronic Composition: Omegatype Typography, Inc.



For related titles and support materials, visit our online catalog at www.ablongman.com.



**Library of Congress Cataloging-in-Publication Data**

Johnson, James E. (James Ewald)
Play, development, and early education / James E. Johnson, James F. Christie, Francis Wardle.
p. cm.
Includes bibliographical references and index.
ISBN 0-205-39479-5
1. Play. 2. Early childhood education. 3. Child development. I. Christie, James F. II. Wardle, Francis III. Title.

LB1139.35.P55J64 2005
155.4'18—dc22

2004053409

Printed in the United States of America

10 9 8 7 11 10 09

*Dedication*

*The authors dedicate this book to their wives Karen, Mary, and Ruth, and to the memory of a good friend and colleague and champion of children and families, Susan Kontos.*

# Table of Contents

## Part II Play and Development

## chapter 4

## Diversity and Individual Differences in Play 85



## chapter 5

## Play's Role in Development 126

## chapter 9

## Enriching Classroom Play: Teaching Strategies and Facilitation Techniques 260



## chapter 10

## Play for Children with Special Needs and Circumstances 285

# Foreword: Play as a Fantasy of Emergency

By Brian Sutton-Smith

One has to be very grateful to the authors of this book for bringing us up to date on all the theorizing and research that have been going on about early childhood play over the recent decades. They make it seem as if we are very close to discovering what play is all about. Indeed, all that is left for my part is to create a fantasy of what play might still be. Let's start by looking at what some of the scholars have been saying these past 200 years. You can look up who they are as you read through the rest of the book. Some say that play is:

1. Energy in surplus, relaxed, or arousing forms.
2. Conation, which is saying that play is about character shown through play treated as causality, practice, effectance, or courage.
3. Emotion, which sees play as an abreaction or as a parody.
4. Evolution, in which play is a recapitulation, civilizing, flexibility, adaptive potentiation, adaptive variability, or the creation of surplus resources.
5. Cognition, where play is envisaged as assimilation, abstraction, subjunctivity, and creativity.
6. Communication, in which play is perceived as signals, frames, and metacommunications.
7. Peak Experience, which is play as self-actualization, as flow and being in the zone.
8. Chaos manipulation, in which play is a preparation for the unexpected in life or a manifestation of unpredictable permutations.

First it is important to realize that all of these concepts can be applied with cogency to some forms of play somewhere. The concepts typically don't have much in common because play itself is a highly complicated phenomenon and has never yet been adequately explained in any agreeable scientific terms. On the other hand, the one thing that most scholars do agree about (and then forget) is that play is primarily intrinsically motivated. That is, they agree that people play mainly because play is fun. Strangely enough, that is not what these scholars are trying to explain; although they all agree explicitly that play is fun, they also agree implicitly that fun is not what matters. What matters to them is what use this fun might be put to for the welfare of the individuals or communities of those who participate, so what I want to do here is to focus on what they neglect and ask rather what this fun is really all about itself in the hope of finding an answer to the meaning of play within that question.

## So What Is Fun?

My first preference is for seeing fun in play as some kind of duality because we say that it is real and not real. It is sense and nonsense. It is profound and stupid. It is rational and irrational. There are always these yin and yang oppositions. Here are the two pieces of evidence that make me feel that such a duality is the right focus if you are hunting for fun.

Play first arose in considerable force in evolution when the mammals began to take the place of the reptiles some 65 million years ago. But at the same time the prior major system of reflexive emotional motivation gave way in part to a new emotional system that was reflective rather than being reflexive. That is, mammals could now react quickly to escape danger as before or they could first consider the alternatives to escape before they decided what to do. One can imagine the everlasting and deathly complexity about which of these two to use on a given occasion. And the fact is that we as humans today still have that problem because sometimes we overreact to a threat without thinking while at others we deliberate too much, and the intruder gets away with it. Our emotional motivation life is always a life of contradictoriness, and that is as true now as it ever was. As creatures we have always existed on the lip of these dualities. It would not be surprising, therefore, that among the mutations that have become advantageous to us in evolution is one that lets us practice at these ambiguities in a way that is safe. My fantasy is that fantasy itself became the mutation that has made living with these maelstroms of emotion more tolerable. In a sense, rehearsing potential disaster in this way has been a kind of inoculation against anger, fear, shock, digust, and loneliness.

The second major fact is that contemporary neurological work on given emotions shows that they have their basis in both the older areas of the brain (in particular, the amygdala) and the modern areas (the forebrain). But some of these emotions are still predominantly in the older areas of the brain, such as shock, anger, and fear, which are more susceptible to reflexivity; these have been termed primary emotions. Others have their main neurological basis in the frontal lobes and are called therefore secondary emotions (such as guilt, shame, and embarassment).

The third part of my fantasy is that play itself is an exhibition of the interrelationships of these two kinds of emotion. In any well-established cultural group, there are forms of play such as hazing, teasing, physical and intellectual contests, risk taking (physical and economic), gross humor, and festivals. In all of these there is always a theatrical usage of the primary emotions, but these are contained within the context of the secondary emotions, which includes established routines, rules, playfulness, ethics, and referees. For example, the pretences of hazing and teasing, which are driven by emotional shocks, playfully parody cultural forms of initiation. They are a parody because they both mimic and mock that which they represent. The fun comes about because of the contrast between the theatrical shocks and the subsequent shared inebriations, which make up for the prior suffering. The suffering of the hazing moves on to the subsequent acceptance into the ecstasies of communality, and the fun of play lies in this contrast between them—the suffering and the celebration. Incidentally, the most successful players are those who presumably develop considerable self-resilience during the play.

If we move on to physical and intellectual contests (e.g., football and chess) that are driven by anger, we find again a parody of life serving combat and predation through the usage of various modulated forms of attack. Again when the players are sufficiently vigilant, there comes the celebration of a game well played or perhaps even a victory that has been won.

In play forms of risk driven by both physical and economic fear (such as climbing Mount Everest or playing poker), we find a parody of overcoming fate by earnest physical preparation or by seeking the luck of the gods. The fun lies in the overcoming of the potential hazards in all of these opportunities, and the outcome is a certain degree of courage required of the participants

In play forms of grossness and profanity driven by disgust, we find a parody of conventional views and conventional behaviors. The fun lies in these immediate mockeries of propriety. The outcome can be a more humorous, imaginative, and iconoclastic reception of everyday life.

Finally, in festivals driven by loneliness, there is a parody of cooperation because the inebriant character of these communities oversimplifies the processes of bonding. Those who succeed, however, may well increase their social abilities.

## Conclusion

It is notable that each of these play forms deals with what in real life would be an emergency, that is, whether one gets to be a member of a desired group, gets to win or lose in skills that seem important, gets to triumph over life's hazards and randomness, gets to laugh and not be depressed by all the proprieties of ordinary life, and finally finds a way to enjoy oneself with other people. Important as all these accomplishments might be, in reality they can be extremely negative in their implication for beginners and amateurs. They are the perils of everyday life, and what play does is render those things that by implication are negative emotionally into performances in the play itself, which turns them into positive accomplishments for the players. And although it is true that these skills that are sometimes developed may have implications for other forms of adaptation, that is not their major point. Their major point is that in play, those negative realities or emergencies that are there simulated are transformed into more comfortable forms of living. Play becomes an alternative reality that, because of its fun, makes it not matter so much whether the rest of life is worth living. People sometimes oppose play because they don't like such negativities being represented in play or anywhere else. If they are not fun-loving themselves, they may also not appreciate the type of strength of living that play makes possible.

Play is at base a kind of courage (resilience, vigilance, iconoclasm, and sociability) that not only protects us from these noted emergencies, but is also, as parodic fun, an antidote to the rest of everyday life with its mortality, accidents, and other occasions of despair. To limit children's play, to overorganize it, and to take away recess play times are to take away children's major means of gaining self-confidence in the face of our turbulent and shared mammal existence.

# Preface

*Teachers need to engage in "observing children as they play and building curriculum that's appropriate for each child from what we see and hear" . . . teachers need to "deeply understand that intellectual development occurs through play. Children integrate everything they know in all domains when they play. Play should have a big place in a curriculum for children from toddlerhood through the primary grades."*

From 1999 interview with Millie Almy, published in January 2000 issue of *Young Children*

There is growing recognition of the importance of children's play in overall development and in the roles of parents and teachers in supporting and scaffolding children's play from the period of infancy on up. Throughout the pages of this book we have sought to relate research and theory devoted to play and development with early education practice and policy. Three major recurrent ideas that appear across the chapters are (1) quality play in early childhood as a prelude to positive functioning later on in development (e.g., imaginative play as a precursor to divergent thinking); (2) play as a way to express individual tastes and interests, a way of becoming a unique personality; and (3) play as a means of connecting with others, of achieving a social sense of self, and becoming a member of a community.

In addition, four broad questions are asked as one reads throughout the text. First, "What is play?" We begin in Chapter 1 by examining beliefs, perspectives, and current issues relating to play. We also tackle the thorny issue of defining play—an endeavor that is not as easy as it might seem. We also discuss the major theories of play, both in Chapter 2 and throughout the book.

Second, "What good is play?" Chapter 3 describes how play develops with age across a number of dimensions, including motor activity, object use, symbolic representation, and social interaction. Chapter 4 explains how play patterns are influenced by gender, personality, race, and ethnicity. In Chapter 5 research is presented on the role of play in a variety of domains of child development.

Third, "How is play affected by different contexts?" In Chapter 6 we discuss the relationship between play and cultural, physical, and social setting variables. In Chapter 11 we examine the effects of popular culture, media, and technology.

Fourth and finally, we address the important question "What is good play and how can we make it better?" Enriching opportunities for play in indoor and outdoor early childhood, school, and nonschool settings is the focus of Chapters 7, 8, 9, and 12. This is where we make direct connections between play research and play practice. We also discuss the important role of parents in supporting, scaffolding, and elaborating play.

Overall, we have tried to convey accurate summaries of complex research areas. We have tried to present a thoughtful and balanced treatment of some difficult and controversial and fascinating issues for which there are usually neither definitive research-based answers nor ready-made solutions for practitioners or policymakers. However, the entire book is also imbued with our deep conviction of the critically important value of play in supporting the total development (cognitive, affective, emotional, social, and physical) of all children.

Over the years, a great deal of time, energy, and resources have been expended across disciplines and across national borders trying to improve understanding and communication of ideas and findings pertaining to theory and practice on play, child development, and early education. The intense interest in this project continues unabated and is likely to grow as we seek to prepare new generations of twenty-first century teachers and children to be bicultural—both global citizens and citizens of particular local cultures.

Play is the universal language of childhood. Play also represents the grammar of each culture. As a form of communication, play expresses a carrier function that seems very similar across cultures; at the same time the content of play, which both reflects and expresses the particular culture, is a metaphor for a culture, a signal that is definable and comprehensible within that cultural community. We cannot help but be struck by cultural differences in play; yet we fully appreciate also the underlying universal qualities in the process of play, such as its fluidity and spontaneity and its changing and multiple forms.

Indeed, children's play is both an end in itself and a means to other ends. Just as it is important to avoid ethnocentricity in viewing children's play, recognizing and appreciating cultural differences as well as similarities, it is likewise important to avoid adult-centricity. We must try to take the child's point of view.

David Elkind (2003) recently distinguished adult-functional versus child-experiential vantage points in viewing children's play. The adult-functional is adult-centric and emphasizes the utility of children's play for some ulterior motive that the adult has, such as play helping the child become ready for school, or to learn how to share and cooperate, or to control impulses and regulate affect. Adult-centric lenses are not invalid or inappropriate ways through which to apprehend children's play; they are just limited. We must also try to put ourselves in the shoes of the children and try to understand what their experiences are when they are playing. We must strive to imagine this. For Elkind, this is the child-experiential perspective. We need to remember that for children, according to Elkind, what makes play genuinely play is that it has no aim other than the experience and the pleasure of the activity itself.

When playing, children are in a special state of being in which they are not concerned about adult evaluations of them or achieving an external goal. They are in a blissful state of play in which external pressures do not matter. Of course, self-imposed pressure to gauge what is within reach and to meet a new challenge is often part of the play experience (e.g., can I climb higher in this tree than I did yesterday?). And, of course, while playing, children may also be achieving adult-centric goals, such as releasing tensions or learning new skills or values, but this is not what is on the minds of the children themselves. We must as adults think about this and respect play and children with commitment to the reality that children are people too. Fundamentally, children play because that is what children do! The need to support the right of children to engage in child-centric play is particularly important today as we in this country and other countries continue to increase academic expectations on young children and as childhood obesity becomes an epidemic.

To conclude, we have two important questions to ask. First, why should anyone read this book? There are many different reasons. One might be that the book is required reading for a course. Perhaps one is intellectually curious about the subject matter, which might be new to the reader. Or the reader might love children and think that this book might assist in nurturing them for a brighter future. Whatever one's reasons, it is helpful to reflect on one's own genuine motivations for actions when embarking upon a new undertaking. In reading this book, what can be accomplished?

Second, how should one read this book? From the start we suggest that the reader should "go meta," so to speak, and think about one's own thinking as one begins to process new information about a topic. Ask critical questions of the text, such as how valid or well-founded generalizations from research studies seem to be. Most critically, what sample was used in the research, and does that sample encompass children from diverse income, racial, ethnic, and cultural backgrounds? Are research findings or suggestions for early childhood practice set forth from within one cultural context reasonable in another cultural context, such as your own? In other words, we recommend that the reader stay active and use imaginative powers and play with the book's content, while reading the text in earnest. Learning and growth in understanding come from being very serious and very playful at the same time! If this is how one reads this book, then we bet that the reader will enjoy and will benefit from studying this book as much as all three of us have greatly enjoyed and benefited from writing it together in our own form of collaborative constructive play!

## ACKNOWLEDGMENTS

This book could not have been done without the help of Angela Packer, who provided excellent technical assistance and support throughout the process leading to the finished product. We are very grateful for her excellent help. We are also very appreciative of Dr. Hey-Jun Ahn, coauthor of Chapter 11, who also provided excellent background research used in some of the chapters of this text.

We would also like to thank the following reviewers for their helpful comments: Diana Ciesko, Valencia Community College; Ramona E. Patterson, South Louisiana Community College; and Regina C. M. Williams, Central Ohio Technical College.

CHAPTER 1

# Beliefs About Play

## INTRODUCTION

Play is not a new phenomenon. People have always played, and children have always played. In fact, most societies associate childhood with play. But what is play? How have attitudes and perceptions of play changed over time, and what is the future of play in postmodern societies? What is the role of play in early education? In this chapter we discuss ideas and attitudes about play and provide an overview of some topics, subtopics, and contexts that are covered throughout the book.

We start with a brief historical peek at play from ancient through modern to postmodern times. Present-day perspectives on play are given from the points of view of children, parents, teachers, and administrators. We then discuss scholarly definitions of play. We attempt to delineate characteristics of play and discuss what we think is the essence of play and three important functions of play. We also compare play with play-related behaviors such as exploration, imitation, and on-task behaviors.

Further, we begin to describe the importance of play in child development and its role in early childhood education. Beliefs about play are formed in context and have a critical bearing on practices and policies that affect children and their play. Accordingly, we discuss several significant play issues and trends, including new brain development research and theories and the rise in organized sports for young children. We gesture toward where play fits into the current national trend involving educational standards and outline the relationship between the growing epidemic of childhood obesity and the need for physical play. Play that is wholesome ➤

is contrasted with bullying behavior, and we discuss the need to guard against well-intentioned school policies concerning bullying that may adversely affect play.

We then discuss new challenges for integrating play throughout early childhood education. Attention is given to how play and our views about play are being modified with technological changes, the effects of globalization on the play of children, and finally how play can help children, given the pressure of longer school days. Many factors influence our thinking about play, what we as adults can do for children's play, and the actual way in which children play nowadays.

### FOCUS QUESTIONS

1. What is play? How is it defined? What might be the essence and functions of play? What are characteristics of play? How does play differ from the nonplay behaviors of children?
2. How have perceptions of play changed over the centuries? What are the differences among traditional play, modern play, and postmodern play?
3. Is play important for all children? How is play important? In a world of academics, TVs, and computers, do children still need to play?
4. Do all the children the world over, regardless of their nationality and culture, play in the same way? Or is children's play governed primarily by cultural contexts?
5. What are the current trends, issues, and direction in indoor and outdoor play for young children? In designs for indoor and outdoor play? Are adult-organized sports for young children conducive to healthy play?
6. How do the views of play differ from the various perspectives of children, parents, teachers, and administrators? What school policies could be antithetical to wholesome play during childhood?
7. How is technology changing the way children play? How is it changing the possibilities for play in early education?
8. What effects is globalization having on the play of children?
9. What are some play applications that can ameliorate stress on children caused by spending long hours away from home during the school day?

## HISTORY AND IMAGES OF CHILDREN AND PLAY

### Ancient and Traditional Times

In Plato's *Republic* the ancient Greek philosopher supported child's play as an important part of learning through experiences. He wrote, "enforced learning will not stay in the mind . . . let your children's lessons take the form of play" (Cornford, 1951, p. 536). The Greek words for play and education were the same (*paitheia*), distinguished aurally by whether the accent was on the second syllable (pie dee′ ah: education) or the last syllable (pie dee ah′: play). Both words derived from the Greek word for child, *pais* (pie ees′). In antiquity it was understood that both play and education were for the young and that they terminated with the passing of childhood. On entering adult society, one had to engage in various competitions, such as the Olympic games, mating games, work, and occupations, to make a living and have a life. The Greek word *agon* (the root of the English word *agony*) meant "contest," which is what preoccupies people when they are no longer young and able or allowed to play (Terr, 1999).

Throughout the centuries notions of childhood, play, and education have remained linked. Sometimes play is seen as compatible with education, as in Plato's case, and sometimes it is seen as being at odds with it, as in the case of the Christian Puritans. Always both play and education have been connected with childhood, although now we certainly recognize the importance of each over the entire life course. We are very familiar with how critical adult education and lifelong learning are in our day and age, and we know as well that we are never too old to play. In fact, we believe that play keeps us young.

Our views of children are related to our views of play throughout American history, and we can sketch changes going from premodern or traditional times (before the nineteenth century) through modern to postmodern times. Historically, in Puritan times and the beginning of the Protestant work ethic, a common traditional image was that children were a seedbed of sin, intrinsically evil or depraved (original sin doctrine), and that the agents of socialization, religious training, and education should be strict disciplinarians and aim to break the will or tame the beast inside human nature (theologically, people were all believed to be part beast, part angel). Play was the enemy, the "left hand of the devil," to be guarded against so that children would focus on family responsibilities, chores, work, and their schooling (to learn to read the Bible).

However, with the Enlightenment and westward expansion on the North American continent, from the early 1800s on, children began to be seen as innocent and as needing protection, as a *tabula rasa,* or blank slate, awaiting imprints from their environments. Although strict discipline remained the norm, a more genuine concern and child-centered sentimentality emerged. Play began to be seen as a positive force for helping children to grow strong and healthy and become full participants in social life.

During this progressive era adults began to take more interest in children's play and helped by creating playthings and areas inside and outside where play could occur. Traditional play, what many today consider wholesome and constructive, often occurred outdoors with pets and with natural objects such as wildflowers, butterflies, or frogs, and children built things out of stones, snow, or wood. Home-made toys such as puppets, dolls, kites, balls, and spinning tops were simple and were enjoyed by all members of the family. Often traditional play involved sports, games, music, folktales, songs, and dance and was seen in communities as part of festivals and special events. Traditional play has been noted to serve group functions and to further ethnic identity (Lee, Hong, Cho, & Eum, 2001). Sedentary or boisterous, solitary or social, play was valued for its contributions to social and physical development (realizing cognitive benefits is a more modern idea). Next to today's postmodern trends toward ever more technological, didactic, academic, and competitive play

(Elkind, 1999), it is small wonder that thinking about traditional play can sometimes evoke a sense of nostalgia in many parents and teachers.

Summarizing a history of premodern play risks making sweeping generalizations. Our sources of information are varied, often suggesting contrasting interpretations and offering different perspectives on both images of childhood and views about children's play. For instance, didactic and prescriptive texts from Puritan and Victorian times often present a cold, austere image of children, an adult-centered and authoritarian approach to education and child rearing, and a view of children's play as unimportant or counterproductive to learning and character formation. Such monolithic accounts of a historical period do not hold, however, when we examine sources such as medical documents or doctor's reports and recommendations for individual children. Here one often detects a more child-centered and humanistic attitude; paintings, too, often depict a different perspective, a kinder rendering of children and their play, as exemplified in the famous sixteenth century painting of Flemish artist Pieter Brueghel, *Children's Games* or in *Playing Children* by eighteenth century Chinese artist Chin, T'ing-Piao (Hsiung, 2000).

## Modern Times

The nineteenth and twentieth centuries have been labeled the period of modernism, in which knowledge was viewed as universal, predetermined, and to be discovered through the rational means of science and technology (Grieshaber & Cannella, 2001). Societal progress and civilization were to be achieved through reason and meeting the needs of every individual in a just and egalitarian society based on reason, research, technology, and social progress.

Examples of modernist universal truths include progress, individualism, rationalism, the elimination of poverty through science and technology, and the Western religious belief of salvation (Grieshaber & Cannella, 2001). In the field of child development and psychology, modernism is seen in the universal acceptance of the theories of Piaget, Erikson, Kohlberg, and other developmental psychologists and the generally accepted philosophies and practices of the field such as developmentally appropriate practice (Bredekamp & Copple, 1997). Many state childcare licensing requirements reflect this view of child development, and the U.S. Consumer Product Safety Commission's playground safety guidelines and Americans with Disabilities Act playground accessibility guidelines share a modernist emphasis on the importance of the individual.

The concept of all children being born with a preexisting program or structure that then unfolds as the child interacts with the environment is a modernist concept. Erikson's and Piaget's stages of development and Chomsky's concept of a language acquisition device are examples of this universal, preexisting structure that infants inherit from their parents. A general developmental progression in thinking, physical development, and even play from the more simple and primitive to the more complex and mature is also a modernist idea. Many believe that this structural view of development is a natural—and maybe even inevitable—result of a time period dominated by rationalism, technology, and the scientific method (Grieshaber & Cannella, 2001). In other words, this view of child development is biased owing to the social and historical context in which it was constructed.

It could also be argued that the universal model of the two-parent family and the predetermined notion that people will grow up and marry other people of the same race (even though race is not biologically determined) are modernist notions. In other words, the belief that there is some universal truth about what was viewed in the nineteenth and twenieth centuries as the ideal family is a modernist one.

The concept of the individual, as expressed in the U.S. Declaration of Independence, is at the heart of modernism. Individual identity is the building block of rational societies, and therefore modernist psychology and education focus on the individual—self-esteem, rationally meeting basic needs, success, and self-actualization (Maslow, 1959). True individuals are able to see truth and real knowledge, despite the radically different contexts they might live in. Thus the last of Kohlberg's stages of moral reasoning—universal ethical conduct—is a true example of the modern individual (Kohlberg, 1976).

The ideal individual is predetermined in the eye of psychology and education, and the role of both these disciplines is to assist, support, and guide the individual to progress along the road to toward this ideal. Young children are viewed as immature and primitive forms of the ideal; education is assigned the function of creating the universal, ideal human being. Consequently, someone who does not meet this ideal—who is irrational, communal, and does not use technology—is not considered desirable and is viewed by society as a failure. The notion of universal academic standards for U.S. schools that every child must master is a good example of the modernist approach.

Many approaches to play discussed in this book—Parten's social play stages, Piaget's cognitive play stages, Smilansky's combination of both, the movement from simple to more complex play, the progression of block play, and so on—all reflect a modernist view of play. The theories discussed in Chapter 2 that postulate play as a preparation for adulthood also fit this idea, because adulthood is presumed to be fixed, universal, and predetermined. The philosophy of play you develop in Chapter 2 might also be based on modern assumptions.

The modernist idea about play that is most open to debate is the concept that children's play is universal. Do children of approximately the same age in the streets of Sao Paulo, Brazil, children washing clothes in the polluted streams of the Highlands of Guatemala, and highly educated children playing on a fancy, brightly painted metal and plastic playground in an upscale area of Palo Alto, California, play in the same way? Is play universal? Modernists would say yes.

## Postmodern Views

A postmodern way of viewing knowledge developed in education during the 1980s and 1990s as a reaction to the modernist view of universal truths and the imposition of those truths on all humanity (Grieshaber & Cannella, 2001). Thus, at its most basic, postmodernism challenges many of the universal truths of the modernist approach. A number of theories fall under this umbrella term, including interpretive theory, critical theory, and feminist theories (Beyer & Bloch, 1996). What all postmodern theories have in common is the notion that truth is relative and subjective.

Of all the postmodern theories, critical theory has had the most influence on education. Whereas postmodern theories as a group challenge rationalism, progress through science and technology, and Western thought in general, critical theory also associates modernism with privilege, power, domination, and oppression by the white ruling classes throughout the world.

In the field of early childhood education, critical theorists challenge our basic knowledge about how to educate and raise children, the theoretical and research underpinnings of our field, constructs such as developmentally appropriate practice (Bredekamp & Copple, 1997), and the power positions of teachers and parents in relation to the lack of power of young children. Critical theorists believe that our view of children is a direct result of the power structures of the historical era in which these views developed—particularly European colonialism throughout the world. Further, critical theorists believe that educators and theorists who did not agree with the modernist approach to early childhood education and development were—and are—marginalized and silenced by the power of the institutional, educational elite.

Critical theorists are particularly interested in diversity and multiculturalism. They view diversity within this structural approach of power and oppression and argue that there are two overall approaches to raising and educating children: a middle-class, Eurocentric American approach and a minority approach (Banks & Banks, 1997; Gonzalez-Mena, 1993; Phillips & Derman-Sparks, 1997). The Euro-American approach is grounded in the Judeo-Christian religions and Northern European values of law, independence, and power. The minority approach is based on group survival, cooperation, and resistance and reaction to oppression. Many argue that the Euro-American approach fosters competition, independence, and power while the minority approach fosters group loyalty, obedience toward and respect for adults and elders, cooperative learning, and learning the role of the individual within the group.

The role of play differs in each of these views. In the Euro-American position play allows children to master skills, develop independence, practice power and control, and gain the skills and abilities they will need to be successful in professional and upper-level positions. For minority children play is viewed either as frivolous—not needed or required for survival—or as a way to develop and coalesce group solidarity, loyalty, and collectivism. Some critical theorists see little value in play for minority and low-income children and therefore see little value to play in the early childhood curriculum.

One example of this perspective is that although minority parents are very concerned about the educational excellence of their children, they are extremely skeptical about the educational value of play. To many, play is off-task and frivolous. And as we discuss throughout this book, many middle-class white parents are also caught up with the emphasis on early academics and early participation in competitive sports. However, in general, middle-class parents see value in play—maybe because the children of the wealthy have always had opportunities to play.

## MULTIPLE PERSPECTIVES ON PLAY

### Children's View of Play

Francis Wardle remembers that when his children were young (three to six years old), they loved to help him in his garden. They helped to break up the dirt, carefully dropped seeds from between their tiny fingers into the rows he scratched with a stick into the ground, and enthusiastically weeded the young plants (often pulling out more seedlings than weeds). They also enjoyed harvesting the ripe radishes, carrots, lettuce, corn, and tomatoes. But as they grew older, they were much less likely to help him in the garden. Apparently, they moved from the view that helping their father was a form of play to the view that helping him in the garden was some kind of work.

But of course, older children still play, as do adults. As we discuss throughout this book, a child's view of what is play and what is not play is based on a variety of factors, including the child's developmental age, the cultural context, whether the event is initiated by the child or imposed by an adult (teacher or parent), and the social context—what influential peers are doing at that time. We have seen children play at doing the dishes, making a pot, painting a picture, building a fantastic castle from Legos, dancing to a drumbeat, and reading a book. We have seen the same children protest doing the dishes, resist an art project, and decline to play with blocks. Dancing to an enticing drumbeat is a lot of fun for a five-year-old, but for a fifteen-year-old preparing a ballet performance involves a great deal of hard, often unpleasant or tedious work—even if the final performance is rewarding.

For the child, then, play is directly tied to our definition of play: nonliterality, intrinsic motivation, process (over product) orientation, free choice, and positive affect (see pages 14–16). From the child's perspective, what is absolutely critical to understand is that each of these criteria changes according to the child's unique view of the world *at the time of the activity.* For example, for one child washing dishes in the sink at home, with bubbles flying and dishes sparkling, might be a nonliteral activity full of positive affect, while to another child it might be a highly realistic (and disliked) chore. A child who chooses to take his dog into the backyard and romp with him will be playing, while the child who is told by his parent to exercise his dog will not. The child who enjoys messing with color pens to make interesting patterns and shapes is playing more than is the child who decides to create a "Welcome Home" sign for her big sister. Although this last activity is self-chosen, it is probably less play and more a kind gesture. And one day a child might love to sit and build with Legos with his buddies but the next day find it a boring process that does not produce a positive affect. Thus play is defined by the individual child within a particular context. Box 1.1 illustrates the idea of play for very poor Maya Indian children living in small villages in the Highlands of Guatemala, in the context of Maya Indian culture.

**BOX 1.1**

## *A Maya Perspective of Play*

**By Francis Wardle**

When I lived in the Highlands of Guatemala with the extremely poor Maya Indians, I observed the children and their play behaviors, and I noticed that play had some interesting functions. First, parents took their children with them to work. There was a school for children in the small mountain village, but there was no childcare, and women worked washing clothes, grinding coffee, weaving clothes to sell, and cooking meals. The younger children of both genders would go with their mothers to work. As the children got older, the boys went with their fathers, the girls with their mothers. They then would find play opportunities to keep themselves involved (Wardle, 1976). The girls would throw soap at each other and splash in the water, as they helped their mothers wash the clothes in the stream. Little boys would sit next to their mother and use sticks to draw in the dirt and dig in the soil.

Certainly, the children were expected to help their parents at an early age—eight to twelve years—but parents seemed to accept and even encourage a certain level of playlike behavior. This was especially true with the younger children.

Adults played with their children. On many an evening the young men would join all the young boys for a rousing game of soccer on the field in the middle of the village. And when we had a full-day fiesta, I noticed that several of the women placed food bowls on their heads as they cooked the recently butchered steer. They were obviously pleased with the fun. A few of the boys and men even played keep-away with some of the parts from the deceased animal.

Also, the children invented a variety of games with bottle caps, sticks, and other found objects. Because they had no TV or toys, they were very inventive in both object play and games with rules. Socially, of course, growing up in a small village, they

➤ The Maya children living in the Highlands of Guatemala invented a variety of games with bottle caps, sticks, and other found objects.

**were simply expected to learn how to get along with each other, follow the highly prescribed gender rules, and defer to authority in the village. It is no coincidence that the village teacher is also an ex-armed official.**

## Parents' View of Play

Clearly, today's parents are being pressured to provide more academics earlier in their children's lives. National, state, and district standards, computer programs, educational games, and advice by experts (e.g., Snow, 2002) to learn specific academic skills—especially literacy at home—all are producing an anti-play view in the minds of many parents (Simons, 2003).

This anti-play view, or at least a neutral view of play, is often exaggerated in parents of minority and low-income children for a variety of reasons. After all, the direct relationship between learning the alphabet song and academic growth seems quite logical to most parents, whereas allowing a child to pull out the pots and pans and sit on the kitchen floor to bang out a fun rhythm does not seem to have any relationship to reading, math, or science. Besides, a cute little toy that teaches the alphabet song is far less of a hassle and less time consuming than letting a child make a big mess on the kitchen floor. Messages that parents hear from educational experts, pediatricians, and the ever-strident voice of toy and educational materials manufacturers is that only educational toys are of any value for their child's future academic success.

This narrow approach to preparing children for school success—understood very clearly by minority and low-income parents as the ticket to their child's entry into the American dream—is reinforced by many multiculturalists and diversity experts, who either imply or state outright that open-ended play is a white, middle-class activity that not only does not apply to minority children, but actually distracts them from more direct and effective ways of developing the skills, attitudes, and defenses they need to succeed in a hostile, white world. Further, as we discuss in detail in Chapter 10, experts in working with children who have specific disabilities or who are at risk of school failure strongly reject a play-focused approach to early learning (Carta, Swartz, Atwater, & McConnell, 1991).

The strong anti–public school rhetoric that is quite popular in this country is often fueled by politicians and demagogues who believe that many of the public schools' problems are caused by too much choice, individualism, diversity, and play. To them the old drill-and-skill approach to learning facts and concepts in a strict, predetermined sequence is the only correct, effective kind of education (Hirsch, 1996). This argument has an especially powerful appeal to parents who learned this way in school and believe that the approach was successful. They reason, "What worked for me will work for my child." Interestingly, although many of these parents were exposed to this approach beginning in first grade, they now want their children to experience this approach beginning in preschool.

All of these pressures, advice, and expert information lead many parents to, at best, doubt the value of play for young children and, at worst, eliminate play from their child's home experience. The continual call for universal preschool (Zigler & Jones, 2002) and the willingness of the federal government and individual state governments to fund educational early childhood programs but not high-quality childcare (Wardle, 2003a) reinforces this academic approach to early childhood development. Finally, many of today's parents of all racial, cultural, and income groups pressure their children's early childhood programs to "not let children play all day," and some experts believe that programs such as Head Start have focused too much on play (Snow, 2003).

## Early Childhood Teachers' View of Play

The view an early childhood teacher will have about play and its value in early childhood programs depends largely on the preparation the teacher received and the teacher's own personal philosophy of play (see Chapter 2). This impact of the teacher's college preparation will depend markedly on whether the teacher attended a program that primarily prepared early childhood teachers or one that prepared elementary teachers with an early childhood certification added onto a primarily elementary certification (Silva & Johnson, 1999). And although early childhood education is now believed to cover the infancy to eight-years-old age range to define the field, many K–12 teachers do not view play as a medium for learning (Bodrova & Leong, 2003).

A variety of studies show a direct link between play in young children and memory, school adjustment, oral language development, improved social skills, school adjustment, and self-regulation (Bodrova & Leong, 2003). In Chapter 5 we explore the positive relationship between play and other academic, social, and behavioral areas, including literacy, symbolic thought, flexible thinking and problem solving, and social competence. Further, as we have already mentioned, developmentally appropriate practice specifically lists play as one of the twelve underlying principles of its philosophy (Bredekamp & Copple, 1997).

But what about the value of play for its own sake, not simply to teach something else? Many observers argue that play is an essential part of childhood in and of itself and that a childhood devoid of play is fraught with scary possibilities for a society (Wardle, 2003a). Some even suggest that all mammals must play just for the fun of it, not to prepare for adulthood or to learn specific survival skills, and that children who do not play will become mentally unhealthy adults (Brown, 1994). It seems that with the pressure to achieve short-term outcomes (social, academic, and behavioral) many early childhood teachers might be forgetting this important aspect of play for young children. Although many early childhood teachers see the critical importance of play in the education and development of young children, the pressure of national and state standards, the focus on early literacy, and the introduction of Head Start academic outcomes and normed tests is leading many early childhood education teachers to change or adapt their positions (Brodrova & Leong, 2003).

## Administrators' View of Play

Francis Wardle's wife taught in a minority public school in Denver, Colorado. On several occasions the school's African-American principal declared in no uncertain terms that children in her early childhood classrooms, funded through Title I and the district general fund, were not going to "waste their time playing." Many administrators of early childhood programs—both public and private—oppose play or see play as simply a rest from important academic activities (Bodrova & Leong, 2003).

There are a variety of reasons for this view. Many public school principals have no background in early childhood education and philosophy, and many directors of other private and public programs often have elementary education, social services, or business backgrounds or are former principals. Additionally, as the result of national standards and local accountability, many districts, such as the Denver Public Schools, have initiated specific academic skill requirements—such as counting and knowing letter-sound relationships—for entry into public kindergarten. This is one of the unfortunate—yet highly predictable—results of Goal I of Goals 2000: Every child will enter school ready to learn (Colorado Department of Education, 1991).

Although these and other specific academic outcomes can be taught in a variety of creative, playlike activities and projects, discussed at great length later in this book, most schools teach these academic skills and concepts in a highly didactic manner (Dunn & Kontos, 1997). And as the push for accountability increases in Head Start (Jones, 2003) and other early childhood education programs (Kagan & Cohen, 2000), this move away from play will surely increase, implemented and monitored by administrators who are most accountable to educational bureaucrats, parents, and politicians.

## DEFINING PLAY

Defining and articulating play are far from easy for at least two different reasons. First, play is abstract and fluid; it is not a concrete object, place, or action. Abstractions such as love, happiness, and play are much easier to exemplify or to illustrate than to define. Years ago, in her book *Psychology of Play*, S. Millar (1968) quipped that play is more like an adjective or adverb than a noun or a verb.

Any activity can be play depending on how we frame it. Our mental approach or attitude toward an activity makes all the difference in the world. Doing your ironing can be play if you are pretending that you are "frying" the bad guys in some fantasy scenario and you are really into it, having fun. On the other hand, playing table tennis is work if you are doing it only because your friend insists and it is really the last thing you want to be doing at the time. In both of these examples, however, note how easily we can imagine a sudden change in the play or work state. Perhaps your friend says something funny, your mood changes, and table tennis becomes fun—you become playful. On the other hand, what happens to your play spirits if you burn yourself while "ironing flat" your mean old boss?

A second reason that play is problematic is its multiplicity of meanings. Play, like love, is a many-splendored thing. The Oxford Dictionary of the English Language lists over one hundred different meanings for play. As a multidimensional and fluid concept play applies in so many different ways in our life and world. From playing a role in society to playing one on stage, from adult recreation to the leisure pursuits of graying Americans, the term *play* shows up repeatedly. And there are so many kinds of play. In early childhood education alone we have role play, rule play, reception play, physical play—and the list goes on.

### Essence of Play

Perhaps it would be helpful to contemplate the absolute opposite of play. What idea comes to mind? We have already alluded to some difficulty in contrasting play with work: One state often morphs into the other; the same activity can be play or work.

Although context, time, and personal variables do influence whether an activity is experienced as play or work, the seriousness and earnestness of work make it a good candidate for what is the opposite of play. Mark Twain said, "Play is what the body wants to do, work what the body is obliged to do." Obligation is serious business; what is done in earnest is not usually construed as play.

Still, we know that sometimes an activity can be genuinely playful but very serious and deliberate at the same time. For example, preschoolers making a fortress with blocks can show intense concentration and persistence toward the task at hand and might even tell you that they are working if you ask them. All the while they are playing and learning about how to get along with one another and about how the blocks can fit together in the real world and also perhaps generating and sharing make-believe ideas in a world of pretend. Play and work often merge, for children and adults. Perhaps John Dewey was correct when he proposed putting play and work on a four-point continuum: chaos, play, work, and drudgery. For Dewey the extremes have no place in the classroom, but play and work certainly do. Good lessons and good learning are deadly serious but very playful at the same time. However, too much work or too much play ruins it, and the activity degenerates into mindless behavior.

Elkind (2001) has noted that play is not identical to work in early childhood education. He bemoans the misunderstanding that has occurred in the field concerning the relationship between work and play attributable to Maria Montessori (1964), who said that "Play is the child's work" (p. 53). Elkind also points out that play is not the opposite of work. Play and work are complementary parts of the adaptational process, which requires both assimilation (play) and accommodation (work). According to Elkind, the proper way to understand the relationship of play and work is to realize that sometimes children's work precedes play, sometimes play precedes work, and sometimes play and work happen at the same time.

When children work before play, their play can be seen as an expression of their mastery. For example, children may work very hard exploring shovels and sand pails and learning how to use the shovels to fill up the pails with wet sand and then how to turn the pails upside-down to make sand cakes. Once these challenging actions are mastered, children are free to incorporate what they have learned in a constructive play episode in which they can vary the size and type of sand cakes. Dramatic play can ensue as the children might pretend to open a baker's shop to sell their wares to make-believe hungry customers strolling along the beach.

Playing takes place before work when a child is attempting to master a difficult emotional situation. For example, in play therapy a child often expresses affect about something for which the child cannot articulate a label or explain verbally. After a feeling is expressed in play, the therapist can help the child work through the problem. In a childcare center, a new child might pretend to lose babies, repeatedly playing this make-believe game with toy dolls that the child scatters around the room. An observant caregiver might recognize the child's need to verbalize and express through play the child's feelings about being left at the childcare center by his or her mother.

Finally, play and work occur simultaneously in games with rules. In learning and following the rules, say, of a board game such as checkers, children are working in the sense of accommodating to the social world of agreed-upon terms for the conduct of the game. At the same time children are playing by enjoying the game, experiencing the thrill of victory and agony of defeat, even though the checkers that are captured or lost have no intrinsic worth or power in the real world. It is the personal investment of transforming the objects of the game into signifiers of importance and power that makes engaging in the activity fun and exciting—playful (Elkind, 2001).

In sum, the essence of play is difficult to define but not so difficult to recognize. Indeed, we think that in the universe of all possible play expression it is not possible to identify one common dimension, even though there are overlapping common characteristics, which we discuss below. Nevertheless, we do contend that whether a play state exists, whether a child or an adult is playing, depends on the inner experience. Inside, we need to be feeling a certain freeness of spirit that allows us to attain a consciousness of being in control that enables us to perform self-initiated behaviors. When we are really playing, we are in a state of mind that gives us freedom to deal with reality on our own terms. Play liberates us for a time from the everyday stress and anxiety that come from living and having to meet the demands of reality or master developmental tasks. Like listening to one's favorite music, play permits us to live in the present moment, to forget the past, and to suspend concern about the future.

## Functions of Play

Play is almost always enjoyable. It is pleasant to step away mentally from pressures to meet social expectations and to have some release from the incessant need to exert the discipline and the self-control that we are asked to maintain in our daily conduct. Because play is in a way disconnected from real-world consequences, the player has less risk and less worry about social evaluation. This quality fosters creativity and innovation of expression and social intimacy.

Of course, play is much more than just fun. Play is needed for a healthy and balanced life. As psychiatrist Lenore Terr noted, play "gives us pleasure, a sense of accomplishment, of belonging" and "without huge risk our cares, worries, sadness, secrets are released" (quoted in Gore & Gore, 2002, p. 222). Play renews our spirits and restores our intellectual capacities. It does for our wakefulness what dreaming does for our sleep. It replenishes psychic energy. For these fundamental reasons play is very basic to our human nature. In fact, evolutionary biologists have noted that playing is one of only three behavioral ways in which primates are phylogenetically superior to reptiles; nursing and audiovocal communication are the other two (Gore & Gore, 2002).

The power of play is seen in how important it is in three general areas that we will be discussing throughout this book: (a) imaginativeness and creative problem solving, (b) identity and self-expression, and (c) social belonging or bonding between people (Brown & Kennard, 2000).

In Chapter 5 we review the empirical evidence showing the importance of playing for the development of creativity and imagination. The second chapter also notes some theoretical evidence for this first proposition about the power of play. Playing is an adaptive mechanism or means by which we have been able to develop and sustain an ability, acquired in evolution, to be always ready for new learning in constantly and rapidly changing contexts. As Al and Tipper Gore (2002) point out, "Play is, among other things, a kind of aerobic workout for the human capacity to change—a freewheeling form of mental, emotional, physical, and spiritual exercise" (p. 216).

In addition to its role in helping us to develop and maintain our creativity and openness, the power of play is reflected by how important it is as a way by which we define ourselves and express our individualities. This second play function is discussed in Chapter 4. Clearly, children have to develop and mature to a given extent before certain play forms of expression are within their capability. However, once these capabilities are attained, variations in play styles and preferences reflect emerging social identies as well as children's unique personalities. Throughout life play affords the opportunity to make personal statements about who you are; it provides a very important means of self-expression. Why do some children gravitate to more risky endeavors outdoors, literally going out on a limb, while others prefer indoor activities, satisfied simply to draw pictures of trees? Why do some adults go for skydiving or scuba diving while others prefer to do crossword or jigsaw puzzles? The rich myriad of play expression possibilities gives everyone the chance to fulfill in a unique way their play needs and to meet their own special play interests.

Third, play can be powerful as an instrument to bring us together as social beings: children and adults, same-age groups or mixed age groups, homogeneous groups or heterogeneous groups with respect to various social markers as race, class, gender, or disability. This theme is treated in Chapters 6 and 10. As important as personal initiative or individual agency are, equally important is our need to bond socially, to relate with others. A sense of belonging or connectedness is a vital aspect of our identities and a basic dimension of human existence. Play serves to promote our sociality, and societies engineer for this, as is seen in so many different culturally specific play activities and events across the life span, whether it is a baby or toddler party, a preschool free play period, recess time on the school playground, a company picnic, or a community festival. Unplanned or spontaneous occasions arise as often, when play serves as a kind of lubricant and glue at the same time, helping to facilitate social interactions and to cement relationships.

## Characteristics of Play

Numerous lists of the essential defining characteristics of play have been suggested by scholars seeking to describe play. Some definitional schemes have approached play by stressing its behavioral manifestations, others by highlighting internal states or dispositions (e.g., playfulness), and still others by emphasizing situational factors. All these approaches to the concept of play are valid and important to varying degrees.

Play is usually characterized by a small number of behavioral and motivational factors by researchers and practitioners alike (Garvey, 1977; Jenvey & Jenvey, 2002; Rubin, Fein, & Vandenberg, 1983), such as positive affect, nonliterality, intrinsic motivation, process orientation, and free choice:

1. *Positive affect.* Play is usually fun and enjoyable; it is usually accompanied by smiles and laughter. Even when play is more serious and intense, children still value the activity. Sometimes play is accompanied by apprehension and mild fear, such as when a child is preparing to go down a steep slide. However, even this apprehension

➤ Positive affect (expressing positive emotions) is a characteristic of play.

seems to have a pleasurable quality because the child will go down the slide over and over again.

2. *Nonliterality.* As will be discussed in detail in the next subsection, play events are characterized by a play frame that separates the play from everyday experience. This essential characteristic applies across all types of play, including rough-and-tumble play, building with blocks, dramatic play, and games. Within this frame, internal reality takes precedence over external reality. The usual meanings of objects, actions, and situations are ignored, and new meanings are substituted. Children adopt an as-if stance toward reality that allows them to escape the constraints of the here and now and to experiment with new possibilities.

3. *Intrinsic motivation.* The motivation for play comes from within the player, and play activities are usually pursued for their own sake. Play does not have to be externally motivated by drives such as hunger or by external goals such as gaining power or wealth. Play offers its own rewards.

4. *Process orientation.* When children play, their attention focuses on the activity itself rather than on the goals of the activity. In other words, process is more important

than product. The lack of pressure to achieve a goal frees children to try many different variations of the activity and is a major reason play tends to be more flexible than product-oriented behavior.

5. *Free choice.* Free choice is an important element in young children's conceptions of play. Children often considered an activity such as block building to be play if it was freely chosen but considered the same activity to be work if it was assigned by the teacher. The free-choice factor might become less important as children grow older. King (1982) discovered that pleasure was the key factor differentiating play and work for fifth-graders, in contrast to kindergartners, for whom free choice was critical (King, 1979).

Freedom from externally imposed rules and active engagement are also often listed as characteristics of play. However, we believe that these two characteristics might be too restrictive because they exclude two important types of play: games with rules (which have external rules) and reception play (in which children are at play mentally but remain physically inactive). We need to think about play from many different angles, each one comprising many different possible ingredients, such as flexibility, quirkiness, spontaneity, nonliterality, freedom, and process orientation. Play can perhaps best be conceptualized as a convergence or intertwining of relevant if not indispensable features or components. Which factor is most central in the sense that it best approximates "pure play"? Box 1.2 explores this question further.

**BOX 1.2**

## What Is the Best Indicator of Play?

Smith and Vollstedt (1985) conducted a clever research study to determine which characteristics of play were actually useful in helping observers identify play behavior. Adult subjects were shown a thirty-minute videotape of young children's behavior, which had been independently rated for the occurrence of play. Before being asked to decide which behaviors on the video were play, different groups of subjects were trained to use a particular characteristic of play as the sole criterion for coding a behavior as play. These behavioral characteristics included *positive affect* (expressing positive emotions), *nonliterality* (pretending), *intrinsic motivation* (undertaken for its own sake), *flexibility* (involving quick changes in activity), and *process orientation* (emphasizing means over ends). In other versions of the experiment, subjects were given more than one criterion to use in coding the children's behaviors (e.g., both flexibility and nonliterality).

The results indicated that *nonliterality* was the most reliable indicator for identifying play. If the nonliterality criterion is used together with positive affect or flexibility, the observers almost always agreed as to whether particular behaviors being exhibited by the youngsters should be called play. Intrinsic motivation was the least helpful indicator; many behaviors performed by children are intrinsically motivated but clearly not play.

On the basis of the results of the Smith and Vollstedt's research, nonliterality appears to be the best litmus test for play. When we play, internal reality takes precedence over external reality, and objects and actions take on new, play-related meanings.

## Play Framing

In addition to defining play and describing the elements or characteristics of play, it is important to introduce and discuss an additional related concept: play frames. Play frames are critical to any analysis of play and playfulness. Bateson (1971) compared the play frame to a picture frame that separates the picture from the wall of a room on which the picture is hung. Play frames set play behaviors apart from normal, everyday nonplay activities. Players, including animals that play, such as the sea otter studied by Bateson, provide social cues to communicate to others how to read their behaviors and how they want others to respond to or treat their actions. Social cues, whether verbal or nonverbal behaviors are part of any transaction between individuals. In play these cues are exaggerated, often with a play face exhibited to let the other know that this is play. In fact, social play is an excellent way to learn how to give and to read social cues.

Play episodes can be viewed in terms of the play frames and the play scripts or play actions that take place within these frames. Play frames and play context are useful concepts because they enable us to talk about not just the play that is going on in a play episode, but also other behaviors that are happening—being displayed by the players around the play itself, as an example. Children often break the play frame to solve social conflicts or to negotiate or plan future play actions. Sometimes play frames are broken to attend to other needs or to listen to the teacher. The ability to maintain play continuity even though there might be frequent breaks in the play frame is an important play skill in its own right. Also, children who are skilled players know how to give and read the social cues that go into navigating across play frames. They know how to enter and reenter ongoing play and how to maintain the cohesiveness of the play episode.

The concept of play frame is also a vital one for play assessment. Observers need to distinguish what is actual play from what is communication about play that takes place outside the play frame. Moreover, this is a needed play concept for adults who wish to facilitate play in children. Some adult roles are done inside the play frame, as when adults are co-players, sharing the play state with the children. Other adult roles are done outside the play context, as when a teacher sets the stage for play by providing interesting and useful materials. Sometimes adults disrupt play, snapping the play frame, by interrupting children at play with some nonplay teacher intervention. This will be discussed in detail in Chapter 7.

## Play-Related Behaviors

When thinking about play and education and child development, especially when seeking to draw some practical applications out of research and theory, as we do in this book, it is necessary to distinguish play from three related behaviors or behavioral constructs: (a) exploration, (b) imitation, and (c) on-task learning.

**Recent Exploration.** Play and exploration are similar in that they are both intrinsically motivated behaviors and not directed by external goals. Previous research, however, has revealed some important differences between these two types of behavior (Hutt, 1971; Weisler & McCall, 1976). Exploration is a stimulus-dominated behavior

**TABLE 1.1 Play versus Exploration**

| | Play | Exploration |
|---|---|---|
| Timing | Follows exploration | Come before play |
| Context | Familiar object | Strange object |
| Purpose | Generate stimulation | Get information |
| Behavior | Variable | Stereotyped |
| Mood | Happy | Serious |
| Heart rate variability | High | Low |

*Source:* Based on research by Hutt (1971), Hughes & Hutt (1979), and Weisler & McCall (1976).

that is concerned with acquiring information about objects and situations. It is controlled by the stimulus characteristics of what is being explored. Play, on the other hand, is organism-dominated behavior, governed by the needs and wishes of the player. Play is concerned with generating stimulation rather than with gaining information. Hutt (1971) explains, "In play the emphasis changes from the question of 'what does this object do?' to 'what can I do with this object?'" (p. 246). Table 1.1 illustrates some of the major differences between play and exploration.

Although play and exploration can be differentiated conceptually, it is often difficult to tell when a child is playing and when a child is exploring. The two states can fluctuate from one moment to the next, especially for infants and animals (Weisler & McCall, 1976). A primary function of play for infants and animals is exploration; in fact the two terms *play* and *exploration* have been combined as exploratory play. Play episodes with older children also often see a mix of play and exploration but usually with a recognizable pattern of exploring before playing, a sequence that can be described as the examine, reexamine, transform cycle.

**Imitation.** Piaget (1962) drew attention to the difference between play and imitation in his research on sensorimotor intelligence and in his general theorizing about the nature of intelligence. Imitation occurs when accommodation takes precedence over assimilation. When imitating, the child bends the self to fit external reality. A twelve-month-old baby might hold an empty cup and appear to engage in pretend drinking, but this could simply be imitation of behavior seen over and over again. The child is adjusting hand and other movements to adapt to the cup so as to imitate drinking behavior modeled by others. Play, on the other hand, occurs when assimilation dominates accommodation. At play the child bends reality to fit the self (wishes, needs, cognitive schemes). For example, the child might take the cup to a doll's face and pretend to give the doll a drink. Here the child is using the cup in a novel way and disregarding the cup's intended use (to hold real water). According to Piaget, play and imitation are complementary processes that are involved in a person's efforts to adapt to the environment. An equilibrated state of adaptive intelligence is achieved when assimilatory tendencies are checked by accommodative ones and the two processes are balanced.

Similar to the relationship of play and exploration, play and imitation often are displayed together in a single play episode, and the two behaviors, while conceptually distinct, are not recognizable as being different. On the surface, in terms of manifested behaviors, they seem the same. Nevertheless, it is important to keep in mind that true play is generative and transformational, with new ideas, thoughts, and behaviors expressed. Imitative play lacks this generative and transformational quality. A child copying statements and actions from a cartoon show, for instance, is imitating rather than playing. Only when a child is actively reprocessing material and is creating something new from the inner workings of his or her being—something different from what is seen in the external environment—can the child be said to be engaging in real play. And it is only when deeply playing that the child reaps the cognitive and emotional benefits of play. We will return to this issue in Chapter 11, in which we discuss play and technology, the media, and popular culture.

**On-Task Behaviors.** It might seem peculiar to bring up for discussion a behavior so obviously different from play. As important as play is in education and development, it is not the only mechanism for learning. Children learn while exploring and imitating, and they also learn by performing on-task behaviors, whether the occasion is following the teacher's directions in a lesson or doing more elaborate self-initiated actions such as when engaged in a project at school. Good early childhood teachers recognize this and have an assortment of play and nonplay elements in the curriculum. As children mature, some nonplay activities, such as ones happening in self-initiated investigations and projects that are on-task behaviors, can also be viewed as a form of cognitive play. Here again we see the interesting dynamic involving what is work and what is play, since we usually associate on-task performance with work, not play. Play and nonplay elements can be mixed in the same experience.

We think it is best to think of play as a continuum of activities from pure play to nonplay and not to make a binary division between play and work. On-task behaviors are placed toward the nonplay pole of this continuum to the extent that doing them is devoid of the play characteristics that we previously discussed (positive affect, free choice, process orientation, etc.). The fact that an activity lacks one or more of these characteristics does not, by itself, preclude the possibility that the child can experience some play states together with nonplay states while performing the activity. As we noted above, at times a child can experience some feelings of being at play and some feelings of being *not* at play at the same time.

In this book any activity with most of the aforementioned five characteristics of play will be viewed as play. Traditional categories of play, including physical, practice, reception, constructive, dramatic, and game play, are covered, as are creative activities such as art and music that have an element of spontaneity (intrinsic motivation), nonliterality, process orientation, free choice, and pleasure. Both *educational play* and *recreational play* are considered. We define the former as being more under the control of an adult (e.g., classroom projects and free-play period activities that are initiated, paced, and terminated by the teacher) and the latter as being more free from adult influence (e.g., some free-play time activities and recess time or break time on the playground). Nancy King (1987) has referred to these two types of play as *instrumental play* and *real play,* respectively, in her discussions of school play. We treat both educational play (or instrumental play) and recreational play (or real play) as important concerns for teachers and parents who interact with the world of children's play.

David Elkind (2003) recently distinguished *adult-functional* versus *child-experiential* vantage points in viewing children's play. The adult-functional perspective is adult-centric and emphasizes the utility of children's play for some ulterior motive such as helping the child become ready for school, learn how to share and cooperate, or learn how to control impulses and regulate affect. Adult-centric or "adultist" lenses are not invalid or inappropriate ways through which to view children's play; they are just very limiting (Sheets-Johnstone, 2002). We must also try to put ourselves in the shoes of the children and try to understand what their experiences are like when they are playing. We must strive to imagine this. For Elkind this is the child-experiential perspective. From this point of view what makes play genuinely play is that it has no aim other than the pleasure of the activity itself. When playing, children are in a special state of being in which they are not concerned about adult evaluations of them or achieving an external goal. They are in a state in which such things do not matter. Like a river, they are caught up in the flow of their own activity. As Winnicott (1971) puts it, "To get an idea of playing it is helpful to think of the preoccupation that characterizes the play of the young child. The content does not matter. What matters is the near-withdrawal state, akin to the concentration of older children and adults. The playing child inhabits an area that cannot easily be left. Nor can it easily admit intrusions" (p. 51). Of course, while playing, children might be achieving other adult-centric goals, such as releasing tensions or learning new skills or values, but this is not what is on the minds of the children themselves. We must as adults think about this, and respect play and children with reinforced commitment to the reality that children are people too!

## CURRENT ISSUES AND TRENDS

Knowledge about development, play, education, and the needs of young children changes over time. Further, as societies change and develop, our view of education shifts and expands. For example, before the creation of personal computers, schools were not concerned with teaching technology. Now all schools include technology in their curricula, and many educators are deeply concerned about the technology divide between low-income children and more affluent children (Wardle, 2003a). New developments, contexts, and research knowledge change and modify our views of play and its role in early development and early childhood education.

### Brain Research

The results of recent brain research are having a radical impact on many disciplines and practices for young children (Shore, 1997). This research has resulted in a vast amount of new information about how the brain works, develops, and is organized and about what is needed to provide optimal brain development in young children

(Shore, 1997). This new research has profoundly changed our view of the interactions and environments needed for the very youngest of our children and has also affected our view of play and its importance during the early years.

Brain research has further solidified the *interactionist* view of development. Results have shown that optimal brain development occurs when the child interacts with the environment and the environment is responsive to that interaction. On the negative side, certain environmental impacts can negatively affect brain development after a child is born. These include stress, boredom, constant chaos, inadequate nutrition, and lack of appropriate stimulation (Shore, 1997).

It is clear that a child who is engaged in a variety of play—object play, physical play, social play, and cognitive play—is developing a variety of important brain connections. Play often integrates a variety of functions. For example, in object play children use their senses of sight, touch, and sometimes hearing; they physically control, manipulate, and arrange objects while they think about various combinations, cause and effect, patterns, and physical realities (will the stack of blocks fall down?). In social play complex language, social give-and-take, and verbal negotiation are added to the mix.

One of the best factors of play is that it is self-correcting. Because play is child initiated and controlled, children will stop playing once the activity is no longer of interest to them. They are no longer interacting with the physical or social environment. We don't have to ask, "Are you still playing?" Either the children will simply stop or they will use the material or social situation in a more complex and challenging way. Thus a child might progress from simply stacking Legos as high as possible to using them to build a house. When the child stops playing, it is clear to the teacher or parent that the child is no longer stimulated by the toys, the social context, or a combination of both.

Thus play keeps children's minds actively involved in interacting with the environment. And because play produces positive affect, these interactions will be pleasurable and without stress. Play is therefore one of the best ways to provide the kind of stimulation, positive affect, integration, and lack of stress that the new brain research calls for in working with young children.

## Outdoor Play

Outdoor play for young children is currently going through at least four distinct trends: (1) the continual upgrade of playgrounds to meet the U.S. Consumer Product Safety Commission's playground safety guidelines, (2) the implementation of the new Americans with Disabilities Act (ADA) accessibility guidelines, (3) a renewed emphasis on physical play because of our increased concern with obesity and childhood obesity, and (4) the elimination of recess from some elementary schools and the reduction of play in some academic preschools and Head Start programs.

One result of the new ADA access guidelines is that more designers are finding ways to create play opportunities close to the ground—what we call a horizontal approach to design (as opposed to a vertical approach). This is because the access guidelines significantly increase the cost of building climbing structures, swings, slides, and other equipment that is located above the ground.

From a pure design standpoint the provision of shade in playgrounds for infants, toddlers, and preschoolers is becoming critical because of the potential for skin cancer. Australia and New Zealand have pioneered this concern because of their proximity to the hole in the ozone over Antarctica. The playground regulations for these countries specify a certain percentage of shade on the playgrounds of early childhood programs and schools.

Finally, there is a move to bring back some of the old traditional games such as four-square, hopscotch and jump-rope, both at home and at school, because of concerns about obesity and a lack of organized physical education activities in many early childhood programs (Simons, 2003).

## Organized Sports

For some time, organized sports for young children in this country have been very popular and seem to cross all cultural and income groups. Soccer, T-ball, girl's gymnastics, basketball, track, swimming, and other sports are all organized activities for young children starting at about age four years. Although these organized sports are not strictly play according to our definition (pages 14–16), organizers have attempted to incorporate more play elements into them to meet the needs of younger players. For example, many young children now play soccer three on three, or five on five (instead of having eleven players on each side) so that each player gets more touches on the ball and to keep the children engaged. And some games for young children do not keep count of the score to determine a winner, thus reducing the competitive nature of the sport. Many believe these organized sports teach our culture's competitive values at a very young age. However, as Box 1.3 suggests, it is not clear to what extent children learn competition from their immediate culture, and to what extent it is biological.

**BOX 1.3**

### *Are All Children Naturally Competitive?*

**by Francis Wardle**

For one school year I had the pleasure of teaching kindergarten children in one of the Bruderhof communities (Wardle, 1997). These religious communities started in Germany between the two world wars. The philosophy of the Bruderhof is based on the New Testament: loving thy brother (and sister) and sharing everything. All adults in the Bruderhof work on jobs they are assigned in the community: the children's house, school, kitchen, toy factory, maintenance, or medical/dental offices. None are paid. All members of the community, including the children, have their basic needs met, such as food, clothing, and household items, on the basis of their needs. Technically, however, everything in the Bruderhof—now eight separate communities—belongs to the group and not to the individual; members don't even own the shirt on their back. All property is held in common, and most meals are taken communally, including the children's. Families are assigned apartments on the basis of their size and needs. All children attend the Bruderhof's children's house, starting at six weeks of age, and then their school through eighth grade. After school and for part of weekends they are also cared for so that their parents can work and go to meetings.

> Thus the entire focus of the Bruderhof is on the welfare and unity of the group and not the needs and wishes of the individual. Families have no TV, and the members entertain themselves with festivals, communal hikes and games, family days, and caring for the physical appearance of the whole community.
>
> With my Bruderhof kindergarten class I played a variety of games from their German, English, and American cultural backgrounds: sing spiels, red light–green light, duck-duck-goose, freeze tag, chain tag, and King Neptune. All the children loved these games, but one boy had a particularly hard time when he was caught out or did not win the game. We played these games on a large slab of tarmac in the middle of a field bounded by woods. There was no fence. After each time this child was called out in a game, he would run off the tarmac and head into the woods. Even by the end of the year he had not learned to lose gracefully, unlike other children, who displayed varying levels of tolerance or enjoyment of the competitive element in game playing.

Some years ago the Dutch soccer federation developed an entire coaching philosophy to make soccer more fun and developmentally appropriate for young children. The Dutch believed that Holland was losing young soccer players because the traditional approach to coaching, which focused on drill-and-skill and adult-directed activities, was turning children away from the sport. They developed playlike approaches to learning specific skills and encouraged coaches to "let them play." The result was that many of the skill drills became more like fun games than like boring chores.

## Obesity

There is currently a health epidemic of obesity in this country that has been well publicized in the local media and professional literature. For example, type II diabetes, which used to be rare in children, is now becoming common (Sutterby & Frost, 2002). Ironically, at the same time this epidemic is rapidly increasing in our society, we are reducing play, physical education, and some sports in many of our early childhood education programs and elementary and secondary schools. While our national government has responded to the problems of substance abuse, including smoking, in our children by funding a variety of studies and intervention programs, our national response to obesity has been to eliminate recess, cut physical education graduation requirements, and allow pizza, hamburgers, and French fries to be sold in many of our schools, including elementary schools. Many school districts have exclusive contracts with soft drink companies to sell their products (which are extremely high in calories) in the schools.

Obesity in our society can be traced to three main causes. First, we engage in too much sedentary activity, including TV watching, computer use, and sitting at desks in school and at work. Second, we do not exercise enough, both as part of our lifestyle and as a means to stay in shape. In this country we seem to have a cultural acceptance of physical inactivity. Ironically, adults in our society seem to prefer to watch professionals engaged in sports contests rather than participating directly in sports and other physical activities. In Europe and South America adults engage in a variety of amateur sports on a regular basis, from soccer to volleyball and cricket. Any casual traveler to these regions will see adults playing these games in parks, village greens, dirt lots, and city plazas. Third, we continue to make food choices that are based on a past lifestyle of high physical activity—such as farming, mining, wood cutting, and cattle herding—in an information society in which most work does not require physical activity. Thus many Americans live inactive lives yet still consume large quantities of the high-calorie food required for active physical work.

The general obesity of our culture has, understandably, filtered down to our children, owing to high-calorie diets, too much sedentary activity, and adult models who are not actively engaged in exercise and physically demanding lifestyles. To offset the problem of obesity in coming generations, we need to work with our children. We need to help children develop appropriate, low-calorie eating habits. We need to provide children with regular physical activity so that they do not develop obesity as children. And most important, we need to develop in children a lifelong disposition toward physical activity—hiking, walking, gardening, swimming, playing games and sports, cycling, dancing, mountain climbing, exercising, and the like. We need to develop people who engage in these activities because they find them pleasurable, rewarding, and worthwhile, not because they have to do them to stay healthy. And we must start this process with our children.

➤ We need to provide children with regular physical activity so they do not develop obesity as children, and so they develop a positive disposition toward physical activity.

One of the best ways to develop a positive view of physical activity in children is to encourage, support, and provide lots and lots of opportunities for physical play. Physical play is enjoyable, develops muscles and gross and fine motor ability, and provides needed exercise. Because it is enjoyable, physical play develops in each child a *disposition* toward physical activity—a positive habit that is continued in the future (Katz, 1985).

For physical play to be effective, it needs to be encouraged from infancy, and its affective nature should be stressed above competition, exercise, or learning to be a team player (especially for children who have not reached the games-with-rules stage). Obviously, a child will not continue to engage in physical activities, especially into adulthood, if he or she develops a negative association with physical play. For example, if a child is always selected last for team games, that child might well associate team sports with a very negative feeling. To keep physical play pleasurable, teachers, physical education directors, and curriculum designers must adhere to the characteristics of play discussed earlier in this chapter; understand the gender issues in play, including different preferences for toys and activities and the different cultural body images of boys and girls, and be aware of the developmental changes that occur regarding play and play preferences as children get older and begin to accept their culture's ideas about work, play, and gender expectations.

## Play and Bullying

The massacre at Columbine High School in Littleton, Colorado, and shootings in several other schools in this country and elsewhere throughout the world were tragedies that many people believe were triggered from a reaction by the perpetrators to constant bullying by the victims. Bullying is now considered to be a real threat to general safety in our schools. Some students in public schools, including elementary schools, feel too scared either to go to school or to go to certain parts of the school (restroom, cafeteria, common social areas, etc). As a result, many states and school districts have initiated a variety of antibullying policies, and the U.S. Department of Education has pressured states and districts to actively address this problem with formal curricula, policies, and procedures.

Children who experience the threat of direct abuse and indirect threats by the bullies are not the only victims of bullying; the bullies are also victims. Thus an effective antibullying policy must address the needs of both the victims and the bullies. As Katz and McClellan (1997) have so well articulated, young children who are not taught appropriate social behaviors are at a very high risk of school failure. These children include those who respond to social conflicts and disagreements by bullying.

The problem with many antibullying programs, as with other school or state education policies, is that implementation is difficult. Francis Wardle teaches college students in Colorado, where the state has mandated that schools create and implement antibullying programs. His students, who are themselves teachers in local public schools, report a variety of problems with antibullying programs, including definitions of bullying and zero tolerance. For example, one school district initiated an antibullying program even before they had defined bullying in the parent and student handbook. Thus parents, teachers, and students were supposed to identify and address bullying without any accepted definition of the behavior. Another school's definition was so broad that it would include aggressive behavior on the football field and in the gym. A zero tolerance policy makes it almost impossible for schools to provide supportive and psychological assistance to the perpetrator; it also makes the consequences of mistakes extreme when program staff make mistakes in judgment or interpretation. For example, a child in a Colorado school was suspended for bringing a butter knife to school to prepare her lunch.

Not surprisingly, the vast majority of bullies are boys (see Chapter 4). Experts attribute this to two main reasons: Boys in our culture tend to be more aggressive and violent, and teachers and administrators tend to assume automatically, when there is a conflict between a girl and a boy, that the boy is at fault. We know that more boys than girls are in special education programs and that boys of any race or ethnicity in general have more difficulty with social adjustment than do girls (Cooney & Radina, 2000). Even among two-year-olds, boys bite other children more often than do girls (Reguero de Atiles, Stegelin, & Long, 1997).

Later in this book (Chapter 4) we discuss gender differences in play. One of the gender differences is that boys engage in far more rough-and-tumble play than girls do (Carlsson-Paige & Levin, 1987; Goldstein, 1992; Smith, 1997). Rough-and-tumble play is a combination of physical, social, and make-believe play. Rough-and-tumble play includes mock wrestling, running, kicking, piling on, hitting, and chasing (Sutton-Smith, Gerstmyer & Meckley, 1988). According to Smith (1997), 5–20 percent of children's play behavior on a playground is rough-and-tumble play.

Because most early childhood programs are staffed by women and most early childhood experts (special education specialists, etc.) are women, there is a strong bias against active, aggressive behaviors and speech (Benson-Hale, 1986; Wardle, 1991). With the creation and adoption of these new antibullying programs, this bias is likely to increase. Very few public school officials and teachers seem to know the difference between real aggression and rough-and-tumble play or to have created an operational definition that distinguishes between the two. To our knowledge no school's antibullying policies attempt to address this distinction. We know of one K–12 school district whose school policy on outdoor activities includes a prohibition against any child touching another child at any time, including—ridiculously enough—a child pushing another child on the swing! Obviously, under this rule, rough-and-tumble play cannot exist. We also know of incidents when children have been disciplined under the antibullying codes for using a finger as a symbolic gun.

We all support school safety and the critical need for each child in our schools and early childhood programs to feel psychologically and physically safe and secure. However, we wonder about the long-term negative effects of curtailing rough-and-tumble play on healthy development, especially of boys. If boys naturally engage in more aggressive or assertive behaviors, at least in this society, should not their play reflect this developmental difference?

## Technology

Many exciting new technological innovations have occurred in recent years that are affecting children's play. For example, new electronic toys are becoming more prevalent and are being made available to younger and younger children. Increasing numbers of young children are also using computers in their homes and schools. And Gameboy® and video game use is more widespread, especially among older children. High-tech toys are often linked to the electronic media and popular culture. How is technology changing children's play? What are the issues and what are the responsibilities of adults?

Smart toys can be defined as play objects that make use of computing power either by connecting to a computer or by having in them sophisticated sensors and electronic circuitry to enrich play (Allen, 2002). Examples include popular virtual pets Shelby© the talking clam and the robot dog Poo-Chi®. These toys seem to have intentions, preferences, and other humanlike traits. Interactive Barney, Me Barbie, and Interactive Yoda are additional examples of this new category of smart toys.

These intelligent toys provide children with a virtual play partner that can interact and convey emotions. Although scripted, intelligent toys show a considerable number of combinations in verbal communication. They encourage hands-on behaviors, are child-directed, and can promote pretending as well as social behaviors owing to their interactivity (i.e., their capacity to interact with the child). A world for play now exists that was not known before the advent of these high-tech toys. Today many children play not only with solid objects in the real world, but also with digital technologies in the computer environment.

Of course, computers themselves also have profound effects on play. There are games, learning programs, paint programs for digital art, and music programs. Digital storybooks exist in abundance that are attractively illustrated and feature interactive activities. All these can engender different kinds of play. In our information age, moreover, a new kind of play that has been seen by teachers and parents has been what children do alone or with peers when interacting with symbols and images on the computer screen. Researchers are beginning to learn more about how simple pretending or more elaborate sociodramatic play, for example, can be stimulated by computer software (Brooker & Siraj-Blatchford, 2002). On-screen activities can serve as a medium for play as children share their attention to what is displayed and use computer content in off-screen play activity.

Improved technology and appropriate adult mediation can help to ensure that computer activities have appropriate amounts of cognitive complexity and high play quality. Just as we should avoid educational software that is merely for drill and practice, we should avoid using computers as simple providers of passive entertainment. Open-ended software, like open-ended toys in general, can have a positive impact on peer interactions and play quality. These and other topics are covered in Chapter 11.

Special forms of play activity and play preferences are emerging with new technology. Children often find modern technological toys more attractive than traditional toys. Seymour Papert (1996) first voiced this challenge: "Our concern must be to ensure that what is good about children's play is at least preserved (and hopefully enhanced) as the concept of 'toy' inevitably changes" (p. 188).

## Globalization

Globalization is the process by which the nations of the world influence one another through the exchange of products and through contacts between peoples of different cultures. Globalization is an age-old phenomenon, but its rate and forms have changed dramatically in recent decades. Trade, immigration, and travel have been joined by movies, radio, television, and the Internet to link people who are at great distances from each other. As never before people are using telecommunications, from e-mail to videoconferencing. Conditions are being created so that more and more people will come to have both a global identity and a local identity (one's own cultural reference group) in the twenty-first century (Arnett, 2002). In this sense we are all becoming more bicultural.

The effects of globalization are seen over a wide spectrum of our lives, including children's play and people's beliefs and attitudes about it. One effect has been increased levels of international discourse about acceptable policies and practices related to children's play. A significant example of this is the effort by the United Nations' Convention of Children's Rights to achieve universal protection and respect for children. All of our planet's children have a basic human right to survive and thrive, including the right to play and express oneself. Global advocacy for children's play has been a core element of the mission statements of a number of international organizations such as the International Council for Children's Play, Playing for Keeps, and the International Association for Children's Play (see Chapter 12). Over one hundred years ago John Dewey opined that one can judge the quality of a nation by the willingness of its citizens to care about other people's children. Perhaps the time will soon come when we will want to judge our world by the willingness of its countries to be concerned about other nations' children.

A number of globalization issues involving play require our thoughtful consideration and action. An educational consequence of globalization facing many teachers of young children in the United States and elsewhere is the growing number of recent immigrant children in classrooms and childcare centers. These children and their families represent a challenge to educators because of cultural and language barriers. Value systems are often in conflict.

Many teachers understand their role in the acculturation process and try to remain cognizant of minority children's cultural roots in the design and implementation of curriculum and instruction that is multicultural. For example, stories, music, dance and songs, and sociodramatic play themes and props related to different ethnic backgrounds are often incorporated into early childhood programs, and children's initial play preferences, nonverbal communication patterns, and social behavioral styles are accepted and supported. At the same time teachers are also aware of the acculturation needs of immigrant children and try to arrange educational and play opportunities that will foster adaptation to subsequent schooling and social life in the main culture—even if the new behavior (e.g., individualized play) is different from what is common in the home culture (e.g., communal play). In the United States, for example, parents of immigrant children report some shifts in their beliefs about play, development, and education as their families become more accustomed to American mores (e.g., Parminder, Harkness, Super, & Johnson, 2000).

Similarly, cultural conflicts induced by effects of globalization are seen in other areas that involve children's play and adults' ideas and attitudes about play. The proliferation of toy industry marketing worldwide, the global spread of media-linked playthings, and the identical and cheap plastic toys children obtain on purchasing child-size meals at omnipresent fast-food chains—all these international trends have caused some consternation in many countries. Important questions include the following: Will the growing popularity of different play forms and objects associated with a new global self-identity cause a harmful shedding of traditional forms of play and games in indigenous cultures and their varied local communities? Will new play behaviors seen in young families so clash with and contradict older play habits as to result in feelings of intergenerational alienation, social erosion in communities, and the eventual extinction of older play and game forms?

A great challenge in the twenty-first century is how to enrich or give positive content to the process of globalization. Internationally, early childhood educators and child development specialists share to a considerable extent a common set of concerns, a defined professional perspective, a conceptual tool kit of ideas and methods of inquiry, and a dynamic and emerging knowledge base. Hence we operate from within our own profession-based cultural sphere and have a specific outlook on issues, trends, and developments unfolding in today's diverse and complex world. Accordingly, we need to continue to network and exchange experiences on a global scale about our specialty area of children's play, development, and education whether we are talking about playground safety, what we can do about childhood obesity, technology, or the invention of toys that are particularly suited for children with special needs.

Finally, how can those of us in this cultural sphere defined by a shared interest in children's play, development, and early education assist (and inform what it means

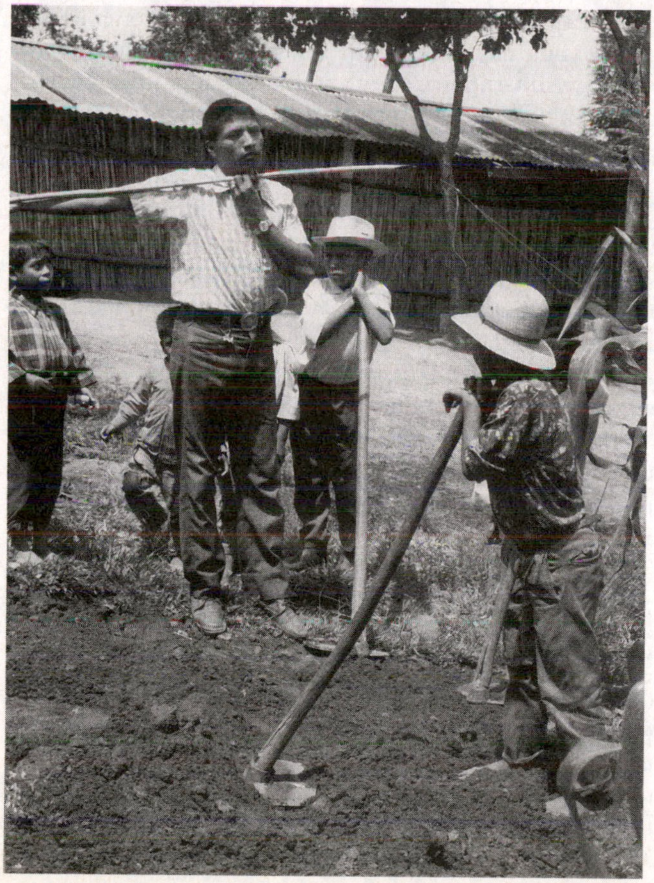

Children of the Highlands of Guatemala are imbued with their indigenous culture. A critical question of globalization is how to preserve these important cultures.

to assist) bicultural identity formation in future generations? Our belief is that in undertaking this important project of our postmodern era, play will be essential. Play possesses protean (after the Greek sea god Proteus, who was able to take on many different forms) adaptive qualities (Vander Ven, 1998). Hence children's play should contribute to the psychological foundation needed to achieve fluid, flexible, and multiple identities—whether bicultural, multicultural, or hybrid—as today's children grow and mature in our new world shrunk by communication and technology.

## Longer School Days

More and more children are spending longer days in early childhood programs, all-day kindergarten, and in-school programs (the traditional school day plus time before and after school in an organized program). At the same time national and state standards are increasing the amount of academics younger and younger children must experience. Further, some states and school districts are using high-stakes tests to measure the learning of these standards; even Head Start has outcomes that are being assessed by national normed tests (Jones, 2003).

Thus our children are spending more time in intense academic pursuits. This necessitates a radical change in our approach to instruction: increasing variety and meaningful approaches, providing continual change of pace and use of different modalities, tapping into all of Howard Gardner's intelligences or talent areas (see Chapter 4) and extensive use of play. During the long day children need variety: individual work, physical activities, quiet activities, creative approaches, and focused learning; student-centered and directed approaches and less didactic instruction; and lots of opportunities for physical and social play—functional, constructive, dramatic, and games with rules (for older children), and solitary, parallel, associative, and cooperative social play.

Play is particularly beneficial during these longer days because of the characteristics of play, including child-initiated, child-directed, positive affect, and nonliterality. Thus play empowers the child to control part of the day himself or herself, which is absolutely critical; it also allows the child to create a fantasy reality that is closer to the child's emotional and psychological needs than the real, politically constructed school environment.

A variety of theories and models are well adapted for this change. One of the best is the Project Approach (Helm & Katz, 2001), which combines child-directed learning with a thematic approach. It also requires lots of hands-on learning with real experiences, use of the community, and parental input. Many of Dewey's approaches are applicable, and the Reggio Emilia approach would work well also (see Chapter 8, pp. 253–254). What is critical is that young children have the opportunity for exposure to new and challenging information and concepts, have plenty of opportunity for hands-on learning and exploration, and then be allowed to practice, manipulate, restructure, and reuse their new learning—what we call play.

Interestingly, at the middle and high school levels across the country the introduction of the block schedule (ninety-minute classes) and the modified block schedule has forced teachers to reject the traditional lecture approach to teaching. Similarly, the increased time young children spend in early childhood programs requires teachers and curriculum specialists to modify what we do with young children. If this is not done, by the time our children reach middle school, they will be so turned off from "school learning" that they will physically or mentally drop out.

## SUMMARY

Throughout the ages adults have formed ideas about play and childhood. These adult conceptions have affected the kinds of arrangements and opportunities for play presented to children. In recent years, there has been increasing recognition of the connection between play and child development, and the relationship of play with early childhood education. However, at the same time, new pressures for academic accountability and other societal trends have created formidable challenges to play's role in education.

We have seen in this chapter a sample of the efforts made to define and articulate play with respect to its characteristics and functions, as well as related behaviors such as exploration and imitation. New research such as the brain development work that has been done that has underscored the importance of the early years, as well as new conceptual analyses and theory construction pertaining to play and its benefits, not just for children but over the life course, adds ever more weight to the proposition that as a species we all need to play. Children need to play, and adults have a responsibility to make sure that they can and do. Unfortunately, this is often easier said than done. Persistent and new challenges must be faced and overcome.

Some of the more significant issues and trends in this regard are identified and discussed in this chapter. Some of these trends appear to be antithetical to play, such as the current push for early reading and academic standards in our schools and some anti-bullying school policies, which can unintentionally undermine positive physical and imaginative play. Reduction of outdoor playground time and recess elimination are yet other negative forces working against positive play in childhood, as can be the rise in organized sports for young children. The childhood obesity epidemic occurring worldwide can be attributed in part to curtailed opportunities for vigorous physical play.

Dynamic developments have affected play. New forms of play have been made possible by technology. New electronic toys, including so-called smart toys, video games, and play in the computer medium, are on the rise. Our beliefs about play, and children's play in particular, have undergone profound alterations in the last decade with the new technology and with globalization. Traditional play and games around the world are endangered by the encroachment of commercial marketing, which pushes for postmodern forms of play and entertainment characterized by competition and technology and fad and fashion and gadgetry. Early educators and others who work with young children and their families face new challenges in our increasingly multicultural world dominated by media influences and popular culture.

## PROJECTS AND ACTIVITIES

1. Find in literature and in art work depicting children at play in the eighteenth, nineteenth, and twentieth centuries, and compare what you infer about past play patterns with current patterns.
2. Visit a toy museum and study toys of yesteryear, noting the kinds of play that are possible with them and noting gender and age differences.
3. Interview a parent or teacher regarding what this person believes play is, the value of it, and what he or she does to influence it in children.
4. Interview children to learn their views about new versus traditional toys.

CHAPTER 2

# Theories of Play

## INTRODUCTION

Why devote an entire chapter to theories of play? Do abstract theories have much to do with how children actually play or how teachers utilize play in early education? These questions reflect the rather negative attitudes toward theory that run deep in American culture and the educational establishment (Beyer & Bloch, 1996). Our response to these questions is simple and direct: Theories about play are important because they are conceptual lenses through which we view play and that directly affect how we respond to children's play behavior (Beyer & Bloch, 1996). Further, knowing and believing the specific theories of play allow teachers to convince the many detractors—other teachers, administrators, and some parents—of the developmental and educational value of play. It makes those of us who believe in the critical value of play sound like we know what we are talking about!

Teachers' and researchers' theories about play influence what they notice when they watch children play, how they interpret these play behaviors, and how they respond to play. For example, several teachers might be watching as a small group of boys engage in a brief bout of rough-and-tumble play. One teacher, who has internalized a implicit theory that "good play" is quiet and orderly, views this play in a negative light. This teacher focuses on the aggressive aspects of the behavior and might think that the activity is actual fighting rather than playful behavior. Odds are high that this teacher will take steps to stop or redirect the boys' raucous play. Another teacher, who has read articles about the social benefits of rough-and-tumble activity and who has formed a theory of play that is influenced by evolutionary psychology, views this play in a much more favorable light. This second teacher notices the positive aspects of the play:

- The boys are inhibiting aggression and are not actually hurting each other.
- They are laughing, smiling, and expressing friendship toward each other.
- They are demonstrating knowledge of the rules for this type of play.

It is highly likely that the second teacher will simply stand back and watch this play episode, rather than trying to intervene or stop the activity.

Theoretical views are firmly anchored to historic, social, and political contexts (Beyer & Bloch, 1996). In this chapter we discuss three groups of theories about play:

- Classical theories, which date back to before the turn of the twentieth century and reflect that era's preoccupation with the theory of evolution and outmoded ideas about the mechanics of energy.
- Modern theories, which have dominated thinking about play during the past fifty to sixty years and place high value on scientific methodology and objectivity.
- Postmodern theories, which are just beginning to influence how play is viewed and reflect current interests in diversity, social justice, and the relative nature of truth and knowledge. These theories of social justice and diversity also apply to education and are therefore particularly relevant to our interest in play.

We hope that in examining this diverse spectrum of thinking about play, the reader will recognize and reflect upon the classical and modern theories that shape their current thinking about play. In addition, we hope that exposure to the newer postmodern theoretical perspectives may lead some readers to question the traditional views of play and education and lead to the development of new ways of viewing play and play's role in early education.

### FOCUS QUESTIONS

1. Why are theories of play important?
2. What are the key differences between classical and modern theories of play?
3. Why are classical theories of play still important today?
4. What are the main differences between modern and postmodern theories of play?
5. What is your own theory of play? To what extent is it based on classical, modern, and/or postmodern theories of play?

## CLASSICAL THEORIES

The so-called classical theories of play originated in European and North American thought around 1900. These theories can be characterized as armchair theories that rely on philosophical reflection and reasoning rather than on experimental research

**TABLE 2.1 Classical Theories of Play**

| Theory | Originator | Focus | Purpose of Play |
|---|---|---|---|
| Surplus energy | Schiller/Spencer | Energy dynamics | To eliminate surplus energy |
| Recreation | Lazarus | Energy dynamics | To regenerate energy expended in work |
| Recapitulation | Hall | Evolution | To eliminate ancient instincts |
| Practice | Groos | Evolution | To perfect instincts needed for adult life |

*Source:* Adapted from Johnson, Christie, & Yawkey, *Play and Early Childhood Development* 2/e. Published by Allyn and Bacon, Boston, MA. Copyright © 1999 by Pearson Education. Reprinted by permission of the publisher.

(Beyer & Bloch, 1996; Ellis, 1973). In addition, these theories reflect the ideas that were in fashion during that period: the notion that human energy has fluidlike properties and early versions of evolutionary theory (Sutton-Smith, 1980a).

The primary purpose of the classical theories was to explain why play exists and what purpose it serves. The four theories can be grouped by their primary focus. The surplus-energy and recreation theories viewed play as a means of energy regulation, whereas the recapitulation and practice theories attempted to explain play in terms of instincts and evolutionary theory. As Table 2.1 illustrates, these pairs of theories had contradictory explanations for how play affects energy and instincts.

## Surplus-Energy Theory

The surplus-energy theory of play can be traced back to Friedrich Schiller, an eighteenth century German poet, and Herbert Spencer, a nineteenth century British philosopher (Ellis, 1973). According to this theory, each living organism generates more than enough energy to meet its survival needs. Any energy that is left over after these needs have been met becomes surplus energy that builds up over time and must be expended. Play, which is viewed as frivolous behavior, serves an important purpose by enabling humans and animals to get rid of this surplus energy.

The surplus-energy theory has a commonsense appeal that might explain why it is still a widely held view. Anyone who has seen young children run out to the playground after a long period of inactive work in a classroom can see the element of truth to this theory. It also explains why children play more than adults (adults take care of children's survival needs, using up their own energy and leaving children with lots of surplus energy) and why animals that are higher on the evolutionary scale play more than lower animals do (the higher animals meet their survival needs more efficiently, resulting in more energy being left for play). However, the theory does have some difficulties. The idea that human energy has fluidlike properties that accumulate and then dissipate is completely discredited, and the theory has difficulty explaining why children continue to play when exhausted.

## Recreation Theory

In direct opposition to the surplus-energy theory, recreation theory postulates that the purpose of play is to restore energy expended in work (Ellis, 1973). According to its originator, German poet Moritz Lazarus, work uses up energy and creates an energy deficit. This energy can be regenerated either by sleeping or by engaging in an activity that is completely different from the work that caused the energy deficit. Play, viewed as the polar opposite of work, is the ideal way to restore energy lost in work.

As with the surplus-energy theory, recreation theory has a certain commonsense quality. If a person gets tired doing one type of activity, it helps to switch to something very different. This theory explains the popularity of adult recreational activities in today's information-oriented society. After a long day of stressful mental activity at one's job, a period of physical activity (such as weight lifting at the gym) or of mental activity of a different sort (such as a game of chess) can be rejuvenating. Early childhood educators have long recognized the principle behind the recreation theory and have structured the school day so that periods of sedentary mental work alternate with periods of active play. However, the recreation theory falsely predicts that because adults work more than children do and have larger energy deficits, adults should play more than children. In our own personal experience, this is rarely the case.

## Recapitulation Theory

At the end of the nineteenth century, scientists discovered that as the human embryo develops, it appears to go through some of the same stages that occurred in the evolution of the human species. At one point, for example, human embryos have physiological structures similar to fish gills. This discovery led to the notion of recapitulation, which maintains that ontogeny, the path of the development of individual organisms, recapitulates or reenacts phylogeny, the *evolutionary* development of the species.

G. Stanley Hall, an American psychologist, extended recapitulation theory to children's play (Ellis, 1973). Through play children reenact the developmental stages of the human race: animal, savage, tribal member, and so on. Hall believed that these stages of play follow the same order that they hold in human evolution. Thus children climb trees (our primate ancestors) before engaging in gang play (tribal humans). The purpose of play is to rid children of primitive instincts that are no longer needed in modern adult life. For example, sports such as baseball enable children to play out and eliminate ancient hunting instincts such as hitting with a club. The primitive quality of some of children's play and games (e.g., rough-and-tumble play) supports this view (Sutton-Smith, 2001), as does the commonly held notion that team sports teach important social rules of life that must supercede primitive individual urges. As with the other classical theories, recapitulation theory also has its contradictions. For example, children's play is very diverse and does not follow an orderly, linear progression. The theory also has difficulty explaining why children like to play with toys, such as cars and spaceships, which reflect modern technology rather than primitive activities (Ellis, 1973).

The current interest to use play to address problems of obesity in young children would seem to be a combination of the surplus energy theory, in that modern people still consume enough food for a physically active farming life yet now lead a much more sedentary existence, and the recapitulation theory, showing that children must play through an active farming stage in their play development to move into the current information age.

## Practice Theory

Philosopher Karl Groos believed that rather than eliminating instincts from the past, play serves to strengthen instincts needed for the future (Ellis, 1973). Newborn humans and other animals inherit a number of imperfect, partially formed instincts that are essential for survival. Play offers a safe means for the young of a species to practice and perfect these vital skills. The purpose of play is to develop skills required for adult life.

The best example of play as a means of practicing survival skills is the play fighting of young animals such as lions. This play develops skills that have obvious utility in adult life. Groos believed that his theory also applied to the play of humans. For example, Groos would contend that when children take on roles as parents during sociodramatic play, they have an opportunity to practice parenting skills that they will need in adult life. Building with blocks and other types of constructive play likely lead to the development of concepts and skills that will be useful during construction activities later in life. Of course, practice theory has difficulty explaining why children engage in the primitive types of play that lend support to recapitulation theory. For example, it may seem hard to imagine how climbing trees prepares one for adult challenges in modern technological societies.

## Connections with Modern Theories of Play

All of the classical theories of play have major shortcomings. They are limited in scope, explain only a small segment of play behavior and are based on outdated, discredited beliefs about energy, instincts, and evolution. In spite of these limitations the classical theories are still important. Many of today's adults subscribe to aspects of these theories, though they are probably not aware of it. For example, many people assume that if children engage in quiet, sedentary activity, they build up energy that needs to be let off through vigorous play. Beyer and Bloch (1996) point out that it is important for early childhood teachers to become aware of these implicit beliefs. They caution:

> Theories and practices often become so widely adopted or taken for granted that they become part of the "common sense" of an activity or organization; they may indeed become part of the "background information" that can be simply assumed. . . . When this happens, teachers' actions guided by such "common sense" will not be the subject of wide-ranging reflection and critique, and possible alteration. (p. 9)

Early childhood teachers need to become critical pedagogists—professionals who continually evaluate and reevaluate the rationale and purpose for what they do with young children. The front end of this process is to seek to know the underpinnings of our implicit beliefs. Then we can modify, improve, or reject them.

The classical theories of play also paved the way for the modern theories of play that we describe in the next section. For example, surplus energy theory paved the way for the attention given to metabolic energy in more modern evolutionary theories of play (Burghardt, 1984). Hall's recapitulation theory stimulated interest in systematically observing developmental trends in children's play, and his stages of play laid the groundwork for modern stage theories of play (e.g., Piaget's theory). Practice theory held that many play behaviors have adaptive significance, an idea that is reflected in more sophisticated form in modern theories of play and evolution (e.g., Bjorklund & Pellegrini, 2000; Sutton-Smith, 1997, 2001).

## MODERN THEORIES

Modern theories of play arose during the twentieth century amid an age dominated by the scientific method and positivism—the belief that there are fixed laws of nature and scientific truths that transcend historical and social context (Beyer & Bloch, 1996). This scientific movement had a tremendous effect on both the nature of theories themselves and the types of research that could be used to investigate and validate theories. Armchair theories and logical reasoning were no longer sufficient. Play theories should be able to explain and predict events and help us to understand the causes of play behavior. A good theory was expected to generate hypotheses that could be empirically verified via experimental research and/or precise observations.

The modern theories of play that arose during this period attempt to do more than simply explain why play exists. They also try to explain play's role in different aspects of child development and, in some cases, to specify conditions that must exist before the play can occur (Ellis, 1973). We have loosely organized these theories by the aspects of development on which they focus:

- Psychodynamic theories: emotional development
- Social learning theory: social development
- Cognitive theories: intellectual development

We also discuss modern versions of evolutionary theory, which cut across all areas of development, and we devote a special section to the theories of Brian Sutton-Smith, the more recent of which provides a bridge into postmodernism.

There are far too many modern theories of play for us to cover them all in sufficient detail in this chapter. Other modern theories, including attachment theory, Csikszentmihalyi's construct of flow, Bateson's communication theory, and arousal modulation theories will be covered in subsequent chapters in the context of topics that relate to each theory.

### Psychodynamic Theories

Psychodynamic theories attempt to explain play's role in children's emotional development. They were among the first modern theories of play and tended to dominate educational thinking about play during the first half of the twentieth century. Sigmund Freud was the founder of the psychodynamic movement. According to Freud (1961), play can help children to deal with unpleasant events and can help prevent these experiences from disrupting the child's emotional development. Play can have a cathartic effect, allowing children to rid themselves of negative feelings associated with traumatic events. Play can accomplish this cathartic function through two mechanisms:

- *Role-switching.* Play allows the child to suspend reality and switch roles from being the passive recipient of the bad experience to being the one who gives out the experience. For example, after being spanked by a parent, a child might spank a doll or pretend to punish a playmate. By reversing roles and becoming the active party, a child is able to transfer negative feelings to a substitute object or person.

- *Repetition.* By repeating a bad experience many times in play, the child divides the experience into small, manageable segments. In this manner the child can slowly assimilate the negative emotions associated with the event.

Brown, Curry, and Tinnich (1971) give an excellent example of the therapeutic value of repetitive play. Their preschoolers watched from their playground as a worker fell twenty feet to the ground and sustained serious injury. Initially, many of the children were deeply disturbed by the incident. They frequently, almost compulsively, engaged in dramatic play themes related to the accident (falling, death and injury, ambulances, hospitals). After many weeks the frequency of such play diminished, and the children no longer appeared to be bothered by the accident.

Erik Erikson (1950) extended the psychoanalytic theory of play by examining its contribution to normal personality development. According to Erikson, play progresses through stages that mirror children's psychosocial development. During the first year of life the child engages in play that focuses on the child's own body and leads to mastery of sensory and motor skills. During the second year the child's play extends to objects and toys. During the preschool years play expands further to include other people and contributes to the development of social skills. Through play children create model situations that help them to master the demands of reality and progress through each of Erikson's psychosocial stages.

As we discuss in Chapter 10, Carl Jung also developed his own version of psychoanalytic theory, which is used in sandplay therapy. Jung's theory focuses on the symbolic processes involved in play.

## Social Learning Theory

Behaviorists such as B. F. Skinner (1974) have demonstrated that behavior is often influenced by subsequent events. For example, if a behavior is followed by a pleasurable consequence, the behavior tends to be repeated. Such consequences are known as positive reinforcement. Behaviors that are not followed by positive reinforcement are less likely to occur again.

The social learning theory of Albert Bandura (1977) utilizes some of the basic principles of behaviorism and adds an emphasis on observational learning to better explain human learning. Bandura (1977, p. 22) states:

> Learning would be exceedingly laborious, not to mention hazardous, if people had to rely solely on the effects of their own actions to inform them what to do. Fortunately, most human behavior is learned observationally through modeling: from observing others one forms an idea of how new behaviors are performed, and on later occasions this coded information serves as a guide for action.

Children, of course, do not learn every behavior that they see modeled by other people. Social learning theory maintains that children are more likely to learn an observed behavior when (a) they perceive that the model has power and status, (b) they detect similarities between themselves and the model, (c) they have an opportunity to code and rehearse the behavior symbolically and then act it out, and (d) the behavior results in positive reinforcement of the model's behavior. According to Bandura, a model can be alive or symbolic (athlete, character in a book, or a TV/video/film character).

These principles help to explain why parents and teachers have such an important role in children's social development: Parents and teachers have power and status, thus children are likely to imitate and learn the behaviors that these adults model. Social learning theory also explains why children tend to learn behaviors modeled by their siblings and other playmates: Peers are perceived as similar to themselves, so children pay attention to the behaviors that are modeled by their playmates.

Social learning theory has led researchers for focus on the effects of parents, siblings, and peers on children's play patterns. These social influences on play are discussed in detail in Chapter 6. In addition, this theory provides a foundation for the connection between play and gender (Curry & Bergen, 1988). Parents treat their sons and daughters differently, reinforcing different types of play behavior and providing different toys and play materials (e.g., Maccoby & Jacklin, 1974; Rheingold & Cook, 1975). And teachers treat male and female students differently. In addition, peers also model and reinforce gender stereotypic behavior during play (Lamb, Easterbrooks, & Holden, 1980). For more information about play and gender, see Chapter 4.

## Cognitive Theories

In the late 1960s, as the cognitive theories of Piaget, Vygotsky, and others gained prominence in the United States, a major shift occurred in play theory and research.

➤ According to social learning theory, teachers play an important role in a child's social development.

Attention shifted from play's influence on social-emotional adjustment to its role in the development of children's thinking. This change was sudden and dramatic. In a historical review of play research, Sutton-Smith (1985) reported that during the 1940s and 1950s, a total of 107 scholarly books and journal articles focused on the connection between play and psychodynamic theory compared to only three works that focused on play and cognition. During the 1960s and 1970s the situation reversed, with only forty-three works on play focusing on psychodynamics and sixty-seven focusing on cognitive development.

**Piaget.** Between 1920 and the early 1950s Swiss psychologist Jean Piaget (1962) crafted a radically new theory of children's intellectual development. His theory, which took hold in the United States during the 1960s, proposed that children go through a series of distinct stages during which their thought processes become increasingly similar to those of adults. During the first two years of life infants' thinking is sensorimotor in nature and is focused on making connections between actions and objects. Their thinking is strictly limited to the here and now. Around the age of two, children develop the ability to use symbols and enter the preoperational stage. They become able to form mental representations of things and events that are not present. Their thinking, however, is not yet fully logical. For example, if water in a tall, thin glass is poured into a short, wide glass, preoperational children will be fooled by appearances into thinking that the amount of water has changed. By the time children are around age seven, they enter the stage of concrete operations in which their thinking becomes logical and systematic. In the water glass example they realize that the amount of water stays the same because while one dimension (height) gets shorter, the other (width) gets wider, or they can mentally reverse the action.

According to Piaget's theory, children engage in types of play that correspond to their current level of cognitive development (see Table 2.2). For example, children under two years of age engage in practice play that consists of repeated physical actions, often involving objects. When children enter the preoperational stage and gain the ability to use symbols, they begin to engage in symbolic (i.e., make-believe) and constructive forms of play. Once they are in the preoperational stage, their logical thinking ability enables them to engage in games with predetermined rules.

Play's role in learning and development in Piagetian theory is somewhat complex. On the one hand, his theory maintains that play, by its very nature, cannot contribute

**TABLE 2.2 Stage/Play Relationships in Piagetian Theory**

| Approximate Age | Cognitive Stage | Dominant Type of Play |
|---|---|---|
| Birth–2 years | Sensorimotor | Practice play |
| 2–7 years | Preoperational | Symbolic play<br>Construction play |
| 7–11 years | Concrete operational | Games with rules |

*Source:* Johnson, Christie, & Yawkey, *Play and Early Childhood Development,* 2e. Published by Allyn and Bacon, Boston, MA. Copyright © 1999 by Pearson Education. Reprinted by permission of the publisher.

to new learning. Piaget (1963) stipulated that for learning and development to take place, there must be adaptation. Adaptation requires a balance between two complementary processes: assimilation, in which the child incorporates new information into existing cognitive structures (often bending reality in the process), and accommodation, in which the child modifies existing cognitive structures to conform to the reality of the physical world. Piaget (1962) viewed play as an imbalanced state in which assimilation overpowers accommodation. This imbalance is most obvious in symbolic or make-believe play, in which children ignore the real identities of objects and use them to represent other objects that suit their play purposes. For example, a rope might be used as if it were a garden hose or a snake. Because of this imbalance between external and internal reality, Piaget maintained that play cannot engender genuine learning.

On the other hand, Piaget also believed that play allows children to practice and consolidate recently acquired concepts and skills through accommodation. Because assimilation is stronger than accommodation, this practice is critical. Piaget considered this practice and consolidation role of play very important because many newly acquired skills and concepts would be quickly lost if they were not repeated and integrated with other skills and concepts during play. In fact, Piaget believed that the process of play both internalized newly acquired skills and concepts, and prepared the child for the next learning spurt. In essence, he thought that play was critical as a condition for learning to occur. So although play does not have a cutting-edge role in new learning, it still has a central function in development.

**Vygotsky.** Lev Vygotsky, a Russian psychologist, believed that play has several roles in cognitive development. At the most basic level Vygotsky (1976) believed that make-believe play has a key role in abstract thought, enabling children to think about meanings independently of the objects they represent. According to Vygotsky, very young children are incapable of abstract thought because for them meaning and objects are fused together as one. As a result they cannot think about a horse without seeing a real horse. When children begin to engage in make-believe play and to use an object such as a stick to stand for another object (e.g., a horse), meaning begins to become separated from objects. The substitute object, the stick, serves as a pivot for separating the meaning "horse" from the horse itself. As a result, children soon become able to think about meanings independently of the objects they represent.

On a second level play can provide a context for socially assisted learning. Vygotsky (1978) distinguished between two levels of development: actual development, the level at which the child can perform on his or her own, and potential development, the level at which the child can perform with help from others. Vygotsky defined the zone of proximal development as the distance between the two. If temporary assistance or scaffolding is provided by an adult or more competent peer, the child is able to engage in activities that he or she could not do alone. This in turn extends the child's knowledge and skills to higher levels. Play is a natural context in which this type of scaffolding can occur.

On a third level Vygotsky viewed play as a self-help tool that promotes learning. He maintained that when children engage in play, they can create their own scaffolding, stretching themselves in such areas as self-control, cooperation with others, memory, language use, and literacy, using private speech to direct, control, and structure their play interactions (Bodrova & Leong, 1996). Vygotsky saw play as a kind of magnifying glass revealing potential new abilities before these same abilities became actualized in other situations. As a result, children engaged in play often seem ahead of themselves developmentally. Play promotes development by serving as a scaffold within the children's zone of proximal development, helping them to attain higher levels of functioning.

**Bruner.** Jerome Bruner's (1972) early theorizing about play focused on how play in childhood contributes to problem-solving abilities that are important later in life. So in some respects his early theorizing is an extension of the classical practice theory of play. Bruner pointed out that in play the means are more important than the ends. When playing, children do not worry about accomplishing goals, so they are free to experiment with novel combinations of behavior that they are not likely to try if they are under pressure to achieve a goal. Once these new behavioral combinations have been used in play, they are available for children to use in solving real-life problems. Therefore play promotes flexibility in problem solving by increasing children's behavioral options. Bruner makes a connection between the adaptive usefulness of play in human development and evolution. He argues that by having a prolonged period of immaturity, young humans have opportunities to develop flexible problem-solving skills through play. This in turn gives humans an advantage over other species. The field of evolutionary developmental psychology has proposed even more immediate adaptive advantages of playful behavior (see Box 2.1).

**BOX 2.1**

### Evolutionary Developmental Psychology

Evolutionary developmental psychology is an extension of Darwin's original theory of evolution that maintains that children face different adaptive pressures at different times in their development (Bjorkland & Pellegrini, 2000). Play is viewed as a mechanism that can help children to meet predictable challenges that arise during childhood. Unlike Bruner's (1972) theory that play helps children to develop flexibility in thinking that will come in handy later in life, evolutionary psychologists believe that play helps children develop specific skills that are useful and adaptive during childhood. For example, Bjorkland and Pellegrini (2000) explain how boys' rough-and-tumble play helps them to learn social signaling, work out issues of peer group leadership, and establish social hierarchies. Thus some of the benefits of play are immediately beneficial for children. They do not have to wait until adulthood to enjoy these benefits.

In his more recent work Bruner (1990, 1996) has emphasized the importance of play in the development of narrative modes of thinking. Bruner maintains that young children organize their knowledge in a sequential, narrativelike manner. This provides a direct connection between play and the verbal and logical parts of cognition. Sociodramatic play involves acting out child-constructed narrative stories. By participating in such play, children have opportunities to learn and perfect their narrative competencies, which in turn may facilitate their narrative thinking abilities.

**Neurobiological Perspective.** Recent technological innovations, such as the PET (positron emission tomography) scan, have enabled neuroscientists to study the brain at a cellular level. Brain imaging techniques allow researchers to record and display three-dimensional, color-enhanced images of the living brain as it processes information. Data from these new technologies have provided researchers with new information about the organization and functional operations of the brain and have led to the establishment of a neurobiological perspective on learning and development (Shore, 1997).

This perspective details the critical importance of the appropriate environmental impact on the brain of nourishment, stimulation, and responsiveness and the negative impact on the brain of lack of stimulation and of inappropriate types of stimulation, such as chaos, stress, and abuse. The brain is made up of brain cells and synapses, the connections between the cells. Most of the cells and synapses develop before birth and during the first three years of life. Together, these make up the neural network. However, the synapses that are used on a regular basis during the first ten years of a child's life through stimulation become permanent; those that are not used are eventually eliminated (Shore, 1997). Thus the first years of life are critical for the development, pruning, and maintaining of the brain circuitry.

For early childhood educators knowledge about how the brain develops suggests these important practices (Shore, 1997):

- Parents and teachers should engage in responsive interactions with their children that match the child's developmental level in all domains.
- Early childhood programs must be safe and without stress and must provide constant, responsive, and appropriate stimulation.
- Society needs policies that support mothers' security and nutrition, high-quality parent interactions, and early childhood programs that match the environment to each child's development.

"Brain research suggests that we have from birth to the age of ten to help children develop the wiring of the brain . . . strengthening the child's neural network then becomes the job of helping him or her make connections between these patterns and relationships and all new information" (Schiller, 1998, p. 50). When children play, they engage in a variety of activities that strengthen this neural network. Play is about the child interacting with the environment—both physical and social. Because children direct their own play activity—from initiating the activity and selecting the materials, place, and script to choosing coplayers and keeping the activity moving—there is always a match between the child and the physical and social environment. Play, by definition, is also interactive. The child responds to the environment, which then responds to the child, who then responds to the altered environment. Finally, one of the greatest attributes of play is its responsiveness. Because play is child directed, it is responsive to the unique needs of each child.

Another aspect of play's importance in strengthening the neural network is that play is an integrative behavior rather than an activity that focuses on one kind of learning. Thus a child who is involved in sociodramatic play uses language, engages in problem solving, develops social skills and competencies, uses abstract (symbolic)

➤ Play is about the child interacting with the environment—both physical and social. Play helps children develop the wiring of the brain.

thought, is emotionally involved in the activity, and uses several of his or her senses. To maximize brain development, the incoming stimulation must match the child's developmental level and should be in as wide an array as possible to nurture the largest number of synapses.

Clearly, brain research supports early childhood programs and homes that encourage and practice complex, rich forms of play. Further, they support environments that help the child progress through the various levels of social and cognitive play, moving to ever more complex and rich interactions between the child and his or her social and physical environments.

## Sutton-Smith's Theories of Play

Brian Sutton-Smith is undoubtedly the most influential play theorist of the second half of the twentieth century. This is reason enough to devote a separate section to his theoretical writings on play. In addition, his theories of play have evolved over the past thirty years, and this evolution in many ways provides a bridge between modern and postmodern theories of play.

Sutton-Smith's (1967) earliest theorizing about play is representative of modern play theories, with an emphasis on play's role in cognitive development. He emphasized the variability of play behavior and its positive impact on creativity and problem solving:

> When a child plays with particular objects, varying his responses to them playfully, he increases the range of his associations for those particular objects. In addition, he discovers many more uses for those objects than he would otherwise. . . . This is to say that play increases the child's repertoire of responses, an increase which has potential value (though no inevitable utility) for subsequent adaptive responses. (pp. 365–366)

Thus Sutton-Smith's early theorizing about play is similar to that of Bruner's (1972) in that both contend that play prepares children for adult life by developing flexibility.

More recently, Sutton-Smith (1998) proposed a more complex theory of play as *adaptive variability.* In this newer theory the variability of play is the key to its function in human development, just as physiological and behavioral variability is central in evolution (Gould, 1995). Because one cannot predict the future, with its radically changing environments, one cannot predict the skills and knowledge needed in those future environments. Therefore the adaptive potential of developing children (or evolving species) requires not exact and precise adaptations that can lead to rigidity of behavior. Rather, adaptability requires great flexibility in behavior or, in the words of Gould (1995), "quirkiness, sloppiness, unpredictability, and massive redundancy" (p. 44), characteristics that Sutton-Smith contends are the hallmarks of play behavior. Thus play is significant in human development because it ensures broad adaptive potential, although the connection between play and adaptation is random in nature and less direct than in his earlier theory.

At about the same time as he put forth the theory of adaptive variability, Sutton-Smith published the *Ambiguity of Play* (Sutton-Smith, 1997), in which he proposed that play theories can be analyzed and better understood in terms of the rhetorical assumptions and values that underlie them. He contends that there are rhetorics of play, each with its own set of values, play forms, and play theories:

- *Play as progress.* Emphasizes that children learn something useful from play. Major disciplines: biology, psychology, education.
- *Play as fate.* Refers to gambling and other games of chance. Major disciplines: economics, statistics, mathematics.
- *Play as power.* Is usually applied to sports and festivals, in which power is wielded or inverted and mocked. Major disciplines: history, sociology, anthropology, cultural psychology, multicultural education.
- *Play as identity.* Is often applied to festivals and celebrations which are viewed as creating group identity. Major disciplines: history, anthropology, folklore.
- *Play as imaginary.* Refers to the improvisation, creativity, and imagination found in the artistic endeavors. Major disciplines: arts (music, dance, visual arts, drama) and literature.
- *Play as self.* Emphasizes the role of play in shaping the personality and in providing peak subjective experience. Major disciplines: leisure studies, psychiatry, therapy.
- *Play as frivolity.* Refers to the activities of tricksters, clowns, and comedians. Major disciplines: history, folklore, popular culture.

Sutton-Smith contends that these rhetorics shape the science that researchers use to study play and greatly influence the way that play is interpreted and understood. He states:

> I wish to suggest that all play investigators tend to group themselves into a variety of persuasive discourses about the cultural value of their particular play science. It has long been argued that the supposedly objective science is not a neutral and value-free phenomenon but exists within a complex value system whose partialities do not derive only from science by itself but derive also from other values within the cultural system and the personality of the scholars. (Sutton-Smith, 1995, p. 277)

This implies that the truth that research reveals about play is relative to the rhetoric to which the investigators subscribe. Thus there are no absolute truths about play behavior—only relative ones. This is one of the key tenets of postmodernism, which is discussed in the next section.

## POSTMODERN THEORIES

Modern theories have, at their core, the assumption that there are universal, unchangeable truths that scientific research can reveal and prove. Postmodern theories challenge this assumption of objective truth, and claim that knowledge is always subjective, influenced by a researcher's values, beliefs, world view, and methodology. Beyer and Bloch (1996) explain:

> What scientists are able to observe depends not only on what is, in some sense, "out there," but on what instruments are available to aid their observations, what patterns of looking they are accustomed to, what purposes and values guide their perceptions and research endeavors, and what research community they belong to. There is more to the activities of scientists "than meets the eye," as what they see, how they see, and along what lines their perceptions and interpretations proceed affect what is regarded as significant. Observing and interpreting are in fact not two, separable activities. As "the known" and "the knower" are two aspects of the same process, a distanced, objective, separate perspective allowing us to see an objective reality becomes a fiction. (p. 20)

Research findings are always contextualized and relative to the researcher's points of view based on the researcher's beliefs, values, and social/political context. To a large extent researchers frame their research within the context of what is important to them: power, racism, developmental trajectories, and so on.

Sutton-Smith's (1997) rhetorics of play, discussed in the previous section, takes this notion of relative truth and applies it to play research. As is illustrated in the example about rough-and-tumble play at the beginning of this chapter, a researcher who views play as progress and another who subscribes to the play-as-power rhetoric could watch the same play episode and come away with vastly different interpretations and findings about play behavior. Possibly, the first researcher views everything from a developmental perspective and the second from the position of power: who has it and who does not.

In the sections that follow we introduce three of these new alternative approaches to play theory: sociocultural perspectives, critical theory, and chaos theory. Although none of these approaches have yielded a comprehensive theory of play, some important progress is being made. We will briefly describe each of these postmodern approaches to theory and highlight early attempts to apply these theoretical orientations to play.

## Sociocultural Perspectives

Sociocultural perspectives have existed for many years in the literature, but only recently have scholars put forth systematic and coherent formulations of this approach to researching and understanding children's play. Also, educators and others who work with children and their families have become increasingly eager to better understand culture in relation to development and behavior. Cultural factors simply cannot be ignored if we hope to build more inclusive theories of learning and socialization and if we wish to provide culturally compatible human services, including early childhood education for diverse groups of children (Roopnarine, Shin, Donovan, & Suppal, 2000).

The notion that human development must be understood in context is often associated with Bronfenbrenner's (1979) theoretical model, which contends that development is a joint function of the person and the environment. Bronfenbrenner's bioecological view posits that it is important to take into account contextual factors ranging from the broader cultural level to the immediate environments of everyday life. These different layers of context interact with each person's individual characteristics.

Examining the similarities and differences across different societies is a cultural expansion of Bronfenbrenner's bioecological model. Whiting and Whitings' (1975) classic "six cultures" research and later work conducted at the Laboratory of Human Development at Harvard (Whiting, 1980) investigated how particular cultural practices and institutions (as well as a culture's history, climate, and geography) are related to specific behaviors such as play. Helen Schwartzman's (1978) anthropological work, which will be discussed in Chapter 6, is a standout example of play research done within the spirit of this tradition.

Recently, play scholars such as Artin Goncu have attempted to articulate what it means to have a sociocultural perspective on play. Goncu and his colleagues see play as cultural activity and interpretation that require interdisciplinary thinking and research in order to grasp the meaning of children's play in a cultural context. Play behaviors are investigated as activities in social contexts that are themselves shaped by economic, social, and political factors operating within the larger culture. In any culture or *cultural community* (i.e., any subset of a culture—usually preferred to the term *culture* so as to avoid a false overgeneralization to a whole culture), we need to find out the significance of play according to adults inside the culture and how beliefs and values concerning play are communicated to children. For example, do adults encourage play, engage in play with the children, or merely tolerate play? These beliefs and values are reflected in the different ways in which adults make available materials, time, and space for children's play or otherwise expend their own energy to have play happen in a cultural community. Finally, sociocultural researchers strive to discover how children represent their experiences of the world in their play. For example, what adult roles and activities do children enact in their dramatic play (Goncu, Tuermer, Jain, & Johnson, 1999)?

The sociocultural perspective not only seeks to illuminate the meaning of play and nonplay behaviors in a cultural community through activity setting analyses, but also attempts to overcome the dualism of the person and the environment by blending them together, with culture as the meeting point of the two. Conventional developmental psychology sees nature and nurture, or the person and the environment, as separate but as interacting with each other. The sociocultural perspective rejects the implied dualism of this interactionism, in which culture is often treated as an independent variable external to the individual. Instead, a person's psyche or consciousness and what's happening "out there" in the environment are viewed as two sides of the same coin. In other words, according to the sociocultural perspective culture happens "between the ears" (in the individual person's psyche) as much as it involves everything that is occurring in the external surroundings. Experiences represent a blending of the person and the context (Shweder, 1991).

A sociocultural approach to the study of play can help us to decide which ideas can be transported from one cultural community setting to another. Also, a sociocultural perspective can help to inform the implementation of culturally congruent curriculum in early education. Knowledge of children's activity settings and awareness that they form a social ecology influenced by broader cultural institutions and values should help to increase positive interethnic communication between teacher and child and between teacher and parent.

## Critical Educational Theory

Critical theory views education (and educational activities such as play) in the broader sociopolitical context of our culture. In particular, critical theorists are concerned with how education perpetuates gender, class, and race inequality in a society (Beyer & Bloch, 1996). According to this view, traditional education benefits the middle and upper classes by conditioning lower-class children to passively accept their lowly position within the world of haves and have-nots. Cultural studies, a branch of critical theory, investigates the power relationships in a culture in order to emancipate its members from the many forms of oppressions that are perceived to exist within the broader American culture. Researchers who hold this viewpoint are less likely to want to improve education as to emancipate members of groups who are oppressed in some way by the educational system (Gall, Borg, & Gall, 1996). Critical theorists favor pedagogical approaches that give children control over their own learning, that are closely linked to their own cultural experiences, and that help children to perceive and address inequalities in their school and society.

Because inequalities in a society are based on power and because schools are an extension of that society, critical theory tends to focus on the locus of power in play activities. Take, for example, how critical theory might view the research of Nancy King (1979, 1982) on children's conceptions of play and work. In her initial study, King (1979) discovered that kindergartners viewed the same activity as either play or work, depending on the locus of control. If children initiated block building on their own and were in control of the building, they thought of the activity as play—consistent with the definition of play we proposed in Chapter 1, in which play is child initiated. If, on the other hand, the teacher ordered children to play with the blocks or told them what to build, children thought of the activity as work.

Interestingly, when King (1982) repeated the study with fifth-graders, she found that choice and control were no longer important in distinguishing between work and play. Fun and pleasure became the crucial variables. If these older students enjoyed an activity, they thought of it as play. King hypothesized that this shift was due in part to teachers' labeling enjoyable academic activities as play. Critical theory suggests a more sinister explanation: Perhaps years of schooling have led these older children to accept the fact that they have little power or control over classroom activities. So fifth-graders have given up on free choice and focus on the emotional outcomes of activities. If a teacher-controlled activity is fun, it is considered to be play.

In a subsequent investigation, King (1987) examined "illicit" play in elementary school classrooms. This is play that happens behind the teacher's back. Examples include passing notes, shooting wads of paper or rubber bands, making faces, giggling, sharpening pencils needlessly, pretending to chew gum, and being intentionally late to class. Teachers try to suppress this type of play but rarely succeed. King contends that illicit play provides children with a sense of autonomy and control in an adult-dominated situation. The more teacher-centered the curriculum is, the more likely children are to engage in illicit play. This is another example of how power relationships can influence children's play activities.

## Chaos Theory

Chaos theory challenges the "modern" conception that the world is orderly, linear, and predictable. In contrast, chaos theory views the world as complex, nonlinear, interdependent, unpredictable, and seemingly chaotic (Goerner, 1994). There actually is order underlying this apparent chaos—a pattern of interrelationships that are constantly emerging and changing—but this order is very difficult to identify and understand.

➤ King (1987) examined illicit play in elementary school classrooms.

Vander Ven (1998) gives the following educational example. A simplistic modern educational assumption is that there is a linear relationship between the amount of time that children spend in school and the amount that children learn. A logical hypothesis emerging from this assumption is that if the school day were lengthened, children's learning would increase. However, chaos theory postulates that many factors besides time in school affect learning, including student engagement, the relationship between what is being taught and cultural values, and occurrences outside of school. Thus it may happen that if students spend the extra time engaging in non-culturally-relevant, passive drill-and-practice activities, children may actually learn less if the school day is extended because they will become less engaged in learning. So the multitude of factors that affect learning give the impression that learning is chaotic and unpredictable, but there really is a pattern of relationship under the surface. Of course, factors affecting cultural relevancy and engagement change, so it is possible that longer exposures to drill and practice activities could decrease learning in other situations. And because a significant percentage of school children fail, it could be argued that if the length of the school day is increased, more children will fail.

Another example of the application of the chaos theory is memory and recall of experience. We used to believe that everyone used the same approach and the same structures to remember new information and that we all follow the same pathways to retrieve information from our memory when needed. Now it is believed that each of us creates our own unique series of webbed pathways in our minds (Ormrod, 1999). Each of us has an idiosyncratic method to store and retrieve information, so comparing the approach of several people would make the process appear to be totally chaotic.

Vander Ven (1998) claims that characteristics of play reflect its "chaotic capacities":

- *Representational/symbolic.* Play allows the player to let one thing stand for another. . . . Play is an ideal medium for representing, and hence experiencing, chaotic content and concepts.
- *Meaning-making.* Through enabling the player to connect various elements of experience, play is personally meaningful and, in a constructivist sense, enables players to make meaning out of their experience as they combine various aspects into larger configurations.
- *Dynamic.* By its very nature play embraces continual change.
- *Connectionist.* Play enables the players to make connections among themes, situations, and persons.
- *Creative.* Play, with its combinatory, integrative aspects, both developing and reflecting divergent thinking, enables creativity to take place in the construction of new patterns and configurations. (pp. 122–123)

Thus play may equip children to thrive in a complex, rapidly changing, chaotic world.

Of course, the degree to which play is adaptive depends on a multitude of factors, making it difficult if not impossible to find direct, simple relationships between play behavior and positive developmental outcomes. Many educators argue that in the information age, it no longer makes sense to learn specific facts and discrete content. Rather, we need to be teaching children how to find, order, and evaluate needed information. The chaos theory of play highlights these skills and dispositions as important.

## Implications for Teachers

As we emphasized in the introduction to this chapter, theories of play are important. Theories of play guide what teachers notice when they watch children play, how they interpret play behavior, and their actions related to play. Also, a teacher's theory of play generally determines whether the teacher believes in the developmental and educational value of play or whether he or she believes that it is essentially off-task behavior. In addition, the theories themselves have some obvious implications for educational practice. Box 2.2 presents a series of "sound bites" that represent the most obvious educational extensions of the theories discussed in this chapter.

**BOX 2.2**

### Theoretical Sound Bites: Some Obvious Implications for Practice

**Classical Theories**

*Surplus energy.* Alternate periods of sedentary activity with periods of active play.

*Recreation.* Provide children with regularly scheduled periods of active, physical play to restore energy expended in mentally taxing, academic activity.

*Practice.* Encourage children to engage in play activities that have direct connections with skills and abilities needed in adult life (e.g., incorporate literacy into dramatic play).

**Modern Theories**

*Psychodynamic.* Encourage children to engage in play themes that allow children to enact powerful roles and themes that help them to work through negative emotions associated with bad experiences.

*Social learning.* Use modeling as a means to enrich and extend children's play.

*Piaget.* Provide lots of time for young children to play so that they have opportunity to practice and consolidate newly learned concepts and skills.

*Vygotsky.* Interact—without direct intervention—with children during play, helping them to do activities that they could not do on their own.

*Bruner.* Encourage children to engage in sustained sociodramatic play to increase their narrative competence.

**Postmodern Theories**

*Sociocultural.* Select play materials and themes paying attention to play and non-play behaviors in activity settings, realizing how cultural values are implicated.

*Critical.* Provide children with choice and some control over classroom activities so that they view learning as play.

*Chaos.* Find ways to reduce structure in the classroom: Create flexible schedules, encourage children to mix and match materials and tools from different centers, use a project and web approach to curricula, encourage children to evaluate their own work, and blur the distinction between work and play.

On the basis of direct personal experience, professional reading, and education, every early childhood educator develops her or his own personal theory of play which usually combines elements from several of the major theories discussed in this chapter, plus some unique ideas. This personal theory then becomes the lens through which each educator views and interacts with play. Box 2.3 presents Francis Wardle's personal theory of play, as presented in his recent book *Introduction to Early Childhood Education: A Multidimensional Approach to Child-Centered Care and Learning* (Wardle, 2003a).

**BOX 2.3**

## Wardle's Theory of Play

**by Francis Wardle**

While I am not recognized as having a specific play theory, I want to present my perspective which incorporates elements of several of the theories discussed in this chapter, plus my own original ideas. First, children progress through stages of play and through levels (complexity) of play. As children master new concepts and practice them through repetitive play, they progress to the next level. In essence, children create their own curriculum. Because children like to learn new information and want to master new tasks (ever watched a child persist in learning to ride a bike?), and because they hate to be bored, children self-diagnose what they know and what they can learn next. Play provides the ultimate curriculum for social, physical, and cognitive advancement. Second, by using materials, interactions with others, and mastery of tasks and skills to progress through levels of play, children develop a sense of control over their environment and a feeling of competence and enjoyment. And play provides a natural integration among all the crucial brain functions and learning domains, an integration that is often missing in teacher-directed instruction. Research shows that integration is very important to brain development (Shore, 1997).

Play is also a very effective way for children to accumulate a vast amount of basic knowledge about the world around them—knowledge needed in language literacy, math, science, social studies, and the arts. When playing with sticks in the sand, a child learns about the properties of sand, how posts are used for building, erosion by water, the effect of moisture on materials, the impact of the wind, and the nature of gravity. A child playing with tadpoles in a pond learns about the cycle of life, the properties of water, and concepts related to water safety and drowning. In sociodramatic play, children experiment with words, phrases, and idioms they have heard and learn more complex ways to express themselves and relate to others.

*Source:* Wardle (2003a).

There are several important advantages in early childhood educators' being aware of your own personal theory of play. First, being aware of your own perspective on play alerts you to what you focus on when you watch children play and, conversely, what you are not attending to. This might lead you to begin noticing important aspects of play that were previously overlooked. Second, this awareness allows you to reflect on some of you personal assumptions and biases toward play and might lead you to challenge and perhaps modify some implicit beliefs. Finally, theoretically awareness might also lead you to discover that some your current teaching practices are not fully aligned with your beliefs about play, and this might result in positive changes in your instruction. Having a solid theoretical framework for play enables you to effectively argue for the value of play with administrators, teachers, and parents. Box 2.4 provides a framework that will help you to identify your own personal theory of play. We encourage you to go through this exercise now, near the beginning of this book, and then do it again when you have finished reading the book. It will be interesting to examine how your views on play have changed as you have learned more about play, development, and early education.

**BOX 2.4**

### Build Your Own Theory of Play

Carefully reflect on these questions:

1. Why do you think children play?
2. What do you believe is the purpose of children's play?
3. How does this purpose work? How does it increase flexibility or imagination, social skills, or whatever you believe to be the purpose of play?
4. What is the relationship between play and learning?
5. To what extent should young children play? For what ages is play important?
6. Should play be encouraged in early childhood programs?

Summarize your responses in five to seven short sentences.

## SUMMARY

This chapter began with a discussion about what theories are and why they are important. We argued that theories are conceptual lenses that influence how we view, understand, and respond to children's play behavior. Theories can also enable one to defend play's role in early education. Therefore it is important that teachers have a well-thought-out theory of play.

Next we presented three major groups of play theories in a rough chronological ordering:

- Classical theories, which date back to before the turn of the last century and are concerned with the overall purpose of play
- Modern theories, which have dominated thinking about play during the latter half of the twentieth century and have resulted in a large body of scientific research on play's role in different aspects of child development
- Postmodern theories, which have recently emerged and reflect current interests in diversity, social justice, and the relative nature of truth and knowledge

Finally, the chapter concluded with a discussion of the practical implications of these theories for early childhood education. We encourage readers to closely examine the theories discussed in this chapter and throughout the book and develop their own theory of play to guide how they view play, facilitate play, and integrate play with the rest of the early childhood curriculum.

## PROJECTS/ASSIGNMENTS

1. Interview a preschool or kindergarten teacher and ask them about their personal theory of play. Does this theory contain elements of classical, modern, or postmodern theories of play?
2. Do the activity, *Build Your Own Theory of Play,* on page 53. Which theoretical perspectives are reflected in your theory?
3. Divide your class into five groups. Have four groups represent major modern play theorists (e.g., Freud, Piaget, Vygotsky, and Sutton-Smith). The fifth group can represent the postmodern point of view. After reviewing your group's theory, pick one student to represent this theoretical perspective. The five "theorists" can then have a debate over the nature of play and its role in development and education.
4. Read an article on play in an early childhood education journal (e.g., *Young Children, Childhood Education, Children and Families, Day Care and Early Education,* etc.). Discuss the theory of play that underlies the article.

CHAPTER 3

# Play Development and Assessment: Birth to Eight Years

## INTRODUCTION

Play and development go hand in hand. In early childhood education and other fields in which young children are the major concern, attention is usually focused on how play contributes to the development of the child. However, before we get to the important question of the function of play (Chapter 5), in this chapter we spotlight the structure of play and its developmental course during the years from birth to eight years. Certainly, we endorse the view that when children are playing well, they are developing well. We need to understand the relationship between play and development and understand how contextual and cultural factors can influence it. We also need to appreciate the nature and extent of individual variation. To achieve these understandings, it is necessary first of all to have a sound grasp of how different play behaviors themselves develop.

In this chapter we trace the development of play behaviors in the motor, the object, and the symbol domains for the individual child, describing major levels and milestones in each general type of play. Social play development is also described, both for the individual child and for the group. Issues concerning peer culture, play transitions, and group entry skills are discussed. Finally, information and suggestions about play assessment and documentation are presented as an important complement to the conceptual and empirical descriptions of play development provided in this chapter.

## FOCUS QUESTIONS

1. What is the typical developmental sequence in physical and motor play, locomotor play, and physical play fighting during the childhood years?
2. What is the developmental sequence in object play during the early childhood years?
3. What are some characteristics of symbolic play development during the early childhood years?
4. How does social play unfold developmentally?
5. What should a teacher realize about children's peer culture?
6. What is social competence? What can the teacher do to help a child with poor play entry skills?
7. What are the purposes of play observation, recording, and documentation? What are some major observation methods to assist play assessment? What is the role of technology?
8. What are some useful ways of communicating play assessment data to other interested adults, such as parents, other teachers, and school administrators?

## PLAY DEVELOPMENT

We believe that there is a two-way relationship between play and development. Development is served *by* play, and development is seen *in* play. But how do we define development? Development means progressive change over time, growth marked by improvement. With development behaviors become more efficient, predictable, and coordinated. In addition, abilities and skills manifest greater flexibility and scope. Development is not simply an additive process showing a quantitative increase in a behavior or an ability. Development is transformational, often involving a qualitative change to a higher level of structural organization and functioning.

An example from the play literature is the developmental sequence from functional to constructive to dramatic play. Change in play to the next level incorporates the elements of the lower levels. Constructive play incorporates the use of functional play skills but elevates the play activity to a higher level in which children are not just playing with the materials but they are using them creatively in combination to achieve play constructions. Constructive play is more than adding up separate functional play acts. Likewise, constructive play actions and products can be integrated into a dramatic level of play marked by make-believe. In this symbolic play level children transform the materials imaginatively and introduce play narrative and pretend themes. This higher level play emerges from and includes but is more than functional and constructive play.

It is important to recognize that development can be long-term or short-term. The above example of a developmental sequence from functional to constructive and then to dramatic play in early childhood can represent long-term development. This is the case when we are thinking of children going through stages in which new play abilities emerge with increasing age. This shift over a long period of time, as in age-related developmental stages of play, is termed ontogenesis. The above functional-constructive-dramatic play sequence can also be an example of short-term development. This is the case when we are thinking of children exhibiting changes in play states. Some changes in states can be discerned over very small periods of time within a single play session. With our example children might initially engage in functional play with materials such as blocks, stacking them up and knocking them down. They might then shift to constructive play in which they use the blocks to build a structure such as a roadway. Once the structure is built, children might then use it as a setting for dramatic play (e.g., pretending to drive toy cars down the roadway). The term microgenesis refers to these short-term sequences in play, consisting of different temporary play states and the transitions between them.

## How Play Develops

Play is a complex phenomenon, and its development is even more complex. In its expression there are recognizable forms or types of play. Multiple forms can occur in the same play episode. Category systems have sought to divide play not only into types, but also into subtypes. Play types and levels have often been arranged or calibrated on an ordinal scale to represent development. Additional play qualities, such as tempo, intensity, and style of performance, have sometimes found their way into the coding schemes invented by play researchers. Because of this complexity, play development is difficult to articulate conceptually and to assess empirically.

Age-related qualitative changes in play during the early years are well documented, such as the Piagetian play stages of sensorimotor play, symbolic play, and games with rules. Developmental changes also occur *within* each play category. The symbolic play exhibited by toddlers, for instance, is much less sophisticated than the symbolic play displayed by the average kindergartener. Play ontogenesis occurs within each play behavior category, and different play forms emerge sequentially, forming more complex developmental patterns. Information about developmental norms and milestones (ontogenesis) in play development is also needed for preparing developmentally appropriate play environments and for making accurate predictions about how children will play, both as individuals and as groups.

Knowledge about short-term play changes within play episodes is useful for anticipating play behaviors and in making situational arrangements or adjustments to optimize children's play in a given circumstance. In ongoing play, for example, teachers may introduce or remove play props consistent with where children seem to be in their exploration and play cycles.

Applying the concepts of play ontogenesis and microgenesis adds to our ability to comprehend and evaluate what takes place sequentially within a play episode—both for the individual child at a certain developmental level and for a group of children of a given age composition. The way in which children in a play group go through play phases or cycles will vary as a function of their developmental ages, the kind of play activity setting they are in, what they are trying to accomplish, and who their playmates are. We need to be adept observers and interpreters of both individual and group play.

### Contexts of Play Development

Descriptions of the development of play found in the literature can often seem too idealized and simple. Previously, descriptions were often linear, one-dimensional, and decontextualized, or isolated from the cultural and peer group settings. Nowadays play experts are more mindful of the ecocultural contexts that influence the developing child. A multifaceted perspective is taken to view play behavior and play development within context, related to situations, culture, language, and the history of social relationships. (See Chapter 6 for further discussion.) Furthermore, knowledge about developmental trends must be integrated with information and understanding about individual differences (Chapter 4), disabilities (Chapter 10), educational interventions (Chapters 7, 8, and 9), and popular culture, media, and technology (Chapter 11).

## DEVELOPMENT OF MOTOR PLAY

Motor play includes all physical play and manipulative play. This includes exploratory play, or exploring one's body, another person's body, or objects in the environment. Sometimes motor play has been called practice play, particularly with reference to infancy and toddlerhood. Second, motor play includes locomotor play, which refers to the use of large muscles and the action of locomotion, or moving about. Sometimes locomotor play has been called physical exercise play. Finally, motor play includes rough-and-tumble play, also called *play fighting* or *roughhousing*. It is more precise to call it physical play fighting to distinguish it from symbolic play fighting, which is seen in war toy play or in video games or computer games with violent themes. However, it is not unusual for physical and symbolic play fighting to co-occur, as when groups of children are pretending to be armies at war in their rough-and-tumble play.

A caveat: Motor play is a broad category or dimension of play. It is the first of four such general categories we examine in this chapter: object play, symbolic play, and social play will follow. An important caveat is that often one or more of these dimensions can apply to any single instance of a play behavior. For example, children often integrate symbols and social behavior into their motor play. Our separation of play into four general play categories is a heuristic device to communicate important information about play development. The four categories also match the way the research literature has generally analyzed play development. Nevertheless, we need to remember that the categories are not necessarily mutually exclusive. Overlap exists and is part of play's complex nature.

### Physical and Manipulative Play

Even the earliest physical and manipulative play requires rudimentary motor skills. The motor abilities of newborns include the general ability to move body parts in an uncoordinated and random way (waving arms or turning the head) and involuntary and finely coordinated reflexes. Healthy human babies progress rapidly to gain control over their bodies, enabling them to be upright, mobile, and able to explore their surroundings in just a matter of months. They can use these new skills as a means to other ends, including goal-oriented activities and play.

During the first year of life infants develop hand skills involving grasping and manipulation that make play with objects possible—and also help babies to acquire informal, practical, or intuitive understandings of objects, actions, three-dimensional space, and cause-and-effect relations. From age one to two years children exhibit ever more elaborate forms of manipulative play; for example, they can turn pages of a large picture book in a variety of ways: from front to back, back to front, one page at time, two pages at a time, and so on. From age two to three years there is rapid physical and manipulative play development. This can be seen both in gross motor activity involving large objects and use of large muscles for mobility and in fine motor activity involving hand muscles, hand-eye coordination, and the use of small objects. This physical and manipulative play progression depends on physical development, experience, and practice.

With age children demonstrate further developmental progression in motor and physical skills and physical play. They can walk and run easily, surely, and with good balance, and they can tiptoe and stand on one foot. Tricycle riding and playing with other vehicles bring great pleasure. Young preschoolers climb by putting one foot on each step. From four to five years of age, children achieve further motor mastery, allowing for greater varieties of play. They can skip, climb, hop, and run. They enjoy chasing games and almost any kind of athletic activity, including rough-and-tumble play. Some children are able to ride a small bicycle equipped with supportive training wheels. Children can button clothing and put puzzles and simple constructions together.

Further physical development from five to six years of age makes possible new forms of motor play: jumping rope, doing acrobatics, and trapeze tricks. With the advances in their fine muscle development, children can cut, trace, draw, paste, and string beads. Many children can use a knife, although they cannot cut very well. Manipulative play overlaps with object play to a great extent.

## Locomotor Play

Running, leaping, and chasing are examples of locomotor play. Running away from or after someone is the most common example of this play. Often faster runners will purposefully slow down (i.e., self-handicapping) and allow themselves to be caught, and there is often role reversal when groups of children take turns pursuing and being pursued. Usually, the locomotor play is of short duration, and the running distance is short.

With increasing age children become more efficient runners, able to reduce extra unnecessary movement while running (Haywood, 1986). Because locomotor play or play chasing often happens independently of play fighting, perhaps it is useful to consider this play on its own merits (Power, 2000). More research studies of play in which this particular play form receives its own billing would be useful, given increasing childhood obesity rates nowadays and the need to do something about this serious social and medical problem.

Power (2000) suggests, in his excellent review of research, that locomotor play (and physical activity overall) increases and then decreases during childhood. This inverted U-shaped developmental trend in locomotor play seems to peak during the school years. For example, Pellegrini (1995) found little differences in play chasing between sixth and eighth graders. By this age chasing occurred with low frequency, compared to findings from a separate study with third graders (Pellegrini & Davis, 1993).

## Rough-and-Tumble Play

Rough-and-tumble play is locomotor play that overlaps with social and pretend play. In rough-and-tumble play the bodies of playmates and the actions of playmates become a focal object of play, and children pretend to hurt each other rather than engaging in real aggression. That is, rough-and-tumble play is play fighting, not actual fighting. This form of play aggression may involve physical movements such as mock wrestling, running, chasing/fleeing, kicking, pouncing, piling on, pushing, open-hand hitting, and poking, as well as loud noises (Sutton-Smith et al., 1988). In a rough-and-tumble play episode typically several children are involved, and there are role reversals—from being the bad guy to being the good guy to being the bad guy again—which allow children to share powerful roles as well as being the hapless victim (Pellegrini, 1991). Gender differences are sharp, as will be discussed in Chapter 4. This is primarily a "boy" form of play.

Play fighting in animals starts sometime in infancy, peaks in the juvenile period, and gradually disappears after that (Power, 2000). This inverted U-shape developmental function also seems to describe what takes place in humans. Rough-and-tumble play first is seen in two-year-olds, increases in frequency of occurrence in early

➤ Rough-and-tumble play is play fighting, not aggression. It is an important play behavior, especially for boys.

and middle childhood, and then drops off in adolescence. It becomes more vigorous and rougher with age (Pellegrini & Smith, 1998).

## DEVELOPMENT OF OBJECT PLAY

By the end of the early childhood period the child shows a great deal of skill in using objects during play. The child is able to use tools, participate in supervised cooking activities, and create elaborate constructions from blocks and other materials. The child can finish rather complicated puzzles and other object displays and often exhibits considerable problem-solving strategies using objects in play, including computers. Furthermore, these skills are frequently exhibited in social settings, requiring additional capabilities.

A theory of play called arousal modulation theory focuses on motivating factors in the external world that stimulate the child to play. This theory is particularly useful for understanding play with objects in a particular situation at a given time. Stimulus characteristics such as novelty, complexity, and manipulability motivate the child to interact with objects. This interaction can take several forms. For example, Hutt (1966), based on Berlyne's (1960) work on arousal and motivation, distinguishes between exploring and playing with objects. Exploration happens when the child seems to be asking the question "What does this object do?" Play occurs when the child tries to discover "What can I do with this object?" In this section, we focus on the latter, in which children play with objects and use these objects in ways in which they were not originally intended to be used.

How are objects played with? There are two dimensions of object play that have been investigated developmentally. First, quality of play has been examined according to how sequenced, integrated, representational, and appropriate the activity is. Second, object play has been studied in children before and after the emergence and consolidation of children's symbolic capacities. The difference between presymbolic and symbolic object play is developmentally significant.

### Object Manipulation and Exploratory Play

As we discussed in the section on motor play, remarkable changes in how babies play with objects occur during the first months of life. There is considerable overlap between motor and object play throughout the early years. As we noted earlier, the newborn is equipped with reflexes and sensory capacities but does not know how to play with objects. Object play develops as a result of experience. Object play during the first year progresses from repetitious and undifferentiated activity to more organized and sequenced action patterns.

Piaget (1962) described the development of mastery or exercise play while advancing his theories about cognitive development during the sensorimotor period. For Piaget objects direct the infant's actions at first and then come under the control of the infant, providing the child with an opportunity to use action schemes. Infants repeat actions on objects and generalize these actions to other objects. Piaget uses two categories of assimilation: reproductive assimilation (repeating actions on an object) and generalizing assimilation (extending these actions to additional objects) to describe this behavior. For example, an infant might repeatedly drop a rattle, varying the height each time (reproductive assimilation), and then do the same type of varied dropping with a small ball (generalizing assimilation). While not goal-directed, these early behaviors are pleasurable, and they define the essence of play for Piaget. During the second year the child is able to construct new schemes from combinations of past experiences. Ritualization and conventional use of objects increase in frequency.

The amount of object exploration has been reported to increase from early life to the preschool and early school years. However, studies that have looked at how much time children spend in exploratory play have reported inconsistent research findings. This seems to be due to differences in the nature of the stimulus items used in the studies. Where more complex objects are involved, there are reported increases in this behavior, and when less complex objects are used, there are reported decreases in exploratory play. Still, a consistent developmental trend in the way children engage in object exploration and play has been found: With increasing age exploratory and playful object use becomes more systematic, orderly, and planned (Power, 2000).

In general, research has indicated that object manipulation during the early years advances from oral (mouthing) or large motor handling of a single object to the coordinated use of both hands and eyes with multiple objects. Manipulative object play becomes more focused and sustained to exploit the object affordances (an object's potential for functional or symbolic use). There is increasing ability to focus on multiple aspects of the same object and to play with more than one object at a time using both hands. Mouthing and large motor actions such as banging decrease (Power, 2000).

The developmental transition of object play into symbolic play or presymbolic to symbolic action schemes has been studied. For example, Fenson, Kagan, Kearsley, and Zelazo (1976) compared the object play from ages nine to eighteen months. Motor schemes such as mouthing and banging objects predominated in the youngest infants. By 13½ months infants used objects functionally, grouping or sorting similar objects and making simple pretenses that were self-directed. Like Piaget these researchers concluded that object play in infancy becomes decentered (less self-centered) and more integrated. There was also an increase in combinational play and a change from functional or motor use of objects to conventional applications.

## Constructive Play

The period from infancy to the preschool years is marked by the child's growing sense of mastery. Children gain greater familiarity with objects and materials through their exploratory and manipulative play and a heightened personal control over their actions on and with objects. They become increasingly able to engage in functional play and constructive play, or play that is in the service of a personal play goal and not simply object exploration or practice play.

On the basis of earlier work of Piaget (1962) and others Smilansky (1968) proposed that functional, constructive, and dramatic play form a developmental hierarchy corresponding to stages of cognitive development. Functional play refers to motor exercise with or without objects, or the use of objects in a stereotyped manner, as children develop. Constructive play is organized, goal-oriented play in which children use play materials to build something. Dramatic play is play that involves role playing and make-believe. Functional play emerges first and is the major type of play during the sensorimotor stage (approximately from birth to age two). After children enter the preoperational stage, constructive play and then dramatic play emerge and become the dominant forms of play. In Smilansky's scheme constructive play is considered to be an intermediary stage between functional and dramatic play. Although not stated explicitly, the rationale for this ordering appears to be the assumption that the symbol use that is evident in dramatic play requires more advanced intellectual skills than does the symbolic activity in constructive play (Christie & Johnsen, 1987).

By age four, constructive play becomes the most prevalent form of play, occupying more than 50 percent of free time in preschool settings (Rubin et al., 1983). The physical environment is partly responsible for this shift from functional to constructive play. The typical early childhood classroom for one- and two-year-olds is equipped with manipulative and functional play materials such as large balls, clay, finger paints, toys for sand or water play, stringing materials, unit blocks, and puzzles. For older preschoolers interest centers and other play areas are equipped with materials that encourage more constructive play, such as Legos and other interlocking building systems (Bronson, 1995). With age children become increasingly capable of building complex structures and of producing recognizable products through drawing, painting, arranging designs, and making small constructions. Moreover, toys and play equipment and computer-related activities (discussed in Chapter 11) are used more and more in preschools and child care centers to challenge young children to interact creatively with the world of objects.

**Play with Blocks.** Block play is common in childhood and represents a major form of object play that reveals clear differences in levels of proficiency. The way children play with blocks has been researched since the early decades of the twentieth century. For instance, Gesell (1940) investigated how young children play with blocks in his studies on maturational timetables. Children from age twelve to eighteen months rarely constructed anything with blocks but instead played with them one at a time, treating them as single units. Between eighteen and twenty-four months of age most children put the blocks in a row or made a simple tower. Three-year-olds usually did both, with the vertical arrangement connected to a horizontal arrangement. Four-year-olds typically built elaborate two-dimensional structures, and five-year-olds constructed more elaborate three-dimensional ones; both these older age groups usually named their finished products.

Gesell's work on how children play with blocks during the early years was confirmed in subsequent research. Block play begins around two years of age and shows increasing complexity, with a shift from vertical to horizontal constructions in the third year and more elaborate constructions such as enclosures made by age four. Block play becomes more representational as the older preschoolers try to build something that is a model of a real-world object (Reifel, 1984).

Reifel and Greenfield (1982) have documented developmental differences in block play by children from four to seven years of age. Block play complexity was indexed by both spatial relationships and symbolism. Reifel and Greenfield developed scales for evaluating the symbolism and the spatial complexity in the block play. Three levels of symbolism were as follows: 0 = blocks treated simply as blocks, 1 = blocks were reported by the child to represent a familiar real-world object such as a house or garage, and 2 = blocks represented a more imaginative or fantastical object, such as a pirate ship or candy machine. Spatial complexity was assessed by examining how well the children integrated the blocks (e.g., joining together arches or bridges) and how well they made geometric planes or represented dimensions with them (e.g., forming lines or rows and surface planes).

Block play is popular among children across a wide age range. How children use blocks and which kinds of blocks and construction materials are used are related to the child's age or developmental status. For example, preschool-age children can master the use of toys such as Lego blocks, Lincoln Logs, and other assorted block-like playthings. They can engage in various activities with these materials, snapping together objects, pressing tubes or bricks together, and the like. Children who are seven and eight years old continue to enjoy these forms of play, but they can also enjoy using tiny screws, nuts, and bolts and playing with battery-powered features of blocks and construction sets (Goodson & Bronson, 1985). Christie and Johnsen (1987) report that older children are more concerned with what they are trying to make than with the process of building per se and that an interest in building with blocks extends well into the elementary school years and serves as a transition to crafts activities. Trageton (1997) also proposed a general shift in the constructive play of preschoolers into arts and crafts and other creative play in primary school. He also noted, as other play theorists have, that children's dramatic play turns into more advanced creative dramatics activities (such as performing skits) as they get older.

**Play with Computers.** Young children are increasingly using and playing with computers. Early computer experience involves learning how to press the keys, push the mouse, turn the computer on and off, use the cursor, run an easy-to-use program, and restart a program. As in any other skill activity that the child is expected to master, it is important that teachers and parents assist the child at first. With increasing maturity children become able to use software programs and computer games with increasing levels of complexity. Children can use simple games and tutorial programs before they can use application or tool programs such as LOGO. The content of these easier programs covers such areas as math, language, and literacy readiness; problem solving; creativity in art, music, and design; logic; and memory. Usually, these programs are storylike and playful and are suited for children in the early years, but others are very didactic and are not developmentally appropriate. More open-ended programs invite playfulness; those designed for practice of didactic materials do not.

Young children use computers in diverse ways, including play. The kinds of play include exploratory play or manipulation and experimentation to investigate computers and programs, especially when they are new. The manner in which young children use new computer software for the first time appears to follow a predictable sequence. Haugland and Wright (1997) outline the stages in computer play as discovery, involvement, self-confidence, and creativity. Computer use by young children is usually a social activity, and some research suggests that the quality of play improves when a peer is present. With a playmate, there is more variety of actions and more pretend themes, and the play tends to last longer (Heft & Swaminathan, 2002). We will discuss these topics related to computer play in more detail in Chapter 11.

## DEVELOPMENT OF SYMBOLIC PLAY

During the second year of life comes the emergence of representational abilities. The infant becomes able to evoke images or symbols derived from imitative activities. This enables the infant to engage in beginning pretense or make-believe play. At first such play is solitary, but with age pretending is done more and more in a social context. Also, children increasingly direct pretend behaviors toward others versus the self, engage in pretend behaviors in which one object is substituted for another, and perform longer, more integrated pretend sequences that are planned. These three developmental trends have been termed decentration, decontextualization, and integration (Fenson & Ramsay, 1980).

Howes, Unger, and Seidner (1989) have described how pretend play emerges and expands during the second year of life. It is very fleeting at first and imitative. Although most of the time early pretending is solitary or part of parent-child play, it may occur in the company of peers. Initial social pretense with another child begins with eye contact while performing a pretend behavior, such as feeding a baby doll. However, before age fifteen or sixteen months children do not usually imitate each other's pretending behaviors. From age fifteen to twenty months toddlers in eye contact often engage in simple pretend and imitative acts, such as pushing a baby doll in a stroller or rocking a baby doll to sleep. Toddlers seem to enjoy imitating each other during this age period. At about age twenty to twenty-four months social pretend is marked by more mutual recognition, such as vocalizing and offering toys to the other child. From age twenty-four to thirty months children will participate in the same theme, such as going shopping with purses, carts, and dolls. At this point there is some decision making about the theme. Then from age thirty to thirty-six months there is heightened awareness of each other and the adoption of social roles and some play negotiation. Role-taking of the other becomes part of the social pretend play.

During the preschool years there is a continuing trend toward more organized symbolic play, often resulting in a replication of reality that is performed in a social context. Piaget's general account of the development of symbolic play has inspired many researchers to study the origin and development of nonsocial and social pretense during the early years. Dimensions of symbolic play that have been studied include (a) pretend actions and objects and (b) role enactments and themes.

### Pretend Actions and Objects

Pretend actions have been analyzed in terms of agent and object substitutions. Babies around twelve months of age usually exhibit rudimentary pretend play involving self-as-agent (Fenson et al., 1976). Examples include pretending to be sleeping or talking on the phone. The behaviors represent everyday experiences, but they are not related to real needs. During infancy and early toddlerhood children become increasingly able to pretend with a variety of substitute objects (such as a block of wood for a bowl of cereal). These simple pretense activities, although unrelated to real needs or wishes, are all self-directed. The child can pretend to eat the block "cereal" but cannot pretend to feed it to another person or a doll. Around eighteen months of age children begin to show outer-directed symbolic activities. Now we see genuine symbolic play sequences unfold, according to Piaget's (1962) meaning of the term. The child pretends that a doll is eating plastic fruit or is talking into a toy phone.

The form and function of substitute objects, as opposed to the real objects they represent, are important to note to judge the complexity of the pretend actions. For example, a rectangular unit block has a shape similar to that of a toy phone, suggesting its use as a substitute object for the phone. Substituting a toy airplane for a phone would clearly be a greater symbolic leap because of dissimilarity both in shape and intended function. As will be explained in Chapter 8, as children grow older, they can use increasingly dissimilar objects to represent other objects. Between the ages of two and three, children begin incorporating imaginary objects and substances into their play (Gowan, 1995). For example, they can shape their hand as if they are holding something and pretend to talk into an invisible phone.

As children develop, they become increasingly able to engage in more complicated and involved pretend-play sequences. Actions are linked meaningfully, and objects are used conventionally and consistently. In the second and third years of life the child is able to perform two or more consecutive acts that reflect a similar theme or topic, such as pretending to cook a meal and then serving the meal to dolls seated around a table. The variety and diversity of such pretend-action sequences increase as the child matures.

A research review of early symbolic play development by Jean Gowen (1995) supports the view that maturation, the individual child's actions on the physical world, and social action all have roles in the emergence and consolidation of symbolic play. As children progress from infancy to the preschool years, their symbolic play (a) shifts from being centered on the self to being centered on others, (b) utilizes more sophisticated make-believe transformations, and (c) becomes more sequenced and better organized.

## Role Enactments and Themes

Pretend actions with objects become more elaborate as the child matures. During the third year another important change occurs for most children. Children begin to engage in role enactment during symbolic play. Role playing is different from the earlier pretend activities with objects in that now the child is able to infer and imagine the role identity behind the pretend actions. The role that is played organizes the pretend actions. Role play typically is more coherent and meaningful than earlier forms of pretending and lasts longer, adding more enjoyment to the pretend activities of the child.

Role play reflects awareness of others and the child's knowledge of role attributes, role relationships, and role-appropriate actions (Garvey, 1979). Role-enactment behaviors are influenced by the player's level of cognitive development and personality (see Chapter 4) as well as by the immediate situation. According to Garvey and Berndt (1977) there are four types of roles: (1) *functional roles* (pseudo-role enactment) are those organized by an object or activity (e.g., pretending to bathe a doll is triggered by the presence of a toy bathtub); (2) *relational roles* (family roles as mother-father-child, wife-husband); (3) *character roles* are either stereotypic (police officer, ghost) or fictional (characters from stories, books, or television or films, such as *Batman*); and (4) *peripheral roles* that are discussed but not enacted (for instance, rescue workers who are on the way to help with an emergency).

Role play is typically connected to play themes. The development of pretend play during the preschool years moves away from highly familiar themes, such as playing house or firefighter, toward play themes that are more fantastic or out of the ordinary (e.g., ghosts and pirates). Children are also interested in enacting roles of characters from fiction as opposed to familiar occupational roles. Potential themes for role enactments become more numerous as children gain greater knowledge about the world they live in—both the real world of everyday living and the events transmitted through books and other media, both fiction and nonfiction.

Another milestone of symbolic play development is seen in the older preschool child who is able to imagine even with no object at all, who is versatile in improvising with props and substitute objects of all types, and who can evoke imaginary situations through words. High levels of symbolic development are seen in the child's being able to take on a variety of diverse roles in collaboration with peers, engaging innovatively and with great enjoyment in sociodramatic and fantasy themes ranging from the most commonplace to the most extraordinary. Concentration, persistence, attention to detail, and seeing the play episode as a whole are other manifestations of symbolic development at an advanced level.

In addition, advanced social pretense is also characterized by meta-communication or meta-play (Howes & Matheson, 1992; Sawyer, 1997). Children periodically take time out from role playing to talk about the play itself. Conversations about the imaginative play, decision making about props and space markers, and role negotiations are common. Children exhibiting complex social play have been characterized by Sawyer (1997) as being similar to an improvisational jazz band, accommodating to the moves of others but doing one's thing, applying different voices in play—actor's voice, director's voice, and so on.

Piaget (1962) and Singer (1973) have speculated that symbolic play becomes internalized during the concrete operational stage of development (age seven to eleven years). This accounts for the rise in daydreaming in school-age children. Daydreaming, a residual of the preschooler's earlier active fantasy social life, continues to exert a positive influence on the children's creativity, imagination, divergent thinking, and operational thinking abilities. Moreover, there are continuing outlets for symbolic play that exist in the form of videogames and fantasy activities for the older child. The disappearance of overt pretense also might be a methodological artifact of the location of researchers' play observations, the vast majority of which take place in classrooms and on school playgrounds, settings that may inhibit overt symbolic play in older children. Findings might be different if observations were conducted at home or in the neighborhood. All three of the authors of this book have seen considerable overt make-believe play by older children in nonschool settings.

## DEVELOPMENT OF SOCIAL PLAY

The sociality of play in early education has long interested researchers, going back to the classical studies of Parten (1932). In a sense, there is a social side to all play. All play originates and unfolds in a social context. Some theorists have maintained that even solitary play is social, in that the child in solitary play has internalized and evokes an imagined play audience (Sutton-Smith, 1979a). As we will see later in the chapter, play assessment routinely takes into account the social dimension, coding play for its cognitive content and its level of social participation. In this section we examine the development of social play in the individual child and also examine social play in relation to group dynamics and social competence.

## Children's Individual Progression in Social Play

Play development in the social domain has been examined in longitudinal research (e.g., following the same group of children for an extended period of time) and in cross-sectional research (examining different groups of children at different ages). In general, as a child grows older, there is an increase in interactive play, with a number of social skills unfolding. As the child's social play becomes more complex, specific social behaviors become more pronounced, such as being able to take turns or to initiate, maintain, or end social interactions. Using language in socially appropriate ways also becomes more developed and elaborate.

Play with objects is a major factor in the development of social play during infancy and toddlerhood (Mueller & Lucas, 1975). Toys can serve as "social butter," facilitating interactions particularly between peers who, unlike adults, are unable or unwilling to make special accommodations or concessions to keep the play going. Toys often serve as entry mechanisms as two toddlers go from parallel to interactive play. Toys mediate social interaction. Studies of social play during the second year of life suggest that children progress to more advanced forms of social play both through toy use with peers and through interaction with peers (Jacobson, 1981).

Children's social play skills continue to grow with age as children mature and gain experience in a variety of social situations. Parten's (1932) classic study established four levels of social play (adapted from Rubin, 1977):

1. Solitary play, in which children play alone
2. Parallel play, in which children play alongside but not with each other
3. Associative play, in which children play and share with each other
4. Cooperative play, in which children have a defined division of labor (e.g., different roles) and a shared purpose.

Parten (1932) also identified two other categories: unoccupied behavior and onlooker behavior, in which the child does not engage in play behavior during free play periods. Parten's research findings showed a developmental progression from solitary (age 2 to 2½ years) to parallel (age 2½ to 3½ years) to associative (age 3½ to 4½ years) to cooperative (age 4½ years) play. This is probably the most widely cited developmental trend in play behavior.

Although there is general agreement on the overall trend toward increases in social play with age, several researchers have questioned the developmental status of solitary and parallel play and have asked whether it is even helpful to propose changes in play in such broad terms. They have recommended a finer, more cogent analysis of play changes in specific social situations.

In a longitudinal study of social play, Smith (1978) reported that although many children followed the trend suggested by Parten, others did not. Older children alternated

➤ According to Mildred Parten, in cooperative play children have a division of labor (different roles) organized around a common goal.

between solitary and interactive play as they outgrew a tendency to engage in simple side-by-side or parallel play. With development comes an increasing capacity to use parallel play strategically to initiate or terminate play with particular play partners (Bakeman & Brownlee, 1980). Some researchers have suggested that perhaps parallel play, not solitary play, is the least mature social form of play (Moore, Evertson, & Brophy, 1974; Rubin, 1982; Rubin, Maioni, & Hornung, 1976). However, many contemporary play researchers or practitioners would not endorse this view. The status of parallel play depends on how it is expressed (i.e., parallel play with awareness of peers versus without awareness) and how it is used in an ongoing play session (i.e., as a bridge between other forms of play). As usual, the development of play is complex and multifaceted.

Solitary play has also been further differentiated by contemporary play researchers as a social or nonsocial play category. Three subcategories of solitary play are now used in research and readily recognized by teachers:

1. *Reticent behavior.* Onlooker and unoccupied behaviors (from Parten's 1932 study) can be reticent behaviors. Unoccupied behavior is when children appear to do nothing and do not seem to be watching others, as in aimlessly wandering around the room. Onlooker behavior occurs when children watch others and seem to take an interest in their play. Reticent behavior may reflect social anxiety and would appear to indicate peer group problems for a child who does a lot of this kind of behavior in an early childhood setting (Coplan & Rubin, 1998).

2. *Solitary-active behavior.* This subcategory includes solitary-functional and solitary-dramatic play. The former refers to being alone and performing repetitive muscle movements with or without an object; the latter refers to engaging in pretense

when alone. Children doing this kind of solitary play often seem to want to play with others but are rejected by their peers. Some researchers have speculated that it is a sign of immaturity or impulsivity or externalizing problems. However, if a child is unfairly rejected by peers and performs this kind of play, it would seem that another kind of interpretation is warranted, one that is more generous to the child and less generous to the peer culture in the classroom and especially to the teacher who would be ultimately responsible for this sad state of affairs.

3. *Solitary-passive behavior.* This subcategory refers to solitary-constructive play. Children are alone making something or doing something that is of interest to them. This behavior seems to be a conscious choice. Children who perform a great deal of this kind of behavior are more object-oriented than person-oriented (see the "Personality and Play" section of Chapter 4). Although such children are generally accepted by others and their behavior would not appear to be a cause for concern (unlike the first two subcategories of solitary play), some research has indicated that children who engage only in this kind of play may be withdrawn, especially if they show symptoms of anxiety in the classroom (Harrist, Zaia, Bates, Dodge, & Pettit, 1997).

Individual differences in these types of solitary play are related to developmental status to some extent, with solitary-constructive play increasing with age and solitary-functional play decreasing, but personality or personal attributes of children would seem to lie behind its variation to a greater extent than developmental age per se (see Chapter 4).

When solitary play is not differentiated into the subtypes listed above, there does not appear to be a developmental trend in solitary play, contrary to Parten's (1932) study. The frequency of solitary play seems to hold up across the early years, the quality improving with age. For example, preschoolers tend to engage in more solitary functional play, whereas kindergarten children tend to do more of the advanced solitary constructive play. Also, it is well known that the physical arrangement of a play setting can influence whether play is solitary or socially interactive. Children's ability to concentrate on solitary play is enhanced by having a play area with physically bounded workspaces, clear paths between play areas, and accessible and appropriate materials (see Chapter 6). Moreover, researchers have demonstrated that the amount of solitary versus social play in a dramatic play center can be manipulated by changing the physical design of the play area (Petrakos & Howe, 1996).

## Group Dynamics

We should not think that the development of play, and social play in particular, is a process that is taking place only in the individual child. Observing individual children at play in various play environments does provide a great deal of information about developmental differences in motor, object, symbolic, and social play. However, important information about play will be left out if we do not also consider groups of children as the target of our search to better understand play and development. Therefore we must strive to know more about peer group dynamics and play. What are the ways in which various social and play behaviors in a peer group fit together over a short period of time during a play episode? How does a particular peer culture in a classroom get formed over a period of time? What impact does a peer group have on children's play on a day-to-day basis? Answers to these kinds of questions interest teachers who try to help create and maintain a community of young learners. Knowing about patterns of group behaviors helps teachers to facilitate play events and help to build overall group cohesion in the classroom.

**Peer Culture.** For Corsaro (1985, p. 75), peer culture is a "joint or communal attempt by children to acquire control over their lives through the establishment of a collective identity." Children learn from adults and peers. They internalize information and appropriate cultural tools from the world of adults. They also actively produce their own peer cultures, which take on their own character. A peer culture, unique to the children who share experiences at school or in a child development program, consists of common activities, rituals, rules, and themes that are based on the children's sense of togetherness.

*Togetherness* means affiliation, a sense of belonging together and being in a social group. Group meaning comes through shared activity, and in early childhood this is often mediated by joint playing in a specified play area, certain physical spaces in a classroom, or a playground. Children in close proximity co-construct their play area, which is established as an imagined reality projected on physical space. In this play area, children share toys and engage in collective symbolism or pretending. Children who are not participating in the play area are outsiders even if they are nearby physically.

Two kinds of activities—play negotiations and play enactments—take place within play areas. Negotiations entail deciding on roles, props, and other collective symbolic meanings within a play script; enactment means actually acting out the script. Negotiation is a form of meta-communication or meta-play that occurs *outside* the play frame, whereas enactment happens *inside* play frames. Some meta-communications negotiate rules and transformations needed for the play activity itself; other meta-communications deal with previous social experiences on which play scripts are based. These meta-communications can be thought of as a kind of play commentary or conversation outside the play scripts and play frame. Enactment and negotiation together help to define three related contexts in a play area: the physical context of space, the social context of communication, and the symbolic context of shared pretend meaning for people, objects, locations, and actions (Janson, 2001).

Peer cultures of young children are characterized by social participation and control. A need to affiliate motivates children to want to partake in community life in the classroom, to share play worlds with playmates. At the same time a need for self-definition and personal meaning motivates children to do their own thing and possibly to try to control others. This is the yin and yang of play. Children must balance social togetherness and individual meaningfulness. Fortunately, many times personal and collective intentions are the same, so what is personally meaningful is also meaningful for the group. Dominant children may persuade other children to go along with them when there is a conflict among children over play intentions. At times a child might leave the group to play alone, or with an adult or other children, as a solution to a conflict between wanting to participate socially and wanting to control or have personally meaningful experiences (Janson, 2001).

Past experiences of children being together in a group, including past play experiences in different play areas shared by children, serve a number of purposes. Common social experiences help children to produce their peer culture. Creating a peer culture is a way in which children are trying to collectively make sense of their socialization experiences at school and is an attempt to muster some influence over their own lives in a world where adults rule.

Peer culture also helps the children to define themselves as a social group, who are leaders, who are followers, who is well-liked, which children are friends. Some social relationships are horizontal peer relations, formed by children of equal status (Janson, 2001). These relationships are characterized by solidarity and mutual trust, by emotional control, and by the coordination of play actions and themes. Vertical peer relations, on the other hand, are formed between children who dominate and those who are subordinated, between those who are assertive and those who are submissive and dependent. Verticality in peer relations feeds a status hierarchy. Power relations in the classroom can have a negative influence on children and can present problems for the teacher who is trying to build the classroom as a community of equal learners.

**Entry Skills and Play Transitions.** What happens today in a play area in which a group of children are playing often hinges on what took place yesterday, in previous play episodes. Play negotiations reflect in part the collective memory of the peer culture. Children's reputations and friendships affect play negotiations. Issues and problems concerning inclusion and exclusion are often seen. Some children are frequently left out or have other difficulties with group play. Teachers who understand peer group dynamics and have their fingers on the pulse of day-to-day, week-to-week activity in play areas will be better able to work with these children.

Research has addressed how young children successfully enter play groups. It has been found that three strategies are typically used. A low-profile way is to simply wait and hover near ongoing play. Eventually, a child might be accepted. Children can also imitate children at play in a play area in the hope of becoming included. Then there is the third strategy: making group-relevant statements and requests. Often this culminates in successful social group interactions.

Rubin, Bukowski, and Parker (1998) have proposed a three-step model in which competent entry into ongoing peer activity requires onlooker behavior, parallel play, and then conversation about play. Robinson, Anderson, Porter, Hart, and Wouden-Miller (2003) put this conceptual model to an empirical test. They investigated the sequential social-play interactions of four-year-old preschoolers during child-initiated play episodes in different activity centers: housekeeping, blocks, and manipulatives. Play in the activity centers was videotaped for thirty minutes on four occasions. For each child present in the center, behaviors were coded in ten-second segments for different social-play states; and data were analyzed to uncover predominant sequential patterns of behavior in the group play. Although boys tended to play more in the blocks activity center and girls more in the housekeeping activity center, the total frequency of different kinds of play displayed across the different activity centers was not significantly affected by gender, socioeconomic status, or kind of activity center. The kinds of play states that were coded included solitary constructive play, onlooker behavior, parallel-aware (with some eye contact) play, and cooperative-social interaction. Results of sequential-lag analyses done to discern temporal patterns indicated support for the three step model indicated above. The children progressed from onlooker behavior to parallel-aware to cooperative-social play to gain entry into play episodes.

This study suggests that if preschoolers have been watching others (onlooker behavior) before playing in the parallel-aware state with other children, cooperative-social interaction will follow. Parallel-aware play is a two-way bridge between various play states. Children who can successfully make transitions using the parallel-aware play state are at an advantage in a peer group. They know how to make relevant comments and how to take the frame of reference of the larger play group as they enter the established play area. Knowing a child's pattern of sequencing behavior in a group play setting may tell us more about the social play developmental status of the child than does having knowledge of the total amount of certain kinds of play the child exhibits.

## Social Competence

During the early years children need to develop the foundation for successful social living. Social competence is required to engage in positive interactions with peers, to become involved in relationships, and to nurture budding friendships. Montagner (1984) has concluded from his research that children who are dominant and aggressive are often not socially adept and tend to be unpopular. The best-liked children, the ones who become social leaders, use affection and power to influence other children. This positive approach tends to be much more effective than using brute force.

Many children who are neglected or rejected by their peers need help to know how to join play and participate in play. Some clues to help teachers assist children are given by the results of research. For example, the study by Robinson et al. (2003) suggests that teachers should focus on the role of parallel-aware activities in the classroom or outdoors. Teachers can attempt to model and scaffold children's transitions between social play states. A child who plays alone with a set of toys can be given a larger set intended for a group of children so that there will be opportunities for modeling and scaffolding transitional strategies. A shy, reticent child might benefit by having multiple sets of props in the dramatic play center so that there are opportunities for several children to engage in parallel-aware activities.

Ardley and Ericson (2002) conducted an interesting case study of a child named Aaron who exhibited an inordinate amount of aggressive play. Aaron was a kindergartner who was from a Quaker family and who seemed obsessed with violent themes in his play and drawing. He did a lot of rough-and-tumble play and symbolic play fighting, pretending to use weapons (his favorite being swords). His dramatic play contained disturbing violent content (cooking babies, blowing up ambulances). He had a great deal of difficulty with play entry. He could not initiate play in a positive way. He behaved inappropriately, grabbing things, for example, even though he really wanted to become part of play groups. His student teacher, Laura, struggled with Aaron's play aggression and wondered about the right thing to do from a developmentally appropriate practices standpoint. Her major concern was her relationship with Aaron. She eventually realized that Aaron needed guidance in how to join in play and was able to help him.

A child like Aaron might be helped through the teacher's modeling and scaffolding or facilitating the parallel-aware play state. Other teacher techniques are explaining to induce social understanding and coaching social skills. Laura chose to initiate with Aaron imaginative play sequences to model appropriate play behaviors. Laura also thought about role playing with Aaron and then discussing with him how it feels being the victim of violent forms of play.

## PLAY DEVELOPMENT FROM AGE SIX TO EIGHT YEARS

Play development is a continuous process along each play dimension: physical or motor, object, symbolic, and social. Because early childhood education extends to age eight years, it is important to continue to trace the stability and change in different kinds of play as the child grows older and attends primary school. This is especially important if we want to include play in the education of children during this important period in their childhoods.

- *Physical play.* School-age children manifest considerable fine and gross motor ability and can be expected to rapidly achieve more mastery in these domains. Their developing large muscle strength and coordination and sense of balance, together with increasing skill and dexterity in use of small muscle, allows for the emergence of new, more sophisticated types of physical play. Older children are attracted to new, challenging activities that provide opportunities for further muscle development and coordination. They spend a great deal of time running, tumbling, and climbing on jungle gyms and swings. Physical exercise play, or locomotor play, and rough-and-tumble play in boys enter a peak period that continues into middle childhood before declining during adolescence. Many children participate in organized sports or other adult-sponsored activities such as dancing and gymnastics. Some children try other difficult physical pursuits, such jumping rope, throwing and catching, and ice skating. Outdoor games such as tag and hide-and-seek are popular.

- *Object play.* Older children's use of objects in play becomes increasingly complex and elaborate. Constructive play is distinguished from the play of preschoolers both by its enhanced sophistication and by the higher levels of social collaboration and pretense. Moreover, older children are more likely to build props and to engage in elaborate planning and negotiation as a prelude to sociodramatic play. They often consume more time and effort in planning their dramatic play than they do actually acting out the episodes.

- *Symbolic play.* Primary-grade children engage in symbolic play with richer texts, more contoured scripts, and more elaborate plots than do younger children. More frequent and higher levels of meta-communication are used to structure and organize play episodes. A lot more stage-managing and directing and redirecting occurs. Older children enjoy ready-made costumes and props but also like to make their own. Many of their play themes are media-linked.

- *Games with rules.* Physical games, various sports, board games, and computer and video games become increasingly popular during grade school years. For six- and seven-year-olds, games must remain rather simple and easy to follow, with few rules and little skill or strategy required for entry-level participation. Older children can often engage in more sophisticated games (e.g., chess) that have greater cognitive and social demands. Strategic planning and genuine cooperation are important ingredients in game play.

## PLAY ASSESSMENT

Play assessment involves gathering descriptive data or information about children's play behavior. By observing children at play, teachers can learn about each child's play development in the different domains: motor, object, symbolic, and social. To plan curricula and effective instruction, teachers must know the strengths and interests and areas of concern for each child being taught. Play assessment can help to provide this information. In addition to guiding instruction, play assessment can show whether children are making progress toward educational and developmental objectives. This achievement information can be shared with parents and school personnel.

Play assessment includes observations and recordings of children's play. Observation methods include narrative accounts, anecdotal records, and vignettes, as well as the use of checklists and rating scales to keep track of how children are playing over time and across different settings. Teachers or researchers who observe children's play can augment their observational accounts, whether written, spoken (into an audio-recorder), or in the form of checklists or ratings, with other representations of children's play—photographs, observer sketches or diagrams, and video recordings. In addition, samples of children's play products can be collected and saved. The teacher can maintain for each child a play portfolio to document growth in skills and abilities as well as a child's changing play interests or activity preferences over the school year.

### Observation Methods

Observing play behavior systematically and objectively is quite different from simply "watching kids play." If the observer knows what is looked for and has the means to record the information and follows a consistent plan or method, then the play observation is systematic. If the observer carefully records the behavior as it occurs, without observer bias or "reading into" the play behavior, and if all children are given equal and fair coverage, then the play observation is objective.

Deciding in advance what you wish to learn about children's play is important, and so is selecting a method that enables you to achieve this purpose. In general, one should try to make the observations in a setting that will allow children to display the full range of their play abilities. This is more likely to be the case when there are ample materials available that are conducive to a full range of play behavior, including motor play (e.g., climbing structures, balls, wheeled toys), constructive play (e.g., blocks, Tinkertoys, Legos), and dramatic play (e.g., dolls, housekeeping props, costumes, theme-related prop boxes).

There also needs to be enough time available for more complex forms of play to develop. If these resources are not available, the absence of these important types of play may be caused by lack of materials or time rather than by lack of play skills. If possible, observe children in both indoor and outdoor settings. Research indicates that some children exhibit higher social and cognitive levels of play outdoors than they do when they are playing indoors (Henniger, 1985; Tizard, Philps, & Plewis, 1976a, b). Delay observations until children have had a chance to get to know each other and get used to the school environment. Children tend to exhibit higher social and cognitive levels of play with familiar peers (Doyle, Connolly, & Rivest, 1980). Observations made at the beginning of the school year can underestimate children's true play abilities. Naturally, this advice also holds true for observations of children who have recently transferred into a classroom.

Observe children's play behavior over time to ensure that it is representative of their typical play behaviors. It is unwise to base decisions about play on a single day's observation. Children might happen to be paired with playmates with whom they do not get along or with play materials that do not match their interests. Illness, problems at home, and other temporary conditions might also influence play on that particular day. Always try to spread observations over as long a period of time as possible to minimize the effects of any transient factors. Two or three observations spread over at least a week would be the bare minimum.

Trawick-Smith (2002) recommends that for play assessment to be culturally fair, observers should carefully note fleeting or embedded play as well. In some cultural groups, traditional play categories such as dramatic play, construction, and games with rules occur sometimes as fleeting behaviors and are often embedded in other play forms. He gives the example that for Puerto Rican children most dramatic play that he observed was embedded in motor play.

## Narrative Accounts

When the observer tries to write down as much as possible about the setting, participants, and behaviors that are observed in a specified place for a given period of time, the observer is using what is called a narrative account method of observation. If one is really trying to record as much as possible in the narrative account, the experience can be frustrating. It is difficult because typically so many behaviors are going on in a play episode. Different general behavioral *states* (e.g., children are running, infants are sleeping) and different specific behavioral *events* (e.g., boy slapped a doll, girl crawled into a box) are all happening at the same time in different parts of the classroom. Singling out one child at a time to observe for a given length of time and targeting certain behaviors can make the use of this method less frustrating. Alternatively, a teacher might observe a group but write down information only about a few chosen behaviors that are of particular interest, such as initiation of play, sharing, bossiness, or choice of same- versus opposite-gendered toys.

Gross (2003) recommends writing down operational definitions of all specific behavioral events that are of particular interest to a teacher or researcher in a given project and to underscore specific instances of them as they appear in the narrative account. Operational definitions have to be precise and clear enough so that different people who are familiar with the definitions and the observational setting will recognize instances of them as they appear in the observational account. The need for interobserver reliability becomes apparent as a requirement for objective observation.

A useful type of narrative account is the anecdotal record. Anecdotal records are brief narrative descriptions of events or incidents that are written down as they occur or shortly after they occur. These records can be used to document significant events that take place during play—events that shed light on children's play abilities and their overall social, cognitive, academic, and physical development. These notes can be written on a piece of paper, index cards, or Post-it Notes. Teachers can also record play anecdotes by speaking quietly into a small hand-held audiocassette player and later transcribing their verbal descriptions. It is useful to date the observations and to identify all children by name.

Christie, Enz, and Vukelich (2003) give the following example of an anecdotal record that a preschool teacher made of a four-year-old Korean girl's play behavior. The girl had been in the United States for only a few months, so the teacher focused on the oral language that she used during play and her skill in using make-believe transformations:

> Name: *Julia* Date: *4/6/95*
>
> Julia observed me making a pretend phone call to Buddy from the post office center. Several minutes later she picked up the toy phone in the housekeeping center and said, "Ring, ring . . . Miss Chari, will you come to my house?" It was her first complete English sentence! (p. 88)

Anecdotal notes tend to be brief, but they can contain a considerable amount of descriptive information: the child's name, date, play setting, and an exact description of the events and products that are observed. In making anecdotal notes, the focus should be on accurate description of what was seen and heard in the play (Vukelich, 1995). Interpretation and evaluation can occur later, after the play period is over and the teacher has time to look over the notes that have been recorded.

Anecdotal notes can be written on a variety of materials. Wood and Attfield (1996) recommend that teachers use sticky notes (Post-it Notes), labeling each note with the date and name of the key student. These sticky notes can later be transferred to student folders, a notebook sectioned off by students' names, or a display board for later analysis. Another system involves taping 3 × 5 inch index cards to a clipboard in an overlapping manner (Christie et al., 2003). Student names are written at the bottom of each card, and the cards are arranged so that the names are visible. When the teacher observes something significant happening during play, she can use this flip chart to locate the child's card and then write the anecdotal description along with the date of occurrence. When a card is full, it is transferred to the teacher's folder for that child.

If it is not convenient to record anecdotal notes while play activities are taking place, the teacher can write a vignette at a later time. Vignettes are recollections of significant events and look much like anecdotal notes, except that they are written in the past tense. Because vignettes are written after the play is over and the teacher is free of distractions, they tend to be more detailed than anecdotal records. The teacher also has time to mention connections between play activities and other things that are known about the child. It is a good idea to write vignettes soon after a play event has taken place. The longer one waits, the more likely it is that important information will be forgotten.

## Technology for Recording Play

Digital cameras are becoming more widespread in early childhood programs, used by both children and teachers to enhance curriculum possibilities and to provide documentation. Digital photographs can be quickly downloaded to the classroom computer and printed out. With typical snapshot sizes (3 × 5 or 4 × 6 inches), quality is often indistinguishable from that of professionally developed film. This eliminates the hassle of having to take film to a store or drop-off point and wait for processing. Digital video can also be uploaded onto computers and then edited by the teacher. Until a few years ago video editing was prohibitively expensive and required special training. New video editing programs, such as *Pinnacle Studio*, are very easy to learn to use.

Photography is also used by researchers and teachers-as-researchers who wish to have a visual representation of play behavior. Images are a rich source of information and can provide some precise details about an event which can supplement other observational data that can be in the form of written notes, ratings, and checklist marks. Some annotated observational notes should always be taken whenever a camera is used. The picture can be shared with another teacher or a parent and can be explored to identify nuances of children's behavior. The emergence of a behavior and its sequence over a short period of time can be recorded with a digital camera. Annotated notes help to recall the meaning of the pictures.

Photographing play should not be a random event. A theoretical perspective should be brought in together with a specific intention whenever a decision is made to photograph. Photographs will be more useful and intellectually meaningful if the photographer was conscious of theory and purpose that guided the picture taking. Play should be photographed at key moments to get the most out of using this observational tool. The photographic moment and the actual picture should offer a point of reflection for exploring movement across levels or states of play, for example.

Videotape equipment, commonly available in homes and schools, is also becoming standard in many classrooms. Like a digital camera, a camcorder can be used both for assessment and instructional purposes. This equipment can be used in several ways to assist the observation of children's play. First, video equipment provides a solution to a major problem associated with play observation: How can a teacher find the time to make systematic observations of play? A video camera can be placed on a tripod, aimed at a play area (e.g., a dramatic play center), and then switched on to record ongoing play without requiring much attention from the teacher. The videotapes can be replayed and viewed later when time permits. Second, video recordings provide a much more detailed record of play behavior than is possible with observation. In addition to showing the type of play, videotapes can reveal the play context, including the materials that children played with, the social interaction that occurred, as well as the nonverbal gestures and oral language that were used during play.

## Checklists

Checklists specify exactly which behaviors to look for and provide a convenient system for recording the presence or absence of these play behaviors. Checklists help to make observation more systematic by focusing attention on specific aspects of play.

They also provide a quick way to record information, making them more time-efficient than narrative accounts or anecdotal records.

A great number of checklists have emerged as an outgrowth of research on the development of play. Many are lengthy and complicated, making them impractical for applications other than basic research. The thirty-category system used by Sylva, Roy, and Painter (1980) in their study of British and American preschools is an example of such a scale. It provides a wealth of data about children's play behavior, but most teachers do not have the time to learn or to use such a complex coding system.

The social/cognitive scale is a popular scale for use with children at both the early childhood and elementary grade levels. It is relatively easy to use, and it provides information that teachers will find to be very useful in enriching children's play experiences. This scale originated in the 1970s when Kenneth Rubin and his associates combined Parten's (1932) social participation scale with Smilansky's (1968) adaptation of Piaget's (1962) cognitive play categories, allowing both dimensions of play development to be assessed simultaneously (Rubin, Maioni, & Hornung, 1976). Rubin modified the scale by collapsing several of Parten's social play categories—associative and cooperative—into one category, group play, to make the scale more reliable and easier to use (Rubin, Watson, & Jambor, 1978). The resulting scale, the social/cognitive scale, consists of twelve play categories plus several categories of nonplay behavior.

To use the social/cognitive scale, first become familiar with the definitions of the various play and nonplay categories. These categories indicate what to look for while observing play. Box 3.1 gives an interpretation of these categories. Note that an additional category—nonplay activities—has been added. Our experience has shown

➤ According to the social/cognitive play scale used to observe children's play, this is group dramatic play.

that many children choose to do activities such as sitting and talking or feeding fish in an aquarium during play periods. The new category enables these types of behavior to be recorded.

**BOX 3.1**

## Social/Cognitive Play Scale Definitions

### Cognitive Levels

1. *Functional play.* Repetitive muscle movements with or without objects. Examples include running and jumping, gathering and dumping, manipulating objects or materials, and informal games (parading).
2. *Constructive play.* Using objects (e.g., blocks, Legos, Tinkertoys) or materials (e.g., sand, modeling clay, paint) to make something.
3. *Dramatic play.* Role playing and/or make-believe transformations. Examples include role playing (e.g., pretending to be a parent, baby, firefighter, shark, superhero, or monster) and make-believe transformations (e.g., pretending to drive a car by moving an invisible steering wheel or giving a pretend injection with a pencil).
4. *Games with rules.* Games involving recognition of, acceptance of, and conformity with preestablished rules. Examples include tag, Mother May I, marbles, checkers, and kickball.

### Social Levels

1. *Solitary play.* Playing alone with materials different from those of children within speaking distance; no conversations with others.
2. *Parallel play.* Playing with toys or engaging in activities similar to those of other children who are in close proximity; however, there is no attempt to play with the other children.
3. *Group play.* Playing with other children; roles may or may not assigned.

### Unoccupied/Onlooking/Transition

Unoccupied behavior, onlooking behavior, moving from one activity to another.

### Nonplay Activities

Activities that must conform to a preestablished pattern, as in academic activities and teacher-assigned tasks. Activities involving coloring books, worksheets, computers, and educational toys (e.g., shoelace boards) are often best considered nonplay in nature.

*Source:* Johnson, Christie, & Yawkey, *Play and Early Childhood Development,* 2/e, p. 233. Published by Allyn and Bacon, Boston, MA. Copyright © 1999 by Pearson Education. Reprinted by permission of the publisher.

To make a permanent record of the play that is observed, we recommend using a two-dimensional grid (see Figure 3.1). The form has a separate box for each of the twelve play categories, allowing the occurrence of each to be recorded, as well as

Name: ____________________ Observation Dates: ____________________

COGNITIVE LEVEL

| SOCIAL LEVEL | Functional | Constructive | Dramatic | Games with Rules |
|---|---|---|---|---|
| Solitary | | | | |
| Parallel | | | | |
| Group | | | | |

| | UNOCCUPIED/ONLOOKING/TRANSITION | ACTIVITIES |
|---|---|---|
| Nonplay | | |

**FIGURE 3.1 Social/Cognitive Play Scale**

*Source:* Johnson, Christie, & Yawkey, *Play and Early Childhood Development,* 2/e, p. 224. Published by Allyn and Bacon, Boston, MA. Copyright © 1999 by Pearson Education. Reprinted by permission of the publisher.

boxes for the two categories of nonplay behavior. A separate form should be used for each child observed.

To avoid observer bias, we suggest that the multiple-scan sampling procedure developed by Roper and Hinde (1978) be used:

1. Shuffle the recording sheets to establish a random order for the observations.
2. Start your observations with the child whose sheet is on top of the pile.
3. Observe this child for fifteen seconds and then place a tally mark in the cell corresponding to the category of play that was observed.
4. After coding the first child's play, place his or her recording sheet on the bottom of the pile and shift your attention to the child whose recording sheet is now on top of the pile.
5. Observe this next child for 15 seconds, code the play, place the recording sheet on the bottom, and so on.

In this manner children are observed in revolving order, each for fifteen seconds. After all of the children have been observed once, begin the second round of observations.

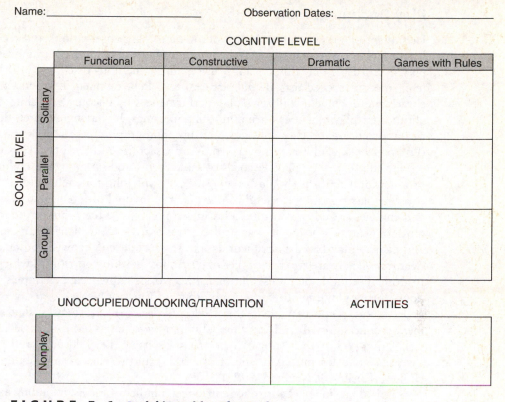

## Play Documentation

Documenting play is an important follow-up to play observations and recording. It is an excellent way to help fulfill the important role of being a communicator about play. Records of play observations, using all the methods discussed in this chapter (e.g., anecdotes, checklists, digital pictures), should be retained. Teachers can also celebrate and document children's play performances by encouraging children to talk about their play activities during morning meetings, by having children dictate stories about dramatic play episodes, and by photographing their play constructions (Polito, 1994). Children can be asked to draw pictures of their play. They can be interviewed about their play. Records of these events and samplings of children's play products and artifacts should be kept in a play portfolio for each child.

The play portfolio is useful to document individual differences in play interests and changes in ability over time. Play in certain areas of the room or indoors versus outdoors can be documented as well. Portfolios are an excellent means to organize and display play-based assessment data to show children's growth and development over time. There are two basic types of portfolios: working portfolios, which are used to store anecdotal notes, observation forms, work samples (e.g., examples of writing done during play), photographs, and other information gathered about each child, and showcase portfolios, which exhibit selected pieces of information that best document a child's growth and learning. Children are often asked to help select the materials that go into their showcase portfolios, causing the children to reflect on their own play and learning (Christie et al., 2003) and to take responsibility for their choices (Roskos & Neuman, 1994).

Individual student's portfolios can take a number of forms, including expandable photo albums, expandable file folders, large plastic boxes with lids, and even gallon-size Ziploc bags bound together with large metal rings (Vukelich, Christie, & Enz, 2002). Dating each item selected for inclusion in a portfolio permits the teacher and child to arrange items in chronological order and show growth over time. Vukelich et al. (2002) recommend that teachers have a date stamp available to facilitate this task.

Cohen (1997) also advocates use of extensive photographing of children at play. The cost of film and developing can be expensive, so she recommends school fundraisers or parent contributions to help. Play panels with photos of children engaged in educational play can be prominently displayed in the classroom on a regular basis, especially during open house. Captions underneath the pictures should be reader-friendly (brief and in large, bold print) and should convey the nature of the play activity and explain what children can learn from the play. Teachers, administrators, parents, and children are thereby afforded an excellent reminder of the importance of play in the curriculum. Play photo albums can also be sent home with children, giving all parents access to information about the values of play.

Cohen (1997) gives the following tips on creating these Reggio Emilia–inspired documentation panels:

1. Focus on children's engagement in meaningful experiences (e.g., a field trip, working with clay, playing with blocks).
2. Select photographs that relate to the experience being described.
3. Provide information related to the process as well as the completed products.

4. Include samples of children's work.
5. Include a verbatim dialogue of children's discussions or responses by parents and/or teachers.
6. The aesthetic presentation of the panel is very important. Use a computer for text and enlarge photos with a color copier. Mount text, photographs, and work samples on construction paper. (p. 64)

Portfolios and documentation panels provide a way to demonstrate to parents, administrators, and policy makers the learning that takes place during play. As will be discussed in Chapter 7, this type of play advocacy is important, given the increased emphasis on standards and accountability in early education.

## SUMMARY

Play development is both microgenetic (short-term) and ontogenetic (long-term). Change can occur over a short period of time in the rhythm and flow play and play-related behavior. Change in how a child plays can also occur over a long period of time owing to maturation and experience. Both types of change are important. Moreover, we should be able to see play development when observing not only an individual child, but also a group of children. The context of play development is significant, such as the influence of type of activity center, age composition of a play group, and cultural membership. Earlier play skills, including physical skills and cognitive-linguistic skills, are precursors to later developing play. Knowledge of developmental sequences helps us to form proper expectations, which are needed to facilitate high-quality play.

Four basic dimensions of play development (motor, object, symbolic, and social) were described over early childhood. Motor play includes object exploration and manipulation, physical activity, locomotor play, and rough-and-tumble play. Motor play development is marked by numerous major motor milestones as children grow physically, become more mobile, and gain greater control, balance, and coordination using their large and small muscles. Object play develops from simple and repetitive motor and functional play routines to elaborate constructive play combinations, including block play and play with computers. Symbolic play advances from earliest imitations of self and others toward more coherent and orderly symbolic play entailing planning and patterning in a social context. Genuine pretense, according to Piaget, commences when the toddler displays outer-directed as opposed to self-directed play behavior. Dimensions of symbolic play include pretend actions, use of objects, role enactments, and themes. By the end of the preschool years, children engage in highly developed sociodramatic or thematic fantasy play characterized by a great deal of meta-communication, a variety of roles with peers, and by concentration, persistence, and attention to detail.

Social play has its origins in the first infant games or routines involving an accommodating partner who compensates for the child's limitations. Objects inspire infants and toddlers to play together but are less important for initiating social play in preschoolers and older children. Social play skills improve with experience in the peer group, where mutual accommodations are required. Peer culture and group dynamics, including entry skills and social competence, are important aspects of social play.

More sophisticated motor, object, and symbolic play is exhibited by children beyond the preschool years. During the period from six to eight years of age motor play advances remarkably, allowing for new play activities using fine and gross motor skills; social play advances as children form peer groups and enter into adult supervised activity; their use of objects in play becomes more elaborate and instrumental; symbolic play takes on additional forms and reaches new heights in sophistication; and games with rules come to the forefront.

Play assessment, documentation, and communication are important adult roles. Play assessment means generating descriptions and records of play which are needed to document activities and progress over time. Play assessment informs our knowledge of individual children and can also be used in curriculum and instructional planning. Information from play assessments can also be communicated to parents, teachers, and school administrators. Play assessments can include narrative accounts, sometimes in the form of anecdotal records or vignettes, as well as checklists. Digital and other kinds of cameras, audiocassettes, and video camcorders are all useful technologies that can enrich play assessment. Observer diagrams and sketches are also helpful, as are samples of play products. A play portfolio compiling all of the above can document play interests and growth in each individual child. This information should be used to plan instruction and to share with others. Documentation panels and photo albums of play can highlight group play as well.

## PROJECTS AND ACTIVITIES

1. Construct a photographic array or collage showing the different types of play and within each category try to display pictures illustrating play development.
2. Visit a playground at recess time at a local public school and systematically scan the play zones and identify occurrences of locomotor play, rough-and-tumble play, and real fighting. Talk with a supervising teacher or teacher's aide about what transpired, asking some questions that are prepared in advance.
3. Visit a commercial pay-for-play establishment and observe play for forty-five minutes using narrative descriptions. Create play categories and definitions for prominent forms of play. Using a prepared coding form and checklist, repeat the forty-five-minute observation. Select a child at random to shadow for ten minutes, and then select another child. Compare results and your experiences using the two methods of observation.
4. Using the social/cognitive system for coding play, conduct observations of free play at a child development center or preschool. Alternate observing an older and younger child. Discuss results with classmates.

CHAPTER 4

# Diversity and Individual Differences in Play

## INTRODUCTION

As we noted in Chapter 1, there are three general ways in which play has value in our lives: (1) as an avenue to help us develop and maintain our creativity and openness, (2) as a way we define ourselves and express our individuality, and (3) as a behavior that brings us together as social beings. Although these three functions are often interconnected, it is the first two functions of play listed above that appear most germane to the present chapter's focus on group diversity and individual differences in play behavior.

Here we first discuss gender difference and play during the early years, then personality as a force affecting play expression, and finally play's relationship to race and ethnicity. All three factors have received considerable attention by researchers trying to adequately understand children's social behaviors and play and by practitioners who have sought ways to promote play that are beneficial to the development and learning of children.

Efforts to support play in children are based on the assumption that children are active players who can benefit from adult support, structuring, modeling, and subtle direction. These efforts at play enrichment are guided in part by the patterns of play development discussed in Chapter 3. These developmental trends provide teachers with a general estimate of children's play abilities and preferences at different ages. When individual differences—gender, personality, race, and ethnicity—are taken into account, we are able to construct a more comprehensive contextual model of children's play. As a result we are better able to foster positive play expression and development. At every age a rich panorama of play patterns can be seen. Our understanding of this diversity of play improves when we consider the importance of gender, personality, and race and ethnicity as variables that affect children's development and behavior in general and their play behavior and interests in particular. With better, more inclusive and complex theories of play teachers are better equipped to enrich children's play experiences.

There are three major analytic approaches or perspectives used to understand children's play in relation to development and education. One approach is the biological perspective, which emphasizes evolution, adaptation, and biological mechanisms or processes that are reflected in such factors as bodily maturity and motor and cognitive ability at different ages. This approach stresses how play is influenced by physical attributes such as sex-linked genes, chromosomes, and prenatal hormones, along with how environmental factors can influence or moderate gene expression. Alternatively, we can seek to explain play through a primarily cultural or environmental perspective. This approach highlights environmental influences and the role of socialization agents as factors affecting children's play. Cultural and psychological functioning are intertwined as societal practices affect the developing child. The third major perspective, the person-centered approach, is based on the fact that it is individuals who generate the thoughts, feelings, and actions connected to play, and it is individuals who experience the play state. This third approach relates to the educational philosophy of constructivism. It rejects the notion that children passively respond to forces of biology or the environment; rather, children are active agents who construct their unique play ideas, tendencies, and behaviors. These three perspectives are interrelated, and each is useful in studying play in this chapter and throughout the book. Given that the focus of this chapter is on individual differences and diversity, the person-centered perspective will be given center stage.

Comprehensive models of children's play and behavior require that we recognize the importance of biology, environment, and person variables and the complex ways in which these factors interact with each other. In other words, how children play can, first of all, be attributable to their developmental status or level of their maturity and the general trajectory of their growth—the pull of the future, if you will. Play can also be related to the immediate environmental contexts within which children play—the "press of the present moment." Finally, play is also related to experiences children bring to their personal play propensities—the force from the past. Researchers, teachers, parents, and others can seek to explain children's play analytically by taking into account the direct and interactive effects of these three factors. It is difficult to construct comprehensive play models to fully encompass these complex variables, and it necessitates that we use our scientific imaginations. But we must do so to avoid using simplistic single-variable theories or one-reason explanations to explain the complexities of children's play.

In today's complex, postmodern world we must also recognize the limits of the strategy of using analytic, rational modes of thought in the service of trying to explain children's play. We should also rely on our poetic imaginations, our intuitions, and our synthetic (as opposed to analytic) modes of thinking to try to understand children's play. We should use what Jerome Bruner refers to as the narrative as opposed to the paradigmatic (i.e., logical-mathematical) aspect of our intelligence. Our goal should be not absolute certainty of explanation, but a pragmatic understanding, a meaningful story about what is going on when children are playing in a given context that will help us know how best to respond.

In this chapter we examine differences in how children play and behave socially, as a function of gender, personality (personal attributes), and race and ethnicity. In the first section boys and girls are compared in terms of physical and motor play and movement, the use of play space, social play development and play in social groups, object play and toy preferences, and quality of pretend play. Parental, peer, and teacher influences are then discussed, and some recommendations are made for both home and school. In the second section the relationship between personality and personal attributes and play during the early years is examined, particular attention being given to play styles and orientations, playfulness, and childhood depression. Environmental factors are discussed, and some recommendations are again made. In the third section racial and ethnic differences in play and environmental influences are examined.

## FOCUS QUESTIONS

1. During the early childhood years, how different are boys and girls in their play behavior? How do they differ in physical play, object play, and pretend play?
2. What are the major ways in which boys and girls differ in social affiliation and communication styles in social groups?
3. What developmental consequences may result from boys tending to stick with boys and girls with girls in play and other childhood activities?
4. What are some typical socialization behaviors practiced in homes and in schools that reinforce sex-typed behaviors and development during the early years? Identify socialization practices that break down stereotypes and treat boys and girls equitably.
5. How do peer groups perpetuate sex-typed play and social behaviors during early and middle childhood?
6. What are major personality differences in play during the early childhood years? What are the different styles of imaginative play? How do these differences develop?
7. How is playfulness defined, and what specific behaviors should we look for to evaluate playfulness in children?
8. How do young children who are suffering from psychological depression play? How does play help these children to cope and adjust?
9. How are race and ethnicity defined, and what effects on play, if any, are attributable to these sociological variables?

## GENDER DIFFERENCES

If you were asked to predict how a particular child would play in a randomly selected situation and you knew absolutely nothing about the child, what would you predict? If you could ask two specific questions about the child, which facts would be most helpful in predicting the child's play behavior? Having read Chapter 3, you might ask the child's chronological or developmental age. But what would be the other fact you would like to know? The child's culture, social class, family structure, or preschool experience? All of these variables are indeed relevant, but knowing the child's gender would seem to be the most useful second piece of information.

Next to developmental age, a child's gender might be the best single predictor of how the child will react in a randomly chosen situation. Throughout life, age and gender account for more of the variability in a person's general behavior than any other pair of personal attributes. Gender is a social marker and a critical individual difference variable that is responsible for a lion's share of the variance in how all of us behave and think over the course of our lives, including how we play. Gender as an individual differences variable must be incorporated into any comprehensive and pragmatic theories of practices we construct to better understand children's play and adult roles in play. Here is a brief review of some conceptual and empirical research on gender and play during early childhood.

## Physical Play

Physical or motor play is defined as gross and fine muscle activity or the use of body parts in play. As we noted in Chapter 3, objects are not the focus of this form of play. However, play equipment, such as large mats, climbing frames, or trampolines, is often used in connection with physical play. Natural features of the environment may also be involved. For example, children can walk along a fallen log, skip across a grassy area, or fall and roll down the slope of a hill.

Gender differences do emerge in physical activity levels around the age of four or five years (Fagot & O'Brien, 1994). Once they reach this age, boys are more active and boisterous than girls are. In New Zealand, Smith and Inder (1993) observed three-and-a-half- to five-year-olds in a kindergarten and a childcare center. Kindergarten boys appeared to be involved in more physical contact. In both the kindergarten and childcare settings, boisterous play was more likely in boys' groups and mixed-gender groups. Girls' groups tended to be quieter and more passive. Choice of indoor versus outdoor play environments was related to gender in this study as well. Outdoor play was more prevalent by boys in kindergarten; girls were more often seen playing inside. In neighborhood settings in Australia this same pattern emerged: boys preferred outdoor environments, and girls preferred indoor environments (Cunningham, Jones, & Taylor, 1994). In general, boys prefer large outdoor spaces to satisfy their needs and interests in high-activity-level behaviors such as playing ball games and running and chasing one another (Frost, Shin, & Jacobs, 1998).

Boys are more active even in relatively sedentary activities. For instance, when teachers ask young children to sit down and draw, it is not uncommon to see the girls taking very readily to the activity and drawing or coloring in a quiet manner. Girls also tend to frequent art tables during free play much more than do boys. Descriptions of boys' responses to being asked to draw include accounts like the following: "They animate their volcanoes and space wars with exploding noises, as if they have jumped inside the pictures" (Paley, 1984, p. 5). Holmes (1992) observed a middle-class kindergarten class of ten boys and eleven girls during snack time. She discovered that all children pretended and told jokes while eating snacks but that only the boys, not a single girl, "fooled around" (e.g., taboo humor) or "goofed off" (e.g., hiding someone's milk or pulling a chair from under someone). Overall, boys' play tends to be more active and rougher than girls' play, involving more physical contact, fighting, and taunting (Maccoby, 1998).

**Use of Space.** Boys and girls differ significantly in their choice of activities and play environments, boys preferring outdoor environments and girls preferring indoor environments (Cunningham et al., 1994). Research also indicates that preschool boys are more vigorous and active than preschool girls in both indoor and outdoor play environments. For example, Harper and Sanders (1975) recorded the total amount of time and use of space by middle-class three- to five-year-old boys and girls over a two-year period. Boys spent more time outside than did girls; interestingly, differences in behavior did not occur between girls who wore dresses and those who wore jeans. It was common to see boys playing outside and in sand, on a climbing structure, on a tractor, and around the equipment shed, and girls playing inside, at craft tables, or in the kitchen. Although there were no sex differences in the percentage of time spent farther away from school buildings, boys used 1.2 to 1.6 times as much space and entered significantly more play areas.

**Rough-and-Tumble Play.** A prevalent type of physical play that appears in early childhood and continues throughout childhood that is gender-related is rough-and-tumble play (R&T). R&T play is not real fighting but one major form of play fighting (other forms include superhero and war toy play). Examples of types of behaviors demonstrated in R&T play include tackling, chasing and fleeing, pushing or shoving, shadowboxing, faking, kicking behind the knee, and grabbing someone's feet on monkey bars. Boys engage in R&T play more than girls do (Carlsson-Paige & Levin, 1987; Goldstein, 1992; Humphreys & Smith, 1984; Smith, 1997). Boys chase one another, wrestle, and struggle, often while pretending to be fictional characters (which overlaps into superhero play). However, Jarrett, Farokhi, Young, and Davies (2001) recently found that more cross-gender R&T play occurred than they expected among first and third graders they observed during recess time at school.

Peter Smith (1997) conducted a series of investigations in England using teacher interviews to obtain estimates of the frequency of occurrence of R&T play and real fighting. His own research and his review of the literature in this area led him to conclude that when direct playground observations are made, real fighting is a rarity, a conclusion that is consistent with the results of the study by Jarrett et al. (2001). In contrast to real fighting, which happens very rarely, R&T play is typically reported happening on the playground between 5 and 10 percent of the time, with a maximum of 20 percent. Boys have been observed in real physical fighting and in R&T play fighting at twice to three times the rate of girls. This gender difference in R&T play occurs across all cultures.

**Real Aggression.** Research focusing on young children has revealed differences in the types of real aggression in which boys and girls engage. In general, boys tend to display more instrumental aggression (e.g., hitting, grabbing, pushing, or otherwise using physical force to obtain a desired object, territory, or privilege during social conflicts). Girls score higher on measures of relational aggression (i.e., indirect or verbal aggression or indirect bullying, such as is seen in ostracism, breaking contact, gossiping, and other behaviors intended to harm another child's peer relations).

For example, McNeilly-Choque, Hart, Robinson, Nelson, and Olsen (1996), in a large multimethod study of 241 preschoolers in Head Start and university-affiliated preschools, reported that girls were more relationally aggressive than boys were on playgrounds. However, boys exhibited significantly more instrumental aggression than did girls. Both kinds of aggression are significant correlates of lower peer acceptance. Note that here we are dealing with real aggression, not the type of play aggression that occurs in R&T. It would be interesting to research whether girls do more verbal or relational play fighting than boys do and whether they do the most of this "verbal R&T" at a later age than the age at which boys do the most of their R&T or physical play fighting.

**Transition to Middle Childhood.** The transition from the preschool to the grade school years is marked by gender-linked developmental transformations of physical and motor play into sports, athletics, and other activities. There is a basic continuity in boys' tendencies to be more aggressive (R&T tends to get rougher) and adventuresome with increasing age and for them to be keenly interested in the culturally assigned notions of power and speed of performance. Girls tend to remain less boisterous and more cooperative and interested in aesthetics and grace in their physical play. For instance, whereas far more boys join Pee Wee ice hockey teams, girls pursue dance and gymnastics groups. Gender-linked behavior does not mean being gender-exclusive behavior, however. Many girls engage in more boy-like activities, and boys engage in more girl-like activities.

In summary, considerable support exists for the assertion that boys, compared to girls, engage in more R&T play and more real fighting (instrumental but not relational) and prefer to use outdoor space. Research is less conclusive concerning level of physical activity, especially at younger ages (Fagot & O'Brien, 1994). Significant gender differences do not appear in total activity level before four or five years of age. Marked variation occurs at each age, making generalizations difficult. During the grade school years, gender-linked trends in physical play are manifested in sports, athletics, and other organized physical activities. Boys' play, compared to girls', is marked by larger play groups, more competitiveness, role differentiation, and rule-governed team play. In general, boys seek more outdoor activity and require more physical space.

## Social Play

In general, sociability does not differ greatly between young boys' and girls' play. Parten (1933) reported that the play scale she developed showed age-related differences but not gender-related differences. However, she did find that two-thirds of the play groups children chose were same-gender groupings and that preferred and favorite playmates were usually of the same gender. Research generally supports Parten's findings regarding the lack of gender differences in the sociability of play. Johnson and Roopnarine (1983) in a review of research concluded that the differences between preschool boys and girls in social play were not significant. Only one study in England reported that girls are ahead of boys in social play during the preschool years (Tizard, Philps, & Plewis, 1976a).

**Play Affiliation.** Others who have researched the social play of young children concur with Parten's observation that same-gender playmates are more common and more compatible than opposite-gender playmates. Sex segregation in play is a consistent finding. Martin and Fabes (2001) reported that in observed peer interaction, 50 percent of the preschool children had same-sex partner(s) and 15 percent had opposite-sex partner(s). The remaining 35 percent of peer interaction occurred in mixed groups. They concluded that young children do socialize with members of the opposite sex a fair amount of time but usually when another member of their own sex is also involved. Maccoby and Jacklin (1987) reported findings from a longitudinal study that showed that preschool children spent three times as much time playing with same-sex as with opposite-sex playmates and that by six years of age this ratio increased to eleven times. Preference for same-gender groupings has been noted by other researchers as well (Fabes, Martin, & Hanish, 2003; Fishbein & Imai, 1993; Hartle, 1996; Moller & Serbin, 1996; Powlishta, Serbin, & Moller, 1993; Ramsey, 1995; Shell & Eisenberg, 1990; Urberg & Kaplan, 1989).

From this research three general assertions can be made. First, sex segregation in play begins during the early years, with the bias against the opposite sex more evident in self-reports (stated preferences) than in actual behavioral observations (Ramsey, 1995). Apparently, even if children show a tendency toward gender-based exclusion in self-reports, they may show much less of this bias in their actual behavior. Attraction to an activity may overrule the urge to live by what they say about wanting to play with only same-sex children. Also, this finding might be due to the possibility that children overstate their gender bias in an interview because of a social desirability factor, that is, to conform to some perceived social norm operating in their lives at this time (e.g., there is "boy play" and there is "girl play," and it is important not to like to play in the opposite way or with an opposite-sex playmate, or at least it is important not to admit it).

Second, girls start to show a preference for same-sex playmates at an earlier age than boys do. Moller and Serbin (1996), in a study of toddlers with a mean age of thirty-five months, found that 62 percent of the girls played with same-sex peers at above chance levels, but that only 21 percent of the males did. However, once gender bias is established, it seems more consistent and rigid in males (LaFreniere, Strayer, & Gauthier, 1984; Powlishta et al., 1993, Shell & Eisenberg, 1990). For instance, in a three-year study of children ranging in age from one to six years, LaFreniere et al. (1984) found that girls typically preferred playing with same-sex peers at an earlier age than boys did. However, at later ages during the preschool years, boys' tendencies for same-sex interaction increased while those of the girls leveled off. In general, for both boys and girls there is a tendency to select same-sex peers as play partners, and this propensity typically increases during the early childhood years, especially for boys (Diamond, LeFurgy, & Blass, 1993; Maccoby, 1990; Ramsey, 1995).

Third, although a bias in children against playing with members of the opposite sex exists across Euro-American, Asian-American, and African-American samples (Fishbein & Imai, 1993), constructive play activity appears somewhat immune to this bias relative to other forms of play (Hartle, 1996, Urberg & Kaplan, 1989). This third assertion, based on the research, reflects the fact that constructive play is usually more structured and more closely monitored by the teacher. For example, Fabes et al. (2003) found not only that mixed-sex group play usually involved nonstereotyped activities (such as the kinds found in most constructive play episodes in early childhood settings), but also that these mixed-sex peer groups typically played near an adult (almost always a female teacher) more than did same-sex or other-sex dyads. Girls more than boys are drawn to their teachers (same-sex adult role models), who often encourage quieter, more sedentary activities such as constructive play. When boys are in these mixed groups, they seem to accommodate to the norms for this kind of classroom activity.

Why young children prefer same-sex playmates is a question that has intrigued researchers and educators alike. Cognitive consonance theory, which postulates that we seek experiences and evidence that conform with our mental models or cognitive beliefs, posits that children first learn their own identity as male or female, and because they value anything associated with their gender, they seek partners "like me."

Another explanation for gender segregation involves the role of toys and activities. This is the gender-typed toy preference theory. Children are drawn to toys they like to play with, toys that are recognized as gender-typed by children as young as two years of age. These preferred toys bring children into contact with peers who like the same toys and activities and who happen to be the same gender. Maybe children tend to play with same-gender play partners for reasons related to a cognitive awareness of one's own gender (with attraction to other children who are the same gender) and to the pull of sex-typed toys and activities (and the compatible play interests of same-gender peers) (Hartup, 1983).

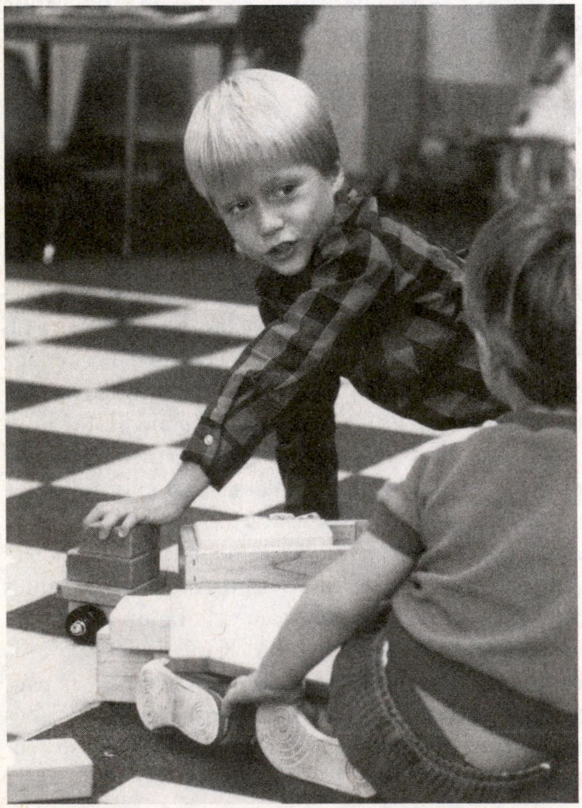

➤ One explanation for gender segregation involves the role of toys and activities. This is called the *gender-typed toy preference theory*.

A third explanation for the emergence of gender segregation in play is known as behavioral compatibility theory (Moller & Serbin, 1996). Contrasting behavioral and social interactional styles are said to be responsible for the gender differences in social play during the early childhood period. For example, some girls may dislike assertive and aggressive behavior in the classroom and therefore avoid boys (unless a teacher is there to mediate the activity, as in typical constructive play). Children gravitate toward other children who exhibit similar styles of play and social interaction. Children feel more comfortable with peers who show behaviors with which they are familiar and to which they can more easily respond. Compatible playmates can more readily build mutually satisfying relationships.

## Communication and Interaction Styles

Research has examined gender differences in interactional style during early childhood as a phenomenon in its own right and for explanations as to why gender segregation is so pronounced in young children. Ideas generated from the research also may turn out to be useful to educators and parents who are concerned about promoting positive behaviors across gender lines—indeed, among all groups of children.

Researchers and educators have recognized gender differences in communication, play styles, and modes of social influence during early and middle childhood for decades. Boys are better known for their more assertive, direct, physical way of obtaining what they want during play and their preoccupation with dominance issues; girls are better known for their more verbal and prosocial manner, their concern about being nice and polite in their behaviors with others, and their use of enabling forms of communication to advance group harmony.

Sluss (2002) examined videotapes and transcriptions of audiotapes that recorded play interactions and that were coded for the play level, block construction complexity, and types of communications of forty-eight four-year olds. These children were playing in same-sex dyads in a laboratory setting using hollow and unit blocks. The children were not familiar with each other before the study. While boy and girl pairs engaged in similar levels of constructive as opposed to functional or other types of play, the girls engaged in a great deal more conversation than did the boys. Their conversations were more complex and lengthier than were those of the boys. Boys were not as cooperative with each other as were the girls, although some boy dyads interacted with nonverbal strategies of communication.

In New Zealand, Smith and Inder (1993) observed the play of younger children in childcare and the play of older children in kindergarten. Mixed-gender play groups were seen one-third of the time, and same-gender play groups were seen two-thirds of the time. Mixed-gender play groups were larger in size, perhaps because children brought same-sex friends with them to combine with the opposite-sex groups. Boys dominated the play in mixed groups, and more conflicts and rejection incidents occurred in these groups than in homogeneous groups, with rates of physical conflicts being higher in the kindergarten setting and with rates of rejection and withdrawal being higher in the childcare setting. These patterns of behavior were seen as evidence of incompatible styles of interaction between boys and girls.

Black (1989) studied same-age, same-gender triads of three- and four-year-old preschoolers as they played together in a university-affiliated preschool laboratory with various toys and materials. Girls, in general, used a smooth style of turn-taking in their play interactions, and their social behaviors were related to each other interactionally and topically. Girls anticipated each other's behaviors, valuing harmonious interaction more than the boys did. Girls' episodes were longer-lasting and more coherent. Boys seemed more interested in having their own way, causing their play to become more fragmented and disjointed. Black's results are consistent with Carol Gilligan's (1982) notion that girls are socialized to roles of nurturance and boys to roles of dominance. This socialization is supported by teachers and parents, who are more likely to assist girls in solving their social conflicts while expecting boys to solve them alone.

Gender differences in the strategy of play interactions is seen in the following: (1) Child A—"Let's play doctors," Child B—"Okay!" versus (2) Child A—"Pretend I am a nurse now," Child B—"My sick baby is sleeping over there." The first interaction reflects a direct strategy; the second represents an indirect strategy. Sawyer (1997) observed indoor free play and found that boys used twice as many direct verbal strategies to enter play but that boys and girls used similar numbers of indirect play entry strategies. Sachs (1987) also found this pattern when he compared pairs of preschool boys and girls playing "doctor" with an assortment of play paraphernalia (e.g., syringe, stethoscope, etc.) related to this theme. The amount of pretend play was the same for boys and girls. However, boys assigned themselves the dominant role 79 percent of the time, compared to 33 percent for girls. Negotiations over new roles were assigned by using both imperatives ("You're the patient") and questions ("Will you be the patient?"). Seventy-two percent of the boys' proposals were imperatives, but only 20 percent of the girls' proposals were.

**Team or Group Activities.** During the early childhood years boys and girls initially seem to have similar interest and participation in games and group activities. As children get older, marked gender differences appear. Boys are much more likely to become involved in large-group competitive play than are girls, who seem more comfortable in a smaller group of children or best friend dyads (Maltz & Borker, 1982; Sutton-Smith, 1979b; Tarullo, 1994). Girls are as concerned about fairness as boys are and have as many conflicts as boys do. However, girls seem more subjective and focused on the nature of social relations, while boys are focused on the activity itself. These trends give boys the edge in certain activities that are hard-nosed and objective, while girls are favored in activities in which sensitivity in social interaction is called for. These are extreme contrasts, and a great deal of convergence can be expected with specific girls and boys. Also, this general pattern may be changing with the trend toward more competitive team sports experiences for girls. We have heard it said more than once that girls can be just as brutal as the boys are in a soccer game, for example. How often we hear referees talking about how vicious the girls are becoming!

In summary, little evidence suggests significant gender differences in levels of social play or sociability, but there is considerable support for the proposition that gender preferences and interaction styles in social play are different for boys and girls. Same-sex playmates are usually chosen, beginning around four years of age and increasing with age. Conflicting play styles are present. Girls tend to be less direct and explicit. Boys are more assertive and dominant. As children grow into the primary grade school years, girls and boys often do not share the same peer culture. Boys' social worlds are more extensive, individualistic, and competitive, and girls' social worlds tend to be more intensive, affiliative, and subjective.

## Object Play

There are significant differences in the kinds of toys young boys and girls use in play. Boys tend to prefer to play on the floor with pushing and pulling toys, blocks, or wheeled toys; girls like to play on a tabletop coloring, doing puzzles, or playing with dolls (Wardle, 1991). How children use toys is linked to the child's gender. Girls show a strong propensity for constructive play, while boys display a greater tendency for functional play. Girls tend to use objects according to a plan, as in completing a puzzle or coloring a page. Boys are more likely to use materials in ways that are appropriate but somewhat stereotyped and repetitious, such as pushing a small vehicle, blowing bubbles, or cranking a mechanical toy (Johnson & Roopnarine, 1983). This gender difference in functional and constructive play relates to differences in active involvement. Preschool girls move objects less and use them more educationally and quietly than do boys (Moore, Evertson, & Brophy, 1974). Tabletop activities that encourage constructive play tend to involve girls and entail sedentary behaviors, while functional play is typically associated with more active movement.

**Toy Preferences.** Toys are gender-typed in our society and in most countries around the world. Gender-role stereotyping of materials and activities appears as early as age twelve months and is responsible in part for the fact that many young boys and girls show well-ingrained toy preferences by three years of age (Sutton-Smith, 1979b). The finding that some materials are more consistently preferred by either males or females has been consistently reported in the play literature for more than seventy years (e.g., Parten, 1933). Girls tend to play more frequently and longer with dolls and art materials; boys prefer blocks and wheeled vehicles.

**Gender Asymmetry.** The literature also indicates that girls seem to enjoy a greater variety of play materials and activities, owing to the gender asymmetry in toy selection by boys and girls. Whereas girls use both so-called boy toys and girl toys, boys are far more likely to shun certain so-called girl toys, such as dolls. This generalization is reflected in a study by Liss (1981) of kindergarten children's play with traditional female, male, and non-sex-typed or neutral toys. Children were observed and rated on appropriate use of a toy, enjoyment, aggression, movement, and nurturance. Boys seemed more familiar with, and enjoyed and played more appropriately with, male and neutral toys, whereas girls played with toys in all three categories. Girls showed more nurturing behavior than boys did, and boys made more noise while playing with toys.

The hypothesis that asymmetry exists in gender-linked toy and activity preferences is supported by numerous research studies. For example, Carter and Levy (1988) asked young children to sort line drawings of a kitchen, a doll, a sewing machine, a gun, a bat, a truck, a balloon, a drum, and a telephone on the basis of which ones they would like to play with. The children were then asked to sort again within the groupings as a measure of flexibility. Boys' preferences were more stereotyped and consistent. Powlishta et al. (1993) observed children who were going on three years old using masculine (e.g., vehicles, balls, Fisher-Price toys) and feminine (e.g., dolls, dress-up items, art) toys. Whereas the girls were inconsistent in their attraction to the male toys, the boys displayed stable differences favoring the masculine items. Interestingly, the girls who played most often with "boy toys" tended to be seen most frequently with girls; perhaps avoiding boys made it easier for the girls to play with their toys, since cross-gender peers tend to inhibit gender-inappropriate play. These trends with respect to toys and play themes (e.g., Smith & Inder, 1993) persist through the early childhood years (Sutton-Smith, 1979b).

## Pretend Play

Research has shown that during the early childhood years boys and girls do not differ in total amounts of pretend play or in their general level of fantasy-making ability (e.g., Connolly, Doyle, & Reznick, 1988; Sachs, 1987). Although gender differences exist in certain aspects of pretend play, such as the interactional styles already described, even more obvious gender differences exist in the content or theme of pretend play. However, there are no gender differences in structural aspects of pretend play, such as its organizational complexity, narrative richness, or transformational quality.

**Object Transformations.** Realistic or representational toys are often used in pretend play: dolls, miniature farm animals, toy soldiers, or toy superheroes (replica objects transformations). Sometimes children play with props that bear little concrete similarity to the imagined object; for example, a large rectangular block is used as a make-believe television set (substitute object transformations). Children sometimes play without a particular object or play prop at all, relying on language and internal imagery to sustain make-believe episodes (pretend objects transformation). Are these object transformation behaviors gender-related during the early years?

Some laboratory research has found that preschool girls are ahead of preschool boys in object transformational abilities. Matthews (1977) reported that four-year-old girls were superior to four-year-old boys in initiating pretend play without relying on concrete props. Boys gradually became less dependent on objects in make-believe play episodes over successive trials, while girls who began at a lower level than did boys and initially maintained a balance between all three types of object transformations later preferred substitute and pretend transformations. McLoyd (1980), in a study of low-income African-American preschoolers, found that girls made significantly more substitute and pretend object transformations than did boys. Fein, Johnson, Kosson, Stork, and Wasserman (1975) found that girls seemed to pretend more than boys during toddlerhood and to become less dependent on realistic concrete props at an earlier age than boys.

These gender differences in object transformation favoring girls tend not to be found in free-play situations in classrooms (as opposed to laboratory experiments). Johnson, Ershler, and Bell (1980) found that preschool girls and boys did not differ significantly in use of objects during pretend-play episodes. Black (1989) reported that triads of preschool boys appeared less dependent on props to initiate imaginative play than did triads of girls, a finding that contradicts the findings of some laboratory experiments.

In summary, the majority of the evidence indicates that girls are ahead of boys in object transformational skills. If this is the case for younger preschoolers, it is probably due to girls' accelerated linguistic and cognitive development. For older preschoolers and kindergartners, however, differences in modes of pretend play are probably more a matter of preference than of cognitive maturity. Neither gender is behind the other in the transformational qualities of their play. Girls and boys have the same symbolic representational capacities, a cognitive parity that also accounts for the apparent lack of gender differences along other structural features of pretend play, such as its narrative script organization (Wolf & Grollman, 1982) and integration (Goncu & Kessel, 1984).

**Role Enactment and Play Themes.** Research evidence suggests that during pretend play girls show a preference for home-centered interests involving dolls, dress-up clothes, and domestic items, whereas boys are drawn to more villainous and dangerous themes and plots and make more use of vehicles and guns (Sutton-Smith, 1979b). Girls tend to portray family characters and to select themes based on everyday experiences; boys tend to participate in adventure themes and to enact superhero roles and appear to be more physically active in pretend play (Levin & Carlsson-Paige, 1994; Paley, 1984).

Research with older girls indicates that they are interested in superhero characters when given the chance to participate in such play (Marsh, 2000). Marsh observed 57 six- and seven-year-olds in an inner-city classroom in northern England. Data were gathered using field notes, video recordings, and a collection of children's writing within a sociodramatic play center that had a "Bat Cave" theme. Drapes and screens helped to create a cavelike atmosphere, and there was a cardboard "Batmobile," and various items representing maps, radios, and the like. Children also had access to a dressing-up rack with various outfits, hats, and masks. There were two desks with writing and reading materials and a computer. Children were shown some videos of Batman and Batwoman adventures and discussed the sexist issues depicted in some of the videos. The children clearly understood that girls could be Batwoman. Data were collected on how often boys and girls went to the Bat Cave over a ten-day period. Not only did the girls frequent the Bat Cave almost as much as the boys did, but girls also showed a great deal of interest, which was recorded by the researcher's field notes and video recordings and in the Batman and Batwoman diaries all the children kept. Marsh concluded that girls did not prefer a male superhero character as found by Singer and Singer (1981) but preferred Batwoman and enjoyed engaging in active and powerful behaviors. A major appeal of the cave for the girls might have been the opportunity to become involved in the reading and writing activities inside this literacy-enhanced sociodramatic play center in a primary school classroom. Also, their attraction to the female superhero figure might reflect the cultural shift toward a wider definition of acceptable feminine roles.

Earlier, Marsh (1999) reported data indicating that although girls were very interested in playing Batwoman, there were some interesting differences in the imaginative play of the boys and the girls. Although girls sometimes mentioned Batman, boys rarely mentioned Batwoman in their literacy production (narrative entries in their Batman diary), and if they did mention her, she was an assistant to Batman.

Further, in their writings and readings the boys described the Bat Cave area as more functional than did the girls. For example, whereas the boys would use the maps and set traps or make lists of things taken by the Joker, girls would write to communicate their feelings to Batman, the police, the victims, and so on.

Bergman and Lefcourt (1994) report a case of a child attempting to integrate both masculine and feminine identifications into the same role play. A little boy, who was under three years of age, enacted the role of a repairman (his father was in the construction business), yet the boy included in his tool kit a vacuum cleaner, which was used by his mother. Thus at times there is no sharp dichotomy; play enactment can occur within an appropriate gender role but can also blend masculine and feminine traits.

Boys and girls choose different kinds of activities during pretend play in part because of differences in interests, temperament, and available shared scripts. Boys soon elect to go beyond the familiar and realistic themes of house, doctor, and school and into the more unfamiliar and fantasy themes of spacemen, superheroes, and different creatures. Girls appear more content to stick with the themes and roles that are popular with all children initially. Howe, Moller, Chambers, and Petrakos (1993) examined preschool children's social and pretend play in the housekeeping center and in other novel dramatic play centers, such as bakery, pharmacy, pirate ship, and fruit and vegetable store. These novel centers were attractive to the boys. Girls preferred the traditional housekeeping centers. The study was done over only a few days. Perhaps girls would have expressed more interest in the novel play centers over time. Although happy in the female-dominated housekeeping area, the girls might want to try out the new play settings after they have been in the classroom for a while. Weinberger and Starkey (1994), in their study of play behaviors of African-American children in different Head Start play centers, also reported that preschool girls preferred the housekeeping center.

In the later early childhood period, overt dramatic play transforms into more covert imaginative or creative play expressions that are appropriate for school-age children, but certain gender-linked pretense play patterns persist. Although the sophistication and complexity of pretense play seen in six- to eight-year-olds do not favor either gender, the content and the themes vary in line with gender socialization. Girls' pretend-play themes and play content continue to reflect their primary concerns and interests relating to nurturance and connection with others, and boys' themes and play content continue to reflect concerns relating to autonomy and power. Play themes in videogames and content in books and toys or from movies and television may be viewed along a continuum of more to less boy-like and more to less girl-like. Boys and girls often pick what play activities to do, what songs to listen to, what roles in classroom skits to enact, what arts and crafts to make, and what hobbies to cultivate along gender-linked lines.

Children from six to eight years of age come into their own as effective storytellers, and their narratives often reveal gender-linked perspectives. Case studies by Tarullo (1994) analyzed the play narratives of seven-year-olds and found that a central developmental task for children of this age revolved around how to balance intimacy, identity, or being connected versus being autonomous, as in conforming to a group or being creative as an individual. Case studies of Eddy and Maggie illustrate how children's stories anticipate the human need to eventually outgrow a polarized gender schema that pits masculinity against femininity. Eddy tells about a neighborhood bully in his story, while Maggie discusses how to confront her friends over a grievance. Eddy fears admitting his anxiety as much as dealing with the bully. His manifest concern is whether he is macho enough, and his latent worry has to do with feelings and vulnerabilities. Maggie fears what might happen if she stops blaming herself and instead asserts herself in public. The manifest issue here is confrontation and potentially damaged relationships with friends; the latent issue for Maggie, according to Tarullo, would seem to be the realization that on a personal level, newly achieved individual assertiveness and feelings of self-reliance can be equal in importance to caring about relationships with others. The findings are consistent with what we know about gender role development in which gender constancy needs dominate at first and children start out in stereotypical fashion. Then, as they become more comfortable with their gender identity, they have less need for behaving in a way that conforms with gender stereotypes. Gender and racial constancy are two huge developmental tasks in early childhood.

Singer (1995) has argued that an important developmental task, which is assisted by gender-linked pretense in its various forms, is to come to grips with the inherent male-female dichotomy within each of us. Boys and girls, men and women, all of us are always battling to balance affiliation needs with autonomy needs. In practice, there is consensus that achievement and affiliation must both be met in human development. Theoretically, it seems that these clusters are not so much opposite ends of one bipolar dimension as two separate unipolar dimensions.

Singer holds that all humans are motivated to make sense of the world and to assign meanings. The *structural features* of pretense play (kinds of transformations, complexity of scripts, organization of the play, etc.) are helpful in achieving this goal of integrating the strange with the familiar, new knowledge with existing knowledge (i.e., accommodation and assimilation). The *content* of the pretense, on the other hand, reveals the child's attempts to cope with these gender-related anxieties concerning linkages and attachment versus power and assertion of individuality. Play themes relating to war (primordial male creature anxiety?) and having babies (primordial female creature anxiety?) might stem from polarized opposites etched in the human psyche from our past as a species on earth (as in the concepts of Jungian racial memories or the collective unconscious). Be this as it may, humans in their life course often do seem to seek to balance agency and affiliation needs, both privately (intrapsychically) as represented in fantasies and publicly (interpersonally) as represented in their ongoing attempts to meet and master real-world tasks. These real-world tasks are also cultural manifestations of what it means to be a girl and what it means to be a boy. Developmental precursors of these strivings for balance may be seen increasingly in the play and narratives of boys and girls growing up.

**Imaginary Companions.** Taylor, Carlson, and Gerow (2001) note that the phenomenon of imaginary companions (pretend playmates) is a misunderstood type of solitary play that reveals a considerable amount about children who have them. Partington and Grant (1984) found that children who create make-believe playmates are most likely to be three-to-six years old, with more girls than boys having such companions. More than half the time imaginary companions are about the same age and the same sex as the children who invent them. Best estimates are that approximately 25 percent of children enjoy this elaborate form of fantasy, and children who have imaginary friends tend to be brighter and to manifest more stable and creative behavior than children who do not. Higher incidence of imaginary playmates has been reported. For example, Taylor et al. (2001) estimate that 28 percent of children have formed imaginary companions by four years of age, with higher estimates for older children (seven years old) and when creating a life-like personality for a special toy is counted as having an imaginary companion.

Dorothy Singer and Jerome Singer (1990) suggest a gender difference in the general incidence of imaginary companionship, but they also note that this difference is not statistically significant. The Singers have reported that for boys imaginativeness and positive affect during free play are positively linked to having an imaginary companion (and are negatively correlated with watching television cartoons). For girls having an imaginary companion was associated with persistence during play and to fewer negative emotional outbursts of anger, fear, or sadness. Both boys and girls who had imaginary companions were more likely to help and share with peers (Singer & Singer, 1990).

Boys were more likely to have animals as make-believe playmates, and girls were significantly more likely than boys to have a male imaginary companion. Only 13 percent of the boys with imaginary friends included any opposite-sex ones; for girls this figure was 42 percent. One-third of the time the children with imaginary companions named them after real people, even friends. Sometimes these imaginary friends come from the media. Again, girls were interested in both male and female characters, such as Bionic Woman, Batwoman, Wonder Woman, Superman, or Batman. Boys selected only male characters (Singer & Singer, 1990), showing the rigidity mentioned earlier in the section on gender differences.

Research by Taylor, Cartwright, and Carlson (1993) and by Gleason, Sebanc, McGinley, and Hartup (1997) are consistent with the Singers' findings linking imaginative play with imaginary companions. Taylor et al. (1993) found that four-year-old boys with imaginary companions were more likely to engage in fantasy play than in reality or object play; Gleason et al. (1997) reported that role play was related to having imaginary companions. The later researchers differentiated between invisible friends and relationships with personified objects and found that children with imaginary companions in the form of personified objects showed a significantly higher levels of role play than did children without imaginary companions. Invisible friends functioned as pretend peers that provided a controllable relationship and a solitary forum to rehearse social skills, whereas personified objects (often stuffed animals) were known by others more and were used by the child across a greater variety of situations, perhaps serving dramatic play purposes to a greater extent than invisible friends.

Partington and Grant (1984) have speculated that imaginary companions might provide an important initial link between fantasy and reality. During their early years, if children have difficulty with roles and rules that frame play episodes with real children, they may gain valuable experience practicing these skills with invented playmates whom they can control. Having imaginary playmates in the primary grades is not considered a positive sign or a negative sign unless corroborating data suggest emotional difficulty. This generalization might not hold across cultural or racial groups.

## Environmental Influences

The first school experience usually is a great homogenizer of individual differences among children. Homogenization refers to the process by which children behave more and more similarly and predictably as they get used to classroom routines and teacher expectations and as they affect one another during the school year. Although considerable individual variation exists in children's initial reactions to the demands placed on them by other children and teachers, patterns emerge in sex-differentiated preschool play in the classroom or childcare center that follow this general homogenization tendency. The foundation for gender-related play patterns is set in the home environment; family influences are the source of initial and persisting variation among children in play interests and behavior that grows during the school year.

Variation exists in how parents socialize young children, and these variations influence children's play. An important source of diversity is the child's gender. Other important child attributes, such as a child's personality or temperament, are also partly responsible for differences in parental socialization practices. Parenting differences also relate to environmental variation due to family and cultural background (e.g., family size, class, race, ethnicity). Further, we know that fathers socialize their children differently than do mothers.

Across cultures, parents, teachers, and other agents of socialization tend to treat boys and girls differently. They encourage boys to engage in stereotypically masculine activities such as block play and rough-and-tumble play and encourage girls to engage in activities such as doll play and helping other people. Parents also assign household chores on the basis of traditional male and female roles, such as asking daughters to wash dishes or to dust and asking sons to take out the garbage or help to clean the garage. Children learn that the world is divided up by gender and, though this is a complex developmental process, come to realize that their gender is a permanent feature of their identity. Children begin to view the world through gender-colored glasses, a biasing tendency to see people and events stereotypically (e.g., remembering a male nurse as a doctor or a female doctor as a nurse).

**Parental Influences.** As we have already suggested, gender-differentiated behavior is first shaped within the family when parents and others in the child's home disapprove of gender-atypical activities and reward gender-typical ones (Maccoby & Jacklin, 1974). Social learning theorists have attested that parents treat their sons and daughters differently (see Chapter 2). They may ignore or discourage doll play by their sons while encouraging nurturing and submissive behavior in their daughters.

Home influences on gender-based play begin soon after an infant enters the family. When the gender of a baby has been determined, even before she or he is born, some parents begin to buy certain gender-linked toys and clothes and might paint the unborn child's bedroom pink or blue. Parents have almost immediate gender-typed expectations of their children. Fathers describe newborn daughters as soft, small, and delicate and describe newborn sons as large and active (Rubin, Provenzano, & Luria, 1974). Children might not actually differ in these dimensions at birth, but parents apparently believe that they do.

➤ In all cultures the influence on gender-based play begins soon after the infant enters the family.

These parental expectations influence the socialization of boys and girls and are reflected in the way parents dress their sons and daughters differently and provide them with different toys early in life. For example, a study by Rheingold and Cook (1975) surveyed the bedrooms of forty-eight boys and forty-eight girls, examining furnishings and toys. The boys' rooms contained more vehicles, educational and art materials, sports equipment, machines, and military toys. The girls' rooms contained more dolls, dollhouses, and domestic toys and were decorated with ruffles and floral prints. These children, between the ages of one and six years, all had their own rooms. Not only did the boys have more toys at every age, but they also had more classes of toys. The boys were given toys that encouraged activities away from the home; girls' toys encouraged home-centered activities.

In addition, parental expectations are transmitted through interaction with their children. Caldera, Huston, and O'Brien (1989) observed mothers and fathers as they played with their toddlers. Female-typed toys were identified as dolls and a kitchen set; male-typed toys were identified as trucks and blocks; and neutral toys were identified as puzzles and shape sorters. Although parents did not openly encourage the use of one type of toy over another, the parents' initial nonverbal responses to the toys were more positive, and they were more likely to become involved in their children's play when the toys were stereotyped for the child's gender.

Moreover, fathers make themselves more available to their sons and interact with them differently than do mothers of sons, mothers of daughters, and fathers of daughters. Lamb (1977) found that fathers engaged their sons in more vigorous and physically stimulating infant games or play routines. Mothers were more likely to engage their infants in conventional activities such as pat-a-cake and to stimulate them with toys and other objects. Although the parents might not be deliberately trying to sex-type their children, these parental actions maximize the possibility for their children to acquire same-sex behavior patterns. These findings lend further support to the contention that parents strongly influence, consciously or unconsciously, the development of gender-differentiated play activities.

Researchers have also examined variation in how mothers and fathers play with sons and daughters. Lindsey and Mize (2001) note that parents as a rule encourage gender-typed play activities in their children, mothers usually engaging their children more in pretense play and fathers engaging them more in physical play, but they also note that the extent to which parents vary in their play with sons and daughters in different situations is not clear. Lindsey and Mize were interested in contextual differences in parent-child play and in how parent-child play may relate to peer play behavior. Results from observing thirty-three mother and father pairs and their five-year-old children in a ten-minute pretense play session (with a set of zoo animals, a cooking set, plastic vehicles) and in a ten-minute physical play session (with a set of Nerf® bats and balls and a large Slo-Mo® ball) revealed context effects on parent-child play. In the pretense play session mothers and daughters performed the most pretend play, and in the physical play session father and son dyads exhibited more physical play than did father and daughter dyads. Parents who engaged in more pretense play with their children had children who engaged in more of this play behavior with peers, and likewise for physical play. These findings suggest that parents may contribute to children's gender-type play with peers.

**Peer Influences.** Considerable gender differences in children's play is seen by three years of age, and these differences are accentuated when children come under the influence of teachers and peers in a classroom or childcare setting. There are also continuing effects of parents and siblings on children's gender-linked play.

Gender differences in group play have been observed in relation to subtle forms of social behavior. Research suggests that gender-differentiated play may be determined in part by responses of peers to children's activities during free play. Serbin, Connor, Burchardt, and Citron (1979) investigated the effects of peer presence on the gender-typed toy choices of three- and four-year-old boys and girls. The experiment consisted of testing the children alone, in the presence of a same-gender peer, and in the presence of an opposite-gender peer. Male- and female-typed toys were presented to the children. Results showed that the probability of play with cross-sex toys was highest for both boys and girls when they were alone and was lowest when they were with an opposite-sex peer. Girls were more likely to play with cross-gender toys than were boys, and examples of "gender-bending" by girls.

Other researchers have found similar tendencies in preschool children. Boys who engage in male-typed behavior receive more positive responses from peers than do girls who engage in female-typed behavior. Peer reinforcement, particularly same-gender peer reinforcement, is also effective in changing children's behaviors to become gender typical (Lamb, Easterbrooks, & Holden, 1980). The male peer group during the preschool years is especially potent in shaping stereotypically male behavior (Fagot, 1981). Children, especially boys, risk ostracism if they fail to conform to peer group standards for play and toy use. Gender doing, not bending, is the norm.

**Teacher Influences.** Overwhelming evidence suggests that the early channeling of children toward traditional gender-typed activities is based on children's experiences as family members. Parents, siblings, and peers lay the foundation for the gender differences that are observed in the classroom or childcare center. By the time they come under teachers' influence, children already seem to possess well-formed notions about gender-stereotyped behaviors sanctioned by our society. The media and popular culture provide continuing influence on children. To what extent do teachers reinforce and further these societal ascriptions? To what extent can and should they try to expand children's play to encompass a wide range of gender play?

Teachers tend to spend more time with children who engage in female sex-typed activity such as arts and crafts and doll and kitchen play. Teachers of young children are, with very few exceptions, females; and preschool-aged girls tend to focus on the same activities. Typical male-typed play behavior such as vehicle or truck play tends not to attract much teacher attention or reinforcement. Boys tend to enjoy playing on the floor with blocks or vehicles, yet many teachers prefer not to spend time on the floor. Girls often are seen as closer to the teacher than boys are and seek structured or constructive play activities far more than boys do (Carpenter, Huston-Stein, & Baer, 1978). Francis Wardle (1991) did a survey of the teachers in his large Head Start program because he was concerned about the high number of boys whom teachers recommended for special education testing. Results showed that teachers not only avoided the block area and science area, but also modeled only traditional female activities in the housekeeping area and rarely played on the floor. Further, woodwork benches that were specifically purchased to increase the range of choices in the classroom were used as teacher desks and fish aquarium stands.

Serbin, Tonick, and Sternglanz (1979) examined the effects of teacher presence in the vicinity of play and the effects of teachers' modeling play with gender-typed toys. The gender of the teacher was systematically varied to examine the influence of this factor on the play of boys and girls. Both boys and girls increased their rates of play participation in response to teacher presence in gender-typed activity areas. The boys were more responsive to teacher involvement in male-preferred activity areas, especially when the teacher was male. Teacher presence and involvement in different locations in the classroom or childcare center can influence children's gender-related play patterns.

Modification of the spatial organization of the classroom can change children's sex-typed play behavior. Children's play experiences will be enriched by increasing the range and type of toys available. Francis Wardle recommends that the housekeeping area be renamed the dramatic play area and that specific male-typed props, such as hard hats, fire hoses, and car tools, be added.

Other educators have suggested that the block areas and the housekeeping areas should be linked so that the areas can be used together, leading to more social interaction with opposite-gender companions. Kinsman and Berk (1979) demonstrated that removal of a divider between the housekeeping area and the block area significantly increased play between boys and girls who had been together one year or less. The removal of the divider also encouraged children to play with toys traditionally used by the opposite sex. Children who had been enrolled in the same center for two years, however, did not change their patterns of play. Instead, some of these children attempted to replace the divider. Nevertheless, this study does suggest that teacher modification of the physical environment can influence play patterns.

Jim Christie also has an anecdote that demonstrates the persistence of gender-typed behavior in spite of these types of environmental manipulation. He visited a kindergarten where the teacher had combined the block and housekeeping areas. Two girls were playing with a dollhouse on the kitchen table, and two boys were playing with a large toy truck and blocks on the floor. The boys brought their truck over to the dollhouse and methodically put all of the dollhouse furniture onto the truck bed and drove away. Then they returned and put the dollhouse on the truck. The two girls, who were watching all this with amazement, asked what the boys were doing. The boys replied, "Robbing the house." The two girls left in disgust.

Teachers may create more egalitarian programs through being more cognizant of the types of social groups that occur in the classroom or center, specifically the opportunities children have for same-sex and other-sex play dyads and mixed-sex group play. Research by Fabes, Martin, and Hamish (2003) recently drew attention to important distinctions between the group dynamics connected with dyadic and peer group play. Variables studied included nearness to adults, behavioral style (how active and forceful), and the stereotyped nature of play activity in different peer play social contexts: same-sex, other-sex, and mixed-sex peers groups. The children who were four years old rarely played during free play in a dyad with an opposite-sex child, but about one-fourth of the time they did play in larger peer groups that included both boys and girls. These mixed-gender peer groups showed less stereotyped play and usually played near a teacher. Children in cross-gender dyads accommodated to each other in that girls with boys tended to be more forceful compared to girl-girl pairs, and boys were less active and forceful when with girls than when in male pairs.

Clearly, individual play patterns are associated with individual child characteristics (gender) and peer group variables (dyad, mixed group). Gender is important in peer relations during early childhood, and teachers may attempt to intervene in ways to affect positively the kinds of experiences children have and the kinds of behaviors and interactions to which they are exposed. However, to do so effectively, teachers must be aware of their own play behaviors in the classroom, whom they play with, and the kinds of play behaviors they model.

## Recommended Adult Roles and Behaviors

We recommend that parents make every effort to treat their sons and daughters equitably in providing them with toys and other play materials, including storage and space for play. Expenditures should be about the same for boys and for girls. Time devoted to playing with sons and daughters should also be equal, and both mothers and fathers should play with sons and with daughters. Finally, and most important, parents should engage their children in play that is both traditionally masculine and traditionally feminine. This means, for example, that fathers not only wrestle with their daughters and play baseball with them, but also sew with their sons and bake cookies with them. No play form or activity should be precluded on the basis of tradition. In the process, not only will parents model and reinforce novel play content and contexts, they will also show children a fresh approach to play. We make these strong recommendations recognizing our culture bias—almost all non-European cultures deeply value traditional gender role expectations.

We recommend that teachers attempt to display the same versatility as we outlined for parents. Teachers should help children to cross the great gender divide in their play. It is okay for girls to be monsters and for boys to be moms. McNaughton (2001) urges early childhood education staff to realize the risks children make when they try to transgress gender lines in their play, risks such as social ridicule and exclusion from the peer group. For the sake of promoting gender equity and out of a concern for human decency, teachers need to minimize the stigma of cross-gender play in the classroom, on the playground, and in other play settings. Again, we recognize how challenging this can be for teachers who have some parents from very traditional cultures tell them, "I don't want my boy cleaning up after snack time, that is woman's work" or "I don't want my boy playing in the dress-up area." We must aspire to worthy values and contend that gender inequality is immoral and that change will come from within traditional cultures to move in this direction.

A key to this needed understanding, according to McNaughton (2001), is to recognize the role of power in children's pretend play. Power is defined as the ability to make things happen; usually, the use of power serves self-interest. The struggle for power is inherent in children's play. It is seen in how children are included and excluded in play groups, who is listened to, who initiates the play, who ends the play, and what objects and activities are selected. In middle childhood and in relatively adult-free settings, same-sex groups are more hierarchical and rigid and demanding (McGuffey & Rich, 1999). However, even in early childhood settings, structured formations of same-gender social groups become established. McNaughton recommends the following steps teachers can take to break down rigid stereotypes in play and to help children expand their play choices:

- Be alert to the power dynamics in children's play, particularly pretend play.
- Be explorative, which means to encourage children to talk about their play experiences, to objectify play experiences. Going "meta" or reflecting on thoughts and feelings in this way enables children to explore their experiences in informal group discussions or in indirect ways as in movement, art, or music activities.
- Be honest, talk about the risks, the advantages, and the disadvantages of being strong, showing weakness, and caring.
- Be proactive and find female heroines and male heroes who transcend gender borders. Expand what it means to be acceptable.
- Be provocative by stimulating discussion about the fact that people have different opinions about gender.
- Be supportive and encourage children to try new things, to feel different at times, to engage in being opposite to the way they are normally, and to have fun trying out new and different kinds of roles.

In addition, we urge teachers to reexamine and expand play options. That means providing more opportunities for different kinds of play. Fixed patterns of gender-differentiated play may be the rule, but preschool children's play patterns can be changed through careful teacher intervention and environmental manipulation.

Teachers should expand dramatic play options. The dramatic-play center in some classrooms is sometimes nothing more than the customary domestic-play area, limited to the kitchen at that. If playing house must be the theme, why not at least provide props representing other rooms, such as the family room or garage? Efforts can be rewarded by enriched group play, benefiting preschool girls and boys alike. Teachers can help girls and boys balance inner needs for achievement and affiliation and become the kind of men and women who will have successful and productive as well as happy and fulfilling lives in the twenty-first century.

Finally, we encourage teachers to continually examine their own play behaviors and other behaviors in the classroom. Do they play only with certain toys and equipment while avoiding other toys and equipment? Do they seem to prefer one gender over the other? Do they spend most of the day involved in certain kinds of play—staying sedentary or moving around? How often do they get down on the floor, play in the water at the water table, or get paint all over their clothes? It often helps to have a colleague or administrator conduct a systematic observation of each teacher, or play sessions can be videotaped by using a camcorder and a tripod. The video can then be viewed, analyzed, and reflected on at a later time.

## PERSONALITY AND PLAY

Personality is often evoked to explain a wide range of diverse behaviors. What do we mean when we use the term? Within the social sciences the concept of personality has taken on the meaning of consistency in certain features of an individual's behavior that persist across a wide range of situations. These individual differences in personal qualities and behavior must be stable over time and cannot be caused by differences in cognitive maturity.

We typically employ the concept of personality to attempt to account for some specific social or personal behavior. Social and personal behaviors vary in their expression from individual to individual. How much of this variation in behavior stems from individual personality factors? How much of the behavior is caused by situational influences? Finally, how much is based on an individual's level of developmental maturity? Children in the same situation and at the same level of cognitive maturity play differently as they attempt to make sense of their worlds and as they grapple with internal psychological conflicts and states. Children express their idiosyncratic preferences and unique personalities in their play. Jim Johnson discusses in Box 4.1 just how complicated it can be to correctly interpret young children's behavior.

**BOX 4.1**

### *Theory-Guided Observation*

Keeping track of how each individual child plays and behaves in a variety of classroom situations is not an easy task, but it is nonetheless the responsibility of every teacher. Each child expresses a unique and budding personality. It is fascinating to see such individual variation in the early years. Noting this individuality becomes particularly important when the time comes for conferences between parents and teachers or in less formal situations when a parent can be informed of a child's progress at school. Often, teachers collect some examples of the child's art work, constructions, and other products for the parent. Long-term projects such as audiocassette logs, diaries, or books of drawings collected over time may also be included. In addition, observations and anecdotes are a common basis of information about a child. Some teachers also keep systematic play records to offer more objective and quantitative information.

The source and kind of observations or information are not as important as what a teacher makes of them regarding a particular child, when considering information to pass on to parents. It is at this point that comprehensive models of child behavior can become useful to analyze what is going on in the classroom. Such models enable teachers to view children through a discriminating lens to acquire a more sophisticated understanding of each child. Thus, the teacher is able to give a more thoughtful and valid account or appraisal of how each child is doing in the classroom.

Consider the following case. Innocently—but harmfully—a teacher told a parent that the parent's child was very shy at school. This surprised the parent to some extent because the child was not shy at home and in other situations. The teacher's remarks troubled the parent. Such labeling, as we know, can influence others and have long-range effects on children. Personality-trait labeling should be used sparingly. The important point about this example is that the teacher used a simple model of the child's behavior in deciding what to say to the parent. It was a one-factor model. That is, the child's behavior was explained by only one factor, the individual difference notion of shyness. It would have been much better if the child's behavior had been considered in terms of a host of factors. It happened that the child was the youngest in the class. Tendencies to withdraw or avoid others, in other words, could be seen as reflecting relative social immaturity or the child's developmental status as much as anything else. It would also have been smarter for the teacher to have noted situational variation in the child's behavior. That is, are there times in the daily schedule of class events when the child appears to enjoy social commerce? When and under what circumstances does the child seem to avoid social interaction or seem to display passivity? Theories and models of child development may seem at times a bit too remote or abstract to be practical, but understood and applied properly, they can be used to great advantage, enhancing the well-being and development of children.

*Source:* Johnson, Christie, and Yawkey, *Play and Early Childhood Development,* 2/e, p. 110. Published by Allyn and Bacon, Boston, MA. Copyright © 1999 by Pearson Education. Reprinted by permission of the publisher.

## Object-versus-People Orientation

One major individual difference in play concerns object-versus-people orientation. Some children are more attracted to activities in which there is a lot of interaction with people. Others prefer solitary activities in which the focus of attention is on objects. In an investigation of the relationship between preschoolers' cognitive abilities and their object-versus-people orientation, Jennings (1975) found a significant difference in children's abilities to perform cognitive tasks involving physical manipulation of materials. Children who spent more time playing with objects did better on tests requiring organization and classification of physical materials. Social knowledge, which differs from a simple preference for social interaction, correlated positively with effectiveness of social interaction. Jennings suggested that object orientation and social knowledge are established early and serve to reinforce cognitive skills related to these orientations. We need to add, however, that there is considerable evidence that a people orientation is a characteristic of interdependent or collectivist cultures, whereas the object orientation is prized in individualistic cultures such as our own. We will return to this important cultural issue in Chapter 6.

## Cognitive Style

In the psychological literature cognitive style has been defined technically as a preferred way of responding to a stimulus and has been considered to be a composite of intelligence and personality. Attempts have been made to study cognitive style in children using the relationship between a child's orientation to objects and to people as a behavioral indicator. Defined as individual variations in preferred ways of responding to a cognitive task, the most widely accepted index has been field independence-dependence (Witkin, Lewis, Hertzman, Machover, Meissner, & Wapner, 1954). The child who is more field-independent has an easier time finding a simple figure within a complex design because he or she is less swayed by contextual factors. The field-dependent child, on the other hand, gets distracted by elements in the total design and often cannot find the hidden figure.

Children who are more field-independent seek out objects to play with, whereas field-dependent children tend to be more people-oriented. The field-independent children's greater success at finding the figure in a design might be due to an analytic style that might make them more likely to learn through observing and responding to physical aspects of the environment. Field-dependent children, with their more global approach, might pay more attention to the social aspects of the same situation (Coates, Lord, & Jakabovics, 1975).

Saracho (1998) reviewed the literature on the play of field-dependent (FD) and field-independent (FI) children and concluded that findings from research studies generally favor FI over FD children in play and social competence and peer status. However, there are some conflicting results, with some studies showing that FD children engage in a wider variety of play. FD children prefer group dramatic play and social play overall; FI children tend to enjoy block building and other forms of constructive and manipulative play. FI children also tend to initiate and communicate ideas more and to assume leadership more than FD children do (Saracho, 1999).

Confident conclusions cannot be drawn about play in relation to cognitive style in young children because it is difficult to obtain stable estimates of this trait in young children. It is difficult to distinguish cognitive style from developmental progression because children in general are becoming more field-independent with development (i.e., less diffuse and global and more articulate and differentiated). The higher-quality play and higher peer status found in FI children may be due to their advanced cognitive development rather than to their field independence considered as a personality or individual difference variable.

➤ Children who are more field-independent seek out objects to play with; field-dependent children tend to be more people-oriented.

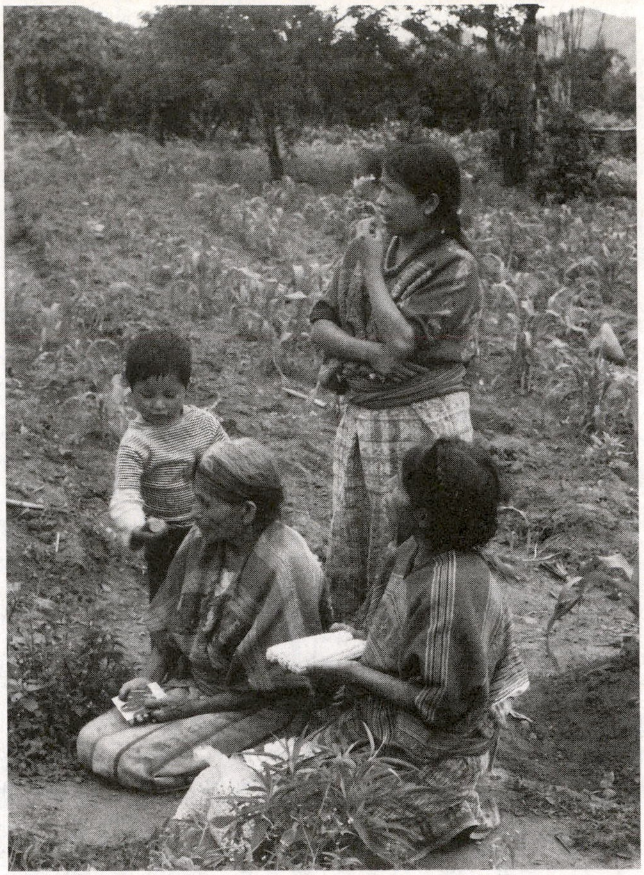

Howard Gardner (1983, 1999) has proposed that children use at least eight different learning styles, or intelligences, which combine concepts of cognitive style, personality, and social orientation. It would only seem logical that a child whose preferred intelligence is interpersonal (relating to other children) will play differently from a child whose preference is spatial (art, architecture, patterns, etc). However, we are not aware of any studies to date that have looked at the relationship between play and learning styles.

## Playfulness

Playfulness is a psychological construct involving individual differences in the disposition to play (Rogers et al., 1998). Researchers have studied playfulness as a personality dimension contributing to observed variations in play behavior and divergent thinking. Playfulness according to Lieberman (1977) can be understood in terms of five traits: *physical, social,* and *cognitive spontaneity; manifest joy;* and a *sense of humor.* Physical spontaneity is seen in exuberance and coordinated bodily movement; cognitive spontaneity in imaginative, creative, and flexible thinking; and social spontaneity in getting along with others and knowing how to join play groups. Manifest joy is reflected in laughter and expressions of happiness and enjoyment. Sense of humor is inferred by behaviors that suggest an appreciation of comedy and fun and a willingness to be teased in good fun. Using rating scales for scoring the play behavior of 93 kindergarten children, Lieberman found that four of the five playfulness traits were very highly related, the remaining trait (physical spontaneity) being less related. Lieberman concluded that playfulness is a unitary personality dimension defined by these traits and correlated with divergent thinking scores, mental age, and chronological age.

Barnett (1991) examined playfulness in kindergarten children in relation to the five dimensions proposed by Lieberman, along with other personality traits and individual characteristics of the children, including gender, number of siblings, and birth order. The Children's Playfulness Scale was used to assess the five dimensions of playfulness, and a second questionnaire was used to assess various other personality traits. Analyses of the data revealed that one personality trait in particular—being confident—significantly correlated with all five dimensions of playfulness. Boys were judged to exhibit physical spontaneity and manifest joy; girls were higher on the cognitive spontaneity dimension.

Other researchers have conceptualized playfulness somewhat differently from Lieberman's original model by evaluating the presence of other elements, such as intrinsic motivation, internal control, and freedom to suspend reality (Bundy, 1997; Creaser, 1990; Morrison, Bundy, & Fisher, 1991; Rogers et al., 1998; van der Kooij, 1989). Each of these three elements, for example, can be represented by a continuum to reflect the extent of the presence of a specific trait in a particular play episode. Intrinsic motivation means that play is instigated internally or by some aspect of the activity itself rather than by an external reward (e.g., being engaged, showing exuberance, persisting). Internal control means the child is mostly in charge of what is going on for at least some aspects of the activity (e.g., assumes leadership, decides, modifies, challenges). Freedom to suspend reality is defined by how close to reality the play episode is (e.g., pretends, clowns, uses unconventional objects). Playfulness is assessed by determining the extent to which these three elements seem to occur in a play transaction.

Another factor discussed by Bundy (1997) in relation to playfulness is play framing, which refers to knowing how to engage in socially expected ways so that the play episode goes smoothly. Bundy's model of playfulness corresponds with both Liebermann's original formulation and Barnett's extension of Lieberman's model in the Children's Playfulness Scale, except for the *physical spontaneity* category. For example, one item in the Children's Playfulness Scale is "plays in physically active ways." Some children who cannot do this because of physical disability are nevertheless very playful. Hence Bundy eliminated physical spontaneity from her model of playfulness.

Some research suggests that playfulness is not the one-dimensional construct originally proposed by Lieberman. Rather, playfulness encompasses at least two fundamental components. One aspect is a cognitive component that may lead to creativity and to the understanding of a joke, for example. The other aspect is the affective component, which is seen in the joy of play and the laughter in a joke. Truhon (1982) modified Lieberman's playfulness scales and observed kindergarten children in solitary play. Each child was also given a battery of creativity tests. Truhon's analysis unveiled a distinction between affective and cognitive components of playfulness: a *playfulness-fun* cluster and a *playfulness-intelligence* cluster. The cognitive and affective aspects of playfulness had different effects on play. The playfulness-fun component measured manifest joy and sense of humor, while the playfulness-intelligence component measured cognitive spontaneity and intelligence.

The Child Behaviors Inventory of Playfulness is a rating instrument used to estimate playfulness in preschool and primary grade children (Rogers et al., 1998). This observational rating instrument has 31 items based on different play dispositions (e.g., intrinsic motivation, process-over-product, flexibility, positive affect, nonliterality) described by Rubin et al. (1983) plus a single global item—"Is playful"—for the raters to use to determine their overall perception of the playfulness observed in a child's behavior. The Child Behaviors Inventory of Playfulness yielded two separate factors in the validation study: *playfulness* and *externality.* Whereas the first factor seemed to indicate overall playfulness, including pretense, active involvement, and so forth, externality appeared to measure the child's dependence on external cues in the environment to guide behavior, recorded through test items such as "seeks approval frequently" and "looks to others to tell him/her what to do." Playful children, in other words, are characterized by their ability for self-initiated behavior and follow-through, without having to rely on reinforcement or approval. They are not high on externality; less playful children are.

An Australian early childhood authority, Barb Creaser, proposed an alternative approach in detailing three different play styles, which are explorers, spectators, and dramatists (Creaser, 1990). Instead of focusing on categories of play behavior or elements of the disposition to play in the individual child, Creaser looked at groups of children engaged in play and observed individual variations in how they approached situations and preferred to interact with others. She was more concerned with what happens during play interaction than with the particular type of play involved. And she believed that what is happening from the child's perspective is more important than what seems to be happening from the adult's point of view. Mental representation and intersubjectivity are involved in all play interactions, including functional and constructive play (explorers), not just sociodramatic play (dramatists), and may be presumed to take place in observational (spectator) activity as well. What is important to remember is that children are active agents and intentional beings. What matters to them when they play? Do we adults make their play more complicated than it really is?

## Fantasy-Making Predisposition

Another individual difference variable concerning play, originally proposed by Singer (1973), is a fantasy-making tendency. Fantasy-making predisposition refers to playfulness that takes primary expression in overt pretend-play activity or in internalized fantasy. Research on this personality variable has relied on observations, projective tests, and oral interviews to assess children's propensities toward fantasy making. Children who are high in fantasy-making show higher levels of imaginativeness, positive affect, concentration, social interaction, and cooperation during play than do children with low fantasy-making tendencies. Children who are high in this predisposition are also more likely to report seeing movement in ambiguous stimulus cards (the Barron Movement Threshold Inkblot series) and report that they see "little pictures in their heads" and say that they have imaginary companions. Their favorite games and play activities involve some make-believe or transformational behavior.

High-fantasy-making children have been found to be better able to control their impulses when forced to wait. These children are less likely to become disruptive or to interfere with others because they are able to engage in some form of imaginative play or to otherwise entertain themselves without overt acting out. High fantasy making is associated with the ability to control impulses and to delay gratification (Singer, 1961). As with field independence, this personality trait might also be conflated with intellectual maturity.

Similar to research on playfulness as an individual difference variable, the early work on fantasy making seemed to indicate that the trait is a unitary one. But subsequent studies have suggested otherwise. Singer and Singer (1980) analyzed a set of 33 variables relating to imaginative play, language, social interaction, affect, and home television viewing. Three factors emerged. One was a general good-humored playfulness across a number of behavior domains; a second identified aggressive interaction associated with television viewing; and a third indexed inner imaginative tendencies and prosocial behaviors. This factor structure was stable over the one-year period of observation. The Singers suggested that manifestations of fantasy-making tendencies, both through play as well as through more inner-directed channels, are the result of a generally positive relationship the child has with the social and physical environment. Like Nina Lieberman's construct of playfulness, Jerome and Dorothy Singer have proposed that the individual difference variable of fantasy-making predisposition is a life-span personality trait (Singer, 1995; Singer & Singer, 1990).

## Imaginative Play Styles

Over two decades ago Harvard's Project Zero researchers unearthed individual styles of symbolic play in early childhood (Wolf & Gardner, 1979; Wolf & Grollman, 1982). In their famous longitudinal study, these researchers found that children have delineated play styles or "modes of behavior remaining consistent across a range of materials and situations" (Wolf & Gardner, 1979, p. 119). Symbolic play was defined as the "ability to represent actual or imagined experience through the use of small objects, motions, and language" (Wolf & Gardner, 1979). The two styles of symbolic play were (a) object-independent fantasy play, in which the child creates imaginary worlds by invoking nonexistent events, roles, and props, and (b) object-dependent pretend play, in which the child creates an imaginary world by ably transforming existing objects and arrangements in the environment (Wolf & Grollman, 1982). These two styles refer to the quality of an individual's behavior, not to the child's developmental level, and are stable across time, not instances of particular periods within developmental levels. Analysis of free-play behaviors of preschool children supports the notion that these stylistic differences persist and characterize children's interactions with materials.

Imaginative elements in play, defined as "vocal or gestural schemes through which a child altered the pragmatic or actual constituents of the ongoing situation"

(Wolf & Grollman, 1982, p. 55), can be grouped into object-independent and object-dependent categories. Object-dependent instances of imaginative play involve existing or actually present events, objects, or people. Object-dependent children make arrangements or patterns with objects and substitute items when actions require props. In contrast, object-independent children often evoke nonexistent elements, sometimes incorporating actual events and objects in interesting and far-fetched ways. For example, a child might incorporate a teacher's coughing into play, making it the roar of a mountain lion in the pretend cave.

Wolf and Gardner (1979) found that young children show a consistent pattern of preferences and characteristic ways of organizing responses with materials and tasks, in both spontaneous play and test situations. These findings were also the basis for conceptually distinguishing the object-independent and object-dependent styles of playing:

- Patterners displayed considerable skill and interest in making patterns, structures, and spatial arrangements with objects and materials and were interested in an object's mechanical and design possibilities rather than in communication or interpersonal events.
- Dramatists, on the other hand, showed a strong interest in human surroundings: what others did and felt and how they could be known.

Dramatists preferred and did well in games, sociodramatic play, and storytelling but often performed poorly when engaged in tasks that demanded close attention to the physical properties of objects. Patterners, in contrast, tended to excel in visual-spatial tasks and in physical relationships between objects. According to Wolf and Gardner (1979), these two distinct styles of play and problem solving are part of children's overall personalities and underlying mental structures.

Matthews (1977) supported the notion of individual differences in play style in her investigation of transformational modes in make-believe play. She pointed out two modes: material and ideational, which are direct parallels of object-dependent and object-independent play styles. A material transformational mode was characterized by the child's active manipulation and reference to actual material in the play environment. An ideational mode involved references, ideas, or mental images of things that are not physically present to the senses. Mathews concluded that familiarity with the play situation increases the use of ideational modes and that preschool girls shift to ideational modes more quickly than do boys.

Research on individual differences in play during the preschool years indicates that there are distinct styles of imaginative play. However, research on the symbolic play of two-year-olds has failed to show differentiated imaginative play styles among toddlers during this developmental period (Frankin, 1985). Perhaps teachers and parents should expect variability within the same child across different play situations and recognize that many young children will exhibit behaviors characteristic of each style. More research is needed on this topic.

## Psychological Adjustment and Depression

As we will discuss in the next chapter, the type of play with the strongest relationship to creativity is pretend play. Just as there are individual differences that emerge in early childhood in pretending, so too is there reason to believe that children vary in creative behaviors. Creativity, like play, is very difficult to define. Usually, it refers to the ability to make original and useful responses. Both cognition and affect are involved in creativity, as they are in play. Cognitive processes involved in creativity include divergent thinking; creativity also involves affective processes, such as affect-laden fantasy. The affective processes, according to psychoanalytic theory, are related to primary process thinking, which consists of affect-laden fantasy and cognition, the content of which is material that is experienced with intense feelings, such as love and aggression. This content is suppressed and stored in an affective system. Individual children and adults vary in the extent to which they can access and control primary process thinking. Those with greater access and control have a richer range of associations, which increases their divergent thinking and creativity (Russ, 1999).

Similarly, children's pretend play makes use of the affective system. Fein (1987) asserted that pretend play is symbolic behavior in which "one thing is playfully treated as something else" (p. 282). For Fein pretense is charged with affect, and pretend play is a form of creativity. Moreover, such play assists in mastering emotions. Slade and Wolf (1994) have argued that affective and cognitive functions of play are intertwined, proposing that "Just as the development of cognitive structures may play an important role in the resolution of emotional conflict, so emotional consolation may provide the impetus to cognitive advances and integration" (p. xv).

More will be said about the relationships among play, affect, and creativity in Chapter 5 as we discuss the benefits of play for development. The interconnections are pointed out here because we wish to draw attention to an important way individual children's personalities begin to vary during early childhood. Differences in the ease with which children can express their budding imaginations in play, the extent to which they are playful, and the level of their fantasy-making abilities all can have important consequences in the lives of young children. In this time in our history when so many young children are under a great deal of pressure—from spending very long periods of time in childcare (which is often not high-quality care), living in high-crime neighborhoods with few safe places to play, growing up in families that are often under extreme financial and psychological stress, and attending early childhood programs and schools that are obsessed with academic standards and testing—it is important for them to have a capacity for high-quality creative and imaginative play. We must do everything we can to help children develop this capacity.

Not very much research has been conducted relating various types of play to behavioral and emotional problems such as maladjustment or childhood depression. Most of the empirical evidence deals with play content, not play type, and comes from clinical studies in which various kinds of play assessment procedures have been used.

An exception is a study by Lous, deWit, Bruyn, Riksen-Walraven, and Rost (2000), who compared the free play, interactive free play, and play narrations of seven clinically depressed preschoolers (admitted to residential and semiresidential institutions) with that of seven nondepressed children. Children in the two groups were matched for age, gender, socioeconomic status, and approximately on educational and cognitive levels. The depressed children showed very little symbolic play across all three conditions of free play, interactive free play (with a warm and friendly but unfamiliar adult), and story narration. They displayed more nonplay behaviors, however, such as orientation to the environment (the play room) and to the researcher (in the story narration condition). Nondepressed preschoolers manifested considerable symbolic play, particularly in the story narration condition in which Lego® dolls were available as props to represent family members and in which the narrative was about waking up, going to school, coming home after school, and going to bed.

Coplan, Wichmann, and Lagace-Seguin (2001) reported that children who engaged in a great deal of solitary-active play (repetitive sensorimotor or solitary pretense) were temperamentally less attentive, more difficult to soothe, and more shy and displayed externalizing problems such as acting out. These children also did more poorly on tests estimating early academic skills, and they had less positive attitudes about school. Other children who had more typical play profiles, including more social and dramatic play, did not exhibit these negative behaviors nearly as much. These findings are consistent with research reporting the negative correlates of immature play patterns, including maladjustment in preschool, of certain forms of solitary play such as reticent behaviors (anxiously watching but not joining play) and externalizing behaviors (repetitive and disruptive dramatizations or sensorimotor activity) (Coplan, 2000). These findings are also consistent with the theoretical notions of Fein and the Singers, discussed earlier. These theorists consider imaginative play and creativity to be critically important personal attributes that develop during the early years—critically important traits that can be construed to be the roots of mental health and social adjustment.

## Environmental Factors and Personality

Child-rearing styles and family structure, among other environmental factors, may influence how children progress through stages of play development and result in individual differences in play expression. Why are some children more playful than others, and how do different children acquire different play predispositions? Why do some children prefer fantasy-based play while others prefer reality-based play? Why do some children like dramatic play and storytelling while others find drawing and clay constructing more to their liking? It is important to realize sources of individual variation in play expression.

Experiences of the young child in the family are vitally important to the development of play behaviors. We know that parents and other significant adults have a very important influence on the child's play. Smilansky (1968) and Singer (1973) have pointed out that young children need a generally favorable home environment and positive relationships with parents for their imaginative play skills to blossom. Children also require specific modeling and encouragement to engage in make-believe play. Dunn and Wooding (1977) and Feitelson and Ross (1973) have elaborated on this idea: Being high versus low in fantasy-making predisposition, as well as the quantity and quality of play a child exhibits, emanate in part from patterns of child rearing and the availability of play space, toys, storage areas, and places for privacy. Box 4.2 discusses two young AfroBrazilian children of about the same age whose play behaviors are nonetheless very different. Since the play environment is the same for both girls, it would seem that part of the reason for this fact is the very different approach of each child's parent to the play setting.

BOX 4.2

## Two Young Children in Belo Horizonte, Brazil

**by Francis Wardle**

During my recent stay in Belo Horizonte, Brazil, I visited an Afro Brazilian dance group with my friend Heloisa. The group works with adolescents from the favelas (slums) and conducts performances of a form of dance that is a combination of *capoeira*—an African-inspired form of fighting—and modern dance. The group practiced in a small room high up over the city that extended out onto a small courtyard. The courtyard was surrounded by a two-foot-high wall and then a high wire fence. While the dancers were practicing, one of the dancers' children was left to essentially entertain herself. She would stand up on the bench to look through the wire fence at the city streets below, pick flowers from a small flower box and then carefully pull the petals of each flower, bang on the various-sized drums along with the drummer, and engage in rough-and-tumble play with a slightly older boy. This very dark four-year-old Black girl had taken off her shoes and was dancing around barefoot, her very curly, free-flowing long hair dancing in the wind. As the adult dancers progressed from practicing and exercising to actually dancing, she would imitate their movements and freely and energetically move to the rhythmic drumbeat.

While the dancers were practicing, one of the dancers' children would pick flowers from a small flower box and then carefully pull the petals off each flower.

> Near the end of the session a new drummer joined the group. With him were his wife and her daughter, also Black. This little girl had straightened hair, a neat, prissy outfit, white stockings, and patent leather shoes. She had a pink bow in her hair. Her mother held her tightly on her lap as she watched the dancers swirl and move to the enticing music. Her mother would not let her play with the other girl, who was about the same age and who was flitting among the dancers, taking an occasional swipe at the drum, then going into the courtyard to continue her improvisation to the music.
>
> The contrast between the two children, who seemed to be of the same racial and economic background, was amazing. Differences in parenting style undoubtedly contributed to the difference in the girls' play styles.

Bishop and Chace (1971) and Barnett and Kleiber (1984) have identified home background factors in the emergence of playfulness in children, using Lieberman's (1977) personality construct. Bishop and Chace found that children who were more playful in performing tasks came from home environments that encouraged playfulness. Barnett and Kleiber (1984) found a similar connection when examining each parent in the family separately but not when looking at them together. These investigators also found gender differences in separate analyses examining additional family structure variables and parental background characteristics. When birth order, family size, and sex of sibling were analyzed to determine their influence on a child's playfulness at school, the investigators found that later-borns were more playful (males only) and that children from larger families were more playful (again males only). Fathers' socioeconomic status was positively and significantly related to playfulness in children; maternal age was negatively and significantly correlated with daughters' playfulness.

These results are complex, and more research is needed to evaluate the contribution of family structure variables to play quality, quantity, and style. The importance of family structure would appear to be considerably less than actual parental practices, particularly during the first and second years of life, when the mother or father provides scaffolding that enables the child to engage in play at the margins of his or her ability (Bruner, 1972).

## Recommendations for Adult Roles and Behaviors

Adults have important roles in the development of play in general. What part do they play in the child's adoption of specific play styles? Little research has been done on this question. It would seem that just as adults influence personality development in general, they can also have a considerable effect on children's play styles. For example, if a parent provides a child with many reality-based toys and puzzles and no materials for dramatic play, we would expect the child to develop an object-based, patterner style of play. If a parent enjoys pretending and sharing a world of make-believe, probably this too would nudge children toward a dramatist play style. Still, there are limits to this type of parental influence. We have all probably heard about the super-jock dad who became extremely frustrated because his son did not have the same interest or ability in sports.

As we have seen, researchers have tried to classify play styles and styles of children's personal expression during the preschool years using dichotomies such as patterners versus dramatists. Children in varied settings no doubt show, in general, consistent patterns of play styles that are representative of each. But although these dichotomies represent extreme opposites, it is more helpful to see them as continuous dimensions, with children's play falling somewhere along them.

Nevertheless, important questions still exist: Should teachers and parents attempt to foster in a child a particular type of play style? Is it better to be a dramatist than to be a patterner? Deliberately promoting a certain style of play is quite possibly doomed to fail or to backfire. There are at least two important reasons to argue against parents or teachers consciously attempting to modify a child's style of self-expression in play (although subconsciously the attempt might still take place).

First, play scholars have stated that play is an ego-building process, the importance of which should not be reduced or tampered with by play theorists and play practitioners. Children at play need to be in control for the activity to be playful, enjoyable, and beneficial. The sense of power, mastery, control, and autonomy accompanying play is integral to play and is too critical to a child's development and well-being to jeopardize through deliberate interventions by adults trying to cultivate a particular play style. As we noted at the beginning of this chapter, one of the three overarching functions of play is individual expression—using play as a medium to find your own true self. The constructivist person-centered view should trump any "biology is destiny" view or a hard-line environmental determinism view. Educational intervention must be respectful of the child and be fashioned in accord with this constructivist person-centered view.

A second case against deliberately trying to influence personality or play styles comes from work done on symbolic development and multiple intelligences (Gardner, 1983, 1999). According to Gardner's theory of multiple intelligences, each child is endowed at birth with specific genetic predispositions that evolve in interaction with environmental events to produce differing levels of talent in specific intellectual areas, or frames of mind, as he calls them. Gardner identifies the following intelligences: (1) logical-mathematical, (2) linguistic, (3) spatial, (4) kinesthetic, (5) musical, (6) intrapersonal, (7) interpersonal, and (8) naturalistic. Each intelligence is a potential, which emerges and is responsive to people and objects and opportunities for learning that are present in the child's world. An educational implication of this theory is that each child in early life becomes "at risk" or "at promise" in each area depending on the kinds and intensities of opportunities and encouragement. An early childhood curriculum should provide a range of play activities that are related to children's interests and emerging abilities and developmental needs. Project Spectrum is a model program in early childhood education that is largely based on this perspective (Chen, 2005).

Because we cannot prejudge the areas in which a child may have particular strength, it would seem much more ethical and appropriate to provide each child with exposure to all kinds of stimulation relevant to each type of intelligence than to provide limited but intensive exposure to selected approaches. Deliberately attempting to foster a particular intelligence or style of play in young children could prevent the child's finding his or her own intellectual, expressive, and creative ways of being, ways that are most natural to the individual child. Because spontaneous playfulness and play in children appear to be so critical for later adjustment and creative expression, we believe that it is best not to interfere. Any intervention that is deliberately programmed to affect a young child's personality or intelligence using play in this way would not be honoring the child as a person worthy of our utmost respect. Sadly, education does not have a good reputation supporting the artist, dancer, or musician in our schools; we say that our children must be readers, mathematicians, and scientists.

## RACE, ETHNICITY, AND PLAY

Throughout this book we discuss a variety of contextual influences on children's play, from the proximity and involvement of adults to the physical environment. Beyond these contexts are what Bronfenbrenner (1979) calls ecological systems: microsystem, mesosystem, exosystem, macrosystem, and chronosystem. We discuss the impact of these systems on children's play in Chapter 6; what is important here is to know that all five of these systems interact to influence children's lives and therefore cannot be considered separately. In the same way, race and ethnicity do not operate independently in affecting children's play behaviors. Wardle (1997) has proposed an ecological theory of seven factors that interact to influence children's development and behavior. These factors are race and ethnicity, culture, socioeconomic status (class), family, community, gender, and ability/disability. Wardle suggests that not only do all these factors interact together differently within each child, but also the impact of each factor changes over time (age) of the child. Further, as West (2001) points out, each child constructs his or her own meaning of all seven factors differently.

Added to this complexity is the very nature of racial and ethnic constructs. It is fairly well accepted today that race has no biological basis and is a sociopolitical construct that differs from society to society and changes over time (Fish, 2002). For example, the U.S. census defines anyone with any African heritage as being African American or Black, whereas in Brazil only people who "look African" are considered *preto* (black) (Fish, 2002). And ethnicity can include a variety of races. For example, the only ethnic group recognized by the U.S. census is Latino, which can be any race, and is primarily *mestizo* (Indian and white) (Wardle & Cruz-Janzen, 2004).

All the above makes any discussion on racial and ethnic influences on children's play quite precarious. Further, when we discuss play behaviors of, say, an African American boy, we must also consider the influence of gender, the environment (home, childcare center, or school), and the impact of African-American parents and/or staff on his play.

### Racial and Ethnic Differences

Two of the most significant developmental tasks for young children (ages 0 to 8) are establishing consistent gender and racial identity. Table 4.1 shows the typical development of a child's racial/ethnic identity plus the child's growing concept of children whose race/ethnicity is different from his or her own (Wardle, 2003a). Because children this age are in the midst of developing a sense of racial and/or ethnic identity and determining the racial and ethnic identity of other children, it is extremely difficult to ascertain the impact of race and ethnicity on young children's play behaviors.

Two things are certainly occurring. First, as with gender identity development, children may use racial labels and same-race grouping as a way of sorting out who they

**TABLE 4.1 Development of Racial and Ethnic Identity**

Developing a sense of racial and ethnic identity is a complex developmental process. In this country children progress through these stages:

**Infancy.** Children can discriminate between dark and light stimuli, dark and light faces.

**3–4 years.** Children can recognize black and white children by physical descriptors but not racial identity and do not know their own racial/ethnic identity. Children are very interested in physical similarities and differences.

**5–9 years.** Children learn to recognize their own racial identity label and develop a beginning awareness of group affiliation. Awareness of group belonging comes after learning group similarities.

**7 years.** Recognition by white children of a Black child (racially) and by Black children of a white child (racially).

**8 years.** Recognition of other ethnic groups (e.g., Native American, Chinese, Japanese, Latinos). Apparently, the salient features are less clear of these children than those of white and black children. Children of this age are very confused about the identity of multiethnic and multiracial children, as is much of society.

**8–10 years.** Develop racial/ethnic constancy and a stronger sense of group belonging. This is more difficult for multiracial/multiethnic children.

*Source:* Wardle, *Introduction to Early Childhood Education: A Multidimensional Approach to Child-Centered Care and Learning.* Published by Allyn and Bacon, Boston, MA. Copyright © 2003 by Pearson Education. Reprinted by permission of the publisher.

are (Sigelman, Miller, & Whitworth, 1986). Second, the natural curiosity of children this age leads them to want to know and play with children they perceive to be different from them (Wardle, 2003b). Clearly, these two factors will have the highest impact on social play and will be evident only in childcare settings and schools that are racially and ethnically diverse. Further, because a child's race and ethnicity are not always physically obvious, especially to other children (some Latinos are white, some Blacks are very fair, etc.), the impact will differ a great deal. Finally, we must consider white privilege and minority marginality, a framework for viewing race and ethnicity in this country that is currently quite popular (Ogbu, 1991; Ramsey, 1998; York, 2003). However, little is known about how these concepts develop, and no developmental timeline exists to describe children's acquisition of these attitudes. Therefore it is difficult to view privilege and oppression as variables in children's play at this point in time.

Within each of the five broad racial/ethnic groups identified by the U.S. census there is a tremendous amount of variability in education, income, recent/past immigration, profession, and language, not to mention the range of different national origins that make up each category. For this reason in this book we make a clear distinction between race/ethnicity and culture.

## African-American Children

Janice Hale (Hale-Benson, 1986; Hale, 1994) has written extensively about African-American children. She makes two overall very significant contributions to our discussion of play and young African-American children. First, she points out that because our definition of play comes out of a white, Eurocentric theoretical and research context, this discussion not only might be biased against African-American children, but also might miss significant components of African-American play. Second, she discusses significant play characteristics of African-American children.

Hale and many other theorists believe play is a direct expression of a child's home and cultural context. According to Hale-Benson (1986, p. 15), some of this context is reflected in the child's African ancestry, which includes the following:

- Folklore
- Dance
- Song
- Motor habits, such as walking, speaking, laughing, sitting, postures, carrying, and singing
- Respect for elders in the family and community
- Magical practices

Hale-Benson (1986, p. 43) also discusses some characteristics of what she views as the typical African-American child:

- Is highly affective
- Expresses herself or himself through considerable body language
- Prefers using expressions that have meaning connotations
- Prefers oral-aural modalities for learning communication
- Seeks to be people-oriented
- Adapts rapidly to novel stimuli

According to Hale-Benson (1986), "we must broaden our conception of play to encompass Black children's expressive style that include a range of behavior, tastes, and preferences that we might not originally include as a part of play behavior" (p. 95). Some of these are movement, dance, music, environmental arts, fashion arts, folklore, and magico-spiritual beliefs.

By *movement,* Hale-Benson means the amount of space used in play and the manner in which it is used, including the ratio of active to passive play. She believes that Black children, particularly males, are very active during play and are penalized for this in school. In dance, Hale-Benson (1986) is referring to "the physical precocity of Black children that has often been observed and reported" (p. 96) and how dance could be effectively used to teach math. In music she is curious as to whether Black children's ability to memorize popular songs can be effectively used in schools and whether the lack of music in our schools negatively affects Black children. Hale believes that Black children's home play environments may give us cues as to how Black children like to learn, such as the influence of certain colors on their learning. To Hale-Benson (1986) "fashion is a very important cultural vehicle for expressing creativity" (p. 97) and should be studied to determine how Black children use it to express their cultural milieu. Maybe this would provide cues for increasing involvement of African-American children, especially boys, in dramatic play. Hale believes that the verbal skills of Black children should be studied to determine how language, words, and cultural expressions are used in games, stories, jump-rope rhymes, and even swear words. Also she believes that we need to find out more about understanding and interpreting the use of fantasy by Black children. As we have discussed throughout this book, fantasy is very closely related to creative thought and cognitive ability.

Hale-Benson (1986) expresses the opinion that children's play has many similarities to spirituality and religion. In play children can achieve a sense of place, they can feel in control of uncontrolled lives, and play gives life a sense of meaning. Further, play has many of the markings of celebration, transcendence, and positive affect. Thus because "investigators have noted a deep concern with the spiritual and supernatural in the creative activities of Black children" (p. 99), we need to examine Black children's spirituality and find ways to encourage it in their play.

## High- and Low-Context Communication

Several theorists and researchers believe that non-European groups in North America use primarily high-context communication—nonverbal cues, contextual cues, traditional and cultural norms—to communicate everything from basic needs to cultural expectations and social rules (Gonzalez-Mena, 1997; Kaiser & Rasminsky, 2003; Lynch, 1998). Kaiser and Rasminsky (2003) point out that in high-context settings, words take a back seat, and "pauses, silences, and indirect ways of communicating, such as empathy, story telling, analogies, or talking around a subjects—are also critical" (p. 54). According to these authors, people from Asia, South Asia, and southern Europe, and Native Americans, Latinos, and African-Americans show a preference for these high-context forms of communication.

This high-context approach to communication differs markedly from the European American, middle-class decontextualized or low-context forms of communication—communication that is direct, precise, and logical and is often done at a distance. In high-context cultures parents and children—even crying infants—often communicate back and forth from a distance (Gonzalez-Mena, 1997).

Clearly, the distinction between high- and low-context communication has a tremendous impact on play, especially social play, sociodramatic play, and the role of the adult in increasing the complexity of play. Further, ideas for using educational play to teach basic educational objectives such as literacy and math skills and concepts will not work as well with children from high-context backgrounds—or at least will have to be radically adapted. And the role of the teacher as play participant and modeler, as opposed to observer or stage manager (see Chapter 7), will need to be modified for children from high-context homes. And, of course, the concept of high-context communication forces us to question whether sociodramatic play as discussed by Smilansky (1968) should be our goal for all children.

## SUMMARY

Studies have shown that boys engage in more rough-and-tumble play than do girls and are more aggressive during play. Beginning around age four, boys are more active and girls are more sedentary during play, but they do not differ in social play development. However, significant gender differences exist in interactional style and in choice of playmates and materials. Boys are more direct in interaction, whereas girls are less rigid in their play selections. Girls are more likely to engage in constructive play and other table activities during early childhood. Moreover, although boys and girls do not differ significantly from one another in imaginative play interest and structural skill, considerable evidence exists that thematic content is gender-typed, with boys being more likely to exhibit individualistic and adventuresome themes and with girls tending to exhibit relational and nurturing ones.

Gender-based patterns in play from birth to age eight years are affected by parents, peers, and teachers. Parental expectations concerning gender-typed play are revealed in different situations provided for boys and girls in the home environment and in interactive patterns. Teachers' presence, play involvement, and their modification of play areas can alter established patterns of play. Wanting to change traditional gender-based play patterns is a matter of an individual's value system, but parents and teachers are urged to treat girls and boys equitably in toy and time expenditures and to encourage a variety of activities through their interactions with children. Adults are encouraged to examine how their own values and biases influence play options for children, particularly play involving role enactments, as children learn social norms.

Individual differences in play during early childhood have been researched in terms of personality as well. Four personal style variables are (1) people-versus-object orientation, (2) playfulness, (3) fantasy-making predispositions, and (4) imaginative play styles. Aspects of playfulness are a cognitive component that may lead to creativity and humor comprehension and an affective component that is seen in the joy of play and the laughter in a joke. Aspects of fantasy-making play include overt imaginative play tendencies and inner forms of fantasy. Styles of imaginative play are object-independent/dramatist versus object-dependent/patterner orientations. Dramatists are less focused on objects in make-believe play than are patterners. Object play varies in action-object combinations, play tempo, elaboration, organization, complexity, and attention span or play persistence—all related to personality and underlying mental structures. Adults must recognize children's striving for independence and personal fulfillment in their play and provide broad support to help them find their own unique talents and preferences.

Race and ethnicity affect child development in general and social identity in particular, but it is difficult to ascertain the influence of these variables on children's play behaviors. African-American family and cultural backgrounds are reflected in certain characteristics of children's play such as its emotional level, body language, and oral expression. Black children's expressive style in play can be seen in movement, dance, music, fashion arts, environmental art, and folk song and story. Variations in communication contexts of different ethnic groups are implicated in children's play and the adults' responses to children's play.

## PROJECTS AND ACTIVITIES

1. Prepare a list of questions to interview children who cross gender borders in their play to discover how they feel about what they are doing.

2. Take a pro and then a con position in the debate on whether children's play is best explained as a struggle for power.
3. Design a dramatic play center that you think will draw children across gender lines.
4. Interview a parent from a minority group and ask about child rearing, play, play provisions and adult involvement at home, and expectations for young children. How different are the answers from your own experiences in your family?
5. From your childhood play memories, construct a portrait of yourself as a player and as a young person. How did your childhood personality shape your play interests? How did your play contribute to your personality?
6. Prepare a pro and a con position for a debate on whether progressive educators should seek to change attitudes and values about sex role socialization in traditional families.

CHAPTER 5

# Play's Role in Development

## INTRODUCTION

For many years play has been regarded as the medium of learning in early childhood. Unfortunately, today this notion is threatened by the rush to academic excellence and to meeting academic standards. This new academic thrust in early education has shifted attention away from play to more direct forms of teaching. In the current educational climate it is important to remember a cardinal principle in early education: Always keep the whole child in mind. We believe that play in early childhood is a learning medium *par excellence*. Play can serve as a vibrant bridge connecting the whole child to school readiness and to meeting, and even exceeding, the new academic standards.

Chapter 2 discussed different theories about the role of play, both in life in general and in child development and learning. In this chapter we further explore the importance of play in development. Empirical research will be cited to buttress the theoretical claims made in Chapter 2. We start with a discussion of brain development and play in order to set our examination of play's role in development on a biological foundation. Play is a mediator of brain development and, by extension, child development. Then we provide a complement to this biological point of view by highlighting the sociocultural perspective on the value of play in development. Here play is seen as a medium of cultural learning and meaning-making.

Many studies have explored the relationship between play and child development. The focus has been on varied dimensions of children's development: cognition, language and literacy, social, and emotional areas. This chapter discusses important concepts and research done within each of these four areas that we hope can provide, when synthesized, information that can be used to explain an integrative "play way" approach to achieving educational and socialization goals during the early childhood years.

## FOCUS QUESTIONS

1. What are three different ways of viewing the relationship between play and development? What are some important concepts and problems that are associated with studying play and development?
2. How are brain development and play related? Why is play a good mediator of brain development?
3. What are universal and culturally specific aspects of play's role in development? What would be the main difference between saying that play serves a role in development that is culturally universal versus one that is culturally uniform?
4. How does research inform the questions of the link between play and cognitive development, between play and language and literacy development, between play and social development, and between play and emotional development?
5. How can playing help to get the preschooler ready for formal schooling? How can playing once in school help the child to meet academic standards?
6. What is good play? How can you explain the importance of play in early education to a parent?
7. What is the relationship between playfulness and imagination and psychological coping and resiliency? How can this relationship be harnessed to help children who are at risk?

## PLAY AND DEVELOPMENT: BASIC OBSERVATIONS

The relationship between play and development can be viewed in at least three ways:

- *Play simply reflects development.* Play behavior can serve as a window on the child's development, suggesting the current developmental status of the child in various domains.
- *Play reinforces development.* Play serves as a context and vehicle for the expression and consolidation of development, providing opportunities for new learning.
- *Play results in development.* Play can serve as an instrument of developmental change; it can generate qualitative improvement in the organism's functioning and structural organization.

Each one of these views is correct to some extent; they are not mutually exclusive ideas about play and development. To decide which answer is best in a given situation, however, additional information is required. We must know what kind of play is involved and which areas and levels of development are under consideration. We must also know the individual child and the context. Sometimes play can result in development; sometimes play reinforces development and learning; and at other times play only serves as a mirror or window on development. Often all three occur simultaneously during play.

An analogy to eating might help us to ask the right questions about the role of play in development. We don't ask whether eating is good for growth and development. We analyze eating into its constitutive caloric, vitamin, and mineral intake. With such analysis we can pose more specific questions about eating and food, such as asking which ingredients are good for specific people under specific circumstances. Fein (1997) suggests that we should approach the general question of play and development in like manner and be prepared to ask sharper, more focused questions like these.

Another basic idea is that play has both short-term and long-term benefits for the child. Some positive effects of play are short-term and can be realized immediately or soon after the play experience. These benefits may persist over time, but often they quickly fade. Long-term benefits of play, on the other hand, last for many years. A sleeper effect is said to occur when the value of prior experiences is not seen until much later. So a sleeper effect is a long-term benefit of play that does not show up for quite some time.

We believe that play can have both short-term and delayed, long-term effects on development. An example of a short-term benefit is the finding by scientists in the former Soviet Union that children's cognitive functioning appears to operate at an elevated level when the children perform play. Manujlenko (cited in Elkonin, 1978) reported greater self-regulation during play than during other times of the day. They reported that a little boy showed a great deal of concentration and attention to detail when playing army—much more so than when he was engaged in school lessons.

The sleeper effects of play are much more difficult to establish with research. Lengthy longitudinal studies are needed to determine such effects with certitude. Researchers have usually extrapolated from short-term studies to make claims about persisting benefits of play. Play intervention studies, for instance, assume that any immediate effects of play training on positive child development outcomes are sustained and even amplified over time in interaction with subsequent experiences. The rationale is that children will benefit from subsequent positive experiences because they were primed by the play intervention, leading to a cumulative long-term effect. Of course, these claims need to be substantiated with longitudinal research, and seldom has this been done (Christie & Johnsen, 1985).

Although positive developmental consequences can be attributable to play, we need to be aware of the so-called epiphenomenon principle—the possibility that it is not play per se but confounding variables such as peer interaction and conflict that are responsible for positive developmental consequences. If play training, for example, results in gains in cognitive performance, these gains may be due to nonplay factors. Indeed, when these epiphenomenon factors are carefully controlled, many of the advantages of play training disappear (Smith, Dalgleish, & Herzmark, 1981).

Another factor complicating the establishment of links between play and development is the principle of equifinality. Equifinality means that specific positive outcomes can happen in multiple ways in an open system (Sackett, Sameroff, Cairns, & Suomi, 1981). Although play might facilitate specific learning or some aspect of development, there are also other ways to obtain the same outcome. In other words, there are multiple avenues or routes to the same developmental destination. This means that play is helpful but not strictly needed. For example, later spelling and writing achieved by preschoolers who were in a literacy-enhanced dramatic play program could also be traced to alternative developmental pathways such as teacher storybook reading or direct instruction. There is no one road to literacy or perhaps to any other positive developmental outcome. An interesting and unanswered question at this point is whether play makes any uniquely distinguishing contribution to development.

## BRAIN DEVELOPMENT AND PLAY

In the first thirty-six months of life the average child experiences so much stimulation that his or her brain makes approximately one quadrillion synaptic connections. From birth a child's mind is primed for receiving and processing new sensations and is ready to try to make sense of all these experiences. A child is prepared for countless encounters with people and things that can be explored with each of the body's senses. The child's freewheeling play experiences help to create this gargantuan number of neural connections. Babies, toddlers, and young preschoolers need to play and explore to construct the richest possible set of synapses, forming the foundation for future brain development. As Sutton-Smith (1998) has commented, "as the brain

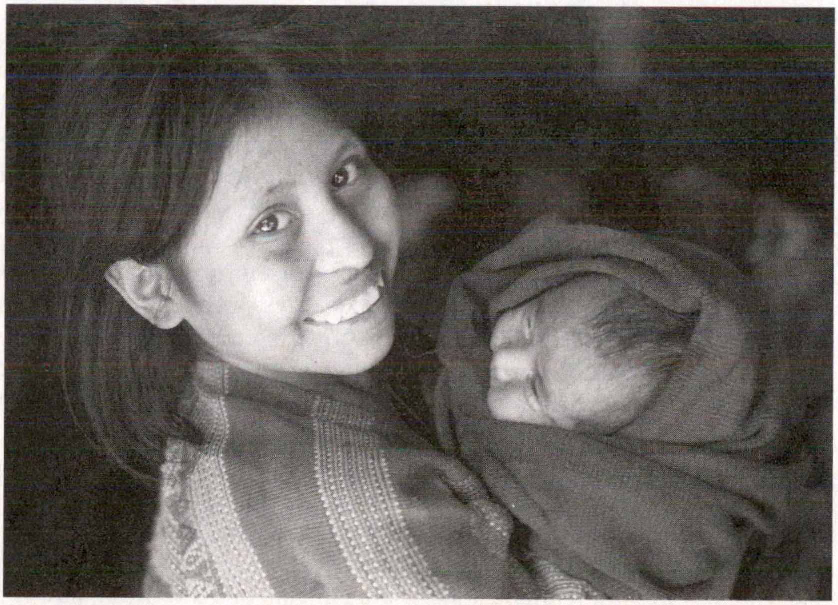

➤ From birth a child's mind is primed for receiving and processing new sensations and is ready to try to make sense of all the child's experiences.

begins in a state of high potentiality, so does play. Play's function in the early stages might be to assist the actualization of the brain potentiality to save in both brain and behavior more of the variability that is potentially there than would otherwise be saved if there was no play" (p. 333).

After age three the nature of brain development changes. The number of synaptic connections does not continue to increase. In fact, there is a drop to about half a quadrillion (i.e., 500 trillion) synapses by age ten years. As the raw *quantity* of connections gets pruned, there is increase in the *quality* of neuronal networking as more complex pathways and patterns and organizational structures are formed. Early synapses that are not used are eliminated as the brain relies on frequently used and increasingly sturdy synaptic pathways that are being established with cognitive development.

Play experiences mediate this brain development, as can other high-quality experiences, first by helping with the creation of the enormous number of synapses that are formed in the first three years and then by helping with the formation of these more complex neuronal structures that are created over the childhood years. For this to occur, play must be meaningful to the child, adding to the child's understanding of the world and ability to adapt to it. Play can then optimally stimulate brain activity and growth and produce a positive change in brain anatomy.

A mediator uses existing neural structures and behavioral systems to receive and process incoming experiences that are developmentally appropriate and enhancing. Play is one of the mediators of brain development. It is able to mediate the development of sensorimotor, social, affective, and cognitive systems because of its intermodal qualities and because the child is intensely active when at play (Bergen & Coscia, 2001). In addition, the play is motivated not by basic needs or drives, but by the intrinsic motivation for the enjoyment of play itself. Play therefore functions as a distinct motivational/behavioral system, according to some psychologists. It has evolved into an independent mechanism by which children can learn, form relationships with others, and develop skills needed in later life (Power, 2000).

When children play, they activate the neocortex (the thinking center of the brain) and the amygdala (the emotional center of the brain), and they integrate connections between these two centers in the developing brain. Strengthening the pathways between the neocortex and the amygdala can favorably affect any behaviors that involve both cognition and emotions, such as problem solving and creative thinking. And when children are engaging in play, their self-motivated behaviors in these affect-cognition areas seem to intensify, while their stress levels seem to decrease. We have never seen children biting their nails or showing other nervous habits while in the play state. But when not playing and feeling stress, they often do. Moreover, if the stress level is too high, the affect-cognitive behaviors, such as creativity and problem solving, can themselves become impaired. Play and these other affect-cognitive behaviors can reinforce each other, as long as there is not too much stress. Too bad the policymakers who want to put ever more pressure on children in schools do not seem to grasp the implications of these important scientific findings.

A useful way to think further about what is high-quality play, and other kinds of high-quality brain development stimulants in general, is to bring into the discussion Bronfenbrenner and Ceci's (1994) bioecological model of nature-nurture relationships and the notion of proximal processes. According to this model, genetic beginnings do not determine developmental ends, even though innate ability potentials do give certain individuals an advantage at the start of life. These innate potentials will be actualized or fulfilled commensurate with the quality of environmental stimulation that is forthcoming. Bronfenbrenner and Ceci speak about this in terms of *proximal processes,* or enduring forms of interaction in the child's environment found in a wide array of activities such as parent-child storytelling, conversations among peers or siblings, problem solving, and, of course, play (Roskos, 2000).

Proximal processes that are favorable to optimal cognitive development (and brain development) are ones in which the child can construct meaning from the experiences. For this to occur, the child must be an active agent in the process. First, there must be choices for the child to make. Second, the social or physical environment must provide informational feedback to the child, which can be used to reconstruct a better working model of the world. For Roskos (2000) these proximal processes are "the pulse of activity—the 'goings on' that bring stability and continuity to daily living at home, play, and work" (p. 129). This is the way genetic potential is realized in human development: There must be an active child and a responsive environment. Because play provides active involvement, choice, and feedback, it can serve as a high-quality proximal process that can stimulate optimal brain development, helping children to reach their full potential.

## CULTURAL LEARNING AND PLAY

Children at play in everyday life and in educational settings are using and developing a wealth of information, skills, and dispositions that have an important role in becoming competent members within their own cultural community. During play they are also engaging in a behavior that is believed to foster cognitive and social abilities that are common across cultures.

Many research studies concerned with play and development were conducted during the 1960s, 1970s, and 1980s when Piagetian theory dominated developmental psychology. Many were conducted in artificial lab settings or in separate spaces set off to the side of a preschool classroom. If the study was a field study seeking to describe play, the subjects usually were White, middle-class European American children, their teachers, and parents. During this period researchers identified a number of developmental correlates of play, personal traits or abilities such as conservation, divergent thinking, and perspective taking. These correlates of play (or the abilities related to play) were typically thought of as universal truths about play and development.

Certainly, a case can be made that much of this earlier research on play and development did yield results that are valid across cultures. The particular content of information picked up while playing would vary substantially across different cultural communities. However, the cognitive-affective abilities used to process the information which were found to be associated with play, such as seriation, conservation, and impulse control, could arguably be the same for developing children around the world. Likewise, recent psychological and educational research linking pretend play with literacy development and the development of theory of mind also seem to assume to an extent that discovered relationships would generalize across cultures.

During the same time that these Piagetian-influenced studies were being done on play and development, research evidence was being gathered in the field of anthropology that was somewhat at odds with their universalistic assumptions and conclusions (e.g., Schwartzmann, 1978). These anthropological studies revealed striking cultural variations in play, differences that could not be easily explained by existing psychological theories. It became obvious that play was not just a matter of individual children developing or individual children being different from each other. A research spotlight was needed to illuminate group as opposed to individual play, play in everyday settings as opposed to lab or school settings, and play in different cultures as opposed to play in the same culture. Research was needed on culturally variable aspects of play and development to go along with the research done on the universal aspects of play and development (Haight & Black, 2001).

Since the 1990s we have seen more research and theory on play and development that recognizes the limitations of the earlier work done in the tradition of developmental psychology. The first rumblings of discontent came from those who championed Vygotsky's theory of play and who insisted that we should realize that play served more than the consolidation and assimilation functions posited by Piaget. As we explained in Chapter 2, play for Vygotsky was a way in which the child could show skills ahead of himself or herself and could "self-scaffold" up to a higher level of development. The social contribution to development was also underscored, with parents, teachers, and other experts able to support and scaffold and facilitate the learning and development of the child during play.

In addition, for Vygotsky development, learning, and play always had to be seen within particular cultural contexts. So-called *natural lines* of development (universal) had to be studied along with *cultural lines* of development (culturally specific). Thus a major goal of research in the Vygotskian tradition is to try to better understand play and development in different cultural contexts. As Haight and Black (2001) note, "Sociocultural approaches have begun to articulate a culturally sensitive theory of play, one that seeks to understand how universal and cultural variable aspects of play interact in specific communities to create distinctive developmental pathways for play" (p. 231).

Vygotsky once gave an example to illustrate how important play is in cultural learning, a story about three young sisters who wanted to engage in pretend play about being sisters. They discovered that it was very difficult or impossible for them to play this make-believe game as long as they were thinking of their actual selves and their actual relationships to one another. They could not make explicit their implicit cultural knowledge of sisterhood. Only when they shifted the game slightly and pretended to be "mean sisters" could they do this. This way it seemed, with the modifier for sisters serving as a releaser of their collective funds of knowledge about this topic, they were able to make use of what they knew about the frames and scripts common in their culture relevant to acting out these pretend sister roles. The cultural meaning of being unpleasant sisters could then be instantiated in their role play.

Play, especially pretend play, contributes significantly to such cultural learning. Children learn a great deal about their cultures while playing. Playing reflects and expresses their cultural knowledge. It is also a way children learn and overlearn (learning and relearning with sufficient repetition that the learning is automatic, that it really sinks into the subconscious) knowledge about cultural norms, expectations, role relations, situation-specific scripts for how to behave, and how important cultural events are framed and played out.

Haight (1999) and Haight and Black (2001) cite some examples to support the view that play may have a universal but not uniform developmental function in cultural meaning-making. Play's function is universal in an important way. It is assumed that all cultures have children who engage in pretend play and that this activity helps children to make sense of their particular culture or helps them to form working hypotheses or cultural models of the ways things are and of the way things should be. But play's function is not uniform across cultures because the meaning-making that comes out of pretending leads to different learning in different cultures. For example, a mother-child pair in Taipei, Taiwan, might enact teacher-pupil exchanges in which the mother steers the child, who is interested in the pretend game, to overlearn social rituals and appropriate conduct in formal social interactions with a person of authority. Meaning-making ties in with internalizing values that are consistent with Confucian principles. Mothers in Chicago, in contrast, might encourage their preschoolers to express their individuality during pretend play, the appropriate value in American culture (Haight, 1999).

These examples suggest that the social function, content, and conduct of mother-child pretend play vary as a function of culture (e.g., Taipei versus Chicago). Play

➤ In play young children have the chance to learn cultural values and cultural knowledge—to construct meaning about what is appropriate in the culture where they live.

helps children to learn their particular culture; cultural meaning-making is a developmental function of play. In play with parents, siblings, teachers, peers, and friends, young developing children have the chance to interpret and reinterpret their cultural experiences. They have the chance to learn cultural values and cultural knowledge and to construct meaning about what it is appropriate in the culture where they live. The role of play in development needs to be seen from this cultural perspective as a complement to seeing it from the biological point of view we discussed earlier concerning brain development and play. In the study of play, as in the study of any social phenomenon, both biology and culture are seen as explanatory givens. Both affect human nature in tandem. Both influence play and its role in development.

## COGNITIVE DIMENSION

### Conceptual Development

Sociodramatic play occurs when two or more children adopt roles and act out a script or story. To engage in this advanced form of pretending, children need to build scripts and use conceptual thinking to impose order and to establish predictable patterns from experience. For example, to act out a fast-food restaurant script, children must be able to reconstruct the correct order of events involved in eating at a restaurant: traveling to the restaurant, waiting in line and placing an order, getting the order, sitting down and eating the food.

Smilansky (1968) has proposed that sociodramatic play helps children integrate experiences that seem unrelated at first, such as selecting menu items and paying money to a cashier in restaurant play. Several research studies have supported this claim. Saltz, Dixon, and Johnson (1977) and Saltz and Johnson (1974) found that sociodramatic play and thematic fantasy play (i.e., adult facilitated role enactment of fairy tales) helped preschool children to connect separate events.

With age and experience, children's conceptual knowledge increases rapidly. Play can greatly facilitate this process. Immature concepts of space, time, probability, and causality can be tested and revised during play. For example, when children wait for their turn to use a toy or to perform their part in a script, expressions such as "in a few minutes," "in a little while," "tomorrow," and even "next week" come to make more sense. Time is often altered in make-believe play episodes, but sequence and structure are often preserved and can become better understood as children engage in play (Athey, 1988).

Recently, Gmitrova and Gmitrova (2003) demonstrated a link between teacher-guided play of three- to six-years-olds and their manifestation of conceptual development. With small groups of children teachers were able to gently enter the playing process, a process known as *bridging* (Fromberg, 2002), and shift the children's cognitive behaviors to a higher conceptual level, "using the powerful natural engine of the free play" (p. 245). Interestingly, teacher-directed play of a whole classroom of children, called frontal play by the researchers, was not related to cognitive behaviors. Perhaps whole-classroom teacher-led play was less effective in stimulating cognitive behaviors because attention to individual differences and peer relations was minimal.

## Thinking and Problem Solving

Make-believe play involves two cognitive operations: decentration, the realization that one can act out a role and retain one's real-life identity, and reversibility, the awareness that one can change from one's make-believe role back to one's real identity at any time (Rubin et al., 1983). Golomb and Cornelius (1977) found that making children aware of the reversibility inherent in their make-believe play helped them to perform better on conservation tasks.

More recently, Wolfgang, Stannard, and Jones (2001) reported the results of following up on a group of preschoolers who were observed playing in 1982 to see how well they did years later in math classes and on achievement tests. Outcome measures for math ability were available for elementary and secondary school years on these children. IQ scores were also available. When the children were preschoolers, their play with blocks was scored on a five-point scale, from "use of materials in a highly insightful way" to "use of materials without regard to physical or representational properties." By controlling for IQ, it was found that the quality of block play predicted math ability at the secondary but not the elementary grade level. The researchers suggested that the nurturing of underlying cognitive structures that came about in the block play that the children did when they were in their preschool years might have promoted the formal operational thinking required in secondary but not in elementary mathematics (algebra and geometry versus arithmetic).

Bruner (1972) has proposed that play contributes to children's ability to solve problems by increasing their behavioral options. As was explained in Chapter 1, flexibility is one of key characteristics of play. Children try many different behaviors while playing, and these behaviors can later be used in solving problem. Several research studies have reported that play promotes children's problem-solving abilities (e.g., Smith & Dutton, 1979; Sylva, Bruner, & Genova, 1976).

Wyver and Spence (1999) conducted a series of three studies to investigate the relationship between pretend play and different types of problem solving in preschoolers. Study 1 investigated the correlations between the types of play that children engaged in and their convergent and divergent problem-solving abilities. Study 2 examined the effects of training children to solve divergent problems on their play behavior. Study 3 turned things around and trained children to engage in sociodramatic play and looked at the impact on children's divergent problem solving. Wyver and Spence (1999) report that their results support "a complex reciprocal causality model in which the development of divergent problem solving skills facilitates the development of play skills and vice versa" (p. 419). Thus there may be a two-way relationship between the two areas of development, each helping the other.

## Divergent Thinking

There are a number of reasons that pretend play should foster divergent thinking. First, in play children practice divergent thinking skills by transforming objects and role playing. Often they are generating different play ideas throughout a play episode, thinking up and deciding on various courses of action. Second, the expression of emotion in play and fantasy may help in the creation of a wider-ranging storehouse of affect-laden associations in the child, and the use of the emotion that accompanies play to access these associations in the child's affect system should facilitate divergent forms of thinking. This is because the involvement of emotions broadens the search process for associations (Russ, Robins, & Christiano, 1999). Third, pretend play is fun, exciting, and often deeply pleasurable. Children can get lost in the flow of the experience, which may stimulate intense engagement and creative associations between ideas.

Correlational research studies have reported a positive relationship between play and measures of divergent thinking. Lieberman (1977), for example, found that kindergartners who were rated high in terms of playfulness scored higher on tests of divergent thinking than less playful children did. Dansky and Silverman (1973, 1975) reported that children who were allowed to play with objects such as paper cups were later able to find more creative, nonstandard uses for these objects. Dansky (1980b) later discovered that free play fostered divergent thinking only in children who regularly engaged in pretend play. He interpreted this finding to indicate that the symbolic transformations that occur in make-believe play may be a key factor in play's contribution to creativity.

Fisher (1992) used meta-analysis (i.e., use of statistical methods to synthesizing numerical information across studies on the same topic) to investigate the effects of play on development. He looked at forty-six investigations done since 1974 dealing with cognitive, linguistic, and social-affective domains. He found that play had a noteworthy effect on divergent thinking, especially in studies focusing on sociodramatic play.

In a longitudinal study, Russ et al. (1999) used the Affect in Play Scale to measure the different emotions in play and play quality in school-age children. Russ found that children's play scores obtained during first and second grade predicted their divergent thinking scores four years later. Higher-quality play in early primary grades predicted creative thinking in the intermediate grades.

Lloyd and Howe (2003) investigated the relationship between different forms of solitary play (solitary-active, solitary-passive, and reticence) and convergent and divergent thinking ability in preschool children. (See Chapter 3 for a discussion of these types of solitary play.) Torrance's Thinking Creatively in Action and Movement Test was used to index divergent thinking ability, and the Peabody Picture Vocabulary Test and another intelligence measure indexed convergent thinking ability. The study also examined the kinds of materials children used in solitary play (open- or closed-ended) and whether their actions were intended or unintended. Lloyd and Howe found that solitary-active players did the best on the measure of divergent thinking and tended to give more unintended uses of play materials (e.g., using puzzle piece as a car). Solitary-active players tended to engage in functional or dramatic play, whereas solitary-passive players preferred constructive play. Given the links between dramatic play and creativity, it is not surprising that the solitary-active players did well on the test of divergent thinking. Pulaski (1974) long ago made the point that some children might need to be alone to practice their creative and fantasy ideas and that this could play a key role in the development of divergent thinking ability.

Other findings on the play-creativity relationship have been less positive. When Smith and Whitney (1987) repeated the Dansky and Silverman (1975) alternative uses experiment using double-blind assessments to control for experimenter bias, they failed to replicate the connection between play and the divergent use of objects.

Dunn and Herwig (1992) found that dramatic play was not related to estimates of preschoolers' divergent thinking and suggested that ecological factors, such as attending a half-day versus full-day early childhood program, might moderate play-creativity relationships. Conceptual problems often beset research on play correlates.

## Theory of Mind

Theory of mind (Leslie, 1987) is an implicit and rudimentary awareness about one's own and other people's mental worlds. It involves understanding the knowledge and beliefs of others and realizing that these might be different from one's own knowledge and beliefs (Smith, 1999). Before four years of age most youngsters seem insensitive or oblivious to their privileged information (knowledge that they have but that another person lacks), thereby preventing them from realizing that another person, who lacks this privileged information, might have a false belief. As children develop their theory of mind, they become more sensitive to the fact that other people have their own minds and perspectives that often are at odds with the children's own point of view.

Smith (1999) has pointed out several reasons why pretend play appears to be a good candidate for facilitating children's theory of mind (ToM):

- Pretend play is absent in nonhuman species, as is ToM.
- Pretend play appears to be present in all human societies, as is ToM.
- Pretend play has a developmental time course similar to that of ToM, developing between the ages of two and six years.
- Pretend play is delayed or absent in autistic children, as is ToM.
- Pretend play may give practice to mental state attribution, which is crucial to the development of ToM.

In research that has examined pretend play and theory of mind development, the latter is usually operationalized as passing the false belief task. In the false belief task a child is shown Maxi, a doll, who conceals a piece of candy in a blue cupboard. Maxi goes away, and during his absence his mommy arrives and moves the candy from the blue cupboard to an adjacent white cupboard. The mommy then leaves the scene, and Maxi comes back. The cupboard doors are closed shut so that the candy is not in the child's field of vision. The child is assumed to have been successfully led to believe that Maxi did not see his mommy move the candy by the way the researcher moved the dolls in and out of the scene. The child is asked, "Where will Maxi look for the candy?" The correct reply is the blue cupboard because that is where Maxi put it and he doesn't know that his mommy moved it.

Research shows that children under four years of age tend to assert that Maxi will look in the white cupboard, egocentrically failing to suppress their own privileged information about what has transpired. Youngblade and Dunn (1995) report that children who did more role enactment play at thirty-three months performed better on this task at forty months of age than did children who exhibited significantly less pretending at thirty-three months of age. Similarly, Dockett (1994) found that children who were trained to engage in pretend play pass the theory of mind task earlier than control group children. Astington and Jenkins (1995) found that pretend-play person transformations significantly correlated with false belief understanding in three- to five-year olds, controlling for language ability and verbal intelligence. Jenkins and Astington (2000), in a longitudinal study, found that theory of mind development in preschoolers and the extensiveness of their pretend-play negotiations were positively related.

In reviewing these and a large number other studies on play and theory of mind, Smith (1999) concluded that evidence supports that pretend play might help to bring about theory of mind, but the current evidence does not support the contention that pretend play is necessary for its development. We concur with this conclusion. We also believe that the nature of the relationship between pretend play and theory of mind might not be a simple one of cause and effect. Both pretending and theory of mind are hallmark abilities of the human species, and more research is needed to acquire a deeper understanding of each of them and their relationship with each other (Lillard, 1998, 2002). Further, Bergen (2002) has pointed out that we still have not seen empirical studies connecting theory of mind to academic skills such as mathematical and literacy abilities. This is odd because both areas—theory of mind and academic skills—would seem to have a lot in common, such as symbolic representation and abstract thinking.

## LANGUAGE AND LITERACY DIMENSION

Play appears to have several connections with oral language acquisition. First, researchers have observed that infants and toddlers frequently play with different aspects of oral language (Davidson, 1998). For example, Weir (1976, pp. 610–611) reported that her own two-year-old child played with (a) sounds by repeating strings of words containing related sounds ("*Babette / back here / wet*") and (b) syntax by substituting words from the same grammatical category ("*What colour / What colour blanket / What colour mop / What color glass*"). Chukovsky (1976, p. 601) reported that his two-year-old daughter played with the semantic aspects of language by telling primitive jokes. After listening to a rhyme in which a dog barks and a cat meows, his daughter said, "oggie—miaow!" and burst into laughter. She had made a joke by intentionally putting together two things that did not go together. In all of these instances the child is focusing on the properties of language and manipulating them in enjoyable ways. Unlike normal language, in which the goal is communicate meaning, here the goal is to have fun with language itself. According to Cazden (1976) this play helps children to perfect newly acquired language skills and increases their conscious awareness of linguistic rules.

Another link is that both pretend play and language involve symbolic representation. In language sound represents objects, actions, attributes, and situations. In play children use objects and actions, as well as language, to stand for other things. Therefore, it is not surprising that symbolic play and language have been found to be related to each other during the toddler years (Bornstein, Vibbert, Tal, & O'Donnell, 1992; Tamis-LeMonda & Bornstein, 1993). In addition, there is evidence that older preschool and kindergarten-age children also gain valuable language practice by engaging in play (Garvey, 1974).

A third connection is that play places heavy linguistics demands on children and prods them to use their maximum language abilities. Children must make intentional use of lexical and syntactical features of language to signify the person, object, and situational transformations that occur in pretense play and to identify and to elaborate on play themes as they unfold during the play episode. Bruner (1983) contends that "the most complicated grammatical and pragmatic forms of language appear first in play activity" (p. 65). In addition to being complex, the language that children use during play tends to be decontextualized (Pellegrini & Jones, 1994). Decontextualized language is language that conveys meaning independently of context (i.e., nonverbal clues). It is marked by the use of rather abstract forms of language, including adjectives, pronouns, and conjunctions. Pretending to call on the phone to order pizza with sausage but not mushrooms, for example, is decontextualized language. The meaning is conveyed in the words said, independent of any contextual cues. Play can strengthen children's representational competence and can help children to overlearn skills needed for comprehending and producing decontextualized texts in later reading and writing academic lessons.

This connection between the symbolic representation in play, oral language, and literacy stimulated interest in play's role in the development of reading and writing. This research got off to a slow start. For example, during the 1970s and early 1980s a few researchers investigated relationships between the amount of symbolic play in which children engaged and their scores on standardized readiness tests that measured abilities that were assumed to be prerequisites to learning to read (Becher & Wolfgang, 1977; Pellegrini, 1980). These early studies provided some evidence that children who frequently engaged in symbolic play also scored high on reading readiness measures. As with all correlational research, however, these studies were not able to determine the causal direction between the two variables. Did engaging in symbolic play promote reading readiness skills (visual memory, auditory discrimination, etc.), or did the readiness skills result in higher frequencies of symbolic play? Or were both areas related to a third variable, such as general intelligence or representational thinking?

The mid-1980s witnessed a major theoretical shift in the field of early literacy. The concept of reading readiness was gradually replaced by a new perspective known as emergent literacy. According to this view, literacy learning began much earlier than had previously been believed and was similar in nature to oral language acquisition. Infants and toddlers observe the literacy that surrounds them in everyday life—bedtime stories, environmental print (e.g., labels on cereal boxes, restaurant signs), and family literacy routines (e.g., looking up programs in *TV Guide,* reading the Bible, writing down phone messages)—and then begin to construct their own hypotheses about the function, structure, and conventions of print. In this process, young children invent their own emergent versions of reading and writing that initially have little resemblance to conventional forms. For example, early versions of writing often resemble drawing or scribbles. As children have opportunities to use these emergent versions of literacy in meaningful social situations, their reading and writing become increasingly conventional.

This new view was prompted in part by a series of case studies in which researchers carefully documented the early literacy development of their own children.

In addition to laying the groundwork for the emergent literacy perspective, these case studies also revealed that young children frequently engaged in emergent forms of reading and writing during make-believe play. For example, Baghban (1984) described how, after returning home from a meal at a restaurant, her two-year-old daughter took on the role of a waitress and pretended to write down her mother's food orders on a notepad. These types of incidents gave rise to the possibility that play had a more direct role in literacy development than was previously believed. Perhaps play offers children opportunities to experiment with, practice, and conventionalize emergent forms of reading and writing.

This direct-link hypothesis resulted in pioneering naturalistic observation studies being conducted in preschool and kindergarten classrooms, such as the studies done by Hall (1987) in England and Jacob (1986) in Puerto Rico. Reflecting the influence of ecological psychology, these descriptive studies were conducted in literacy-enriched play centers that contained materials that created an environmental impetus for play-related reading and writing activities—pencils, markers, notepads, signs, menus, and so forth. Data showed that when given the opportunity, young children eagerly incorporated literacy props into their dramatic play.

These pioneering studies really caught the attention of early literacy researchers in the United States. A series of studies on literacy-enriched play centers revealed that this type of intervention led to large increases in emergent reading and writing activity during play (e.g., Christie & Enz, 1992; Neuman & Roskos, 1990, 1992). These literacy-rich settings also appeared to enhance the duration and complexity of young children's dramatic play episodes (Neuman & Roskos, 1992). So infusing literacy props into dramatic play settings appeared to be a win-win situation: Literacy activity increased, and the quality of children's play improved. (See Chapter 7 for more information about literacy-enriched play centers.)

Initial attempts at linking children's play in print-enriched setting with gains in literacy development were mixed. For example, Neuman and Roskos (1990) found that adding literacy materials to play centers resulted in a significant gain in preschoolers' scores on Clay's Concepts about Print test, but Christie and Enz (1992) failed to replicate this finding. However, more recent studies have shown convincingly that as children play in print-enriched settings, they do learn to read the words that are present in centers (Neuman & Roskos, 1993; Vukelich, 1994). For example, if a restaurant play center contains several signs (e.g., "Paula's Pizza," "Place Your Order Here"), children will often learn to recognize these printed words. In addition, Neuman and Roskos (1997) present strong evidence that while engaging in literacy-enriched play, young children develop strategies such as self-checking and self-correction, which will later on have an important role in reading comprehension.

On the theoretical front, attention shifted away from Piaget and an emphasis on symbolic representation to social-interactionist aspects of Vygotsky's (1978) theory and his concept of the zone of proximal development, in which adults or more competent peers help children to engage in activities that they cannot do on their own. Researchers used this construct as a rationale for investigating the effects of adult support on children's behavior in literacy-enriched play settings. Results of several intervention studies indicated that adult scaffolding combined with literacy-enriched play settings increased the amount of literacy activity during play (Christie & Enz, 1992; Morrow, 1990).

The mid-1990s marked the beginning of a third generation of research on play in literacy. This new wave of studies revisited some earlier connections and examined these in more depth while expanding the scope of the literacy-play interface to include a broader age range and sociocultural and ecobiological factors. For example, Rowe's (1998) carefully designed ethnographic study of toddlers' book-related play is a good example of the search for earlier connections between play and literacy. She investigated how two-year-old children used play to remember and make sense of books. Some of the children's book-related play appeared to have a key role in comprehension, helping the children combine ideas, feelings, and images from books with their own prior knowledge to create meaning.

The Vygotskian notion that social interaction between individuals during play can serve as the source of literacy knowledge has also been refined and expanded. Whereas earlier studies focused exclusively on teacher-child play interactions, the third generation of literacy-in-play studies have also examined how children can appropriate literacy knowledge and skills while playing with parents and peers. For example, Christie and Stone (1999) investigated how multiple-age grouping in a play setting allowed children to teach one another about literacy. Findings showed that the collaborative literacy interactions that occurred during play were more complex than Vygotsky's concept of the zone of proximal development would lead one to believe. Although a majority of the joint literacy learning conformed to the zone construct, flowing from older or more competent "experts" to younger or less able "novices," a sizable number of collaborative interactions in both groups were multi-directional, with the "expert" and "novice" roles not firmly set.

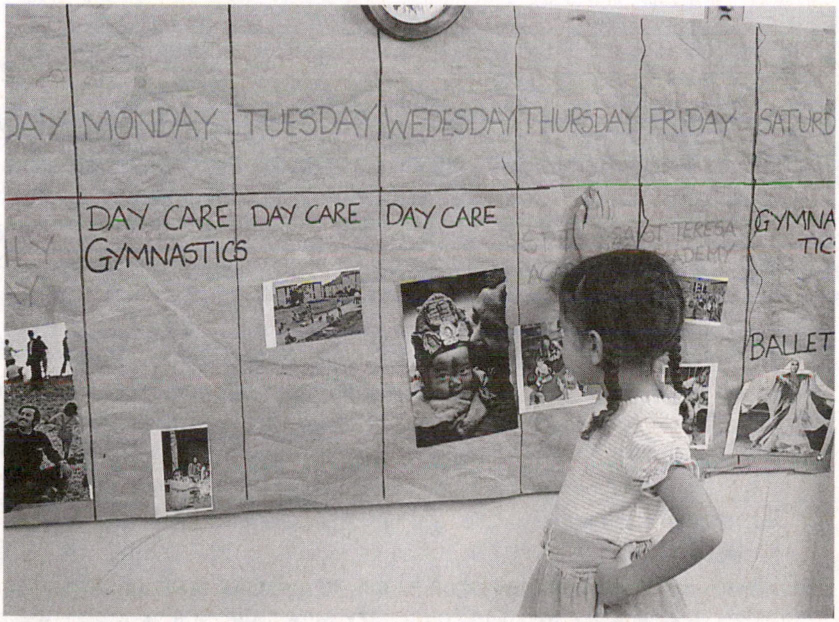


➤ The relationship among play, literacy, and the physical environment has been found to be much more complex than was previously assumed.

Finally, the relationship among play, literacy, and the physical environment has been reexamined and found to be much more complex than was previously assumed. Earlier studies assumed a unidirectional relationship between the play and the environment, with literacy-rich settings influencing children to incorporate literacy into their play. Several third-generation investigations have embraced Bronfenbrenner's (1995) basic concept of the person-environment dynamic, namely, that individuals both shape and are shaped by their surroundings. Play is viewed as a system of activity that arises from individual intentions as well as setting influences both near (the immediate surroundings) and far (socially held views of play). For example, Han (2002) has examined how preschoolers' individual play predispositions (the *dramatist* and *patterner* play styles described in Chapter 4) interact with the physical and social environment of the classroom to determine the nature of literacy-related play. Sonnenschein, Baker, Serpell, and Schmidt (2000) focused on macro-level sociocultural influences, examining how family income influenced parents' views about literacy and play. Low-income parents tended to have a skills orientation that favored drill-and-practice activity, whereas middle-income parents favored an entertainment orientation that valued activities that made literacy fun and enjoyable (e.g., play, storybook reading). These parental attitudes in turn appeared to influence the children's access to various forms of home literacy activities. Longitudinal data showed that children who grew up in homes with an entertainment perspective toward literacy were more likely to develop phonemic awareness and a positive orientation toward print than were children who grew up in homes that emphasized a skills perspective toward literacy. The discussion in Box 5.1 supports the value of the entertainment orientation for school readiness.

**BOX 5.1**

## School Readiness and the Educational Value of Play

School readiness and "leaving no child behind" are two sides of the same coin. We want all children to be able to benefit from instruction when they start elementary school. Unfortunately, the number of children in our country who are not prepared for school is alarming. According to our best research estimates, well over 20 percent of our children are ill-prepared for what will be expected of them when they reach the kindergarten classroom. To experience initial success, children need to be ready to follow simple instructions, to share and cooperate, and they need basic expressive and receptive language skills. Yet research shows that 34 percent of kindergartners have difficulty recognizing letters, 25 percent experience peer problems, and 25 percent show difficulty persisting on tasks (Singer & Bellin, 2003). Many of these children in this "at risk" category, moreover, demonstrate superficial knowledge of academic content that can be misleading. For example, if asked to recite the alphabet, they can effortlessly and without error give the singsong version, but they might think "ellemeno" is one of the letters of the alphabet, and they will not know or be able to recognize letters in isolation. If asked to count, they can produce rather rapidly the correct sequence "*123456* 7 8 9 10," but if asked how many fingers are being held up or to count out a select small number of objects from a larger group, they cannot succeed.

A major theme of this book is that when play is in the classroom, good things happen. Good things can also happen when play is an important part of the child's life before he or she gets to the classroom door. Symbolic abilities and social competence, for example, are two general characteristics needed for school readiness, and both are promoted by sociodramatic play. Good-quality child development centers and preschool programs recognize sociodramatic play as a developmentally appropriate means to prepare children for subsequent academic learning once the school bell rings.

Dorothy and Jerome Singer of Yale University have been doing a great deal over the years to help teachers and parents realize the promise of play for children's learning and development. For example, they recently came out with a brand new book for parents and teachers, *Make-Believe: Games & Activities for Imaginative Play* (2001). The book is a how-to guide with more than 100 games and activities for parents and teachers to use to promote a sense of play in young children (two to five years old) and to enrich their developing imaginations. In addition, the Singers' ideas have been used in the creation of video-based programs for training parents and other caregivers to engage preschoolers in guided play and learning games that can strengthen school-readiness skills. Language use, counting, colors, and shapes are some of the school readiness skills targeted, as are motor skills (using school supplies), social skills (civility, emotional literacy, school citizenship), and creativity.

*Circle of Make-Believe* is one of two video-based programs that have been developed (the other is called *Learning through Play for School Readiness*). *Circle of Make Believe* is an interactive video-based program for parents and other caregivers of three- to five-year-olds that can be used in Head Start centers, families, home care, and preschools. Seven different learning games are illustrated on video (demonstrated by real people—actual parents, preschooler, and teachers), each conducive to play activity and each supportive of school readiness. For example, in "Where Is My Kitten?", children use a kitten puppet (a cat face drawn on a paper plate) and pretend binoculars to practice words that describe spatial relationships: *on top of* and *under, in front of* and *behind.* In the very popular "Restaurant Game," which revolves around a story of a make-believe birthday party at a restaurant, children play the roles of waiter or waitress, birthday person, and party guests. Here the video engages viewers through real-time, interactive challenges to practice the skills modeled in the game, such as "reading" a pretend menu, politeness, sharing, counting, and setting the table with placemats and plates, glasses, bowls, cups, and so on. The play-based program is an excellent illustration of adult-guided play to foster school readiness and is clearly the one we would favor over a drill-and-practice method of teaching phonics, for example. More information on *Circle of Make-Believe* can be obtained by from http://homepage.mac.com/mediagroupct/circle_mb/index.html or by e-mailing MediaGr@aol.com.

## SOCIAL DIMENSION

Creasey, Jarvis, and Berk (1998) contend that a two-way relationship exists between play and social development: the social environment influences children's play, and play also acts as an important context in which children acquire social skills and social knowledge. We agree with this assertion. As we discussed in Chapter 3, group play demands high levels of social competence. Children learn attitudes and skills needed for this play from their parents, teachers, and other children. Play has a key role in social development by providing a context in which children can acquire many important social skills such as turn-taking, sharing, and cooperation, as well as the ability to understand other people's thoughts, perceptions, or emotions. In the sections that follow we will examine both sides of this interactive relationship.

Of all the social abilities required for group play, the most basic is the ability to understand the rules of play. All social play is rule-governed. Even simple games that parents play with their babies, such as peek-a-boo, demands that participants follow the rule of turn-taking. In sociodramatic play the rules become much more complex. For instance, when children adopt a role, their behavior must be consistent within that role (Garvey, 1974). If their behavior becomes inappropriate, such as a baby acting like a adult, the other players will usually issue a sharp reprimand ("Babies don't act like that!"). Unlike games with rules, rules for group dramatic play are not set in advance; rather, the rules are negotiated and established and sometime changed by children during the course of the play. Even when school-age children engage in games with preset rules, the rules are frequently changed by players, particularly those who have more power and skill (Freie, 1999). This conscious manipulation of rules provides an opportunity for children to examine the nature of rules and rule-making. Therefore play is a context in which children not only learn specific rules such as turn-taking, but also learn about the meaning of rules in general. As we noted earlier, children learn about this in the context of their own culture; they are interpreting and commenting on their own culture, indicating their understanding of it. They are engaged in cultural meaning-making.

Significant positive correlations have been reported between the frequency of group dramatic play and measures of peer popularity and social skills (Connolly & Doyle, 1984; Rubin & Hayvern, 1981). Perhaps these correlations are due to the high social demand of this complex form of play. Garvey (1974) notes that to successfully engage in group dramatizations children must first agree on who will adopt each role and on the make-believe identities of objects and actions. For example, in a gas station/mechanic's garage dramatization they might agree that Barbara will be the mechanic, Judy will be the cashier, and Ben will be the customer who arrives in his car. It might then be decided that a discarded milk carton will represent an oil can and that a pencil will be used as if it were a tire gauge. The children must also make cooperative decisions about the story sequence. Barbara, Judy, and Ben might agree that first, the customer will by some gas; next, the mechanic will add some oil and check the tires on the car; and finally, the customer will by some snacks in the convenience store part of the gas station. These plans can be altered during the course of the play. Perhaps the children will decide that Ben's car needs a complete engine overhaul. This type of joint planning requires give-and-take and cooperation. Children who do not choose go along with the group's consensus are often excluded from the play, and cooperation is rewarded by inclusion in the play. So there are powerful social incentives to negotiate and cooperate during sociodramatic play.

Rough-and-tumble (R&T) play has been found to correlate positively with social cognitive ability and popularity in older children (Pellegrini, 1995). Perhaps this relationship is due in part to the cognitive/kinetic perspective-taking required by this type of play (see the next section). In a qualitative study of R&T play of seven boys from six to nine years of age, Reed and Brown (2000) demonstrated that this play form was conducive to expressions of caring and intimacy. Perhaps the boys exhibited caring and showed concern for each other because they recognized in themselves and others the human body's limitations and vulnerabilities to the kinetic challenges experienced in R&T play. Sheets-Johnstone (2002) theorizes that the recognition that others are as vulnerable as you are, which children can acquire in R&T play, is a kinetically learned moral precept of the first order and might very well be an important source in the beginning of social morality, a foundational principle not just for play and games, but for life.

As was the case with cognition, causal relationships between play and social competence are difficult to establish. Several researchers have conducted training studies in which children were taught to engage in sociodramatic play. Results showed that play training not only resulted in gains in sociodramatic play, but also led to increases in positive peer interaction and cooperation (Rosen, 1974; Smith, Dalgleish, & Herzmark, 1981; Udwin, 1983). These findings support the position that engaging in group dramatic play promotes the acquisition of social skills. However, other epiphenomena associated with the training, such as adult or peer interaction, might have contributed to the gains in social competence.

Sawyer (1997, 2003) has provided a theoretical lens and research data pertaining to the connection between play and social cognitive development during the early childhood years. Sawyer compares group pretense play to a jazz band that engages in a great deal of improvisation. Children's play motifs (which are shared collectively and come from the children's local peer culture and popular culture, such as the latest superhero movie) are similar to the jazz musicians' riffs or figures. These are employed to reach shared understanding between players and afford opportunities for variation, repetition, and embellishment during play episodes.

Much implicit knowledge is shared by child players, just as occurs in a jazz band of accomplished adult musicians. According to Sawyer, the expressed play script and frame are merely tips of the iceberg. Underneath the surface there exists a great deal of potential material for mutual play due to the shared peer culture. The challenge is for players to integrate performances that are individualistically inspired with the ongoing group performance. There is an opportunity for children to learn to balance their budding individual creativity with group demands so as to be able to do their own thing while at the same time blending in with the group play. Sawyer claims that skill at group pretense in childhood may foreshadow skill in verbal conversation later in life. Box 5.2 suggests an approach to sharing with parents an understanding of the many benefits of play.

**BOX 5.2**

## *Communicating the Value of Play to Parents*

Not surprisingly, some parents are perplexed by the importance put on play by early childhood educators. Many parents recognize that there is a place for play in the daily life of children but question whether play is overemphasized in school and worry that perhaps their own children will pay the price. They might fear that without a clearer commitment to academics in the early childhood curriculum their children's preparation for formal schooling will be less than optimal. It is important to know how to communicate to parents the value of play in development and education.

Home and school relationships are especially important in early childhood education. Teachers must be responsible for maintaining positive communications with parents. To be successful, teachers need to recognize and keep in mind several basic facts about families. Of course, in today's pluralistic society there are many kinds of families, differing in culture and ethnicity, family structure, social class, and so forth. Teachers also need to remember that parents are busy people who are sharing their children with educators. Parents know their own children very well and can communicate what they want for them. In the school-home partnership parents need to have some ownership of educational goals for their children. The skillful teacher will try to share information, enlist parental cooperation, and help parents to view themselves as collaborators in educational endeavors.

A number of important general messages about the value of play should be shared with parents. Many of these have been discussed in this chapter. For example, teachers can provide information about what the research literature says about the importance of play in cognitive development and literacy development, especially the benefits of social play and pretend play. Fact sheets can be prepared as separate handouts, or the information can be included in a brochure or parent newsletter. The classroom's website and other information sources can be made available for parents who are interested in pursuing the topic further.

In addition to general play information it is worthwhile to share specific concrete examples of children's play in the program. Parents need to be informed about how children are increasingly choosing more challenging and meaningful play, how their play is lasting longer, and how it is reflecting higher-level language, social, and cognitive abilities. Parents need to be informed about how children are getting better at solving problems, are using richer speech, and are including more reading and writing activities in their play (even if their reading and writing are unconventional emergent versions). Be sure to mention how children's pretend play reflects their experiences, including their vicarious experiences in the world of literature. Tell the parents about their children's growing knowledge about events and their improved thinking skills as these are seen in their sociodramatic play. Parents can be informed about children's increasing social competence and how their play negotiation skills reflect and contribute to this important development. Parents need to learn about children's improved artistic expressions, block constructions, and story-making efforts, not just in the real world of the classroom, but also in the medium of computer technology. These specific play examples can come from play assessment and play documentation, activities that are part and parcel of a good early childhood program as we saw at the end of Chapter 3.

Even with general information sheets and examples of play in classroom websites, photo albums, videotapes, and the like, some parents might still not be convinced about the value of classroom play. Parents from different cultural backgrounds or different racial and ethnic backgrounds often do not have the same belief and value system as the early childhood teachers. Some parents from different cultural backgrounds may understand the rationale for the play-based early childhood program but still not buy into it for reasons having to do with an opposing value system and different priorities. When this happens, the teacher must look with wise eyes at the play of the children who have concerned parents and start to build a bridge to the parents' beliefs by showing an appreciation for the parents' point of view.

Williams (2002) discusses how having these wise eyes might work in practice, in a case study about a three-year-old African-American girl named Andi and her mother, Mrs. Smith. At Parents' Day at Andi's preschool one of the critical events reported was how Andi wanted to pretend to feed the baby on the floor in a make-believe play session and how Andi's mother disagreed with eating on the floor, pretend or not. Andi's mother wanted to intervene, become spokesperson for reality, and weave in and out of play to teach lessons in self-care, home care, and care of others. She viewed the pretend-play context as a chance to teach rules about appropriate behavior, realizing, as many traditionally minded parents do, that this is better than straight lecturing.

The teacher with wise eyes is not dismissive of Mrs. Smith's more directive play facilitation style, even if it is not the one recommended by the mainstream early childhood education professional community. The teacher with wise eyes, according to Williams, realizes that there is not necessarily one best way for the child to play or for the adult and child to play. It is not just a one-way street between the expert teacher and the novice parent. Teachers can and should learn from parents too. Together they need to engage in honest conversations and small group discussions with others about the similarities and differences between home and school play. To strengthen the partnership between the parent and the teacher, a bridge must be built between the home and the school that is based on open communication and respect.

Trust and care must be manifest in the teacher-parent relationship before beliefs and attitudes can change in either party. For parents who want an academic early childhood program, teachers need to communicate general and specific information about the benefits of play in the context of an honest and trusting partnership. By giving parents information and examples of educational play done at school, teachers can recommend the same at home—not as a substitution or replacement for the educational activities already taking place at home, but as a supplement. It is not an either/or proposition but a both/and one. Often the teacher can change curriculum and instruction in the classroom in response to what is learned from parents about families' funds of knowledge.

## EMOTIONAL DOMAIN

### Affect Regulation

Affect regulation includes inhibitory control that begins to emerge as the child nears his or her first birthday. There are temperament differences in the ability to control impulses, making it more difficult for some children than others, but all children must learn conscious regulation of affect and conduct. Not succeeding in this important developmental task does not bode well for school readiness. Social competence, on which so much of school readiness depends, requires affect regulation, as do so many of the other social and academic skills needed to be a good student. Children who do not succeed in this critical developmental task of early childhood, sometimes called *disinhibited* children, are at risk to develop externalizing problems such as conduct disorders and attention deficit/hyperactivity disorder.

On the basis of what we discussed earlier in this chapter about brain functioning and development, play and affect regulation are related theoretically. Play is under the control of the child, and challenges and affect levels are experienced at the moderate level. This provides opportunities for fine-tuning emotional control and gaining mastery over impulses to act out. Acceptance by peers during social play hinges on such emotional control. Self-regulation is aided by internal imagery and language and private speech, which accompany a great deal of playing.

Elias and Berk (2002) explored the potential link between sociodramatic play and self-regulation. In their short-term longitudinal study, fifty-one middle-income three-

➤ In a study by Elias and Berk (2002) results showed that complex sociodramatic play predicted self-regulation during cleanup.

and four-year-olds were observed in their preschool classrooms, and incidences of complex sociodramatic play and solitary-dramatic play were coded. The children were also observed during circle time and cleanup time to assess self-control in regulating emotions. Observations of play and cleanup and circle time occurred twice, four or five months apart. Children's temperament or natural inclination toward being impulsive or nonimpulsive was assessed by having mothers or fathers complete the impulsivity scale of the Child Behavior Questionnaire. Results showed that complex sociodramatic play predicted self-regulation during cleanup time, especially for children who were temperamentally high in impulsivity. Solitary-dramatic play was negatively correlated with improvement in cleanup time performance. The researchers noted the potential of sociodramatic play to foster children's self-regulatory development.

## Coping and Resilience

Play is a medium that is self-enabling, and play and fantasy give the child a chance to be powerful and the master of circumstances. Sutton-Smith (1980b) discussed the way in which role reversal in play can foster a sense of control and autonomy in the child. Consider a child who is dropped off at school or a childcare center day after day by a parent who hurries off to work. The child has no choice in the matter. The parent decides what happens and is in total control of the entire situation. But in play the child can reverse roles and pretend to leave dolls or teddy bears at a pretend childcare or nursery, thereby recapturing a little of the loss of control experienced in real life.

Therefore playing is intimately related to the expansion of a sense of self as an autonomous and functioning person who can influence surrounding events. Through play the developing identity of the child emerges. The child forms a secure position and from this position of strength is able to achieve empathy for others and other positive behaviors.

One can argue that children growing up in our times are under more stress than ever before. Certainly, many children who are privileged and buffered are spared the worst, but many other children feel the full impact of the economic and psychological stresses that are so pervasive in today's society. We firmly believe that play can help children—and grown-ups too—deal with stress. Behaviorally and on the level of brain functioning, play entails both affect and cognition. Defensively, play can help one to deal with stress as a diversion from reality; it also can serve cathartic functions that help to heal past psychological wounds. Play can also help one to mount a good offense against stress by facilitating the development of coping skills and resiliency.

In Chapter 4 we mentioned that we should help children who live under very stressful conditions develop their playfulness to the fullest extent. We cited Sandra Russ's (1999) model, which claims that because affective and cognitive components are intertwined in play and in creativity, play can help children to cope and be resilient. According to Russ's model, the two global personality traits of tolerance of ambiguity and openness to experience are related to affective fantasy in play. These two traits can be viewed as behavioral manifestations of a person's underlying affective process. Russ's model assumes that these specific affective processes and personality traits promote creative cognitive abilities, including social problem solving and coping.

This working together of emotional functioning and cognitive structure has been cited as especially significant in creativity. Singer and Singer (1990) have developed a cognitive-affective framework in which access to emotion affects developing cognitive structures and developing cognitive structures affect access to emotions. Children who are more imaginative in their play are more open to their affect system and are thus able to develop a more elaborate and richer storehouse of affect-laden symbols and memories. The collection of symbols and memories in turn can foster a child's divergent thinking ability. This is because having a more elaborate storehouse allows for greater manipulation of images and ideas; one can draw on a wider range of mental associations or connotations to solve problems and cope with stress (Russ, 1999).

Children who suffer hardship and turmoil in their lives, economically or psychologically, are certainly at risk, but they are "at promise" too. They are at promise for becoming, when they grow up, competent individuals and even perhaps among the most imaginative and creative people of their generation. Arguably, on the basis of the theory we have just described, they could very well have a more elaborate storehouse of affect-laden symbols and memories in their affective system than have children who are not growing up under such emotional turmoil and adversity. Accordingly, their potential for creativity, imagination, and innovation might be promisingly high, higher than those of other children. The biographies and autobiographies of successful and creative adults who had very difficult and tumultuous childhoods give some credence to this idea.

Coping is being able to think of things to do in problem situations. If imaginative and creative play promotes divergent thinking and divergent thinking helps one to think of things to do in problem situations, then imaginative play is connected with coping skills. Russ (1998) also notes that the transformational abilities in pretend play could also lead to more flexibility in thought later on, another coping skill that can help one to break out of rigid maladaptive ways of thinking. In addition, play interventions that aim to improve imaginative play skills may increase access to emotion-laden memories and lead to greater expressiveness and consequent reduction in anxiety.

Resilience requires the development of strong coping skills because resilient children are the ones who beat the odds and succeed despite exceptional hardships relating to poverty and/or parental maltreatment. Resilient children have other personality characteristics as well, such as having likable personalities, realistic goals, and strong motivation to succeed. They also usually have one or more trustworthy adults in their lives (Masten & Coatsworth, 1998). Resiliency may be aided by play intervention because resiliency requires coping, and coping can be improved by play and its effects on the cognitive and affective components of coping skill.

The play of children and their unfolding play lives, alone and with others, are instrumental in the construction of their narratives about themselves and the formation of their private personalities (Singer, 2003). Resilient children may benefit from the kind of play lives they are leading, even if others cannot see what is going on. According to Singer and others, if the affective system remains in disarray or in a non-integrated state, then children who are at risk remain so. However, with help from trusted adults, children may become at promise as their affective system becomes more integrated and controlled. This leads to the following:

- Improved autonomy or active agency, independence, and a sense of purpose and direction

- Improved emotionality, or the ability to control impulses and delay gratification in striving after goals with great persistence
- Improved subjunctive thought, or the ability to explore the possible and the fantastic

All three—autonomy, emotionality, and subjunctive thought—seem to be very important qualities for resilience. Resilient children need to form a sense of purpose and determination, and they must know how to regulate affect and sublimate their energies to persist in working toward future goals. Subjunctive thought is vitally important as well, being needed to create a vision for the future that resilient children must be constructing for themselves. These visions often must be created under dire circumstances and often must be maintained even after many setbacks, as resilient children cope and dream for a brighter future. We believe that with the power of play and fantasy, more children who are at risk can become at promise and can realize in their adult lives the fulfillment of their childhood dreams.

Teachers possess both book and professional knowledge from practical experience that tells them that play is indeed important for all young children to succeed in school. Box 5.3 can help them better explain their beliefs about the developmental and educational significance of play.

**BOX 5.3**

## Play as a Medium for Bridging the Whole Child to Academic Standards

Does play, as a centerpiece of learning in early childhood education, have to be replaced or reduced in the curriculum now that academic standards are the topic of the hour? There is no doubt that national and state standards exert pressure on early childhood education and on education in later grades as well. Standards are statements about what children should know and be able do at different grade levels. They represent an effort to increase accountability for teaching and learning. Standards have made educators much more conscious of educational outcomes. The focus has shifted from "What did I teach?" to "What did the child learn?"

In one way, standards do not seem to apply to early childhood education, especially at the pre-K level. The reason for this bold assertion has to do with the way early childhood education views the teaching and learning relationship as it applies to our school's youngest learners. Standards assume a "Teach now, learn now" model, a commonsense coupling of the input of teaching and the output of learning. In fact, many early childhood teachers might agree with this coupling, finding it reinforcing to see immediate results of their teaching efforts. Certainly, most teachers today would reject the opposite model: "Teach later and expect learning later." This second model is maturational, a "Let Mother Nature take her course" view. It was popular in the past and can still be found in some early care programs that nurture but do not teach.

Fortunately, there is a third alternative, the model that we believe is characteristic of high-quality early childhood programs. Here the motto would be "Teach now and expect learning later." This means that teaching and enrichment in early education are not usually expected to show results right away in any specifiable learning manifestations in the child. But this does not mean that the child is not benefiting from being in the early education program. A great deal of the learning that occurs during the early years is emergent in nature. There is not always a specific outcome. Skills and abilities are in a process of formation, and there might not be any ready-made performance indicators to reliably tap the learning that is taking place. Given this complicated state of affairs, the teaching strategy of choice is to expose children to, and familiarize them with, a great deal of information, skills, dispositions, and concepts without expecting any immediate proof of learning. It is assumed that this early educational enrichment is benefiting all the children, perhaps in different ways, and will have measurable effects in the future.

We believe that the third model is best for early childhood education because it shows respect for the whole child, a very important value in early education. Early educators want to put off formal evaluation because such evaluation can induce anxiety and lead to negative dispositions, such as an attitude represented by the statement "I am not a good learner," or, as one child who was retained in kindergarten said, "I'm a flunky." In the third model the teacher teaches without expecting the child to show specific learning right away. Learning is viewed as long-term and cumulative and as the result of increasing maturation in interaction with high-quality learning experiences. High-quality learning experiences require a great deal of nondirective teaching, and when directive teaching is also used, as it many times should be, all the teaching activities need to occur in a relaxed, low-key atmosphere.

The third model is also recommended because the other two are very flawed. The "Teach later and expect learning later" model is a cop-out and is irresponsible in the sense that the teacher is not teaching. And the "Teach now, learn now" model can be antidevelopmental, and seeking immediate proof of teaching can cause long-term harm. The third model does not have such flaws and is also most compatible with play-based early childhood education.

Play-based early education is an essential feature in any high-quality early childhood program. Educational play—providing for it, facilitating it, assessing it, and documenting it—is very consistent with this "Teach now, expect learning later" model. If this is the case, then how can play serve as a bridge between the whole child, so important in early education, and meeting academic standards? The secret is to have the right attitude about standards, to realize that just because they do not originate from within our model of teaching and learning is not any reason to feel threatened or to believe that sound early childhood education is not meeting academic standards. A high-quality program with educational play and with intellectual and social enrichment at its core is providing many opportunities to master the knowledge and skills contained in academic standards. Meeting and exceeding state learning standards can be a purposeful, rewarding, and enjoyable experience for teachers and children in a program in which the process of playing, exploring, learning, practicing, and interacting is at the center of the curriculum.

However, teachers have a responsibility to know how to relate state learning standards with play and other learning activities in the classroom. It is important for teachers to know the standards and to recognize how different play activities are directly or indirectly related to them. Many behaviors of children at play can be interpreted as learning continuum indicators leading to meeting state learning standards. For example, it is not difficult to see how acting out a fairy tale in preschool can help to prepare children to meet a state learning standard requiring that third-grade children identify literary elements in stories, describing characters, setting, and plot. It is also obvious how opportunities for constructive play with blocks serves well a learning standard in math in areas of counting, grouping, and ordering. Teachers should familiarize themselves with state learning standards and practice discerning elements in the curriculum that relate to them. In addition, play and play-related behavior assessment and documentation and the assessment and documentation of other activities in the classroom should be geared to capture not just learning products, but also emergent learning processes that are relevant to state learning standards.

## SUMMARY

The relationship between play and child development can be viewed in these ways: Play reflects, reinforces, and/or results in development. Possible general and specific benefits of play on child development and well-being can be immediate or can be delayed, even operating as sleeper effects that do not show up for many years. All these possibilities fall under the second and third positions. Complications ensue in linking play with development in accordance with the epiphenomenon and equifinality principles. The former posits that often other factors that occur along with play and not play per se are responsible for the purported benefits of play; the latter posits that even when play is convincingly shown to be implicated in an important child outcome such as literacy attainment, there are always presumed to be other pathways to the same developmental endpoint.

A case can be made for the importance of play in child development by using both biological and cultural arguments. Neuroscience has recently provided evidence and theory in support of play-mediated brain development. Play helps the brain to form dense synaptic connections by involving different brain areas for emotions, language, thinking, and sensory and motor actions. Sociocultural theories have argued that an important function of play is to help children to learn and understand their own particular culture.

In addition to its link with brain development and cultural learning and meaning-making, research studies have indicated that play is related with cognitive, language, social, and emotional developmental domains. Qualitative research has become more common in addition to quantitative work in pursuing the significance of play in child development. Considerable empirical research exists that is consistent with theories of the role of play in development covered in Chapter 2. Play at a minimum reinforces cognitive development with respect to representational competence, operational thought, and problem solving. Play seems even more strongly connected with decentration and perspective-taking and also appears to be a causal factor in the development of divergent thinking and theory of mind abilities. Language development is closely associated with cognitive growth, and play has an important role in the child's use of language in their emergent literacy development. Research suggests that play in early childhood can have valuable outcomes later on in school in areas of reading and writing.

The literature shows the importance of play for social development and emotional development. Play is related to social skills and social cognition (perspective-taking and theory of mind) and is vitally important in self-awareness, emotional differentiation, and regulation. The child's sense of reality and being and the child's trust and hope in the future, as well as the child's management of stress, are linked to play behavior and experience. A holistic, integrative approach to play and child development enables us to best appreciate play's significance, thereby improving our theories of practice with respect to the roles of the adult in children's play, and our abilities to explain to others the place of play in children's lives and in early childhood programs. Clearly, play and playfulness can be valuable in specific interventions to help young children to learn and to cope, perhaps even assisting in resiliency, as well as valuable for school readiness and for meeting and exceeding state learning standards in general.

## PROJECTS AND ACTIVITIES

1. Using this textbook and other books about play, form teams and go on a scavenger hunt to see how many different benefits of play you can find that have been stated in various ways by different authors. Do a content analysis of the different ways to form a smaller number of distinguishable categories.
2. Interview a teacher at the pre-K, kindergarten, and primary levels asking about the value of play in child development and the value of play in the classroom. Analyze, interpret, and share results with classmates.
3. Obtain a copy of your state's learning standards and try to think of different kinds of play activities that would help meet those standards.
4. Interview a child at each of ages six, nine, and twelve years (or roughly those ages) and ask them about their play—the different kinds they do in different locations, with different people—and why they engage in the different kinds of play. Do they think that play does them any good, or is it just for fun as far as they are concerned? Analyze, interpret, and share results with classmates.

CHAPTER 6

# Play Contexts: Physical Environment, Social Ecology, and Culture

## INTRODUCTION

In Chapter 3 we pointed out that scholarly accounts of the development of play have often been criticized as being too linear and simplistic and devoid of the intricacies needed to be adequate descriptions or explanations of play expressed at different age levels. Foremost among various criticisms that have been levied is that theories of play development have been too idealized and isolated from cultural and community settings. To properly understand children's play in our rapidly changing, complex, and pluralistic world, we need conceptual frameworks that are 'recursively interactive and multidimensional' (Monighan-Nourot, 1997). We need conceptual frameworks that fully take into account play contexts.

Proclaiming that we must understand play in relation to contexts might appear trite at first. After all, isn't it essential that "all human behavior must be understood relationally, in relation to 'its context,' as the expression goes" (Cole, 1996, p. 131)? However, we think that this is not a trivial point. In this chapter we first discuss the meaning and significance of the concept of context, prescribe some guidelines for a cultural-contextual approach to the study of children's play, and sketch a general conceptual model for play-environment relations. Next, we discuss three general topics that fall under the rubric of play contexts: (1) the physical environment and play, which consists of geography, climate, and locations and domains of play, including communities, neighborhoods, and schools; (2) social ecology and play, where we put the spotlight on family dynamics and social class influences; and (3) culture and play, including time as a context variable and the effects of culture ➤

on play. Throughout the chapter we suggest some ideas for translating theory and research on play and context into educational practice and policy.

## FOCUS QUESTIONS

1. What is a cultural-contextual approach to play? Why is it necessary to take this approach to play, development, and education?
2. What effects do climate and geography have on children's play?
3. How do the kinds of neighborhoods and communities children live in expand or limit play possibilities and affect the quality of play displayed by children?
4. How do space and indoor designs in schools affect play?
5. What are parental and sibling influences on children's play?
6. What does the way children play tell us about their cultures? Or, to put it the other way around, what in a child's culture dictates the way he or she plays?
7. What professional dispositions should the early educator have with respect to play and cultural differences? What are some classroom applications?

## CULTURAL-CONTEXTUAL APPROACHES TO PLAY

There are at least four different ways to think about the relationship between the child and the environment. First, we can study children's behavior and development, including play, from a biological-maturational point of view. This means that the environment is important only insofar as it provides opportunities for the child to practice skills that emerge with maturation. Second, we can adopt an environmental-learning perspective that assumes that the environment has an overwhelming influence in shaping the child's behavior and development. Third, a framework labeled interactional can be applied to our thinking about child-environmental relations. In this framework behavior and development are the result of the joint influence of the child and the environment. Theorists Gesell, Skinner, and Piaget, respectively, are associated with the above three approaches.

An approach called cultural-contextual, sometimes referred to as the sociocultural perspective (see Chapter 2), is the fourth way to think about the developing child and the environment. In this approach development and the environment are blended with culture into an inseparable whole. The elements—development, environment, and culture—are combined and do not function as separate entities (just as the atoms of hydrogen and oxygen can no longer function as discrete elements once they are combined into a water molecule). Behavior and development, including play, are conceived to be part of an emergent process comprising biological, social, and cultural factors. Culture is a medium that creates conditions for growth and development in which there is a dynamic interaction between the child and the environment. How this dynamic complex interaction gets played out is different in different cultures (Cole, 1996). Child, environment, culture—this has sometimes been called the Vygotskian triangle, for Lev Vygotsky, who helped to establish this perspective.

The cultural-contextual approach to viewing play blends development, environment, and culture into an inseparable whole. Play is an outgrowth of this cultural context.

## Meaning of Context

The term *context* has been defined in two general ways. First, there is the idea that context is that which surrounds; second, there is the idea that context is the whole situation relevant to a particular behavior or event. The first one, that which surrounds, is the definition that is most familiar in education and the social sciences. It is the one compatible with the interactional model of person-environment relations noted above and the one that is often represented by a set of concentric spheres for different levels of context, such as in Urie Bronfenbrenner's ecology of human development:

- *Microsystem.* The patterns of activity, roles, and interpersonal relations experienced by a developing person in a given setting with particular physical and material features.
- *Mesosystem.* Interrelationships among microsystems, such as relationships between home, school, and neighborhood.
- *Exosystem.* Linkages and processes taking place between two or more settings that indirectly influence the process within the immediate setting in which the developing person lives (e.g., workplaces of parents, school boards).
- *Macrosystem.* Broad factors such as cultural norms and values, the economy, and politics (Han & Christie, 2001).

According to this meaning of context, external forces within different levels are seen as surrounding and engulfing the individual child. There are layers of contextual influence, with more general and inclusive levels setting the conditions for what can take place in lower levels of context but without directly causing events that take place there. For example, political ideologies and educational philosophies and policies at the macrosystem of context (e g., the neoconservative rationale of the soft bigotry of low expectations for selecting a tougher approach to teaching, learning, and evaluation) influence reading curriculum in classrooms but do not dictate entirely specific proximal processes within the microsystem of a classroom (e.g., particular teacher-child interactions).

Context also can mean the total situation or that which weaves together (i.e., Latin *contexere,* which is defined as "to weave together"). This way of thinking about context fits with the cultural-contextual approach defined earlier. Context is not defined as a set of containers for development and behavior (e.g., Bronfenbrenner's Russian nesting dolls). Rather, context is the connected whole that gives coherence to the parts. A play context, for instance, would be the totality of the situation in which a playing child *constructs* for himself or herself. A relational interpretation of the mind or the psyche is at work here, as the psychological experiences take precedence over external factors. The boundary between the child and the world is not clear-cut. There is not an inside and an outside; both are part of a system. Culture and context are happening between the ears, so to speak. The mind is in culture, and the culture is in the mind.

This second definition of context does not require that we dismiss external reality as a figment of our imaginations. We do live on the planet Earth, and there is gravity, and the velocity of light is a constant. What is required, however, is that we can accept the belief espoused by historian and philosopher of science Karl Popper that we all live in three worlds, not one. We all live in a world of material objects and space; we all live with the reality of our very own subjective mental states; we all live together in a shared symbolic world of collective meanings (Popper & Eccles, 1977). An infant playing with a rattle is holding a real, material object and is located at a real time-space coordinate. The infant is experiencing a subjective mental state of sorts, and the child is situated in a family, community, and culture with which he or she will increasingly come to communicate and share meanings.

Understanding play as cultural activity and interpretation is the central aim of the cultural-contextual approach to the study of play. This approach is synonymous with the sociocultural perspective, which views the child as an active agent who learns and develops through his or her own agency and through interaction with adult mediators. Individual action and social mediation are inherently related in the process by which the inter-mental becomes intra-mental. For example, from parent-child pretend play the child first experiences a state of intersubjectivity. The child appropriates transformation actions from the shared pretense and uses them intramentally, having gained facility in doing so from the earlier social encounters involving guided participation. The child's internal cognitions have a social origin: they derive from interpersonal and cultural processes.

Playing happens in a context that is called an activity setting, the unit of analysis for those play theorists who hold the sociocultural view. Activity settings refer to repeatedly occurring child-in-context situations that are important in socialization and development. Indoor free-play periods in an early childhood educational program are a school-based activity setting, with the reoccurring patterns of play actions happening there influencing the learning of social skills, and so on. Sociocultural research usually has examined activity settings and behaviors in situ—they are part of everyday life important in a cultural community. Artificial settings and short-term laboratory research are avoided in favor of naturalistic observations, intensive interviewing, and longer-term investigations.

Barbara Rogoff (1995, 2003) analyzes play (or any other important cultural action) as an activity setting in which playing is occurring. She examines the processes of play in an activity setting through three different lenses: community, interpersonal, and personal. To understand the processes involved in any ongoing play activity, Rogoff does *not* divide up characteristics of the individual children by level. Sociocultural activity is seen as a totality by looking through the personal lens, the interpersonal lens, and the community lens. The totality of these three levels is always there in the sociocultural activity. Only the focus of the analysis changes, depending on which lens the observer picks up and peers through. Some aspects of the social phenomenon come to the foreground and others must remain in the background only because not everything can be studied at once.

Therefore the second meaning of context (e.g., the totality of the situation, or that which weaves together) is implied in performing a sociocultural analysis; that is, culture is a system of meanings and is not something outside and surrounding the child and acting as an independent variable or an external cause of the child's behavior and development. The playing child and the play context are treated as a seamless whole. Sociocultural analysis seeks to understand how interlocking persons, dyads or groups, and communities or cultural institutional aspects "transform as they together constitute and are constituted by sociocultural activity" (Rogoff, 1995, p. 161).

## Guidelines for the Study of Play in Context

There are five guidelines for research on play from the sociocultural perspective (Goncu et al., 1999). First, how does a cultural community's economic structure influence the availability of play opportunities as one type of activity for the children in the community? Both play and nonplay behaviors should be included in any study because in some cultural communities play is perhaps not as important as other behaviors of children, such as doing household chores. These behaviors must be examined as activities in social contexts, which themselves are shaped by economic, social, and political factors operating within the larger culture.

Second, research needs to shed light on the meaning and significance attributed to play by the adults inside the cultural community. What are their beliefs about play and the value of play? What beliefs do they have about when, where, and how parents and other adults should actually play with children? Cultures vary on whether a parent can act like a peer in play with his or her children.

Third, research needs to illuminate how adult values are communicated to children. How are community values about play conveyed to children? Within a given cultural community, have the adults set up special times and places for children's play? Are there media messages? How do the adults help children play, if they do? Are they actually playing with children? Repeated, sustained observations and interviews in naturalistic settings are ideal for obtaining needed data to begin to answer these questions.

Fourth, understanding children's play requires examining how children represent their worlds in play. When children play, play represents their cultures. Therefore we must study play in relation to nonplayful aspects of culture. What adult roles do children adopt? What types of events are represented? How do they symbolically represent their lives? How is the physical, social, and symbolic environment used? How are play actions and accompanying operations expressed in various environments? How are children transforming meaning and conserving meaning across play media and contexts, and what does this information tell us about the development of imagination and creativity? Here again, naturalistic observations and interviews are best for seeking the answers.

Fifth, investigators must use interdisciplinary thinking and multiple research methods to illuminate children's play in the cultural context. What are play's economic, cultural, educational, and psychological contexts in a given culture? An array of research tools are needed to obtain information on multiple levels—from historical and archival analysis to understand labor relations and economic structures, for example, to interview and observational methods to understand how adults think about play and how children actually play and represent adult life in their play. In sum, following the above five general guidelines can help researchers to demonstrate that play is a cultural activity and represents as well a player's interpretation of his or her culture.

## General Model for Play-Environment Relationships

Figure 6.1 shows a general model for a cultural-contextual study of children's play. This general model represents major categories of factors operating on both macro and micro levels about which information is needed to understand play in context. At the foundation are ecocultural factors, which are the history, climate, and geography of a given culture that influence its sociocultural systems and institutions. These systems and institutions create the political, economic, social, and educational scripts for learning and development. The inner psychology of agents (values, attitudes, beliefs) and cultural working models (action plans) of members of a culture are in a process of dynamic reciprocal relation over time with the sociocultural systems on the one hand and with the generation of physical-material, temporal-spatial, and interpersonal activity settings on the other hand.

As is shown in Figure 6.1, also linking inner psychology of agents and activity settings are cultural working models or "blueprints for action." Cultural working models are how individuals in the cultural community personally represent for themselves within their own belief system, how they think things are in their culture, and how they would like them to be. Hence they give rise to goals and intentions and are the motivating force leading to actual behaviors and events and objects in activity settings. Activity settings, which require analysis in terms of actor-participants, task-activities (e.g., chores, schooling, caregiving, play), and scripts (i.e., norms for self-expression, motives, and goals related to salient cultural values), are the various contexts for children's play and nonplay experiences that impact development. In turn, the life course developmental manifestations of children, including play actions, affect the transactions occurring between social systems and also affect the thoughts and actions of caregivers and the activity settings they influence.

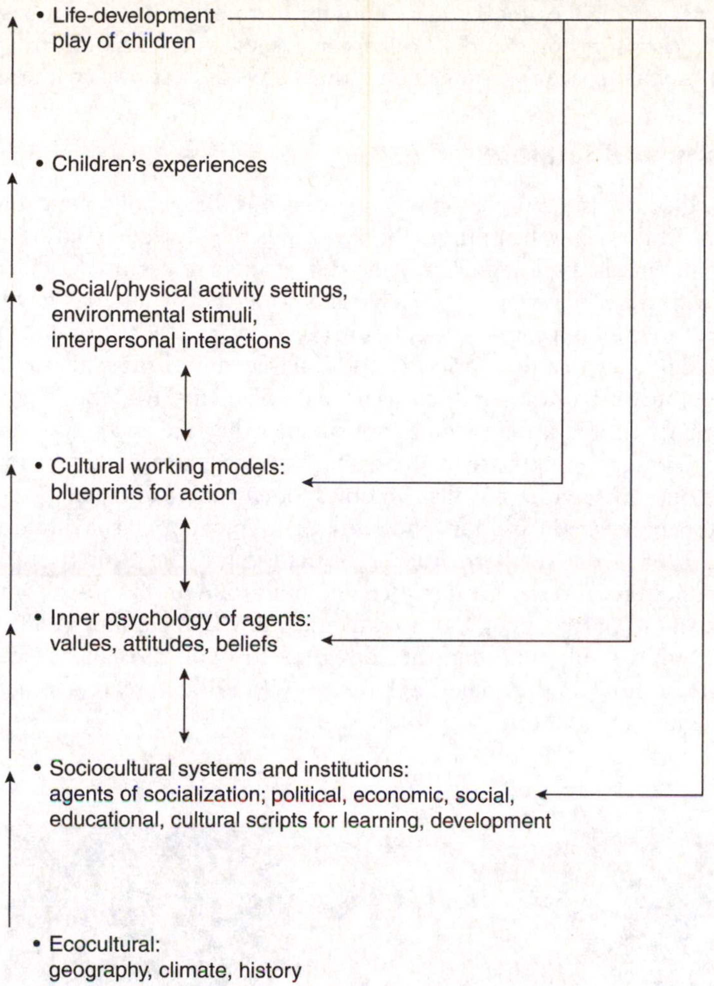


**FIGURE 6.1 Conceptual Framework for a Macro-/ Micro-Level Analysis of Play-Environment Relations**

Hence this general model suggests that to properly think about play-environment relations, or play in context, requires broad consideration of macro-level and micro-level factors, physical environments and social environments, group processes and individual processes, ideational variables (beliefs, attitudes, values, ideas) and behavioral variables. The relationship between play and context is far from simple!

## PHYSICAL ENVIRONMENT

The physical environment comprises micro-level, inanimate aspects of settings that can affect behavior. It includes broad factors such as climate, geography, and the physical characteristics of neighborhood and community settings. It also encompasses the specific characteristics of home and school settings such as the amount of space that is available, how that space is arranged, and the materials that occupy the space.

## Geography and Climate

Francis Wardle has visited Brazil on several occasions. Brazil, of course, has a tropical climate. One of the things he noticed about Brazil is the very open nature of the buildings, especially public buildings. Roadside restaurants are essentially large, tiled roof structures with their sides open to the elements. University buildings have classrooms and hallways that are arranged around central courtyards that are totally open to the outdoors and filled with a rich variety of colorful trees and shrubs; no doors, windows, or walls separate the hallways and rooms from the elements. And the airport in Brasilia is so open that visitors are never quite sure whether they are inside or outside. For example, all the ticket counters are in an area under a large overhanging roof but totally open to the outdoors, with no walls, windows, or entrances and exits.

This flow between the indoors and outdoors, typical of warm climates, contrasts with the approach of Northern Europe, Canada, and the United States. In these countries buildings are carefully designed and built to maintain warmth in cold, winter months and to protect people from rain and snow (Greenman, 1988). In much of the United States public buildings are designed to maximize air-conditioning efficiency in the summer. In these geographic areas we build to create distinct separation between the indoors and outdoors.

➤ In warm climates public buildings provide for a natural flow between indoors and outdoors. In cold climates buildings are carefully designed to maintain warmth in the cold winter months.

This separation is clearly seen in our early childhood buildings and public schools and can also be seen in program philosophies and practices. What occurs indoors is meaningful and educational; that which occurs outdoors is recess, recreation, between classes, and off task. (We discuss the use of the outdoors extensively in Chapter 12.) Further, some early childhood and school buildings are designed in such a way that they feel like a fortress, disconnected from the potential hostile surroundings, giving children the message that "it's all a jungle out there and not for me" (Greenman, 1988, p. 100). Francis Wardle, who covers the nation designing playgrounds, has observed that the state licensing requirements calling for continuous, four-foot-high fencing around playgrounds has resulted in chain link fences around playgrounds that make the playground "look like a cattle feed lot or a jail." Greenman (2003) says that they look like squirrel cages.

Some early childhood buildings have indoor/outdoor transition areas built into their overall designs. These are areas that have a roof (an overhang of an existing roof or a roof made of translucent materials to let in light), a floor of treated wood or an outdoor carpet (Astroturf), open walls, and direct access to the classrooms and the playground. The access to the classroom is through large, sliding doors; the access to the playground is open. These are areas where playing children use hollow blocks, woodworking tools, materials for large art projects, riding toys, and large balls and a variety of hardy plants are used as screens. These transitional areas also provide needed shade for the hot summer days and provide a method to cool off the building from the hot summer sun. Although Bruderhof communities (a religious organization with a long history of early childhood programs) are located in England and on the East Coast of the United States, their children's houses (childcare centers) are all built with transition porches. This is a result of the Bruderhof's history in Paraguay, South America (Rudy Hildel, personal communication).

New early childhood and school buildings should have at least large roof overhangs to protect children from inclement weather, provide shade during the hot part of the year, and keep the entire building cooler during the hot days of summer (Greenman, 1988). Further, early childhood and school buildings need windows (yes, there are new schools with no windows), and the windows must open to the elements to provide sound, smell, and air circulation. As anyone who has worked in a controlled environment knows, when the air conditioner fails, life in a children's program becomes intolerable (Greenman, 1988).

Climate, of course, affects play—especially outdoor play—in other ways. Schools and early childhood programs in cold and/or wet climates cannot use the outside as often as those in mild climates, and many of these programs do not have adequate indoor space for gross motor activities. In inclement climates programs must also deal with increasing parental pressure not to allow their children to play in wet and cold conditions. One wonders whether one cause of the American problem with childhood obesity is the unwillingness of some parents to let their children play outside in "bad" weather.

## Neighborhoods and Communities

Family and school settings, which we will discuss later in this chapter, are of course very important influences on children's play, but they do not exist in isolation. Families and schools are part of neighborhoods and larger geographic communities that exert influence on families and schools and the children growing up in them (Burton & Price-Spratlen, 1999). Children's experiences can be very different from one community to the next, even within distinct neighborhoods in the same community (McDevitt & Ormrod, 2004).

Some neighborhoods and communities, whether urban, suburban, or rural, have many features that are assets for play and child development; others are lacking in developmental assets and seem to have "play allergies." Even communities with relatively plentiful economic and social resources may be adverse to play if adults fail to connect with children and if neighborhoods try to be child-proof. For instance, urban and suburban life today often removes children from public spaces and public life, putting them in segregated age cohorts and adult-organized and -controlled activities. If they want to promote positive play, communities need to adopt policies that are child-friendly.

Furthermore, with changing lifestyles and changes in family structure from extended to isolated nuclear families and from two-parent to single-parent families and with the erosion of some communities owing to extreme poverty, crime, and institutional and family disintegration, many neighborhoods are no longer vibrant social entities. Some communities are clearly dangerous or "socially toxic" environments (Garbarino, 1995). Many communities and the neighborhoods that make them up have been trying to rebuild. A battle cry in some places has been "Let's take the neighborhoods back for families!" Efforts also are needed to make more families functional and engaged.

It is understandable that many neighborhoods and communities that have been dispirited and neglected want to be healthy and whole again. They want to bounce back and construct a new community mosaic from its broken fragments. To succeed in rebuilding for families, communities, and neighborhoods requires, among other ingredients, a replenishment of social capital. Social capital refers to the existence and the availability of human energy that can be harnessed to help out in social situations; it refers to having trustworthy relationships. Etzioni, cited in Gore and Gore (2002), defines community as a "web of relations among individuals that often criss-cross and reinforce one another" (p. 294). The quality of the social fabric of a community or neighborhood depends on its social capital. There must be a shared intergenerational commitment to support children and youth by making where they live a safe place and one that is conducive to their learning and development (Furstenberg, 1993).

External assets must also be present to create play-friendly neighborhoods. Children need to feel support and empowerment, know that there are expectations and limits, and be able to realize their creativity, energy, and playfulness in specific and tangible activities and programs in their neighborhoods and communities. Vacant lots turned into play spaces, parks, playgrounds, recreation centers, and public library children's programs are welcomed external assets. They are especially welcomed by low-income families who cannot afford to travel or pay admission prices for museums, pay-to-play environments, and other commercial initiatives such as amusement parks and theme parks (see Chapter 11).

Even with the best intentions the play potential in many neighborhoods remains quite limited. There have been pervasive social changes in our modern and postmodern times away from valued communal sociability to individualism. Because of congestion, crime, or lack of adult supervision, many children do not venture forth into neighborhood parks and playgrounds to engage in social play, especially younger children who in earlier times were often seen in mixed-age peer groups in which older children often kept an eye on younger children. Recreation centers and libraries might not be open at the right hours for many families. And in most communities there are just not that many natural outdoor spaces for play that can be found anymore that are safe and appealing to children. So we see many children staying at home, watching television or playing video games. Unfortunately, when they get older, some of these children vandalize and destroy neighborhood play environments.

Even in rural areas there has been a narrowing of play habitats. Beach (2003) studied two rural communities in Maine, observing the play of children and interviewing adults about their memories of how they played when they were children of the same age and in the same locations as the children she observed. She found that over time there was a drastic reduction in common areas for play. A local pasture where kids had played in former years was now a residential area, and a favorite vacant lot was gone. Play was reduced in other ways as well. A whole network of secret pathways or shortcuts through the neighborhood was gone, replaced by parking lots, bank buildings, and "No Trespassing" signs put up in some yards. A child-centered universe with child-to-child mutuality and initiative and with only indirect and supervisory (watchful eye) adult presence and influence, fondly remembered by some of the elderly interviewees, was no more. It was fractured by new economic developments that had taken place in these rural communities. Beach suggested that this change is adversely affecting the neighborhood play of today's generation of children.

On a more positive note efforts are currently under way in some communities to restore safe, stimulating neighborhood play settings for children. Johnson, Christie, and Yawkey (1999, p. 281), citing Rivkin's (1995) work, describe some of these projects:

- *Greenways.* Corridors of protected open space that connect parks, playgrounds, nature reserves, rivers, and historic sites with each other and with people's homes.
- *Urban initiatives.* Projects such as the Revitalizing Baltimore Program that attempt to make cities safer and better places to live and play.
- *Child-aware land development.* Planned communities that set aside undeveloped "wild areas" for children to play.
- *Calming traffic.* Altering roads (narrowing, adding trees and other plantings, lowering speed limits) to reduce traffic speed and to make streets safer for play.

## Space: General Considerations

Growing up on a farm, Francis Wardle loved the freedom of open spaces. He remembers that he and his brother led their six ducks from their cage up on the plateau, down the hill, and across the village to an area where they had made a little pond by damming up the stream. He also remembers running through the bracken, tall pink flowers, and underbrush to find a hiding place for a game of hide-and-seek. And he remembers walking along the edge of sugar beet, hay, and wheat fields. But his favorite exploration of the outdoors was climbing Titterstone Clee Hill, the local "mountain." In England open moors—areas of gorse, heather, short-cropped grass, ice-cold streams, and granite outcroppings—surround most hills. There are no fences, and the land extends up to the horizon. Francis loved climbing Titterstone because he never knew what was over the horizon; there was always another surprise.

The use of space has always been part of the human condition. In the early years of this country people with means would always leave Philadelphia, the capital, in the summer to avoid yellow fever epidemics (McCullough, 2001). People who could afford farms and ranches were viewed as superior to those who had to remain in cramped cities. Even today, many Americans consider suburban lifestyles to be better than city dwelling. However, such preferences differ from culture to culture. To many Scottish people, living in a tightly squeezed rowhouse on a select street in Edinburgh was considered the pinnacle of power and prestige.

In 1969 Edward T. Hall wrote *The Hidden Dimension,* which examines how dimensions of space and our cultural backgrounds mediate our perceptions. For example, Hall suggests that in the United States, where status is not determined at birth, one's address is an important clue to status, whereas in England, where status is assigned at birth, where one lives is much less important. In Arab countries "spaces inside their upper middle class houses are tremendous by our standards. They avoid partitions because they do not like to be alone. . . . Their way of being alone is to stop talking. Like the English, an Arab who shuts himself off in this way is not indicating that anything is wrong or that he is withdrawing" (Hall, 1969, pp. 158–159).

On a recent trip to the United Arab Emirates Francis was surprised to see a small, open, meticulously maintained area in the middle of the local playground where people took off their shoes and then knelt and prayed to Allah at the appropriate time every day. Clearly, residents of the United Arab Emirates have no problem engaging in what many Westerners consider the very personal activity of prayer while physically surrounded by playing children.

Most space is designed for a specific function or functions, for example, to buy and sell products in a store; to get and pay for gas in a gas station, along with drinks, candy, and cigarettes; and to socialize and relax in the family room at home. The function of a space is based on how it is set up and experiences we bring to that space. Someone who has never seen a car's gas tank get filled will not understand the functional nature of a filling station; further, in this country most people now fill up their own tanks, whereas in Brazil, because of the cheap labor pool, someone else does this for them. For one child the kitchen's function might include playing with the water in the sink, while for another it is a place to stay clear of, especially when someone is cooking.

There is always a human factor in the use of space. Francis Wardle remembers observing small Mayan children intently copying a lesson from the board onto their little slates with small stubs of chalk. They were sitting in a thatched shelter in the middle of a field, no different from all the other wall-less structures that had been quickly erected after the earthquake that had destroyed most of the permanent buildings. The lack of a functional "school" building did not seem to bother them because adults who were intently trying to learn the same lesson surrounded them.

Children have not been culturally conditioned to view space the same way adults have. Further, children experience the world, including space, differently than adults do. A young, sensorimotor child experiences the world through his body and his actions—by touch, smell, crawling, running, sitting, and so on. Greenman (1988) comments on these age-related differences in perceptions of space: "We, who do not inhabit the floor, undervalue the hot, sunny spot on the floor that draws cats and babies. We are not drawn to the pile of dirt or the hole, to the puddle or dew, or to the rough spot where the plaster is chipping away that beckons small fingers" (p. 21). Children, of course, look at the potential of space to enjoy what comes to them naturally: run, play in the water, stack the blocks, bang on the kitchen utensils, or examine the sun reflecting off the crinkled aluminum foil. They have no concept of what the space is designed for—its utilitarian use—and they do not care.

To maximize play possibilities for children, a variety of contexts must be in place. It is easy to separate out the physical environments (space, spatial arrangement, etc.) and the human environment (teacher modeling, setting up the environment, structuring activities, etc.). What is more difficult is to view this issue in a holistic manner; after all, for teachers and caregivers to be effective, they need physical environments that are conducive and supportive of teachers' working, interacting, and playing with children. Jim Greenman (1988) attempts to do this under the title "what children need":

1. *Places rich in experience.* Children need lots and lots of opportunities to explore the natural and human-made world: water, sand, stones, leaves, rotten fruit, animals, trees, sticks, trees, places to hide, blocks to stack, rope to swing on, paper to draw and paint on, and music to make and listen to. Further, they need to be able to manipulate these materials: move the sand in a wagon, play in the water with funnels and tubes, bang on the pots and pans to make music, and walk barefoot through the mud. Childhood is about expanding one's world, including the physical world. Experiencing all these materials can only enhance play, often play with these very materials.

2. *Places rich in play.* Good environments for children must be specifically designed to encourage play. This, among other things, suggests children need environments with enough space for physical and rough-and-tumble play, appropriate materials for dramatic play, and enough materials to encourage play across all domains.

3. *Places rich in teaching.* Children need places where teachers structure, model, and extend play and where teachers set up environments that encourage all sorts of play. "Children need teachers who know what children need is to have their questions answered, not the teachers'. Teachers who stimulate more questions than they directly provide are truly teaching" (Greenman, 1988, p. 33). In later chapters we discuss at length ways in which teachers can help children move to more complex and sophisticated levels of play; this will be particularly helpful for teachers working with children who have a variety of disabilities.

4. *Places rich with people.* Early childhood programs are taking the place of children's experiences in neighborhoods, on the farm, and in local stores and shops. We do our young children a tremendous disservice if the only people they see on a regular basis are teachers and caregivers. We must bring plenty of people—diverse in race and ethnicity, age, profession, and ability and disability—into our programs, and we must take children out into a variety of stores, workplaces, and community social environments.

Clearly, people are critical for play. They provide role models, characters for sociodramatic play, ideas for all sorts of constructive play (gardening, building, making bread, doctor's office, tortilla factory, etc.), and opportunities for children to represent the ever-expanding and diverse social world through their play. Because children play at what they experience, we need to find ways to expose them to a variety of human interactions.

5. *Places to be significant.* Children need to feel important. Children used to have the responsibility to care for animals, water garden plants, and do chores on the farm. (4H members still follow this approach of responsibility and care.) Children need to engage in activities in which others depend on them—the family, community, neighbors, people in nursing homes, and so on. From a play perspective this sense of responsibility will help children to change roles in their play, help them to nurture younger and less sophisticated players, teach them how to set up the environment to enhance their play, and show them how to return play materials to their storage places.

## Space and Indoor Designs in Schools

In Chapter 12 we discuss the need for children to have enough space to do what children like to do: run, climb, tumble, throw, ride, slide, jump, and build. But beyond this obvious need for space is what space allows children to do: shout, sing, scream, squirt water, change their physical elevation and perspectives of the world, experience hiding places, take risks, investigate, and so on. And because most young children are in Piaget's sensorimotor stage or preoperational stage, they need space to move their bodies and space to investigate and manipulate lots and lots of real, concrete materials. However, it is also possible to have too much space. In his playground work throughout this country Francis Wardle has seen preschool playgrounds that are so large that teachers could not supervise children without either restricting them to certain areas or yelling at them, and children could not easily engage in social play.

This question of space is a critical concern because all state licensing standards stipulate the minimum number of square feet allowed per child, both indoors and outdoors, depending on the child's age. (See Box 6.1.)

**BOX 6.1**

### How Much Space Is Needed for Play of Preschool Children?

Spatial density is the amount of space available per child in a play setting. A formula to determine this is as follows:

Spatial density = (area of room – unusable space)/(number of children)

1. Determine the room area by multiplying width × length.
2. Determine the unusable space by determining the size (length × width) of furniture and areas that cannot be used for play (narrow spaces between furniture, etc.).

3. Determine the total usable space by subtracting unusable space from total room area.
4. Finally, calculate the spatial density by dividing the results of #3 by the number of children who are in the room.

For example, for a room 20 × 20 feet, with fifteen preschool children calculation would be as follows:

Room area: 20 × 20 = 400 square feet
Total unusable area: 60 square feet
Spatial density: 400 – 60
340 square feet ÷
15 (number of children)
Play density per child: 22 2/3 square feet

The Children's Environmental Project recommends that there be at least forty-two square feet for what they consider "child activity space" (Greenman, 1988). Smith and Connolly (1980) determined that reducing space from seventy-five square feet per child to twenty-five square feet per child reduced the amount of gross motor play; reducing the density to fifteen feet per child resulted in a reduction of group play and an increase in aggressive play.

So how much space is needed? Is the loss of gross motor play significant, especially for boys, who are more physically active in their play and who are more often labeled as having behavior problems?

*Source:* Johnson, Christie, and Yawkey, *Play and Early Childhood Development,* 2/e. Published by Allyn and Bacon, Boston, MA. Copyright © 1999 by Pearson Education. Reprinted by permission of the publisher.

**Spaces for Children to Play.** Early childhood programs are challenged to provide spaces that optimize young children's growth, development, and learning. And because we deeply believe that all young children should experience a vast array of play opportunities in their programs and schools, the physical environment should be designed to maximize play. As research has demonstrated, the environment not only supports certain kinds of children's play behaviors, but can also encourage negative behaviors and cause fatigue, frustration, and even aggression (Kritchevesky, Prescott, & Walling, 1977; Prescott, 1994).

One of the great challenges of creating optimum environments for young children is the conflict between home environments and institutional environments (Wardle, 2003a). Home environments tend to be ones that are familiar to children and whose function is to make family members feel comfortable, prepare food, wash clothes, and entertain. They tend to be fuzzy, familiar, somewhat disorganized, somewhat unsafe, and personalized. Preschool environments, on the other hand, tend to be downward extensions of schools—straight, long corridors; tile floors; high ceilings; windows out of the reach of children; large bathrooms; extremely safe; and identical-looking rooms.

Considerations for the design of institutional environments are safety, ease of cleaning, ease of maintenance, cost of heating and lighting, ease of supervision, and regimentation. Further, most architects who design early childhood facilities are trained and experienced in designing schools and other large public buildings for adults. Fire, health, safety, and building codes are all based on a long history of school buildings. Early childhood programs are relatively new in this country, and designing and building facilities especially for this age group is even more of a recent phenomenon (Wardle, 2003a). In the past many programs were hosted in church basements and old school buildings.

**Setting up Environments for Play.** In general, environments that encourage play share certain characteristics. We consider the following to be the core requirements for classroom play spaces:

- Enough materials for every child to use.
- Ease of selecting and returning materials. This requires storage that is close to where materials will be used, at the children's level, and organized in a way that makes sense to the children.
- A range of different kinds of materials, different levels of materials, and materials of different complexity (see Chapter 8).
- Enough space. Clearly, different kinds of play and play materials require different kinds of space; for example, playing with table blocks requires far less space than playing with hollow blocks. However, we should not force children to play just with tabletop blocks (and other materials that take little space) because of the amount of space we provide. There also needs to be enough space for adults to become actively involved in the play and for a child in a wheelchair or a child who needs special adaptations to participate as well.
- Permission to make a mess. The environment must be one in which some mess is acceptable (Greenman, 1988). Therefore areas used for play should not be next to the computer or reading area—and maybe not next to the principal's or director's office!
- Permission to make noise. Lots of play creates a certain level of noise: children conversing with each other in dramatic play, blocks falling and hitting each other in block play, and children engaging in arguments and discussions as they define roles and scripts for a play episode. There are quiet forms of play, but we do children a disservice if we limit play to the kind that makes little noise.
- Ease of supervision. Playing children often need adult help to resolve problems—who will take which role, how materials can be shared, children who may be too aggressive or loud, and so forth. Also, children sometimes need help in using materials safely and appropriately (this is especially true in the woodworking area); therefore areas for play must be easy to supervise by teachers and caregivers.
- Relatively easy to keep clean. As we have already suggested, play can be messy. Therefore we need to find ways to control the mess. These include placing the art area next to fresh water and a sink, providing a resilient and easy-to-clean surface under the sand/water table, and making sure the block area has industrial carpet. Community Playthings makes lofts and nursery gyms that come with detachable carpets that can be removed and cleaned in a washing machine.

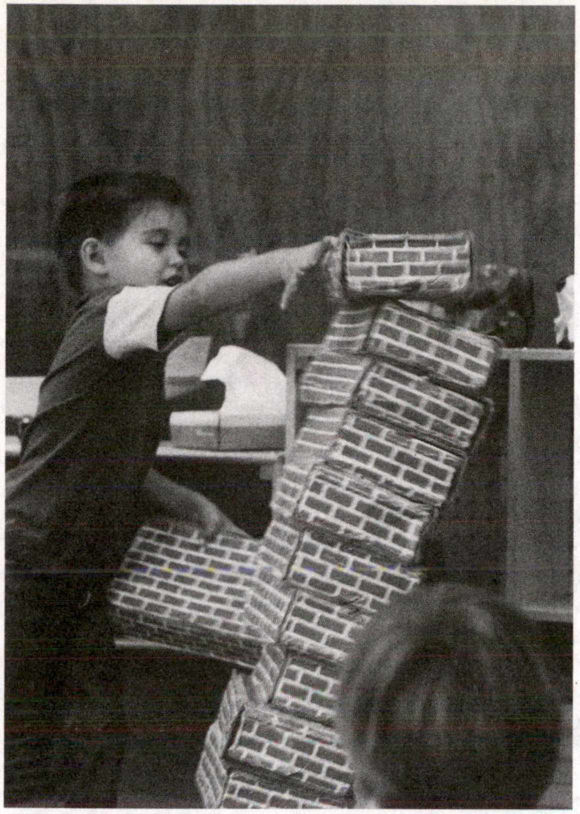

➤ Environments for play must be places that allow children to make a noise—like that of blocks falling in the block area.

- Change and variety. Children are consistently seeking out novelty and stimulation (Berlyne, 1960). Because children are spending more and more time in child-care programs, schools and after-school programs, we have an obligation to continually change the play environment. One of the best ways to do this is to have flexible learning centers. Every classroom should have several rotating centers that change periodically. And, of course, the permanent centers should be changed continually according to the program's curriculum, children's changing experiences in and out of the center and school, and the basic need for change and variety.

## Learning Centers

Many programs for young children arrange their space in a variety of learning or activity centers. These centers are defined areas that contain materials designed to help children learn different concepts and skills. Ideally, as children interact with these focused sets of materials, they will discover key concepts, either on their own or with help from the teacher or peers. As Johnson et al. (1999) point out, "If centers are set up properly and if an effective management system is established, the classroom environment does much of the 'teaching'!" (p. 249).

Some typical centers for preschool and kindergarten classrooms (many also work for older toddlers) include the following:

- *Art area.* This area includes easels, a variety of paints and paper, and a variety of pens, chalks, and more advanced media for older children. The art area needs to be on a tile, linoleum, or plastic-covered surface and near a sink.
- *Music area.* This area usually includes a listening area, a variety of music instruments, a CD player, and in some programs (e.g., British infant/primary programs) a piano.
- *Dramatic play (housekeeping) area.* This is the traditional housekeeping area, with child-size furniture, dolls, clothes, and props. As we discussed in Chapter 4, the area needs to include furniture, props, and clothes that boys tend to play with.
- *Block area.* Most block areas are centered on a large collection of unit blocks. A carpet surface in the block area radically reduces noise.
- *Math manipulatives.* A variety of math manipulatives, measuring instruments, and opportunities to collect, sequence, order, group, and categorize objects must be included. Often a math area will also have ongoing problems and activities that children can try to solve.
- *Literacy area.* A good literacy area has listening tapes, lots of environmental print, a variety of writing and printing instruments, lots and lots of different books, and ongoing literacy projects, such as a wall newspaper, a class book, and opportunities for publishing.
- *Woodworking area.* In Chapter 8 we discuss specific materials for the woodworking center, and safety rules. Needless to say, this area needs to be away from any quiet areas and must be easy to supervise.
- *Loft.* Programs often use lofts for a reading area on the top and a dramatic play area underneath. The area underneath can also be a nice, quiet retreat for children who want to get away for a while.
- *Computer center.* Haugland (1997) believes that computers need to be integrated into the classroom, not be placed in a separate technology lab. The location of the computer in the classroom is critical. It must be placed next to electrical outlets and phone or cable for Internet connection and away from dust, water, and glare. It makes sense to put the computer area next to the literacy area or even in the literacy area.
- *Sand/water table.* This area needs to be on a tile, linoleum, or plastic-covered surface and must be easy to supervise. It needs lots of space and easy storage (maybe underneath).
- *Tabletop center.* A variety of puzzles, tabletop games, tabletop blocks, and the like can be arranged in this area.
- *Science center.* A science center must be next to an outdoor window or in an indoor/outdoor transitional area. A good science area includes growing plants, a variety of weather measurement tools, possibly insects or bees, and hands-on

manipulatives—pulleys, levers, cogs, prisms, electrical circuits, and the like. Solar energy devices can also be used to create light, power toy cars, and so forth. Some programs, of course, also have fish and a variety of other pets.

Programs with indoor/outdoor transition areas or a large concrete slab outside the classroom can create other centers:

- Woodworking area (moved from inside)
- Larger, more diverse art area (big pieces of butcher paper, large chalk for different surfaces, etc.)
- More sand/water opportunities
- Hollow blocks and constructive building materials
- Riding toys

In addition to these permanent centers, the classroom should contain one or more temporary or rotating centers that change periodically. In Chapter 7 we discuss creating temporary theme centers to encourage play activities that teach specific educational goals, such as literacy. For this approach to work most effectively field trips or classroom visitors are needed to create initial interest and motivation, and the rotating center needs to be carefully designed to encourage the targeted play activities. Whole curricular approaches, for example, the project approach (Helm & Beneke, 2003), provide a sophisticated methodology that includes carefully constructed theme centers. A few ideas for rotating theme centers include (Christie, Enz, & Vukelich, 2003; Johnson et al., 1999):

- Post office
- Grocery store
- Restaurant
- Doctor's office/veterinarian's office
- Airport
- Library
- Gas station/garage
- Police station
- Space station
- Bakery
- Fire station
- Fast-food establishment
- Pizza carryout
- Factory making cars, tortillas, newspapers, and so on (places where the children's parents work)

By changing the theme periodically, teachers ensure that all children in the classroom will have opportunities to engage in dramatic play that matches their personal interests and life experiences.

## Arranging Space

In arranging classroom space for toddlers, preschoolers, or school-age students, the first considerations are practical: where are the exits, bathrooms, windows, outlets, water sinks, and so on? Next, on the basis of the location of these physical constraints, decisions should be made regarding practical placements of areas, such as the following:

- The art area goes next to the water source.
- The computer area is placed away from water and glare and next to outlets (electrical and Internet).
- The science area should be placed near windows so that plants can be grown.
- The sand and water areas must be over tile, linoleum, or plastic.
- The quiet areas should be situated away from bathrooms, exits, and noisy activity settings.
- The loft must be placed away from windows and ceiling lights.

The distinction between open and closed spaces also needs to be taken into account. Open spaces allow students to move easily from one learning area to another but also seem to encourage gross motor activities and rough-and-tumble play (Moore, 1987; Sheehan & Day, 1975). Screens, partitions, and dividers help to close areas off from each other and reduce noise and visual distractions (critical for child with attention deficit/hyperactivity disorder). Small areas also create a more intimate atmosphere and may encourage social and cooperative play and verbal interaction (Field, 1980; Moore, 1987; Sheehan & Day, 1975).

There are many ways to enclose areas in a classroom. Moore (1987) suggests that these areas be well-defined behavioral settings that are "limited to one activity, with clear boundaries from circulation space and other behavior settings, and with at least partial acoustical and visual separation" (p. 60). Furniture (shelves, etc.), dividers, plants, low walls, storage bins, or display areas can be used to create this separation. (Community Playthings has a product called Playscapes that connects existing furniture and room characteristics to create well-defined physical areas.) One of Francis Wardle's Head Start teachers created boundaries using colorful streamers hung from the ceiling. Symbolic cues also work well and make it easier for teachers to supervise.

However, care must be taken to create openings where areas can cross over to integrate with each other. When Kinsman and Berk (1979) removed a barrier between the block area and the dramatic play area, boy-girl play increased, there was more integration of materials across the two areas, more boys played in the dramatic-play area, and more girls played in the block area.

Moore (1987) studied preschool environments that were classified from poorly defined spatial areas to well-defined areas. In classrooms with well-defined areas children engaged in more exploratory behavior, social interaction, and cooperative play, and teachers were more involved in helping and supporting children's play.

Carving the classroom up into well-defined, partitioned areas limits the number of children who can physically be in any one area at a time. This necessitates a classroom management system to make sure areas are never too crowded. One of our favorite solutions is a hook and name tag system. Hooks are placed by each classroom area, with the number of hooks specifying the number of children who can play in the center at one time (four hooks = maximum of four children). When children choose an area, they place their name tag on an open hook. If all the hooks are used, they must wait until someone leaves the center and a hook becomes available. Other systems include having a set number of tickets for admission to popular areas or placing signs over areas that specify maximum numbers; these signs usually feature the word for the number (*four*), the numeral itself (4), and some type of pictorial representation of the amount.

In 1977 Walling engaged in what we now call an action research project (Kritchevsky et al., 1977). She identified a problem in her preschool classroom of three- and four-year-olds, and set out to fix it. In her classroom Walling was concerned about the amount of aggressive behavior and rough-and-tumble play during free-play time. She also noticed that her children rarely used the dramatic-play center or engaged in dramatic play. She believed that the problem was caused by her classroom layout (see Figure 6.2):

- There was too much space in the center of the room.
- The various play areas were not well defined, opening up into the rest of the classroom.
- Some areas, for example, the block area (loud) and the book area (quiet), conflicted directly with each other.
- There were no defined pathways, so children would go through play areas to get from one area to another.

Walling then decided to see whether changing the spatial arrangement of her classroom would address these issues (see Figure 6.3). In this new arrangement Walling made the following changes:

- She moved tables and added dividers to break up the large open space in the middle of the room.
- She created pathways through the classroom.
- She physically defined the housekeeping area and other areas.
- She moved areas next to areas with which they were more compatible, such as the block area and the dramatic play area.

Results of these changes included increased playing in the dramatic-play area and block area and a decrease in rowdy and aggressive behavior. Therefore Walling could spend less time addressing disputes and disciplining children and more time interacting with them in their play.

On the basis of a variety of studies (Kinsman & Berk, 1979; Moore, 1987; Sheehan & Day, 1975; Smith & Connolly, 1980) and Walling's action research, we recommend the following strategies for teachers who want to arrange and rearrange their classrooms or who want to troubleshoot environments that are not working:

- Break up large open areas with dividers and furniture to discourage running and rough-and-tumble play. However, these dividers might need to be moved for whole-group activities (e.g., reading, classroom visitors) and large motor activities, such as dance.
- Use physical cues (e.g., furniture, dividers) and symbolic cues (e.g., print, pictures, streamers) to clearly define separate play areas.
- Place complementary areas, such as blocks and dramatic play, next to each other.
- Place areas that need water near the water source and sink.
- Place areas that tend to be messy on hard surfaces that are easy to keep clean.
- Place conflicting areas (e.g., noisy/quiet, wet/dry) away from each other.
- Be sure there are clear pathways between classroom areas and ample space by entrances and exits.

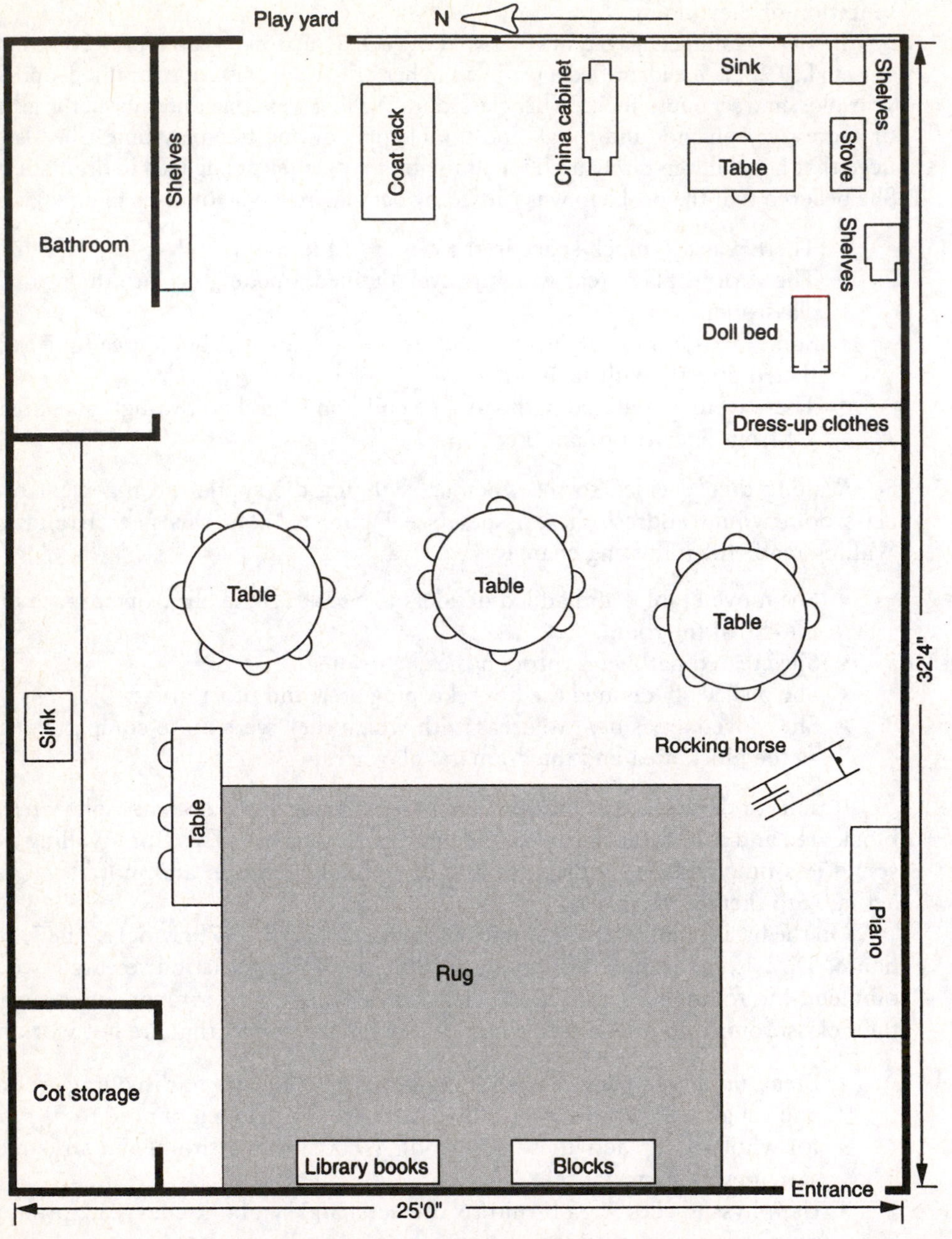


**FIGURE 6.2 Walling's Original Room Arrangement**

*Source:* From Kritchevsky and Prescott (1977, p. 50). Adapted in Johnson, Christie, and Yawkey, *Play and Early Childhood Development,* 2/e. Published by Allyn and Bacon, Boston, MA. Copyright © 1999 by Pearson Education. Reprinted by permission of the publisher.

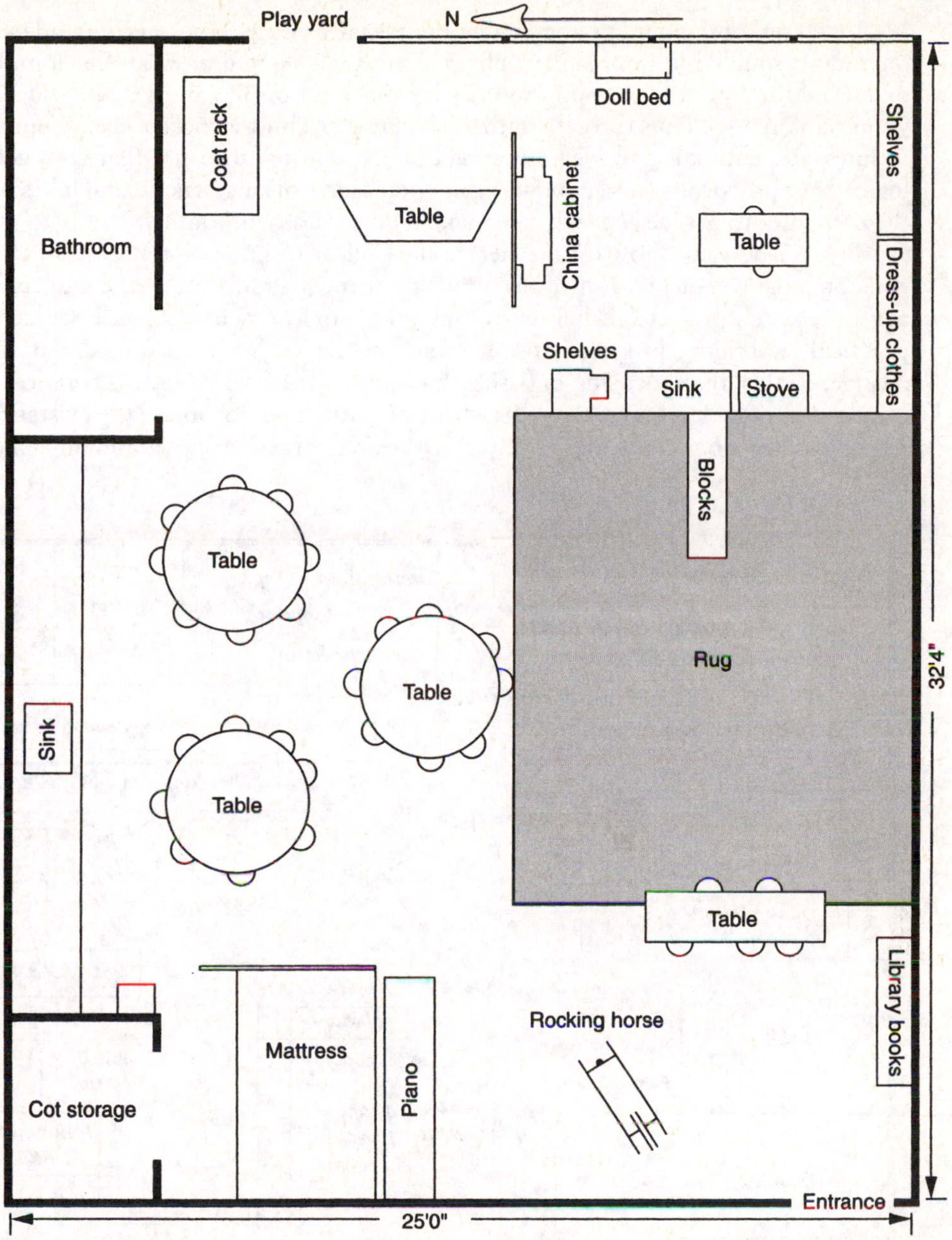


**FIGURE 6.3 Walling's Revised Room Arrangement**

*Source:* From Kritchevsky and Prescott (1977, p. 51). Adapted in Johnson, Christie, and Yawkey, *Play and Early Childhood Development,* 2/e. Published by Allyn and Bacon, Boston, MA. Copyright © 1999 by Pearson Education. Reprinted by permission of the publisher.

Figure 6.4 illustrates a classroom arrangement that is based on these principles.

One note of caution: young children, especially young boys, need an adequate amount of rough-and-tumble play, physical movements, and physical freedom. Frequent indoor and outdoor opportunities for this kind of play must be provided for young children—infants through third grade. Further, children need to be encouraged to integrate materials and ideas from all centers, not just the ones that go together logically or practically (for example, print out pictures of cars, trucks, and bikes from the computer to get ideas of what to make on the woodwork table).

Box 6.2 describes how the teachers at the College of Education Preschool at Arizona State University, with help from faculty member Pradnya Patet, conducted an action research project on their early childhood environment. Action research is a practical experience in systematic problem solving designed to result in positive change. Rather than focusing on issues and questions of a broad or theoretical nature, this approach requires the researcher to identify and document the existence of a problem in his or her setting. The teacher/researcher then proposes and implements

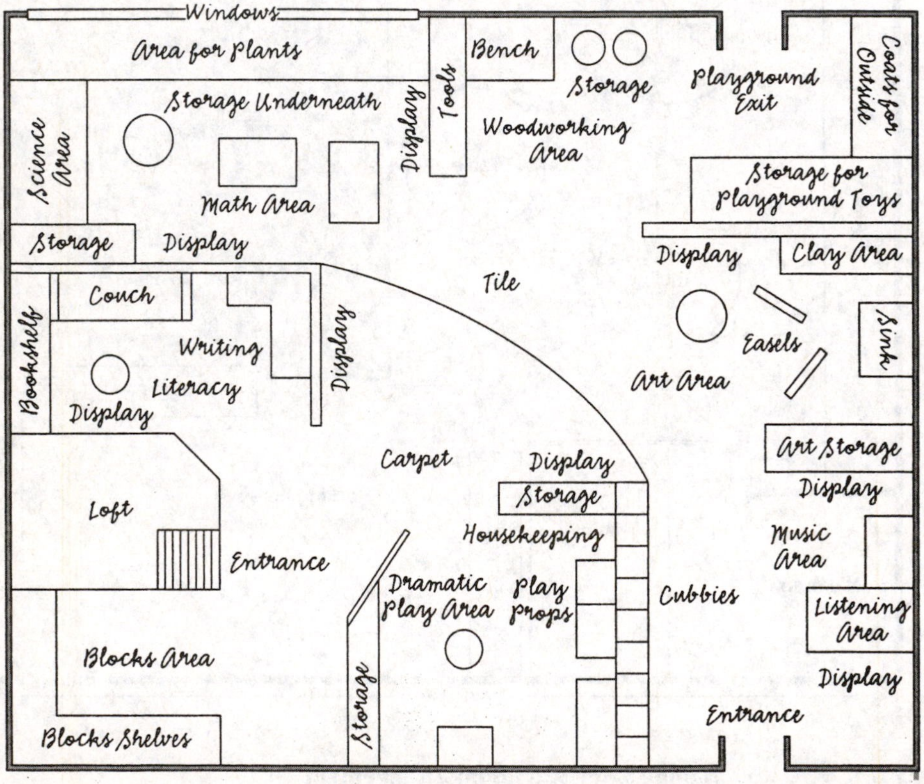


**FIGURE 6.4 Possible Room Arrangement for a Preschool Classroom**

*Source:* Wardle, *Introduction to Early Childhood Education: A Multidimensional Approach to Child-Centered Care and Learning*, p. 141. Published by Allyn and Bacon, Boston, MA. Copyright © 2003 by Pearson Education. Reprinted by permission of the publisher.

a plan to solve the problem or improve the situation. Finally, the teacher/researcher determines whether the solution worked. The advantage of action research is that practitioners can have a direct, positive impact on their practice; the disadvantage is that it lacks the objective controls of more traditional research approaches.

**BOX 6.2**

## *Designing Physical Spaces to Enhance Play and Development*

**by Pradnya Patet**
***Arizona State University***

With a strong interest in children's negotiation skills I set out to observe pretend play in the College of Education Preschool at Arizona State University. Surprisingly, there was very little interaction among the children, despite a wide variety of materials. My attention was instantly drawn to the room arrangement, the subspaces, and the amount of materials in the room. The teacher and I relocated one shelf to another part of the room, and almost immediately a brief period of cooperative play emerged.

Inspired by the educators in the preprimary schools of Reggio Emilia, who pay considerable attention to design in their classrooms (Tarr, 2001) and often refer to the environment as the "third educator" in conjunction with the two classroom teachers (Gandini, 1998, p. 177), I proposed to the preschool staff the use of a conceptual model grounded in Christopher Lowell's (2000) seven layers of design. With the intent to "create a template that would work regardless of floor plan, budget, and individual taste" (p. 7), Lowell gives seven specific sequential steps or layers to develop physical environments, which I applied to an early childhood setting. In addition, a few conversations and reflections later, we decided to translate our ideas into an action research project.

On the basis of a preliminary interview with each teacher about the kind of play that she wanted in the classroom and a report of trouble spots and favorite areas, I created a floor plan using Lowell's seven layers (2000). These layers as applied to the early childhood classroom are

1a. *Architectural elements,* or built-in features such as windows, electric outlets, and built-in cabinets that we have no control over.
1b. *Paint/wall color.*
2. *Installed flooring,* usually a combination of tile and carpet in a classroom, often fixed because of budget constraints.
3. *Upholstered furniture,* or cushiony, plush furniture and materials that enhance the softness of the room.
4. *Accent fabrics/area rugs.* Given the safety hazard of flowing fabric in a classroom, I consider this layer to include artificial windows, bulletin boards, or any elements that add dimension to the room or make certain features of the room pop out.

➤

5. *Workhorses,* or non-upholstered furniture such as tables, shelves, and other furniture that can be moved around.
6. *Accessories,* or play materials and displays of children's work and pictures, which constitute almost 90 percent of the early childhood classroom.
7a. *Plants,* whether real or silk, to add some ambience and, in the case of real plants, enhance responsibility and nurturance in children.
7b. *Lighting,* the balance between dark and bright areas in the classroom. These layers interact to create a cohesive whole and cannot be viewed separately.

Several educational researches have advocated the importance of considering aesthetic elements such as color, natural lighting, and varied textures (Greenman, 1987) and creating homelike environments with pillows, plants, and accessories such as flower vases and tablecloths (Hay-Cook, 1996; Tarr, 2001), as well as arranging furniture in a way that clearly defines the space for a particular activity (Kritchevsky et al., 1977; Loughlin & Suina, 1982). We used these ideas as we focused on the holistic effect generated by the seven-layer model. In rooms designed around the seven layers two things happen. First, the entire room flows from one area to another with subtle boundaries. This flow generates a sense of inner equilibrium much like the comfort one experiences in a house where one room flows into the next despite its unique decor. This is primarily why, despite the uniqueness in the design of each of our preschool rooms, all the teachers reported that they noticed a sense of calmness in the children. Second, the play props (accessories) get a meaningful, holistic, and realistic context and therefore stimulate connected thematic play rather than mere functional play. Following are three examples of how we embedded the seven layers in our design and how children reacted to the change.

**Example 1**

Along a rectangular strip of approximately 30 × 12 feet in an L-shaped room we created subtle boundaries to separate a noisy block area from a quiet reading area.The blocks, confined naturally to the carpeted area, flowed into a car floor mat that partially covered the tiled floor and transitioned smoothly into a cushioned space under the unmovable fish tank table, which was positioned perpendicular to the wall. This natural and subtle boundary with a crawl-under option further connected the next carpeted area, ideal for quiet table toy play and reading.

Children began to extend their block play into themes of transportation and to extend the floor mat itself with accessories organized in the shelves aligned against the wall. The cushions under and around the fish tank table encouraged children to crawl through the table tunnel and to quiet down and to sit and watch others play on both sides. The quiet atmosphere was further accentuated by a focal point that we created with the nearby window. A tall silk plant on the side, an artificial bird cage dangling down, and a footstool against the wall underneath drew children to look out the window and engage in quiet conversations. These behaviors were a definite change from the previous ones in which activities occurred unrelated to the neighboring areas and were sustained primarily in the block area, leaving the other play areas unused. Cooperative play increased.

**Example 2**
In another room, when the loft stairs were allowed to lead into the kitchen and the loft was stocked with soft cushions, stuffed animals, and books, the children perceived the kitchen as part of a whole house. The redesign of our kitchen added a whole new dimension to the children's play. We anchored the whole area on the tiled portion of the room with an artificial window over the sink, a pegboard with screws to hold up pans and oven mitts, an ironing table with a real wall telephone near it, flower vases, and a table set with a few plates and cups.

All of a sudden, children were planning tea parties, cooking and serving, having dialogues on the phone while ironing dolls' clothes, and pretending to be cats looking for food. This was a dramatic change from the prior parallel and associative play that had dominated this area.

**Example 3**
The flow in the third room was created by a diagonal arrangement that directed the children to move into an area that was not clearly visible from the entrance. Different types of accessories and work surfaces such as magnetic pieces, a Plexiglas table, a weaving board, and a clay area were distributed strategically throughout the room to encourage children to pause and play as they flowed from one area to the other.

The teacher noted that "the material [was] the same but the presentation was different," and so children found something to engage in at every part of the room. Children who had chosen water colors all year were now drawing, making designs with magnets, and reaching out to explore other materials.

**Conclusion**
Overall, children's play seemed to reach more complex levels intellectually, socially, and emotionally. They began to notice, appreciate, and participate in classroom design. We found that aesthetically pleasing spaces encouraged children and adults to stay in them longer and therefore sustained their activity and took them to higher play levels. Meaningful conversations emerged in such environments, and the quality of play blossomed. "No space is marginal, no corner is unimportant and each space needs to be alive and open to change" (Cadwell, 1997, p. 93) because "children behave in ways suggested by spatial contents and arrangement" (Kritchevsky, Prescott, & Walling, 1999, p. 152).

Acknowledgement: I would like to thank the Arizona State University, College of Education Preschool staff—Gerri Fredette, Nancy Siket, and Rosa Teran—for their valuable contributions to this project.

## SOCIAL ECOLOGY AND PLAY

Children perform or fail to perform certain kinds of play because of environmental conditions. Physical space and time for play are important for the development of play skills. Children need objects, including natural ones such as stones, twigs, cornstalks, and walnuts, as play props to trigger and sustain their imaginations. Climate, geography, communities, and neighborhoods help to define these environmental conditions. The context of children's play includes community and neighborhood, space, and preschool and school environmental design variables, as we have just discussed. It also includes families, parents and siblings, as social agents that affect the expression and development of children's play.

## Family Dynamics

An abundance of factors helps to determine the kinds and quality of play a child will experience growing up and how playful and creative a person may become throughout his or her lifetime. Many of these early childhood influences emanate from within the family context, as we saw in Chapter 4, where we discussed the influence of home background on gender and personality, and as we will see again in Chapter 10 when we discuss families and children with disabilities.

How parents interact with their children can have a lasting effect on the kind of person the child grows up to be. According to Csikszentmihalyi (1990), the family context promoting optimal experience, which he refers to as "flow," has five features: clarity of expectations, focusing on the present, giving children choices, trusting children, and giving them challenges. The presence of these five features makes for an "autotelic family context" because they provide ideal training for enjoying life. The term *autotelic* derives from two Greek words—*auto,* meaning "self," and *telos,* meaning "goal"—and refers to intrinsically motivated behavior. For Csikszentmihalyi this type of behavior constitutes a "flow experience." In the state of flow, as in the state of optimal play, experiencing life is its own reward.

Unfortunately, there are forces at work that run counter to the types of family dynamics that promote creative play and flow experiences. Many parents are worried that schools and society at large seem to value only performance, particularly academic achievement but also musical and athletic performance that is excellent. Accordingly, they socialize their children to excel in these areas and perhaps also try to teach them how to deal with all the stress that is generated in the process and that is felt by the children and their parents alike.

This new type of performance anxiety is also affecting parent-teacher relationships. Brown (2003) reports a trend toward increasing parental worry over play-based curriculum in early childhood, especially in low-income and minority families. Parents have been increasingly asking pre-K teachers not to play so much with the children, especially in the spring of the school year in the weeks just before the time when kindergarten screening is scheduled. They want to make sure that their children can perform academic skills. In theory, these parents might understand and even endorse the belief that play is important in their children's learning and development. But living this value in practice is another matter. Competing values that can stand in the way include wanting their children to fulfill school expectations and to meet or surpass school definitions of academic success.

## Parental Influences

Parents in many families also experience a shortage of time for everything they have to do as parents plus the added stress from the role strain due to competing career demands. Purchase of toys and enrolling children in organized activities often are done to compensate for the lack of parental play time with their children. This is unfortunate because most children would rather have high-quality play time with their parents rather than more new toys or organized activities. We are in favor of more maternal and paternal leave time from work and flexible, family-friendly work schedules. This is because we believe that the best toy is the parent, especially during infancy and toddlerhood. Older children also benefit from having their parents freed from some of their job and career stress. This way parents can better attend to their children's play needs, such as by helping them network with friends when transportation is needed, taking more time for family vacations and recreational activities, and playing games and sports together as a family.

Research indicates that children can benefit a great deal from parent-child play. Advantages include positive effects on children's language, symbolic representation, exploratory behavior, attachment to parents, and social relationships (Damast, Tamis-LeMonda, & Bornstein, 1996; Haight, 1998; MacDonald, 1993). Parent-child play during infancy and the toddler years also helps to prepare children for later play and social interaction with their peers after parents lose the distinction of being their child's primary playmate.

In many Western cultures maximum benefits are believed to occur when parents aim for mutually interactive play with their infants and toddlers and accommodate to them a great deal. Researchers have described parents as warm, nondidactic, and verbally responsive when playing with their young children (Shine & Acosta, 2000). This helps young children to develop rudimentary play skills. Many parents have a knack of providing children with appropriately challenging play experiences that nudge children to the next level of development (e.g., Vygotsky's zone of proximal development). Many parents also deliberately seek to foster in their young children a sense of playfulness and fantasy-making skills (Haight, 1998).

These parental play behaviors with the child are, of course, culture-bound (Roopnarine, Lasker, Sacks, & Stores, 1998). How, when, and where parents play with their children vary considerably across cultures. In many cultures we do not see the phenomenon described above—that is, the American parents seeking to use pretend play or physical play with their young children as a way to enhance child development. In the parent-child context in developing cultures and in minority families within the American culture, play is often embedded in work activities and combined with direct teaching of information. Parental behaviors reflect their beliefs, which are shaped by sociocultural forces operating in cultural communities. Parental behaviors in playing or not playing with children and variations in parent-child play are manifestations of parental belief systems, which in turn are the result of sociocultural determinants, such as social class and culture (see Figure 6.1).

Although studies have suggested that there is little if any parental participation in play with their children in some cultural communities or families, this does not imply that the parents of these children do not play with them. This seems very unlikely, given that parent-offspring play is found in many animal species and would appear to be a universal human parenting trait that is selected by evolution. Children growing up in certain minority groups in the United States, or in other cultures such as the Mayan (Gaskin, 1999) may experience parent-child play in different ways. Perhaps a great deal of parent-child play occurs in private contexts, such as at night before sleeping or at other quiet family times (see Maya perspective on play, p. 7).

## Sibling Influences

Sibling relationships within the family enter into the family dynamic and affect the play of children. Sibling play and social interaction in general differ from parent-child patterns of behavior and also differ from peer relationships. Moreover, the study of sibling effects has been complicated by ordinal position and child spacing and gender effects (Oden & Hall, 1998).

Siblings are not as likely to accommodate to a younger child's play behaviors as parents are and do not strive for mutuality. Often the older brother or sister of a toddler or young preschooler plays in a parallel play fashion with the younger sibling. A certain amount of sibling rivalry can be expected, with feelings of jealousy or envy precluding sharing toys and playful cooperation at times. As children get older, tensions can rise, and an ambivalence can set in about doing things together. Parents can help by not comparing children or showing favoritism. Even when sibling relationships are very positive, parents should expect the highs and lows of close intimacy and secret sharing on the one hand, and play disruption and hostility on the other hand. Even when things turn bad and siblings are fighting, they do stick up for one another and defend one another when attacked by a person outside the family. A considerable degree of stability in how siblings get along seems to be the rule. If siblings are close when they are young, this tends to persist into adolescence (Dunn, 1992).

Gender and ordinal position must be taken into account in thinking about how siblings play. Same-sex sibling dyads, for instance, compared with opposite-gender sibling pairs, are known for being competitive. Same-sex siblings also engage in more gender-stereotypic play (Stoneman, Brody, & MacKinnon, 1986). Older siblings, of course, tend to be more dominant. The younger brother or sister usually welcomes teaching and managing attempts by older siblings.

Other family variables as well can moderate sibling interactions, including play behaviors. If children are more than four years apart, they will have much less in common then if the spacing between them is less. This is not only because they grow up being in different developmental stages (e.g., when one is a preschooler, the other is in elementary school), but also because they are in different generation cohorts (e.g., the difference in being born in the middle 90s versus the late 1990s). Social-historical periods separated by even a few years can be quite different from each other in today's fast-changing world. For example, what is happening in terms of fads, fashions, jokes, and preferred recreation emanating from forces within the popular culture and affecting children's play can be remarkably discordant (see Chapter 11).

Cultural differences are seen in sibling play as well as parent-child play. For example, Mayan mothers tickle and jounce their toddlers but do not otherwise engage in play because they have to go to work in the fields. The role of playmate belongs to the sibling or cousins (Rogoff & Mosier, 1993). This is a common finding in many developing cultures in which older children supervise younger children and engage in work-play, that is, embedding play events within work that has to be done by the children in a cultural community (Haskins, 1999). Still, mothers might be more inclined to stimulate pretend play in young children than siblings are. Perez-Granados (2002) reported in a study of families of Mexican descent that mothers of two- to three-year-olds were more likely to suggest pretend play (e.g., going on a picnic) with a set of food props than were four- to six-year-old siblings, who labeled objects for their younger siblings but did not try to engage them in much conversation, as mothers did.

## PLAY AND CULTURE

In Abu Dhabi, the capital of the United Arab Emirates, a sign hangs outside a city park that reads "Garden is for ladies and children. No entry for boys aged more than ten years." In the highlands of Guatemala girls and boys as young as eight years old are expected to help their parents in working in the fields, grinding coffee, and preparing meals, and girls as young as five and six years old help to wash clothes in the stream. But these children do not seem to have our Protestant concept of work, often playing tag through the corn, splashing each other with water in the stream, and running around between the adults as they prepare the meal on a community fiesta day. And sometimes the adults drop their work and play with them.

Culture affects everything we do, including play. However, like play, culture is very difficult to define. We know what culture does: It structures our experiences, sets our goals, defines our roles, and determines our values. Religion, home language, ethnicity, education, income, and national identity all relate to culture. But we also know that all cultures are dynamic (they change over time), that the impact of culture is different for different people (for example, a woman in the United Arab Emirates as opposed to a man), and that cultures rub against each other and change as a result of this contact. Hoijer (1954) explains that "No culture is wholly isolated, self-contained, and unique.

Sign outside a public park in Abu Dhabi, United Arab Emirates.

There are important resemblances between all cultures—resemblances that stem in part from the fact that all cultures are built around biological, psychological and social characteristics common to all mankind" (p. 94). And people can, to some extent, change their cultural context. For example, an Arab family that comes to the United States will maintain some of their cultural identity and values, such as their religious practices, but probably will have little trouble allowing their children of both genders to play on U.S. playgrounds. A Mayan family that immigrates to this country will probably retain their Cachiquel language and other cultural aspects, but will have little trouble moving from a work day that goes from sunup to sundown to a traditional eight-hour work day.

And let's be clear that although race and ethnicity, as we said, are a part of culture, they do not by themselves define culture.

**BOX 6.3**

## Houses and Culture

**by Francis Wardle**

During the devastating 1976 earthquake in the Highlands of Guatemala many of the beautiful adobe houses with orange ceramic tile roofs were destroyed. Therefore one of the central relief tasks was to rebuild the homes of the poor Maya residents. I was a member of a team from the Mohawk Indian Reservation who traveled to the Highlands to help build new homes, but most of the rebuilding was done by a team from Canada.

As a gift to help the devastated country (and as a way to rejuvenate the Canadian lumber industry), Canada donated tons of chipboard (a premade plywood) and building lumber to Guatemala. Teams of Canadians set up a "factory" on the local soccer field to create prefabricated houses, which were then erected by the local residents to replace their picturesque adobe homes.

Maya Indians are small, hard-working people. Their small, low-ceiling homes have thick mud walls to keep out the mountain cold and damp, and the tiled roof has a convenient space between the roof and the top of the wall to let out smoke from the cooking fire and to create a breeze in the hot summer months. Doors and windows are small to keep out the cold. Wood is very scarce in the mountains and is reserved for the cooking fires. Using wood to heat the home is considered wasteful. The houses are quite small, and often people sleep together to stay warm.

Western buildings are designed around 4 × 8 foot modules; all plywood, wallboard, and chipboard come in 4 × 8 (or 4 × 16) sizes. Most 2 × 4s–the pieces of structural lumber used to frame buildings–are precut to fit these modular sizes. Therefore the standard height for most Western rooms is 8 feet. These units have developed over time to match the average size of Northern Europeans and North Americans and to match our geography and climate. For example, unlike in Guatemala, houses in Europe and North America need heating (and often air conditioning) and therefore are heavily insulated and have heating systems. Houses in Central America and Brazil are generally not heated and are open to the elements.

The houses the Canadians built were based on these 4 × 8 dimensions, with chipboard walls and corrugated tin roofs. (They were not strong enough to hold tile roofs.) Further, the Canadians believed that the locals should cook their meals outside of these homes, in a kitchen. The local people found these buildings cold and impersonal, and the smoke from their cooking fires had no place to go. Many of the families ended up using their new buildings as a place to dry their laundry and remained living in the little shacks they had built after the earthquake.

## Culture and Play

One of the most interesting and controversial questions in psychology and child development today is whether there are universal behaviors, learning sequences, developmental schedules, and growth patterns or whether all factors around growth and development are a direct product of a child's cultural context. Many scholars believe that there are no universal norms and expectations, that children develop characteristics their culture supports and reinforces, and that gender roles and cognitive abilities are based only on cultural expectations (Kaiser & Rasminsky, 2003). Of course, this question also covers play: To what extent are children's play, play patterns, and developmental sequences universal, and to what extent are they culturally bound? And, as we suggested earlier, culture encompasses a variety of variables that interact in unique ways: race and ethnicity, language, group affiliation, and income. Therefore part of this discussion is whether play is a function of privilege and middle-class status.

For us these questions have extreme importance because much of this book is based on the belief that what we know about play—different kinds of play, the progression from simple to complex play, the relationship between play and learning, and how to use play to assist children in learning school-related skills, facts, and concepts—is sufficiently universal that teachers can use it to help children learn and develop. But the central question is whether these constructs that we discuss are of value to all children or just to children from a specific cultural context. As our early childhood programs and schools become ever more diverse, the answer to this question is obviously critical.

Clearly, the culture of this country and many Western societies emphasizes education, provides a clear distinction between work and play, and places extreme importance on individualism and consumerism. Further, these societies view childhood and education primarily as a preparation for a successful and productive adult life. Is our discussion of play—research, philosophies, theories, and practical advice—of value only to children living in Western societies and children who belong to the mainstream culture in those societies?

**Animals Do It.** Young monkeys that were studied in Africa engage in an entire range of rough-and-tumble play—chasing, rolling over in the dirt, wrestling roughly, and attacking—but never really hurting each other. Other monkeys would join the game (Blurton-Jones, 1976). It has been hypothesized that young animals use play to practice social and fighting skills and to develop the strength and endurance they will need to survive as adults (Brown, 1994).

However, Brown also believes that animals play just for the fun of it. In a *National Geographic* article he describes a husky dog and a polar bear, two normally antagonistic species, apparently playing with each other—and returning to play with each other on a regular basis. He describes how a raven in Wales slides down a snowy bank on its back, walks back up the hill, and repeats the process several times and how young Japanese macaque monkeys make snowballs by rolling them along the ground the way children do and then proudly display their snowballs to each other (Brown, 1994). And we all know that most dogs—and not only retrievers—love to play at retrieving balls, Frisbees, and objects thrown into the water and that cats like to play with string and toy mice.

Because animals do not exist within a cultural context, it seems that play in animals is universal. And according to Boulton and Smith (1989) rough-and-tumble play has been observed in children in Japan, Kenya, and Mexico, as well as in every income and ethnic group in North America, Europe, and Australia.

**Are Cultures So Different?** Hall (1977) calls Western Europe, North America, Australia, and Canada *low-context cultures* and Asian, African, southern European, and Latin American countries *high-context cultures.* Low-context cultures value the individual over the group and value individual independence and success as the highest possible virtue. The American Declaration of Independence's statement that "all men are created equal" and have a right to "Life, Liberty and the Pursuit of Happiness" is an example of this value, as is Maslow's (1959) hierarchy of needs, which identifies self-actualization at the pinnacle of a person's development. Low-context cultures focus child rearing and education on "teaching their citizens to assert themselves, take initiative, explore and achieve" (Kaiser & Rasminsky, 2003, p. 54).

High-context cultures, on the other hand, view individuals as being interdependent on each other and on being primarily members of a group—extended family, community, ethnic or racial group, and so on. The individual's worth and status are based on his or her contribution to the group, and harmony and group consensus are valued. Individual achievement, especially when it conflicts with group values, is viewed as selfish and a rejection of the group (Kaiser & Rasminsky, 2003).

Clearly, play has completely different functions in high- and low-context cultures. In high-context cultures play focuses on cooperation, sharing, group loyalty, and learning to subsume individual needs and wants to the collective good. Group games are used to help children understand their role within the larger group. On the other hand, play in low-context societies focuses on developing individuals' skills and competencies, individuality, leadership, self-expression, and continually pushing children toward independence (Kaiser & Rasminsky, 2003).

**Is Play Universal or Cultural?** We believe that play—in a variety of forms and expressions—is one of the fundamental things all children do, with a few exceptions that are based largely on physical disabilities. However, we also believe that how this play is expressed depends on the child's cultural context. Cultures that value verbal expression, fantasy, and imaginative play will encourage that kind of play, and cultures that value physical movement and manipulation of real objects will place more value on functional and constructive play.

Although this idea is fairly simple and logical, a difficult question presents itself: In highly pluralistic countries such as Canada, Brazil, the United States, and much of Europe, should we in early childhood programs and schools encourage the kind of play we believe will help children be successful in school and eventually in life? If so, what kind of play is this? Although most educators and researchers now believe that no one cultural context is better than another and therefore no one kind of play is best, we do have a responsibility to prepare all of our children to maximize their potential within the greater society. It would be nice and satisfying to simply support the notion that children living in different cultural contexts should engage in play that is consistent with their culture, but is this fair to the children?

For example, Francis Wardle recently provided training to Head Start staff on the Seminole Indian Reservation in Oklahoma. One of the participants asked the provocative question, "How can we teach early literacy to our children when we are an oral society that does not read? Where are our children going to see the critical modeling of reading, when our parents do not read at home?" Because literacy is now a focus of Head Start and the Federal No Child Left Behind Act, this question is critical. Whereas the Seminole people would seem to provide a high-context cultural environment for their children, Head Start is a federal program that reflects the cultural values of a low-context culture. And for Seminole Indian children to succeed, they must be able to function effectively in the mainstream American culture.

## Cultural Influences on Play

Research on children's play in other countries around the world in the past has been undertaken to test the universality of stage theories of play development or the prevalence or even existence of certain play states such as symbolic or pretense play. Ethnographic anthropological research such as that compiled by Schwartzman (1978) has proven useful for dispelling certain myths such as that children's early integration into the adult world of work precludes having a play life or that having toys designed for pretend play and having same-aged peers are necessary conditions for social pretense. Imaginative play expressions occur cross-culturally with clear differences in themes, content, and play style and tone.

Research studies have revealed the enormous variation across cultures in the content and style of children's play and how play affects and is affected by cultural context. This research can be divided into three categories:

1. Investigations that have described play and related behaviors in specific cultures (e.g., deMarrais, Nelson, & Baker, 1994).
2. Studies that have compared the play of children in different countries—for example, Taiwan and the United States (Pan, 1994; Tobin, Yu, & Davidson, 1989).
3. Research on the play of immigrant children attending preschools or childcare programs in a new culture—for example, the play of children who have recently immigrated to the United States from Korea (e.g., Farver, Kim, & Lee, 1995; Farver, Kim, & Lee-Shin, 2000).

To illustrate research on play in a specific culture, consider the work of deMarrais et al. (1994) on Yup'ik Eskimo girls. This study, based on ethnographic interviewing and participant observation, illustrated the importance of "storyknifing" in the mud for the enculturation and development of young girls from six to twelve years of age living in villages in southwestern Alaska. As the researchers noted, as the afternoon sun warmed the muddy banks of the river, girls would engage in storyknifing for up to three hours. Storyknifing provides an activity setting that helps the girls learn from older peers cultural knowledge about kinship patterns, gender roles, and community norms and values. It also helps the girls to consolidate through play and story expressions their understandings and feelings about their culture and promotes the learning of skills, habits, and attitudes relevant to the culture in which they live.

The second type of play and culture research is represented by the cross-cultural comparison done by Pan (1994), who contrasted the play kindergarteners in Taipei with the findings of Rubin et al.'s (1978) earlier study of the play of comparable U.S. children. The observation procedures and the way in which the play behaviors were coded were similar across the Pan and Rubin studies. Pan's results showed that constructive play was commonplace in both countries but that group-dramatic play was more prevalent in the U.S. sample: It occurred twice as much in preschool and three times as much at the kindergarten level. Parallel-constructive and interactive games with rules were more prevalent in the Taiwanese sample. Pan traced some of these differences in play patterns to maternal attitudes toward play in the two cultures.

Play research of the third kind, focusing on immigrant children, is exemplified by the study by Farver et al. (1995). These researchers examined cultural differences in three- to five-year-old Korean- and Anglo-American children's play behavior. The Anglo-American children engaged in more social pretend play, whereas unoccupied states and parallel play were more common in the Korean-American children. On the surface, it appeared that the Anglo-American children were engaging in more sophisticated play. However, Farver et al. also observed that the Korean-American children would offer objects to initiate play and were more cooperative than their Anglo-American counterparts, a finding that is consistent with their high-context cultural values of interdependence and field sensitivity.

In her comprehensive book *Transformations: The Anthropology of Children's Play* Schwartzman (1978) provided an abundance of rich ethnographic data about the play of children from non-Western, less technologically and economically advanced societies. She noted that ethnographic studies that have reported a paucity of play among children in rural Egypt and Kenya and among the Kurdish Jews in Israel did not have as their primary focus children's play, let alone types of play. She warned that the absence of evidence from these studies is not evidence of absence. According to Margaret Mead (1975), "Students should be warned that one can never rely on a negative statement that any toy, any game, any song is absent just because it is neither witnessed nor recalled by adults" (p. 161). More recent ethnographic accounts (Roopnarine, Johnson, & Hooper, 1994) suggest that children from diverse cultures participate in a wide variety of play forms, play that is often combined with work (e.g., Bloch & Walsh, 1983).

Differences in imaginative play between Western and traditional societies may well relate to what Sutton-Smith (1972) called differences between "ascriptive" and "achievement" game cultures. Children who belong to an ascriptive culture engage in play that is imitative but not transformational and that relies on the use of realistic toy representations rather than improvised ones or none at all. In other words, children in ascriptive game cultures imitate the behavior of their elders; they replicate but do not transform. In contrast, the imaginative play of young children in achievement cultures is replete with make-believe transformations that are more flexible and diversified (subject-object, object-object, and self-other transformations).

Sutton-Smith and his colleagues over the years have described differences in imaginative play styles related to cultural factors. For example, ethnographic work by

Sutton-Smith and Heath (1981) analyzed two styles of imaginative behavior, which they called *oral* and *literate*. The oral style of imagination is usually of a rhetorical type that is embedded in verbal communication between the central performer and the group. In cultures in which the literate style predominates, imagination is often used in solitary situations and stresses detachment from the mundane world and the conjuring up of things that are not present. Sutton-Smith and Heath suggested that what appear to be developmental deficiencies in imagination might be differences in imagination style.

In the American middle-class today, play and the toys that are manufactured to support play of young children are generally thought to be necessary for the stimulation of early cognitive and social development, which is believed to be useful for success in school and later life. Pretend play is particularly valued, and such play is seen as a particularly appropriate activity for adults to engage in with children. However, in other cultures such play might be looked on as a natural but inconsequential aspect of childhood (e.g., Haskins, 1999), and manufactured toys and time for play might be nonexistent, with adults not even part of the participant structure (Roopnarine et al., 1994; Schwartzman, 1978). Clearly, cultures vary in how adults see children's play and whether and how they might participate in it.

**BOX 6.4**

## History, Religion, Economics, Politics, and Play in Taiwan

In traditional Chinese culture education is regarded as a most important ladder to the achievement of higher social status and economic advancement. The ancient sages' sayings are well known: "All things are beneath contempt, only education is to be esteemed"; "Only if you suffer can you surpass others"; "You must study well to rise to be an official"; "Diligence has its own reward; play has no advantages." Parents judge children's achievement from their performance on academic work using a narrow definition of success. By tradition children learn by being told and by being shown how to do things. They learn from didactic instruction, a mimetic as opposed to a transformational approach to learning (Gardner, 1989). The Chinese language system biases one toward mimetic instruction, since it requires memorization of thousands of Chinese characters and training in stroke sequences. Parents learned this way when they were young. Other factors affecting parents' expectations for their children include the government's exam-oriented educational system and peer pressure from their social network. Parental choices and decisions for children's learning (i.e., selections of kindergartens, enrollment in out-of-school programs, and work at home) affect children's play and their right to play.

Chang (2003) found that children's play is affected by the school they attend. She studied two classrooms in depth, using ethnographic research methods, and discovered quite a contrast in the children's play opportunities and play behavior. Children in the "Exploratory Learning kindergarten" played at school and even invited their parents to engage in pretend play at home. But children enrolled in the "Efficient Learning kindergarten" had no time scheduled for play, and the small number of available toys were almost always off limits, kept high up on a shelf. Interestingly, some children dared to take risks to play when the teacher was busy correcting or preparing worksheets. Even though there was a paucity of play materials in the classroom, children still made use of objects to play, such as transforming the straps of schoolbags into horsewhips and pretending to be horsemen or to drive carriages or using a string as a phone line to initiate a conversation or a chalkboard eraser as a cell phone.

Chang found that parents in Taiwan often sent their kindergarten children to after-school programs to practice academic skills or to take lessons in the arts, such as piano, drawing, or dancing. These children had quite a busy week, with little time for play. The parents felt strong traditional cultural pressures to help their young sons to become dragons and their young daughters to become phoenixes (*"Wan tsu chen lung"*). They were very concerned about their children's readiness for elementary school. Parents often supervised their children's academic work at home. The work at home decreased time for children to play.

Chang's research uses a sociocultural approach to the study of play and culture. Basic to questions about education in Taiwan and in other Asian societies is an understanding of traditional cultural values centered on Confucianism. According to Confucian philosophy, the ultimate goal of socialization and education is maintaining natural and social harmony, and to achieve this, one must first cultivate oneself, then harmonize one's own family, and then help to govern one's state well. The end is to be able to manifest one's bright virtue to all in the world. The traditional educator's responsibilities include being a role model of virtue, helping students to cultivate themselves, and delivering external knowledge. Academic emphasis in Taiwan derives from the combination of Confucianism and contemporary political will and ideology (Yang, 2002). Incorporating educational play will always remain an uphill struggle for kindergarten teachers in the traditional Taiwanese cultural context.

## EDUCATIONAL APPLICATIONS

We have noted in this chapter that the form and content of children's play are influenced by a range of context variables, including cultural and social class factors. We would like for all children to be able to play to their fullest potential, and we believe that for this to happen, we must be cognizant of the content of each child's own real-life experiences and provide play opportunities that are in line with children's backgrounds. Carefully observing and listening to children playing at school is an important first step. Teachers can also use partnerships with parents to better understand children's diverse backgrounds. Parents can help teachers to set up culturally appropriate play activities at school. An enriched, culturally appropriate program can facilitate play, peer relations, and friendships among diverse children, teachers, and parents.

### Parental Input

Welcoming input from parents and creating working relations with them fosters greater multiethnic perspective-taking skills (Hyun & Marshall, 1997). Beyond becoming more knowledgeable about different lifestyles, languages, and cultures—and attaching positive value to this—teachers need to promote empathy and perspective-taking ability, both in themselves and in children. The ideal is to successfully navigate together the diverse cultural landscape of today's pluralistic society. Communication and empathy go together and lead to detailed, intimate knowledge of the whole child and the family. This is needed for a better understanding of intragroup variation, both as an antidote to stereotyping and as a critical ingredient of any curriculum that hopes to become anti-bias (Derman-Sparks, 1989).

## Curriculum Adaptations

In addition to positive dispositions towards diversity, teachers need to plan and implement changes in their programs to accommodate this diversity. Curry (1971) provides an excellent example of a curricular adaptation, albeit an accidental one. She relates how a group of Navajo (Dine) children were not engaging in sociodramatic play at all in the housekeeping center of a middle-class-oriented preschool center. The housekeeping center was set up with the child-size furniture arranged at right angles to the wall so as to set the area apart from the rest of the classroom. As we explained earlier, this type of partitioning is commonly recommended to make the dramatic play area well defined and set apart from the rest of the classroom. However, this particular group of Navajo children happened to live in traditional circular hogans, in which all of the furniture was arranged against the wall. As a result, the children did not connect the housekeeping center with what goes on in their own homes. One day, unintentionally, the toys were left against the wall after cleaning. The Navajo children then vigorously engaged in sociodramatic play. The props were in the position where the children were used to seeing them in their circular hogan homes!

Another example of culture-sensitive teaching comes from an anecdote shared by Patricia Monighan-Nourot (1995) about Sysavath, a little girl newly arrived from Laos. One day, Sysavath entered her preschool classroom with a baby carrier on her back. Her baby doll had Asian features. Throughout the school day Sysavath took the "baby" along as she participated in program activities with the teachers and the other children—from easel painting, to water table activities, to block play, and so on. The opportunity for Sysavath to mother her doll this way helped her become acclimated to the program and find a sense of belonging and mastery. It gave her peer group recognition too. Sysavath's mother was asked for replicas of the cloth baby carrier so that others could share in this new play in the classroom.

Early childhood education that is multicultural integrates play throughout the program much as it does multiculturalism itself; they are not add-ons but are essential dimensions of the inner workings of overall curriculum. Creating mutually directed activities in which adults negotiate and share power with children is integral to culturally responsive teaching (Stremmel, 1997). Children's knowledge, culture, and life experiences are taken seriously and are allowed to affect the curriculum and teaching, as in the examples above. Children inform us about themselves and their backgrounds and cultures through their play.

Play, culture, and curriculum can come together in numerous ways, including free play and structured play. In general, free play should have available objects and symbols in the environment that show each child that his or her own culture is respected and validated. Parents can be consulted and invited to share materials and accessories that would be useful for free play: items such as jewelry, costumes, scarfs, clothing, props for foods, music, toys, puzzles, and games. These multicultural materials should always be present, although specific items can be changed through rotation on a regular basis.

Teachers must be ready to intervene whenever necessary to foster multicultural competencies and attitudes during free play. For example, if the teacher sees children who are playing restaurant express a cultural stereotype such as "All Chinese like rice and all Mexicans like beans," the teacher would suggest that some Mexicans do not like beans more than rice and that some Chinese like beans (Boutte, Van Scoy, & Hendley, 1996). Teacher interventions are required to counteract in children or other teachers any biased behaviors or words, as well as any expressions of the superficial tourist approach, which fails to recognize intracultural variation and individual differences.

For structured play multicultural theme boxes can be employed (Boutte et al., 1996). Theme or prop boxes contain toys and other objects related to a particular theme such as beauty shop, barber shop, or bakery. For example, a multicultural theme box for a bakery would contain simulations of baked goods representing different cultures (e.g., tortillas, baklava, pita, challah) with cookbooks, magazine recipes, and pictures used to reinforce diversity, as well as different kinds of cooking and eating utensils from different countries.

In conclusion the role of the teacher is critical in making the curriculum work to achieve multicultural ends through play-related means. Teachers must remain vigilant and know when and how to intervene during play and other times of the day to promote empathy and friendships among children. Teachers need to be ready to facilitate and to guide different kinds of play that serve various socioemotional needs of the children and also cognitive and language growth.

## SUMMARY

This chapter has taken us on a rather ambitious exploration of play and context. We have given a broad treatment of context, discussing its meaning with respect to the sociocultural or cultural-contextual approach to play. In this approach context refers to the totality of the situation, or that which weaves together. A general model of play and environmental relations was proposed that included ecocultural variables of geography, climate, and history; sociocultural systems and institutions; and beliefs, attitudes, values, and behavioral variables. This general framework suggests connections among various topics in the play literature and is a way to orient ourselves to the contents of this chapter that cover a range of context variables relating to physical environments, social ecology, and culture.

After discussing geography and climate as contextual variables influencing children's play and play spaces, the importance of neighborhoods and communities was noted. On this level of context we saw that social capital and the presence of external assets such as parks and recreation centers can have a favorable impact on children's play and development. Children need play habitats that are rich in experiences and have ample room for vigorous physical play and a sufficient amount and variety of appropriate materials.

Additional concerns arise in applying contextual principles for purposes of maximizing the positive play potential of children in preschool and school settings. Teachers need to plan and implement indoor space for play with attention to additional matters such as supervision of children and maintenance of equipment and playthings. There needs to be variety, choice, and accessibility responsive to children's needs and interests within the different learning or activity centers of a program. Ideas were presented for arranging and changing spaces in indoor child program environments to enhance play and development.

The social ecology of family contexts is very influential for play behavior and development. Dynamics within the family that are conducive to play and flow were described as autotelic. Autotelic family contexts provide children with positive feelings, challenges, a sense of purpose, and empowerment. Many parents are caught in conflict over wanting to promote play and wanting to meet demands for academic mastery. Parent-child play reflects parental beliefs and cultural values. Within families siblings are also potent influences on children's play.

Cultural variables relate to play behavior and development. Cultural-contextual frameworks help us to understand environmental settings and the dynamic reciprocal relationships among social and physical situations, cultural influences, and human development, behavior, and play. Teacher and parent beliefs and attitudes influence play environments and opportunities. Variation in children's play within sociocultural groups are mediated by teacher and parent variables.

Opportunities and motivation for various kinds of play expression are related to cultural differences in adult ideas and values about play. Notions about cultural deficits in regard to children's play are rejected in light of concepts from within the cultural-contextual framework. Empirical work on play of children in other countries, international comparative studies, and research on immigrant groups in the United States demonstrate strong support for the notion that children's play is influenced by culture, supporting a cultural difference (not deficit) notion.

Educators are responsible for promoting early childhood education that is multicultural and antibiased. Teachers' beliefs, attitudes, and practices concerning children's play and diversity and their curricular planning are important for achieving the goal of having all children play up to their potential, thus serving their education and development. Practical suggestions were presented to increase our sensitivity to children's diverse home backgrounds and to ensure better continuity between home and school environments. Specific modifications of classroom curriculum and environments in free play and structured play can stimulate multicultural play in children.

## PROJECTS AND ACTIVITIES

1. Prepare a thematic play prop box that contains materials and activities that are related to a specific culture.
2. Remembering the neighborhood and community you grew up in, list play opportunities that were there and favorite play habitats. Observe the current situation, and compare the play and play habitats of children now to what existed when you played in the same neighborhood and community.
3. Design an indoor play space that you think embodies the most important principles of environmental design favorable to play behavior and development.
4. Should low-income children or children from minority backgrounds be encouraged to play in certain ways? Have a class debate.

CHAPTER 7

# Educational Play

## INTRODUCTION

> After chatting with the school principal, I finally get to Bob's Grade 2 class by 9:30. As I walk through the door, the sight dazzles me. Five groups of children are working in investigative play groups with dry cells, buzzers, low-wattage light bulbs and switches. . . . I take in the overall scene first and then edge over to the group of five children working near the window, using dry cells and a light bulb. While they have not articulated the hypothesis, I can see that they are implicitly testing the idea that an increase in the number of dry cells strung together will increase the brightness of the light. They try increasing the number of batteries to three, and the light brightens. A shout goes up from the investigators. They begin to rewire with four dry cells. By this time, their enthusiasm has attracted an audience of children from some of the other groups, who come over to observe. The four-cell hypothesis is supported, accompanied by shouts and laughter. "Try six," one observer offers, while others go back to their groups to test the same hypothesis. (Wasserman, 2000, pp. 21–22)

Play advocates claim that play-based learning activities, such as those in Bob's classroom, offer distinct advantages over more direct types of instruction. Rather than passively absorbing information and memorizing facts, children have opportunities to construct their own knowledge about electricity with help from their peers. Because concepts are connected with enjoyable play, children will tend to develop positive attitudes toward academic learning. No rewards or reinforcement are needed to get the children to learn science. Play is intrinsically motivated. In fact, when the recess bell rang in Bob's classroom during the electricity experiments, the children responded in a collective wail, "Oh, Mr. Sinclair, do we *have* to go outside today?" (Wasserman, 2000, p. 22). Imagine the different response if the second-graders had just spent an hour reading a chapter about electricity in their science textbook and then filling out a factual recall worksheet.

The concept of play-based education is not new. It can be traced back to the original play pioneers of early education—Jean Jacques Rousseau (France), Johann Pestalozzi (Switzerland), and Friedrich Froebel (Germany)—who had considerable influence on the beginnings of formal preschools during the sixteenth and seventeenth centuries in Europe (Glickman, 1984). In the United States educational play got off to a later start and has come in and out of fashion. A number of "play" schools were established in the early 1910s, such as Carolyn Pratt's famous school in the Greenwich Village area of New York City. The trend toward educational play accelerated during the 1920s and 1930s with the rise of the Child Study Movement, "progressive" education, and John Dewey's experimentalist philosophy of education (Glickman, 1984; Varga, 1991). Play then faded during the general shift toward conservatism following the Second World War. Play-related teaching strategies came back into favor during the "radical" 1960s with curricula such as inquiry-based science and new math, only to fade again under the onslaught of the back-to-basics movements during the late 1970s and early 1980s (Glickman, 1984).

Today, play remains in the center of early childhood curriculum (Drake, 2001; Fromberg, 2002; Van Hoorn, Scales, Nourot, & Alward, 1999), with attempts to even extend educational play into the primary grades (Kieff & Casbergue, 2000; Wasserman, 2000). Three factors are responsible for the efforts to keep play in education:

- *Developmentally appropriate practice.* As defined in the influential position statement by the National Association for the Education of Young Children (NAEYC), developmentally appropriate practice occurs when teachers provide learning environments, materials, and activities that match the teachers' observations of children's emerging cognitive, social, emotional, and physical development. One of the guiding principles in the NAEYC position statement is that play is at the heart of developmentally appropriate practice and should be a key instructional strategy during the early years (Bredekamp & Copple, 1997).

- *Constructivism.* The constructivist model of learning asserts that learning is an active, social process in which children build their own understandings based on experience. Bredekamp and Copple (1997) explain that "children need to form their own hypotheses and keep trying them out through social interaction, physical manipulation, and their own thought processes—observing what happens, reflecting on their findings, asking questions, and formulating answers" (p. 13). Play activities offer an ideal context for this type of active, social learning to occur.

- *Self-regulation.* Increasing attention is being given to the development of self-regulation, the set of abilities that enable children to control their behavior, engage in positive interactions with others, and become independent learners (Bodrova & Leong, 2003; Bronson, 2000). Play's intrinsic motivation and collaborative nature make it ideal for promoting this important aspect of learning.

Educational play proponents argue that carefully planned play experiences can provide developmentally appropriate opportunities for children to construct academic knowledge and skills. In addition, educational play has the added bonus of helping children become self-motivated learners.

The academic play movement, however, faces stiff opposition from two contradictory forces. The most formidable of these is the current standards movement, in which the federal and state governments and local school districts are establishing statements about what children should know and be able to do before they are permitted move on to the next level of schooling (Hewit, 2001; Morrison, 2001). This movement is accompanied by an essentialist philosophy of education that is currently embraced by the general public and by many school administrators. This philosophy, which underlies the current back-to-basics movement, maintains that the primary purpose of education is for teachers to transmit essential knowledge and skills to students (Glickman, 1984). Direct instruction has long been the method of choice for accomplishing these essentialist goals, whereas play has been dismissed as being ineffective and a waste of time. As a result, teachers face pressure to replace play-oriented activities with more direct forms of instruction that can quickly help children to meet academic standards.

The other source of opposition consists of play proponents who believe in the value of free play. These play advocates worry that play is undermined and disrupted when it is used to achieve academic ends (e.g., Götz, 1977; Sutton-Smith, 1987). Sutton-Smith has been one of the most vocal critics of instructional play activities. He once commented, "It is better to encourage children to play amongst themselves than to infect them with our own didactic play bumblings" (Sutton-Smith, 1990, p. 5). Postmodern theorists and early childhood education reconceptualists are also concerned that when play is focused on future academic outcomes, the joy and value of the here and now of play might be lost (Tobin, 1997).

The forces that oppose academic play raise contradictory objections. On the one hand, many politicians, school administrators, and members of the public worry that academic play activities are too playful and are not an efficient means for children to acquire the knowledge and skills set forth in state education standards. On the other hand, some free-play proponents claim that educational activities in these programs are not really play at all but rather are work disguised as play.

This chapter examines these conflicting perspectives in an effort to sort out the value of mixing play and educational goals. We first look at the pros and cons of educational play. Next, we examine specific examples of educationally oriented play activities, ranging from academically enriched play settings to activities on the playground. Finally, we discuss some of the barriers that teachers face when attempting to use educational play and offer some strategies for overcoming these barriers.

## FOCUS QUESTIONS

1. What is educational play?
2. When does the use of play to teach specific academic skills and concepts cross the line from play to work?
3. With the current emphasis on standards and accountability, can we afford to use play to teach academic skills, especially in kindergarten and the early grades?

4. Because many minority parents are very concerned about their children's academic progress and seem to prefer direct instruction, is it appropriate to use educational play in predominantly minority programs, such as Head Start?
5. How can we prepare future teachers to know how to engage in educational play?

## THE VALUE OF EDUCATIONAL PLAY

At first glance, the term *educational play* would seem to be an oxymoron. Play, as we have discussed at length in this book, has many characteristics that place its focus on the child: motivation, choice, the child's sense of reality, and the positive affect of the child. Education, on the other hand, tends to be external of the child: standards developed by content experts and imposed by state governments; curriculum consisting of planned instructional sequences developed by experts; and instructional strategies that are defined and selected by the teacher.

So what is educational play? We can arrive at a definition by examining the two components: education and play. Education, of course, has a wide variety of definitions. But most of these definitions include the notion of educational goals: the intended outcomes of education (Wiles & Bondi, 1998). Thus education is about achieving something at some end point—end of a curriculum unit, end of Head Start, end of first grade, or, ultimately, graduation from high school or college. These goals are often academic, such as math, literacy, and science, but also include things like problem solving, independent thinking, and making decisions responsibly. Play, by contrast, refers to activities that are nonliteral, intrinsically motivated, self-initiated, and/or more concerned with means than ends. Educational play, then, is linking educational goals, objectives, and outcomes to one or more of the significant characteristics of play.

The concept of educational play is paradoxical and controversial. To give balanced coverage, the following sections examine both the advantages and disadvantages of using play to accomplish educational goals.

### Advantages of Educational Play

Play provides two vital functions in children achieving educational goals: learning general strategies, skills, and attitudes from play itself, such as problem solving, creative thinking, positive self-esteem, and divergent thinking, and using play as a vehicle to learn other, more specific skills, such as playing a geography game to learn the names of states and their capitals, learning numbers while enjoying a game of hopscotch, and using dramatic play to increase literacy skills. All these outcomes can be taught without using play. So the question is "Why use play?"

In general, the key advantage of linking educational outcomes to play is that it enables us to teach specific educational goals through a vehicle that is, from the child's perspective, inherently self-motivating. The use of play answers one of the central dilemmas of education: how to motivate children to learn. With play teachers do not have to motivate the child because play is intrinsically motivated. More specifically, the characteristics of play, discussed in Chapter 1, make play an excellent medium for all sorts of educational learning.

**Positive Affect.** As we discussed in Chapter 1, positive affect—enjoyable, fun, full of smiles and laughter—may be one of the central characteristics of play. If children are exhibiting these characteristics, then they are most likely playing. They continue to play because it is fun, so the activity becomes self-motivating. This is one of the key advantages of educational play. If we can make education fun, children will engage in it without us having to provide other forms of motivation (rewards, punishments, threats, etc.).

Making educational activities fun can be a challenge. The concept of fun varies, depending on children's age, personality, and life experiences. What is fun for one child (e.g., playing at a water table) might not be fun for another child who has to wash dishes at home as a chore—or, worse, a punishment. We have all heard elementary school teachers bemoan that with the popularity of video and computer games and fast-paced TV programs, it is much more difficult to provide children with educational activities they view as fun.

**Free Choice.** Another characteristic of play is free choice. King (1979) found that kindergarten children believed that an activity such as block building was play if it was freely chosen by the children but work if assigned by the teacher. According to King, this choice versus teacher assignment duality is particularly important during the early years. It would seem that as children grow older, they shift from the choice versus teacher assignment paradigm toward culturally approved views of work and play. Indeed, in a later study, King (1982) found that fifth-graders considered an activity to be play if it was enjoyable, regardless of whether it was freely chosen or assigned by the teacher. But with younger children, free choice is an important criterion for play.

The concept of free choice is sometimes more a matter of belief than reality. If young children believe that they have made a free choice to engage in a certain educational activity, they will see it as more play-like, even if their "choice" is somewhat limited. Lickona (1983) gives an example of the power of choice in his book *Raising Good Children*. Although his example is about behavior, it illustrates the point. Lickona insisted that his young son hold his hand every time they crossed a street together, for obviously safety reasons. So every time they came to a street, Dr. Lickona grabbed his son's hand, and his son fought to take it away. Finally, Dr. Lickona had an idea and said to his son, "Choose which hand you want to hold as we cross the street." His son immediately put his small hand in his father's, and they peacefully crossed the street together. His son believed that he had a choice, and that was what mattered.

Choosing empowers children. Choosing which educational activity they will participate in makes children feel important and invested in the activity. In addition, choice helps to ensure that the activity is appropriate for the child's interests and abilities. When children select and pursue a play activity, the child is declaring that the activity fits into his or her zone of proximal development—often near the bottom of this zone. Then it is up to the teacher to scaffold the play to enable the child to learn the educational outcomes and to nudge the child toward higher levels of performance while at the same time making sure the activity both remains within the zone of proximal development and maintains enough of the characteristics of play that the child still feels that it is play and not work.

**Nonliterality.** In play children define the play frame on the basis of their unique experiences and view of the world. Within this play frame, attempts at academic learning become meaningful to the individual child. Writing may become meaningful to four-year-old John as he "writes" the various names of different pets for his imaginary pet store, using scribbles to represent writing. Within the play frame personal meaning takes precedence over external reality. So to John (and perhaps his playmates) his scribble writing signifies real writing. Not only does this unique context provide meaning to children's academic efforts, but it also shows the teacher how John is beginning to understand the important functions of print. In addition, John begins to view himself as a writer, increasing his motivation to learn about literacy. Play's make-believe characteristic lets him get off to an early start at being a writer.

**Means-over-Ends Orientation.** We have all seen young children work enthusiastically together to build an elaborate fort, only to pull it apart and build another one. This is because children enjoy the process of play; they are not primarily focused on achieving a product or achieving a goal. Even if they do care about the product, such as the fort, the end result (what it will look like and can do) will likely change during the process of play. This means-over-ends orientation allows children who are involved in play to focus on risk taking, experimentation, and seeking and trying out alternative approaches. There is no best way, no one correct approach or perfect product that must be produced, and the children are not going to be judged on the end product of their play.

This process-oriented characteristic of play is tremendously valuable for learning educational skills and outcomes. We know one of the reasons that young children are so good at learning second or third languages is because they take a low-risk approach to the process, whereas teens and adults are very uptight about making mistakes. Children who are learning educational concepts and skills through play are not focused on getting the right answer. Instead, they are interested in messing around with the new information: pushing it, manipulating it, trying a variety of combinations, and seeing what they can do with the new knowledge. Play provides a low-stress climate that encourages creative problem solving, divergent thinking, and risk taking.

**Making Learning Meaningful.** According to Barell (1995), "Personal meanings are those concepts, ideas, facts, and feelings that directly relate to our sense of self, and to our general attitudes, dispositions, and habits of mind" (p. 271). Personal meaning can make it easier for children to retain and retrieve new knowledge. This is because we store new information in our long-term memory in association with related pieces of information that are already in our memory (Mayer, 1996). If this new information is somehow tied to one's own unique experiences, it is learned and retained even more effectively. A research study by Rogers, Kuiper, and Kirker (1977, as quoted in Ormrod, 1999) demonstrated that only 3 to 7 percent of new information that was unrelated to what students already knew was remembered; 13 percent of information that was related to past knowledge was retained, and 30 percent of information related to the individual student's unique experiences was remembered. Meaningful learning allows new information to be organized in the context of previously learned information, and if that previously learned information is personally meaningful, the new information is learned and retrieved even better. Further, early childhood professionals know that facts learned in isolation, outside of meaningful context, are easily forgotten (Jones, 2003).

Play enables the child to assimilate incoming information into existing knowledge and to make that information personally meaningful. The nonliterality of play discussed previously creates a play frame in which internal reality takes precedence over external reality: The usual meanings of objects are ignored, and new meanings are substituted. These new meanings are imposed by the child on the basis of the child's set of personal experiences, feelings, and aspirations. For example, Jim Christie observed a group of preschoolers engaging in airport play at a dramatic-play center. One of the children who was working at the check-in counter declared that he would make tickets for the airplane. He tore a sheet of construction paper into small pieces and wrote the letter "T" on each piece. These were then distributed to the other child players and the teacher. These "passengers" then gave the make-believe tickets to a flight attendant in order to get on the plane (an elevated loft with several rows of chairs). To the child ticket-maker and to the passengers these pieces of paper represented real airline tickets. It is likely that several of the children remembered the "T"-ticket connection, building valuable knowledge about letter-sound relationships.

**Balancing the School Day.** In Chapter 2 we discussed a variety of theories of play, including the surplus-energy and recreation theories. The surplus-energy theory argues

➤ Play enables the child to assimilate incoming information into existing knowledge and to make that information personally meaningful.

that animals and people use play to get rid of built-up energy that has not been used in survival activities; the recreation theory argues that play replenishes energy lost through work and purposeful activity. Although we have critiqued both of these theories, they do seem to make sense on a very basic level: Children need a variety of activities and intensities throughout the day—quiet activities, movement, intense learning, more relaxed experiences, teacher-directed learning, groups experiences, and so on.

As we have already discussed at length throughout this book, the school day is becoming much more intense, with more demands to learn more academic skills and information. In addition, for many of our children the school day has been greatly extended. These children attend programs before and after their traditional school day. Because of demands from parents and administrators, many of these before- and after-school programs focus on academic instruction. Play provides a wonderful way to balances this longer and more intense school day—to provide the shift from intense, often teacher-directed instruction to more student-directed, pleasurable, less intense experiences. Educational play also ensures that the classroom objectives can be met while providing our children with their needed diversity of experiences, interactions, and intensities throughout the school day.

## Potential Disadvantages of Educational Play

One reason educational play is not as widely used as we believe it should be in early childhood programs and elementary schools is because it does not fit neatly within what many view as the traditional educational enterprise. Just as the characteristics of play can enhance teaching and learning, these same characteristics can sometimes impede the educational process. In the following subsections we discuss some potential disadvantages of academic play.

**Progress Is Difficult to Document.** Public schools are under more and more pressure to document student progress. Politicians who allocate tax money to public schools and the public at large expect that students will meet grade-level standards in each academic subject area. These standards were developed by national professional organizations (the National Council of Teachers of Mathematics, National Association for the Education of Young Children, International Reading Association, etc.) and then adopted or modified by state departments of education. Local school districts then adopt these standards and develop policies based on student progress in each content area. In some cases, as in Texas and Colorado, state-mandated tests are used to report progress to the public on these standards.

Accountability is about documenting progress. When children play, it is very difficult to document exactly what they have learned. A classic case is vocabulary. Curriculum designers and specialists usually include learning new words as an indicator of content learning. The assumption is that if you know the meaning of a word, you also know the complex ideas it represents. Playing with words generally does not teach children one-to-one correspondence between a word and its official definition; rather, play can help children learn how to use words flexibly, constructively, in various contexts, and under various circumstances. Bruner calls this "building ideas" and "problem solving" with the ideas words represent (Bruner, 1972; Sylva, Bruner, & Genova, 1976). This higher level of vocabulary learning is very difficult to test or document.

It seems that most tests evaluate the basic knowledge level of Bloom's taxonomy—the bottom, basic recall level. Play, on the other hand, teaches children the higher levels of application, synthesis, and analysis (Bloom, 1956). Thus there is often a mismatch between what accountability tests measure and what children learn from play.

**Some Children Avoid Hard Work.** Learning takes persistence, attention, focus, and often hard work. Not all learning is pleasurable, and students need to understand and accept this fact. In an age of computer games, fast-paced, attention-keeping videos, and attractive TV fare for young children such as *Sesame Street* and *Learning between the Lions,* many children grow up believing that life is generally pleasurable and that they need to make little effort to be entertained or educated. Further, as we have moved from an agrarian economy in which young children were expected to work hard on the family farm to a culture in which many young children engage in no work of any kind, the view that life should be easy and enjoyable has been reinforced. Teachers often report that children refuse to do certain tasks because they are "boring," "no fun," or "too hard." One obvious disadvantage of educational play is that it can reinforce the belief held by many children that education should always be enjoyable and that effort and hard work are not needed to learn and grow.

**Play Takes Too Much Time.** Francis Wardle recently read the homework policy of the Denver Public Schools as part of a project of one of his graduate students. In part, the policy argues that there is not enough time in the school day for children to learn everything they need to know and therefore homework is needed to lengthen the school day. If public schools believe that they do not have enough time to teach everything a child needs to learn during the school day, it is easy to see how educational play gets shortchanged. Play takes time. In fact, Christie and Wardle (1992) suggest that play activity usually requires thirty minutes at a minimum. Many of the types of educational play described later in this chapter require even more time to set up and carry out. There is no question that the same academic skills and concepts could be taught faster by using direct teacher instruction. It is easy to see why administrators and teachers, who face increasing demands to improve children's academic achievement, find the short, direct approach extremely attractive and tend to shy away from time-consuming educational play activities.

**Teachers Are Unprepared to Use Play.** The first item under Standard II, Promoting Child Development and Learning, of the Guidelines for Preparation of Early Childhood Professionals (NAEYC, 1996a, p. 71) states, "Teachers Understand the Central Role of Play in Child Development." This standard goes on to state that teachers must know how to include play within their daily curriculum for young children. The problem is that many early childhood teachers have degrees that are essentially elementary education degrees, with a couple of early childhood education classes added. Silva and Johnson (1999) reported that principals prefer to hire teachers with K–6 certification rather than a preschool–third grade certificate to teach young children because this provides them with more flexibility to move teachers within the school. As a result, many kindergarten and elementary-grade teachers have little or no teacher preparation in the advantages and uses of play to teach educational goals and objectives.

Additionally, the current emphasis on academic standards encourages teachers to use direct instruction rather than play to learn fundamental educational skills and concepts (Jones, 2003). As a result, teacher education programs and inservice professional development programs need to focus on increasing teacher's knowledge of the importance of play and educational play strategies (Benham, Miller, & Kontos, 1988; Bowman, 1990).

**BOX 7.1**

## Convincing Teachers of the Value of Educational Play

This document can be used to stimulate discussion in a teacher preparation course or it can be handed out to teachers in an early childhood program or school.

**Why Educational Play?**

With the increasing pressure on schools to teach content standards and be accountable to the public, is there still a place for play in early childhood and elementary school programs? How does play help to teach the standards we are all required to meet?

- *Provides meaningful learning.* Students who learn new concepts, ideas, and vocabulary in a context that is meaningful to them will learn these concepts more easily and retain them longer.
- *Provides practice.* We all know that children need to practice new skills and concepts to be able to internalize and use this new learning. Play provides wonderful opportunities to practice in a variety of ways.
- *Enables children to control.* More and more children lack control over any part of their lives. Some children have carefully choreographed schedules that take them from school to sports or childcare and then run them home to repeat the schedule. Other children come from such chaotic and disorganized homes that they lack any control of their physical and social environment. Play gives children the control they so desperately need and often lack.
- *Develops flexibility and creativity.* Higher-level thinking skills and problem-solving abilities are required in an ever more complex world. Therefore children need to learn to be creative and flexible thinkers, and play teaches children to apply newly learned skills and concepts in a variety of situations, in new combinations, and in different contexts. This skill then transfers into problem solving and creative thinking.
- *Makes learning fun.* Although not all learning can be fun and children obviously need to learn to engage in challenging learning activities, it is also important to make learning pleasurable so that children will continue to learn, and it is important to keep more students in school. After all, the average kindergarten student has at a minimum twelve years of school ahead (and a three-year-old has at least fifteen years), and if a child dislikes school, chances are he or she will not succeed or will even drop out of school.
- *Provides a break from intense school activities.* All of us need to take a break from intense, focused activities, and children are no different. As we increase

pressure on them to learn academic skills, we must allow for periodic relief, rest, and relaxation: play.

- *Allows children to move.* All young children, especially young boys, need lots and lots of opportunities to move around. Their bodies are not mature enough to stay quiet and seated for long periods of time, and their minds lack the power of concentration needed for long, uninterrupted activity. Play enables us to meet the need all young children have for physical activity; educational play allows us to meet this need while also teaching and reinforcing educational skills and concepts.

As we place more and more pressure on our youngest students to succeed academically, we need to increase the regular play opportunities for these children in the early childhood program and school. We should also encourage parents to encourage their children to play at home.

**Play Creates Conflict with Parents.** We have discussed throughout this book the opposition to play by many parents. Research has shown that parents tend to value academic knowledge and skills more than early childhood teachers do and that this tendency might be more common in minority and low-income parents (Dunn & Kontos, 1997). Although parents often believe that there is no place for any kind of play in their child's program, they may accept play as a break from hard academic work or as a time to gain energy for academic pursuits. An elementary school in Colorado recently introduced yoga as a tool to provide this needed break and revitalization. But many parents do not believe that learning important academic skills and concepts should be pleasurable or meaningful. They view their child's education through the lens of the memory of their own educational experiences. Unfortunately, these memories can sometimes be distorted. For example, many parents started school in kindergarten or first grade, yet they often transfer these memories to their children's preschool experience; or parents might tend to remember many of the more negative experiences from their early education and believe that this is simply the way it is supposed to be (Wardle, 2003).

The use of extensive educational play in early childhood programs can at best cause misunderstanding on the part of parents and at worst cause disagreements that lead to a child's being removed and placed into a more rigorous program. As we have discussed elsewhere, this is true of both middle-class and low-income parents. Therefore there is a pressing need for teachers to educate parents about the value of educational play. Box 5.2 (page 145) contains a number of suggestions on how to accomplish this, including play fact sheets, newsletter items, and documentation of classroom play activities (e.g., photographs and videotape). Kieff and Casbergue (2000) also suggest that teachers involve parents in the development of academically enriched play centers by sending home lists of needed materials and having evening or weekend work parties to set up the centers.

## Considering the Pros and Cons of Educational Play

Given that this is a book about play and education, it will probably not come as a great surprise that the three authors all believe that the advantages of educational play outweigh the potential disadvantages. The key is for teachers to take steps to maximize the positive features of educational play and to minimize the negative ones. Here are some examples of how this can be done:

- *Provide a balance of educational and recreational play.* King (1987) has identified two positive types of play that are found in schools: instrumental play, which is educational play that is used as means for helping children learn academic skills and knowledge, and recreational play, which is free play that occurs outside the classroom at recess and before and after school, such as games (e.g., jacks, hopscotch, tag), sports (e.g., kickball, soccer, tetherball), and rough-and-tumble activity. It is important that children at all grade levels have ample opportunities to engage in both types of play—play to learn and play to have fun. This meets the objections of both the academic essentialists (provided that the educational play is focused on skills and knowledge included in educational standards) and the play purists. A box feature by Rebecca Lamphere in Chapter 12 discusses some of the challenges to keeping time for recess—the main avenue for recreational play—in the school schedule.
- *Make educational play challenging.* Educational play experiences can be fun and challenging at the same time. Many of the play experiences described in the next section require considerable effort and attention from children. Even if a play activity is at the low end of child's zone of proximal development, Chapter 9 details a number of ways in which teachers can get involved in the activity and up the ante to make the activity more challenging for more capable children. This eliminates the potential problem of play eroding children's work ethic.
- *Use play as a context for authentic assessment.* Although some types of skills and knowledge do not lend themselves to play-based assessment (such as the vocabulary example earlier in this chapter), many do. Play both promotes and reflects development. Teachers need to take advantage of this reflective quality of play. As we detailed in Chapter 3, educational play activities provide many opportunities to observe, document, and assess what children know and can do. For evaluating higher-order types of thinking skills, play can often provide more accurate information than standardized tests.

## TYPES OF EDUCATIONAL PLAY

Educational play experiences are designed to help children learn academic skills and knowledge and strengthen cognitive processes and self-regulation. In the sections that follow we describe four basic types of academically oriented play activities: academically enriched play centers, games, simulations, and playground activities. Both early childhood and primary-grade examples will be given for each type of educational play.

### Academically Enriched Play Centers

Dramatic play centers are areas of the classroom that are designed to stimulate sociodramatic play. A well-designed dramatic play center can provide children with opportunities to develop oral language, cognitive, and social skills. The basic ingredients for developmentally stimulating dramatic play setting are a well-arranged space for play (Chapter 6), theme-related props (Chapter 8), adequate play time (Chapter 9), and appropriate forms of teacher involvement in play (Chapter 9).

The learning potential of sociodramatic play centers can be greatly expanded by adding one more ingredient: academically related props and materials. The home or housekeeping center, for example, is typically equipped with miniature wooden or plastic kitchen furniture and appliances, dolls, and other domestic play props. Kathy Roskos (2001) gives an example of how a traditional home corner can be enriched by adding a variety of home-related literacy materials:

> Boost the amount of print in the play space. You can do this by:
>
> - Including an abundance of environmental print, such as grocery packages, coupons, a calendar, emergency number decals, magazines, recipe cards, telephone book (a smaller, local one), and other print we see around us everyday.
> - Providing writing utensils, such as pencils and markers, assorted paper and notepads, play money, blank recipe cards, greeting cards, envelopes, storybooks (to read to dolls), cookbooks (for kids), a message board, magnetic letters, and the like.
> - Labeling objects and play things, such as on/off knobs on the play stove, places for dress-up hats and coats; baskets for fruit and vegetables; and other storage containers and shelves.
> - Displaying print and messages gathered from other activities, such as language experience charts from day trips, recipes from whole class cooking, enlarged versions of upcoming community events, collages of logos and labels (made by children), and children's work. (p. 72)

The literacy enrichment strategy can be applied to other dramatic play themes, from the grocery store to a mechanic's garage (see Table 7.1). Using the strategy with a variety of themes increases the range of literacy activities and routines to which children are exposed and also increases the likelihood that the play will match the interests of individual children.

Descriptive research shows that this print-enrichment strategy is effective in increasing the range and amount of literacy behaviors during play, thus allowing children to practice their emerging skills and show what they have learned (Morrow & Rand, 1991; Neuman & Roskos, 1992). The gains in literacy activity during play tend to be quite large. For example, Neuman and Roskos (1992) reported that the average number of literacy behaviors per play session increased from 1.7 to 7.3 for children in the print-enriched play setting versus an increase from 1.4 to 1.5 for the control group. Evidence is also accumulating that this strategy helps children to learn important literacy concepts and skills, such as knowledge about the functions of writing (Vukelich, 1993), the ability to recognize play-related print (Neuman & Roskos, 1993), and comprehension strategies such as self-checking and self-correction (Neuman & Roskos, 1997).

In addition to these gains in literacy, the print-enriched play setting strategy has been found to enhance the quality of children's dramatic play. Detailed analyses of videotaped play sessions in the Neuman and Roskos (1992) study revealed that the literacy prop group's play sequences were eight times longer and much more complex than those of the control group. These effects were maintained over the entire seven months of the study, indicating that novelty of the literacy props was not a factor.

**TABLE 7.1 Props for Academically Enriched Play Centers**

| | |
|---|---|
| *Business Office* | *Gas Station/Garage* |
| Pencils, pens, markers | Pencils, pens, markers |
| Notepads | Employee name tags |
| Telephone message forms | Signs ("Gas," "Pay Inside," "Regular $3.00/gallon") |
| Calculator | Cash register |
| Calendar | Cardboard gas pump with numbers for prices |
| Typewriter | Notepads (for work orders and receipts) |
| Stationery, envelopes | Credit cards and play money (child-made) |
| File folders | Empty product containers (oil bottles, auto parts) |
| Wall signs ("Open/Closed") | Auto repair manuals |
| Order forms | Road maps |
| *Restaurant* | *Post Office* |
| Pencils | Pencils, pens, markers |
| Notepads | Stationery and envelopes |
| Menus | Stamps |
| Wall signs ("Deli," "No smoking") | Mailboxes |
| Bank checks | Address labels |
| Cookbooks | Wall signs ("Line Starts Here," price list) |
| Product containers | Scale for weighing mail |
| Coupons | Cash register |
| Cash register | |
| *Grocery Store* | *Veterinarian's Office* |
| Pencils, pens, markers | Pencils, pens, markers |
| Notepads | Appointment book |
| Bank checks | Wall signs ("Waiting Room," "Keep Pet in Carrier") |
| Wall signs ("Supermarket") | Patient charts |
| Shelf labels for store areas ("Meat") | Prescription forms |
| Cash register | Pet care brochures |
| Product containers | Empty pet food bags and boxes |
| Newspaper ads and coupons | |
| *Airport/Airplane* | *Library* |
| Pencils, pens, markers | Pencils |
| Tickets | Books |
| Bank checks | Shelf labels for books ("ABCs," "Animals") |
| Luggage tags | Computer |
| Magazines (on board plane) | Wall signs ("Quiet," "Reference") |
| Air sickness bags with printed instructions | Library cards |
| Price lists, schedules | Checkout cards for books |
| Maps | Cash register (for fines) |

Thus it appears that the print-enriched play setting strategy creates a win-win situation: Children gain valuable literacy experience, and the quality of their play improves.

The academic enrichment strategy also can be used with other subject areas, such as mathematics and science. Van Hoorn, Scales, Nourot, and Alward (1999) give an example of how a teacher added numeracy props to grocery store play center to help her students meet the school district's kindergarten mathematics standards:

> According to her district's kindergarten math curriculum, Marilyn is expected to teach rote counting and recognition of numerals from 1–20. She also decides to experiment with turning the dramatic-play center into a store. In addition to a balance scale, she is lucky enough to obtain an old hanging scale. She includes a Bates stamp with numbers that the children can rotate and change. She has several hand calculators and an old adding machine borrowed from a third grade teacher. She also includes tubs of small objects, like Unifix cubes, that can be sold. She is delighted to find that she now has a use for out-of-date coupons and the weekly ads from local supermarkets. The pictures and numbers make the messages understandable for customers. The store is now open for business! On opening day, workers and customers discover that Marilyn has forgotten an important component: They need money. This leads to a group project making bills and coins. (p. 175)

Marilyn has designed a play setting that provides opportunities for children to recognize numbers and to count—important objectives in her kindergarten math curriculum. She uses this play center as an alternative to more traditional forms of instruction, such as direct instruction and worksheets. The addition of math-related props transformed the center into an ideal environment for her students to learn about numbers and counting.

Play centers can be enriched to promote learning other curriculum areas such as science and social studies. Roskos (1994) helped two kindergarten teachers develop play settings that were closely connected with science content presented in whole-group instruction. For example, during a six-week unit on winter, the teachers taught children how to read thermometers and how to record information using symbols for degrees. To connect this content with play, the teachers supplied dramatic play centers with various types of thermometers, notepads and pencils for recording data, materials for an experiment measuring the temperature of water under different circumstances, lab coats for dress-up, and printed matter related to the topic of measuring temperature. Children's play in these academically enriched play centers was videotaped and analyzed. Results showed that a majority of the children's interactions were related to the content-oriented activity available in the centers (e.g., using thermometers). What was more impressive, the children's engagement in these content-oriented activities persisted across the entire play period. The children did not shift to off-task activities such as visiting with friends or other forms of play. Roskos (1994) concluded that "the combination of setting cues (e.g., the 'lab'), objects (i.e., the experiment, paper and writing tools), and opportunities for peer interaction around a common purpose appeared to create sufficient conditions for enjoyment that urged children to persist in the content-focused task as a form of play activity" (p. 10).

Jarrett (1997) describes a number of ways to incorporate science and mathematics concepts into dramatic play centers. She includes lists of props for setting up a math/science-oriented doctor's office, supermarket, zoo, and museum. For example, she recommends that the following materials be added to a "fix-it shop" play center: simple tools, such as screwdrivers and adjustable wrenches; fasteners, such as nuts, bolts, and glue; old appliances such as toasters and door bells; batteries and wires; and low-voltage light bulbs, such as those used in flashlights. Jarrett warns teachers that this center will require more supervision than other play settings. She recommends cutting off electric cords before allowing children to play with appliances. She also warns against allowing children to disassemble television sets or computers because of the danger of shocks even when the items are unplugged.

## Games

Games are activities "in which an individual or team of individuals play or compete against one another with an agreed-upon set of rules, a limited time, and a means of scoring" (Clegg, 1991). As we discussed in Chapter 3, games are a cognitively advanced form of play that require children to conform to external rules. Piaget (1965) studied the development of children's game-playing abilities by asking them to teach him how to play marbles. He found four general stages in children's game play: (1) motor and individual play, during which children explore the properties of game materials; (2) egocentric play, during which children begin to try to follow other people's rules without much success; (3) incipient cooperation, in which children see the necessity of following rules; and (4) codification of rules, in which children learn to

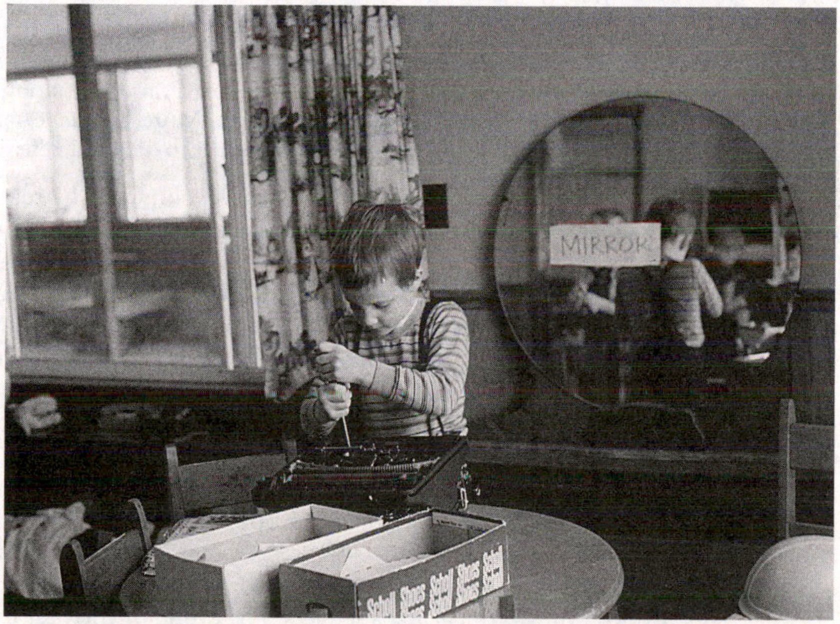


➤ Jarrett (1997) recommends that old appliances and simple tools such as screwdrivers be added to incorporate science and math in dramatic play.

establish elaborate systems of rules and can come to agreement when disagreements arise about rules. The last two stages emerged quite late in Piaget's research—incipient cooperation at age seven to eight and codification of rules at age eleven to twelve, although DeVries (1998) reports that she has observed these stages years earlier with children who had considerable game-playing experience.

From a developmental perspective, "Games are an ideal candidate for an intersection between formal school and children's play" (Fernie, 1988, p. 7). Games can offer a highly enjoyable means for children to learn new academic skills and to practice skills that have already been taught. Of course, games need to be tailored to the children's developmental levels. Very young children are often frustrated by the external rules of games. However, Kieff and Casbergue (2000) explain that simple motor games such as Ring Around the Rosy and Duck, Duck, Goose enable young children to gain experience with rule-bound activity in an enjoyable situations. With age and experience, children become able to enjoy manipulation and coordination games (e.g., tiddlywinks), card games (e.g., old maid), board games (e.g., Monopoly), knowledge games (e.g., Junior Scrabble, Trivial Pursuit), computer and video games (e.g., Super Mario Brothers), strategy and fantasy games (e.g., Risk, Dungeons and Dragons), and competitive sports (e.g., baseball, Ping-Pong) (National Toy Council, 1997).

Games can help to promote general development. For example, DeVries (1998) discusses how group games promote children's self-regulation and social and moral development by "providing a context in which children can voluntarily submit themselves to rules. Children are free to exercise their autonomy by choosing to play and choosing to follow rules" (p. 412). Kieff and Casbergue (2000) explain how group games also promote language development and perspective taking:

> Every game with rules requires children to come to a shared understanding of how the game will be played. Often significant negotiation among players is needed when children have differing interpretations of particular rules; this negotiation always entails discussion and explanations of points of view. More language may be used when differences cannot be resolved, and children turn to an adult referee. (p. 189)

They point out that these games also promote social development by requiring children to share, take turns, cooperate, be sensitive to other players' viewpoints, and delay gratification.

Games can also be used to promote the learning of academic skills and knowledge. Casbergue and Kieff (1998) offer a number of examples of how traditional games, such as jacks and marbles, offer children opportunities to learn basic concepts in mathematics and science. For example, when children play jacks, they must constantly use concepts of addition, multiplication, and division to determine which jacks to pick up. Casberque and Kieff explain that the game of dominoes focuses children's attention on one-to-one correspondence, the concept of higher and lower numbers, and basic counting skills. Marbles provides opportunities to learn basic science concepts such as trajectory and velocity.

In addition to traditional games, games can also be specially designed by teachers to provide opportunities to learn academic skills. Some of the best examples of instructional games are contained in the constructivist mathematics curricula developed by Constance Kamii (1985, 1989). Take, for example, Hundred Board, a game from Kamii's (1989) second-grade mathematics program that consists of a blank

10 × 10 grid and 100 tiles numbered 1 to 100. The tiles are placed upside down, and each player selects eight tiles and keeps them face up in front of him or her. One of the remaining tiles is turned up and placed in its appropriate space on the grid. For example, 68 would be placed six rows down and eight columns to the right. The players then take turns placing tiles on the grid that touch a side or corner of a tile that is already on the board. For example, if 68 is on the board, then 57, 58, 59, 67, 69, 77, 78, and 79 can be played. The game helps children learn about our base-10 number system and provides experience with finding numbers that are one more, one less, ten more, or ten less than a given number.

Kamii and Lewis (1992) explain the advantages of using games over traditional drill-and-practice worksheets:

> 1. *In games the motivation to work comes from the children.* Children beg to play games. In contrast, most children complete worksheets because they are externally motivated by games or stickers or afraid of consequences such as missing recess. . . .
> 2. *In games children invent their own strategies and ways of achieving their goals.* If children play a board game with one die, for example, we simply introduce a second die and let them figure out what to do. . . . When worksheets are used, children repeat the same kind of calculation over and over, with only slight variations. Worksheets thus promote mechanical repetition and mental passivity. . . .
> 3. *In games, children supervise and correct each other.* If one player takes a 3 and an 8 in Tens [a card game in which players can only use pairs of cards that make a total of 10], for example, another player is likely to object immediately. Immediate feedback from a peer is much more effective than worksheets corrected by the teacher. Worksheets are usually returned the next day, and young children cannot remember and do not care what they did yesterday. (pp. 90–91)

In effective educational games the natural activity of game playing is linked to the academic curriculum. Unfortunately, in our work-dominated elementary schools many "educational" games violate basic principles of play and games. Kieff and Casbergue (2000) provide an example of a first-grade teacher's treasure hunt game, which was intended to help children learn sight words from the school district's reading program:

> I made a simple Treasure Hunt game board with thirty squares drawn along a curving path decorated to look like an underwater scene, and also constructed a simple spinner. I used some Disney *Little Mermaid* characters on both the board and the spinner since I know how popular the video is with children this age. I taught the children how to spin and then move the correct number of spaces. . . . When the children landed on a space with a treasure chest, they got to pick a card from the treasure pile in the middle of the board and then read the word written on the card. If they read the word correctly, they got to put the card in their treasure pile. If they could not read it, the word had to go back into the pile. (p. 17)

It turns out that this "game" was not very successful. The children did not want to play the game. When forced to play it, they used the game pieces in an inappropriate manner. In the teacher's own words, here is what happened:

> They argued about everything: whose turn it was, what number the spinner was really pointing to, whether a spin counted or not, even what word someone had said when he had tried to read a card!

> Even worse, they didn't stay focused on the game. I'd see them grabbing the spinner and flicking it to see who could make it go the fastest. Other times, they'd take turns just spinning to see who could get the highest number, and not even move their pieces or try to read the words. Once, I saw them using the cards to try to build homes! They seemed to do everything *but* play the game like it was supposed to be played. (Kieff & Casbergue, 2000, p. 18)

The problem with the treasure hunt activity is that it is not a real game. Rather, it is an example of a pseudo-game. Fernie (1988) points out that these gamelike activities are not truly games for the following reason:

- The rules were not negotiated or agreed on by the players; rather, they were set by the teacher.
- Peer interaction is replaced with a public performance (reading the card).
- The playful tension of winning or losing is replaced by the serious adult standard of "right" and "wrong" answers.

In addition, the activity relied on external motivation and did not involve any real fantasy. It is interesting that the children managed to turn the treasure hunt activity into a real game on their own—by coming up with their own rules and outcomes (e.g. the person who can spin the spinner the fastest is the winner).

## Simulations

Simulations are games that are based on a model of a real situation and are designed to teach principles that operate in that situation (Clegg, 1991). Role playing is used to increase students' personal involvement in the activity. In genuine simulation games players act out well-defined roles and encounter decision-making situations that require them to choose from designated options. There are also less structured simulations that give players more control over their roles and actions.

Simulations are particularly well suited to the elementary grades. They tend to be more complex than dramatic play and other types of games and lend themselves to teaching academic concepts and skills. Because the players engage in role playing and fantasy, elementary-grade students regard simulations as being playful and fun. The role-playing feature of these complex games also leads to high levels of engagement and effort.

As we will discuss in Chapter 11, high-quality computer simulation games have become available in recent years that can help children learn academic skills and content. *Sim City,* the pioneer among this type of computer game, can help students learn a variety of social studies concepts encompassing government and economics. Players set up their own city—buy land, build roads, set up utilities, establish businesses, confront environmental issues, conduct elections, and so on—and encounter situations that are very similar to real life. *The Sims* and *Sims2* are extremely popular "spin offs." In *The Sims,* players create an entire neighborhood of Sim-people and have an opportunity to control many aspects of their lives. *Sims2* takes the simulation to the next level and allows players to direct the journey of their Sims' lives over the span of their entire lifetime, from infancy to adulthood.

**BOX 7.2**

## *Some Educational Simulation Software Programs*

**Sim City 4**
Publisher: Electronic Arts
Ages: 9 and up
Academic area: social studies
One of the best-selling simulations of all time, Sim City gives children the opportunity to be a mayor and run the major aspects of a city government. Players can zone different parts of their city to control for growth and determine where specific city services such as hospitals and schools are located. A local newspaper provides updates on the city's progress and the mayor's popularity, and maps and graphs show how the city compares to neighboring communities with respect to variables such as property values.

**Oregon Trail II—Anniversary**
Publisher: Riverdeep
Ages: 10 to adult
Academic subject areas: history, geography, and social studies
Players take on the roles of pioneers during the 1800s and choose to travel on one of three trails: the Oregon, Mormon, or California Trail. Players also can select their level of expertise as a Greenhorn, Adventurer, or Trail Blazer to vary the difficulty of the adventure. Players also have the option of keeping an online journal of the activities and characters that they meet.

**Where in the World Is Carmen Sandiego? (Deluxe)**
Publisher: Broderbund
Ages: 9 to adult
Academic subject areas: history, geography, and social studies
Carmen Sandiego, a supercriminal, and her band of thieves are stealing treasures from all over the world. Players take on the role of detective and try to gather evidence to identify the thieves and where they are located. Players use a map and a geography book (provided) to plan their chase. When players have sufficient evidence, they make an arrest and take the thieves to court. In addition to learning about geography, players also learn to take notes, use reference materials, and analyze information.

*Source:* School District #42 Project Files, Educational Software/CDs and Peripherals. (n.d.). Retrieved July 18, 2003, from http://www.schdist42.bc.ca/ProjectInfo/Reviews/edsoft3.html#SC2000+

Of course, simulations are not limited to computer software. Teachers can create their own simulations to teach academic skills and concepts. Jim Christie recalls that when he taught fourth grade in the 1970s, a fifth-grade teacher at his school used an elaborate simulation to teach social studies content. The simulation started with a giant map of an island being put up on a classroom wall. The students then imagined that they were passengers on an airliner that had crash-landed on the island. The survivors had the task of creating a community and setting up a government. Over the course of the simulation, which lasted about six weeks, the students learned many important social studies concepts and research skills.

More than two decades later, Jim Christie visited the Hazelwood Infant School in Manchester, England, to view literacy-enriched play centers. One of the intermediate-grade teachers had set up a real estate agency in her classroom as part of a simulation to help students learn reading, writing, and mathematics skills. The students pretended that they were real estate agents and selected properties in their neighborhood to list and sell. They visited the buildings and homes and gathered information so that property spec sheets could be prepared. This involved taking photographs, measuring room dimensions, researching ads in the newspaper to determine selling price, and so forth. This simulation, which integrated all aspects of the academic curriculum, was very popular with the students—and very educational.

## Playground Activities

The possibilities of educational play on the outdoor playground are endless. The secret is to provide activities that are developmentally appropriate and that conform to at least some of the characteristics of play. Free choice, process orientation, and positive affect are three good indicators of whether the child is involved in play. Teachers need to know their children well enough to select, create, and model meaningful activities. Here are a few general ideas for encouraging educational play on the playground.

**Science.** Obviously, the ideal place to study science is outside! After all, science is about studying natural phenomena, including what Forman and Kuschner (1984) call transformations—growth, dying, decomposing, drying, changing shape in the wind, erosion processes, the path the snake makes as it glides through the sand, the slow unfolding of new leaves in the springtime, and so on. And because young children are natural scientists—wanting to know why, how, how much, and for what purpose—science, young children, and the outdoors are a perfect fit.

Another important aspect of science is the scientific method, which involves creating a hypothesis and then making observations to prove or disprove the hypothesis. These processes can be developed with young children on an outdoor playground. Teachers can help children to carefully observe natural phenomena: the way the sun moves across the sky, the changing length of shadows, how vegetables grow, and so on. Hypothesis testing is simply making predictions on the basis of these observations. Teachers can promote hypothesis testing by asking questions such as "How big do you think the corn will get?" "How many eggs do you think are in the magpie's nest?" "Will it rain this afternoon?" and "Whose car will go down the slide the fastest?" Then, of course, the teacher needs to help children carefully observe what happens and then decide, on the basis of these observations, whether or not their hypotheses were correct. It is obvious how easy it is to make this process a game; it is also obvious that many of these activities can take on playlike qualities if the teacher is sensitive to the child's need to control the activity, enjoy it, and keep the focus on the process. This is easy because most of science is about process.

Although science outdoors can capitalize on observing natural phenomena, outdoor play can also help children to understand physical science: damming and redirecting water; making slopes with boards, crates, and small cars; using boards and other loose parts to study leverage; and the use of wheels to move heavy objects (wagons, tricycles, etc.). Here are a few specific ideas that Francis Wardle has developed for including science in the outdoor playground:

- *Sundial.* Create a sundial with children by selecting a flat area that is located away from traffic and in the sun all day. Then place a five-foot pole in the ground in the middle of the area. The pole can be a broomstick, 2 × 4, dowel, or similar object. The main thing is that it is straight. Observe the shadow of the pole every hour, and mark the concrete or surface in some way. Write on these markers the hour for each position. Then have the children tell time when they come out to play or during their play time.

- *Shadows.* When the sun is low, have children stand against a solid object in a line to cast their shadow on the ground. Measure the length of their shadow with a tape measure, then record the length of the shadow on a sheet of paper. Graph the results.

- *Weeds.* Pick a section of the garden that you and the children weed regularly. Pick another section that is not weeded. Have children observe the different results of the weeded and unweeded sections on the growth of the flowers and vegetables. Talk about the results.

- *Birds.* Leave birdseed on a bird feeder away from noise and children. Help children to quietly observe the birds as the children first come to the playground. Note the names of the different birds that use the feeder, and record these on a chart. Older children can record the birds that stay all year and those that migrate in the spring and fall.

- *Planting vegetables or flowers.* Any activity in the garden that involves planting vegetables and flowers, caring for them (weeding and watering), and harvesting the ripe fruit and mature vegetables creates opportunities for scientific inquiry. What is important is to help children observe what is going on: the initial shoots as the seeds germinate, how plants grow from day today, why we have to weed and water plants, the formation of buds and flowers, holes and cuts in leaves from various pests and birds, the development of seeds and fruits, and so on. Good scientists are good observers. Help children become good observers of the world around them.

- *Velocity.* Have children select a variety of things that roll on an incline: small cars, balls, cotton spools, round blocks, beads, and so on. Take these objects and toys to the slide, and have one child situated at the top of the slide. Have this child pair off different items and toys and let them roll down the slide. For each race, have the other children at the bottom of the slide declare the winner. By a process of elimination, determine which of the objects and toys goes the fastest. Ask the children to speculate why it was faster than the other objects or toys.

➤ Any activity in the garden that involves preparing the soil, planting vegetables and flowers, caring for them, and then harvesting the ripe fruit and vegetables creates opportunities for science inquiry.

## Math

Math is not just about numbers. It is about quantity, relationships, patterns, and measurement. It is about shapes, volume, area, and length. And it is about timelines, graphs, patterns, sorting, and categories (National Council of Teachers of Mathematics, 2000). Here are some specific ideas that Francis Wardle has developed to encourage mathematical play in outdoor settings:

- *Collecting stones.* Have children collect as many stones on the playground as they can in ten minutes. Help students count their stones to see who has the most. Help students line up their stones according to size, from smallest to biggest. Then have the children split their stones into two groups: small stones and big stones.
- *Hopscotch.* Draw a hopscotch design on the concrete or asphalt with chalk. Draw numbers in the squares. Teach children the traditional hopscotch game.
- *Traffic signs.* Have children help make speed limit signs for the tricycle or bike path. Dowels, old mop handles, 2 × 4s, or similar objects make good sign posts. The actual sign itself can be made from cardboard or thin plywood. Make speed limit signs for 5 mph, 10 mph, 20 mph, 15 mph, and 30 mph.
- *Charting tomatoes.* There are many math activities that can be done in the garden. Children can count the number of tomato plants that have been planted. Put

this amount on a chart near the garden (one that will not wash away in the rain). When the plants begin to bear tomatoes, count the number of plants again, then count the number of tomatoes that are picked from each plant. Show on your chart the number of tomatoes from each plant by drawing a small tomato next to the plant. As you add tomatoes, you begin to create a bar graph. On the basis of this graph, see which plant produces the most tomatoes.

- *Market.* On a parent day, create a market to sell produce and flowers from the garden. Have children help make price tags for each product: "Tomatoes, 5¢ each," and so on. You can give out paper money to parents or use real money and have the children sell their vegetables.

- *Racing against the clock.* Set up a course on the grass with a beginning line and ending ribbon. Have volunteers run as fast as they can from the start line to the finish line. Use a stopwatch to record their times. Keep a list of names and times. Then, with the children's help, graph the results on a large piece of paper. If students enjoy this activity, repeat it with variations: skipping, hopping, running backward, and so on.

- *Measuring rainfall.* Buy a rain gauge from a hardware store. Set it up in a playground area away from activity. (In fact you could create a whole science area in a corner of the playground.) After a heavy rainfall, check the amount of rain in the gauge. Help the children see the measurements on the container and begin to understand that the more rain that falls, the fuller the container; the fuller the container, the more rain that fell.

**Literacy.** The outdoor playground lends itself well to all sorts of writing and reading activities. Playground equipment manufacturers have been aggressively marketing "learning panels," many of which include alphabet charts (Wardle, 1994). As we will explain in Chapter 12, these are rather artificial add-ons that do not lend themselves to being incorporated into children's play activities. Here are several more effective ways to incorporate literacy into outdoor play:

- *Outdoor writing.* Have children practice writing letters, numbers, shapes, and patterns on the sidewalk with paint or chalk.

- *Signs.* Help children to make signs for outdoor dramatic play centers (e.g., McDonald's) and traffic signs for tricycle paths.

- *Obstacle course.* Paint obstacle courses on the sidewalk with written directions ("Start here," arrows, "Do not enter," etc.).

- *Dramatic play.* Have children take on the role of police officer and write tickets for speeding tricycles. Other outdoor roles that encourage literacy include nature scientist (take notes about plants, insects, and other living things found on playground), mechanic (write up repair bills for fixing tricycles), forest ranger/game warden (citations for illegal activity), and the like.

- *Story reading.* Good books should not just be used indoors. Find a quiet spot under the tree or on the picnic table, and read to those who want to listen. Set a specific time every day when children know that you will read, a time when they are tired of running and climbing and are ready to settle down.

- *Story drama.* Encourage children to reenact stories in outdoor settings. For example, after *The Three Billy Goats Gruff* is read indoors during storybook time, a bridge could be built on the playground, using loose parts (crates, a large board, etc.). The children could then reenact the story, taking turns being the billy goats and the troll. Or *Little Red Riding Hood* can be acted out with the grandmother being located in the playhouse and children creating a forest by using loose materials (old cornstalks, sticks, etc.). The possibilities are endless. By acting out these stories, children internalize the ideas, use words from the book, and learn the sequence of events—all critical prereading skills.

## BARRIERS TO EDUCATIONAL PLAY

Early childhood education is built on a long-established tradition that play has a key role in learning and development. As was illustrated above, a variety of forms of educational play can be used to promote academic learning. However, previous observational studies in England (Bennet, Woods, & Rogers, 1997; Moyles, 1989) and in the United States (Polito, 1994) have revealed an apparent gap between rhetoric and reality concerning the role of play in some preschool and kindergarten classrooms. In these studies, teachers stated that play was valuable and had an important role in their curriculum. However, the teachers' actions often revealed that play was secondary to activities that they themselves supervised and directed.

Bennett et al. (1997), for example, conducted an extensive, year-long study of nine early childhood teachers in British schools to investigate factors that might be contributing to this gap between rhetoric and reality. The teachers filled out preobservation questionnaires about their intended goals for play activities. Next, researchers made visits and videotaped classroom play activities. Finally, the teachers were interviewed while they viewed the videotapes of the play that took place in their programs.

The teachers indicated that they had a strong commitment to using play as an integral part of the curriculum. They believed that play provided ideal conditions for learning. Observation, however, revealed that in spite of their strong commitment to play, the teachers undervalued their role in play and focused their attention on more formal, worklike activities. Interviews revealed that this devaluing of play was often caused by constraints of time, space, teacher-child ratios, and curriculum pressures to teach basic skills and the teachers' own beliefs that adults should not intervene in play. In addition, the teachers often made unrealistic assumptions about how children would respond to play activities, overestimating or underestimating children's competencies or the degree of challenge presented by the play context. This further undermined the teachers' confidence in using play as a learning medium.

Today many schools are experiencing pressure to provide teacher-directed instruction, cut out recess and the arts, and standardize curricula and evaluations. In schools everywhere, even in Head Start, tests are mandated to measure success in meeting learning objectives and outcomes (Jones, 2003). As the focus on academics and standards increases, the time and resources devoted to play decrease, even though, as we have discussed in this chapter, play can be used very successfully to promote academic learning.

We believe that the major cause of this anti-play shift across all levels of schooling is the widespread belief that if teaching is not didactic (direct instruction by experienced, knowledgeable teachers) and if learning is not hard work (unpleasant), children's academic achievement will suffer. "They are just playing" is an emotionally loaded phase that implies many things: Because play takes little effort and is pleasurable, it cannot be important (learning); because children can play without expert adult direction, it cannot be education; and because young children choose to play and will often play to avoid work, play can impede education. And the famous quote attributed to Montessori—"play is children's work"—only confuses the issue and leads to work being disguised as play.

Thus the major barrier to educational play—held by many educators, parents, administrators, politicians, education policymakers, and even some children—is the belief that play is the opposite of teaching and educational learning. This belief leads to the unfortunate conclusion that to increase teaching and educational learning, we must reduce or eliminate play and play opportunities (Jones, 2003).

Aside from this general anti-play sentiment, the reduction of play and play opportunities in early childhood programs and schools occurs differently and for different reasons at preschool, kindergarten, and early elementary levels based on specific standards for each age level, the education of the teachers, parental expectations, and the expectations of other stakeholders for each age group. In the following section we examine some potential barriers to play at each of theses levels. Then we suggest several strategies for overcoming these barriers.

## Preschool Barriers

With the new emphasis on school readiness promulgated by the Goals 2000: Educate America and No Child Left Behind federal education acts, Head Start, private, and school-based early childhood programs are all under pressure to replace play with more important "learning" activities (Bodrova & Leong, 2003; Jones, 2003). Many school administrators have even interpreted the new literacy initiative created by the International Reading Association and the National Association for the Education of Young Children (IRA/NAEYC, 1998) as a mandate to require increased direct instruction and to decrease play. While the implementation of standards at the K–12 level is reducing play for elementary children, the push to get children ready for the K–12 academics is reducing or eliminating play at the three- to five-year-old level.

Another barrier is that many early childhood educators lack understanding of developmentally appropriate practice (DAP) in general and play's role in DAP in particular. Earlier in this chapter we noted that one of the underlying principles of DAP stresses the importance of play (Bredekamp & Copple, 1997). However, research by Dunn and Kontos (1997) suggests that most early childhood programs do not effectively implement DAP and that only 33 percent of the early childhood programs they observed were truly play-based. Francis Wardle has discovered from teaching early childhood practitioners that although DAP is on the lips of most of his students, many cannot describe what it really is. This includes being able to describe the importance of play in the early childhood curriculum. If early childhood practitioners do not fully understand the need for play or its important role in DAP, how will they defend it in their programs against the pressure of administrators, politicians, and parents?

A third barrier concerns attitudes about educating children from minority groups. There is naturally a deep concern in this country regarding the academic achievement gap between Black, Hispanic, and Native American students and White and Asian students (Bowman, 2003). This has led many parents and educators to assume that black and Hispanic students benefit more from direct instruction than do middle-class children (Gonzalez-Mena, 2001; Snow, 2002) for a variety of reasons. We have already discussed that Head Start has recently introduced very specific educational outcomes that will be assessed through normed tests (Jones, 2003). Although these outcomes can be taught through developmentally appropriate practices, including play, the tendency is to use direct teacher instruction, especially by teachers who are not well versed in DAP. Francis observed a Head Start program for Black children in Louisiana in which the teachers were teaching to the test, using direct instruction and rote memorization. The teachers firmly believed that this was the best approach to helping their students get ready to succeed in school.

## Kindergarten Barriers

The barriers to educational play in kindergartens include all the ones discussed for preschools plus the added problem that kindergarten is now being considered part of the elementary grades—with all that this implies. In Chapter 12 we will discuss how innovative kindergarten playgrounds, which were brought from Germany as part of the kindergarten movement in the United States, became sterile and unsafe as the kindergarten movement became absorbed by the local public schools (Frost, 1992). Unfortunately, this is also occurring with play in kindergartens, as schools push the academic curriculum down into the kindergarten years. Public kindergartens now have very specific academic outcomes—including counting, alphabet knowledge, and phonics skills—that must be learned by the end of the school year and, in some cases, that are used to judge teacher performance and even pay. Many principals see no need for play in kindergarten classrooms (Bodrova & Leong, 2003). This clearly has a very negative impact on the use of play in most kindergarten classrooms.

## Primary Grade Barriers

In Chapter 12 we will discuss the low priority that is given to play in elementary schools and even the elimination of play from some school days altogether. Klugman (1990) reported that only 9 percent of principals surveyed believed that play has an important role in a third-grade curriculum, and this study was conducted before the inception of the current standards movement! Francis Wardle teaches elementary school teachers in a master's-level program in Denver, Colorado. Colorado is one of the states that has adopted statewide content standards and now administers a yearly test to determine student performance on those standards. His students—elementary teachers in local public schools—report extreme tension, heavy emphasis on direct instruction, and schoolwide pressure to perform well on these standardized tests, all of which leave little room for play. As might be expected, Francis's students who are training to be school counselors report higher incidences of school anxiety, referrals, and other problems in children.

In addition to this intense pressure to teach the basics, other barriers to academic play in the early elementary grades include the following:

- Lack of time in the schedule for play, caused in part by the short periods of time in the curriculum devoted to any one discipline
- Lack of appropriate space to play
- High teacher-student ratios
- Lack of needed materials
- Messy materials and activities that are not allowed in many elementary classrooms (Goldhaber, 1994)
- Lack of parent and administrator support for play

On the plus side, a body of research on teaching the basics, including math, science, and literacy at the elementary school level, is challenging traditional approaches to teaching these subjects (e.g., Perlmutter & Burrell, 1995). This research suggests that more developmentally appropriate and challenging methods often are more effective than traditional teacher-directed instruction and memorization. One example is a math activity that teaches students all sorts of shortcuts to basic multiplication facts and then has them engage in the game Beat the Calculator. In this game students use their newfound skills to do multiplication tasks much more quickly than they can do them with a calculator. This approach teaches math facts and also teaches children they do not always need to depend on a calculator. Another example is using jump-rope routines to teach basic math facts.

## Overcoming Barriers

Many of the barriers discussed above are beyond the control of teachers. Teachers cannot do much to turn back the current standards movement or the mounting pressures to increase academic achievement. However, educators can work to eliminate the most serious barrier of all: the general negative attitude about the educational value of play. We can also work to increase our colleagues' knowledge about educational play and DAP and take steps to refute the notion that low-income and minority children have a special need for direct, didactic forms of instruction.

First and foremost, we need to be more vigorous advocates for educational play, at both the early childhood (Hewit, 2001) and elementary grade levels (Stone, 1995). We need to do a better job of disseminating research that shows that play can promote academic achievement (Johnson, 1994). As is evidenced by the hundreds of studies cited in this book, a robust body of research supports the educational value of play. This research also has revealed the most effective play-based teaching strategies. This research needs to be made known to preservice and inservice teachers, parents, administrators, and educational policymakers. Jim Johnson (1994) recommends that we not only use the traditional venues of textbooks and academic journals, but also utilize the popular press, radio (e.g., National Public Radio), and television. The Internet is another promising medium for spreading the word about the educational effectiveness of play.

Dunn and Kontos (1997) recommend that teachers share with parents research on the effectiveness of DAP and play. This information needs to be coupled with findings about the negative effects of an overemphasis on academic skills, namely, increased stress and restricted emotional development. Dunn and Kontos (1997) point out that:

> Taken together, the research favors developmentally appropriate practice. In general, child-initiated environments were associated with higher levels of cognitive functioning. Coupling this information with the findings on stress and motivation, provides a strong argument for developmentally appropriate practices, especially for low-income children—the very children whose parents may prefer academically-oriented programs. (p. 12)

Stone (1995) suggests that teachers go a step further and become open advocates for play by vigorously planning for educational play experiences and taking steps to make parents and administrators aware of these activities. She recommends that teachers post information about the value of play in a prominent place in the classroom and label play centers with benefits that children will gain from experiences at each center. Teachers also need to collect artifacts (e.g., writing samples) and take photographs to document the learning that occurs through educational play. Stone recommends that teachers involve parents in educational play activities through informative newsletters and by inviting parents to help plan and provision play centers. Finally, Stone (1995) suggests forming play support groups in which teachers "share information, exchange ideas, and confirm beliefs" (p. 54) about educational play.

Moyles (1989) has an even more radical suggestion for parent involvement. She believes that "parents are particularly predisposed to understand play and its learning potential if invited to curriculum or topic sessions in school and allowed to experience themselves some of the [play] materials and resources that children use" (p. 158). She recommends that these educational play activities be designed for adults rather than expecting parents to play like children. For example, she recommends that parents play with a Hundred Board (described earlier, in the section on educational games) and discover what pattern emerges when every *n*th (third, fifth, etc.) space on the board is covered. She reports that many parents find this surprisingly difficult—and educational.

Teacher education programs also need to pay more attention to educational play. Jim Johnson (1994) points out teacher preparation programs need to do more to familiarize future teachers with play theory and research. The programs themselves need to "become more developmental in their approach to preparing new teachers, as well as showing greater understanding and greater respect for the playfulness inherent in all good teaching and learning" (p. 616). In other words, teacher educators who are play advocates need to practice what they preach.

Finally, teachers need to be more active and intentional in their use of play. Bennet et al. (1997) found that the most successful play activities involved active teacher participation. Teacher involvement and planning appeared to lessen the impact of constraining factors and to promote student learning. Learning was facilitated when teachers outlined expectations for the activity and assisted children in articulating what they learned from the play. Here are some of the recommendations that Bennett et al. (1997) make for improving the quality of play in schools:

- Integrating play into the curriculum through clearly specified aims and intentions. . . .

- Making time for quality interactions to enhance learning through play.
- Recognizing opportunities for teaching through play rather than relying on spontaneous learning.
- Providing a structure for review time so that children become more consciously aware of what they are doing, learning, and achieving in their play. (p. 130)

## SUMMARY

This chapter has examined the controversial subject of educational play: using play to help children achieve educational goals. The advantages and disadvantages of linking play and education have been discussed. On balance, we believe that pros outweigh the cons, particularly when teachers carefully plan academic play experiences and make sure that these experiences are aligned with academic standards. Examples of four major categories of educational play were presented: academically enriched play centers, games, simulations, and playground activities. We also presented an impressive body of research that supports the educational effectiveness of these forms of play. Finally, a variety of barriers to educational were discussed. Although some of these barriers, such as the current standards movements, are beyond teachers' control, we suggested a number of ways in which negative attitudes and lack of knowledge about educational play can be dealt with. Most important of all, teachers and teacher educators need to become more active advocates for educational play, making the parents, other teachers, administrators, policymakers, and the general public aware of the many advantages of using play as a learning medium.

## PROJECTS AND ACTIVITIES

1. Select an objective from a curriculum for children in kindergarten through third grade in any subject area. Develop a way to teach this objective using educational play.
2. Interview a preschool teacher, a kindergarten teacher, and a third-grade teacher regarding the place of play in their curriculum. Compare and contrast their responses.
3. Interview a parent of a child in preschool. Ask the parent questions regarding his or her beliefs about play and learning. To what extent does the parent believe play is an important part of their child's learning?
4. Observe two Head Start programs, one for primarily minority children (Black, Hispanic, and/or Native American) and one for predominately White children. Study the extent to which each program includes educational play. Compare and contrast the differences.
5. Interview a teacher in a pre-K, kindergarten, or first- through third-grade classroom regarding his or her philosophy about educational play. Then observe them in the classroom for an extended period of time. Does the teacher practice his or her philosophy?

CHAPTER 8

# Enriching Classroom Play: Materials and Curriculum

## INTRODUCTION

This chapter deals with two important influences on classroom play: materials and curriculum. Play materials have a significant influence both on the type of play in which children engage and on the content of that play. For example, if a classroom contains large quantities of blocks and building sets, children are likely to engage in a large amount of constructive play. If the classroom also has lots of miniature road signs and toy vehicles near the construction materials, children are likely to incorporate roads, gas stations, and other transportation content into their constructive and dramatic play activities. Other materials, such as tumbling mats, will encourage children to engage in functional-motor forms of play. Teachers need to carefully plan the types of materials that they make available for play because these materials will shape the types of play that occur in the classroom.

The school curriculum is another *potential* influence on classroom play. Curriculum refers to a school's course of study—the academic subject areas, objectives and goals, instructional strategies, learning activities, methods of evaluation, and so on. We highlight the term *potential* because it is up to the teacher to decide how much influence curriculum will have on children's play activities. If the teacher makes an effort to connect play and the academic curriculum, the influence can be profound. For example, if the class is engaging in a project to learn more about community helpers and is taking field trips to fire and police stations, having police and fire personnel visit the classroom, and is being read books about these professions, the teacher could set up the dramatic and constructive play areas to encourage children to play out what they are learning. When these types of play-curriculum links are established, the curriculum will have a major influence on play content. On the other hand, the same teacher could isolate play from the curriculum and not make any adjustment to the play areas or make any other kinds of connection. In this instance the curriculum would likely have a minimal influence on play content. After a field trip to the fire station, children would be motivated to engage in firefighter-related forms of play, but the materials would not be present to facilitate this type of play.

We believe that it is best to provide children with opportunities to make connections between developmental enrichment, academic activities, and play. Curriculum-related play allows children to work through and consolidate the new concepts and skills that they are learning. In addition, play creates a context in which children can learn from each other and receive support from teachers. Of course, children must choose to engage in such play. They should always have the option of choosing other types of play that fit with their current interests and play needs.

This chapter begins with a discussion of our beliefs about the relationship between play materials and development. We then examine several key characteristics or dimensions of play materials, including open or closed, simple or complex, soft or hard, and cultural relevance. These characteristics cut across the various categories of materials and can be useful in selecting play materials for different purposes. Next we discuss the different types of play materials that are available, ranging from realistic replica toys to natural materials such as sand and water. Then guidelines are presented for selecting materials for children of different ages. Finally, we explore the relationship between play and curriculum and describe the role of play in several widely used early childhood programs, including Montessori, Reggio Emilia, High/Scope, and Bank Street.

## FOCUS QUESTIONS

1. Discuss the two-way relationship between play materials and child development. What practical importance does this conception have for educators?
2. If you were starting a new school and had a limited budget, what would be the first three types of play materials that you would purchase? Explain these selections.
3. Discuss how the dimensions of open or closed and simple or complex play materials affect children's play behavior.
4. Distinguish between curriculum-generated play and play-generated curriculum. What are the two functions of curriculum-generated play?
5. How have different early childhood education model programs incorporated play?

## RELATIONSHIP BETWEEN PLAY MATERIALS AND DEVELOPMENT

We believe that there is a two-way relationship between play materials and children's development. Play materials can indirectly and directly facilitate development by encouraging children to engage in specific types of play. At the same time children's level of development influences the types of materials that they choose to play with.

Research has convincingly demonstrated that certain types of materials elicit specific forms of play. For example, theme-related collections of props, such as a cash register, empty product boxes, a miniature shopping cart, and play money will likely encourage children to engage in dramatic play with a store theme. Materials can also have a substantial effect the social quality of play. Some materials such as puzzles tend to encourage solitary play, and others types of materials such as large hollow blocks tend to encourage group play. Thus we can be fairly certain that play materials can *indirectly* affect children's growth by stimulating developmentally important types of play.

Proving *direct* connections between play materials and development is more problematic. To date, research has failed to provide firm evidence that play materials have a direct effect on development (Almqvist, 1994; Sutton-Smith, 1985). Lack of research evidence, of course, does not mean that this relationship does not exist. It is possible that the same issues discussed in Chapter 5 that make it difficult to prove that play in general has an impact on development, including sleeper effects (benefits do not show up for a long time), the epiphenomenon principle (other variables connected with play also influence development), and equifinality (play is just one of many pathways to development), also create problems proving that play materials influence development. The relationship may be there, but it might be so complex and complicated by other factors that it can be extremely difficult to substantiate with our current methods of research.

Sutton-Smith (1986) reminds us not to get too discouraged by these research difficulties. Common sense dictates that if children spend lots of time interacting with various play materials, some general learning and development are bound to take place. And as we explained in Chapter 5, it is quite likely that children learn specific concepts while playing with certain play materials. For example, when preschoolers play in literacy-enriched dramatic play areas, they have an opportunity to learn about the practical functions of print (Vukelich, 1993).

## CHARACTERISTICS OF PLAY MATERIALS

In her book *The Right Stuff for Children Birth to 8: Selecting Play Materials to Support Development,* Martha Bronson (1995) provides an extensive and expansive list of play materials for each age group, beginning with infants through children twelve years old. These recommendations must, of necessity, first consider safety (choke hazards, flammable materials, etc.), then the developmental needs and interests of children.

When Francis Wardle worked in the Guatemalan Highlands, he observed Mayan children playing with bottle caps, soap, leaves, and sticks. This type of play with everyday types of materials is not unique to the Mayan culture. Many children in the United States have enjoyed playing a game that is sometimes known as Pooh sticks, in which they drop sticks into the stream on one side of a bridge, then rush to the other side to see whose stick has "won the race." We have also seen children play with sticks in the sand, pebbles in the water, and flower petals in the grass.

However, we in this country (and in many other nations) have become fascinated with "educational" play materials. Probably the first educational materials were Friedrich Froebel's "gifts." His ten gifts were a collection of balls; wooden blocks; wooden cubes, rectangles, and pyramids; mosaic tiles; sticks and rings; and colored beads. These materials were designed to achieve specific goals consistent with Froebel's educational philosophy. Perhaps the most popular example of these types of educational play materials today can be found in authentic Montessori programs.

But what exactly makes a toy, material, or piece of equipment educational? And is there a conflict between educational materials and play materials? As we discuss throughout this book, there is currently such an emphasis on teaching isolated educational outcomes during the early years that many people now expect all learning and play materials to further specific academic outcomes. For example, parents might see far more value in a toy that matches phonemic sounds to visual displays of each letter than in constructive or make-believe forms of play. Essentially, educational toys and materials are those that claim to promote adult-defined educational outcomes (Wardle, 2003a). However, as we discuss throughout the book, children's play is about children's realities and fantasies, not adults' wishes.

A good toy or play material challenges, involves, stimulates, and engages a child's imagination (Wardle, 1999a). Good toys encourage complex play and can be used in a variety of ways. The best examples are blocks, crayons and paint, tools to use in sand and water, and the like. Other good play materials—toy cars and trucks, dolls, dress-up clothes and props, child-size furniture, and large cardboard boxes—encourage complex language use and the development of abstract thought and imagination. Balls, wagons, blocks, dolls, swings, and the like encourage social play. Good play materials also teach a variety of problem-solving skills, help children to enjoy physical activity, and encourage a variety of forms of expression and representation (Wardle 2003a).

In the sections that follow, we examine several characteristics or dimensions of play materials that influence their impact on children's learning and development. These dimensions include open versus closed, simple versus complex, soft versus hard, and multicultural.

## Open and Closed Materials

Open or low-structure play materials are those that offer children many ways to engage with them. For example, children can play with sand, water, or clay in a variety of ways, depending on the children's maturity and experience playing with these materials. Closed or high-structure play materials, by contrast, can be used in only a very limited way. For example, a jigsaw puzzle has only one correct solution, and a realistic replica of an airplane is difficult to use to represent anything but an airplane. Similarly, most Montessori equipment must be used in one prescribed manner. Closed materials have the potential to build in children a sense of mastery; however, because of their limited range, children often become frustrated or bored when playing with such materials.

There are some play materials that fit midway along the open/closed continuum. Legos and Tinker Toys are good examples of materials that fit this middle ground; they have specific physical properties that dictate how they can be used—for example, you cannot roll a block—yet they are flexible enough to provide for a wide range of play. Early childhood programs need to provide open materials, closed materials, and materials that lie somewhere between (Prescott, 1994). However, because many children who spend most of their day either in a childcare program or in in-school and after-school programs must do so many things to meet the needs of others (parents, teachers, etc.), providing open-ended toys gives these children a sense of control that they need (Wardle, 2003a).

Considerable research has been conducted on the realism of dramatic play props, which is one aspect of the open/closed dimension of play materials. Realistic replicas of objects, such as a miniature spaceship, are considered to be closed in that the toys' realism dictates their use in play. It is difficult to use a toy spaceship as anything but a spaceship. Unstructured materials, such as blocks and cardboard boxes, are considered to be open in that they can be easily used to represent a variety of objects.

A series of studies conducted during the 1970s and 1980s reported that realistic, highly structured props facilitate make-believe in younger (two- and three-year-old) preschoolers (e.g., Jeffree & McConkey, 1976; Johnson, 1983; McLoyd, 1983; Olszewski & Fuson, 1982). This is hardly surprising. Children in this age range are in the process of acquiring the representational skills needed for make-believe. It stands to reason that realistic replicas of theme-related objects will help toddlers to get started in dramatic play.

With increasing age children's representational skills grow to the point at which realistic toys are no longer required for engaging in make-believe. The research on toy structure and older children's dramatic play is contradictory. Some researchers have reported that realistic toys interfere with the imaginativeness of kindergarten and primary-grade students' pretend play (Pulaski, 1973). On the other hand, Trawick-Smith (1990) found that children between the ages of three and six years exhibited more make-believe with realistic play props than with less realistic toys. These mixed findings (and common sense) imply that teachers should provide preschool- and school-age children with a mix of realistic and less realistic play props. Realistic props will stimulate dramatic play in children with less developed symbolic capabilities and in children who simply prefer these types of props, whereas unstructured, open materials increase children's play options and can be used to represent a wide variety of objects.

## Simple and Complex Units

Considerable research has been conducted on how the amount of toys and equipment available in a setting affects children's play behavior. In general, findings indicate that there is an inverse relationship between the amount of equipment available and the level of social interaction in children's play (Johnson, 1935; Smith & Connolly, 1980). Decreasing the amount of materials in a setting brings about increased social interaction of both a positive nature (cooperative interactions, sharing) and a negative nature (aggression). Children either share or compete for the limited play resources. Increasing the materials has the opposite effect, reducing both aggression and cooperative interactions. When there is an abundance of play materials available, children tend to focus on the materials rather than on each other.

Focusing solely on the amount of materials available, however, may be misleading. The relationships between materials are also important in determining how much children can do with any given set of materials. Elizabeth Prescott (1994) has developed a way of describing these relationships using a three-tiered model, from simple to complex to super complex:

- A simple unit is a toy or material that has a single manipulative component, such as a pile of sand without anything added.
- A complex unit combines two related materials, such as a pile of sand and a plastic shovel, bucket, and funnel.
- A super-complex unit combines three or more interrelated materials, such as a pile of sand, a variety of sand toys, and water.

Kritchevsky, Prescott, and Walling (1977) devised a numerical way to determine the number of units (simple, complex, and super-complex) needed per child. They assigned a simple unit a value of 1, a complex unit a value of 4, and a super-complex unit a value of 8. Here is an example of how this system can be used to analyze the materials in an outdoor area:

| | | |
|---|---|---|
| 10 vehicles | simple units (1) | 10 |
| 1 rocking horse | simple unit (1) | 1 |
| 1 balance beam | simple unit (1) | 1 |
| 1 jungle gym with boxes and board | complex unit (4) | 4 |
| 1 sand table with water and tools | super-complex unit (8) | 8 |
| | Total play units | 24 |

If twelve students are playing in this area, there would be two play units per child. The number of units per child required depends on the activity, goals, and level of teacher direction and control. However, it is clear that less than one unit per child will force children to share (or compete for) materials, and a one-to-one ratio will provide almost no choices, because all options will be taken by other children. The more play units per child there are, the more choices there are and the less potential for conflict or need for teacher involvement.

As Kritchevsky et al. (1977, p. 17) state, "The amount to do per child in a space can be increased most readily either by scheduling smaller groups of children in the space, or by adding complex and super complex units" (p. 17). Clearly, for this approach to work, teachers need to encourage children to combine materials, equipment, and found objects in creative and innovative ways. For example, children can use wood from the workbench and yarn from the art area to stake flowers and tomatoes; combine writing instruments from the literacy area, art materials from the art centers, and wood from the woodwork area to create artistic plaques; and so forth.

An issue related to the amount to do per child concerns the concept of "overstimulation." Is it possible to have too many materials and too many things to do in a classroom? Many early childhood teachers are concerned that too many play materials can lead to overstimulation and hyperactivity. As Francis explains in Box 8.1, understimulation and boredom are much more pressing concerns.

**BOX 8.1**

## Unpacking Overstimulation

**by Francis Wardle**

In almost all my early childhood classes, one or more of my students brings up the need to prevent overstimulation. They might say, "So-and-so said it's very important not to overstimulate the infants" or "The environment must be very carefully and deliberately ordered so that children do not get overstimulated." Closely related to this concern is what seems to have become an early childhood mantra: Children need a specific, consistent daily schedule to give them a sense of security and order (leading sometimes to bizarre infant and toddler schedules).

Ironically, although the discussion of overstimulation comes up in every class, the topics of boredom and understimulation never come up! Considering what the new research on brain development has shown us about the critical importance of appropriate and multisensory stimulation of infants and young children (Shore, 1997), this is quite surprising, and quite disturbing.

When my students bring up the issue of overstimulation, I suggest that they observe children in a large toy store. Talk about an overstimulating environment for children! These stores are full of all sorts of shiny, flashy, attractive toys that all focus on initial interest so that children will persuade their parents to buy the toys. Many toy makers really do not care whether these toys have much prolonged interest, and many of the toys do not. (Box 8.5 discusses initial and prolonged interest in toys.)

But my observations in toy stores are that the children's behavior is not at all overstimulated. Children walk into the store, grab their parents' attention, and then march right to the toy they want their parents to purchase for them. Generally, they are so focused on their goal that they are not at all distracted or overstimulated by other toys. These children have learned to discriminate between relevant and irrelevant stimuli; the relevant ones are about where to find the toys and how to convince their parents to buy it, the irrelevant ones are about everything else. We live in a country where each of us must ignore lots and lots of irrelevant stimuli. (Count the number of commercials you see and hear on your way to work or college in one day!) What we must do is help children be selective and discriminating.

We need to provide environments that never bore children, and we need to help children select what they need from the environment. Ways to do this include the following:

Provide children with lots of choices.

Provide environments with lots of complex, challenging, and open materials.

Provide lots and lots of opportunities for play.

Help children return used materials to their rightful places.

Help children structure their own environments.

Provide lots and lots of field trips (focusing on specific stimuli within the disorganized, multistimulus world).

Provide a classroom environment with variety: brightly lit to dim, shadowy areas; a variety of colors and color intensities; lots of different smells, textures, sounds, and tastes (Phipps, 1999).

Model using materials in a variety of constructive ways.

Help children plan activities (High/Scope's "plan, do, and review" approach is one example).

Make lists of things needed for projects; this works well with a theme or project curriculum.

When children appear bored, do not tell them what to do next, but help them select the next activity.

Have flexible, open-ended daily schedules.

## Soft and Hard Materials

Throughout this book we have discussed the fact that many children are spending more and more hours every day in early childhood programs, schools, and afterschool programs. In Chapter 6 we discussed how these environments often stress the institutional aspects of schools and childcare buildings: lots of hard surfaces that are easy to keep clean and bright. The problem is that hard surfaces take their toll on human bodies because they do not respond, change, and adapt to our unique, soft, round shapes. Most people, when they come home after a long, tiring day at work, choose to lie down on a soft sofa, not on a hard wooden chair or bench.

Hard surfaces in early childhood programs and schools cause children to fatigue and get stressed and tired (Prescott, 1994). Furthermore, hard materials always require children to adapt to them and always to use them in a certain way. By contrast, softer materials such as sand, paints, clay, and water will respond to whatever a child is feeling at that time. Maybe the child feels like simply pounding the clay to release frustration that has built up during the day, or maybe the child is ready to delicately shape the clay into a beautiful pot or statue.

Therefore, according to Prescott, young children need lots of soft materials: stuffed dolls and animals, pillows, carpets, beanbag chairs, soft blocks, water, paints, clay, play dough, dirt in the garden, and the like. There is no need to worry about supplying hard materials, as they are always present in abundant quantities.

## Multicultural Materials

As the diversity of children and families we serve in our early childhood programs and schools continues to increase, we have a responsibility to provide activities and materials that are multicultural. Clearly, many of the basic materials for infants through third grade are culturally neutral: paints, clay, crayons, balls, math manipulatives, measurement instruments, mirrors, rattles, wagons, bicycles, building blocks, and so on. These basic play materials are relevant to children from almost any cultural background. Efforts to try to make such materials relevant to specific groups of children are humorous at best and potentially counterproductive. For example, when Francis Wardle worked as the education director for a national childcare provider, he received some "multicultural blocks" with words in different languages reproduced on their sides.

However, as children begin to use play materials that depict people (e.g., dolls) or that contain pictures of people (e.g., puzzles), attention to diversity becomes important. This is also true for dramatic play materials—dress-up clothes and dramatic play props—and books. In general, toys and other materials should both reflect the diversity of all the families using the program—race, ethnicity, gender, culture, family structures, profession, disabilities, and so on—and expose children to people with whom they have no contact in their daily lives (Wardle & Cruz-Janzen 2004).

Some specific guidelines to make sure toys and materials are truly multicultural include the following (Wardle, 2003a):

- Materials should increase each child's self-acceptance, knowledge, and understanding of his or her heritage and identity by showing the child's culture in a positive light.
- Materials should increase each child's acceptance, knowledge, and understanding of people who are different from him or her by showing those people and their cultures in a positive light.
- Materials should expand children's view of the world and people in the world.
- Materials should address a variety of areas of diversity at the same time, such as gender, disability, and family structures.
- Materials that expose children to diversity should be integrated within the whole program and its curricula, not isolated in a token manner.
- Diversity represented in materials should be realistic and authentic, such as Native Americans in real jobs with contemporary clothes rather than dancing in headdresses.
- Materials should continually challenge every kind of stereotype, be it that women can only be nurses and men cannot be nurses, that Asian boys are always good at math and Black boys are always good at athletics, or the like.
- Materials need to emphasize diversity within large groups and not convey the idea that all African-Americans, all Latinos, all women, and so on look the same and think the same.
- Materials should emphasize the choices, freedoms, and uniqueness of each individual, who have attributes from a variety of diverse groups (gender, race, etc.).
- Materials should never convey that one group is somehow better than another group. Unfortunately, if certain people are not represented in play materials, this invisibility is a powerful indicator of lack of importance (Wardle & Cruz-Janzen, 2004).
- Materials must not exclude any person or any part of a person; thus multiracial and multiethnic children and their families must be represented as

unique individuals, not just part of the minority parents' cultures (Wardle & Cruz-Janzen, 2004).

## TYPES OF PLAY MATERIALS

There are various ways to categorize play materials. In the sections that follow, we group play materials into categories that describe their characteristics (e.g., replica toys) or denote their intended use (construction toys). However, it is important to keep in mind that these are adult categories, and children will use materials in ways that meet their specific purposes (Sutton-Smith, 1986).

### Replica Toys

Replica toys are miniature versions of large objects and people. Some are real objects, such as cars, people, and animals; others are familiar objects from books, TV programs, and films (Disney characters, superheroes, etc.). These toys encourage dramatic play and can be used creatively with a variety of other materials (blocks, art materials, sandbox, etc.). Replica toys can be used both indoors and outside on the playground.

**Animate Toys.** These are toys that represent people, animals, and other creatures, made of either plastic or some cuddly materials; examples are rag dolls and stuffed animals. The affinity young children have for these toys have made them a marketing bonanza for fast-food chains and TV and movie companies. The ability of the

➤ Replica toys are miniature versions of large objects, people, and animals.

preoperational child to attribute lifelike properties to animate objects makes these toys popular with children up to about age seven years.

**Transportation Toys.** These include miniature trains, cars, trucks, wagons, and ships. These often are used in conjunction with a variety of accessories (garage, etc.) and block sets. Popular building systems, such as Legos and Duplos, have added a variety of transportation toys to their lineup to go along with the cities, train stations, space stations, and other such things that children build with basic blocks. Wooden train sets are particularly popular with young children.

**Dramatic Play Props.** These are materials that children use to enhance their dramatic play. They include a variety of hats, clothes, and shoes; kitchen utensils; miniature furniture; child-size baby carriages and cradles; toy phones; and a variety of dolls. As we have discussed elsewhere, these props tend to be slanted toward girls' interests. Teachers should make an effort to include a variety of male-oriented props, to encourage more boys to engage in dramatic play.

As a rule dramatic play props should not be used in the outside playground because they can cause a variety of safety hazards (for example, dress-up clothes can catch and strangle a child climbing on outside equipment).

## Educational Toys

Educational toys are designed to teach specific educational objectives or outcomes. These might be social (self-help skills of lacing a shoe board), physical (fine motor skills of putting beads on a string), cognitive (one-to-one correspondence of matching cards with uppercase and lowercase letters on them), or affective (learning about feelings through the reading of a particular book). Examples of educational toys include the following:

- Puzzles
- Alphabet cards, blocks, and books
- Stacking toys
- Geo-boards and other pegboard games
- Stringing toys
- Nesting boxes
- Lacing boards
- Zipping boards
- Phonics games

As we mentioned earlier in this chapter, Froebel probably started the craze for educational toys with his ten gifts. Montessori reinforced this idea of education play in her curriculum (sandpaper letters and the pink tower being two of her best-known play materials), and the current early academics movement is making these materials more popular than ever.

Although well intentioned, educational toys have several shortcomings. First, as we mentioned earlier, children might not use the toys as manufacturers intend (e.g., they might use the strings on a lacing board as make-believe snakes). Second, the material simply might not be properly designed to teach the targeted skill or concept (e.g., blocks with alphabet letters on them teach children how to play with blocks, but they do not teach the alphabet). Because of these limitations, we believe that these didactic toys should be used in moderation in classrooms. As Damon (2001) has pointed out, everyday objects can be used to teach young children all the basic math skills and concepts needed to be successful in school. If this is the case, why do we need these didactic toys? Educational toys, in general, should not be used on the outside playground because their parts are easy to lose and the toys can easily get damaged by rain and sand (sand acts like sandpaper on surfaces).

## Construction Toys

Constructive play is extremely popular for young children and is the favorite kind of play on playgrounds for preschoolers (Ihn, 1998). Although children can use sticks, stones, art supplies, and other miscellaneous materials for constructive play, construction toys are designed specifically for this type of play.

**Unit Blocks.** These are the standard block sets made from carefully finished hardwood (usually maple or beech) found in many early childhood programs. They are called unit blocks because their lengths are based on a single unit, and then other blocks are two times the unit, three times the unit, and so on. Even the round pillars are proportional to this basic unit. The blocks are made with such precision that they enable a child to, say, combine six half-units to match a three-unit-long block. Angles, ramps, and large, flat boards are added to these units for increased versatility.

The unit approach allows children using these blocks to learn a variety of math skills, from multiplication to fractions; their basic format enables children to create a vast array of complex patterns, games (marble shooting is a favorite), and complex buildings. Box 8.2 explains the stages of block building that children typically go through. A good unit block set is a must in every early childhood programs, and ample amounts of blocks are needed to maximize their use.

**BOX 8.2**

### Stages of Block Building

All children progress through specific stages as they use blocks in play. Except for stage one, this is also true for older children who have not experienced block play. However, older children progress through each stage quicker than younger children.

*Stage one.* Blocks are carried around but are not used for construction (very young children).

*Stage two.* Building begins. Children mostly make rows, either horizontal (on the floor) or vertical (stacked). There is much repetition in this early building pattern, which is basic functional play with blocks.

*Stage three.* Bridging: Children create a bridge or portal by using two blocks to support a third. In architecture this is known as the post-and-lintel system.

*Stage four.* Enclosures: Children place blocks in such a way that they enclose a space. Bridging and enclosures are among the earliest technical problems children have to solve when playing with blocks, and this happens soon after a child begins to use blocks regularly.

*Stage five.* With age children become steadily more imaginative in their block building. They use more blocks and create elaborate designs, incorporating patterns and balance into their constructions.

*Stage six.* Naming of structures for dramatic play begins. Before this stage children might have named their structures but not necessarily according to the function of the building. This stage of block building corresponds to the "realistic" stage in art development.

*Stage seven.* Children use blocks to represent things they know, such as cities, cars, airplanes, and houses. They also use blocks to stimulate dramatic play activities: zoo, farm, shopping centers, and other locations.

*Source:* Wardle, *Introduction to Early Childhood Education: A Multidimensional Approach to Child-Centered Care and Learning.* Published by Allyn and Bacon, Boston, MA. Copyright © 2003 by Pearson Education. Based on Johnson (1996).

**Table Blocks.** These are small, unitized blocks that can be used on table surfaces and are made of hardwood or plastic. Legos and Duplos are good examples. They tend to encourage fine motor development and can be used in much smaller areas than unit blocks. Children playing with table block tend to make less noise than children playing with unit blocks. (In Chapter 4 we discussed why girls tend to play with table blocks while boys tend to play with unit blocks, for complex reasons having a lot to do with female teacher preferences.)

**Large Hollow Blocks.** These are large enough that children have to use both hands to carry them. They are made of wood, plastic, or cardboard. Because of their size they are particularly good for building dramatic play structures: houses, forts, spaceships, and so on. The weight of the wooden blocks both develops muscle strength and coordination and requires children to work together to carry the larger blocks. Large hollow blocks are great for outdoors, especially on a concrete slab in the playground, but the wood will deteriorate in bad whether, so if they are used outside, they must be brought inside at the end of the day.

**Foam Blocks and Plastic Crates.** Several companies make large blocks of plastic foam and durable vinyl. These are large, soft shapes that can be used in gymnastics activities (tumbling) and are particularly useful in working with children who have specific physical disabilities. They are also great for providing progressively difficult physical challenges for toddlers. Large plastic crates designed primarily for storage work wonders for construction play in the outdoor playground. And because plastic does not deteriorate outside, they can be left on the playground.

**Reusable Materials.** "Junk" materials such as old lumber, boxes, empty egg cartons, Styrofoam packing peanuts, and other discarded materials can make excellent unstructured play materials. As Walter Drew explains in Box 8.3, some early childhood educators are forming partnerships with manufacturing companies to make these materials readily available to schools.

**BOX 8.3**

## *Reusable Resources and Creative Education*

**by Walter F. Drew, Ed.D., Founder**

***Reusable Resources Association***
***Institute for Self Active Education***

Creative and energetic teachers have been collecting and reusing scrounged materials for years. Teachers know that children develop a unique sense of self-worth from being creative. However, creative hands-on activities are often hampered by a lack of good materials. Yet within every community there is a wealth of material resources that remains untouched. This discovery has led to an exciting partnership that has businesses, schools, and parents working together to help our children and our environment.

Local businesses and industries are donating a continuous supply of free materials, referred to as "impaired assets," that they no longer want. Reusable resource centers receive these overruns, rejects, and obsolete supplies, including such diverse materials as Mylar, foam, fabric, felt, wood, wire, tile, plastic pieces, and paper. A growing network of over 100 centers then make these materials available for teachers to promote constructive play and enhance our children's educational experiences.

These centers benefit a wide audience. Goods that have lost usefulness for the business community are now enabling educators to provide valuable resources that stimulate innovative, creative hands-on play and learning across the curriculum. These centers provide homes for unused materials, and the ethics of reuse and recycling are promoted. It is truly a win-win situation.

**The Process: Get the Stuff and Play**

"I gathered a variety of materials from our local Resource Center . . . squishy foam, odd-shaped plastic pieces, flexible colored tubes, felt circles, metallic gaskets, and other discarded items donated by businesses," comments Beth Scarborough, an early childhood special education teacher in Brevard County, Florida. "My goal was to inspire investigation, creative thinking, and the development of inventive language skills. Adapting and using what I learned during a professional development play workshop, I simply said to my children, 'Here are some materials that I know you have never seen before. Play with them, move them around and explore them, and see what you discover!' I observed and photographed the children and recorded their comments as they worked in small groups investigating, comparing, and talking about the different attributes or properties of materials, . . . matching objects by color and texture, whether the objects are rough or smooth, thick or thin, heavy or light, which ones roll or stand alone, . . . the children are working together creating categories and systems for organizing and in the process developing their higher order thinking skills. At the same time, they are also learning to appreciate the environmental and educational benefits of collecting and reusing materials that were once wasted and bound for the landfill."

**Transforming a World View**

"Reusable resource centers have the potential to fundamentally transform the way people, children and adults, think about materials," suggests Michael Ohlsen of the Florida Department of Environmental Protection. "These centers are redefining what waste means and seeing any material for its creative possibilities. It's comforting to imagine the future of our environment emerging under this new paradigm."

It is not simply that the materials are free that makes them valuable to educators. It also is their unusual quality, which provokes hands-on inquiry and experimentation across the curriculum, from mathematics and science to art and reading. Children, especially between the ages of three and nine, need to explore the world directly and apply their intelligence and creativity to problems they encounter. When children explore materials using their hands, they become totally absorbed in their own creative being. The unique, open-ended nature of reusable materials gives children access to the inner power to create at their own fingertips.

**Resources for Teacher Education**

"Most people don't even know that such materials are available and how little they cost, yet when given a chance to explore them, they immediately sense their value in enhancing creativity of persons regardless of age," comments Dr. Rolf G. Schmitz, Director of the Muskingum College's Master of Arts in Education in Ohio, which has for six years integrated reusable resources in its Masters of Education Early Childhood Summer Training Institute. "We need to offset the sedentary effects of being glued to an electronic device and instead enhance kinesthetic potentials inherent in multimaterials and multidimensional creations."

Jane Wiechel, President of the National Association for the Education of Young Children, believes that "through the world of reusable resources children have the opportunity to explore the depths of their imagination. It is through this process that children become actively engaged in the process of learning. By constructing their own experiences and sharing their ideas with each other as well as with adults, learning becomes an exciting and provocative experience."

Recycled materials help teachers to express their own ingenuity and creativity. Teachers experience a deep satisfaction when they see their children actually achieving through active exploration and experiencing the joy of learning.

**Integrating Reusable Resources: The Teacher's Role**

The problem-solving act of transforming concrete objects into unique organizing designs, of making physical patterns or orderly three-dimensional systems, is a creative, intellectual process engaging the whole child. Through the active use of the senses, children discover their own creative potential and gain a feeling of mastery and self-fulfillment. This simple underlying concept provides the basis to fully appreciate the benefits of using reusable resources as in the classroom. The teacher's role in supporting this process is to do the following:

- Select reusable materials that enhance the learning of the lesson's particular concepts and skills
- Focus on the respective curriculum learning goals or standards
- Provide time and space for exploring the materials
- Observe and document the experience carefully as part of the reflection process
- Interact thoughtfully to ensure student focus and attention to relevant content and encourage thinking about what is happening
- Encourage children to document or represent their construction/play experiences with words, drawings, and three-dimensional collage
- Coach children to reflect and describe their experiences as a way of identifying interests and questions for further exploration

**How the Play Experience with Reusable Resources Touched My Teaching**

"Several years ago, I attended the Play Experience workshop at the NAEYC Annual Conference," writes Sandra Waite-Stupiansky, kindergarten teacher and Professor at the Miller Laboratory School, Edinboro University in Pennsylvania. "During the several hours together, we played with a wide range of reusable materials, ranging from long ribbons of different textures to cardboard tubes to Styrofoam shapes. I remember playing silently by myself as soft music played in the background. I connected with others who played alongside me, even though we had never met before. This whole experience awakened my childhood juices for playing. Those delightful times when there were no pressures to perform or hurry to get from one event to another, no standards of right versus wrong ways to do things, and few external rules. Our only mandate by the play experience folks was to play.

"At the end of the session, the leaders invited us to fill a bag with the reusable materials and take them with us (for a nominal fee). I stuffed my bag with round, blue Styrofoam pieces that resembled hockey pucks in size and shape. I selected these materials because they would fit into my suitcase without adding too much weight, plus I knew my kindergartners would love them.

"I was right! When I presented the round blue blocks to the kindergartners, they knew just what to do with them. They made them into food items in the dramatic play center. They built elaborate structures out of them that looked like pyramids. Together we made a hockey rink out of a plastic tarp and they played hockey using the blue Styrofoam pucks, small hockey sticks, and makeshift goals.

"Each year since that time, the children have come up with different ways to use the blue blocks. My class last year worked for several weeks making a 'Cookie Castle' out of them. Each day they would add a little, change their design, or rebuild it from scratch. They made signs that said 'COOKE CASOL' and placed them strategically beside the 'DO NOT TOUCH' sign. I truly believe that their creation was stimulated by these interesting blocks that some industry was going to throw into the landfill somewhere! In the hands of these children, the discards became a magical castle!

"The wonder of the reusable materials (other than their price!) is the way they become so many different things in the hands of the folks who play with them. The fluidity of the materials and their interesting textures and shapes stimulate the creative juices. It's hard to believe that such valuable materials would be pushing up dirt somewhere if the folks from the Reusable Resources Association didn't save them!"

For information contact:
Reusable Resources Association
P.O. Box 511001
Melbourne Beach, FL 32951
Tel: 321-984-1018
Fax: 321-984-9090
Email: dr-drew@earthlink.net

## Gross Motor Toys

These are designed to foster large muscle development and coordination. For older children they also encourage social play and constructive play (e.g., children pull each other on wagons; wagons, wheelbarrows, and toys trucks are used to carry dirt or other materials from one building site to another). Many of these toys are used almost exclusively outside because of the space needed and sometimes because of the noise they generate. These include (for infants to children age eight) in no specific order:

- A variety of rubber, plastic, and leather balls of different textures, weights, and sizes
- Push and pull toys
- Single-axle and swivel swings
- Stationary riding equipment
- Riding trucks, tractors, trains, etc.
- Wagons, wheelbarrows, and carriages
- Tunnels, slides, and low platforms
- Low riders and tricycles
- Bikes
- Rocking horse or rocking boat
- Plastic bat and ball
- Jump-ropes*
- Slides, rails, ladders, platforms, monkey bars, and steps
- Scooters
- Balance beams
- Basketball hoops, volleyball nets, soccer goals, etc.
- Hopscotch, four square, etc.

## Games

Older preschoolers begin to enjoy simple games, such as bingo and matching cards (turn-ups). They graduate to simple board games, including Chutes and Ladders, con-

*Ropes must be very carefully supervised on the playground because they can cause a trip hazard and can cause strangulation on the climbing equipment.

centration, dominoes, and (by age eight) checkers. And, of course, kindergarten and elementary age children love a range of outdoor games, including various forms of tag, basketball, soccer, baseball, red light/green light, red rover, prisoner's base, and so on (Wardle, 2003a).

Teachers should modify the rules of commercial games and help children invent their own games. Of course, teachers also must be aware that children of this age are experiencing a struggle between their egocentric nature and the group requirements of games with rules. So learning to play games will be challenging but also developmentally rewarding.

## Real Materials

Real materials are objects from the real world that children use for play, such as sand, water, art materials, literacy materials, and wood. All these materials are enhanced by a variety of accessories and tools—shovels and pails in sand, woodworking tools, brushes and scissors for art materials, and so on.

**Sand, Water, and Mud.** Children love to play in sand, water, and mud. When Francis taught in the kindergarten program at the new Meadow Run School, the children would spend hour on hour damming up the streams in their outdoor environment (Wardle, 1995). Sand, water, and mud are particularly attractive because they are so versatile and because children can make such a mess with them—surely a basic right of childhood! This messiness makes these materials particularly appropriate for outdoor playgrounds. In addition, these materials are extremely versatile because they have no predefined form and can be shaped and molded by the containers in which they are placed.

Adding all sorts of tools to these basic materials greatly increases their potential (Prescott, 1994). Some suggestions by Hill (1977) and Crosser (1994) include the following:

- For sand play, add shovels and pails, funnels and sifters, bulldozers, dump trucks, road graders, molds, cookie cutters, magnifying lenses, and magnets.
- For water play, add funnels, plastic tubing, squeeze bottles, soup ladles, large spoons, jars, margarine tubs and other containers, sponges, egg beaters and kitchen whisks, Popsicle sticks, fishing bobbers, and food coloring (especially fun if you also add Crisco, since oil and water do not mix).

Of course, as Prescott (1994) suggests, combining sand and water is also great. Children can also add objects made from the woodworking bench (boats), art area (signs on top of the sand castle), and literacy materials (names of boats, advertisements on boards next to the highway in a sand city, etc.).

**Art Materials.** A great deal has been written about the use of art and art materials by young children (Arnheim, 1969; Dewey, 1934; Engel, 1995; Gardner, 1980; Read, 1943). Needless to say, most educators and developmental psychologists believe that young children should have lots of opportunities to engage in a variety of art activities—to explore materials and tools; develop self-expression; learn preliteracy (especially pre-writing) skills; and find a variety of ways to represent their experiences, feelings, and the world around them. Art materials for young children include the following:

- Finger paints, pudding, and shaving cream (to use for painting)
- Paints, beginning with tempera and moving to watercolors and even acrylics
- Clay, play dough, and plastic clay
- Plaster of Paris and papier maché
- A variety of paper of different colors, textures, and weights
- Crayons, felt pens (large and fine tipped), and chalk (different colors and different sizes)
- A variety of yarns and fabrics
- A variety of found materials for collages
- Stencils and prints of all kinds and shapes
- Scrap wood, cardboard, and plastic foam

**Literacy Materials.** In Chapter 7 we discuss in detail a host of ways in which literacy activities can be included in play: adding theme-related materials to dramatic play centers, including home, store, post office, airport ticket counter, doctor's office, and restaurant settings. In addition, literacy materials can be added to almost any play activity:

- Making labels for seeds planted in the garden
- Making traffic signs for the tricycle path in the playground
- Adding a blueprint, sales brochure for a house, and a "For Sale" sign in the block area
- Placing a poster of different trees with their names next to them in the woodworking area

**Woodworking Materials.** Young children absolutely love woodworking. (See Box 8.4 for safety tips.) Soft pinewood can be collected from local lumber and hardware stores, and foam scraps can be obtained from arts and crafts stores and furniture factories. An assortment of other materials and accessories should be added:

- Various shaped and sized pieces of plywood and Masonite
- Dowels of different diameters
- Hinges, bolts, and latches
- Yarn and fabric
- Paints
- Several different size "C" clamps
- 35mm film containers (the lids make wonderful wheels)
- A variety of nails, including furniture tacks (big, shiny heads)
- Wood staples of various sizes, screws, and bolts

Basic hand tools for this age include saws (cross-cut and ripping saws), hammers, screwdrivers (regular and Phillips), drills (center and brace and bit), pliers, wrenches, Sure forms, and various grades of sandpaper.

BOX 8.4

### Woodworking Safety Tips

No more than two students should work at the workbench at one time.

Provide enough tools for each student doing woodworking.

Make sure the workbench is secure and steady; it must not bounce or rock.

Provide constant adult supervision.

Keep the workbench surface clear of tools, wood, nails, and other supplies that are not being used.

When a child is drilling or sawing, the piece of wood must be secured in the vise grip or with a "C" clamp.

Children working at the workbench should be totally concentrating on what they are doing. Remove a child who is tired, distracted, fooling around, frustrated, or fighting.

Children using tools must wear protective goggles.

Have a well-equipped first-aid kit on hand.

Make sure tools are used only appropriately (don't use a hammer to break stones, saws to cut apples, etc.).

Make sure storage for wood and tools is close by and easy to access.

*Source:* Wardle, *Introduction to Early Childhood Education: A Multidimensional Approach to Child-Centered Care and Learning.* Published by Allyn and Bacon, Boston, MA. Copyright © 2003 by Pearson Education.

## SELECTING PLAY MATERIALS

Selection of play materials is based on a variety of factors, including the children's developmental age, budget, and program goals and objectives. Companies that sell toys and educational materials provide lists of materials for new programs that are starting from scratch (for example, Community Playthings' *Equipped for Play*). State licensing regulations stipulate kinds and amounts of materials for different ages, and accreditation criteria specify the types and approximate amounts of materials that should be in each classroom area (NAEYC, 1998).

There are also a variety of helpful books, including *The Right Stuff for Children Birth to 8: Selecting Play Materials to Support Development* by Martha Bronson (1995); *Planning Environments for Young Children: Physical Space* by Sybil Kritchevsky, Elizabeth Prescott, and Lee Walling (1977); *Caring Spaces, Learning Places: Children's Environments That Work* by Jim Greenman (1988); *Selecting Educational Equipment and Materials for Schools and Home* by Joan Moyer (1995);

➤ Selection of play materials is based on a variety of factors, including children's developmental age, budget, and program goals and objectives.

and two books published by the U.S. Consumer Product Safety Commission: *Which Toys for Which Child?: A Consumer's Guide for Selecting Suitable Toys: Ages Birth through Five* (1993) and *Which Toys for Which Child?: A Consumer's Guide for Selecting Suitable Toys: Ages 6 through 12* (1994).

## General Guidelines

Box 8.5 provides specific criteria for selecting materials. In general, programs should provide materials to encourage all kinds of play:

- Physical or motor or functional
- Social
- Constructive
- Dramatic play
- Games with rules

Also, schools should provide toys and materials that children do not have at home. This requires a needs assessment or survey of your children. Finally, because more and more children are spending more and more time in early childhood programs, a wide variety of materials must be selected. When children spend up to ten hours a day in one program, they must have materials that continually challenge, excite, extend learning, and provide novelty. Play materials and choices for half-day programs are completely different from those for programs that run eight to ten hours a day (Wardle, 2003a).

The authors of this book also believe that young children need lots and lots of materials that provide opportunities for them to be creative, solve problems, and use materials in innovative and unusual ways. We also believe that children can find a great deal of pleasure, and learn many skills and concepts, using natural and basic materials: sand, water, stones, sticks, dirt, found objects, recycled materials, leaves, pieces of clean wood, pots and pans, rope, and so on.

**BOX 8.5**

## Selecting Toys and Play Materials

**Does the toy have high initial interest?**
Initial interest is created by novelty, attractive physical characteristics (color, shiny, frilly, strange noises, etc.), and interest to the child (matches the child's likes, the child's friends have one, the child saw it on TV).

**Does the toy have high prolonged interest?**
Everyone has heard stories of the expensive holiday gift that was ignored by the child in favor of the box it came in. The box had high prolonged interest. Toys that have high prolonged interest include blocks, crayons, balls, Duplos, and dolls. These toys are flexible enough that children can use them in a variety of ways.

**Can the toy be used with minimal adult supervision?**
Toys should not incorporate adult rules, need constant attention to solve conflicts, or require close adult supervision to prevent misuse or breakage.

**Does the toy strengthen self-concept?**
Dolls that reflect the children's cultural and physical characteristics are a good example. Can the children positively identify with the toy?

**Does the toy strengthen the child's respect for others?**
Does the toy expose children to diversity in nonstereotypical ways?

**Does the toy teach alternative ways to solve conflicts and arguments?**
Many video games and other toys teach children that force is the way to solve problems. Good toys provide children with a different approach: teamwork, give and take, and so on.

**Is the toy durable?**
Will it withstand constant, active use by children? Will it last over time? If designed for the outside, will it last outside? Can it be easily repaired?

**Is the toy versatile?**
Can it be used in many ways? Can a child impose his or her meaning on it? Examples are blocks and dress-up clothes.

**Is the toy adaptable and progressive?**
Can it be used by children at a variety of different levels? Can one child use it in progressively more complex ways? For example, Lego blocks can be grouped by color, used to build simple constructions, and used to construct a futuristic space vehicle or a replica of a complex castle from a book.

**Is the toy easy to keep clean?**
Can it be sterilized in the dishwasher? Can the cloth components (e.g., dolls' clothes) come off to be easily washed? Does it resist dirt?

**Does the toy strengthen social relationships?**
Balls are usually more fun when played with by more than one child, as are large blocks. A swivel swing requires more than one player to be fun.

**Does the toy arouse imagination and creativity?**
Dramatic play materials are a good example. Enough toys must be provided, and the environment needs to encourage creativity and imagination. Play periods also have to be long enough for complex play to be planned and carried out.

**Does the toy encourage intellectual development?**
Are language, grouping of similar objects, labeling, and comparisons encouraged? Is basic knowledge taught?

**Is the toy safe? Can it easily become unsafe when broken? Can the child easily replace the toy to its correct storage place?**
Toys with lots of little parts are difficult to restore.

**Is the toy developmentally appropriate?**
Children develop progressively though physical, social, and cognitive stages. Toys should match these stages.

**Does the toy encourage constructive play?**
Constructive play involves making things. Examples are blocks, woodworking, painting, and crafts.

**Does the toy convey to the child a sense of quality?**
Is it well made? Does it feel solid when picked up? Does it look like someone took care in making it? Does it keep its appearance over time?

**Does the toy encourage large and small muscle development and eye-hand coordination?**
Not all toys in a program will meet all criteria, but all toys should be developmentally appropriate, safe, durable, and easy to clean and require minimal supervision. Other criteria encourage more extensive use of toys and self-concept development. Make sure the program has toys that cover all the other criteria. Do not overemphasize one area.

*Source:* Wardle (1993).

## Materials for Different Ages

In her book *The Right Stuff for Children Birth to 8: Selecting Play Materials to Support Development* (1995), Martha Bronson lists some materials for each age group. As we have already pointed out, the two major criteria for selecting these materials are safety and developmental level. In this section we list a few of the materials that are appropriate for each age group. Clearly, there is a vast range of choices, which also depend on the program's specific curriculum. Additional materials are progressively added to each age level.

**Infants (Birth to Twelve Months Old).** Because infants are in Piaget's sensorimotor stage, they love to follow moving mobiles with their eyes, enjoy batting and kicking at objects, and like rattles and bells. Mirrors are great at this age because infants can keep themselves interested by continually moving; and because they are attracted to faces, they like to look at their own face. A few dolls and stuffed animals work, and balls and push toys can be added as they get older.

Outdoors, infants are also fascinated by things that stimulate their senses: wind chimes, leaves that filter the sunlight, water reflecting the sky, and playing with rattles and other sound-making toys on a blanket beneath the tree.

**Toddlers (One to Three Years Old).** Sand and water toys, cars and trucks, simple lightweight blocks, and sturdy books can be added, along with riding toys, push-pull toys, big balls, and music-making toys. At the older end of this age range, dress-up materials, housekeeping furniture, miniature people and animals, unit block sets, and a water table should be added. Include simple puzzles and pegboards, simple games, stacking blocks, beads for threading, a variety of art materials, musical instruments, and more books. Care must be taken to make sure all small parts pass the choke test.

Because toddlers are learning to walk, then run and climb, basic climbing structures should be provided, both inside and in the outside playground. These should include ramps, tunnels, steps, and a basic slide.

**Preschoolers.** Add to the materials already discussed hand puppets, hollow (large) blocks, science and measuring materials, a large variety of puzzles, and more materials for sand and water play. Specific science, math, literacy, and art materials should be added, along with more musical instruments, more complex puzzles and games, and a variety of gross and fine motor materials, such as beanbags, balls, jump ropes, beads, and strings. Lots of different props need to be added to the dramatic play area, depending largely on the experiences of the children who attend the program.

And, of course, a vast array of books must be provided: picture books, nursery rhymes, Dr. Seuss books, how-to books, sports books, and books in foreign languages if the program teaches a second language (Wardle, 2003b).

The outdoor playground should include swings, climbing structures with ladders, steps, tunnels, and slides; wagons, tricycles, and low riders; a variety of sand and water tools; and a vast array of loose parts.

**School Age (Kindergarten to Third Grade).** Materials for school-age children need to add complexity and challenge. Additional art materials include clay and other media that expand the children's art activities—collage, printing, book making, use of computer art, photography, and so on. Math manipulatives, measuring equipment, materials to learn about money and telling time, all sorts of science materials (related to weather, the solar system, plants and animals, the human body, and ecology), and a variety of developmentally appropriate computer programs should be added. A variety of writing tools (e.g., pens, pencils, stencils, old typewriters) and different surfaces to write on should be included.

Gross and fine motor materials begin to shift to specific cultural sports such as soccer, basketball, baseball, and gymnastics, along with simple and more challenging gross motor materials and equipment.

Books at this age should include both story texts and expository texts and should include a vast range of content and subject matter. One of Francis Wardle's graduate students conducted an action research project on the fact that her male kindergarten students lagged their female counterparts in reading. As she explored the problem, she discovered that almost all her books were about subjects girls like, such as fantasy stories, fairy tales, and cute animals, but very few were of interest to the boys, such as sports, transportation, how things work, and wild animals. At this age care must be taken to select a variety of books, including multicultural texts (Wardle & Cruz-Janzen, 2004).

## PLAY AND CURRICULUM

*Curriculum* is one of those terms that is widely used but that does not have an agreed-upon definition (e.g., McNeil, 1990). In this book, curriculum is a school's course of study: the academic subjects, objectives and goals, instructional strategies, learning activities, methods of evaluation, and so on. In other words, curriculum is the entire academic program—what gets taught (content) and how this content is taught and assessed. We will examine the interplay between play and curriculum at a general level by examining overall play-curriculum relationships and at a more specific level by examining the role of play in several widely used early childhood education programs.

### Play-Curriculum Relationships

The relationship between play and curriculum can be analyzed along several different dimensions. First, one can examine the *amount* of relationship between play and the school curriculum. One will typically find one of three patterns:

- *Isolation.* Children's play activities are completely separate from the rest of the curriculum. For example, the class might be engaging in a unit or project on transportation and also engaging in literacy and mathematics activities. The dramatic play center is set up as a traditional housekeeping corner, and the block center contains no transportation toys. No attempt has been made to add literacy or numeracy materials to either play center. Under such conditions it is highly unlikely that the children's play activity will have any relationship with the ongoing study of transportation or contain any of the literacy or numeracy content that children are currently learning. There is a complete disconnect between play and the curriculum.

- *Juxtaposition.* Children are presented with play opportunities that are related to the academic curriculum (or curriculum activities that are related to play), but no attempt is made to take advantage of these relationships. Continuing with our transportation unit example, the teacher might set up a transportation-related dramatic play area and put some transportation toys and props (e.g., miniature road signs) in the block play area. The teacher does not draw children's attention to these props or make any connections during circle time, storybook reading, or small group instruction. Children have opportunities to play out what they are learning about transportation during play, but they must do this on their own (with perhaps a little help from their peers).

- *True integration.* The teacher provides connections between play and curriculum and makes a concerted effort to exploit the learning potential of these connections. Returning to our transportation unit example, the teacher would set up a transportation-related dramatic play center (e.g., a gas station or mechanics garage) and add theme-related props to the block area. The teacher would also draw the children's attention to possible transportation play opportunities and connect children's play activities to academic content. For example, after reading a book to the class about a mechanic, such as *Sylvia's Garage* by Debra Lee (2002), the teacher might suggest that the children engage in some of the same activities as mechanic Sylvia (putting oil the car's engine, checking the tire pressure) when they play in the gas station/garage play center. Or the teacher might point out that one of the children checked the tire pressure of a car during yesterday's play.

One can also examine the *direction* of the relationship between play and the curriculum: Curriculum can generate or influence children's play activities, and children's play behavior can help to determine curriculum content. Van Hoorn, Nourot, Scales, and Alward (1993) have labeled these relationships as follows:

- *Curriculum-generated play.* Play experiences are provided to help children learn academic concepts and skills. The academically enriched play centers discussed in Chapter 7 are examples of this approach. Play centers are equipped with theme-related literacy and mathematics materials that help children incorporate reading, writing, and numeracy activities into their play. Curriculum-generated play gives children an opportunity to consolidate and practice concepts and skills that are learned in the academic curriculum. In addition, this type of play gives teachers an opportunity to observe and assess what children have learned and retained from instructional activities.

- *Play-generated curriculum.* Curriculum activities emerge from the interests that children reveal during play. For example, if children express interest in gardening during play (e.g., pretending to plant and grow flowers or vegetables), their teacher could take advantage of this interest by planning a project or unit that focuses on how plants grow. This could include field trips to a nearby garden, science experiments (e.g., growing lima bean seeds in a Zip-lock bag), setting up a class garden on the playground, and reading books about plants and gardening. Projects and integrated units tend to be much more successful when they focus on things that children really want to learn about. Play can offer a perfect opportunity for teachers to discover these high-interest topics.

## Role in Early Childhood Programs

Play is very important in the major models of early childhood education. Model programs are examples of high-quality practices, and each has distinctive features and different orientations to incorporating children's play into the curriculum. Here we will briefly examine three well-known models that are European in origin and three that developed in the United States. All have been widely disseminated worldwide, being imitated or adapted to indigenous cultural communities in developed and developing countries.

**Montessori.** Maria Montessori (1870–1952), Italy's first female physician, developed a well-known model of early childhood education originating with Casa dei Bambini (Children's House) in 1907 for impoverished children ages four to seven years. To this day, mixed ages are a hallmark of the Montessori model. She is credited with inventing special materials that are self-correcting as children play and work at their own rates in the areas of art and music, language, science, geography, practical life, and the education of the senses (sensorial materials).

The environment is viewed as an extra teacher in a Montessori classroom, with the actual teacher, or "directress," serving as the keeper and custodian of the classroom environment. The teacher shows children how to use materials correctly, observes children, and encourages children to use the materials independently without teacher interference. There is great respect for the unique individuality of each child. There are four kinds of materials in a Montessori program:

- Practical life activities and materials are divided into four areas: care of the environment, self care, life skills, and grace and courtesy. Various materials used for practical life include pouring items such as water and beans, tweezers and eyedroppers for transferring, dressing frames, jars with lids, and nuts and bolts.
- Sensorial materials are also called "materialized abstractions," "keys to the universe," and "paths to culture." These attractive materials are arranged from simple to complex, have a single built-in concept, and are self-correcting, such as precut shapes and inserts to teach shapes. Children learn abstract concepts such as seriation, classification, and resistance from concrete materials such as cylinder blocks, the pink tower, color tablets, and the fabric box.
- Academic materials are for language, writing, reading, and math and cover a variety of cognitive skill and concepts. Examples of these materials include bead frames, cubes for learning powers, sandpaper letters, and movable alphabet letters.
- Cultural materials include those related to the arts, science, and social science.

Montessori education for young children emphasizes children's active involvement with the materials, independence from the teacher, individualization of learning, and the importance of the prepared environment. The wide range of materials cover many domains of learning and are used in a sequenced series as children work with them at their own pace. A sense of order is very important in the Montessori classroom. Maria Montessori believed that this sense of order was necessary for creativity. However, critics have pointed out that her materials, her "pedagogical devices," cannot be used creatively because they are used in a predetermined order and are self-correcting. Also, Montessori education has been associated with lack of fantasy play; she believed that the low-income children whom she first taught in Rome many years ago needed order, control, and realism in their play and work at school much more than they needed fantasy play. Many programs today, however, do offer some time and space for sociodramatic play as a complement to the Montessori curriculum. This concession is made in response to the weight of evidence that says such play is important in early childhood.

**Reggio Emilia.** Reggio Emilia, named after a city in Northern Italy where it began right after World War II, is not a model program in a strict sense, with set methods, teacher certification, and an accreditation process. However, it is a distinctive approach with a strong vision of the child. Its founder, Loris Malaguzzi (1920–1994), espoused social constructivism as in the work of Piaget, Vygotsky, and Dewey. He saw the child as a future citizen and protagonist, a human being who is very resourceful and involved in becoming a producer in society.

Visitors to Reggio Emilia schools encounter a very aesthetically pleasing environment. There are many photos of children at play and other scenes from school life. Many plants are there, and displays of children's work. Inside the classrooms are large spaces for work and play, with many elegant displays of the products of the children's activities. Transcriptions of conversations by children and teachers are also posted, as are descriptions of the teacher's purposes for various short- and long-term projects. From this the visitor can surmise that documentation is a distinguishing characteristic of the Reggio Emilia approach to early education, along with artwork, aesthetics, and a close relationship with parents and the community.

Creative expression is the primary activity in the curriculum. Great credence is given to the idea that children have considerable potential and openness and want to communicate and express themselves using the hundreds of languages of childhood. These languages include sculpture, shadow play, collage, music, dramatic play, painting, words, and pantomime. Creative, artistic expression is a way of knowing and ties together other aspects of the program. Children learn by finding ways to communicate their understandings, their ideas. Reggio Emilia schools have an art studio on the premises, and a special art teacher, a professional artist, to work with the children.

Many play opportunities exist. Teachers respect children's play and provide plenty of time, space, and materials. There are dolls and housekeeping items, large and small blocks, puzzles, and the like. The environment is organized to invite high-quality play and extended involvement with materials, often in small groups. Teachers believe that playing helps young people practice and elaborate their developmental skills and cognitive abilities. Often children are videotaped or photographed while playing. Sometimes their play verbalizations are audio recorded. Teachers use these data to engage children in conversations to learn more about their thoughts and feelings or to discuss among themselves or with parents. The atmosphere of the classroom is playful and uplifting, with zest for life and creative expression.

**Waldorf.** The Waldorf early childhood classroom is an extension of the home, in design, function, and atmosphere. Daily chores, which were the rhythm of traditional family and community life, show up in the Waldorf early childhood education program and provide a sanctuary for children. Part kitchen, part playroom, the physical environment is marked by delicate odors, fresh flowers, curtained walls, subdued lights and colors, and simple and natural furniture. When children arrive in the morning, they can find an open place to play and can use screens, blocks, tables, and lengths of cloth to make their own play environment.

Rudolf Steiner (1861–1925), who founded the Waldorf model of education after World War I in Germany, emphasized two valuable ways in which young children develop a sense of community. One is imitation, and the other is play. Young children are naturally inquisitive about the work of adults and want to imitate what they see to deepen their own understanding. So Waldorf teachers consider it very important to give children something valuable to imitate. They engage in the work of the home or classroom, such as mending classroom materials, preparing food for snacks, polishing tables, washing floors, and caring for the plants that adorn the windowsills. Each of these tasks is rooted in meaningful, day-to-day necessity. The children are not coerced to do this work alongside the teacher but are always welcomed when they decide to imitate the teacher's behaviors. This self-initiated imitation enables children to learn to do their part for the classroom community and to learn to rely on others.

Play is a very important way by which children develop a sense of community. Play provides safe opportunities to practice social interactions. Children can try out different roles, work through conflicts, and attempt various methods of communication, all under the pretense of play. Social play allows children to practice their social skills and to learn how to function within a group. Lengthy periods of time designated for true imaginative play in the Waldorf classroom permit children to *experience* community in a protective, aesthetically pleasing setting while strengthening their emotional maturity.

In addition to sufficient time and appropriate space, children have open-ended materials for play. They do not have prestructured play environments such as post office, hospital/medical center, or castle, nor are there many ready-made toys such as police cars or fire engines. Waldorf believes that play materials must have open-ended potential. Few realistic props are found. Even dolls have featureless faces. Children must have the opportunity to transform, not simply use materials that were preformed by adults. Plenty of blocks of wood, ribbons, and baskets with shells and driftwood, for example, are in the Waldorf early childhood environment.

Teachers respect play and children's privacy and seldom intervene to try to extend play with the teacher's aims in mind. Play is seen as a manifestation of the children's will and as coming from their inner needs, which arise from their impressions from their experiences, such as seeing workers repairing a road or hearing a fairy tale told by the teacher. Very rarely, if ever, does a teacher try to turn a child's play into a lesson.

**The Project Approach.** The project approach has a long tradition in American progressive education, going back to John Dewey and his Laboratory School at the University of Chicago in the late nineteenth century and early twentieth century. The project approach is not an early childhood education model or curriculum, technically speaking. But it is part of the curriculum for three- to eight-year-olds in many schools. Projects are an in-depth investigation of a worthwhile topic by a class, a group, or even a single child in a program. A project complements other aspects of the curriculum. For preschoolers projects are a more formal complement to their informal and play activities; for older children they are a more informal complement to their more formal academic instruction.

Projects serve well the goals of early education. They are multifaceted enough that individual needs and interests can be met, and positive affect and dispositions are fostered. Many concepts and skills, including research and computer skills, are developed when, for example, a classroom conducts a project about a local pond or about a school bus. Projects usually take at least two weeks to complete, and some last for months. Children learn to represent and communicate the results of their research endeavors. They learn to work as a team and to respect individual differences in knowledge and ability. Many program curricular aims and state early learning standards can be met by doing projects.

Children's play interfaces with the projects method in a number of different ways. First, teachers can get ideas for projects from watching play; projects are a stimulus for play-generated curriculum. For example, a teacher might discuss with the children the prospects of doing a project on hair or head coverings after seeing children's enthusiastic responses to playing barbershop, beauty parlor, or hat store. Then in the early phases of project work children could be asked to draw pictures and make up stories from the previous experiences with barbershops, beauty parlors, or hat stores. Children might be asked to dramatize these experiences. The project method then goes into an in-progress stage that involves fact-finding field work, research, and field trips, as well as recording and organizing information. Projects may culminate in a variety of ways, some of which may involve play behaviors. For example, a kindergarten class might make up a story and enact a script involving barbershops or beauty parlors. Music, dance, and movement activities might evolve in doing a project, as well as art and constructive play activities.

Another way in which play relates to the project method is as a substitute for embarking on a project. Katz and Chard (2005) suggest giving children opportunities for spontaneous dramatic play around a theme in which children show great interest but that the teacher does not think is a good topic for an in-depth, long-range project. A movie might stimulate high interest in pirates, for instance, but the teacher might decide that doing a project on this topic would not meet educational, developmental, or moral goals. The teacher might believe that it is not worth the time and energy required for the sustained effort a project demands and that there are better topics to pursue. So the teacher would let the children play pirates without its being part of a project, to show respect to the children's interests while at the same time taking responsibility for the children's education.

**High/Scope.** This well-known model originated in Ypsilanti, Michigan, in the 1960s under the direction of David Weikert. The curriculum is cognitively oriented and was influenced a great deal by the theory of Jean Piaget. From the start the High/Scope program served low-income children, and over the years it has become the curriculum of choice for many Head Start programs in the United States and many early education programs in developing countries. High/Scope does not require specialized play and learning materials as Montessori does, for instance, and can use whatever materials are available on location, including inexpensive, natural, and found objects. Consistent with Piagetian theory, emphasis is put on the child as an active agent in his or her own development.

A prominent characteristic of High/Scope is the daily routine, which aims to provide a consistent, secure, and controlled environment for the children to help them develop confidence in the adults around them and a sense of responsibility for their own actions. Teachers see themselves as participants in the children's experiences, asking open-ended questions to stimulate conversations and encouraging children to make choices and become involved in play activities in an open-framework environment. The High/Scope daily schedule includes large and small groups, snack time, and so on, as other early childhood education programs do, but also includes as its defining feature the "plan, do, and review" activity period:

- *Plan.* During the planning phase the children state their intentions. Expressing choices is done by pointing or saying a word, short sentence, or detailed description, depending on the child's ability. Programs use various external mediators to facilitate this process.
- *Do.* This is a long period of active play when children execute their plans. Interestingly, this period is called "work time" in many High/Scope classrooms. A range of play and work opportunities exist during the doing phase, as well as other times during the daily schedule. Curricular categories include movement, music, creative representation, seriation, classification, time, space, number, initiative and social relations, and language and literacy. Each category is subdivided into specific experiences; for example, creative representation includes draw and paint; pretend and role play; and object constructions with blocks, clay, and other materials.
- *Review.* Once things have been put away, the children have review time, when the teachers guide them to reflect on the play and work experiences that they executed during the doing phase of the daily routine. Children think about their accomplishments and respond by naming playmates, recounting problems encountered, dictating a story, or simply telling what they did. Recall strategies can include drawing pictures, reviewing their plans, verbal recall, or making models.

High/Scope has documented its effectiveness in longitudinal evaluation research, which shows life and school successes of its preschool graduates (Weikert & Schweinhart, 2005). The program attributes its success to its emphasis on developing competences in children, getting them to try things, and getting them to trust adults. Play in this model is viewed primarily as instrumental to the achievement of intellectual and social aims set by the teachers, unlike Waldorf's and Reggio Emilia's views of play as arising from the inner needs of the children.

**Bank Street.** The Bank Street College of Education in New York City has long been associated with a developmental-interaction approach to early education. The Bank Street approach highlights the fact that child development is an interaction among various dimensions of development, such as social, emotional, and cognitive, as well

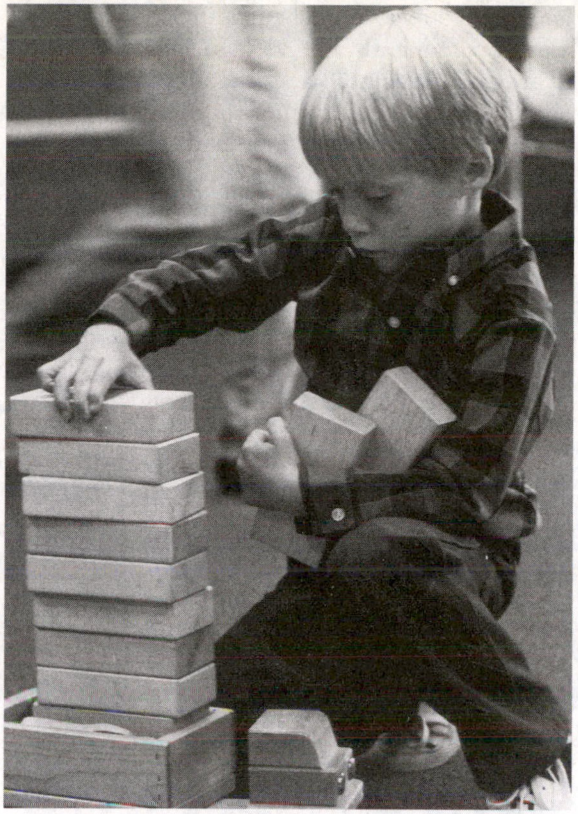

➤ The Bank Street approach to early childhood curriculum uses open-ended materials such as unit blocks, for which it is famous.

as an interaction between the child and significant others in the environment. Child development is seen in dynamic terms and in a social context.

Social studies is the core of the curriculum as children are encouraged to learn about the relations between and among people, and connections with the environment and history. Experiences in democratic life are emphasized. Literacy, math, and other subjects are integrated with social studies. It is assumed that the what and the how of learning are interconnected (Cuffaro, Nager, & Shapiro, 2005) and that children learn from experience. For experience to be educative, there must be active involvement by the child, and there must be continuity with past and future experiences. The teacher is a guide who links the child's world with the material to be covered in the curriculum, which includes practical and academic skills. The teacher strives to meet each child's developmental needs while creating a democratic, humane, and cognitively demanding classroom.

Play is incorporated into this approach as an integral part of the curriculum. Time and space are appropriately allocated for constructive and dramatic play. Imaginative and artistic expressions and representations are advanced by the presence of open-ended materials such as unit and hollow blocks, for which Bank Street is famous, as well as clay, paint, water, sand, paper, crayons, and wood. More structured materials include puzzles, weaving, books, writing materials, and computers.

Dramatic play centers and dress-up clothes are available for sociodramatic play. There is time for children to actively explore materials, to take trips, and to work together on different activities in small groups. There is also time for rooftop outdoor play on a daily basis, weather permitting.

Play is also integrated with other aspects of the curriculum. Daily classroom life often benefits from field trips and visitors and other resources, and content from these opportunities often find their way into children's literacy activities and artwork, as well as play. For example, children can nonverbally express their thoughts and feelings with paint, wood, paper, and crayons, or they can express their experiences and satisfy their inner needs through other types of play, including pretend play. The Bank Street curriculum is holistic and emergent at times, as when a theme such as a hurricane comes up to hold the class's interests and to generate and to link various learning and play experiences for a period of time. Play is seen both from the child's experiential point of view and from a more functional perspective, including being a means for individual social-emotional and intellectual development, as well as for fostering skill and understanding of democratic group living.

## SUMMARY

Materials and child development stand in a two-way relationship with each other. Materials can directly or indirectly facilitate specific areas of the child's development, such as literacy, cognitive, or language. At the same time the child's level of development influences the types of materials he or she chooses to play with. Materials can be used to enhance play behavior in the classroom or center. The potential of materials and the curriculum to positively influence learning and development depends on the teacher. Teachers should seek to make connections between enrichment activities, academic learning in the curriculum, and children's play to maximize the benefits.

Play materials for children in early childhood education programs come in many varieties. Key dimensions or characteristics of them include open/closed, simple/complex, soft/hard, and multicultural. Types of play materials include replica toys, animate toys, transportation toys, dramatic play props, educational toys (puzzles, blocks, books, zipping boards, etc.), and construction toys (unit blocks, table blocks, large hollow blocks, foam blocks and plastic crates, building sets, gross motor toys, games, art materials, literacy materials, and woodworking materials). A good toy or play material encourages complex play, stimulates the imagination, and can be used in a variety of ways and combinations and in more sophisticated play; it must also be safe and developmentally appropriate. Materials should be conducive to a broad and deep play experience. Guidelines for selection of materials can be found in books, state licensing regulations, and accreditation criteria.

Curriculum refers to the totality of experiences in a program, the enrichment, academic, and play content. Teachers should deliberately use curriculum aspects in relationship to one another. Curriculum can enrich play; play can enrich curriculum. There are three patterns in the amount of the relationship between play and the school curriculum: isolation, juxtaposition, and true integration. Two patterns in the direction of the relationship are curriculum-generated play and play-generated curriculum. In curriculum-generated play, play is provided to reinforce the curriculum (e.g., academically enriched play centers). Here two functions are served: Children can consolidate learning, and teachers can observe play as assessment to determine learning levels and any needed curriculum modifications. In play-generated curriculum, curriculum emerges from interests revealed in children's play. A variety of ways in which play can be incorporated into a early childhood program are illustrated by specific well-known approaches or models. The Reggio Emilia model views play as arising from the needs of the child, whereas High/Scope and Montessori are more representative of an instrumental perspective. Bank Street and the Projects Approach reflect both perspectives. Each of these programs has distinguishing features that set it apart from the others, and the programs suggest a range of ways in which children's play can be incorporated into the early childhood education curriculum.

## PROJECTS AND ACTIVITIES

1. Obtain a toy catalog, and cut pictures out and group them according to the types of play materials discussed in this chapter.
2. Select six play materials from Activity 1, and analyze each material for play potential and make age recommendations.
3. Bring to class a really worthless toy that you bought at a local store and tell why you believe this is one of the world's worst toys.
4. Visit a preschool or kindergarten classroom, and observe the curriculum in operation. Give particular attention to how, when, and where children play. Analyze the relationship between play and curriculum to determine whether it is an example of isolation, juxtaposition, or true integration.

CHAPTER 9

# Enriching Classroom Play: Teaching Strategies and Facilitation Techniques

## INTRODUCTION

A group of four-year-old preschoolers has decided to take a make-believe train trip from Phoenix to France. They first decide to make the corner loft into the train. They tell the teacher their plan, and he helps them move some chairs to the loft so that the passengers and crew have a place to sit. The children also decide that they need some signs to designate the identity of the train and to regulate the behavior of the passengers. So they ask their teacher to help them make two signs: "Train" and "No Smoking." The children dictate the words for the signs and tell the teacher what type of illustration to make (e.g., a cigarette with a line through it for the "No Smoking" sign). One boy makes his own sign, "No Ghosts," using scribblelike writing and a picture that looks more or less like a ghost (with a line through it, just like the teacher's signs). He declares that this is so that no "ghostes" will come on the train. All three signs are put up on the side of an elevated loft that has become the train. While waiting for the teacher and one last passenger to get on board, three of the boys lean over the side of the loft and start reading the signs: "No Smoking," "No Ghosts." However, they cannot figure out what that last sign says. Pointing to the "Train" sign, they ask, "Teacher, what's that say?" The teacher responds, "That's the train sign you asked me to make." One of the boys responds, "Oh, yeah . . . Train!"

In this vignette the teacher is very actively involved in the children's play. He helps them to set the stage for their train dramatization by assisting with moving the chairs to the loft and by helping to make the signs that the children want to put on the train. In addition, he gives them assistance in reading the one sign that they cannot figure out on their own. This is a good example of a teacher providing scaffolding that creates Vygotsky's (1978) zone of proximal development and enables children to do things that they are not quite capable of doing on their own.

We believe that when teachers skillfully support and extend children's ongoing play, both play and learning are enhanced (e.g., Neuman & Roskos, 1992). However, there is an art and a science to play facilitation. If not done appropriately, teacher involvement can disrupt and impede children's play endeavors and their learning (e.g., Schrader, 1990). In addition, there is a longstanding tradition in early childhood education for teachers not to interfere in children's play, stretching back to the psychoanalytically oriented writings of Susan Isaacs (1930). This might explain why a recent investigation of fifty African-American Head Start teachers' beliefs about play revealed that although almost all the teachers highly valued play in the classroom, a majority responded negatively to a vignette, similar to the one above, in which a teacher intervened and helped some preschoolers make play money for a grocery store dramatization (Spielberger & McClane, 2002). Advocates of teacher involvement in play have some steep hurdles to overcome.

In this chapter we explore ways in which teachers can effectively facilitate children's classroom play by providing adequate time, preparatory experiences, and appropriate types of involvement in play. We closely examine the debate surrounding teacher roles in play, and we describe roles that research has shown to enhance play and roles that should be avoided. Finally, we discuss how teachers can link play with academic instruction through use of curriculum connections and guided play.

### FOCUS QUESTIONS

1. What are your views on the teacher's role in play?
2. Why is it important for teachers to provide adequate time for play? How much time is needed?
3. What are preparatory experiences? How can these experiences help to facilitate children's play?
4. What are appropriate roles for teachers in play? What are some inappropriate roles?
5. How can teachers effectively link play with ongoing academic instruction?

## PROVIDING ADEQUATE TIME FOR PLAY

One of the most important aspects of facilitating high-quality classroom play is to provide adequate time for children to play. Cognitively complex forms of play, such as sociodramatic play and constructive play, require a considerable amount of time to plan and carry out. To engage in sociodramatic play, children need time to recruit other players, negotiate the roles to be enacted, agree on the story line to be dramatized, designate the make-believe identities of objects, and construct props that will be used in the dramatization. It has been our experience that these preparations often take far more time than the actual time required for children to act out their stories. Complex constructions can also take hours or days to complete.

Research has shown that lengthy play periods are required for these complex, sustained types of play to flourish. For example, several studies have found that preschoolers engage in higher social and cognitive forms of play during thirty-minute play periods than during fifteen-minute sessions (Christie, Johnsen, & Peckover, 1988; Tegano & Burdette, 1991). During the longer play periods, children were more likely to engage in sociodramatic and constructive play, whereas during the shorter periods the children tended to engage in simpler forms of play, such as functional (motor) play and nonsocial parallel-dramatic play. During the shorter play periods the children also engaged in more nonplay activities (e.g., unoccupied, onlooking, and transition behaviors).

What lies behind this relationship between time and play complexity? On the basis of our experiences observing children at play, we have several hypotheses:

- *Sociodramatic play.* When play periods are short, children often have to stop and clean up just after they get started acting out their stories. Sometimes they have to quit before they have even finished their preplay preparations! When this happens a number of times, children tend to give up on group-dramatic play and settle for less advanced forms of play, which can be completed in short periods of time.

- *Complex constructive play.* Brief play periods are also not conducive to complex constructive play. Children are just getting involved in a construction when it is time to clean up and put the materials away. After a number of such experiences children may abandon this type of play completely, resort to stacking blocks up and then knocking them down, or resign themselves to building very simple structures. In this latter case many important benefits of extended constructive play— planning, persistence, cooperation, and problem solving—are lost. The opportunity for the constructive play to evolve into dramatic play is also greatly reduced.

How much time is needed for play? Christie et al. (1988) and Tegano and Burdette (1991) showed the advantage of having play periods last at least thirty minutes. Our own experience indicates that even longer periods are often required. Jim Christie spent a semester observing a preschool classroom that had rather generous, forty-minute play periods (Enz & Christie, 1997). Even with this amount of time the four-year-olds had often just finished preparing for a dramatization when it was time to clean up. Fortunately, the teachers were flexible and would let the children have an extra ten to fifteen minutes to act out their dramas. When it comes to time for play, the longer the period, the better.

Finding time for play in the busy school day can be a daunting challenge. The back-to-basics movement and the accompanying pressures to devote more time to structured academic activities have made it difficult for many early childhood teachers to schedule adequate amounts of time for free play (Christie & Wardle, 1992). In addition, externally imposed time constraints, such as arrival and departure times and lunch periods, have to be accommodated (Wien, 1996). We are aware of some kindergarten classes that have play periods that are only ten to fifteen minutes long or that permit free play only during before-school transition periods. We have also visited preschools with similar lack of play time.

We have several suggestions on how teachers can carve out enough time for high-quality play:

1. The ideal solution is to have a regularly scheduled, thirty- to sixty-minute free-choice or center period every day during which play is one of the options that children can choose. This might require examining the daily schedule to create more play time. Perhaps naptime can be shortened, lunchtime can be curtailed, or other schedules can be adjusted to free up time for play. If several brief play periods are scattered throughout the school day, consider combining them into one longer period. Such a schedule would be more conducive to the occurrence of advanced forms of play.

2. Make better use of available time by having a flexible schedule that can adjust to unexpected events and children's interests and ongoing activities. Wien (1996) conducted a qualitative study of how three preschool teachers structured their daily schedules. She found that two teachers followed rigid "production schedules," in which the schedule was the dominant determinant of events in the classroom. This resulted in fragmented, brief periods of play. Another teacher was much more flexible and constantly adapted her schedule to fit her goals and the activities of the children. As a result, when children were engaged in rich, sustained play, she juggled the schedule to permit them to finish their play activities.

3. Allow complex, sustained play to roll over to the next day. This usually involves some relaxing of the usual cleanup rules. For example, if a child is in the process of building a complicated block construction, a special tag can be placed on the structure, and it can be allowed to stand until it is completed the next day. Similarly, if children have assembled and constructed a set of props for a sustained dramatization but the story has not been completed by cleanup time, they can be allowed to store their props in a special place and continue with their story the next day.

Christie and Wardle (1992) present several other suggestions for making sure that all children have ample opportunity to engage in sustained play. First, teachers should avoid scheduling play solely as a before-school transition. Many children arrive just minutes before school starts, thus missing out on opportunities to engage in advanced forms of play. Second, teachers should ensure that support staff (therapists, psychologists, etc.) do not pull the same children out of play periods on a regular basis. All children, including those with special needs, benefit from sustained, enriched play experiences.

## PREPARATORY EXPERIENCES

There is an old saying that children play best at what they know best. The basic principle underlying this saying is that conceptual knowledge is a key ingredient in rich play. Conversely, if children have very limited knowledge of a topic, it is difficult for them to engage in play relating to that topic. Here is an example. When Jim Christie conducted his first study on literacy-enriched play centers (Christie & Enz, 1992), one of the theme centers was a bank. It turned out that this center was a total disaster. The preschoolers did not know what to do when they were trying to play in the center. As a result the children's attempts at dramatic play were unfocused, disjointed, and usually very brief. By interviewing the parents, Jim was able to discover that very few of the children had even been in a bank. What they had experienced was their parents using the drive-up teller. As a result of this insight, the play center was changed to a drive-up bank, and the children's play flourished.

This type of mismatch between children's prior knowledge and play themes can be avoided by the use of **preparatory experiences**—experiences that children have before they begin to play. Teachers can help to clarify children's understanding of themes and roles by providing relevant experiences such as field trips, classroom visits by people in different occupations, and books or videos about different jobs. A field trip to a nearby bank, for example, could have been used to acquaint the children in Jim's study with what goes on inside a bank. Alternatively, a bank clerk and/or a bank officer could have visited the class and explained what they do in their job, or a children's book about a bank, such as *Bank Tellers* by Katie Bagley (2001), could have been read to the children. Smilansky (1968) found that these types of preparatory experiences greatly increased the effectiveness of her sociodramatic play training procedures. Table 9.1 lists preparatory experiences that can be used with a variety of dramatic play themes.

## TEACHER INVOLVEMENT IN PLAY

Teacher involvement in play has long been a controversial subject. As we mentioned at beginning of the chapter, there has been a longstanding tradition in early childhood education that teachers should not interfere in children's play. This tradition stems back to the psychoanalytic view that play's main function is to enable children to work out their inner conflicts (Isaacs, 1930). According to this view, the teacher's role was to set the stage for play and to observe children's play closely for clues about their emotional adjustment. Teachers were cautioned never to interfere with children's play because such interference might disrupt play, inhibit children from revealing their true feelings, and reduce play's therapeutic benefits. The results of Spielberger and McClane's (2002) recent research on Head Start teachers' attitudes about play show that this hands-off attitude still persists today.

Beginning in the 1960s and 1970s, forces emerged to challenge this noninterventionist stance toward teachers' roles in play. Starting with Smilansky's (1968) pioneering research in Israel, a series of play training studies demonstrated that adults could help low-income children learn how to engage in sociodramatic play and possibly lead to gains in play-related areas of development (Trawick-Smith, 1998). Around the same time Vygotsky's (1978) notion of the zone of proximal development rose to prominence, suggesting that adults could help young children engage in advanced forms of play that children could not do on their own. In addition, a series of studies conducted in preschools in Britain indicated that teachers were not interacting very much or very well with children during play, resulting in a preponderance of immature forms of play in classrooms (Sylva et al., 1980; Tizard et al., 1976a; Wood, McMahon, & Cranstoun, 1980). During the 1990s a series of qualitative studies focused on specific roles that teachers adopt during play and identified spe-

**TABLE 9.1 Preparatory Experiences**

| Theme | Field Trip | Classroom Visitor | Children's Book |
|---|---|---|---|
| Post office | Post office | Mail carrier | Janet and Allen Ahlberg, *The Jolly Postman* (Little, Brown, 2001) |
| Grocery store | Supermarket, convenience store | Store manager, cashier | Bill Grossman, *Tommy at the Grocery Store* (HarperCollins, 1989) |
| Restaurant | Ethnic restaurant, fast-food restaurant | Waiter, chef, crew, manager | Douglas Florian, *A Chef* (Greenwillow, 1992) |
| Doctor's office | Doctor's office, hospital | Doctor, nurse | Martine Davidson, *Rita Goes to the Hospital* (Random House, 1992) |
| Airport | Airport | Pilot, ticket agent | Byron Barton, *Airport* (Harper & Row, 1987) |
| Gas station | Gas station | Attendant, mechanic | Debra Lee, *Sylvia's Garage* (Wright Group, 2001) |
| Police officer | Police station | Police officer, dispatcher | Marianne Johnson, *Let's Visit the Police Station* (Powerkids, 1999) |
| Space | Planetarium, observatory | Astronomer | Ian Graham, *The Best Book of Spaceships* (Kingfisher, 1998) |
| Firefighter | Fire station | Firefighter | Robert Munsch, *The Fire Station* (BT Bound, 1999) |

cific roles that appeared to enhance children's play-related learning (Enz & Christie, 1997; Jones & Reynolds, 1992; Roskos & Neuman, 1993). As a result of these influences, there was a shift toward acceptance of appropriate forms of teacher involvement in play.

Most recently, the rising influence of postmodernism and the reconceptualist movement in early education have resulted in a new force opposing teacher intervention in play. Proponents of postmodernism object to the notion that teachers should attempt to shape children's play so that it conforms to the teachers' preconceptions of "good play." Brown and Freeman (2001) explain:

> Postmodernists empower children, believing that they alone are uniquely capable of choosing personally meaningful occupations. They resist efforts to shape or control children's freely chosen activities by creating constraints about the materials, themes, or time devoted to play. (p. 261)

Postmodernists are concerned that teachers' efforts to influence play will be at odds with children's actual inclinations and interests. Thus the pendulum might swing back toward opposition to teacher involvement in play.

We begin this section with a brief review of research on play training and teacher involvement in play. Next, we provide concrete descriptions of positive teacher roles that have been found to facilitate play and negative roles that can disrupt and impede children's play efforts.

## Research

In the review that follows, we make a distinction between two types of research on teacher involvement in play. First, we examine play training studies, in which a special intervention is used to teach children play skills, usually those associated with sociodramatic play. This special intervention is either delivered by a researcher or by teachers who have received special training. Play training is an add-on to what teachers are already doing in the classroom. The second group of studies, which focus on teacher roles in play, examine how teachers normally interact with children during play. No special training or extra intervention is involved.

**Play Training.** Play training occurs when adults teach children how to engage in sociodramatic or other mature types of play. Interest in this type of training was initially sparked by a study conducted in Israel by Sara Smilansky (1968). She had observed that children from low-income North African and Middle-Eastern immigrant families engaged in far less sociodramatic play than did middle-class Israeli children. Because these immigrant children were also experiencing academic difficulties in school, Smilansky hypothesized that their school problems might be caused by their inability to engage in sociodramatic play. To test this hypothesis, she conducted a study in which large numbers of low-income preschool and kindergarten students were assigned to four treatment groups: direct experiences, such as field trips; play training; combination of play training and direct experiences; and control.

The play training, which was administered by the children's regular teachers, involved two types of intervention:

- *Outside intervention,* in which the adult remained outside of the play episode and used coaching to encourage play behaviors
- *Participation in the play* (inside intervention), in which the adult took a part in the children's play and modeled desired play behaviors

Results showed that both the play training and the combination treatments were very effective in increasing the amount and quality of the children's sociodramatic play. Both treatments also appeared to improve some aspects of the children's cognitive performance. Simply providing extra direct experiences, on the other hand, had no effect on the children's play or their cognitive abilities. Smilansky concluded that it was lack of knowledge of specific play skills, rather than inadequate experiential background, that kept many low-income children from engaging in sociodramatic play.

Beginning in the 1970s, U.S., British, and Canadian researchers conducted a number of play training experiments. These studies used either of two types of training strategies:

- *Sociodramatic play training.* Variations of Smilansky's outside intervention and participation-in-the-play strategies described above.

➤ In studying sociodramatic play, Smilansky hypothesized that school problems of low-income children might be caused by an inability to engage in sociodramatic play.

- *Thematic-fantasy play training.* A more structured type of training in which an adult helps children to enact fairy tales (e.g., *The Three Pigs*) or other repetitive stories. The adult reads the story, assigns roles to the children, and helps them to enact the story by prompting and at times by taking a role in the dramatization.

The results of play training research, on the whole, have been quite positive. Findings indicate that both sociodramatic play training and thematic-fantasy play training are very effective in increasing low-income children's participation in sociodramatic play (Christie, 1983; Dansky, 1980a; Saltz, Dixon, & Johnson, 1977; Smith, Dagleish, & Herzmark, 1981). In addition, both types of play training has been found to lead to gains in measures of intellectual and social development (Burns & Brainerd, 1979; Dansky, 1980a; Hutt, Tyler, Hutt, & Christopherson, 1989; Saltz et al., 1977). Thematic-fantasy training has been also linked to gains in various measures of story comprehension (Pellegrini, 1984; Saltz & Johnson, 1974; Silvern, Taylor, Williamson, Surbeck, & Kelley, 1986).

At the same time that these positive findings were being reported, other researchers pointed out several serious methodological weaknesses in play training studies (Christie & Johnsen, 1985; Smith & Syddall, 1978). One common problem has been the failure of experimenters to control for the effects of peer interaction and adult tutoring that accompany play training (Smith et al., 1981; Smith & Syddall, 1978). The possibility exists that the social and cognitive benefits of play training were caused by social interaction rather than by the play component of the training. From a theoretical perspective this is a serious weakness because it prevents the findings of play training research from being used as evidence that play has a causal role in cognitive development. From an applied perspective this limitation is less worrisome. Teachers are likely to be pleased with the finding that play training fosters increased amounts of sociodramatic play and produces gains in various aspects of social and cognitive development. Perhaps it is this pragmatic stance that sustained interest in play training, as witnessed by recent studies (e.g., Bondioli, 2001) and Trawick-Smith's (1998) recent review.

**Teacher Involvement in Play.** Beginning in the 1970s, British and American researchers began to investigate what teachers do while children are engaging in play. Initial findings indicated that teachers only spent between two and six percent of their time actively involved in children's play (Sylva, Bruner, & Genova, 1980; Tizard, Philps, & Plewis, 1976a; Wood, McMahon, & Cranstoun, 1980) and tended to restrict their involvement to a very superficial level (Hutt, Tyler, Hutt, & Christopherson, 1989). Similar findings of low levels of teacher involvement in play continued through the early 1990s (Farran, Silveri, & Cupp, 1991; Shin & Spodek, 1991).

More recently, researchers have reported increased amounts of teacher involvement in classroom play:

- Erwin, Carpenter, and Kontos (1993) reported that preschool teachers were engaged in facilitating play 27 percent of the time
- Grinder and Johnson (1994) discovered that childcare providers assisted in play 39 percent of the time.
- Kontos (1999) found that Head Start teachers spent 85 percent of free-play time helping children get involved in play and facilitating play. Most of this teacher involvement occurred in the constructive play (41 percent) and manipulatives (20 percent) areas of the classroom. Teachers spent relatively little time (12 percent) interacting with children in dramatic play areas.

It is possible that this large increase in teacher involvement in play has been caused in part with the growing acceptance of the concept of **developmentally appropriate practice,** which holds that early childhood curricula and teaching practices should match the developmental needs and characteristics of young children (Bredekamp & Copple, 1997). One of the basic tenets of developmentally appropriate practice is "the need for teachers to engage in supportive, responsive interactions with children during play" (Erwin et al., 1993, p. 2).

Research on *qualitative* aspects of this increased teacher involvement in has been less positive. For example, Kontos (1999, p. 379) reported that although Head Start teachers did spend a lot of time interacting with children during play, "the excerpts from the transcripts reveal that the conversations are not exactly filled with rich, stimulating content. . . . Clearly, there is room for growth in the area of quality." Earlier studies reported that teachers focused almost exclusively on cognitive aspects of play, such as children's use of materials, toys, or ideas (Erwin et al., 1993; File & Kontos, 1993). Support for social aspects of play, such as facilitating peer interaction, accounted for only two percent of play time in both studies.

Grinder and Johnson (1994) also reported some negative findings about the quality of teacher play interactions. Although the teachers in this study provided positive support for play 39 percent of the time, they spent another 27 percent of their time engaging in "play-interfering" behavior. These negative forms of interaction included distracting play, instructing, conversing, taking over play, inopportune questioning, and commanding.

In summary, the results of research on teacher activity during play periods have been mixed. Recent studies indicate that the *amount* of teacher involvement in play is increasing, but there are also growing concerns about the *quality* of this involvement.

A second group of studies have examined the outcomes of teacher involvement in play. Again, the findings are mixed, as one might expect, given the uneven quality of this involvement. Positive findings include the following:

- *Duration and elaboration.* Observational studies of British preschools revealed that children's play episodes lasted twice as long and were more elaborate when a teacher was involved than when the children played only with their peers (Sylva et al., 1980).
- *Social interaction.* Farran et al. (1991) reported that teacher involvement was associated with increased participation in social forms of play. Cooperative play, the highest category in Parten's (1932) social play hierarchy, occurred *only* in the presence of a teacher.
- *Cognitive activity.* Howes and Smith's (1995) large-scale study of 150 child-care programs revealed that positive teacher interaction was associated with higher levels of cognitive activity during play.
- *Literacy activity.* A series of studies have investigated children's play in literacy-enriched play settings (see Chapter 8). Results have shown that teacher involvement results in increased amounts of reading and writing behavior during play in these settings (Christie & Enz, 1992; Morrow & Rand, 1991; Vukelich, 1991).
- *Oral language.* Teachers who spent more time interacting with children during free play or small group activities also spent more time engage in cognitively challenging and pretending talk with children (Smith & Dickinson, 1994).

On the other hand, studies have also reported negative effects of adult involvement on play. Tegano, Lookabaugh, May, and Burdette (1991) reported that when kindergarten teachers imposed a high amount of structure on construction activities by presenting models to copy or by giving instructions, the amount of constructive play decreased, and nonplay activity increased. File and Kontos (1993) found that when teacher involvement is heavily biased toward cognitive aspects of play, the social quality of play often suffers. Finally, a number of other researchers have reported incidents in which overzealous teacher intervention disrupted children's ongoing play activities (Jones & Reynolds, 1992; Schrader, 1990; Wood et al., 1980). For example, Manning and Sharp (1977) reported an incident in which a six-year-old girl was playing with some shells in a sand tray, making up a pretend story. The shells represented people and trees, and the girl's finger was a make-believe cat. A teacher aide intervened by trying to draw the girl into a conversation about the pattern she was making with the shells: "Those shells are very pretty, aren't they? Doesn't the sand feel soft and smooth on your fingers—is it tickling? You have made a lovely pattern. Have you finished or are you going to put more shells or something in it?" (p. 18). This intervention disrupted the make-believe context or frame of the play, causing the girl to stop playing altogether.

The mixed results of the research reviewed in this section points out that *how* teachers interact with children during play is more important than *how much* they interact. Positive findings show that when teachers get involved in play in appropriate ways, children's play experiences can be enriched, and other positive outcomes, such as increased social interaction and cognitive activity, can occur as well. On the other hand, if teachers intervene in a heavy-handed or insensitive manner, play can be seriously disrupted. Effective play involvement is a challenging skill, requiring teachers to walk a "fine line between responsive and intrusive interactions" (File & Kontos, 1993, p. 15).

A third strand of research has sought to identify the different roles that teachers can adopt during play and to determine which roles have positive effects and which have negative effects on play. In the sections that follow, we discuss the facilitative and precarious roles that have been identified by this research and end with a discussion of why teachers need to be flexible how they interact with children during play.

## Facilitative Roles

Research has revealed that teachers assume a variety of roles when interacting with children during play (Enz & Christie, 1997; Roskos & Neuman, 1993). As we illustrate in Figure 9.1, these roles form a continuum from no involvement to complete domination of play. The roles in the center of this continuum have been found to be the most effective for enriching the quality of children's play and encouraging play-related literacy activities: observer, stage manager, coplayer, and play leader. The roles on the extreme ends of the curriculum tend to have negative effects. We describe the positive, facilitative roles in this section and then address the precarious and risky roles in the next section.

**Onlooker.** Onlookers serve as an appreciative audience for children's play activities. When in the onlooker role, teachers position themselves near the play space (but not actually in it), watch children as they play, nod or give other nonverbal signs of approval, and make occasional comments to the players. However, onlookers do not join in the play or do anything to enhance or disrupt the ongoing activity. The following vignette, from the Roskos and Neuman (1993) study, illustrates the low-key onlooker role:

> Several children are playing in the book corner, leafing through books and talking about the pictures in their books. Betty [the teacher] is sitting at a table nearby, watching the children with their books. She rests her chin in her hands, looking on with a smile. . . . She comments to the group, "You're having fun with your books. Aren't you having a good day?" The children look up at her momentarily, then continue to handle the books, pointing at the pictures. (p. 86)

The onlooker role has several important advantages. First, by paying attention to play, teachers let children know that their play activities are important. Second, the

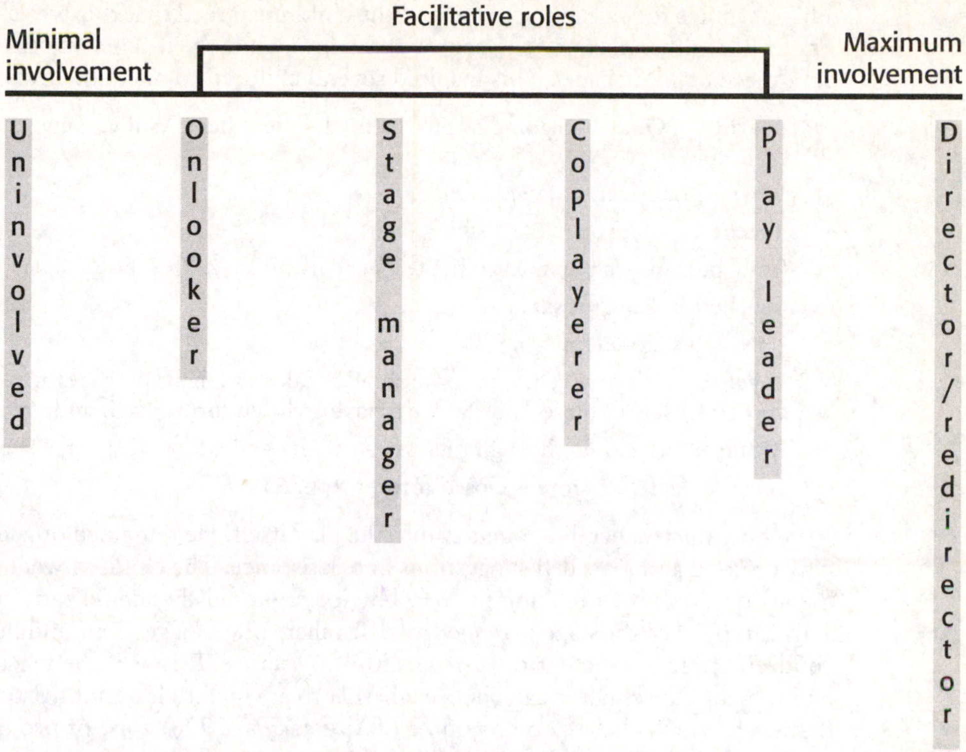


**FIGURE 9.1 A Continuum of Teacher Roles in Play**

➤ Effective roles are in the middle, whereas the roles on either end tend to have a negative effect on play

observation that accompanies the onlooker role informs teachers about what is going on in children's play. This information allows teachers to make informed decisions about when more direct forms of involvement, such as the stage manager, coplayer, and play leader roles, are needed. Observation also allows adults to tailor these more direct forms of involvement to match children's current play interests and activities. As explained in Chapter 3, play observation can allow teachers to assess children's play development and their social-intellectual development as well.

**Stage Manager.** Like onlookers, stage managers stay on the sidelines and do not enter into children's play. But unlike onlookers, stage managers take an active role in helping children prepare for play and offer assistance once play is under way. When in the stage manager role, teachers respond to children's requests for materials, help the children construct costumes and props, and assist in organizing the play set. Stage managers also may make appropriate theme-related script suggestions to extend the children's ongoing play. Kontos (1999) found that this was the most popular role for Head Start teachers, accounting for 47 percent of their activity during free-play time.

Enz and Christie (1997) provide an example of a teacher taking on the stage manager role while several preschoolers are playing toy store. The children began their play by gathering toys that they wanted to sell. The teacher suggested making a list of things for sale in the store, and the children agreed that this was a good idea. The children then dictated the names of the toys while the teacher wrote them down on a piece of chart paper. This inspired several children to make their own signs:

> **Teacher:** Okay: I'm going to put the toy list right here. Will you give me a piece of tape, Joey?
>
> **Joey:** Look what I signed.
>
> **Teacher:** Oh, you made a sign. Great!
>
> [Joey puts his sign up next to the teacher's list. It says, "KZ FR."]
>
> **Teacher:** What's it say?
>
> **Joey:** It's closed forever.
>
> **Teacher:** Oh-oh! Well, maybe we should make one that says the store is open. Can you make one of those, too? So we'd have a closed forever sign and an open sign.
>
> **Monica:** [Leans in through the store window and addresses Joey] I need a hat.
>
> **Joey:** Hey! This store is closed forever! (pp. 65–66)

Note how the teacher did not enter into the play itself. He remained outside the store play episode and provided suggestions and assistance. The children went along with the suggestion about making the list, but Joey ignored the idea of an "open" sign. This is typical of the stage manager role. Teachers offer suggestions and help, but the children are free to accept or disregard this assistance. It is as if the teacher floats a balloon, and the children can choose whether to grasp onto it or not. Also notice how the teacher provided a good example of Vygotsky's (1978) zone of proximal development, helping the children make the toy list that they could not make on their own. This scaffolding prompted Joey to make his own sign using invented spelling.

**Coplayer.** The coplayer role differs from the two preceding roles in that the teacher actually joins in and becomes an active participant in the children's play. Coplayers function as equal play partners with children. The teacher usually takes on a minor role in the drama, such as a patient or a passenger on a plane, leaving the prime roles (doctor/nurse, pilot/flight attendant) for the children. In enacting this role, the teacher carefully follows the flow of the dramatic action, letting the children take the lead most of time. In being the children's play partner, opportunities often arise for the teacher to model sociodramatic play skills such as role playing, make-believe transformations, and peer interaction strategies (e.g., how to enter into an ongoing dramatization). Kontos (1999) found that this type of play enhancer/playmate role (which also includes the play leader role described in the next section) was popular with Head Start teachers, accounting for 38 percent of their time during play. So preschool teachers are not shy about joining in children's play.

Roskos and Neuman (1993) present a vignette that recounts one preschool teacher's experience in the coplayer role:

> I ask Megan and Supraja if they want to play "making dinner." They say "Yes." . . . I sit at the table and I ask, "What's for dinner?" Megan begins looking for a bottle for the baby. Then she says she has to vacuum before dinner and begins propelling the toy vacuum around the area. Meanwhile, Supraja says she's making dinner. She points to the back of a box, points with her finger and pretends to read. She says, "We need a

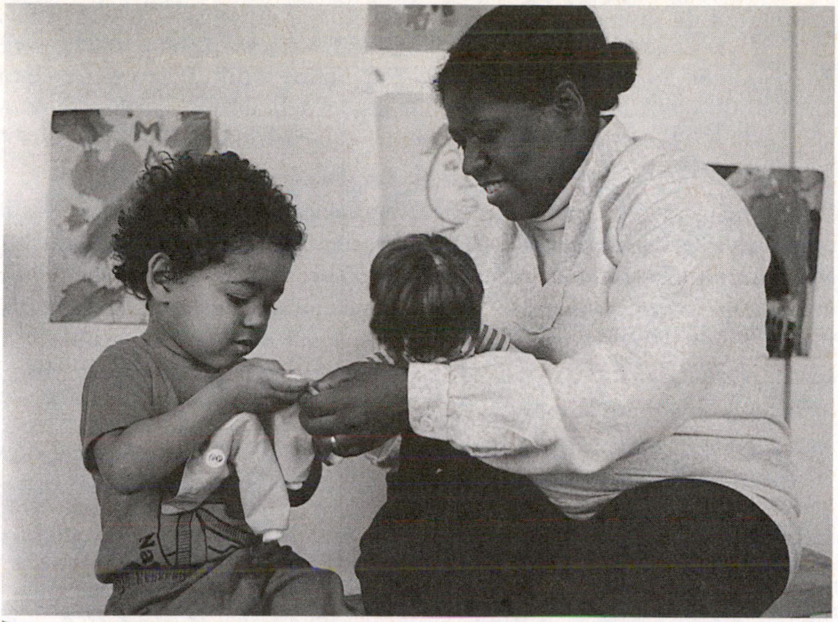

➤ In a coplayer role the teacher actively joins in and becomes an active participant in children's play. Coplayers function as equal partners with children.

> mixing spoon" and begins stirring some "food" in a pot. I say, "Is that a good recipe? I hope so. I'm really hungry." She looks at the back of the box again as if reading and wags her head back and forth. "Yup. It's good." She gives me a plate and says, "It's macaroni and cheese and eggs." I say, "Thank you," and start to eat. But they say, "Stop! Stop! You have to wait until everyone has their food." So I wait. (p. 87)

In this example the teacher initiated the play episode by inviting the children to play "making dinner." However, once the play started, the locus of control shifted to the children. The children determined what was for dinner and when it should be eaten. While in her make-believe role, the teacher subtly influenced the course of the play by asking about dinner and stating that she was hungry. She also modeled make-believe with regard to objects and actions by pretending to eat the invisible food.

**Play Leader.** As in the coplayer role, play leaders join in and actively participate in the children's play. However, when teachers are in the **play leader** role, they exert more influence and take deliberate steps to enrich and extend play episodes. Teachers do this by suggesting new play themes and by introducing new props or plot elements to extend existing themes. Adults often switch to this role when children have difficulty getting play started on their own or when an ongoing play episode is beginning to falter.

Kitson (1994) recommends that when children lose interest in a drama, the teacher should refocus the children by adding tension to their story. He gives the following example of how he intervened with a group of nursery children who were acting out a story about building a house:

> After sorting out what had to be done, the work started. It was not long before the children began to lose concentration in the "building" as there was little to hold their

> interest. In dramatic terms, there was little or no tension. It was at this point that intervention was needed. I then pretended to receive a phone call from the boss who was going to come round and check up on our work. We would have to make sure that the house had been put together properly. Immediately, the children were drawn back into the fantasy play and found a renewed vigour and purpose, created by the injection of tension. (p. 97)

In the following example, recorded in the Enz and Christie (1997) study, a group of preschoolers were making a pretend plane trip to Florida. The drama got off to a good start as the children prepared for takeoff and got their make-believe plane up into the air. After the meal had been served and naps were taken (it was a "sleeper" flight), the children began to lose interest. The teacher, who was in the role of passenger, reenergized and extended the drama by interjecting tension into the plot by mentioning rough weather and the possibility of a plane crash:

> **Teacher:** The wind is blowing and the plane is bouncing up and down. Oh, the plane is bouncing.
>
> **Channing:** Don't worry. We have [air sickness] bags.
>
> **Joey:** This airplane's going around and around.
>
> **Channing:** We had better get our stuff.
>
> **Teacher:** Are we going to evacuate the plane? Okay, let's land. Maybe we'll have a crash landing. Let's land the plane. [Children start screaming.]
>
> **Teacher:** Crash landing! Oh—crash landing!
>
> **Joey:** Okay, guys, let's get off the plane now.
>
> **Channing:** Okay, let's abandon ship.

The play continued for many more minutes as the children got off the plane and discovered that they had crashed in a Florida swamp. The teacher enlivened the plot further by adding another crisis for the children to contend with: alligators!

## Precarious Roles

When it comes to adult involvement in play, either too little or too much can have negative consequences. Problems can occur either when adults are totally uninvolved in play or when they get too involved and take over control of the play or try to redirect toward academic goals that are not connected with the play.

**Uninvolved.** Research in preschool settings has revealed that some teachers tend to ignore the play that is occurring in their classrooms (Enz & Christie, 1997; Sylva et al., 1980; Tizard et al., 1976a; Wood et al., 1980). These teachers use play periods to prepare for upcoming activities, do paper work, and to chat with other adults. Enz and Christie (1997) found that when teachers adopted this uninvolved role, children tended to engage in large amounts of functional motor play and rough-and-tumble activity. When children engaged in sociodramatic play, the episodes were simplistic and often quite raucous, featuring themes such as monster, superheroes, or dogs versus cats (the girls' favorite). The boisterous nature of this play had the unintended result of forcing the teachers to be safety monitors who attempted to curb undesirable or unsafe play behaviors. When the teachers acted as safety monitors, they spent a considerable amount of time issuing verbal warnings ("Don't run," "Stop pushing"), intervening to settle disputes, and taking measures to ensure the children's safety.

**Director.** At the other end of the involvement continuum is the director role, in which the adult takes over control of children's play. When teachers take on the role of director, they remain on the sidelines and tell children what to do while playing. Enz and Christie (1997) give the following example of a preschool teacher who used the **director** role to encourage the children to enact a birthday party.

> **Teacher:** Brittany, come here. Do you get to wear a party hat? Would you like to wear this? This is the special one for the birthday person. Could you put that on? It's like a crown.
>
> **Brittany:** No. [Responding to the hat idea.] I already have this [referring to her hair ornament].
>
> **Teacher:** Can you make us a sign for November? We have to pretend it's your birthday. [Brittany goes to get paper to make a sign.] Let's make a sign. [Teacher begins passing out clay for the cake and candles.]
>
> **Brittany:** Real candles?
>
> **Teacher:** Paco, Paco. Do you want to make the cake? Who wants to make the cake?
>
> **Brittany:** Not me, I'm the birthday girl.
>
> **Teacher:** But see, lookit. She's gonna put candles on the cake, too. Real candles! How about if we make two cakes? Paco, you make one. You get one candle. Everyone gets a candle. And then, Joseph, you get one, too. You have to make the cake. Make one, make the cake. Take the candles out. Make the cake first, and then we'll put the candles on. Where's that "November" sign? (68)

The children responded to this excessive direction by sneaking away to other areas of the classroom. Within a few minutes, only one child remained—Paco, an English language learner who seemed to enjoy being told what do to during play.

**Redirector.** A related role—the redirector—occurs when play is used inappropriately as a medium for academic teaching. When in the redirector role, teachers remain outside the play and ask questions aimed at suspending make-believe and interjecting reality into the play episode. Wood and his associates (1980) reported that this role, which they referred to as "spokesman for reality," was used frequently by teachers but had mixed results. Sometimes the children's play was not seriously disturbed by the adult's reality-oriented comments and questions. The children would come up with thoughtful answers to the questions and continue on with their play. On other occasions the adult's intervention would seriously disrupt the make-believe play frame, causing the children to stop playing. The example cited earlier in this chapter, in which a teacher aide disrupted a girl's pretend play with sea shells by trying to get the girl to discuss the shells' physical characteristics, illustrates the potential negative effects of being a spokesman for reality.

Schrader (1991) gives another excellent example of a preschool teacher using the redirecting style. In this episode Angie was engaged in a dramatization in the home center that centered on phone conversations when the teacher approached and tried to get her to write a letter to the Easter Bunny. Because this had nothing to do with their ongoing play, the teacher's involvement was more disruptive than beneficial:

**Angie:** (*Sits at table in house, handles papers, uses phone*)

**T:** (*Talks across the room.*) Are you ready to um . . . to write your letter for Easter?

**Angie:** (*No response.*)

**T:** I'll come over and we'll write for Easter. (*Goes to house, sits with child at the table.*) Now, do you write a letter to the Easter Bunny?

**Angie:** (*No response.*)

**T:** I wonder what he would do if we wrote a letter to him.

**Angie:** (*No response.*)

**T:** Do you think that he'll like to get a letter?

**Angie:** (*No response.*)

**T:** I think that he would. Let's . . . You write a letter, and I'll write a letter to him. Okay? . . . Now what are you going to say to the Easter Bunny, Angie?

**Angie:** I don't know. (*Shrugs shoulders.*) . . .

**T:** (*Makes cursive-like lines on paper as she talks.*) "Dear Easter Bunny, I will be at my house on Easter Sunday. I will still have company at my house. I hope you will leave me some Easter eggs . . . I love you Mr. Easter Bunny. Okay then, you write your letter. (*Points to Angie's paper*).

**Angie:** (*Watches teacher, does not write*) . . .

**T:** Okay. What are you going to say in your letter, Angie?

**Angie:** I can't think of anything. (pp. 207–209)

As a result of this interaction, Angie's play was completely disrupted, nor did she engage in any meaningful literacy activity. The basic problem is that the activity toward which the teacher was trying to steer Angie was completely unrelated to Angie's ongoing play.

As we will discuss in the next section, teachers can successfully link play with academic instruction. However, to be successful, this play-based teaching should differ from the redirector strategy in two ways:

1. The instruction must related to and extend ongoing play. In the preceding example the teacher might have suggested that Angie write down phone messages because Angie's current play centered on the toy telephone in the home center.

2. The teacher should tread lightly and make suggestions that the children are free to accept or reject. This allows children to remain in control of their play. To return to the balloon metaphor used earlier, the teacher could float the suggestion that Angie might like to write down phone messages for other family members. If Angie chose not to grab onto this balloon, the teacher should just let the idea float away. As the Easter Bunny example above illustrates, pressing the matter and insisting that children redirect their play usually does not work.

## Flexibility

There are two keys to successful teacher play involvement. First, teachers need to use the facilitative roles described above, and avoid the precarious ones. Second, teachers need to be flexible in their play interventions and choose the role that best fits with children's ongoing play interests, styles, and activities. Roskos and Neuman (1993) observed six experienced preschool teachers and found that they used a repertoire of roles—onlooker, coplayer, and play leader—to enrich children's dramatizations and to encourage literacy-related play. These veteran teachers switched roles frequently, depending on the children who were playing and the nature of play. The teachers' ability to switch roles to fit the children's play agenda appeared to be as important as the specific roles they used.

## LINKING PLAY WITH INSTRUCTION

Chapter 7 discussed educational play in which play activities are used to help children learn academic knowledge and skills. In this section we examine another approach for using play to promote learning: making direct links between play and academic instruction. This involves three strategies: making connections, guided play, and play-based assessment. These linkage strategies can help to align play activities with the rest of the school curriculum so that play reinforces and extends academic instruction.

### Making Connections

The easiest, simplest, and least intrusive way to maximize play's instructional impact is to connect the types of educational play described in Chapter 7—academically enriched play centers, games, simulations, and playground activities—with other parts of the curriculum. Actually, this is just basic good teaching. Children are likely to learn more from a series of connected activities than from a set of activities that have no relationship with each other. Connectivity enables learning activities to reinforce and build on each other. The result is an integrated educational experience in which the whole equals more than just the sum of its parts.

Achieving play-curriculum connections simply requires instructional planning. When selecting themes for academically enriched play centers, for example, teachers can link the center theme with an ongoing project/unit or with instruction in one of the subject areas. For example, if the class were involved in a unit on transportation, the dramatic play center could be temporarily transformed into a transportation-related setting (or series of settings): gas station, mechanic garage, airport/airplane, bus station, and the like. This enables children to act out and work through the knowledge that they are gaining about the topic of study. The play center can also help get families involved in the curriculum study. A note can be sent home, asking families to donate props from the new play center. This keeps families informed about the purpose of play activities and provides opportunities to make connections between play and children's cultural backgrounds.

Recently, Jim Christie visited a Head Start classroom that was engaging in a unit on automobiles and other wheeled vehicles. The teacher temporarily transformed the home center into a combination gas station and mechanic's garage. The parents, the majority of whom were native Spanish speakers, enthusiastically responded to the teacher's request for theme-related props. Some of the donations included real auto repair manuals, funnels (for pouring make-believe oil into engines), tire pressure gauges, and a broken scooter for the mechanics to repair. Several Spanish-language magazines and books were also donated.

To build the students' English vocabulary, the teacher was using a number of uncommon automobile-related words during story reading, discussions, and small-group instructional activities: *speedometer, hood, dashboard, gauge,* and so on. The play center offered an excellent context for the children to use these words in their own speech—both the English words used by the teacher and the words' Spanish translations (which the children figured out together or with help from their families). The play center offered an excellent opportunity for the teacher to assess the children's vocabulary growth and how well they understood the activities and routines that take place at a gas station and mechanic's garage.

The success of this play-curriculum strategy is highly dependent on the origins of the curriculum unit or project. If the unit or project originates from children's interests, then the play center will likely be successful. In the example just given, the teacher decided to do a unit on automobiles because a number of children expressed keen interest in this topic and wanted to learn more about cars and other types of vehicles. The teacher then used this child-generated theme to teach skills that the children needed to learn. Because they were interested in cars to begin with, it is hardly a surprise that the children greatly enjoyed playing and learning in the theme center.

These types of play-curriculum connections can be made with other forms of educational play. For example, if the math curriculum is stressing counting, the children can be encouraged to engage in games that involve scorekeeping, such as bowling or beanbag tossing (Trawick-Smith, 1994). The teacher can supply paper and markers and encourage the children to keep score. Of course, the actual scorekeeping will vary, depending on the children's age and mathematical development. Trawick-Smith (1994) gives an example of how two six-year-olds came up with completely different systems for scoring a game of bowling that the teacher had set up in a math center:

**Child A:** (Having just bowled) There, I got a lot of 'em!

**Teacher:** (Sets paper and markers down at a nearby table) If you want to keep score in your game, you can use these.

**Child A:** Okay! I'll write down how many. (Counts the number of pins he has knocked over) Four! (Writes a 4 on a sheet of paper)

**Child B:** It's my turn. (Bowls once, knocks over three pins. Gets the ball back and bowls again, knocking down four more. Standing close to the pins he rolls a third time, and the remainder of the pins fall)

**Child A:** C'mon. It's my turn.

**Child B:** (Ignoring child A, making his own score sheet) Okay, I'll put a three. (Writes this on paper)

**Child A:** Ah. You wrote a three?

**Child B:** Yeah. I rolled it once, and I rolled it again, and I rolled it again. Three.

**Teacher:** I see. It took you three times to knock them down.

**Child B:** Yeah. (To his playmate) It's your turn. (p. 165)

The children continued bowling for quite a while, each using their own scoring system. Both were getting valuable counting practice, reinforcing the teacher's mathematics instruction.

## Guided Play

Guided play is play that is structured to directly teach academic skills and concepts. As such, guided play is actually a blend of play and academic work. Because it is structured by the teacher and has a preset outcome or outcomes, it lacks some of the key characteristics of play. However, guided play often involves make-believe and can be quite fun and enjoyable. As discussed in the section on precarious roles, caution is needed in applying any strategy that uses play to accomplish nonplay outcomes. The guided play strategies described are intended to *supplement* the regular child-centered play experiences that children have in the classroom and on the playground. Guided play is not intended to be a replacement for real play. What it does replace is more traditional forms of academic instruction.

**Before-During-After Strategy.** Instructional activities can have more of an impact on learning if they are logically sequenced and connected with other learning experiences. The before-during-after strategy provides a simple means to accomplish this instructional integration. This strategy is commonly used with story reading, in which the teacher does one or two activities *before* reading to engage children's interest in the book, then pauses occasionally *during* reading to point out new vocabulary or to get children to make predictions about what might happen next, and finally engages children in a discussion and perhaps some type of response activity (e.g., art, drama) *after* reading to help deepen their understanding of the story.

The same strategy works very well with dramatic play. Box 9.1 presents an example of how one preschool teacher used the before-during-after strategy in connection

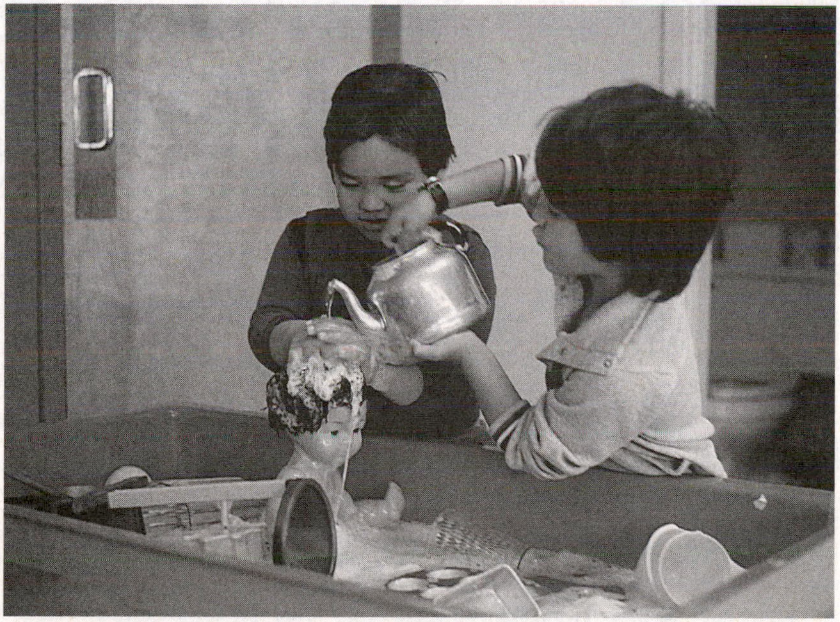

➤ In guided play, the teacher first observes children at play to learn their current play interests and activities.

with an academically enriched play center to help children learn new vocabulary and phonological awareness skills. In addition to this guided play, the children had many other free-play experiences during the day. Rather than replacing child-initiated play, this structured play activity was used to replace direct instruction on beginning letter sounds.

**BOX 9.1**

## Guided Play to Explore New Words and Their Sounds

**by Kathy Roskos, James Christie, and Donald Richgels**

With the teacher's help, the children are creating a gas station/garage play center as part of an ongoing unit on transportation.

**Before Play**

The teacher provides background knowledge by reading *Sylvia's Garage* by Debra Lee, an informational book about a woman mechanic. She discusses new words, such as *mechanic, engine, dipstick,* and *oil.*

Next, the teacher helps the children plan the play center. She asks children about the roles they can play (e.g., gas station attendant, mechanic, customer) and records their ideas on a piece of chart paper. She then asks the children to brainstorm some props that they could use in their center (e.g., signs, cardboard gas pump, oil can, tire pressure gauge) and jots these down on another piece of chart paper. The children then decide which props they will make in class and which will be brought from home, and the teacher or a child places an *m* after each make-in-class item and an *h* after each "from home" item.

During the next several days, the teacher helps the children construct some of the make-in-class props, such as a sign for the gas station ("Let's see . . . gas starts with a *g.* Gary, your name also starts with a *g.* Can you show us how to write a *g*?).

The list of "from home" props is included in the classroom newsletter and sent to families.

**During Play**

The teacher first observes the children at play to learn about their current play interests and activities. Then she provides scaffolding that extends and enriches children's play and at the same time teaches important literacy skills. She notices, for example, that the mechanics are not writing out service orders or bills for the customers, so she takes on a role as an assistant mechanic and models how to write out a bill for fixing a customer's car. She monitors her involvement to ensure close alignment with children's ongoing activity.

**After Play**

During small group activity time, the teacher helps children with a picture-sort that includes pictures of people and objects from their garage play. They sort the pictures into labeled columns according to beginning sounds—/m/ (e.g., *mechanic, man, map, motor*); /t/ (e.g., *tire, tank, top, taillight*); and /g/(e.g., *gas, gallon, garden, goat*). They explore the different feel of these sounds in the different parts of their mouths. They think of other words they know that "feel" the same way.

After modeling, the teacher gives a small deck of cards for the children to sort, providing direct supervision and feedback.

*Source:* Roskos, Christie, and Richgels, The Essentials of Literacy Instruction (2003, p. 59). *Young Children 58*(2): 52–60. Reprinted with permission from the National Association for the Education of Young Children.

**Play-Debrief-Replay.** The play-debrief-replay strategy, originally developed to teach primary-grade science (Wassermann & Ivany, 1988), has been extended to other curriculum areas, including mathematics, social studies, and literacy (Wassermann, 2000). It is based on the assumption that children learn most effectively in situations in which they have choices, challenges, and opportunities for creative and investigative play. The strategy involves having children (1) play, engaging in play activities that provide intellectual and creative challenges; (2) debrief, reflecting on their play investigations and identifying what they have learned from the experiencing; and (3) replay, engaging in further play activities that encourage continued reflection and learning.

Wasserman (2000) has identified the characteristics of play activities that yield significant conceptual growth:

1. Investigative play tasks are open-ended. They do not lead students to "the answers."
2. Play tasks call for the generation of ideas, rather than the recall of specific information.
3. Play activities challenge students' thinking; indeed they *require* thinking. Higher-order mental challenges are built into each play task.
4. Play activities are "messy." Children are, in fact, playing around. Learning through play is nonlinear, nonsequential. . . .
5. Play tasks focus on "big ideas"—the important concepts of the curriculum—rather than trivial details.
6. Each play task provides opportunities for children to grow in their conceptual understanding. When children carry out investigative play, they grow in their ability to understand larger concepts.
7. The children are the players. They are actively involved in learning. They are talking to each other, sharing ideas, speculating, laughing, and getting excited about what they found. They are not sitting quietly, listening to the teacher's thinking.
8. The children are working together, in learning groups. Play is enhanced through cooperative investigations. Cooperation, rather than competitive individual work, is stressed. (pp. 27–28)

The vignette at the beginning of Chapter 7, in which the second-graders in Bob's classroom are conducting experiments with dry cell batteries, light bulbs, and buzzers is an excellent example of the play phase of this strategy. Small groups of children playfully investigated the effects of connecting different numbers of dry cell batteries together. As a result of this initial playful investigation, several of the groups discovered that, when more dry cells were connected together, the light bulbs shined brighter and the buzzers buzzed louder.

After cleanup the teacher Bob gathered the children together in a large group and initiated the debriefing phase of the strategy:

**Teacher:** Tell me about some of the observations you made as you investigated with your dry cells.

**Frank:** We were tryin' to see if the light would get brighter if we put more batteries on.

**Teacher:** You added more batteries to see if that would make a difference.

**Frank:** Yeah.

**Teacher:** And what did you observe?

**Kuldip:** When we put four cells, the light got brighter. We wuz goin' to do it with six cells.

**Teacher:** You have a hypothesis about what might happen with six cells.

**Kuldip:** It would be very bright. Real bright.

**Teacher:** The more cells, the brighter the light. Is that your theory?

**Kuldip:** Yup!

**Teacher:** I wonder how it happens? How do you explain it?

**Sarah:** Well, I think you got more power there. You see there's power in the cells. So if you have more cells, you get more power and that makes the light brighter. (Wasserman, 2000, p. 23)

Note how this debriefing discussion makes the children aware of the hypotheses they were testing and the principle they discovered. Bob doesn't evaluate the children's ideas as being right or wrong (which they often are). Instead, he listens to their ideas and plays them back so that the children can process and evaluate their own ideas. Wasserman points out that during these debriefing sessions the teacher usually raises at least one puzzler question that might stimulate further investigation when the children turn to the replay phase with the same materials during subsequent days. For example, Bob might ask the children how the battery–light bulb and battery-buzzer setups were similar and different, or he might ask where the power in the battery comes from.

During the replay phase the children continue to play with the same materials. They continue on with their initial experiments, try to find answers to the puzzlers asked by the teacher, and engage in new, more elaborate experiments. Children have many opportunities to work together to discover basic principles of electricity. They are learning basic science concepts and the scientific method of developing and testing hypotheses in a playful context.

**Paley's Story Play.** Vivian Paley (1981) has developed a form of guided play that combines storytelling, writing, reading, and drama. The teacher helps children create their own scripts, which they then act out. Children first take turns dictating stories; they each tell an oral story that is tape-recorded and later written down by the teacher. The teacher reads the stories aloud to the class, and then the children work together as a group to act out the stories. This strategy promotes many aspects of children's social, oral language, and cognitive development. In particular, it helps to develop their narrative skills. Over time their stories become better organized and increasingly complex.

In her book *Boys and Girls: Superheroes in the Doll Corner,* Paley (1984) gives an example of a story written by one of her kindergarten boys:

> Superman, Batman, Spiderman, and Wonderwoman went into the woods and they saw a wicked witch. She gave them poisoned food. Then they died. Then Wonderwoman had magic and they woke up. Everybody didn't wake up. Then they woke up from Wonderwoman's magic. They saw a chimney and the wolf opened his mouth. Superman exploded him. (pp. 50–51)

The boy's story has a rudimentary narrative plot: The main characters encounter a problem (dying as a result of eating poison), an attempt is made to solve the problem (magic), and there is a resolution (waking up). Then a new problem comes along (the wolf), and the narrative cycle continues. Also note that this child has incorporated superheroes from popular media along with elements from classic fairy tales to build his story: finding a cottage in the woods (*Hansel and Gretel*), a witch who gives poisoned food (*Snow White*), and a wolf and a chimney (*The Three Pigs*). Of course, when the children in the class acted out this simple story, it became much more complex.

Fein, Ardila-Rey, and Groth (2000) have developed a version of Paley's strategy that they call *shared enactment.* During center time, the teacher positions himself or herself in the classroom writing center (a center that contains materials to write with and to write on) and encourages children in the center to tell him or her stories. The teacher writes down the children's words verbatim. When a child finishes telling the story, the teacher asks whether there is anything else the child wishes to add. The teacher then reads the story back to the child to make sure that it matches the child's intentions. The child then decides whether he or she wishes to share the story with the group. If the child does, it is put in a special container called the "story box." Later, during shared enactment time, the teacher reads the story to the class, and then the story is dramatized. Fein and associates (2000) describe how a typical shared enactment session unfolds:

> The children gathered along two sides of a large space used for circle time and the teacher sits among them. The empty space before them became the stage. The teacher summoned the author to sit by her side and read the story out loud to the group. The teacher then asked the author what characters were needed for the enactment. The author identified the characters (often with the eager help of other children) and chose a peer to portray each one. When the actors had been assembled, the teacher read the story slowly as a narrator would, stopping to allow for action and omitting dialogue so that the actors could improvise. The players dramatized the story, following the lead of the author who acts as director. At the completion of the enactment and the applause, another story was selected for dramatization. (p. 31)

Fein and her colleagues used the shared enactment procedure with a class of kindergartners twice a week for twelve weeks and found that this form of guided play resulted in a substantial increase in narrative activity (story enactment and storytelling) during free play. The investigators noted that this brief play intervention appeared to penetrate the daily life of the classroom and promised to make important contributions to the children's narrative development.

## SUMMARY

This chapter has explored ways in which teachers can enrich and extend children's play experiences. First, we examined the topic of time and explained why it is important that children have long, uninterrupted periods of time in which to plan and carry out their play. When children have adequate time, they tend to engage in complex, challenging forms of play. Several strategies were presented for carving out time for play from the busy classroom schedule.

Next, we discussed how teachers can use preparatory experiences such as storybook reading, field trips, and classroom visitors to build children's knowledge of the roles, objects, and routines associated with different play themes. These types of experiences increase the knowledge base that children draw on during play, increasing their play options. The result is richer, more complex play.

We then addressed the issue of teacher involvement in play—a very controversial subject. Advocates maintain that teacher participation can enrich children's play experiences and can maximize play's impact on intellectual and social development, whereas opponents maintain that teachers often disrupt or inhibit play activities and reduce children's opportunities to learn during play.

We believe that there is merit to both positions. Teacher involvement can have positive and negative effects on play. The crucial variable is *how* teachers become involved in play. If teachers interact with children in a sensitive, responsive, and supportive manner, play can be enhanced. On the other hand, if teachers take over the control of play, provide too much structure, or interrupt play for academic purposes, play will usually suffer. We described a continuum of teacher play interaction styles, separating the facilitative roles (onlooker, stage manager, coplayer, play leader) from the precarious ones (uninvolved, director, redirector).

Finally, we examined several ways in which teachers can link play with instruction. Strategies include making connections between play and the academic curriculum and using guided play strategies such as before-during-after and play-debrief-replay. These instructional forms of play are intended to be a supplement to, rather than a replacement for, child-initiated play.

## PROJECTS AND ACTIVITIES

1. Discuss the pros and cons of adult involvement in children's play. What is meant by the idea that *how* the adult becomes involved with children at play is more important than *how much* they get involved?
2. Make a poster illustrating the continuum of adult involvement in children's play. Highlight the points along this continuum that are most fruitful for enhancing children's play.
3. Arrange to visit and observe a preschool classroom or childcare center and observe teacher and child interactions during indoor and outdoor play time. Focus on specific teacher behaviors, and note how many different types of facilitative or precarious teacher behaviors occur and what the children's reactions are to them.
4. Interview a child five years of age or older about how he or she likes adults to behave when the child is playing. Share answers in class discussion.

CHAPTER 10

# Play for Children with Special Needs and Circumstances

## INTRODUCTION

We believe that play is not only important for typically developing children, infants to age eight, but also critical for children with a variety of disabilities. Certainly, the role of supporting, enhancing, and extending play in children with disabilities requires extra effort, knowledge, and commitment on the part of caregivers, teachers, and parents. Unfortunately, children with disabilities often do not have lots of play opportunities in the classroom and on the playground—or even at home. This has a variety of causes, including lack of adequate teacher training and equipment that does not make accommodations for these children's special circumstances. Even procedures that are specified in special education laws can work against the optimum inclusion of play for children with disabilities.

Play theory and research inform special education, even as there are serious obstacles to overcome in translating our knowledge into policies and practices. In this chapter we begin by examining some of these barriers to play in special education programs. Next, we note the value of play for children with disabilities and discuss the effects of disabilities on play, the importance of inclusive education, adaptive equipment and environments, play as a context for instruction, family involvement, and play-based assessment. Play therapy is then discussed, a number of different approaches being noted and one approach, sandplay therapy, being discussed in some detail, along with implications for early childhood education. Finally, we turn to child life programs, which are designed to help support and maintain children's development and well-being while the children are in hospital settings. Again, implications for early childhood teachers are noted.

## FOCUS QUESTIONS

1. Why is there a conflict between the educational philosophies used to teach typically developing children and those used to teach children with disabilities?
2. How does the requirement to write an individual family service plan or an individual education plan sometimes negatively affect the use of play with children who have disabilities?
3. Why is play particularly helpful for twice exceptional children and other children with disabilities who need constant challenge and stimulation?
4. What are some simple adaptations for children with specific disabilities?
5. What are some elements of successful parent-child interaction with respect to play and a child with disabilities?
6. Why is play a particularly good vehicle for assessing the needs of young children with special needs?
7. For what particular disabilities is play therapy effective?
8. What are some ways teachers can help a child who must be hospitalized?

## PLAY AND SPECIAL EDUCATION

The contemporary approach to working with children with disabilities in our early childhood programs reflects changing views of children, families, and education. At the end of the nineteenth century and the early part of the twentieth century there was an increased interest in young children in Europe and this country, illustrated by the popularity of the German kindergarten program, the international Montessori and Waldorf approaches, the creation of the Bank Street College Child Study Institute, and the inception of various early childhood professional associations and journals (Wolery & Wilbers, 1994). Additionally, educators such as John Dewey stressed the importance of individual children's unique experiences in structuring curricula, as opposed to the traditional view that curricula must be imposed by society.

The 1960s saw the culmination of the civil rights movement, educational results of *Brown* v. *Board of Education of Topeka,* and increased advocacy for the rights of disenfranchised groups, including people with disabilities. Multicultural education developed as an effort to reform schools to be responsive to each of these groups (Banks & Banks, 1997). Also in the 1960s the counterculture challenged the way we had always done things in this country, including the way we educated our children. The federal Head Start program, created in 1965, furthered our belief in the importance of young children and the need to address specific needs of certain populations—in this case, low-income and minority children. Later Head Start was mandated to serve children with disabilities, and in 2002, 13 percent of Head Start children served throughout the nation were children who had disabilities (U.S. Department of Health and Human Services, 2003).

Theoretical views of ability and education also changed, from a reliance on maturation and biology to a view that environmental impact was increasing powerful. Bronfenbrenner's ecological theory gained importance, stressing both the systems in which children function—homes, communities, and programs—and how these systems interact to support each other and the lives of children (Wolery & Wilbers, 1994).

Starting in 1968 with the Handicapped Children's Early Education Program, a variety of federal laws were passed to address the role of education in the lives of children with disabilities. These laws developed both out of the civil rights legislation, and also as the result of an increasing belief in education as the great equalizer of American democracy—the belief that through education, anyone can succeed. These laws culminated in the 1990 Individuals with Disabilities Education Act (IDEA) that provides free education to children with disabilities, infants to age twenty-one. The IDEA law stipulates very specific activities that must occur to meet the needs of children with disabilities. Goals of IDEA are as follows (Wolery & Wilbers, 1994, p. 20):

- To support families in achieving their goals
- To promote children's engagement, independence and mastery
- To promote children's development in key domains
- To build and support children's social competence
- To promote children's generalized use of skills
- To provide and prepare children for normalized life experiences
- To prevent the emergence of future problems and disabilities

For every child who is diagnosed with a specific disability or multiple disabilities an individual family service plan (IFSP) or an individual education plan (IEP) must be developed. These are formal, written documents that specify the responsibility of the early childhood program in serving the child. The type of plan is based on the child's age. IFSPs are developed for children under age three, IEPs are written for children aged three years old and older. Box 10.1 lists information that should be included in an IEP. IFSPs developed for infants and toddlers are broader and less specific than IEPs.

**BOX 10.1**

### *What Should Be Included in an IEP*

- The children's present level of educational performance in every area
- Goals of educational performance to be achieved by the end of the school year
- Short-term objectives that lead to achieving the annual goals
- The specific educational services needed, including the kind of program needed and any adaptations required
- The length of time services will be required
- The extent to which the child will be involved in regular education programs

- A justification for the type of educational placement the child will receive
- The individuals who are responsibile for implementing the program
- A way to determine whether short-term objectives are being achieved

*Source:* Wolery and Wilbers (1994).

As a result of the laws and amendments regarding the education of children with disabilities, these children and their families have certain rights, including the following (Wolery & Wilbers, 1994):

1. Each preschool child with a disability must have an IEP or IFSP.
2. Children must be placed in the least restrictive, appropriate environment. To the extent possible, and making sure the child benefits, services must be provided with nondisabled children.
3. Parents control the process; they must be consulted during every part of the process, including evaluating the child, developing the IEP or IFSP, and placing their child in a program.

More and more early childhood programs are enrolling children with disabilities and/or keeping children once they have been identified. In a study reported by Wolery et al. (1993), 58 percent of programs that enrolled children with disabilities enrolled children with speech/language impairments; 31 percent enrolled children with developmental delays; 24 percent enrolled children with behavior disorders, 21 percent enrolled children with physical handicaps, and fewer than 15 percent enrolled children with mild, moderate, or severe mental retardation; visual impairments; hearing impairments; or autism. Thus while more and more programs are enrolling children with disabilities, they tend to enroll children with less severe conditions. Inclusion "assumes that all children should be served in the same programs they would have attended if they did not have disabilities" (Wolery & Wilbers, 1994, p. 8) and is based on the belief that all children belong together.

Clearly, play has a central role in an early childhood or school environment that includes children with disabilities. However, because some children with disabilities often have difficulty playing at the same level as their peers (discussed later in this chapter), teachers and providers must take specific steps to make sure that children with disabilities can benefit fully from play with nondisabled peers. For children with disabilities to fully benefit from classroom play in inclusive settings, they need help in the form of adaptations, modeling, and direct intervention.

## Value of Play for Children with Disabilities

Clearly, play provides a variety of extremely beneficial opportunities for children with a range of disabilities. The extent to which a disabled child can play and the level and kind of play—physical, social, cognitive, simple, complex—depend on both the child's disabilities and the amount and quality of their previous play experiences. With this in mind, here are some of the specific benefits of indoor and outdoor play for children with disabilities:

- Play provides a low-risk environment in which children with disabilities can develop and improve social skills.
- Children with disabilities have a vast array of emotional, psychological, social, cognitive, and physical needs that are identical to those of normally developing children. Play allows children with disabilities to meet these diverse needs.
- Play encourages both the social and physical integration of children with special needs within the program (Chandler, 1994). Physical integration of special needs children is simply a result of their being included in programs with typically developing children; social integration occurs as they learn to interact with other children and as the other children learn to accept them as coplayers.
- Play provides a sense of success. Whereas much of a special education student's daily program focuses on specific goals and outcomes developed by experts to target their weaknesses and teach needed basic skills (Carta, Schwartz, Atwater, & McConnell, 1991), play allows these children to be successful on their own terms. Because playing children determine their own goals and outcomes, their success is largely assured, and their sense of accomplishment has been guaranteed.
- Play encourages independence. A common tendency with special needs children is to help them too much, and in some cases these children have even learned to act helpless and dependent (Chandler, 1994). Children with disabilities need to be encouraged to do things for themselves. This requires risk-taking, challenging themselves, and results that are not measured, criticized, or punished—an ideal recipe for play (Wardle, 1998).
- Play emphasizes children's strengths. All children with special needs also have special strengths. Because of its flexible, child-centered nature, play is an ideal context for these strengths to come to the fore. Performance is high when evaluation anxiety is low or nonexistent, as is the case when the child is at play.

## Barriers to Providing Play Opportunities in Special Education

Unfortunately, several barriers exist that make it difficult for play to have a key role in early childhood education programs. We deal with these issues up front in this chapter because play will not gain its rightful place in early childhood special education curricula unless these barriers are adequately removed or circumvented.

**Bias toward Direct Instruction.** In 1987 the National Association for the Education of Young Children (NAEYC) published *Developmentally Appropriate Practice* (Bredekamp, 1987). This document was an attempt to articulate the current knowledge about developmentally appropriate practice (DAP) for working with young children in our early childhood programs. A decade later, the DAP document was revised by Bredekamp and Copple (1997). The concept of DAP is based on many of the theories discussed throughout this book, including those of Piaget, Bruner, Vygotsky, and Erikson. Therefore it is not surprising that play has a key role in DAP. In fact, one of the twelve "principles . . . that inform developmentally appropriate practice" is that "play is an important vehicle for children's social, emotional and cognitive development" (Bredekamp & Copple, 1997, p. 14). Thus the philosophy of DAP explicitly includes play.

Although DAP is professed to be the leading early childhood philosophy in this country, research has shown that in practice it is not (Dunn & Kontos, 1997), suggesting as few as one third of programs studied actually implement DAP. Further, as the national trend toward standards and accountability continues to push academics farther and farther downward, it appears that fewer early childhood programs will be truly developmentally appropriate (Wardle, 1999c).

Special education approaches in early childhood programs are even less developmentally appropriate than regular programs. In fact, many experts in special education believe that the developmentally appropriate practice "may not be sufficient as guidelines for planning, carrying out and evaluating early childhood special education programs" and that "it (DAP) falls short as a standard of effective programming for young children with disabilities" (Carta et al., 1991, p. 59). The most obvious conflicts between a philosophy espoused by DAP and one advocated by early childhood special education (ECSE) approaches are according to Carta et al., 1991, as follows:

- The explicit mission of ECSE programs is to produce outcomes that would not occur in the absence of intervention and teaching.
- The major goal of ECSE is early intervention, especially in providing basic skills that form the foundation for more complex skill acquisition and educational opportunities.
- For these children direct adult intervention is often necessary to guide their behaviors and structure beneficial opportunities.
- The IDEA law requires teaching plans based on goals and objectives, which are based on children's strengths and weaknesses and on acquiring skills needed for future success.
- Traditionally, ECSE programs have emphasized skill acquisition and making best use of instructional time, whereas DAP programs have stressed skill generalization and use of the least intrusive and most natural techniques. ECSE programs tend to stress and emphasize rapid skill acquisition.
- Teachers of children with disabilities might need to provide direct instructional strategies to help these children initiate activity, use materials appropriately, and make choices.
- Young children with special needs must be provided with services that are beneficial, and programs serving these children must prove that these benefits are being achieved. "This is perhaps the area of greatest discrepancy between what is required in early childhood special education programs and the guidelines of Developmentally Appropriate Practice" (Carta et al., 1991, p. 63). Programs serving special education students must show that the programs are moving the children forward toward their goals and outcome.

The basis of the ECSE philosophy is the belief that direct intervention targeted to specific, individual needs is required to improve the child's development more quickly than would occur without direct intervention (Odom & McEvoy, 1990; Peterson, 1987).

**BOX 10.2**

## *Head Start and Special Education*

**by Francis Wardle**

When I was a Head Start director, my staff worked very closely with the local public school to provide services for our children with disabilities. We developed a contract with them whereby their special education teachers helped us to diagnose the Head Start children who failed our screening instrument. The special education teachers then provided services directly to children in the Head Start classrooms. In return, the local school counted our children in their annual federal count (the number used by the federal government to reimburse local districts for services to children with disabilities). The public school teachers also taught our teachers how to work with each child, depending on the child's disability.

This relationship caused considerable tension within the Head Start program because of the competing philosophies between Head Start and public school special education. Head Start uses a comprehensive, whole-child approach to education, development, and family support. Further, our program had recently adopted the High/Scope curriculum, which emphasizes student choice and developmentally appropriate practice. On the other hand, one of the public school special education teachers working with the Head Start children insisted on using a highly teacher-directed approach not only to teach skills listed in the IEP, but also to accomplish the general goals of the class (teaching the alphabet, rote counting, etc.). As the Head Start director I was very concerned about this approach, not so much because it was inappropriate for the individual child, but because it modeled an approach to early childhood education that we, as a program, had fought long and hard to discourage.

As anyone who has worked in an early childhood program is aware, there is an automatic tendency toward the direct instruction of discrete academic skills, especially in programs that hire low-income, often poorly prepared teachers (Wardle, 1996b). Because the special education teacher was a certified public school teacher, she acted as a very powerful role model for my teachers, who at best had a Child Development Associate (a field-based credential). Even after intervention from the classroom teacher and the director (me), the special education teacher would not modify her approach. Part of the problem was that she had been taught that her approach was appropriate. Another was that she believed she knew more about working with children with disabilities that we did. Eventually, I asked this teacher to leave our program.

The differences between the overall philosophies of DAP and ECSE can produce tremendous amount of conflict, miscommunication, and distrust (see Box 10.2). Duplication of services—for example, Head Start and the state-funded preschool program for students at risk—and turf issues also restrict the full inclusion of children with disabilities in programs for typically developing children.

**Preparation of Early Childhood Teachers.** College and university training programs for regular early childhood and elementary teachers and for special education teachers are often segregated from one another (Wolery & Wilbers, 1994). Faculty members who prepare general early childhood and elementary teachers often lack knowledge and experience in working with children with special needs; therefore these prospective teachers receive little, if any, instruction in meeting the unique needs of these children. Further, special education students receive little training on basic issues of child development, DAP, and the role of play in development (Odom & McEvoy, 1990). Many special education teachers in public schools have not received training on the value of play and often teach within an educational climate that places ever more emphasis on academic attainment, in which play is often considered little more than off-task behavior (Strain & Smith, 1993).

## Effects of Disabilities on Play

IDEA established the legal parameters that schools must follow to meet the needs of children with disabilities. IDEA uses 13 categories to label various forms of disability: deafness, dual sensory impairments, hearing impairments, mental retardation, multiple handicaps, orthopedic impairments, other health impairments, serious emotional disturbances, specific learning disabilities, visual impairments and blindness, traumatic brain injury, autism, and speech and language impairments. Many states use the all-inclusive term *developmental delay* to specify a whole range of young children with disabilities (Wolery & Wilbers, 1994). A variety of other terms are also used to describe certain disabilities. In examining the effects of different disabilities on children's play behavior, we will use the terms defined by IDEA.

**Deafness and Hearing Impairments.** Children who are deaf or have hearing impairments seem to engage in typical play during the sensorimotor period, but after age two, as language develops, these children show delays in symbolic play and social play years. For example, children with hearing problems tend to engage in more solitary and parallel play than do other children. Because much of play is social, this can have a profound negative impact on children's play experiences and on their social development. Further, because children who play together initially engage in meta-play exchanges (e.g., conversations in which they set up the play episode with roles, scripts, and contexts), deaf and hearing-impaired children tend to miss out on this important part of play. As a result, they have limited responses to other playing children in both the planning stages and the actual play activity, and nondisabled children might think disabled children are not interested in playing with them or are simply no fun to play with. One solution would be to teach all children sign language, including children who are not hearing impaired.

**Orthopedic Impairments.** Children with a variety of physical impairments, such as cystic fibrosis, spinal bifida, muscular dystrophy, or an injury due to an accident, are included in the orthopedic impairments category. Clearly, the impact of the child's disability on play depends on its severity and the extent to which it limits movement and mobility. Fine and gross motor limitations will affect playing with materials and toys and engaging in active play on the playground. Children who become dependent on others to accomplish simple tasks can become increasingly passive in play and in

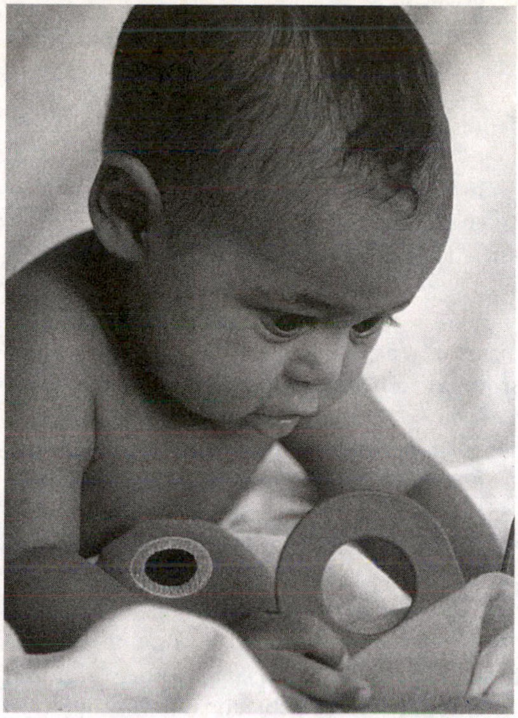

Children who are deaf or have hearing impairments seem to engage in typical play during the sensorimotor period, but after age two, as language develops, they show delays in symbolic and social play.

using self-help skills (Greenberg & Field, 1982). Lack of mobility and the extent of the child's adaptive equipment can also affect a child's interaction in social play. For example, if a child plays in the dramatic play area while in a wheelchair, this can influence the child's interaction with other players. Physical disabilities that affect speech will also have an impact on communicating with other children. Finally, children's ability to engage in fine and gross motor activities has a direct impact on their sense of self-confidence because of body image and the children's perception of their physical abilities as it compares to other children.

However, caution must be taken not to assume that one form of disability necessarily affects all play. For example, a child in a wheelchair might be an expert in puzzles, chess, and playing with blocks; a child with cystic fibrosis might be brilliant at word games. And use of assistive devices and computers adds play options.

**Health Impairments.** Clearly, there is a whole range of different health problems that affect children, from mild to severe. One of the biggest problems with health-impaired children is that they might miss much of formal early childhood education involvement because of frequent hospital and clinic visits. Therefore they might not have learned appropriate ways to initiate and prolong play with other children, or they might not have had the opportunity to progress adequately through the social and cognitive stages of play. Finally, because they are often cared for and attended by adults, their behavior might be more adult in nature—and thus less playful—than that of other children their age.

Attention-deficit hyperactivity disorder (ADHD) is considered a health impairment. Signs of ADHD in a child include the following (Whaley, reported in Peterson, 2001):

- Fails to give close attention to details or makes careless mistakes in schoolwork or other activities
- Has problems sustaining attention in tasks or play
- Does not seem to listen when spoken to directly
- Does not follow through on instructions and fails to finish schoolwork or homework
- Is easily distracted
- Fidgets with hands or feet or squirms in seat
- Leaves his or her seat in the classroom or other situations in which remaining seated is expected
- Runs or climbs excessively when it is inappropriate to do so
- Talks excessively
- Blurts out answers before questions have been completed
- Interrupts or intrudes on others

The fact that many of these behaviors are evident in typical preschool children illustrates that many children, especially boys, are mislabeled as having ADHD (Berger, 2003). Further, the characteristics of the ADHD child suggest these children might have some difficulty playing. Their apparent need for constant stimulation lends itself to frequent opportunities for playing with objects and lots of hands-on activities; their short attention span, impulsivity, and ease of distraction suggest difficulties in sustaining play. In addition, this syndrome can affect social play because other children might get upset with the ADHD child's constant need for change and stimulation. Outdoor nature play may help improve these behaviors (see p. 333).

**Visual Impairments.** Blind children have little motivation to reach out and use objects and toys in front of them because they do not know that they exist. Once they have objects in their hands, they explore the items through touch, smell, and taste and do not readily let go of them. This behavior often becomes repetitious and predictable. As a result children with visual impairments are often delayed in the exploration both of toys and the environment. Further, blindness or severe visual impairment means that children cannot see and imitate the play modeling of other children and adults, resulting in more isolated, solitary play and less complex play. Consequently, the cognitive, social-emotional, motor, and language skills that are acquired and practiced through play are all negatively affected for children with visual impairments, depending on the degree of their disability (Lander, 1993).

**Autism.** Autistic children often have impaired communication, and may engage in repetitive behaviors and use toys in inappropriate ways. Children with autism may demonstrate behaviors that are antithetical to play, such as rocking movements, head banging or shaking, finger flicking, hand flapping, and the flicking of objects close to the face (Lander, 1993). These behaviors make it difficult for children to engage in both object play and social play. As a result, both their social play and cognitive play tend to be less advanced than those of normally developing peers (Baron-Cohen, 1987). Language and "theory of mind" struggles also affect their social pretend play.

**Mental Retardation.** Mental retardation may have a biological basis or be caused by negative environmental factors, such as drug and alcohol use by the mother during prenatal development. Although children with developmental delays in cognition appear to progress through the same sequence of development as children who do not have developmental delays, their play is characterized by reduced use of language, less sophisticated representational (symbolic) play, and a limited selection of play materials (Li, 1981). They engage in more unoccupied behavior and stereotypical play behaviors and often focus on the exploratory behaviors that usually precede true play. These children need help to move beyond exploration to more advanced forms of social and cognitive play.

**Social-Emotional and Behavioral Disabilities.** Clearly, the impact that emotional and behavior disabilities have on play depends on the kind and severity of these disabilities. Most children don't like to play with aggressive children. Children who are frequently removed from play activities because of misbehavior do not have enough interaction to develop both appropriate social skills and complex social behaviors. In fact, one of the most negative things that occur in many early childhood programs is that the children who most need to learn how to engage in prosocial interactions are punished for their inappropriate behavior by being removed from a social situation. How can a child who continually gets into fights and arguments with other children learn prosocial skills if he or she is always in time-out? Children with emotional problems may have difficulty staying with a play activity or might not have the security needed to engage in the kind of risks play behaviors require; they may be less sophisticated in both cognitive play levels and social play levels.

Katz and McClellan (1997) argue that children who struggle with social interaction need immediate and continual intervention to make sure they learn to engage in positive interactions with peers and adults.

**Twice Exceptional Children.** There are gifted children who have disabilities, and there are children who have disabilities who are gifted. Whitmore (1981) suggests that there are at least half a million gifted K–12 students who have special needs. Clearly, there are also large numbers of children below age five who fit this pattern. These children are called twice exceptional (Whitmore, 1981), and there are many factors that affect their play behaviors. One of these is that most of these children are identified with only one label, either with a disability or as being gifted; another is that typical learning behaviors of gifted children directly clash with common approaches used to work with children with disabilities (Karnes, 1979). Gifted children dislike repetition, out-of-context learning, and reinforcement for no apparent reason. They like challenge and out-of-the-box thinking and often fail easy tasks while mastering complex ones (Silverman, 1989). Therefore typical special education strategies, such as using small, carefully sequenced tasks and external reinforcement, are anathema to many twice exceptional students. Box 10.3, which recalls an episode of the TV program, *The Simpsons,* illustrates what can happen when activities are not designed to meet the needs of twice exceptional children—both their giftedness and specific disability.

**BOX 10.3**

### *Bart Simpson, a Twice Exceptional Student?*

**by Francis Wardle**

My favorite TV show is *The Simpsons,* largely because of Bart's antics at school. As an educator, I value Bart's ability to humorously highlight some of the things we do wrong in schools. For example, I remember the episode in which Bart's family had recently moved, and Bart was placed in a special education class. Although the program never said what Bart's disability was, my bet is that it had to do with behavioral difficulties. But on the basis of his very strong verbal skills and his ability to copy lines and lines of "I promise not to . . . ," Bart is probably twice exceptional.

In the episode with Bart in a special education class, the teacher is teaching three or four students letter-sound correspondence. She carefully and deliberately teaches each child the letter and its corresponding sound. They learn the sound-letter combination of two or three letters, and then the teacher says, "We'll continue with the next letter tomorrow."

Bart responds to this announcement by the teacher, to no one in particular (as he tends to do), "Let me get this straight–We are behind the rest of the other children in our grade, and this is how we are going to catch up?!!!"

Bart's comment illustrates the downside of the reductionist approach to special education, especially for children who are mentally bright or who need challenging and stimulating lessons and activities. Although it makes sense to isolate a child's specific areas of disability and target them for improvement, children with disabilities need a whole-child approach to meet all of their cognitive, physical, emotional, and social needs. In fact, because being labeled with a special need is often very negative in our culture, these children need lots and lots of opportunities to be successful–socially, physically, and/or cognitively, depending on their specific disability. What they don't need is to be treated as if they are disabled or delayed in every area. Most children with disabilities are perfectly normal or even advanced in most of their abilities. We need to respect this fact.

## Adaptive Equipment and Environments

Classroom furniture, educational equipment, instructional materials, and toys are designed and made for children who approximate the norm in physical, social, and emotional development, abilities, and behaviors. Manufacturers of these products very carefully study demographic and anthropomorphic information—the average physical size of children at specific ages—when designing their products. Further, with the overall acceptance of DAP as the desired, albeit not universally practiced, early childhood philosophy, early childhood materials are targeted to the "average" child. It is, of course, also a cost issue. When children differ from the norm in physical, social, and emotional abilities, giftedness, and specific learning challenges, the average, mass-produced, and mass-marketed equipment no longer meets their needs.

Changes and adaptations made to materials and environments obviously depend on the specific disability or disabilities the child may have.

**Attention-Deficit Hyperactivity Disorder.** ADHD children often are easily distracted, like to debate rules and expectations, and can become easily bored. Some of these children are gifted, which increases their potential for boredom, their ability to challenge rules, and their dislike for order (Clark, 1997). These children need to be provided with an environment that minimizes distractions—a setting that is well-defined, partitioned, and located away from windows and other distractions. They also need many opportunities for hands-on, integrated, project-related activities. Make sure that when a task is completed, there are other activities the child can immediately select without a lot of downtime, which is when these children can easily get into trouble. Instructions should be simple, sequential, and very easy to follow. Make movement from one activity to another simple and clear, and place areas of sequential activity next to each other. Rules also should be simple and repeated often. If possible, children should participate in making these rules. Provide multiple modes of communication, such as oral, written, and visual symbols. Access to higher-order activities, such as using computers, should not depend on successful completion of lower-level activities. Also, nature and greenery exposure is calming.

**Children with Visual Challenges.** Make sure all sorting games allow children to sort and classify by touch. Make magnifiers available for when a child might need one (e.g., when playing with puzzles), provide big brushes for painting activities, and encourage lots of play with objects. Always offer children the opportunity to feel objects that are being used in play. When any changes are made in the play environment, such as the addition of a new piece of equipment or rearrangement of the room, let the child touch the changes that have been made and walk the new routes. On the playground, provide sound indicators that enable the child to know where safety issues exist (the swings) and where play activities are located.

**Children with Hearing Challenges.** Use picture charts for directions and rules when needed. Limit noise that can interfere with the child's decoding of information, such as traffic noise and noise from other children's activities. Send written notes home to reinforce verbal instructions given to children. Provide sign language materials, and give rules and instruction in sign language to all the children. Many programs have successfully taught sign language to all the children in the program, which increases play between children with a hearing impairment and the other children.

**Children with Physical Challenges.** Provide specialized seating that gives the child needed support when engaging in all activities, such as water play, art, and blocks. This might require especially designed equipment or adaptations of equipment, for example, altering the height of the surface to match the correct height for the child. Several companies, including Rifton Equipment, provide a variety of supports and adaptations. Large brushes and large paper should be used for art projects, and unit and large hollow blocks should be provided for constructive play for children with fine motor challenges. Individual sand and water tubs can be available for children who cannot comfortably gain access to larger tables, but these children should still be encouraged to play with other children. Adjust the environment so that children with physical challenges can play with other children. For example, provide extra room in the dramatic play area for children in wheelchairs. Table 10.1 lists other ideas and adaptations for children with a variety of disabilities.

**TABLE 10.1 Modifying Activities for Children with Disabilities Depending on the Disability and Its Severity**

**Space**

Entrances and areas need to be wide enough for wheelchairs and walkers. Too small spaces cause aggressive behavior; too large spaces reduce social interaction. Specific space alternatives might be needed for a particular child.

**Materials**

As we have discussed elsewhere, a large variety of materials are needed to encourage play. Graduated challenge is particularly important for children with disabilities. Toys that can be used in a variety of ways are practically effective; toys that require cooperation between children encourage social play. Start with toys and activities the child enjoys playing with.

**Specially Designed Assistance**

Use of various assistance techniques discussed in this chapter. Other ideas include modeling, verbal guidance, physical assistance (actually holding the part of the child's body used to manipulate the toys), and use of visual cues (e.g., a picture of a child using the toy).

**Time**

Children need enough time for play episodes to develop. Some children need extra time to practice newly learned skills. Where appropriate, give the child with a disability the material first, or get him or her ready for the outside first. When children are deeply engrossed in play, the scheduled time should be adjusted. Many children with disabilities also require very specific transition approaches (as do all children).

**Directions**

Most toys and materials provide their own cues for how they should be used. However, some children with disabilities need assistance in using toys and materials. To do so, the teacher should (a) get the child's attention, (b) use vocabulary the child can easily understand, (c) break directions down into small steps (d), combine instruction with demonstrations (manipulation), (e) ask questions to validate the child's level of understanding, (f) have the child repeat the direction, (g) and physically assist the child but remove assistance once it is no longer needed.

**Special Positioning and Assistive Technology**

Positioning involves where a child should be located for a task, and whether the child should be standing, lying, sitting, etc. Adaptive equipment helps children with motor impairments by facilitating movements and providing the best position to perform the activity. Various adaptations include adapted toys, computers and computer programs, adapted seats, mobility and standing devices, and various ways to assist the child's communication.

*Source:* McCormick and Feeney (1995).

**Outdoor Play.** In Chapter 12, which concerns outdoor play environments, we discuss the new Americans with Disabilities Act (ADA) access guidelines for early childhood playgrounds. Table 10.2 provides some ideas for specific adaptations on the playground. The National Center for Boundless Playgrounds is a nonprofit organization that facilitates the design and development of play environments so that all children can play together. Boundless Playgrounds works with communities to provide fully integrated playgrounds that are accessible to all children. For instance, one piece of equipment in a Boundless Playground is the Boat Swing, which is made to accommodate two children in wheelchairs and six children without them. The eight children can all swing together.

**TABLE 10.2 Planning Guide for Outdoor Play Adaptations Examples for Two Children**

| Activities | Child Who Is Blind | Child Who Has Autism |
|---|---|---|
| Transition to the playground | Upon entering the playground, give child verbal directions about where friends and equipment are located; use sighted guide (peer or teacher) to help child move to area of choice. | Prior to entering playground, tell child he is going to playground next; give him a ball to carry outside and repeat, "We are going outside now." |
| Gardening | Orient child to garden area verbally and physically; describe other children's activities (watering, digging) and offer choices for participation. | Create a physical boundary around garden area (fence or other physical structure); establish for child a specific area in which to dig, plant, and water |
| Water table | Tell child which materials are in the water table, where materials are located, which friends are present, and what they are doing. | Model ways to use materials and describe what you are doing or what the child is doing. |
| Balls | Use adapted balls with beeper noise inside; place ball under child's hands rather than pulling child's hands to ball. | Communicate rules and boundaries clearly when playing with balls and repeat in different ways, as needed. |
| Climbing equipment | Alert child to any potential safety concerns (bumping head) and describe the location of possible danger. | No modification necessary (but monitor activity for safety) |
| Sandbox | Tell child which materials are available and who is playing; be aware of potential need to facilitate child's entering and maintaining play with peers. | Limit number of toys/materials available to those specifically of interest to the child. |

*Source:* Flynn and Kieff (2002, p. 23), Including *Everyone* in Outdoor Play. *Young Children* 57(3): 20–26. Reprinted with permission from the National Association for the Education of Young Children.

## Play as a Context for Teaching

The premise of this chapter is that children with diverse disabilities can benefit immensely from play, play activities, and interventions by teachers to enhance the quality, complexity, and duration of their play. Providing specific adaptations, as we have discussed, is one approach to meeting this goal. However, this by itself is not enough. Children with disabilities need to be directly taught many things, and play can be an excellent context for this instruction. Wolery and Wilbers (1994) discuss various considerations for teachers working with children with disabilities. Some of these considerations fit comfortably within our overall definition of play; others are significantly teacher directed and should be used only to teach the child a specific skill needed to enhance his or her play.

**Physical Space and Materials.** Many children with disabilities function very well within the overall early childhood environment. However, changes, adaptations, and alterations will need to be made for children with specific disabilities. For example, a child in a wheelchair will require more space in areas such as the dramatic play area and at tables, counters, water tables, and other places where the wheelchair must be able to go underneath. Children with limited vision need a highly ordered and predictable environment and a teacher to show them initially where equipment and materials are situated.

Because play is such an important medium for learning about the world, children who do not play with toys and materials might need help in doing so (Bradley, 1985). Teachers might need to directly show children how to stack, bang, shake, push, pull, and manipulate toys, or they might use one or more of the teachers' roles in play techniques discussed in earlier chapters (e.g., become a coplayer and model how to use the materials). Children need large enough chunks of time to fully engage in and benefit from play; children with disabilities might need even more time, as it takes them a while to initiate play and engage in exploration.

Play can also be used to implement the specific goals of a child's IEP or IFSP. For example, children who need to increase their positive interactions with other children should be encouraged to use dress-up clothes, balls, dishes, wagons, seesaws, blocks, dolls, trucks, cars, and all sorts of games (Wolery & Wilbers, 1994). However, we caution that high-quality play and play materials for all children, including play of children with disabilities, should minimize adult intervention and the need for adult control, direction, and assistance. If teachers need to initially provide direct intervention and instruction, they also need to be very adept at reducing their involvement and encouraging the child to lead. Box 10.4 describes the experience of Francis Wardle, one of the authors, who contracted polio as a young child in England. He believes his family and school's emphasis on physical activities and outdoor play greatly enhanced his rehabilitation.

**BOX 10.4**

### *Play and Disability*

**by Francis Wardle**

The dark Shropshire (near the England/Wales border) night was illuminated by the flashing ambulance lights. I was scared, not so much from pain as from having to leave my family and friends. I was a very shy five-year-old who had spent his whole life in a very secure, insulated community. Now, suddenly, I was being rushed off with several of my peers to the hospital.

My friends and I had contracted polio. Although it was 1953 (the year of the development of the polio vaccine), the vaccine had not yet reached England. I spent the next two months in a hospital a long way from home, being visited by my mother every other Sunday.

Polio causes atrophy of the skeletal muscles. My right calf muscle never developed beyond that of a five-year-old. Also, because my other leg continued to grow, my right leg is significantly shorter than my left leg. When I got out of hospital, I was fitted with a platform shoe to compensate for my shorter leg. But because I loved to go barefoot and was extremely hard on shoes (I still am!), I soon learned to ignore the shoe with a platform and just went barefoot or wore regular shoes.

My teachers expected me to be fully involved in physical activities and did not allow other children to tease me. All my physical activity enabled me to compensate in many ways for the lack of a calf muscle. In fact, I became so good at soccer that I played freshman soccer at college and so good at dance that I joined several performance dance groups, including Fiesta Mexicana, the Magic Tortoise Company, and the Kansas City Ballet.

My polio leg limited me in some ways. In soccer I was quite slow; and in dance I could never plié—a necessary requirement for many dance steps and all jumps—because of the shortened tendon in my calf muscle. But these limitations never affected my love of soccer, dance, cycling, and hiking.

**Social Aspects.** How adults interact with children during play and the manner in which children are grouped affects the social interaction and overall development of children with disabilities. Wolery and Wilbers (1994) present some guidelines for teachers working with children who struggle in their play:

- Respond to the child's behavior and shifts in behavior.
- Encourage and support a child's purposeful interactions with the environment.
- Play with objects that the child has chosen to play with, and follow the child's lead in interaction.
- Observe the child and imitate his or her behavior.
- Increase the duration of interactions by taking turns and expecting the child to continue.
- Repeat the child's sounds and phrases.
- Take your time, and wait after each time you act, allowing the child to respond.
- Respond within the child's zone of proximal development (e.g., present challenges that can be accomplished with your help).
- Try to play at the same level as the child, and view the play from the child's perspective.
- Be sensitive toward and supportive of the child's attempts to extend interactions.

In most cases young children with and without disabilities do not engage in high levels of interaction with one another unless encouraged and supported in doing so

➤ Wolery and Wilbers (1994) present guidelines for teachers working with children who struggle in their play, including "taking your time and waiting each time you act" and, "increasing the duration of the interaction by taking turns and expecting the child to continue."

(Guralnick, 1981; Odom & McEvoy, 1988; Wolery & Wilbers, 1994). Further, typically developing children seem to prefer to play with children who are similar to them—usually the greater the difference, the less likely the interaction (Guralnick, 1981; Stoneman, 1993). However, certain strategies often work to increase interactions between typically developing children and children with disabilities who are not engaging in social interactions. One of these is to encourage small group activities and to have some children in these groups who are competent in the activity. Children with disabilities view these competent children as role models. Another approach is placing children into mixed age groups. Children with disabilities increase in general developmental progress and communication skills when in mixed age groups (Bailey, Burchinal, & McWilliam, 1993).

**Children's Preferences.** As we have suggested, children who play at preferred activities with favorite toys are more engaged and purposeful in their play (Dyer, Dunlap, & Winterling, 1990). This is what we typically refer to as meaningful learning. Thus we should encourage children with disabilities to make their own choices, but also find ways, through modeling by adults and other children, for example, to increase the child's range of preferred play materials and activities.

**Structuring Routines.** Capitalizing on necessary routines, such as diaper changing, eating, and walking to the bus, has long been a favorite technique used by good early childhood teachers to increase growth and development in a variety of areas, including language, cognition, and adult-child interactions and bonding. This same approach can be used effectively with children with disabilities, using two techniques: naturalistic time delay and transition-based teaching. Naturalistic time delay is a technique involving identifying times in routines when adults provide direct assistance. The teacher then purposefully delays that assistance for a few seconds while expecting the child to initiate the language associated with the routine. The teacher provides a model of the language if the child fails to do so and praises the child when the language is forthcoming (Wolery & Wilbers, 1994, p. 116).

Transition-based teaching requires identifying skills a child needs to know, then asking the child to perform that skill before moving on to the next activity. For example, a child who has completed a puzzle might be asked by the teacher to put the puzzle away, to ask another child whether she or he wishes to play with the puzzle, or to ask another student whether he or she has finished playing with the puzzle before moving onto the next activity. These skills should be play-related.

**Structured Play Activities.** Certain kinds of behaviors and play behaviors are more likely to occur in some activities than others. For example, play activities in which teachers help children to set up the dramatic play by supplying roles, theme, and/or a script can increase social interactions of children with and without disabilities (Dekylen & Odom, 1989). Affection training is an approach designed to increase children's physical and social contact. In typical group activities such as Hokey Pokey, the instructions are changed from "Put your right foot in, put your left foot in" to "Put your right hand on your friend's head, put your left hand on your friend's back," and so on (Wilbers & Wolery, 1994, p 118). These social and physical play contacts transfer to increased social contacts during free play (Brown, Ragland, & Fox, 1988).

## Families and Programs for Children with Disabilities

Working closely with parents and families has always been a central component of early childhood philosophies and programs, going back as far as Froebel and Pestalozzi. In more recent times, one of Head Start's major goals is to involve parents in the education of their children, and a significant number of today's early childhood programs are parent-run cooperatives (Wardle, 2003a). Further, as Powell (1998) has suggested, our methods of working with families have changed to a view of early childhood programs as family support systems that function as modern-day versions of the traditional extended family. For a variety of reasons, including the increased diversity of the students and families they serve, schools are also attempting to increase their partnership with families (Wardle, 2003a).

Relationships between families of children who have special needs and early childhood programs are built on this new model. On the basis of the early success of Head Start and the theories of Bronfenbrenner (1979) and others, professionals now believe that an essential component of early intervention is working with the child's family (Wolery & Wilbers, 1994). Efforts include providing parenting skills, teaching parents how to implement specific educational program goals, and teaching behavioral management strategies. Family support activities are based on the belief that families of children with disabilities face special challenges; support services therefore focus on issues related to caring for children with disabilities, such as parent support groups, providing information and knowledge of how to access community services, resources and referral programs, parent-parent networks, and transition services (Wolery & Wilbers, 1994).

**The Role of Parents in Early Intervention Programs.** Professionals working with children with disabilities must make family support the primary goal of early intervention. To this end, the following guidelines are important:

- All professionals working with children with disabilities must support the family in their efforts for the child and empower the family to eventually function independently without professional assistance.
- Professional services must be tailored to meet the unique culture and set of strengths, values, skills, expectations and needs of each family.
- Families have a right and a responsibility to play the primary role in determining the nature and extent of services provided for them and their child, a concept that is included in the law. Parents are consumers of all available services and need to be educated in selecting and using these services.
- The system must help parents to make sense of the various community services for their child and help them to use these services to their full potential. Agencies must find ways to coordinate their services and make sure these services are family-friendly (Wolery & Wilbers, 1994).

**Play within the Family.** Because we believe that play is critically important for all children with disabilities, regardless of the kind or severity of the disability, we believe that families should play often with their children. Several ideas can help to encourage this concept:

- Families should be taught the educational and developmental value of play, both for the child's specific disability and to support their overall development.
- Families should be provided with specific play-based activities and techniques, such as scaffolding and modeling, to encourage play, and families should be helped to implement these techniques.
- Provide family play groups and instruction on how to make these effective.
- Provide ample play opportunities in the child's program. If the child splits time between a therapeutic or special education program and regular program, the specialized center should model the value of play by providing lots of play opportunities.
- Provide parent training and sessions at parent conferences dedicated to play in families of children with disabilities.
- Provide direct, simple, and accessible (in the parent's language, easy to read, illustrated) parent communication about ways to support family play.
- Provide training for professionals who work with families of children with disabilities on the value of play both in a program and in the family, and provide specific ways to encourage play at home.

Not only does family play help children with disabilities to grow and develop, but it also provides wonderful opportunities for the family to enjoy each other, to relax, to be less task-oriented, and to strengthen the bond between parents and their children with disabilities. Because living with children with disabilities is often very stressful, this is important. Often parents need help to become a skilled play partner, as discussed in Box 10.5.

**BOX 10.5**

## Encouraging Parents to Play with Their Children

Parents need to learn how to become sensitive and responsive play partners with their child with special needs. What constitutes sensitive and responsive play intervention strategies that parents can learn to employ? For Joan Goodman (1992) it is solving the problem of "take" in play. To illustrate, consider the following scenarios:

1. A child is removing animals and blocks from a shelf. The parent suggests building a zoo with the blocks and animals. The child, who is interested in removing and lining up, cannot participate in the zoo construction. The parent picks up an animal, pokes it in the child's stomach, and says, "Monkey is going to get you." The child giggles. The parent then tries to retain the child's attention by constructing cages with the blocks and putting an animal in each.

2. A child spontaneously moves a car back and forth without releasing it from his hands. The parent, having successfully gotten the child to roll cars to her, asks, "Will you send me the big car or the little one?" No response. "The small car or the police car?" No response.

In each of these cases there is a great psychological distance between the parent and the child. The parent in both examples is trying to expand play to a symbolic level that is much higher than what the child initiated. Neither parent is tuned into the child's play (and mental) state or appreciates what the child is doing. Moreover, in these two cases the parent seems to be pushing for symbolic play. Each time the child loses interest and the activity becomes the parent's play, or the episode terminates. Such intrusions can be seen as another kind of inappropriate "play redirector" in the above intervention (see Chapter 9) found all too often in early education programs.

Careful observation of the child's play and the child's responses to the parent's suggestions are needed for parent play intervention to be effective. For example, play shifts in response to parental interventions are inconsequential to the child's learning and development unless there is "take." *Take* is defined both in the sense of mutual engagement (i.e., both the parent and the child being on the same wavelength) and in terms of the parent's suggestions being permanently incorporated into the child's behavioral repertoire. On-the-spot imitation and forced compliance are not take. Rather than trying to get the child to accommodate to the parent's play idea about a road for cars, the parent could attempt either *horizontal* or *vertical expansions* close to the meaning or intentions of the child's original play actions. Empathy for the child and respect for play are shown when the parent accommodates to the child by showing or asking the child to perform simple action variations of the cars play—from different spatial locations or with different amounts of pushing, all following a back-and-forth, up/down routine as an example of *horizontal* expansion.

*Vertical* expansion extends play by going from the back and forth, up/down schemata to other concepts that are known to be achieved at approximately the same developmental level, such as open/close, give/return, and raising/dropping.

Misreading a child's play intentions is common in cases in which a child is four years old chronologically but mentally only twenty months. It is easy to make the mistake of assuming an interest in and a capacity for symbolic play. Parents need to support their child's level of play and guard against hurting the child's self-esteem by making frustrating and unrealistic demands. Playful parenting (or teaching) includes knowing play facilitation strategies and knowing how to scaffold the child's play, and this requires knowing how to solve the problem of the match between the child's interest and ability and the challenge offered from the parent or teacher, or the problem of take in play, as Goodman called it.

**Play Groups.** Mother's-day-out programs were originally created to enable children to spend time socializing with other children of the same age on a regular basis. These groups are still popular for stay-at-home mothers. Interestingly, one effective approach to increasing father involvement in early childhood programs is having family play times at the program, in which families are invited to use the facility and materials to engage in play activities together (Cunningham, 1998, 1999). Further, the notion of family play groups has expanded in a variety of directions. For example, most families that home-school their children are also members of home-schooling associations, which provide regular opportunities for the children to engage in social activities with other students, including play.

During the 1970s, 1980s, and 1990s a large network of interracial support groups sprang up throughout the country. As a direct result of the increase in interracial families and biracial and multiracial children and a new awareness of the identity needs of these children, interracial support groups served a variety of functions. One of the main purposes of these organizations was to provide a regular play group for biracial children to play with other biracial children of the same age (Brown & Douglass, 1996). This served a critical function because biracial children tend to be marginalized or simply invisible in early childhood programs and schools (Wardle & Cruz-Janzen, 2004).

Other play groups exist for families of children who were born premature at the same time, adopted children, and families who emigrated recently from other countries. A long-standing play organization for children with disabilities and their parents is Lekotek discussed in Box 10.6.

**BOX 10.6**

### Lekotek

A Lekotek (*Lek* means play in Swedish and *tek* means library) is a resource center for children with disabilities and their families. Originating in Stockholm in 1963 by a small group of parents and teachers, the first Lekotek operated from an apartment where parents and children began to meet to exchange toys among themselves and to offer each other socio-emotional support. From this grass-roots beginning has developed a worldwide network of play libraries serving the needs of children with special needs. The first Lekotek in the US was opened in Evanston, Illinois, in 1980 by Sarah deVincentis (Sinker, 1985). Evanston serves as the national Lekotek Center with a current nationwide network of 46 Lekotek centers and 18 Compuplay sites.

Lekotek uses family-centered play as the primary way to facilitate the inclusion of children with special needs into the full range of family and community life. Currently, Lekotek's operations include monthly center-based play sessions and a toy-lending library for children from birth to eight years old as well as outreach services to families through inclusive play groups, home visits, toy making workshops, and family literacy programs.

Lekotek play leaders facilitate family play sessions once a month using specially adapted and off-the-shelf toys selected for the individual child. Emphasis is on creative use of materials and social interaction among family members and, most important, enjoyment. Experiencing success and having a positive experience are utmost goals. Monthly, the family borrows a number of toys for home enjoyment. Chosen toys are ones the parent had seen the play leader use and feels comfortable using to expand the child's play. Siblings, grandparents and neighborhood children are encouraged to participate in play sessions to maximize transfer or carry-over to the child's home and community environment.

During the one-hour session, play leaders usually employ about seven or eight toys preselected with the child's ability in mind to provide stimulation to the developmental progress. The relaxed, close atmosphere that prevails seems to foster the growth of familial bonds. The orientation is very child-centered, for instance, a game of catch that degenerates to simple throwing by the child can be salvaged by the play leader who grabs a box as an open container to turn the activity into a simple form of "basketball." By accommodating to the child in this sensitive and responsive way, the play leader is scaffolding the play episode and elevating the child's behavior to a more mature level through the energetic and clever use of attention recruitment and maintenance strategies. One parent remarked (McLane, 1984):

> At Lekotek, I learned the joy of playing with my child. . . . The Lekotek leader looked at my child as though he had no handicap. She took all of the positive things about him, all the good things, and never said "you can't do this" or "you can't do that." "You *can* do this." The atmosphere was so relaxed and so tranquil. . . . The Lekotek leader is not judging you. And not judging your child. . . . They taught me how to play with my child again. . . . I had forgotten the more natural kinds of things to do with my child. . . . They taught me how to enjoy my child. It was like seeing my son for the first time.

Lekotek libraries in the US contain more than 50,000 toys. In addition to commercial and educational toys, the libraries include especially designed toys and ones adapted with special switches and motors to accommodate youngsters who are physically challenged.

Compuplay centers, which are run in conjunction with Lekotek centers or independently, have play sessions that allow children and their families to learn through play with computer programs and equipment. An extensive inventory of interactive software programs for diverse ability levels are available for preview and home loan. Compuplay's goal is to use technology to compensate for physical limitations and to help children have control over their environment.

Lekotek also has a toy resource helpline to help family and friends choose toys to buy as gifts for children with disabilities. For individualized assistance in selecting appropriate toys and play materials one can call toll-free the Lekotek Resource Helpline 800-366-PLAY (TTY 847-328-0001) Monday through Friday from 9:00 A.M. to 4:00 P.M. (central time). www.lekotek.org

*Source:* Johnson, Christie, and Yawkey, *Play and Early Childhood Development,* 2/e, pp. 170–171. Published by Allyn and Bacon, Boston, MA. 

## Play and Assessment

Assessment and children with disabilities go hand in hand, from the initial screening that alerts professionals to potential problems to continual efforts to assess progress in achieving the children's IFSP or IEP goals and objectives. A variety of assessments are used with these children, including screening, diagnosis, eligibility for special services, instructional and program planning, placement, monitoring program effectiveness, and overall program evaluation.

**Play-Based Assessment.** Play-based assessment is very effective for many of these functions with young children because they are truly authentic assessments, and because they match up well with the NAEYC/NAECS/SDE recommendations. Specific questions help us understand these recommendations (Hills, 1993):

- Are the assessments based on the goals and objectives of the program?
- Are the results of the assessments used to benefit the children—to create plans for individual instruction, improve instruction, individualize instruction, and so on?
- Do the assessment address all domains—social, emotional, physical, and cognitive—as well as students' feelings about learning?
- Do the assessments rely on teachers' regular observations and record keeping of children's everyday activities and performances, reflecting behavior over time?
- Do the assessments occur as part of the ongoing life of the classroom?
- Do the assessments use multiple sources of information about children: teachers' interviews, parent input, children's work, and observations?
- Do the assessments reflect individual, cultural, and linguistic diversity?
- Do children appear comfortable and relaxed during the assessments?
- Do the assessments focus on strengths and capacities, not just weaknesses?
- Are children given opportunities to evaluate their own learning?
- Do the assessments determine both what children can do independently and what they can do with constructive support?
- Are assessment results used to assist in instructional planning?

Play-based assessments meet many of these recommendations, largely because play is a low-risk activity. (There are no right or wrong answers; no one is telling you what to do and what not to do.) There are a variety of play-based assessments, including Developmental Scale of Infant Play (Belsky & Most, 1981), Play Assessment Scale (Fewell

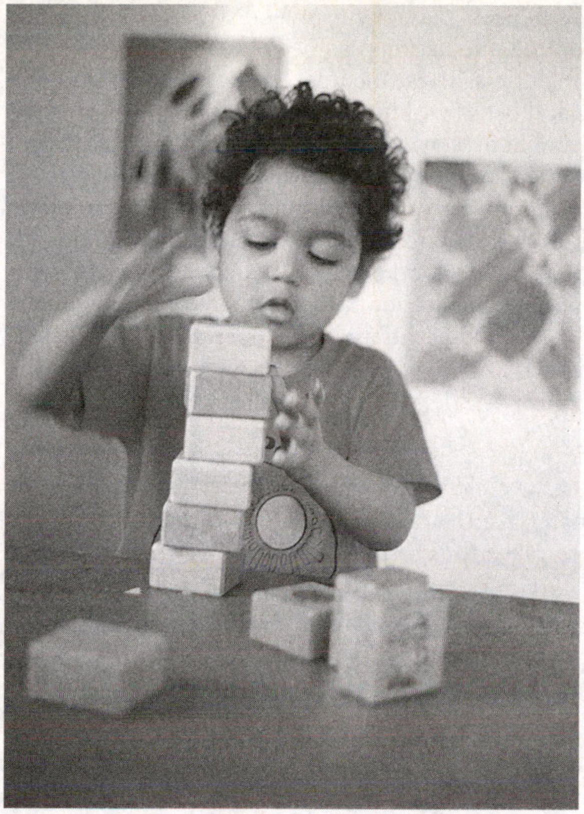

➤ Play-based assessments are very effective with young children, because they are truly authentic assessments, and because they match up well with NAEYC/NAECS/SDE recommendations

& Rich, 1987), and the Transdisciplinary Play-Based Assessment (Linder, 1993). A brief description of Transdisciplinary Play-Based Assessment is provided here.

**Transdisciplinary Play-Based Assessment.** Transdisciplinary Play-Based Assessment (TPBA) was developed by Toni Linder to use with infants to children six years old. The method is appropriate for typically developing children, children at risk, and children with disabilities. The cognitive, social-emotional, communication/language, and sensorimotor domains are assessed, and the data that are collected can be interpreted for a variety of purposes, included the development of a child's IFSP or IEP (Linder, 1993).

This assessment involves a team of professionals who see and evaluate the child during a play session. Although the team comprises professionals from various fields, each person on the team must be knowledgeable of all the domains being assessed and know how to evaluate the child on each domain. The team includes the child's parent(s) and at least three professionals: speech therapist, occupational or physical therapist, and a teacher or psychologist. Additionally, a social worker, psychiatrist, or eye specialist might be included, depending on the specific needs of the child. One of the team members is the facilitator; another explains the process to the parents and facilitates their involvement in the assessment.

TPBA is conducted in a well-equipped play environment, a naturalistic place where the child's authentic behavior and interactions can be assessed by the team, including a variety of toys and play materials. These include dramatic play props such as small tables, chairs, sink, stove, doll beds (traditional housekeeping props), dress-up props, phones, blankets, miniature houses, garages, farm sets, dolls, a traditional block set with cars and trucks, a variety of blocks, and a well-equipped art area. A sand and water table, an area with manipulative toys and puzzles, and gross motor equipment such as steps, balls, balance beam, and tricycles round out the equipment.

The assessment itself has six phases, which take sixty to ninety minutes to complete: unstructured facilitation, structured facilitation, child-child interaction, parent-child interaction, motor play, and snack. Observational guidelines are used to assess and score their observations, and observational worksheets, provided along with the test, are used to record these scores. If possible, each session should be videotaped.

- *Phase I: Unstructured facilitation (20–25 minutes).* The facilitator engages the child in unstructured play, allowing the child to lead the activity. The child is free to choose different play areas and materials; the facilitator develops rapport with the child while encouraging the child to play at his or her highest level.
- *Phase II: Structured facilitation (10–15 minutes).* In this phase play materials are still used, and the activities need to be as playlike and child-initiated as possible, but the facilitator asks the child to perform specific tasks and asks the child questions, with the purpose of addressing cognitive areas, language, and activities that were not displayed during Phase I.
- *Phase III: Child-child interaction (5–10 minutes).* Here the child plays with another child in unstructured play. The other child should be of the same sex and developmental level and familiar to the child being assessed. The purpose of this phase is to observe and assess the child's social development. The facilitator generally follows the child's lead but will initiate interactions between the two children if none occurs naturally.
- *Phase IV: Parent-child interaction (10 minutes).* In this phase, one or both parents play with the child, as they would do at home. After five minutes of this play, the parent(s) tell the child that they are leaving but will return shortly. The child's response to this separation is observed, as is the child's behavior when the parent returns after a few minutes. Then the parent performs a more structured, unfamiliar, and challenging task with the child, and the child's behavior is observed.
- *Phase V: Motor play (10–20 minutes).* Initially, the child engages in unstructured motor play with various pieces of motor equipment; then the facilitator directly has the child involved in activities that were not evident in the unstructured play. The physical therapist may also join the session at this time to collect additional data on the child's physical development and abilities.
- *Phase VI: Snack (5–10 minutes).* At this time the child may be rejoined by the child he or she played with during Phase III. The team is interested in the child's social interaction, self-help skills, and adaptive behaviors.

After the play session is complete, the team analyzes the videotape, correlates their observations and scores with each other, completes the summary sheets, and develops preliminary recommendations that are put into a formal report (Linder, 1993). This report is then used for the development of an IEP, IFSP, or diagnosis of a specific disability or is used as input for program options and design.

## PLAY THERAPY

If the basic parameters of play are in direct opposition to the more behavioral and reductionist approach to children with disabilities, then the theoretical basis of therapy is even further removed. Theorists such as Sigmund Freud, Carl Jung, Virgina Axline, and Carl Rogers are even less compatible with the ECSE view of working with children who have disabilities. There are a variety of reasons for this, many being the same reasons the special education field questions the value of play. Because therapy—except behavioral therapy—deals with nonobservable changes in a child, it is difficult to set goals and objectives, chart progress, and be accountable. However, play therapy is a legitimate process that is used by many professionals working with children with a variety of disabilities, especially those related to abuse, sexual abuse, neglect, dysfunctional homes, separation, anger, and being in foster and adoptive care.

In play therapy the child is encouraged to play out feelings, conflicts, and problems (Axline, 1969). Play is used because it is a natural process of self-expression for children, enabling the child to engage in a pleasurable, self-directed activity while the therapist observes and interprets the child's behavior. Play therapy in a subset of therapy that also includes art therapy, music therapy, and even therapy riding on horses.

There are different kinds of play therapy, but they all have several things in common. First, all play therapy assumes that everything said and done by the child in the play session has meaning to the child. The challenge for the therapist is to decipher that meaning and then to determine its effect on the child's behaviors, especially the targeted behaviors the therapist is addressing in the session. Second, all play therapy involves a therapist, although in filial play therapy the therapist is the parent. Although play therapists come from a variety of disciplines and have different training, according to Virginia Axline (1969), a play therapist must:

- Have a warm, trusting relationship with the child
- Accept the child as he or she is
- Be sensitive to the child's feelings and be able to reflect those feelings back to the child
- Understand that therapy is a slow process
- Provide only those guidelines needed to create a positive relationship between the therapist and child and those needed to handle reality (not making a mess, time, etc.)

There are a variety of approaches to play therapy, including the following:

- *Psychoanalytic approach.* In this approach, the therapist interprets the child's play and words to determine insights into the child's unconscious conflicts. The therapist rarely directly intervenes but reflects on the child's play in statements such as "You seem to be very angry with that doll." This approach is quite popular in the dramatic play area in many preschool programs, especially in therapeutic preschool programs.

- *Play group approach.* In the play group approach, group dynamics is added to the process, revealing how well children play together and how well they address their feelings toward other children.
- *Behavioral approach.* This approach is not strictly a play therapy approach because the therapist is very much in control of the session. The therapist uses behavior conditioning to change the child's behavior, in the hope that when the child returns to the situation that caused the problem (say, fighting with peers while playing), the behaviors that were learned in the session will transfer and the child will no longer engage in problem play.

## Sandplay Therapy

Sandplay therapy is one kind of psychoanalytic play therapy. It is discussed here to illustrate the considerable therapeutic value of play and to familiarize students with an approach that might be used with some of their children. Clearly, teachers are not qualified to conduct specific play therapy. Sandplay is based on the theories of Swiss psychiatrist Carl G. Jung, a contemporary of Freud, who was also concerned with the subconscious and the effect of the subconscious on a person's behavior. Jung viewed the unconscious mind as containing forces that drive the individual towards wholeness, growth, and potential (Allan & Brown, 1993) and as a self-entity that can heal itself. He believed the state of a person's psyche is revealed through dreams and the creative process, including play with objects and symbols.

In Jung's view, the psyche is made up of the ego (conscious mind), the personal unconscious (a collection of unconscious personal experiences), and the collective unconscious (a collection of various archetypes). To Jung people are continually involved in a struggle of opposites, the conflict between the external world of family, school, peers, work, and so forth, and the inner world of feelings, wishes, and emotions. With a person or child who is in Jungian therapy, the therapist helps the client balance these two opposite forces by helping the client to develop new attitudes toward self, others, and the world around him or her.

In sandplay therapy the process of playing with objects in the sand enables the person's inner unconscious content to be expressed at the conscious but nonverbal level. Thus sandplay allows for a broader, more revealing look at the unconscious than is possible through just words (Kalff, 1993). The therapist interprets the symbols that are evident in the child's play, which are multidimensional and represent a cluster of emotions and experiences. (Kalff, 1993).

In sandplay therapy a child selects miniature figures that he or she wishes to play with and then creates a scene in a sand tray, a large container filled with sand. Box 10.7 lists some of the miniature figures used in sandplay therapy. The child can choose to work in dry sand or wet sand. The therapist provides no direction, other than to indicate that the child is free to make anything—there is no right or wrong approach. Some children talk to themselves throughout the session; others work silently. After the child has left, the therapist takes a photo of the sand tray and then replaces the miniature figures on their shelves. During the session the therapist sits quietly a little distance from the child, providing emotional support and a physical presence but no guidance or interpretation. The aim of sandplay therapy is to offer a truly safe place for the psyche's own healing (Family Psychological Consultants, 1992).

BOX 10.7

## Sandplay Objects

*Animals:* Wild, domestic, forest, prehistoric, fantasy, farm
*Insects:* Butterflies, caterpillars, bees, spiders, daddy longlegs, etc.
*Birds:* In flight, on nests, ducks, eagles, peacocks, etc.
*Sea creatures:* Dolphins, fish, sharks, whales
*Reptiles and amphibians:* Alligators, crocodiles, frogs, lizards, snakes, etc.
*Buildings and bridges:* Castles, forts, houses, schools, teepees, hogans, etc.
*Monsters:* Dragons, sea monsters, fantasy monsters
*Barriers:* Fences, screens, walls, signs, etc.
*Eggs and food:* All cultures
*Plants:* Trees, palm trees, flowering trees, flowers, seaweed, cacti
*Mountains, caves, volcanoes*
*Vehicles:* Buses, cars, fire trucks, police cars, emergency vehicles, etc.
*People:* Multicultural, multiage, action figures, fighting figures, both genders
*Spiritual symbols:* Candles, icons from different religious, goddesses, gods, etc.

*Source:* Family Psychological Consultants (1992).

The therapist interprets the child's sandplay over a number of sessions. According to Kalff (1993), the therapist should use four functions to make these interpretations: thinking (rational), intuition, feeling, and sensation. Although some of the interpretation is based on the process of the child involved in creating the scene, most is based on an interpretation of the sandplay scenes. Some of these interpretations are based on the following (Kalff, 1993):

- The therapist's feeling response. What is the therapist's response, either to the scene as a whole or to the individual elements: cold, warm, sad, confused, etc.?
- Use of space. How has the child positioned the miniatures in the tray: covering the whole space, clustered in clumps, concentrated in certain areas, etc.?
- Use of wet or dry sand.
- Shapes in the sand and the arrangement of objects. Do curves and circles predominate, or straight lines and angles? Further, are the objects freely distributed or placed in strict, geometric patterns?
- Use of figures. What figures are used, and what is the symbolic value of those figures?
- Placement of figures in space. What is the proximity of objects to each other, what is the distance between them, and do they logically relate to each other, or are they unrelated to each other?

- The context of the whole process. The individual scene must be viewed within the context of scenes that came before and ones that come afterward which is determined from the photographic record.

All the miniatures that are used in sandplay have symbolic value based on fairy tales, mythology, religion, and dreams. Box 10.8 explains some of these symbolic meanings.

**BOX 10.8**

### *Symbolic Meanings Used in Interpreting Sandplay*

*Water:* Freedom, emotionality, anxiety, primitive, sadness, regression
*Soldiers:* Conflict, aggression, life/death issues, force
*Animals (domestic):* Family, dependency, compliance
*Car:* Mobility, power, travel, family, escape
*Dolls:* Self-identity, regression, friendship, closeness, siblings
*Monsters:* Fear, unknown, friendly, secretive, power, fantasy, aggression, revenge
*Teddy bear:* Warmth, nurturing, security, compliance, protection
*Female:* Issues with mother, teachers, sisters, aunts, etc.
*Baby:* Nurturing, siblings, competition, regression
*Males:* Issues with father, brother, teachers, etc.
*Thermometer:* Crisis, need for help, need for choice, sickness
*Dinosaurs:* History, death, power, fear, survival, loss, extinction
*Sunglasses:* Hiding, avoiding, distance, safety

*Source:* Family Psychological Consultants (1992).

The sandplay therapist uses his or her interpretations of the child's sandplay sessions to determine progress, provide support, and help the child move toward more control of issues of concern. Choice of the use of sandplay for specific children with specific disabilities is based on the therapist's judgment. Only people who are trained in sandplay therapy are qualified to use this approach.

## Group Play Therapy

Group play therapy for children is a social and psychological process in which children play with each other in a playroom. The purpose is for children to develop individually and in positive interactions with other children. In group play therapy children learn by observing the interactions and play behaviors of the other children in the group. Then, in the secure, nonevaluative environment, they try out and practice these new behaviors. The hope is that they will then engage in more prosocial play activities in their life outside of therapy. There are no group goals in play therapy, and group cohesion and solidarity are not required for progress (Landreth, 2002).

Group play therapy is often used in conjunction with individual therapy; it is also used in many school settings as a way to provide therapy to a group of children who are dealing with similar issues.

## Filial Therapy

The history of child therapy has always involved some attempt to teach parents how to act as therapists at home (Landreth, 2002). The value of using parents as therapists is based on the emotional bond between the parent and child, which is potentially much stronger than the bond between the therapist and child. Filial therapy uses play as the means to facilitate interactions between the parent and child, and to build up the relationship between them (Landreth, 2002). Filial therapy is typically used with children two to ten years old and is a weekly play session that focuses on the child's play. The focus of these sessions is to use the relationship between the parent and child to produce change and growth in the child. "The objective is to help the parent relate to the child in ways that will release the child's inner directional, constructive, forward-moving, creative, self-healing power" (Landreth, 2002, p. 370).

The parent is taught how to create a supportive, nonevaluative climate and then to allow the child to take the lead in the special play sessions. The parent learns how to take the child's perspective and to respect the child's effort to grow and self-heal. In the thirty-minute sessions the child initiates and directs the play activity and is free to express himself or herself in any way the child chooses—within obvious reasonable limits. During the play the parent affirms and empowers the child. The play session is structured in this way:

1. The child leads the play, and the parent follows by verbally reinforcing and reflecting on the child's play. The parent does not make suggestions or ask questions.
2. The parent's major task is to empathize with the child's thoughts and feelings and to observe the child.
3. The parent verbalizes the feelings experienced by the child.
4. The parent sets—and reinforces—limits regarding time, caring for and not breaking toys, and not physically hurting the parent (Landreth, 2002).

Toys to be used for filial therapy include play dough, crayons, paper, scissors, baby bottle, rubber knife, doll family, doll house with furniture, toy soldier, car, Tinker Toys, doctor kit, Band-Aids®, play money, rope, tape, a Bobo inflatable doll, hand puppets, domestic and wild animals, ring toss game, and masked figures. These toys do not have to be new and should be used only during the play session. The play sessions should occur at the same time every week at an uninterrupted time period (no TV, phone calls, etc.), and in an appropriate place but not the child's room. Parents must be trained to work with their children; the filial therapy model provides parent training by a play therapist in small groups in conjunction with the parents working with their child. A ten-week model is considered to be ideal and has shown positive results both in changing the parent-child interaction style and in changing specific child behaviors (Landreth, 2002). Often the overall parenting style changes as a result of these sessions.

➤ Filial therapy teaches parents how to play with their children.

Filial therapy enables the professional to provide direct and specific parenting instruction to the parent and also provides the parent the support required. Further, it provides a nondirective, play-based approach that targets emotional and psychological issues of the child while encouraging parents to move to a more supportive, nonintrusive approach to working with their child.

## Early Childhood Teachers and Play Therapy

Although, as we have said, teachers are not qualified to conduct therapy with children and parents, ideas taken from play therapy can help teachers in working with their children with disabilities. To this end, teachers should do the following:

1. Understand the value of play therapy and provide a supportive, risk-free, unstructured environment in which similar processes can occur in their classroom and playground.
2. Advocate for play therapy intervention for children with disabilities whom they believe would benefit from this kind of intervention.
3. Encourage parents of children with disabilities to engage in all sorts of play with their children at home.
4. Convince parents of the important value of play, both at home and in the early childhood program.
5. Make a wide range of toys and play materials available to the children at all times. All play therapy involves a variety of toys and play materials. And because toys and play materials are both culturally specific and relevant to each child's experimental context, teachers should make sure the materials reflect both genders and the cultures and experiences of all their children (Wardle, 2003a).

Of most importance, play therapy makes it clear that children need a variety of noneducational toys (ones that do not have specific educational objectives in mind) and lots of time to simply engage in free play. Finally, play therapy provides a variety of ways in which teachers can support children in play and help them progress without direct intervention (verbal reinforcement, reflection, modeling, and simply being physically present while children play).

## CHILD LIFE PROGRAMS

Play theory and research have generated many useful ideas for teachers to apply in early childhood education and in special education and play therapy. Similarly, child life programs have benefited from research on children's play and the roles of the adult.

Child life programs serve hospitalized children. There are now over 400 such programs in the United States and Canada. They are available in a variety of hospital units, including intensive care, pediatrics, emergency departments, and outpatient clinics, as well as serving children with long-term conditions in home care and child care programs. The American Academy of Pediatrics Committee on Hospital Care (1993) has recommended that adequate play facilities under the direction of child life specialists be part of all pediatric settings (Hartley, 2002).

Child life programs have a long and honorable history going back to the early decades of the twentieth century, having evolved from play programs for hospitalized children that were operating as early as 1917. The movement became firmly established in the 1950s and 1960s with the pioneering efforts of women like Mary Brooks and Emma Plank, who considered it mandatory for the medical profession to respond to the need for play in children who had to adjust to hospitalization (Thompson & Stanford, 1981).

Child life specialists are members of an interdisciplinary health care team who help children who require treatment and hospitalization. They embrace the value of play in service to children who are hospitalized, seeing play as an activity that is essential and not merely a diversion or a pleasant extra. Play empowers children to become active participants in the hospital rather than the passive recipients they often are. Play is also valued because it is a window on the child patient's thoughts and feelings, giving useful information to adults caring for the child. Also, play can help patients deal with the unpleasantness of their situation. Play allows for social interaction, enabling life and social development to go on, and losing oneself in a play state can be a relief from stress and a chance to forget and think about better days ahead.

Being in the hospital is a very frightening experience that can easily impede play and development. The child specialist works to overcome these psychological barriers to play, as well as the physical ones related to being in a wheelchair or being bedridden because of traction, sometimes encumbered with intravenous (IV) lines. Adaptations are made so that opportunities for play can exist in the hospital to the extent that they are medically permissible. For example, a young child with an IV line might visit the hospital playroom under the supervision of a child life specialist or parent to explore the play area and watch other children playing or play to some extent alone or with others. Child life specialists foster play that is rich and varied, is developmentally appropriate, and accommodates to the child's medical condition.

Physically attractive playrooms are valued as a haven by children in a hospital, where parents and children also benefit from contact with other families and gaining support from their peers. Much can be learned about the concerns of families and the needs, anxieties, and play styles of hospitalized children by observing parent-child play interaction in the playroom.

Playrooms in hospitals are designed for directive and nondirective play and informal discussion. They often have child-size furniture and toys, including toy medical kits; Lego doctor, nurse, and family figures; and video games. A main feature of child life programs is that they are equipped with toys to meet varied developmental needs, individual interests, and play preferences. Space must be adequate and accessible for children in wheelchairs or children who are rolled in on a bed.

The playroom requires a great deal of management, which is often delegated to a staff assistant who provides general developmental and diversional play (Hartley, 2002). This enables child life specialists to be free to prepare children for medical procedures and to work with parents and children who need their support. Play with dolls and medical instruments is used to promote developmentally appropriate learning and coping strategies. Parents are enlisted as co-helpers so that child life specialists can serve more families.

Individual rooms and hallways and other areas of the hospital can also be play spaces. Child life specialists help patients visit each other's rooms to play and share art projects, game play, favorite stories, or puppet shows. Boxes of play materials that are often seen in waiting rooms of doctor's offices and clinics are placed in hallways to encourage play and to stimulate social interaction. Children are encouraged to use materials that encourage self-expression, such as puppets, musical instruments, art supplies, dolls, and dramatic play materials. Child life specialists provide children with many opportunities to express feelings, and they let children know that it is all right to have all sorts of feelings—that these are normal and acceptable. The child life specialist's services and observations in the different settings are documented and included in the child's medical record (Hartley, 2002).

Hospitalized children often exhibit so-called medical play. For instance, some children enjoy using real medical equipment such as IV lines without needles, stethoscopes, and casting materials, though some children find real material too threatening and prefer miniature replicas to enact medical play themes. Both these opportunities allow children to open up and vent their fears and anxieties. Medical play allows a chance to master feelings about being in the hospital and to overcome fear of medical equipment.

Important changes are occurring in child life programs that reflect changes in today's health care system, including a response to a variety of cost-cutting measures. For example, there is more outpatient care, and children who remain in hospitals longer are usually more acutely ill or immobile and thus less able to play. There is also less time for play in groups in hospital play resource rooms; increasing use of technology with patients in monitoring their care affects play opportunities, and opportunities for play in the hospital appear to be in a process of being squeezed out.

Professionals in child life today are mounting a counteroffensive to return high-quality play to the hospital. They are decentralizing the hospital playroom, assembling play kits that can be brought to children inside and outside hospitals, including home visits. Alliances are being formed with other professionals who are in contact with chronically ill children to bring to them high-quality and sustained play opportunities in new and different ways. Parents, teachers, and siblings are included in play plans. Amid these changes in child life programs, a strong belief in the benefits of play for hospitalized and outpatient children is maintained.

Teachers of young children in various early childhood programs can help children who are chronically ill or scheduled for long-term hospitalization, as well as help families better cope with this stressful and disruptive experience. Assistance can be accomplished in the form of anticipatory and follow-up classroom activities to lessen the discontinuities brought on by a child's leaving a program and reentering a program. Both the hospitalized child and his or her peers will benefit. The teacher needs to work carefully with the child's family to share information and develop strategies to reduce the likelihood that the hospitalized child will suffer from the negative behavior of peers toward him or her after the child returns to the class.

When a child is hospitalized for an extended time, the teacher can make arrangements to coordinate with the child life specialist to keep abreast of mutual activities to the degree appropriate. Technology can be used as a means of communication by the enterprising teacher and by the child life specialist for the benefit of the hospitalized child. Furthermore, teachers can plan a field trip to a local hospital, possibly the one the child will attend, as an invaluable experiential base for sociodramatic play or other activities and as an excellent anticipatory socialization experience for children who need to spend some time in a hospital. Children's books such as *Curious George Goes to the Hospital* are excellent for this as well.

## SUMMARY

Strong tensions exist over the place of play in early childhood special education. These tensions result from differing theoretical and philosophical foundations and programmatic purposes in the fields of special education and early childhood education. We believe that early childhood education, with its tradition of holding children's play in high regard, can help special education teachers make better use play in planning and implementing educational activities for all children. Nondirective play-based interventions are needed. More effort is required to help parents of children with disabilities know how to play with their children and foster their children's play. Teacher preparation programs in special education and early intervention need to give more attention to these topics. Regular early childhood educators also can learn a great deal from their special education counterparts to better work with exceptional youngsters in inclusive settings.

Young children with a variety and range of disabilities can benefit enormously from play, but changes are needed to make this happen, including improved preservice and in-service personnel preparation and increased collaboration between regular teachers, special educators, other professionals, and parents. The special education field needs to shift from a dependence on a reductionist paradigm to working with children with disabilities to a more constructivist approach, especially for children who can benefit from integrated and challenging approaches to their learning and development.

The field of play therapy also is undergoing change and development. Therapists are increasingly using new techniques in their work, such as sandplay therapy, with children and families with mental, emotional, and psychological problems. Although early childhood teachers cannot directly practice play therapy, they can refer families with troubled children to play therapists and can implement programs that are intrinsically therapeutic for all children, programs that afford opportunities for spontaneous play and free expression. They can encourage parents to play with their children.

Child life programs are another field in which play is very important, and teachers and other professionals need to be aware of the needs of hospitalized students. For all children with disabilities, including those in early intervention, child therapy, or hospitals and child life programs, parents and families must be fully involved.

## PROJECTS AND ACTIVITIES

1. Observe children with disabilities who are mainstreamed into a regular early childhood program. Interview the teacher about the child's disability and ways in which the teacher is adapting materials and instruction to meet the child's need.
2. Why is play critically important for young children with disabilities? List some specific reasons.
3. Suppose you have a child with a learning disability in your class who has trouble playing with the other children. What are things you can do to help this child improve his or her ability to play?
4. Find a private therapist who uses play therapy with children. Interview the therapist, and describe the technique(s) used.
5. Go on a web-based treasure hunt to locate several children's hospitals, and use the information you find on the Internet (and any other sources you can find) to rate the hospitals for how well they seem to be prepared to meet the play needs and interests of hospitalized children. What criteria will you use in rating the hospitals? What is the rationale of your rating system?
6. Go to a waiting room in a clinic or doctor's or dentist's office, and evaluate the kinds of play provisions that exist. Do naturalistic observations of how the toys are used and how the children behave with one another and with their parents. Record and interpret your observations.

### Resources

Lekotek:
**www.lekotek.org**

Toys "Я" Us/Amazon.com:
**www.Amazon.com (go to "Toys & Games")**

Assistive technology:
**www.assistivetech.net**

Association for Play Therapy, Inc.:
**www.a4pt.org**

National Center for Boundless Playgrounds:
**www.boundlessplaygrounds.org**

CHAPTER 11

# Popular Culture, Media, and Technology

## With Hey-Jun Ahn

## INTRODUCTION

In Chapter 6 we discussed play contexts and presented a general model of play-environmental relations that is consistent with the interpretation of context as that which weaves together or the total situation in relationship to the playing child. A major topic was culture, and we implied that an apt metaphor for culture is a garden in which children grow and develop. Culture as a garden puts emphasis on the fact that we can look on culture as a medium in which the forces of nature interact with the forces of nurture. To get a total picture of how culture operates in relation to play and child development requires that we envision the dynamic interplay between macro- and micro-level influences. We need to recognize that reciprocal relationships exist among cultural institutions (such as the government and the economy and a culture's educational system) on the one hand, and adults' play beliefs and practices, play activity settings, and children's play behaviors on the other hand. We believe that our role as responsible teachers and parents in this culture garden is to tend to the most important crop of all that we are raising: our children.

For most of this book the garden metaphor for culture seems best. This is because we in education are very concerned about the development and growth of children. We want to provide challenging enrichment that is developmentally responsive to the unique needs, capabilities, and interests of children. However, there are other metaphors for culture that are also useful. In this chapter we shift metaphors and compare culture to a gladiator's arena in which power relations get played out and to a foaming sea of semiotics in which symbolic meanings swirl about (Packer & Tappan, 2001). These additional metaphors are useful because in this chapter we broaden the discussion about play contexts begun in Chapter 6 to include a consideration about how the popular culture, the media, and technology all affect children's play and development. Popular culture, media, and technology interrelate and are laden with power issues and symbolism, even as they can still be garden tools, returning to the first metaphor for culture.

Many of the topics we present in this chapter are ones about which there are ongoing critical debate and concerns. For example, are the media-linked, marketing tie-ins such as superhero toys, which are known to encourage aggressive play, appropriate for young children? This is a very controversial subject in early childhood education. Some claim that playing with these kinds of toys, known to foster violent themes in play episodes, legitimizes brute force as a way to get what you want, an approach that is in direct opposition to what is taught in most early childhood programs. As those who favor critical theory (see Chapter 2) are quick to point out, economic institutional power is used to manipulate children and their parents into buying these toys by linking them to television shows and movies. Culture is a garden, but it is also saturated with invisible lines of power relations. It is sometimes useful to apply this concept when trying to understand cultural phenomena.

Similarly, the metaphor of culture that evokes an image of a sea of semiotics or symbolic messages can also be useful. Current thinking about what culture is rejects the idea that it is an independent variable or an external factor impinging on the individual. Culture is now defined as a system of meaning. Play as a meaning-making activity for children was discussed in Chapter 5. Children are constructing meaning on a personal level about the physical world and the social world. They are trying to understand nature and the world of objects, their own mental life, and their communications with others and the social worlds that they share. The popular culture, the media, and technology bombard children with an incessant flow of symbolic messages that have cultural and developmental significance. Children actively interpret cultural symbols, artifacts, and tools and assimilate them through the use of play and other behaviors.

When it comes to children's play and development, there are positive and negative sides to popular culture, the media, and technology. Both sides are discussed in this chapter. We believe that thinking about culture as a garden, as an arena of power relations, and as a sea of semiotics can be usefully applied to these topics and will contribute to a more complete understanding of children's play within the contexts of today's postmodern, postindustrial world.

## FOCUS QUESTIONS

1. What is your vision of children growing up today? Is it a hopeful one? What do we want for our children and our future? How does play help children live in a changing world? In what ways can play help children to prepare for the unknown future?
2. What features of popular culture today are impediments to healthy, wholesome play? What can parents and teachers do to help buffer the negative effects? Can certain elements

of popular culture serve to enrich play? How can teachers use popular culture in the classroom?

3. How can children's play and development benefit from child-care programs, affiliations with organized religion, children's museum and libraries, nature centers, and zoos? What are adult responsibilities here?
4. How is children's play affected by social tragedies such as acts of terror and when disasters strike? What purpose does play serve? What are the adult responsibilities in these situations?
5. What are the adverse effects of the television media on children's play? In which ways does television have a positive influence? What must parents and teachers do to ensure this?
6. How have movies and VCRs affected children's play?
7. In what ways have new technologies altered our definition of a toy?
8. What kinds of computer programs are good for children's play? What is known about how children play with computers?
9. Do children play any differently with traditional versus technology toys?

## POPULAR CULTURE

Ours is a dynamic, turbulent, and troubled time. Raising and educating children in the twenty-first century presents many challenges. Our nation overwhelmingly believes that it is harder to raise children now than it was when today's parents were children. This alarming conclusion comes from a recent survey conducted by Leo J. Shapiro and Associates (Shapiro, 2003). A U.S. national representative sample of 450 households was interviewed by phone in February 2003. Respondents were 177 nonparents, 82 fathers, 83 mothers, and 108 grandparents. Respondents were asked, "Thinking about the world in general, compared to when you were a child, do you feel it is easier or harder to raise a child these days than when you were a child?" They could answer "easier," "same," "harder," or "much harder." For the four respondent groups listed above, the percent of "much harder" replies were 37 percent, 48 percent, 62 percent, and 78 percent, respectively, and "harder" replies were 75 percent, 86 percent, 92 percent, and 98 percent, respectively. Grandparents and mothers were more likely to say that it was "much harder" than were fathers and nonparents.

The respondents in this survey who answered "harder" or "much harder" were asked what makes them feel the way they do. The most common responses were that the world is dangerous (i.e., terrorism 20 percent, drugs 17 percent, violence and crime 13 percent, society/everything 8 percent, bad morals 7 percent, schools failing/no God in schools 6 percent, and peer pressure 6 percent) or that TV, movies, and the Internet tell things children should not know (21 percent). Other reasons included not enough money (17 percent), no child discipline allowed (14 percent), and children who are spoiled (9 percent). Eighty-five percent of all respondents said that violence is more of a problem today than it was when they were a child, and this has to do more with media exposure to violence than to anything else (about 40 percent). Concern was expressed about all forms of media exposure, including too much violence on TV, movies, videos, video games, CDs, glamorization of violence, violent action figure toys, scary movies, movies with wrong ratings, frightening images, violence in the news, and wrestling on TV.

Two strong historical trends are currently affecting popular culture. One was discussed in Chapter 1, namely, globalization. We live in a rapidly changing and shrinking world brought on by economic development, technological advances, and political changes. People and knowledge from all around the world are much more connected than ever before because of greatly enhanced transportation and communication. Accompanying globalization is the spread of capitalist economy, the "McDonaldization" of the world, with the ever-increasing importance of corporate internationalism. Spreading capitalism is leaving its fingerprints all over many aspects of life in different cultures, and some people fear that it can lead to an economic takeover of the cultures themselves. That is, capitalist economies spawn capitalist cultures, resulting in an erosion of values, traditions, and the quality of life.

A related trend is the spread of secular humanism and democratic values to many places around the globe. Modern and postmodern secularism conflicts with religious traditions and creates cultural wars, if not some actual wars, in different places in the world. Religious traditions, as with other cultural traditions, put value on basic virtues and shared principles, whereas secularism values rational, technological problem-solving science, change and progress, and individual rights. Traditionalists seek what is good, true, and beautiful. Secularists also aspire toward the good, the true, and the beautiful (morality, science, and the arts), but they are open to different ideas about them and are not so convinced that there are absolute standards for judging (postmodern thinking). Modern secular thought tends to be more open-minded and inclusive. It is cosmopolitan, humanistic, rational, and scientific. It emerged from the Enlightenment in Northern and Western Europe about three centuries ago in reaction to superstition and ignorance in religious tradition and the parochialism of the time. The downside is that secularism carried to the extreme can lead to a lack of principles and core values and can leave people feeling adrift and disconnected from their roots and traditions. Postmodern thought believes that people need to retain their own ethnicity and sense of tradition as well as adapting to the realities of cultural diversity and worldwide developments, keeping track of where they have been while also sorting out the best new ideas and ways of doing things (Shweder, 2003).

Popular culture reflects the processes of globalization and secularization. It is the tempo of our times. It's the buzz out there. It is pushed by market and media forces, with capitalist media themselves driven by marketing forces. Individualism and materialism prevail. For example, MTV culture for teens and youth epitomizes popular culture for this age group, as does the hip-hop culture of music and music videos. Popular culture seems to say, "Life is great when you accelerate." "What's hot, and what's not?" is an important question for those who are engaged with popular culture, who take popular culture seriously, and who use it as a social barometer for their worth and well-being. What is stimulating, expedient, and efficient is at least as important as what is good, true, and beautiful; in fact it often defines what is good, true and beautiful. Peer group pressure mediates the strong effects that popular culture can have on developing children and youth. This youth culture is directly tied to marketing and money and targets the young, who have lots of expendable income.

Many families and probably most teachers try to critically deconstruct popular culture. They try to be discriminating about what news reports to believe and about what politicians say, and they do not want to be gullible targets of sales pitches and advertisements. They understand that the life they want for themselves and their children requires constant vigilance against the destructive influences of commercialism. They do not want their children to be at the mercy of the latest consumer fads and fashions, succumbing mindlessly to a materialistic way of life, or to become hedonistic pleasure seekers living for the moment. And most parents and teachers deeply understand that success in this culture requires children to learn to delay gratification and set long-term goals—things that run against the grain of popular culture. They certainly do not want their children to be exploited or harmed.

In Chapter 6, in which we discussed social ecology, family dynamics, and children's play, we described the autotelic family context and recommended it for parents who wish their children to be imaginative, creative, and playful; to be able to live life to its zenith; and to experience states of flow. Children in these families have been nurtured to set their own goals and to follow through in work and play to achieve them. We believe that parents and teachers should encourage children to develop a sense of inner direction and self-control that can mediate positive work and play habits and serve as a shield against popular culture.

In Chapters 2 and 5 we discussed theories and research showing that play contributes to the emotional, cognitive, physical, social, and overall development of the child. Genuine, deep engagement in play, in particular, helps children in many ways. We cited research and presented arguments that play can help children to cope and be resilient in today's difficult world. Throughout this book we have developed the theme that adults can help children reap the promises of healthy, self-directed play—promises that include knowing one's self and others better; heightened creativity, imagination, and problem-solving skills; and greater emotional, personal, and spiritual well-being. Being self-motivated and having the will power to control one's experiences, being able to arrive at and maintain a sense of contentment, having confidence and a good moral compass, and being a compassionate and loving person—these are possible for our children when the power of play is unleashed and channelled in a positive way. We believe that this is possible, even in the face of all the challenges posed by popular culture, mass media, and technology. But we need to find ways to both reduce the negative impacts of popular culture, media, and technology and at the same time identify and use their possibilities for enrichment.

## Family Life and Public Places

"The buzz out there," what we have labeled popular culture—that is, what is out there and is readily accessible or available in daily life—is not favorable to child development, learning, and moral and spiritual well-being. One reaction to popular culture by some schools and families is to develop in children a respect and joy of more permanent forms of culture: the performing arts, education, learning, and various intellectual and physical pursuits. This can offer an alternative and help to take children away from the lure of the cheap thrills and from a dependence on the immediate satisfactions offered by popular culture. A second solution is to teach spiritual or religious values to help the next generation maintain perspective in the face of secularization and the onslaught of popular culture. A third approach is to expose children to popular culture in moderation and to help them deconstruct the negative aspects of popular culture.

**Childcare.** Families are not alone in being responsible for our children, although they often might feel that they are. In addition to schools, another important social institution that affects the next generation is early childhood programs. As institutions of early childhood education, childcare programs and preschools are situated between the private, intimate sphere of family life and the public, economic, and government spheres of the workplace and the state. Dahlberg, Moss, and Pence (1999) have proposed that childcare and preschool programs as institutions of early childhood education serve economic (capitalism) and national (progress) aims; they are located in the economic domain and in the domain of the state. They also meet the very basic needs of working families. But they can also be situated in a different domain: civil society.

Civil society is a sphere of social life that is public, unlike the privacy of the intimate sphere of the family, but it is voluntary, unlike the spheres of the state and the economy. Civil societies exist in the spaces of voluntary associations among people who want to engage in a common activity with a shared focus. Civic associations, clubs, special interest groups, and the like are forums in civil society. The public life that goes on here is different from that of the marketplace and the affairs of state.

Childcare and preschools can also be such forums or public spaces in civil society, according to Dahlberg et al. (1999). They can be places in which children and adults can come together to participate in significant projects. As envisioned by these authors, the focus would be on developing collective action and the spirit of democracy and on seeking the realization of the good life in the present. This focus would complement but not replace the customary national and economic goals of early childhood institutions, which are future progress and productivity. As such, childcare and preschool can be places for children to live their childhood with the help of teachers and parents working and playing with them (Greenman, 1994). Quality would be defined very locally in terms of how well stakeholders of a specific program—the children, their teachers, and their parents—engage in discourses of meaning-making. This would be seen in the teaching and learning projects and in the play experiences. The model balances respecting the child in the present as a person and preparing the child for future adulthood, supporting the contention of the great British educator Lord Nuffield that the best preparation for adulthood is a rich and meaningful childhood. And this model is compatible with the idea of play as cultural meaning-making.

Childcare and preschool programs as public places that currently follow this model would appear to be few and far between in the United States. Those that exist have been recognized for their ties with the Reggio Emilia and Waldorf models of early childhood education from Europe, the British infant and primary programs, and some re-emerging private Froebelian kindergarten programs (see Chapter 8). Nevertheless, the idea of transforming the institutional role of early childhood education in society is provocative. The kinds of social relationships and projects, including play, that are suggested seem worthy of emulation. A child-experiential perspective on play, as opposed to an adult-functional one, is reflected in this model (see Chapter 1). There is a primary concern placed on present-tense living and on emergent processes, not on preparing the child for the future (national progress goals and early childhood standards) and not on serving teachers' needs for gainful employment and parental needs for childcare so that they too can work for pay (economic goals). This model is a hopeful one because it is democratic and collective and defines quality in a way that is different from the technical and managerial ways now prominent in the government and in the marketplace. As such, the model is an idealistic alternative to the usual ways of viewing the purpose of early childhood institutions. Dahlberg et al. are critical theorists in early childhood education, and their perspective is postmodern; their views may prove influential in the years ahead in how childcare programs and preschools are run for parents and young children. Their view also parallels the views of many professionals and practitioners in the early childhood field, who are aghast at the current wave of accountability, standards, tests, and developmentally inappropriate activities.

**Places of Worship.** Other public places where families frequently go are churches, temples, synagogues, gurdwaras, and mosques. Yearnings from the innermost chambers of the human heart give rise to these places of worship where people congregate to practice organized religion.

Sigmund Freud wrote in his *Civilization and Its Discontents,* "The communal life of human beings had, therefore, a two-fold foundation: the compulsion to work . . . and the power of love." When asked what was needed to live a happy and productive life, Freud said, "Lieben und Arbeiten" ("loving and working"). Playing—or, in German, "Spielen"—should be added to this list of fundamental human activities. David Elkind (2003) has said this, Lenore Terr in her book *Beyond Love and Work* has said this, and we have been hinting at much the same throughout this book. When thinking about what it means to be a complete person, being able to love, to work, and to play certainly do come to mind as general categories of fundamental human activity.

But something still seems to be missing for many people. Mature adults love, work, and play and also take a walk of faith, a spiritual journey, or some other important quest in search of meaning in the experience of life. Not everyone testifies to a belief in an ultimate reality, a supreme being. Shakespeare had Hamlet say, "To be or not to be, that is the question." Here the question is to believe or not to believe. Everyone is faced with this question. Answering it in some fashion and acting on it would seem to be a fourth fundamental human activity, one that has implications for personal and communal life.

Places of worship as sacred forums in civil society can be oases in the desert of secular life. They can serve as sources of spiritual renewal and strength, which help people cope with the demands of hectic, everyday living. Joining an organized religion can provide social and moral support to families, social capital made available through congregational membership. Religious instruction and practice and application found here also can help to shield children and parents from the adverse effects of secularism in general and popular culture in particular.

Places of worship of world religions serve many roles, foremost of which is to worship Deity and to have one's faith affirmed. In addition to this religious role, they provide instruction for adults and children and provide facilities and activities for the local community. Social, educational, and community functions typically are held in rooms, halls, or buildings that are separate from the place where religious services are conducted. Kitchens are used to prepare meals, and separate rooms usually exist for play groups, youth groups, and clubs. Places of worship are family resource centers where friendships are formed. In some locales the existence of synagogues and gurdwaras can help to reinforce the social identities of the Jewish and Sikh communities, for example.

Usually, recreation and play opportunities exist in abundance on their premises. Play spaces include outdoor playgrounds and ball fields, and a wide range of provisions for play are found indoors in nurseries, as well as for use in classes. Religious curricula and instruction for children often incorporate educational play materials and activities, such as the use of puppets and felt boards to tell stories and relate messages with a religious theme. Many sports, music, dance, gymnastics, and arts and crafts programs for boys and girls of various ages are connected to organized religion. For example, Jim Johnson's son Clayton played in a local church's tackle football league with over 150 children from ages six to thirteen years. The program is in its tenth season. Families also network with one another to support peer relations for their children, making available additional play opportunities.

It is unfortunate that racial and ethnic segregation occurs so frequently in places of worship. To the extent that an in-group versus out-group mentality is reinforced, organized religion can influence the development of negative play attitudes and habits.

**Children's Museums.** In the past twenty years the number of children's museums, both national and worldwide, has been growing remarkably. They provide a new kind of play and learning environment for an increasing number of children and families—ideals that museums like the London Science Museum and the Chicago Museum of Science and Industry have provided for several generations of happy, inquisitive youngsters. They are an attractive feature in many communities, and visiting them is a very popular family activity for those who can afford admission (Dierking & Falk, 1994). Classroom visits are also very popular and provide many low-income children, who otherwise might not have a change to go, with an opportunity to visit them. Unlike traditional museums, where paintings and sculptures are on display to see but not to touch, exhibits in children's museums invite active hands-on participation by those who attend. Also proliferating are exhibits and discovery centers for children that are found in other types of museums, science centers, and libraries.

It is a good thing that children's museums are becoming an ever more common feature in our social landscape. They are for playing and wandering around in, exploring and wondering, satisfying curiosities, taking risks, using one's imagination, and showing persistence. When more and more of the outside world is becoming inhospitable and inaccessible (because of pollution, street crime, etc.), and opportunities to mess around in sheds, garages, and attics and basements are often limited in the name of hygiene and safety, where can children go to rummage, explore, and discover, and learn about things? Children's urge to explore and find interesting things to poke at can be satisfied through a visit to a local children's museum (Fasoli, 1996).

According to Forman (1998), the characteristics of a good exhibit in a children's museum are that they are interactive, participatory, and hands-on and they focus on something that is interesting to a particular age group. Children require control over events and should be able to discern the purpose of the activities in an exhibit. The built-in structure of activities should allow for a level of exploration, experimentation, construction, and problem solving that is developmentally appropriate for the intended age group. And a number of children should be able to use many of the exhibits at the same time.

Many exhibits are relevant to science education and invite behaviors ranging from exploratory play and discovery to complex and creative constructive play. For example, youngsters might be invited to an inventing lab to use various gadgets and gizmos to get an alarm clock to work to wake up a sleeping lion, or to travel back in time on a dinosaur expedition to explore an excavation pit.

Other subjects are also commonplace, such as art education, social science, or citizenship education. For example, children and parents might be given basic cardboard boxes to transform into original artworks or welcomed into an exhibit that is a multimedia, interactive experience to learn how to recognize and respond to prejudice and discrimination. It is not uncommon to find, for instance, a climbing apparatus made of tubes, rafters, and ropelike tunnels set to a theme such as outer space or under the sea to stimulate vigorous and exhilarating physical and mental play. Or there might be a games area with oversized chess, checkers, and dominoes sets; tabletop and wall games; and bowling and hopscotch.

Hands-on exhibits provide delight for families, encouraging cooperative play, creative problem solving, classification and sequencing skills, and reading and mathematics. Children benefit the most when a feeling of playfulness accompanies the use of the exhibit's materials. A good exhibit is one that kids want to go to, and once there, provide so much fun that they do not realize that they are learning something.

Children's museums are public places where families and schools can go for children to enjoy and to learn. Often teachers tie in visits with specific curriculum aims and structure the experience more than parents would. In fact, when families visit, parents are encouraged to let the child take the lead in going through the exhibits. Parents should see what interests the child, what the child is looking at and enjoying, and then respond to the child's choice. Parents need to be alert and engage in meaningful conversation, asking questions and answering the child's questions. Parents can draw relationships between experiences at the exhibits and other experiences in life for the child and can imagine and role play together and explore ideas. Exhibits encourage the child to play and get involved, and parents can enrich this by trying to get their children to think more about what they are doing. Sometimes this takes the form of director/redirector; at other times the parent may be a co-player with the child (Chapter 9, p. 271). Forman (2000) urges parents and teachers to help children construct meaning from their involvement with the exhibits in children's museums.

Sometimes this can be easier said than done. Some research suggests that parents and children seem to exhibit different tendencies when they visit children's museums (Shine & Acosta, 1999, 2000). Children generally like to engage in pretend play and to explore materials; parents like to teach concepts related to materials and to guide children's social and self-regulatory behaviors. Shine and Acosta have observed parent-child interaction in children's museums and have found that they are usually short-lived and sporadic; children do not always welcome intrusions into their play and other self-initiated behaviors. Often there appears to be a disconnection between what the child is doing and what the parent wants the child to do. For example, Shine and Acosta (2000) reported that in a grocery store exhibit, children tended to play without explicitly organizing roles, scripts, or activities. Parents tended to remain outside the play frame, directing, prompting, and guiding the child at play. Few extended sequences of pretend-play interaction were observed in this study. This lack of mutual pretend play contrasted with other studies that have examined parent-child pretend play at home (e.g., Haight & Miller, 1993). Shine and Acosta (2000) learned from follow-up parent interviews that parents wanted to progress beyond play, to teach their children. Perhaps they felt a duty to do so because of the setting they were in. Many children's museums market themselves to parents by stressing the educational value of their programs. Also, parents noted that they felt exposed by being in public.

Many exhibits do invite children to learn, to explore, and to make discoveries while engaging in pretend play. Parents can participate in this more fruitfully if children's museums would provide more private, smaller, and enclosed areas for pretend play, equipped with costumes and props suited for adult use. Perhaps signs can be posted to remind parents to enter into pretend play and to encourage them to go beyond a prescribed play script (Shine & Acosta, 2000).

It should be noted that many children's museums reinforce aspects of popular culture. Because many exhibits are funded by local corporations, a product tie-in often exists; for example, the Denver Children's Museum has for years had a fantasy play Safeway. The same museum has also used local professional sports figures to engage children in a variety of science and math activities (height, strength, leaping ability, etc.).

**Libraries.** Children's libraries have been around for many years as special sections of public libraries; nowadays, they have many exciting and innovative features that make them even more attractive to parents with young children. Many children's libraries now have print material in Spanish, French, and some Asian languages in addition to English. Libraries also lend audio and video cassettes of children's books and movies, and many have toys. Librarians are available to find the right book or to assist parents and children in the use of computers and children's software programs. Special programs include regular story hours for toddlers and older age groups.

When children are very young, it is best to begin a home library. Small children benefit by having even a shelf or two of some books that they can handle freely. Infant books need to be highly durable. Encouraging young children to touch, smell, and even taste books will facilitate their forming strong attachments to books and eventually a love of reading. Parents should treat books gently and with respect so that their children will see and imitate this.

In the past parents usually started going to children's libraries when their children were at least toddler age—often later, when they entered school. Recently, however, many libraries have initiated programs for infants. New parents receive library information kits through hospitals, adoption agencies, and prenatal classes. One popular program called "Catch 'Em in the Cradle" provides information on how to stimulate language development through games, songs, and other play activities for infants. Lists of recommended books for babies are provided. Parents are often invited to come to story hour no matter how young their child. Parents can learn nursery rhymes, songs, fingerplays, and other activities that they can use to foster their child's development at home. Toddlers, age eighteen to thirty-six months, are the first age group specifically targeted in story hour. Read-aloud programs are simple and help to socialize children into a group activity, seated with parents. Songs are simple and repetitious, such as "The Wheels on the Bus." By the time children are three to six years old, they like to be in groups, and parents do not have to stay with their children throughout the activities, which may include puppet shows, arts and crafts, films, and reading programs. Special visitors, magicians and clowns, and costumed adults (e.g., Clifford, Raggedy-Ann) make their appearance at times. By ages seven and eight years, programs aim at motivating reading as an enjoyable activity. Discussions and presentations by the children themselves become part of the special programs put on by children's libraries. Computer software programs and educational use of the Internet are of particular interest to this age group as well.

Both children's museums and children's libraries are family-friendly public spaces that have a lot to offer young children that stimulates their enjoyment and learning. Play and other educational activities that can result from their use can serve as a constructive alternative to the passive amusement and the much less positive pursuits that are promulgated by popular culture. In both cases, however, these programs must understand the basic value of play and avoid the temptation to teach instead of play.

**Nature Centers and the Outdoors.** In *The Sense of Wonder,* Rachel Carson wrote, "The years of early childhood are a time to prepare the soil." From nature emerges a sense of wonder, joy of discovery. E. O. Wilson's biophilia hypothesis posits that we are hard-wired to love life and be attracted to nature. It is a good thing to take children outside and experience nature as often as possible. Children learn about living creatures, bugs and worms, plants, life, and decay. They learn about streams and ponds, about the wind and rain, the sky and clouds. And as children are learning about all these aspects of the natural world, having their eighth intelligence (naturalist) nurtured, they are also learning to overcome their fears and become more secure and confident. They can learn positive values and habits that can prove influential and inspirational for a lifetime. Respect for nature and the environment as well as healthier living can both result.

Unfortunately, children have fewer spontaneous encounters with nature than previous generations did. According to the Wisk Active Play Survey (2003), out of 830 mothers who were sampled, 70 percent indicated that they played outdoors each day when they were children; only 31 percent of these mothers could say the same about their children today. Traffic, more people, less play space, less free time, air and water pollution, living near toxic waste sites, emissions from cars, crime, and danger all work against children going outside to play and to enjoy nature (Rivkin, 1995). This confinement to human-built environments, as opposed to the natural environment, and the inactivity and the sedentary, passive play that this breeds reduce children's opportunities to learn about nature. It also is responsible in part for our cultural diseases of childhood obesity and attention-deficit hyperactivity disorder (ADHD).

A central reason for this shift is that no one is marketing the outdoors to children and families because no one makes money from it. However, many companies market to children and their families computer programs, video games, "educational" TV shows, and educational toys (usually used indoors), because these are profitable products.

Schools, families, early childhood teachers, and a concerned citizenry have been responding to this problem by creating more opportunities for young people to enjoy and learn from nature and the great outdoors. In addition to naturalizing school grounds with gardens, wildlife habitats, and other nature-based enhancements, there has been an increase in nature centers, zoos, arboreta and other special places, and informal learning settings in communities and countrysides where teachers and parents can take children for environmental education. Although play might not be the primary focus of these efforts, indirectly there is an effect: the quality of children's play and school performance often goes up as a result of these enrichment experiences with nature. Nature is relaxing and can help to restore attention and focus and can help to relieve mental fatigue. It is inspirational, often stimulating creative energies. Unlike print and electronic media, which use only two of the human senses, environmental education and play engender perceptual learning through seeing, hearing, smelling, touching, tasting, and motion. And kids are motivated to learn new words and facts about what they have directly experienced with enjoyment and usually great interest. They are motivated to engage in pretend play and constructive play and art projects linking their natural environment experiences to the indoor early childhood education curriculum.

When young children are taken on trips to nature centers, chances are that they will encounter a great many interesting things as they walk along trails, explore fallen logs, and go up to the edge of a pond, climb rocks and hills, and crawl under shrubs and through vines. There is an abundance and great variety of things to notice and collect. Children can be prepared to get the most out of the visit by having on waterproof boots, wearing a magnifying glass on a cord around the neck, and having a strap-on bag for collectibles. Adults accompanying children should help children to notice things, pointing out the kinds of seeds and leaves, the bugs under the rock, the fungus growth on the fallen log, the moss and fern, the birds and animals, the sky and clouds, the different kinds of animal tracks, and the rings on the tree stump. Remembering shared conversations and having collections and photographs to take back to the classroom will help to tie together the outdoor field trip and the play and learning curriculum inside the school or center. Chapter 12 provides additional suggestions about the use of the outdoors and integrating the outdoors with program goals and objectives.

Zoos for children are great places to learn and have fun. Family zoos are specifically designed to be enjoyed by young children, so it is not surprising that different play opportunities abound. Zoos, like nature centers and children's museums and libraries, are refreshing alternatives to the experiences children have when they are being shuffled between organized music and sports lessons or when they are parked in front of the TV or computer. Zoos are places to reconnect with nature and the animal kingdom and to learn and to have a good time as well. Children can touch armadillos and feed goats, examine animal X-rays, dress up like a bug or a bird, pretend to be a veterinarian, finger paint in the mud, and explore a stream. Trained staff members help children relate to nature on an emotional level as well as intellectually.

➤ Zoos are places to reconnect with nature and the animal kingdom. Children can touch armadillos and feed goats.

Staff know the research that says that conservation-friendly adults had positive experiences with nature during childhood and were often nurtured by someone who cared about the environment (Damato & Love, 2002).

Too many of our children—as many as 8 percent in urban settings—are diagnosed as having attention deficit hyperactivity disorder (ADHD) and are treated with medication when there might be a better solution. Naturalizing or greening school grounds (i.e., providing more greenery) and other play areas, giving children more time to enjoy them when at school, and taking children to nature centers and zoos certainly seem to be better responses. It might be no coincidence that far more boys than girls are diagnosed with ADHD and that boys seem to be have a particular affinity to outdoor activities and play. Perhaps boys' lack of access to the outdoors is partially responsible for their ADHD.

"Greenness" seems to have a positive effect on children's behavior. Wells (2000) found that children who moved from barren areas to homes with views of nature showed better attention after the move as measured by tests of attention. Taylor, Kuo, and Sullivan (2001) found that children diagnosed with attention deficit disorder (ADD) exhibited less symptomatic behaviors after playing in green areas. They suggest that greening schoolyards might reduce the incidence of ADD/ADHD.

## Schools

Teachers are very concerned about the negative effects of popular culture, media, and technology, as are some parents, and wish to neutralize these effects through education and by offering uplifting cultural experiences to stimulate physical and intellectual growth (Levin, 2003). Many curricular projects and activities, including those that have a high number of play elements, require planning, reflection, and persistence, thus promoting work habits and patience. These dispositions and work/play styles may help to counterbalance children's tendencies to be impulsive, wanting their needs immediately gratified, and other undesirable consequences of popular culture, media, and technology. When children are intellectually mature enough, teachers also try to get them to be more thoughtful and critical about the messages they receive from popular culture and more discerning and astute in interpreting all the various meanings and symbolism (Levin, 2003). This helps to immunize them from the harmful effects of popular culture, media, and technology.

In addition, some teachers have tried to use popular culture to educational advantage in the classroom (Dyson, 2001). Children have a strong interest in singers, football heroes, movie and TV stars, and cartoon characters. Many of their experiences derive from popular culture; they like media programs and characters and related merchandise—superhero figures, books, toys, and clothing. A lot of what they read might come from books and comics based on popular cultural icons and media and computer sources. Many children frequent fast-food restaurants, shopping malls, and places of entertainment, and companies marketing to children use these icons to access this huge, lucrative market. Children's script and text knowledge bulges with the effects of these experiences, even though most childcare and preschool centers, places of worship, and many homes have shunned or ignored the realities of these experiences. For Dyson and others it is best for teachers to acknowledge this reality and to help children put their school learning into perspective, to build on what they already know. However, teachers must be highly sensitive to parents who conscientiously protect their children from these negative influences.

Dyson (2001) investigated how popular media influenced literacy in early childhood in a case study of a six-year-old child named Noah. During morning composing time, Dyson noted how Noah, like others in his first-grade classroom, frequently wrote and spoke about characters from popular culture and the media. Media texts from movies, cartoons, and songs mingled in his imagination with performing literacy activities, storytelling, drawing and playing at school. One morning Noah wrote a story about Donkey Kong, from a video game. Donkey Kong is an animated gorilla and a rowdy character. The case study demonstrated how Donkey Kong texts can become integrated with other texts, such as Little Bear, whom Noah met in small group reading instruction.

Over time Noah wrote more and more extended prose and did a lot of action-packed drawing, even making "moving pictures" by drawing on separate cards or sheets of paper a number of slightly different events in succession. Noah also made more discriminating choices in constructing texts and communicating with others about these constructions. He combined media and genre in his productions and reproductions, transforming and translating meaning. This demonstrated for Dyson the development of literacy in media saturated times, how popular culture can benefit teachers, students, and classroom learning. The case study revealed a child's symbolic playfulness and social resourcefulness in deliberately making multimedia compositions in different symbolic forms. Teachers can use media figures to foster literacy development—and playfulness and imagination too. Mutual benefits should ensue in connecting literacy and play competence.

In Chapter 4 we gave another example of the positive use of popular culture in education by describing Marsh's (1999, 2000) research on the positive effects on literacy from having a Batwoman and Batman headquarters as a literacy-enhanced dramatic play center in a second grade classroom.

Not all agree with this merging of education and popular culture. Many argue that one of the purposes of early childhood programs and schools is to extend children's experiences beyond popular culture to more meaningful and richer scripts, icons, and cultural content.

## Terror, Violence, and Disasters

Children's play is important and vital to their development and well-being. This is more true now than ever before, at least in our lifetime, given the horrific event of September 11, 2001, and its aftermath: the war on terror and Sudan, invasion of Iraq, and so on. Many children worldwide, from Bosnia to Rwanda, have long experienced and continue to experience death, terror, and even child slavery. Given the state of the world during wars or when catastrophes or disasters hit, children need to find ways to work out the violence and destruction they see in the media or in real life. For most children play and art expression are helpful in this process.

Until recently, although we knew a great deal about the effects of personal tragedies on young children and how to help them, little was known about how tragedies were experienced collectively, in a community or on a national or global scale. Now, however, we see a growing literature on this topic. Van Hoorn and Hesse (2003) have created an archive of children's reactions to the traumatic events of September 11, 2001, gathering teacher reports and anecdotes of children's behaviors and examples of children's drawings. They organized a group of teachers and researchers to share and discuss the findings at a meeting of the National Association for the Education of Young Children (Van Hoorn & Hesse, 2003). Some young preschoolers thought that hundreds of planes crashed into the towers because they saw the replay so many times on TV. Other reports included the observation that for weeks after 9/11, groups of kindergarten children crashed blocks and toy planes into towers they had built, with firefighters and ambulances coming to the rescue. Six months after 9/11, second graders in one school renewed their concerns, mentioning Ground Zero and talking about the smell of dead bodies. Commemorative TV coverage might have triggered this.

In these violent, media-saturated times, according to Diane Levin (2003), we need to listen to young children and help them cope. Play and art, in addition to conversation, are very important means by which we can learn from young children. Parents and teachers need to find out what children are picking up from the media about violence and the way people treat each other. Adults need to be there for children when the issues get raised, and adults must try to influence what children are learning. We cannot avoid this responsibility because it makes us feel uncomfortable. The late Fred Rogers wisely noted that nothing really should be an unmentionable, something you do not want to talk about with a child when it comes up. For a grown-up to act that way would be even more frightening for the young child than the scary topic, need, or worry the child expresses. Children must feel and be assured that it is okay to talk to parents and teachers about issues that disturb them, and parents and teachers need to know developmentally appropriate ways to respond.

Levin's book *Teaching Young Children in Violent Times* (2003) includes a chapter on helping children to deal with violence in the news. Guidelines for conversations are given, as are suggestions for how to use art and play to help children work out violent and disturbing content. Levin recommends that parents and teachers listen and ask questions and respond to the issues that children share in their conversations with adults about violent content. Adults need to support children, provide information, and help children feel safe. Adults should not try to give a lot of information or the "correct answer" and should see the discussion as part of an ongoing process.

Artwork or drawing and dramatic play are concrete ways in which children attempt to render meaningful their experiences in real life or from the media that are emotionally disturbing to them. Play and art are creative forums to express and work through feelings and ideas about violence seen in the news or in everyday life. After 9/11 a lot of block play involved miniature people being buried, even children burying themselves with blocks, pretending to be dead (Levin, 2003). In their play, art, and writing children vent feelings and try to come to grips with what has happened, why there are bad guys, and what makes them that way. Often children try to transform negative events into positive ones, trying to make things better. For example, children might rebuild the twin towers of the World Trade Center.

Levin recommends that teachers and parents watch children's play carefully and not be taken aback by thematic violence and destruction in play and art, because this is a normal response of children to having witnessed or having heard about traumatic events in the media or real life. If play gets too dangerous or frightening, teachers should intervene and redirect the behavior. It is not hard to extend play in a positive way, for example, by suggesting that rescue workers come to the scene of destruction. After the play episode there should be a discussion to reinforce feelings of security and safety and to clear up misconceptions. Teachers should try to teach peaceful alternatives to the harmful learning that results from children's exposure to a violence-saturated media.

Winter, Surr, and Leaf (2003) have discussed how young children can be helped when disaster strikes a local community, whether it is an act of God or human-made. Disaster Child Care (www.disasterchildcare.org) volunteers, in cooperation with the American Red Cross, to bring to the aid of a stricken community a warm, comforting presence and a supply of Kits of Comfort. In each Kit of Comfort is a set of materials for art and play. Activities can be quickly set up for rice or water play, bubble blowing, puzzles, dolls, stuffed animals, puppets, and cars and trucks. These supplies and any usable materials that are available on site, such as empty chairs and tables and boxes, can make up the Disaster Child Care center. The focus is on calming the children and allowing them to express their feelings through art, play, talking, and writing.

Erik Erikson (1972) has noted that a sense of hope undergirds human development across his eight stages of psychosocial development, from trust versus mistrust to wisdom versus despair. Children's play in response to violence, terror, death, and destruction helps them emotionally by enabling them to work through their experiences and try to regain some sense of control or understanding of the world. It also allows them, according to Piaget, to process the experience within schema they already have. In their play and art expressions violence is replayed and repeated but also often transformed as children want to make things better.

In *The Uses of Enchantment*, Bruno Bettelheim (1975) argues that fairy tales and fantasy literature play an important role in stabilizing children's identities and meeting their emotional and psychological needs. Of his famous children's series *The Narnia Chronicles*, C. S. Lewis once said, "I am aiming at a sort of pre-baptism of the imagination" (Sayer, 1988, p. 192). Bauckham and Hart (1999) speak of imagination and fantasy in arousing and enabling hope: "The quest for meaning, truth, goodness and beauty is closely bound up with hope as an activity of imagination in which we seek to transcend the boundaries of the present, to go beyond the given, outwards and forwards, in search of something more, something better, than the givens afford us" (p. 52). The best and truest fantasy and imaginative play, down deep, perhaps does much more than serve emotional and psychological needs. Perhaps they evoke, and to some degree satisfy, spiritual longings.

## Commercialism

About 100 years ago, British historian Arnold Toynbee coined the name "the Industrial Age" for a big change that had been unfolding in the Western world for nearly a century. Big changes in history alter the way we think and act. However, they unfold gradually over time and have a way of creeping up on us until we suddenly realize that something new has arrived on the world scene. Now too, for about 100 years, a new form of capitalism has been gestating, and we are suddenly realizing that a big change is on us. Postmodern society is postindustrial, an information age brought on by the computer revolution. It is also called the "age of access" (Rifkin, 2000). Whereas the industrial age viewed material production and consumption as its main business, the age of access sees services, information, and human time as its main business commodities.

In this new era that we are entering, we are increasingly replacing traditional social relationships with money-related types of human arrangements, buying experiences that before were provided for free. During the industrial era people bought material things, but experiences were usually centered on human activity that flowed freely from associations with family, friends, and others in society. People were responsible to one another out of deeply held values and shared commitments to family, community, and culture. In contrast, the paid-for experiences that are increasingly sought today are based on commodified relationships, in which, from the beginning, it is understood that the purchased experience will be expedient, superficial, and short-lived and that a social distance will remain between parties. Whether it is drop-in care for your child, a kennel for your dog, someone to manage your child's birthday party, or a personal assistant to do the shopping, the obligations in the shared experience are spelled out and represent an exchange of money, not feelings of faith, empathy, and solidarity.

The experience industry or experiential commerce is upon us. Travel and tourism remain a leading industry in the world even after 9/11, with revenues in the trillions of dollars—more than those of the information industry. Shopping centers and malls are now entertainment centers, fun places to go to see the latest at the IMAX theater, the cinema complex, the video game arcades, the theme clubs. People seek destinations for virtual reality simulation and go online to become part of a new cyberspace culture. We can buy the time and attention of lifestyle designers to arrange our homes, select our clothes, and help us entertain. Health consultants and trainers can be hired to help us lose weight and keep fit.

In the 1980s and 1990s deregulation and reduction of government services and functions in this country began. In the United States, the government has given over to the private sector garbage pickup, utilities, transportation, prisons, and communication. Less government money is devoted to parks and recreation. Our national parks are impoverished and deteriorating, with needed improvements long awaiting the required attention, and fees have been radically increased to cover those costs. With the reduction of traditional culture and government, what is left is a vibrant commercial sphere with its commodified relationships taking over a great deal of human life. To the extent that this means fewer close, warm human relations, one may worry whether civilization as we know it can survive this big historical change. An advocacy group called Stop Commercial Exploitation of Children exists that champions children's causes in the face of this onslaught (www.commercialexploitation.org).

**Pay-for-Play and Other Organized Activities.** So many experiences can be purchased in the cultural marketplace, including human services and time for children. Increasingly, paid-for experiences for our children have been sought, and commodified relationships have been formed to which our children are party. Children are enrolled in all kinds of after-school programs—athletics, music, arts, and lessons of various sorts. Many children have very little time for spontaneous play. For young children make-believe play and games are important activities. To the extent that adult-organized activities interfere with this, there is cause for concern.

When at home during their formative years, privileged children might have a bedroom that is equipped not only with a television and a VCR/DVD player, but also with a Gameboy, video games, and a computer. When away from home, these children can be taken to pay-for-play places at the mall, special destinations, theme parks, fancy motels, and other vacation centers. Carnivals and amusement parks are other fun places to go. To the extent that these less than desirable play forms interfere with positive play, there is cause for concern. There is also the question of why more appropriate play environments are not provided for our children.

**Toy Marketing.** The time is long past when families could go to the toy shop down the street and see individual toys displayed neatly on the shelves and be attended by a patient shopkeeper ready to help parents and kids make the right decisions about which toys to buy. Toy stores today are huge places with long aisles and boxes piled high and are usually part of a national or international conglomerate. The sheer quantity of merchandise is overwhelming. And families no longer purchase toys for their kids just on special occasions such as birthdays and holidays, but buy them year round. Toy makers have found ways to reach children and to get them to urge their parents to buy the latest toys, and we are being inundated with new products at a brisk pace. Retail sales of toys are in the billions of dollars a year.

Every February in New York City the American International Toy Fair takes place, hosted by the Toy Industry Association. It is the largest toy trade show in the western hemisphere, with approximately two thousand manufacturers, distributors, importers, and sales agents from thirty countries represented. New toys and entertainment products are showcased in a large exhibition hall and are seen by the thousands of people who attend the event, one that stretches over several days. There are special feature sections for collectibles, dolls, and other kinds of toys; a game zone; a model and hobby pavilion; and international pavilions. Every year certain familiar toys remain popular, such as Barbie dolls, and new, exciting surprises appear. In recent years, for example, exhibitors have displayed such technological marvels as Vmail, which allows children as young as five years old to send their own computer voice mail, and various plush dolls with built-in chips that allow the dolls to talk. Many products are technological or novelty playthings and appeal to the child's sense of fantasy and desire for immediate pleasure. Positive developments include a tremendous increase in diverse and multicultural toys, including dolls.

As we discuss throughout this book, parents want their children to engage in productive, purposeful play because they see this as a way for the children to prepare for a complex and changing future. Parents are often drawn to so-called educational toys, such as Intelli-table, which uses a built-in computer to teach children about colors, letters, numbers, and music. They listen to child development experts and early childhood educators and also seek out open-ended toys that are conducive to discovery and complex inventive play, such as construction sets or blocks. At the same time parents believe that childhood is a time for imagination and that children need to be sheltered from the adult world, with some autonomy from parental and teacher authority. Parents are susceptible, then, to their child's request for those toys that are flashy and appeal only to childish imaginations and that parents know are not good for the child's development. Many times parents cave in and purchase such toys out of concern about peer group pressure on their child and because they want their child to be happy. Many parents also believe that they cannot go against the popular culture.

Toy makers realize that parents will usually follow the child's lead when it comes to buying a toy and hence make sales pitches directly to children through newspaper and magazine ads, toy catalogs, ads on cereal boxes, and TV advertisements during children's television shows. Many toys are media-linked, such as superhero figures that are stars of cartoon shows. Because the primary aim of the toy industry is profit, toy makers are typically not shy about pushing toys that many educators would not recommend.

Some toy makers promise instant gratification to children, presenting toys in sparkling packages and misleading TV commercials. They also misrepresent the educational value of many toys to anxious parents. They produce lines of toys, such as certain dolls, action figures, and other fantasy toys, that are ever changing and require constant additional purchases to keep the plaything or play set current and enjoyable. Many children are being socialized by these elements of popular culture and the media into wanting things and experiences. Once this consumer bug infests one's consciousness, it is hard to ever be really satisfied. Francis discusses how his family sought to moderate the effects of popular culture in Box 11.1.

**BOX 11.1**

## *Barbie Dolls*

**by Francis Wardle**

My wife is a product of the women's movement of the 1960s. While in college, she was actively involved in several feminist projects and lived with other female students in a sort of collective. I have three sisters who all grew up to be very strong, independent individuals. Of our own four children, three are girls. So we were very committed to raising them to become strong, independent women.

When our girls were young, they played with Lego sets, made projects on a woodworking bench, and played with a rag doll made by one of their aunts and carefully selected Black dolls. I even built an indoor climbing play area for them in our third-floor apartment in Kansas City. And my children helped me till the soil, plant the seeds, and harvest the various vegetables from the gardens I planted every year.

As they grew older, the three girls participated in a variety of athletic activities, including gymnastics, soccer, lacrosse, and track.

We were committed to carefully limiting their exposure to popular culture. TV watching was regulated; at that time we did not have a computer, and we refused to buy video games for our children. We also made sure our girls did not play with Barbie dolls. We deeply believed that Barbie dolls present an unreal standard of female beauty and teach girls that their physical appearance is far more important than any other of their attributes, including intelligence, education, and hard work.

However, our youngest daughter, RaEsa, not only really wanted Barbie dolls to play with, but also was a very social child with lots of girlfriends. Although she could never convince us to buy her a Barbie doll, she was able to get some of her friends to lend her several of their dolls. We did not have the heart to tell her that she could not play with them.

One day we were surfing the TV channels and stopped momentarily at the Miss America pageant. While we were watching the program, RaEsa walked by the TV, noticed what was going on the TV, and declared in absolute disgust, "How horrible—those ladies on the show look just like Barbie dolls!"

We can't always protect our children from contemporary culture. Further, children construct their reality in a variety of ways—sometimes in ways we adults do not expect. It seems that RaEsa used the Barbie dolls as symbols she could use to engage in fantasy play with dresses and gender roles and to create social interactions in her solitary play. She was the youngest child, and her older sisters no longer played with dolls.

As a result of playing with Barbie dolls, RaEsa became very interested in fashion, using it in several of her high school art projects. But she never wished to look anything like Barbie, and she has expanded her horizons beyond typical female goals and occupations. For example, her favorite artist is Joseph Cornell (a man), and her career choice is forensic psychology.

The toy market in our mass consumption economy reaches out to potential customers through advertisements in the media and by including miniature versions of their toy lines in children's meals in fast-food chains. Usually, these toys are inspired by characters in the mass media, often from the latest hit movie for children. These miniatures create a demand for the real thing at the store. The toy market also tries to make going to the store more appealing. In leading toy stores a recent trend is to provide space for parent-child play, children's birthday parties, parenting classes, play areas for kids, eateries, and even barbershops for children. The Toys "Я" Us company has a new "imaginarium" division, which was installing over 1100 imaginariums in their toy stores globally in 2003. These are 3000-square-foot padded interactive areas for play, exploration, and social interaction. The intent is to motivate children to think and imagine within these play areas.

Through all of these extras, some with educational value, this toy company hopes to make its stores more than toy stores; they are to be a kind of family center where various parent and child needs can be meet. Of course, the bottom line remains the bottom line, and the skeptic might say that this is consumerism in the guise of education. It is hard to picture a family making many trips to the store, participating just in the educational activities, and then coming home without a toy for the child. McDonalds and other fast-food places have used playgrounds and toys as a direct enticement for families with young children for many years. How many of these families go there and never buy a Happy Meal?

## PLAY AND THE MEDIA

Children today grow up in a media-saturated environment. Of the several important forms of electronic media that affect the play and development of young children, the most influential is television. Music, computers and computer games, movies, and video games account for the rest (Gentile & Walsh, 2002). The electronic media might seem to be an easy way to keep children busy for unwary parents and educators, but some significant dangers accompany this convenience. For instance, heavy television

➤ How does the play behavior of these children in Guatemala, who have no TVs, computers or video games, differ from the play behavior of children from industrialized societies?

viewing poses threats to children's physical development. The incidence of obesity is highest among children who watch four or more hours of television a day and lowest among children who watch an hour or less a day (Crespo et al, 2001). In another study of preschoolers a child's risk of being overweight increased by 6 percent for every hour of television watched per day. If a child had a TV in his or her bedroom, the odds of being overweight jumped an additional 31 percent for every hour watched (Dennison, Erb, & Jenkins, 2002). Excessive viewing of television programs such as sitcoms can rob children of precious time for more productive play experiences (Powell, 2001).

Another potential negative influence on play behavior is excessive exposure to violence in television, videos, and movies. Buchanan et al. (2002) examined the relationship between aggression and media violence and found that children who watched more television and played video games more often were more likely to infer hostile intent from the actions of others, even when the intent was ambiguous and might be benign. These children tend to assume the worst in their interactions with others. By being exposed to violent media, children's perception of hostility from the outside world seems to be influenced in a negative way. In addition, children who spend more time engaged in these media forms tend to have less parental supervision.

## Television

Television still dominates children's media life. Current estimates suggest that American children, between the ages of two and seventeen, watch an average of twenty-five hours of TV each week, and almost one in five watch more than thirty-five hours of TV each week. Twenty percent of two- to seven-year-olds have TVs in their bedrooms. On average, children who have TVs in their bedrooms watch 5.5 hours more TV each week than do those who do not have their own TV. The amount of viewing is related to parental education; parents with less education report that their children view significantly more TV than what parents with more education report. The amount of viewing is also related to parental income; lower-income parents report that their children watch significantly more TV than what higher-income parents report. Not surprisingly, the amount of television watching is negatively related to school performance (Gentile & Walsh, 2002; Mahoney, 2000). Of course, it is important to remember that correlation does not imply causality. The amount of television viewing is likely related to a host of other variables that may affect children's academic performance.

**Negative Effects.** In preparing their book *Who's Calling the Shots?,* Nancy Carlsson-Paige and Diane Levin (1990) interviewed many parents and teachers and found that they reported that their children's play has been greatly influenced by TV. Teachers reported that children imitated aggressive scripts from television, showing little evidence of original or creative play. Levin (2003) reported teachers' concern that superhero play abruptly ends when someone gets hurt. Children who appear to be most obsessed by war and superhero play are likely to have the hardest time engaging in creative and imaginative play of their own scripts. Other researchers have noted similar findings. In a naturalistic study of four-year-olds on a preschool playground, Shin (1994) found that boys imitated the aggressive behaviors of Saturday morning cartoon superheroes. They knew all the characters' names and what weapons they possessed, and they strongly identified with the characters' aggressive behaviors.

Carlsson-Paige and Levin (1990) have traced the influence of television programs on children's toy culture and their play from the time when the Federal Communications Commission first eliminated the government regulations that once existed to maintain high-quality programs for children and to control advertising targeted at children. Program-length commercials that market television programs and products together became legal in 1984 when advertising time restrictions were eliminated. This deregulation led to TV programs produced by toy makers with their toys as aggressive television characters. By the fall of 1987, 80 percent of all children's television programs were produced by toy manufacturers. In 1993 the sale of TV action figures equaled the sale of children's books! And the link between toys and TV characters was left virtually unaffected by the Children's Television Act of 1990, which continued to allow manufacturers to market toys during children's television shows. Ever since deregulation hundreds of parents and teachers have reported adverse effects on children's play (Carlsson-Page & Levin, 1990).

It is possible that media-linked toys interfere with the expression of generative play. Many educators and concerned parents worry that play influenced by the link between the media and the toy industry is not play behavior at all, but merely imitation. Children simply imitate what they have watched on television using toys that limit their imaginations, namely, action figures and other realistic items. High-level dramatic play is essential to the healthy development of children because such play is assimilatory and transformative for the child, allowing for creative self-expression or working through of past experiences. Although imitation is useful as a beginning point in play, it can interrupt the benefits of play if children get stuck on imitation and do not transform and digest what they copy from scripted television shows.

Carlsson-Page and Levin (1990) recommend that adults seek to help children convert low-level, highly stereotyped behaviors into higher-level transformational play instead of ignoring or forbidding thematically aggressive and imitative play behavior. For instance, teachers can help children to make up their own stories about their favorite characters from a TV program or can urge them to draw or to cut out pictures from magazines to make a book based on a TV show. Levin (2003) also addressed this growing concern of teachers of young children about violent media-influenced play by reminding us that simply enforcing a "no war play or pretend fighting" rule brings a constant struggle. Rather, teachers need to provide much more direct help. One teacher described her intervention to children's disruptive play:

> In desperation, I decided if you can't beat 'em, join 'em! So I tried to get more involved with the play one day when Jules was using a block as a gun and several times had his friends fall down as if they had been shot. I put a block up to my mouth as if it were a walkie-talkie and said, "Calling Officer Jules, Calling Officer Jules. Someone is hurt! We need to get help! We need an officer to help us over here!" At first, Jules kept shooting with great relish saying, "He's the bad guy, he has to be shot." I talked into the walkie-talkie, "What did he do to be bad, Officer Jules?" Jules paused, then reported he had robbed a bank. With the walkie-talkie to my mouth I suggested, "We better get him to jail if he's robbed a bank." By now, as Jules continued shooting, two other children had grabbed blocks as walkie-talkies and reported they were coming to

> take the robber to jail. Jules came over to join them at the large appliance box in the dramatic play area which quickly was designated "the jail." (Levin, 2003, p. 84)

The teacher in this example used open-ended questions and modeled how to use play materials such as a block as a walkie-talkie. This kind of approach helps the children to develop a cops-and-robbers script of their own design. Jules seemed to become less obsessed with violent gun play.

Not all play experts are as concerned as Carlsson-Paige and Levin are about media impacts on children's play. For instance, Sutton-Smith (2004) noted that each new cohort of children receives new toys, scripts, and characters from their generation's popular culture that they then incorporate into their play episodes:

> When the focus is on children in their own playground, while there is still an impact of popular media figures on play and games whether from books (Harry Potter) or cards (Pokemon) or media singing contests, the children assimilate them to being the kinds of contests and central person games that have always been an essential part of their peer play. They are forbidden to bring the Pokemon cards to schools, so instead they enact the characters that are on the cards. Again what was once the exhibitive girls' game of being voted the best "statue" now becomes a similar exhibitive game of being the best contest singer. For boys Harry Potter already has so many of the attacks and escapes and magic that have always been a part of children's traditional imaginative contestive play forms that it is easy to assimilate it to playground social play. See *Children's Games of Street and Playground* by Iona and Peter Opie (1969) which is very much of a Potter book. In addition there are the articles pointing out that the most important thing about games, including computer games, is their own microsystemics. (Foreword for book: *Toys, Games and Media* edited by Goldstein, Buckingham, and Brougere)

Sutton-Smith grants that today's mass media entertainment industry exposes a wider audience of young children to aggressive fantasy scripts than ever before. However, these are variants of the cops-and-robbers and cowboys-and-Indians motifs that were popular with earlier generations of children. Children imitate only what serves their overarching play purposes. These earlier forms of "good guy versus bad guy" play were also based on media. Goldstein (1995) agrees with Sutton-Smith and argues that there is little evidence that children play in a worse or less imaginative fashion today than they did in 1984. Interviews with parents and teachers and direct observations and interviews with children in future research might help to inform this debate.

Does TV cartoon violence adversely affect children's moral understanding and behaviors? Peters and Blumberg (2002) reviewed the research on the topic and concluded that as long as young children understand the difference between consequences of cartoon violence and real-life transgressions, then the impact of cartoon violence is not as serious as is commonly believed. However, adults' role in helping children to interpret the violence in popular cartoons is important. Peters and Blumberg urge adults to watch television with children and to comment on program contents and to model and discuss morally acceptable alternatives to resolving conflicts. Potentially harmful television content can become teaching opportunities to help children learn moral lessons applicable to situations in real life. This is similar to Levin's urging adults to help children play more imaginatively in response to TV. Whether media helps or hurts kids depends on mediation by parents and teachers. It is too bad that most parents almost always see TV as a babysitter and not as an experience to share with their children.

**Positive Effects.** Television can be a positive addition to children's development. Young children enjoy stories portrayed through real people, high-quality animation, or storytelling. Some TV programs are creative and memorable. Nature and travel programs can show children sights they might not otherwise see. A great deal of information can be transmitted via television. Prosocial messages can be conveyed, as well as violence, stereotyping, and consumerism. There are advantages to TV but only if the medium is used wisely by teachers and parents.

One-year-olds have been known to wave and say hi to people they see on TV. They also pick up emotional messages displayed on TV. In one study, one-year-olds sat watching a twenty-inch television set and viewed a twenty-second video of an actress reacting to toys with different affective expressions. When the infants had a chance to play with the same toys, they avoided the toy to which the actress had responded negatively and played happily with the one to which the actress had responded positively. At two years of age, children watch television and already have preferences for certain shows.

Howard and Roberts (2002) studied twenty children averaging eighteen months of age watching *Teletubbies* footage. *Teletubbies,* produced in England, is the first TV show for the under-twos. The show has costumed characters (Tinky Winky, Po, etc.) who are life-size and have the head-to-body ratio and simple linguistic communication styles of very young children. Each episode is set either in the Tubbydome or in the rolling landscape outside, which is futuristic and has a periscope that comes out of the ground to ask questions or make comments on the action. There is a sun that has the face of a real, chortling baby and a whirlygig that emits sparkling lights at the beginning and end of each episode. In one episode Tinky Winky and Po played a drum with magic qualities: Every beat caused a visible change in the landscape, such as a flower changing color with each beat or a cloud moving. All episodes are child-centered and playful with repeated images and sounds.

Howard and Roberts videotaped each child watching the show and jointly studied the child's behavior in connection to what was seen on screen from the TV show. They found that children usually exhibited rapt attention together with physically active behaviors while watching *Teletubbies*. They displayed pleasure and cognitive responses, such as frowns of concentration when something puzzling happened on the show (e.g., the drum with magic qualities). Parasocial responses were fairly frequent, that is, joining in with what is happening on screen or interacting with the characters. Parasocial responses were both physical (e.g., clapping, waving goodbye) and verbal (e.g., talking to characters, answering questions). Howard and Roberts concluded that there should not be moral panic about putting toddlers in front of the TV set; quite to the contrary, young viewers do interact meaningfully with the text and are developing skills and dispositions that will help them be future savvy operators in our pervasive media environment. Most adults who watch this show, however, cannot relate to it, so this show does not lend itself easily to shared parent-child viewing and adult mediation. Also, unlike Mister Rogers and Barney there is no adult or authority figure on the program, which young children need.

Some people believe that TV can stimulate imaginative play and creativity. This belief rests on the fact that TV content does get incorporated into children's play. Also, current theory about media effects assumes that viewers are actively engaged in exploration and mental activity when watching TV. Children watching television are not comatose; there is not necessarily a harmful, deadening effect. Nor are they necessarily mesmerized; there are mental and physical responses, such as toddlers waving bye-bye to the Teletubbies.

Nevertheless, there is little evidence that television watching in general stimulates play, imagination, or creativity (Valkenburg, 2001). Perhaps educational viewing might stimulate children's imaginative play and creativity, especially when programs are specifically designed to foster imagination. An important research goal is to try to learn how TV can influence imaginative play and how it can be used to try to promote richer play. Research needs to pay attention to child characteristics. For example, perhaps TV is effective in affecting imaginative play for children of a particular developmental level or play style (see Chapter 4). Maybe TV can have important benefits but only if parents or teachers also try to influence pretend play based on TV shows. Specific content of TV shows also needs to be studied for possible differential and interactive effects on play and imagination (Valkenburg, 2001).

Some researchers believe that television can be used to facilitate play competence in children. Common elements between pretend play and television, such as visual fluidity, time and space flexibility, and fantasy-reality distinctions, make this a reasonable hypothesis. Program content can provide ideas for pretend play, assuming that the TV show is comprehensible to young children. Also, adult mediation seems essential for any positive impact that TV might have on imaginative play and creativity (Singer & Singer, 1990). During the early years adults can help children to view programs more actively and also gain social understanding. For instance, Singer, Singer, Desmond, Hirsch, and Nichol (1988) reported that parental discussion with young children about TV shows facilitated in children a better appreciation of the distinction between fantasy and reality.

In addition, some children's shows have been reported to advance children's prosocial behavior and imaginative play. *Mister Rogers' Neighborhood* is an outstanding example. This show has reached millions of children over the years with the expressed intent of meeting the threefold needs of every child: hope, trust, and imagination (Collins & Kimmel, 1996). The late Fred Rogers helped children to understand the world through the use of warm eye contact and his slow-paced, soft-spoken manner of communication. This occurs for part of each program in the reality mode, when Mr. Rogers deals with factual information conveyed through visitors, field trips, explanations, music, and the like. The remaining part of the show is in the fantasy mode, when the red trolley takes the audience to the Neighborhood of Make-Believe, which is peopled by puppets ruled by King Friday. Feelings, attitudes, and social behaviors are explored and processed on a symbolic level in this segment of the show, in which the significance of pretending is explicit.

Educational TV shows with a specific focus on pretending have the potential to facilitate imagination in children. Play intervention experiments using *Mister Rogers' Neighborhood* demonstrated that the television show by itself had little holding power over children in a group setting. Singer and Singer (1976) reported that children found peer interaction more appealing than watching *Mister Rogers' Neighborhood.* But the Singers reported that adult-mediated television viewing (an adult helping children to pay attention to certain aspects of the program) improved imaginative play. Friedrich and Stein (1975) found that the most reliable positive effects on preschool play occurred when television was combined with having a teacher actively tutor children at play. Other research by the Singers and associates at Yale University further suggests an association between home viewing of *Mister Rogers' Neighborhood* and children's dispositions to play imaginatively. Other work is examining *Barney and Friends,* another popular show for preschoolers that also puts the accent on the importance of make-believe (Singer, 1995). These TV shows affirm the value of pretending during the early years and cast a positive light on what electronic media can contribute to children's play. Again, adult mediation at home (which unfortunately seems rarely to happen) and at school would seem critical.

## Other Forms of the Electronic Media

Ever since the VCR became widely used in American families in the 1980s, parents have been buying videos for their children in increasing numbers. The family video business is lucrative. The biggest-selling video of all time is the movie *The Lion King,* with more than thirty million copies sold. As with television, the movies and home videos influence the play and development of children.

Children love to watch their favorite movies endlessly. Hey-Jun Ahn's five-year-old daughter Hyunjae has watched her favorite Disney princess movies over and over again, to the point at which she is able to recite almost every important line (see Box 11.2). She likes to act like a princess after watching a movie. Yoffe (2003) reported the results of a national survey showing that 70 percent of parents of two- to four-year-olds said that their child watched a video more than once. With parents of older children, ages five to seven years, the number decreased to 61 percent. Only 34 percent of parents of eleven- to fourteen-year-olds reported repeated viewing.

**BOX 11.2**

### Raising a Young Daughter in Media-Saturated Times

**by Hey-Jun Ahn**

My daughter, Hyunjae, is five years old. When I had a girl, I decided to raise her not as a girly girl. My husband even told me that he was not going to buy any dresses for her. We wanted to have a girl who is strong, brave, smart, and independent. Well, that is what we hoped.

When Hyunjae was around three, I bought a DVD of Disney's *Snow White and the Seven Dwarfs.* I remember that I read a newspaper review of the DVD version of this movie. The review was pretty favorable, and I thought it would be nice to move Hyunjae on from her favorite *Teletubbies,* since she was already three.

I did not know that Hyunjae would love *Snow White and the Seven Dwarfs* so much. She asked me to play the movie over and over again. I was grateful that I did not have to rewind it repeatedly, since it was on a DVD. Soon she memorized some lines and scenes. For example, she liked to pretend that she was Snow White being deserted in a dark forest. Her teachers told me that she screamed and would run around in her childcare center classroom. And she liked to pretend to clean up the floors like Cinderella, from another movie. She asked me to call her "Cinderella," just as the mean stepmother and stepsisters do in the movie.

Hyunjae's interest in the princess theme expanded to other movie characters. Ariel from *The Little Mermaid,* Belle from *Beauty and the Beast,* Sleeping Beauty, and of course Cinderella became her favorite role models. She wanted to be like them. She had to have a hairband because Snow White had one. She insisted on wearing a dress every day, even when it was very cold outside. She also began to draw princesses. I was surprised that she remembered, and still remembers, all the details of each one of the princesses' outfits. It did not take long for me to realize that there was lots of merchandise based on movie characters. Princess costumes, backpacks, lunch boxes, pencils, clothing, stickers, watches, bedding, shoes—you name it! Every time we went to shop, Hyunjae picked up something she had seen on television or in a movie and asked me to buy it. I always tried to reason with my daughter about purchasing toys. Reciprocal conversations with regard to appropriate choices of toys and a rationale for the selection do not always work. Sometimes it is hard to resist "Mom, can I have this doll? PLEASE?"

Hyunjae seemed to be frustrated after finding that all princesses have blond hair and blue eyes. Finally, I found out that there was one Disney movie whose main character is an Asian woman, named Mulan. One day Hyunjae asked me, "Mom, is Mulan Korean, like me?"

"No, Mulan is a Chinese," I answered.

"Oh! No! Then I want to be a Chinese girl like Ellen or Amy," cried Hyunjae, naming Chinese girls in her childcare program.

"No, you can't be a Chinese because you were born in Korea," I told her.

She was pretty upset for a while, realizing that she can't be a Chinese like Mulan even if she looks very similar to a Chinese.

I think children can learn a lot about different cultures by watching a movie like *Mulan.* Movies have a powerful impact on children's image of world. Although I don't like the hidden message of many princess movies—that a woman's ultimate goal is to meet a prince and live happily ever after—it is difficult to ignore peer influence. I bet every girl in Hyunjae's kindergarten class has at least one toy or item of merchandise related to a princess or Barbie. Now I know how difficult it is to keep the balance between children's needs and those of parents' in this media era. Hyunjae knows that I am not going to buy her another princess doll because she already has them all. But she still asks me when we shop, "Mom, can you buy this on my birthday? PLEASE?"

Although there has been little research on the effects of the repeat syndrome (i.e., watching the same video or movie over and over again), children seem comforted and even seem to acquire a deeper understanding of the text from repeated viewing of their favorite movies. Replaying a favorite video can help to create a pleasurable mood and trigger positive emotional memories because children know what will happen and feel safe by knowing the results. Replaying leads to overlearning scripts, to having story lines really sink in. Overlearned scripts may be readily incorporated into children's own pretend-play scenarios and artwork when the children are away from the electronic medium. The good teacher knows how much children love their favorite book to be read repeatedly, and a song to be sung repeatedly—often to the total boredom of the teacher!

Movies and videos that are made especially for young children often have characters who reflect a concern for fostering positive social behavior in children. Plots or story lines are sometimes simple and repetitive and provide good material that is appropriate for later make-believe play by young children. There are action-adventure movies and videos as well as television programs with such scripts. These can greatly influence children's pretend play. However, superheroes and supervillains are also very popular and are used in children's role enactments. Adults should shape and redirect children's reenactments of the content from such movies to match more acceptable play patterns and cultural norms (Levin, 2003). Watching movies and videos or television might seem to be a passive activity, but viewing can affect play at a later time by triggering the imagination, especially with support from teachers and parents who can serve as play facilitators. What is required is that we share these media experiences with children. The acts of watching can themselves be forms of play. When children participate in these media activities, they not only get an escape from reality in some sense, but also are enjoying what they are doing at the time. This physically passive but mentally active form of play is called reception play.

## TECHNOLOGY

Remarkable new possibilities now exist for play, made possible by technological progress. Jim Johnson remembers how, as a child, he wished there was an electronic toy that could play chess. He remembers being told how unlikely that would be, that the game is too complicated, and being asked whether he would settle for checkers, a more likely invention in his lifetime. Now, a generation or so later, we have Deep Blue defeating the Russian world champion Gari Kasparov at the ancient royal game! Technology has affected the play by people of all ages, from the software, or "lapware," available for children as young as nine months of age to the sophisticated technology that allows older people to have a multisensory play experience in a three-dimensional virtual reality space. Some of these effects have been positive; some have been negative.

Certainly, important new questions have been raised about children's play and the role of the adult because of the great impact of technology on our lives. Here we present information on technology and children's play, development and early education in relation to computers, video games, computer games, and computer toys.

### Computers

Computer games and other activities represent one of the most important forms of children's involvement in information technology. Computers are in schools and libraries and in many early childhood programs. In August 2000, fifty-four million, or 51 percent, of American households had purchased one or more personal computers. Since 1984, the first year in which the Census Bureau asked about computer ownership, there has been more than a fivefold increase in the proportion of families with computers. Among school-aged children, two out of three students have access also to computer at home; four out of five students actually use a computer at school (Newburger, 2001). Greater access is also a worldwide phenomenon. For instance, Kishimoto (2002) found that more than 72 percent of Brazilian kindergarten classrooms have computer materials that aid visual, sound, and audiovisual communications. Note that in Brazil *kindergarten* is the term used to describe private early childhood programs; the poor attend very badly equipped programs called creches.

Haugland (1999) reported that many children are using computers, either at school or home, for at least fifteen minutes a day, and many children spend forty-five minutes or more on the computer daily. However, there is a tremendous technology divide: Poor and minority children tend not to have access to computers.

Despite the common use of the computer by young children, not all educators and researchers recommend that young children use computers. Pendleton (2001) argues that the fast pace and ever-changing visual stimulation of computer games and software are causing damage to children. She recommended that adults select toys and games that provide children with the maximum opportunities to enjoy childhood and to think creatively. Cordes and Miller (2000) warned that emphasizing the use of computers in childhood can place children at increased risk for injuries, visual strain, obesity, and other consequences of sedentary behavior. They urged reduction in computer use because young children are not emotionally, socially, morally, or mentally ready to be restricted to the constraining logical abstractions that computers demand. A sedentary approach to learning, and one that uses only two of the human senses, is also not good for developing children. And Haugland (1999) recommends that children under age two should not use computers at all.

Although available evidence regarding risks and benefits of children's computer use is controversial, how children should use computer is less debatable. Silvern (1998) recommends that teachers of young children not use computers for practice of didactic materials, such as electronic books and drill-and-practice worksheets. Instead, teachers should encourage children to use developmentally appropriate programs to help them find a challenging match between their abilities and attitudes and the demands and expectations of the computer environments. Computer use should also not be used as a reward; nor should its withdrawal be used as a punishment (Wardle, 2003a).

Tremendous strides have been made in computer hardware and software over the decades of the 1970s, 1980s, 1990s, up to the present. Programs for young children at the beginning of the computer age seem feeble by today's standards. They were very limited in graphics, were heavily textual, and were mainly of the drill-and-practice variety, coming out of a discipline called computer-assisted instruction. Today computers are, by comparison, much more powerful and faster. We have high-speed DVD/CD-RW combo drives, monitors, and printers capable of generating tens of thousands of colors, and computers with internal sound sources, including voice activation, and access to the Internet.

Great strides have occurred in our understanding of young children's ability to use computers in early childhood education. Earlier there was concern about the developmental appropriateness of computers, given that computer-based activities were considered to be symbolic and not concrete. But as Clements and Nastasi (1993) note, "what is 'concrete' to the child may have more to do with what is meaningful and manipulable than with its physical nature" (p. 259). Our children grow up in a computer age. They are very familiar with this new technology. There is even lapware for babies and parents to use. Children's manipulating symbolic content on a monitor with a mouse-driven cursor has become a routine experience comparable to actions on any other concrete object. There is growing acceptance that it is appropriate to use computers with children.

Questions still exist about how, when, and why computers can support play, creativity, and learning. For example, Elkind (1996) has cautioned that the way in which children use computers should not be taken as an estimate of their cognitive maturity. Children might appear more advanced than they really are when using a computer. Manipulating computer icons with a mouse is not the same behavior as concrete operational thinking (e.g., the ability to cross-classify or solve conservation of quantity problems). Moreover, computers and technology cannot fulfill most social and emotional needs. Elkind maintains that computer use should not be a substitute for traditional play activities such as drawing, pretending, and block building and that computers should not be viewed as an alternative for teacher interaction. Computers and software are possibly a supplement or complement to other activities and materials. Teachers should seek ways to integrate computers into the curriculum to serve overall educational goals within a program and to integrate with other learning centers.

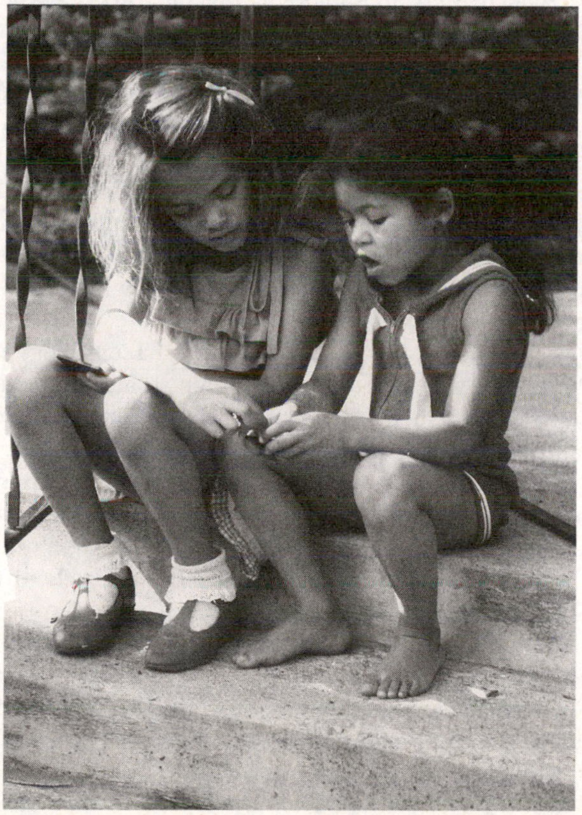

Not all educators recommend computer use for young children. Computers cannot fulfill many social and emotional needs of young children.

Some kindergartens in Brazil have a separate computer room in a school building, but the high-quality kindergartens have integrated spaces within classrooms with areas for reading, building, arts, and dramatic area. For the computer to be used as a means to develop language and communication among children, they need to be located in the language area, next to the books and paper (Kishimoto, 2002). Haugland (1999) also suggests that computers be in the classroom, not in a traditional technology lab. Trageton (2002a, 2002b) in Norway echoes this need for classroom integration of computers and is also a strong advocate for the use of simple word processing. As a computer tool, word processing is a open-ended creative plaything with endless possibilities for children with the help of teachers. They can publish books, classroom newspapers, and magazines. Trageton (2002a 2002b) also recommends vigorous outdoor pretend play to inspire playful computer writing in the classroom.

**Software Quality.** How should adults provide appropriate computer experience for young children to optimize their play and development? The issue of high-quality software is a major concern for teachers and parents of young children. According to Liang and Johnson (1999), the quality of software can be evaluated by considering four factors: problem-solving orientation, developmental appropriateness, playfulness, and incorporating new technologies. Haugland adds a cultural diversity standard to her software assessment tool. Software that is targeted at children needs to be problem-solving-oriented and open-ended. Software should provide microworlds where children have choices to explore and opportunities to follow their curiosity and make things happen. Programs should not be drill-and-practice because these closed-ended programs limit children's initiative and decision making. Open-ended programs do not ask children to determine a single right answer. Rather, they encourage children to explore and to extend their thinking (Fischer & Gillespie, 2003). Software that facilitates children's playfulness also stimulates imagination, creativity, challenge, and curiosity. Open-ended software allows children to engage in creative play and conversation (National Association for the Education of Young Children, 1996b). In addition, open-ended software has been found to elicit more cooperative behavior among children than drill-and-practice programs have (Chen, 2002).

Also, according to the NAEYC's Position Statement on Technology and Young Children (NAEYC, 1996b), software should have content that is reflective of real-world models and diverse cultures, such as multiple languages, mixed gender, people of color, differing ages and abilities, and diverse family styles. Positive benefits to children are believed to be more likely when the child is in control, with expanding complexity or graduated challenges inherent in the program. It is also very important that programs have clear and easy-to-follow instructions for software use and guidelines for linking software programs to other curricular activities (Haugland & Wright, 1997; Wright, Shade, Thouvenelle, & Davidson, 1989).

Current software is graphics intensive and capable of showing realistic scenes and colorful animations with much less reliance on text. Accordingly, a great deal of current computer software is developmentally appropriate and capable of independent use by children during the early childhood years, especially when a childproof interface program is available that can serve as a protective buffer between the young child and the hard drive's filing systems (Shade & Davis, 1997). One of the greatest educational advantages of computers is the way they can be used by children with a range of disabilities, from physical challenges to learning disabilities. Programs can be tailored to match each child's IEP. It is also critical that programs give every child the opportunity to explore and use the computers, not simply the compliant child or the child who has a computer at home.

**Playing with Computers.** Haugland and Wright (1997) outlined the stages of preschoolers' computer play. When they encounter computer software for the first time, most children seem to be following stages: discovery, involvement, self-confidence, and creativity. Children at first investigate specific features of the program and engage in a certain amount of exploratory play. This is followed by use of the program, at first tentatively and with teacher's scaffolding, and then more independently as the child's confidence grows. Finally, the child uses the computer program independently and in a creative fashion.

In one rural Head Start classroom, Fischer and Gillespie (2003) observed that children displayed a great deal of social interaction while working with computers. This classroom had learning centers built around technology. Five laptop computers, one desktop computer, and programmable Lego bricks allowed children to sit near each other. In one case three children set up their laptops next to each other. Fischer and Gillespie asserted that this layout facilitates peers helping as well as conversation about what each child is trying to create. Also, teachers' guidance seemed to be critical in order to capitalize on the rich social context offered by computer usage, not to mention the necessity of having enough computers to go around. Children can learn cooperative behaviors, such as sharing ideas, problem solving, and conflict resolution strategies.

Playing with a computer can provide children with opportunities for rich social interactions, giving the lie to the concern that computers isolate children from one another. It is not uncommon to see children watching other children playing and commenting on other children's action and children helping out one another at the computer. Children are more likely to ask their peers next to them rather than to ask the teacher. However, conflicts related to turn-taking and use also happen, usually because there are not enough computers. Sometimes these conflicts are resolved by the children, but teachers are needed to intervene at other times (Heft & Swaminathan, 2002).

Computers can stimulate pretending in young children. Simple acts of make-believe to more elaborate sociodramatic play can be triggered by events unfolding on the computer monitor. On-screen activities serve as a medium for play as children first share together their joint attention to what is presented and then use computer content in off-screen play activity (Brooker & Siraj-Blatchford, 2000). For example, children might see balloons flying on screen and begin to pretend to chase invisible balloons around the classroom. On-screen images might be playfully smacked, talked to, or scolded, or other parasocial behaviors can occur. A play theme of a grocery store or a food court might occur in the dramatic play center after the use of software that had food content. Brooker and Siraj-Blatchford reported how food items such as apples and pears were frequently grabbed from the screen and effortlessly integrated into other classroom play activities, with children pretending to share the food and licking their lips after pretending to eat the food displayed on the screen.

## Video Games

The video game industry has grown into a multi-billion-dollar market over the past decade. The sales of video games were $20 billion in 2004; over 280 million units were sold in 2000 alone ($6 billion). It is estimated that 60 percent of all Americans, or about 145 million people, play video games on a regular basis (Children Now, 2001). With rapid technological advances, young children are drawn to video games by the combination of their visual attractiveness and interactivity or potential for social interaction—and peer pressure.

There may be some benefits to playing video games that are nonviolent. Hypotheses advanced over the years by researchers such as Greenfield (1994) are that video games promote hand-eye coordination, visual scanning, auditory discriminations, and spatial skills. These hypotheses lack convincing empirical support. Some studies have found that playing video games can improve children's visual attention, spatial iconic skill, and computer literacy. On the other hand, the use of educational games, which are almost exclusively sold for the PC, have been shown to help improve academic performance (Children Now, 2001).

On the negative side, a host of studies have found relationships between playing video games, particularly those with violent content, and unhealthy outcomes, such as social isolation, obesity, belief in gender stereotypes, and increased aggressive feeling, thought, and behavior (Anderson & Bushman, 2001). In fact, unique interactive capabilities and reality may make them likely to adversely affect children's attitudes, beliefs, and behaviors—more so than traditional forms of media.

In *Fair Play? Violence, Gender and Race in Video Game,* Heintz-Knowles and Henderson (2001) examined the top-selling video games for each of seven different game systems. First, they found that most video games (89 percent) contained violent content, almost half of which was serious in nature. Killing was almost always presented as justified, sending the message that violence was an acceptable way to achieve one's objectives and that players could be heroes by using violence successfully. These findings are particularly alarming because some children may internalize these messages and act them out aggressively or they may become desensitized to violence. Others who come from violent neighborhoods may come to believe this violence is acceptable.

Second, Heintz-Knowles and Henderson also found that video games tend to reinforce gender stereotypes. Female characters accounted for only 16 percent of all characters, and these few females also were likely to scream and wear revealing clothing. Males were more likely to engage in physical aggression. Such biased portrayals send negative and misleading messages to children—that there are certain ways that males and females are supposed to look and act.

Third, video games also contain very little racial diversity. Nearly all heroes were white; African Americans and Latinos were typically athletes. Asians and Pacific Islanders were usually wrestlers or fighters. These kinds of racial images and stereotypes adversely influence children's attitudes toward people of other races. In addition, children of color feel devalued or ignored because of limited and stereotypical representations of people from their own racial group, or they come to believe that the only legitimate occupation for them is to be athletes or fighters. Rarely cast as champions, rescuers, or heroes, people of color are often portrayed as no more than muscular brutes, exotic fighting machines, or athletes displaying near-supernatural ability. Victims of aggression in video games are often minorities, and humor is present in many cases to trivialize the consequences. The Lion & Lamb Project exists for a number of reasons, including to bring attention to the hateful play that today's video games make possible (www.lionlamb.org).

Teachers and parents admit that it is very hard to ban children from playing video games, even as the adults worry over the possible negative influences. Video games, as a form of the electronic media like computers, are interactive, in contrast to television, radio, and movies, which are all essentially one-way communications. The combination of visual attractiveness and the potential for interaction is very appealing. Most children prefer video games to academically oriented computer programs. For this reason also, there is a strong need to develop appealing educational and nonviolent, nonsexist video games. An advocacy group called Teachers Resisting Unhealthy Children's Entertainment (TRUCE) campaigns against media violence and entertainment (www.truceteachers.org).

Dorst (1999) demonstrated that children's play can be influenced by video games. He reported that school-age children reframe the video game "Super Mario 5" in a playground game involving roving around and encountering and surmounting obstacles and barriers. In this video game children fight a variety of dangerous creatures, acquire artifacts that give them enhanced powers, enter "warp zones" that allowed special movements, and traverse boundaries from one imagined world to another. Dorst found that although children moved around the playground and acted out the kinds of encounters and events that appeared in the video games, they also seemed to improvise, elaborate, and include more imaginative ingredients in their play than are found in the video games. For instance, the children added putting themselves "on pause," which required freezing the action as one can do with a key on a control pad. Children also "collectively mapped the playground in terms of correspondences between mundane physical features such as bike racks and jungle gyms and the imagined landscape of a particular fantasy world"(Dorst, 1999, p. 270). The children's play reflected a blending of video game content (ideas or images of the animated figures moving about a fantasy landscape beset with obstacles and adversaries) with children's fantasies when engaged as players in the playground game inspired by the video game (Dorst, 1999).

## Computer Games

Computer games can include games played on computers as well as games played on specially designed equipment, such as video game consoles, hand-held machines, and video arcade equipment. Analyses of the cognitive and perceptual-motor aspects of these games reveals that many require a high level of skill and that players elect to meet increasing challenges. Many consumer games have violent images in common with TV and overlapping with the concerns about video games we discussed previously. Simulated violence is a prominent feature of many games.

Durkin and Barber (2002) found that sixteen-year-olds who play computer games scored better than did peers who never played computer games on several measures, including positive school engagement, positive mental health, self-concept, friendship network, and activity involvement. Durkin and Barber also reported that computer game players report greater family cohesion than do those who do not play, contrary to the speculation that computer gaming is a solitary activity that reflects a lack of social skills.

There are many computer games that are constructive and prosocial and have educational value. For example, children can build zoos, amusement parks, and aquariums in various ways that are aimed at making a profit. These computer games invite creative and imaginative play. Parents can help younger children learn to use such computer games to promote learning, positive play experiences, and development. Even games with some violent content can serve some purpose for children in terms of helping them feel some power and control over events. Sometimes the violent aspects might not be the primary feature motivating play, but merely an incidental feature. Winning or succeeding in the computer game play might be much more important. Of course, parental guidance is required so that such content does not exceed acceptable boundaries.

## Computer Toys

The concept of children's play has changed considerably with the advent of new technologies in toys. Electronic toys not only serve as catalysts for new forms of play, but also can influence the content of more traditional forms of play, particularly dramatic and constructive play. Technological advances in toy manufacture bring significant opportunities and challenges to early childhood education. Parents and teachers need to know how to use technology to promote learning, enrich children's play, and protect children from possible negative influences. Parents and teachers need to maintain a balance between the traditional toys and the new digital ones.

Electronic toys include technology-enhanced battery-operated toys and toys with computer chips installed that make the toys talk or act in certain ways. These toys have become popular with affluent parents and children, but there are few studies on how children play with these toys and how these toys affect children's play. Whether such electronic toys hamper or facilitate children's play creativity and channel their play in ways either prosocial or anti-social is not clear.

Levin and Rosenquest (2001) have suggested that parents and teachers should be concerned about the increasing use of electronic toys; electronic toys are limited and repetitive, and children are likely to become bored soon after starting to play with one of them. Levin and Rosenquest also claim that children's development can be negatively influenced by playing with these toys because the toys do not encourage creative play. They note that open-ended opportunities for creative play can be considerably reduced by the programmed vocalizations of mobile phones, by scripts embedded in talking dolls, and by music that is only a push-button away in an electronic toy. Also, such toys, with their strong initial appeal and attractiveness due to fancy gadgetry, might spoil children, who might then find other, ordinary toys less appealing. However, studies are needed to confirm or refute these assertions.

On the other hand, Marsh (2002) has presented a case that electronic toys can have a more positive impact on children's play. Toys have always been social markers that reflect sociocultural practices and the values of the society. Immersed in this multimedia world, children should experience diverse ways of learning and playing, including the use of media and electronic toys. Marsh also claims that it is hard to find studies that provide confirmation of the hypothesis that use of electronic toys by young children produces any negative effects on play or development. More research is warranted on the effects of technology-enhanced toys.

Bergen (2004) has recently conducted a study to investigate preschoolers' play with talking (computer-chip enhanced) and nontalking rescue heroes, when the children were either alone or with a playmate. Children were videotaped playing for fifteen to twenty minutes with toys (talking and nontalking versions of firefighters and police) and blocks in two sessions one to two weeks apart. Bergen found that children who were presented with the talking toys used language narratives that were similar to those of the children with the nontalking toys. In addition, the two groups of children did not differ from each other in use of language and actions relevant to the themes of the pretend play. Bergen concluded that play was not stifled by the talking toys' special features. After repeating some novel phrases and sounds made by the talking toys, the children seemed to take control of the play and did not simply imitate. Children sometimes also created original texts in play, such as pretending that the rescue workers' backpack was a pillow for resting on a picnic or a television (using the little screens on the backpacks) to watch when it was time to go home and go to bed. Most of the time the children's play was prosocial, although not all of it was channeled by the talking toys' prompts. Children's cognitive, social-emotional, and language abilities were on display as they played with both sets of toys, and having a playmate resulted in richer play under both toy conditions: technology-enhanced or not.

Teachers and parents need to become more knowledgeable about electronic toys. For instance, toys that make music have preprogrammed tunes that can be played by pressing the right buttons or keys. Sometimes there is a delay in tone after the switch is pushed, which might be confusing to a child. In general, these musical activities can offer the child a way to discover a sense of rhythm that is not likely to be discovered with simple band instruments. Computer toy versions of musical instruments sometimes lure children into musical appreciation and interest, while other children might see and use them as just noisemakers. Adult mediation of children's play likely makes an important difference.

Two additional issues need to be considered. First, with the ever-decreasing time and opportunities children have for play, for a variety of reasons discussed throughout this book, do electronic and technology toys take time away from more traditional forms of play? If so, is this bad? Second, although just one form of technological play might well encourage all the same creative and self-control aspects of good play, what happens if all of a child's play opportunities are electronic: computer games, video games, electronic toys? Do the children then have the reserve of experiences and behaviors they need to engage in complex, high-quality play? Obviously, research is needed to answer these questions.

## SUMMARY

Many aspects of today's society can make it difficult to help the next generation become the kinds of people who are likely to be humane, productive, inventive, and playful. Popular culture, the mass media, and technology appear to generate impediments to creative play and child development. This presents real challenges to parents and teachers, who need to realize that culture is not just a garden but also an arena of power where self-interest, domination, and exploitation abound and a sea of semiotics with whirlpools of symbolism and meaning can interfere with socialization goals and healthy child development. For example, much in postmodern civilization engenders a superficial, materialistic, and hurried lifestyle with ever-increasing demands for immediate gratification. Schools and families must seek ways to shield young children from the most adverse consequences and try to find constructive alternatives and uses of technology, media, and popular culture.

Living in today's society, families with young children intersect with a variety of public places, among which are childcare programs and schools, places of worship, children's museums, children's libraries, nature centers, and zoos. Here parents can find many needed allies to help them ward off the adverse effects of popular culture, mass media, technology, and commercialism; they can provide children with opportunities for wholesome play and learning and, by doing so, nurture positive behaviors and dispositions in young children.

Teachers and parents of young children who are concerned about play, development, and education must stay mindful that we live in an age of access. We must guard against the negative effects of entering into commodified relationships and money-related arrangements in which experiences of all kinds are purchased for children. Children need close, warm relationships with significant others and shared experiences; they should not be overscheduled in adult-organized activities at the expense of spontaneous play. And they need positive play, not negative, passive play that can result from living in homes with too many TV sets, computers, and video games or from being taken too often to carnivals, amusement parks, and other pay-for-play destinations that can be found in our communities and neighborhoods. Children also need adult protection from exploitation from the toy industry; when purchasing toys, parents must balance their desire to see their children happy with a concern for what is good for the children.

Today's mass media also present formidable challenges to parents and teachers who want good play and positive child development and education for their children. Media saturation can result in much unwelcome exposure to content showing violence, stereotypes, consumerism, and other inappropriate messages. Cultural diseases of childhood obesity and epidemic rates of ADHD are perpetuated by overuse of the electronic media; other causes include lack of opportunities for physical play and few experiences in nature or in the outdoors. Parents and teachers need to know how to rechannel and enrich children's play that is negative and destructive and reflects the influence of exposure to violence and other disturbing content in media, including the news. Positive effects can result when the TV program is educational and intended to foster the imagination and when there is adult mediation, discussion of program content, and facilitation of play.

Computer technology holds great promise as an aid to education of children of all ages and can be appropriate in early childhood education to foster positive play and child development. Concerns that computers pull children away from peers or traditional activities appear to be unfounded; developmentally appropriate software with open-ended content can encourage play, cooperation, and creative problem solving. Use of such software and tool programs, including playful writing with word processors, can be a complement to other curriculum for young learners and can lead to high-quality play.

Video games, like TV, have the potential to foster passivity and negative values. There is also some evidence that these games can stimulate positive play outside their virtual reality in school-age children. Technology and media can be used by children as they construct meaning of their culture through generative rather than imitative play behaviors. This two-sided play scenario is also the case in the use of electronic and computer toys. Children can use these technologically advanced toys in a very limiting and repetitive way. However, there is also evidence that children can incorporate them as tools for their imaginative play in ways that were not necessarily intended by the toy industry that produces them.

## PROJECTS AND ACTIVITIES

1. Draw one picture or diagram that illustrates culture as a garden of growth, another that shows culture as an arena of power relations, and a third that depicts culture as a sea of symbolism. Do this in connection with young children in today's world. Be able to explain the usefulness of each metaphor for culture.
2. Take a pro and then a con position in the debate on whether electronic toys for young children are appropriate playthings in early childhood settings.
3. Design a computer center in an early childhood educational setting that you think will facilitate high-quality make-believe play and also further children's emergent literacy development.
4. Interview a teacher at each of the pre-K, kindergarten, and primary levels, asking about the value of technology in children's play and the impact of technology in the classroom. Analyze, interpret, and share your results with your classmates.
5. Visit a library or computer store, and study children's software. Analyze a small random selection of the available software by the standards of problem-solving orientation, developmental appropriateness, playfulness, cultural diversity, and incorporating new technologies.
6. Visit a children's museum, zoo, library, nature or environment center, or a place of worship to learn about types and quality of play opportunities for children. Report your findings to the class.

CHAPTER 12

# Outdoor Play

## INTRODUCTION

Playgrounds are a place where children's play can take off and flourish. Good outdoor playgrounds are large enough and designed in such a way that children's play can be fully expressed. Children can make a mess, run, jump, and hide; they can shout and whistle, and they can explore the natural world. In this chapter we briefly look at the history of playgrounds and discuss the various kinds of contemporary playgrounds. We discuss a variety of factors that determine the quality of a playground for young children, infants to eight-year-olds, including design, equipment, safety issues, accessibility guidelines, and adult supervision. Particular emphasis is placed on how playgrounds must encourage all forms of play, the critical need to develop a disposition toward outdoor physical activities in our young children, and a caution against making outdoor play too academic and too teacher controlled. We also briefly discuss ways to extend outdoor play beyond the playground. Finally, we discuss global issues of outdoor playgrounds and international safety guidelines.

## FOCUS QUESTIONS

1. Why is recess being eliminated from some of our public schools?
2. Why is obesity becoming a national health epidemic?
3. Why is it important for children to engage in different kinds of play on the playgrounds? How should playgrounds encourage diverse forms of play?

4. Are infant/toddler playgrounds needed? What makes these playgrounds different from playgrounds for preschool-age children?
5. What are the various roles for adults on playgrounds?
6. Should specific academic equipment, such as learning panels, tick-tack-toe panels, and alphabet reproductions, be included in outdoor playgrounds? What is their value, if any?
7. As we increase academic standards for our children, isn't it only natural to reduce their opportunity to play and divert scarce resources to focus only on academic activities?
8. How is outdoor play for young children qualitatively different from indoor play?
9. Why are specific safety guidelines needed for playgrounds? Should these guidelines be implemented globally?

## HISTORY OF PLAYGROUNDS

Francis Wardle remembers that when he was in elementary school in England (fifty years ago), the equipment on the playground was composed of a massive jungle gym with ropes, ladders, overhead bars, and climbing poles that rose fifteen to twenty feet into the air, and a large giant stride, a piece of play equipment that has ropes or chains radiating from a central pole. These ropes are attached to a mechanism at the top of the pole that turns as children run round the pole, holding onto the end of a rope. Once

➤ When playing on a giant stride, children hold onto chains or ropes, run around the pole, and then fly into the air.

they get up to speed, the children jump off the ground and fly in the air. However, the giant stride was continually off limits because too many children broke their arms playing on it. Beyond these large pieces of equipment the teachers had set up some old round army tents under large shade trees. The children would spend hours digging the ground from under these tents, creating their own forts and houses.

## Parallel Historical Movements

The history of playgrounds in the United States follows four general strands: kindergarten, nursery school, park, and elementary school playgrounds. Although each of these types of playgrounds developed as an extension of the theories and practical applications of their time, companies that manufactured and sold playground equipment greatly influenced playgrounds, and there was naturally some interface between all four kinds of playgrounds.

Initially, U.S. playgrounds developed from the outdoor gymnasium concept developed in Germany in the first decade of the 1800s (Frost, 1992). These playgrounds emphasized physical exercise and activity, a longstanding German tradition that, unfortunately, culminated in the Hitler Youth movement of Nazi Germany. In 1821 the Latin School in Salem, Massachusetts, developed its own outside gymnasium; in 1825 an area for outdoor play and gymnastics, equipped with German-type equipment, was developed at the Round Hill School in Northampton, Massachusetts (Frost, 1992).

Another outdoor play idea also originated in Germany. During the 1880s piles of sand were placed in public parks in Berlin, and the Sandgarten ("sand garden") movement was born. This idea soon found its way to the United States, and in 1897 the famous psychologist G. Stanley Hall wrote the book *The Story of a Sand Pile,* discussing the developmental and psychological merits of sandplay for children. (In Chapter 11 we discussed the topic of sandplay therapy, an extension of this idea.)

**Kindergarten Playgrounds.** Froebel, the father of the kindergarten, always emphasized the value of outdoor play for children (after all, *kindergarten* means "children's garden"). His playgrounds were nature itself—streams, tree trunks, gardens, dams, areas of grass to play games, and trees to climb—based on the ideas of Rousseau and Pestalozzi. Froebel also believed that outdoor play was essential for the child's total physical, intellectual, and moral development, not simply for physical exercise. Froebel's gifts, specific educational toys that Froebel developed, were also added to the playgrounds as play materials and loose parts. By the turn of the nineteenth century many U.S. kindergartens had adopted this Froebelian idea of playgrounds.

Although kindergarten playgrounds were based on this concept, elementary school playgrounds were not. And as the popularity of kindergartens grew in this country, they became more and more like regular schools, including their playgrounds. By 1925 the better kindergarten playgrounds, which had not succumbed to the public school approach, included the following:

- Woodworking
- Paper construction
- A variety of toys for dramatic play, including playhouse, housekeeping, toys, carts, wagons, and play stores

- Balls of all sizes, slides, swings, seesaws, ropes, ladders, and sand piles (Frost, 1992)

**Nursery School Playgrounds.** The nursery school movement in the United States and northern Europe developed separately from kindergartens. In the 1920s these programs stressed play as central to a child's development and created indoor and outdoor environments to facilitate play. Extensive indoor and outdoor playtime was provided, and, even compared to today's programs, "the total array of materials and certain program practices were impressive" (Frost, 1992, p. 118). However, just as with kindergarten playgrounds, safety was of little concern in these playgrounds. They consisted of natural grassy areas with plants and trees to emphasize contact with animals and nature, a playhouse, and a wading pool. Commercially made jungle gyms, slides, and swings were also included. Although the nursery movement tended to express the philosophy of Dewey and Montessori, the playgrounds were greatly influenced by Froebel.

After the 1920s the philosophical belief in the central role of play in development kept the focus of nursery playgrounds on the whole child. Nursery school playgrounds also began to address safety issues, such as providing soft surfaces under equipment and reducing the heights of much of the equipment. In the 1940s and 1950s paved areas for wheeled toys, gates and fences for safety, shelters for inclement weather, and a combination of play surfaces were added. Today nursery schools, what we now call early childhood programs, continue to take a far more holistic approach to play—physical, emotional, creative, social, and cognitive—than park and public school (including kindergarten) playgrounds do.

**Park Playgrounds and School Playgrounds.** In 1889 a free playground for men and boys was opened in Charlesbank, Massachusetts. In 1909 Massachusetts passed a law requiring all towns of over 10,000 to establish public playgrounds (Frost, 1992), and the playground movement in this country was launched. The sandgarten idea was expanded to sandplay areas in these city parks. By 1909 the Playground Association of America had changed its philosophy of outdoor play to go beyond just physical fitness to include a variety of what it considered social aspects of play: cleanliness, politeness, friendships, obedience, loyalty, justice, and truthfulness (Playground Association of America, 1909/1910).

In 1905 thirty-five cities in the United States had established supervised playgrounds, and by 1909, 336 cities had created park playgrounds, which all included sand gardens, ten-foot-high rope swings, sliding boards, giant strides, teeter-totters, ring toss games, and a variety of balls, bats, beanbags, and nets (Frost, 1992). Equipment was made of steel, wood, or iron. Toilets, drinking fountains, shade, seated areas, shelters, storage, landscaping, and lighting for nighttime were also included. Play leaders were considered essential for the supervision, organization, and administration of playgrounds (Frost, 1992). These playgrounds were often overcrowded, equipment was extremely high and dangerous, and the surface under the equipment was usually hard.

It seems that public school playgrounds during this time took the worst from the park playgrounds, a situation that many people believe is still all too true. Most public school playgrounds provided minimum opportunities for play, and exercise equipment that was provided tended to be extremely dangerous, often over fifteen feet high, with asphalt or concrete underneath. Merry-go-rounds and seesaws were also dangerous and often caused broken arms. Many people believe that school playgrounds were designed and built primarily for the use and convenience of the janitor, especially with regard to ease of maintenance and keeping order (Frost, 1992). Even today this is the chief concern of many public school administrators, maintenance supervisors, and building managers.

## Eras of Playground Equipment

As we discussed earlier, specific playground equipment, manufactured and sold by commercial playground companies, has had a tremendous impact on playgrounds. The development of this equipment can be broken into four general eras.

**Manufactured Apparatus (1910–1950).** In 1910 manufacturers of playground equipment provided a variety of items made of steel, iron, and wood and featured a variety of glossy catalogs from which to buy this equipment. Equipment for children under ten years of age included ten-foot-high rope swings, sliding boards, giant strides, teeter-totters, and a collection of balls, bats, nets, beanbags, and the like. Additionally, public playgrounds and school playgrounds included very high climbers, swings, monkey bars, and other dangerous equipment, all set in concrete or asphalt. Play leaders (supervisors) were a critical part of park playgrounds, which also included shelters and seats. When cars became popular, school and city playgrounds had to be isolated and protected from the streets by being placed in separate locations and behind fences and gates.

**Novelty Era (1950s–1960s).** By the 1950s the official playground movement had morphed into a recreation movement (Frost, 1992). Physical fitness, aesthetic quality (what the playground looked like), and equipment manufactured by play equipment companies drove design and practice; child development needs were not of central concern.

Novelty and fantasy structures began to be added to playgrounds. In 1952 Philadelphia developed sixty theme playgrounds. A Dennis the Menace playground was constructed in Monterey, California. In East Orange, New Jersey, two fourteen-foot cabin cruisers were added to a constructed lighthouse, jetty, and dock to create a nautical playground. In the 1960s rocket play structures inspired by the space race sprang up around the country (Frost, 1992). Although swings, slides, climbers, and the like remained popular, they often also took on the look of various fantasy characters, animals, rockets, and so forth. This kind of equipment is still very popular in Brazil and is seen in the expansive Sarah Kubitschek Park in Brasilia, Brazil (Wardle, 2001).

**Modular Equipment (1970s–1990s).** During the 1970–1980s modular wooden equipment dominated the manufactured choices; then in the 1980s powder-coated metal and polyurethane equipment became popular. These modular structures combined the physical activities of slides, swings, and a variety of climbing opportunities

➤ In the 1960s, rocket play structures, a form of theme playgrounds, inspired by the space race, sprang up around the country. These structures are still popular in Brazil today, seen here in Sarah Kubitscheck Park in Brasilia.

with dramatic-play houses, forts, and hiding places and the constructive play of sand and loose parts (Wardle, 1997). The swivel swing (single-axle swing), a tire suspended horizontally by three chains or cables, became popular at this time.

Public park playgrounds were dominated by architecturally impressive designs, natural environments, and aesthetic layouts, with inadequate fixed equipment purchased from manufacturers catalogs. According to Bruya and Langendorfer (1988), public school playgrounds were a national disgrace, with static, often unsafe equipment that stressed physical activity. Most of these playgrounds contained rows of very high swings, massive jungle gyms, and single, high slides. Many of these school playgrounds still exist today; the Denver Public school playgrounds still, incredibly, include giant strides. Many schools also began to include wooden modular equipment.

Although early childhood programs often reflected some of the above realities, they were more creative and appropriate for the needs of young children, and manufacturers began to design and buy equipment specifically for this age child, although these were initially simple junior versions of elementary school equipment (Wardle, 1997). Early childhood programs were also much more likely to include natural elements of trees, water, and gardens; to include tricycle and wagon paths; and to provide a variety for loose parts.

**Modern Era: Safety and Accessibility.** The modern era of playgrounds—in parks, schools, and early childhood programs—is dominated by the influence of the U.S. Consumer Product Safety Commission (CPSC) guidelines and the ADA accessibility guidelines. Although both of these documents are technically guidelines (not laws), they have been unilaterally adopted by most play equipment manufacturers, many schools, and state child care licensing agencies. These guidelines have been accepted because they are effective publicity tools for playground equipment companies and because they are a good defense in liability lawsuits (Frost & Sweeney, 1996).

According to Frost and Sweeney (1996), "The frequency of playground lawsuits is growing rapidly throughout the United States. Practically all the litigation involves very serious injuries, ranging from fractured limbs to brain damage and deaths" (p. 15). Playground injuries occurred most often at public school playgrounds, followed by those at public parks and childcare centers.

These injuries and the resultant lawsuits, which are most often settled out of court, are leading to inspection and upgrading playgrounds, including making them conform to the national CPSC standards (Frost & Sweeney, 1996). However, in states where schools have immunity from legal liability for playgrounds (e.g., Texas), little is being done. It is interesting to note that of 190 cases of severe playground injuries studied by Frost and Sweeney, 94 percent involved violations of these national safety guidelines (53 percent due to lack of absorbent materials under the equipment). We will discuss these specific safety guidelines later in this chapter.

One unfortunate result of the trend toward safety is the abolishment of swings from some schools and early childhood programs, even though, according to Frost and Sweeney (1996), injuries on swings, like most injuries, are caused by falling onto hard surfaces. On a recent visit to Texas a Head Start director told Francis Wardle that Texas Licensing was considering banning swings from all early childhood playgrounds; other programs have pulled out swings, allegedly on the advice of early childhood experts. Another result of these guidelines is that modern playgrounds need much more space, and are more expensive to create and maintain.

For a variety of reasons, wood has been rejected as a material for park playgrounds and public school playgrounds. Some early childhood programs still use wood, especially programs in which parents and volunteers help to build the equipment. Plastic has gained a tremendous hold, with whole lines of preschool equipment made totally of plastic (for example, by Little Tikes, a division of Rubber Maid). Most equipment for public schools and parks is now built of a combination of metal and plastic. Although public school playgrounds still emphasize physical activity, ease of supervision, and minimal maintenance, the combined units of the modular era have found their way into many public school playgrounds.

Beginning in the 1970s, teaching specific academic goals entered the minds of some school playground designers. Playground surfaces were painted with world maps, the alphabet, numbers, words, and other specific academic skill instruction. This idea quietly crept into preschool equipment designs, with a resultant plethora of learning panels (Wardle, 1994). These panels are still very much available and are aggressively marketed by playground equipment representatives as methods to teach children academic and preacademic skills for school entry and academic success. With the advent of national school standards and the current emphasis on academic knowledge and skills at lower and lower levels, public elementary school playgrounds and early childhood playgrounds are returning to this notion of painting words, letters, numbers, and the like on their playgrounds.

The more creative and innovative early childhood programs struggle to meet the safety and accessibility guidelines while trying to stay true to the developmental needs of young children. However, playgrounds are still very much the orphan child of any program. Francis Wardle has visited a variety of early childhood education programs across the country in his role as a playground consultant, and even in brand-new early childhood buildings the playground is almost always an afterthought. Even many campus childcare programs, used by colleges that train our future early childhood teachers, have playgrounds that can only be described as embarrassing to the field.

### Cultural Issues

Clearly, playgrounds develop out of a culture's view of childhood, education, and the role of the outdoors in supporting childhood and education, not to mention a historical context. Further, outdoor play and playgrounds are embedded within each culture. For example, Mayan children who live in remote villages in the highlands of Guatemala freely use the entire village, ball field, streams, and mountainside as their outdoor playground (Wardle, 1977). There is no need for a separate playground. These children live in a village where everyone knows everybody, there are no roads and road traffic, fences do not exist, and public pathways twist throughout everyone's private land. Children simply run into the soccer field to play catch, jump over the stream, and climb the trees next to their house.

In the public city parks in Abu Dhabi, the United Arab Emirates, a neatly constructed and maintained prayer area is included as part of the playground so that people who cannot get to a mosque can still observe their religious obligations. And in Brazil's large cities, parks such as Sarah Kubitschek Park in Brasilia are absolutely huge, and the children are carefully observed and monitored by the maids all middle-class families hire to care for their young children. When one of the authors commented to a teacher in a private preschool in Diamantina, Brazil, that the playground was very dangerous (it had concrete under all the equipment), the teacher commented, "But we always provide very close supervision" (and they did!).

Playgrounds in the United States vary markedly owing to a variety of ecological and cultural factors. For the preschool and school at New Meadow Run, in rural Pennsylvania, the entire 120 acres of woods and wetlands attached to the school was considered the playground (Wardle, 1995). In contrast, playgrounds in crime- and drug-infested inner-city areas must have high fences, lots of security, and indestructible equipment.

## PURPOSE OF OUTDOOR PLAY

There are two fundamental reasons why outdoor play is critical for young children in our early childhood programs and schools. First, many of the developmental tasks that children must achieve—exploring, risk-taking, fine and gross motor development, learning vast amounts of basic knowledge—can be learned (or can be most effectively learned) only through outdoor play. Second, our culture is taking outdoor play away from young children through excessive TV and computer use, unsafe neighborhoods, busy and tired parents, educational accountability, elimination of school recess, and academic standards that push more and more developmentally inappropriate academics into our early childhood programs, thus taking time away from play. The following sections (based on Wardle, 1996–2003) describe the main reasons why outdoor play is critical for the healthy development of young children.

## Physical Exercise

Children need to develop large motor and small motor skills and cardiovascular endurance. Gallahue (1993) provides a comprehensive discussion of the motor development and movement skill acquisition of young children, which must be encouraged in outdoor playgrounds. Extensive physical activity is also needed to address a growing obesity problem in American children. According to Gabbard (2000), 25 percent of children in the United States are obese. Obesity leads to type II (adult) diabetes in children as young as age five and can cause increased risk of early heart disease and hypertension in children and young adults (Perry, 2001; Stoneham, 2001). According to Sutterby and Frost (2002), the increase in child obesity is caused by an increase in caloric intake and a decrease in physical activity. For most children outdoor play offers an opportunity to engage in vigorous physical activity. Further, according to Sutterby and Frost (2002), physical activity is much more effective than dieting for preventing and combating obesity. (However, one of the great outcomes of vegetable gardens in playgrounds is teaching children appropriate dietary habits and choices.)

## Enjoyment of the Outdoors

Outdoor play is one of the things that characterize childhood. And as Lord Nuffield once said, the best preparation for adulthood is to have a full and enjoyable childhood. Thus childhood must include outdoor play. Children need opportunities to explore, experiment, manipulate, reconfigure, expand, influence, change, marvel, discover, practice, dam up, push their limits, yell, sing, and create. Some of our favorite childhood memories are outdoor activities. This is no accident. Francis Wardle remembers damming up the little stream below his house for his brother's ducks, digging a fort into the side of the bank behind the house, and building treehouses and drainage ditches to divert the constant English downpours. To him, childhood and the outdoors are synonymous.

## Learning about the World

Outdoor play enables young children to learn lots and lots and lots of things about the world. How does ice feel and sound? Can sticks stand up in sand? How do plants grow? How does mud feel? Why do we slide down instead of up? How do I make my tricycle go faster? How does the overhang of the building create a cool shade from the sun? What does a tomato smell and taste like? What does a chrysalis change into? Do butterflies have to learn to fly? Much of what a child learns outside can be learned in a variety of other ways, but learning it outside is particularly effective—and certainly more fun! In the outside playground children can learn math, science, ecology, gardening, ornithology, construction, farming, vocabulary, the seasons, the various times of the day, and all about the local weather. Not only do children learn lots of basic and fundamental information about how the world works in a very effective manner, they are more likely to remember what they learned because the learning was concrete and personally meaningful (Ormrod, 1997).

## Learning about Self and the Environment

To learn about their own physical and emotional capabilities, children must push their limits. How high can I swing? Do I dare go down the slide? How high can I climb? Can I go down the slide head first? To learn about the physical world, the child must experiment with the physical world. Can I slide on the sand? Can I roll on grass? What happens when I throw a piece of wood into the pond? Is cement hard or soft to fall on? An essential task of development is appreciating how we fit into the natural order of things—animals, plants, the weather, and so on. To what extent does nature care for us, providing water, shade, soft surfaces, and sweet-smelling flowers? And to what extent does it present problems, such as hard surfaces, the hot sun, and thorns on bushes? We can discover this relationship with the natural world only by experiencing it as we grow up, develop, and interact with the natural environment.

## The Surplus-Energy Theory

As we discussed in Chapter 2, the surplus-energy theory of play hypothesizes that play allows people to release pent-up energy that has collected over time. Many teachers and administrators believe that after intense (and often inactive) academic classroom pursuits, children need to "let off steam." To some extent, educators also believe that outdoor play enables children to "recharge their batteries," to reinvigorate themselves by engaging in a very different activity from their classroom experience. This recreation theory of play enables children to get ready to return to the important work of academic learning. These theories view outdoor play as an essential component to academic learning, not as an important activity in its own right.

## Health

Everyone who works with young children in early childhood programs and schools knows how quickly bacteria and viruses spread in these environments. One way to reduce the spread of infection is through lots and lots of fresh air. Outdoor play enables the infectious agents to spread out and be dissipated; it also enables children to get fresh air and exercise and be less constrained than they are in the classroom (Aronson, 2002).

Outdoor play also enables children to enjoy the natural environment and learn to seek out exercise, fresh air, and activity. There is something fundamentally healthy about using the outdoors. Thus outdoor play develops a disposition for the outdoors, for physical activity, and for caring for the environment. Children who engage in lots of physical activities at school tend to engage in more energetic activities at home, while children who have childcare and school experiences that lack active physical activity, engage in more sedentary behaviors at home, such as TV watching and computer use (Dale, Corbin, & Dale, 2000). Children who learn to enjoy the outdoors have a much higher likelihood of becoming adults who enjoy hiking, gardening, jogging, bicycling, mountain climbing, or other outdoor endeavors. This is critical as obesity becomes an ever-greater national concern and as we must all learn to care for and protect the environment.

### Allowing Children to Be Children

To use open space to fulfill basic childhood needs—jumping, running, climbing, swinging, racing, yelling, rolling, hiding, and making a big mess—is what childhood is all about! For a variety of obvious reasons, many of these things cannot occur indoors. Yet children must have these important experiences. Today children's lives are more and more contained and controlled by small apartments; high-stakes academic instruction; schedules; tense, tired, and overworked parents; and fewer opportunities to be children. Outdoor environments fulfill children's basic needs for freedom, adventure, experimentation, risk-taking, and just being children (Greenman, 1993).

Children need the opportunity to explore the unknown, the unpredictable, and the adventurous. They also need to be able to wonder at nature, from the worm gliding through the newly turned dirt in the garden to the monarch butterfly emerging out of the chrysalis and gracefully fluttering away in the summer breeze.

## DIFFERENT KINDS OF PLAYGROUNDS

In the first section of this chapter we discussed the history of playgrounds in this country by focusing on playground movements and trends during different eras. In this section we examine the different types of playgrounds that also developed over time but are still available, ranging from traditional playgrounds characterized by metal climbing equipment and hard surfaces to truly modern playgrounds.

### Traditional Playgrounds

Traditional playgrounds are those that you and we remember from our school experiences. According to Frost and Klein (1979, p. 60), traditional playgrounds "provide the usually concrete/steel jungle." The equipment usually consists of swings, slide, jungle gym (monkey bars), seesaws, and a merry-go-round. The design and equipment on these playgrounds were dictated largely by the wishes of the school and early childhood programs for ease of supervision and a minimum of maintenance. Further, the equipment only met the physical play needs of children. Although hard surfaces were provided for various ball games, such as basketball, four square, and tether ball, these playgrounds generally did not include any components that could be moved by children and had no sand and water, gardens, or absorbent materials under the equipment. Ground surfaces were usually concrete or asphalt—or just plain dirt. Many such playgrounds still exist, particularly in parks.

Most schools today provide fall zone materials under equipment and use more modular and safer climbing equipment with slides, ladders, steps, bridges, and various learning panels, but the focus is still on physical play, ease of supervision, and maintenance. Further, as the practices of Greeley, Colorado, and the Denver public

➤ One advantage of creative playgrounds is that parents and other volunteers can help in building them, thus reducing costs. This playground is being built for a community college childcare program.

schools illustrate, engineers, architects, and school principals, not child development specialists and educators, make all the decisions about school and early childhood playground design and equipment.

## Creative Playgrounds

Frost and Klein (1979) define creative playgrounds as being "constructed primarily from scrounged materials such as tires, lumber, telephone poles, railroad tires, cable spools, and scrap metal. The construction often incorporates existing commercial equipment and purchased or free equipment. The playground includes permanent equipment, provisions for sand and water play, and an array of loose parts to accommodate all forms of play" (p. 131). Creative playgrounds are collaborative efforts between a program, parents, and the community. They capitalize on free and inexpensive materials, volunteer labor, and community support. Community groups such as the PTA, scouts, and various volunteer groups often assist. Box 12.1 reports on a playground project built by the Ault, Colorado, Head Start program in 1973.

**BOX 12.1**

### *Head Start Parents Build a Playground*

The Head Start program is located on the ground level of an old house, right on Main Street, which has been remodeled into a classroom and a kitchen. . . . Although the

Head Start program has done a nice job of remodeling the inside of the house, the back is an empty yard.

We decide to find out whether parents would be interested in helping us design and build a playground in the back yard. Several fathers are recruited to help us. Because all the parents are involved in farming, they have access to a variety of materials and tools, and have carpentry and masonry skills needed to build a playground.

We set to work on the playground. A dump truck delivers a huge tire from a road grader, which we will fill with sand to make a sandbox; a group of fathers drop off several cable spools, and the rest of us diligently transform a fire escape to the upstairs apartment which is empty) into a slide with a big curve at the bottom. By the end of the day we have transformed the empty backyard into a fun playground for a group of Head Start children.

*Source:* Wardle (1973).

Creative playgrounds link different single pieces of playground equipment into large linked structures, which often include platforms, ladders, slides (a whole variety, including roller slides and wide slides), bridges, swings, a variety of tire nets and climbing apparatus, climbing ropes, steps, and pulley slides, all in one unit. The purpose of these linkages is to increase play opportunities. For example, building a platform also creates a playhouse underneath, and providing a bridge linking two platforms can become a play event unto itself (Frost & Klein, 1979). Also, linking equipment acknowledges and supports the incredible social nature of most young children's play, allowing children to play together on a variety of equipment. As we discuss in a subsequent section on modern playgrounds, some of these linkages can cause safety problems and have been scaled back in modern playgrounds.

## Adventure Playgrounds

C. T. Sorensen, who observed that children playing near traditional playgrounds preferred playing with the scrap materials left over from the new construction rather than the newly finished playgrounds, developed the first adventure playground in Denmark in 1943. The concept quickly spread throughout England, Denmark, and Sweden. According to the London Adventure Playground Association (LAPA), an adventure playground is a place where children are free to do many things that they cannot easily do elsewhere in our crowded urban society—they can build houses, dens, and climbing structures with recycled materials, have bonfires, cook in the open, dig holes, garden, or just play with sand, water, and clay. The atmosphere is permissive and free. Each playground has two full-time leaders in charge who are friends of the children, and who help them with what they are trying to do (Jago, 1971).

An adventure playground is a large (one-third acre to four acres) fenced-in area that includes lots and lots of scrounged materials, gardens, tools and hardware, a main building and restrooms, and a construction area, animal areas, a separate area for children under age five, flat grass area for games, and fire pits for children to do their own cooking. A critical part of the playground is the play leader, who provides supervision, must be a jack-of-all trades, and must love working with children (Frost & Klein,

1979). Adventure playgrounds never fully took off in the United States for a variety of reasons, including the lack of group leaders in most park playgrounds, not to mention reluctant supervision by teachers on school playgrounds, liability issues, safety concerns, local zoning and architectural codes, and health laws. However, many elements of good modern early childhood playgrounds, discussed below, come directly from adventure playgrounds.

## Modern Playgrounds

Although traditional playgrounds did not meet the play needs of young children and were very dangerous (Frost & Klein, 1979), creative playgrounds had problems of their own, including extremely high maintenance (because found equipment and materials quickly deteriorate), difficulty of supervision (lots of places to hide), liability concerns, and safety problems (due to splinters in wood, old materials, and lack of knowledge of basic safety issues by designers and builders).

Modern playgrounds are the answer to these problems. Driven by the CPSC guidelines, liability concerns, and advances in playground equipment construction and design, good modern playgrounds also meet the fundamental play needs of children, infancy through school age. These playgrounds combine the best of traditional, creative, and adventure playgrounds. Elements from traditional playgrounds include swings, slides, monkey bars (for older children), climbing nets, and ladders (Frost & Klein, 1979). Because of CPSC safety guidelines, modern playgrounds isolate certain equipment, especially swings (traditional swings and swivel swings). Important ideas taken from adventure playgrounds include the belief that active supervision of playgrounds is required at all times (Hudson, Mack, & Thompson, 2000); the use of a variety of challenging, complex, and ever-changing loose parts scattered throughout the playground; and the inclusion of vegetable and flower gardens for preschool and school-age children (Dunbar, 2001).

Ideas taken from creative playgrounds include a central climbing structure, a variety of play surfaces, and additional equipment, including tires, culverts, and slides on a bank or elevated area (Frost & Klein, 1979). The use of extensive, winding tricycle and wagon paths can also be attributed to creative use of pathways in creative playgrounds. Many modern playgrounds include expensive climbing units made and installed by a variety of national and international playground equipment manufacturers. The use of absorbent materials under all equipment and other safety improvements come directly out of the increased concern for children's safety (discussed later in this chapter). Because of liability and maintenance concerns, community-built playgrounds that use recycled materials and equipment are becoming scarce.

**BOX 12.2**

### *Building a Playground in Brazil*

I gaze at the sun-drenched slab of concrete surrounded by an eight-foot wall, site of the proposed playground. I'm in the middle of Brazil! Actually, I'm 350 miles north and inland of Rio de Janeiro.

I was asked to travel to the town of Sete Lagoas (Seven Lakes) by Bryan Cooke, a member of Partners of the Americas, who sponsored my trip. Partners of Americas is a Kennedy-era program, now independently funded, that matches people and projects between states in the United States and Latin America, to provide a two-way exchange of ideas, expertise and goodwill. My state of Colorado is matched with the large Brazilian state of Minas Gerais, where Sete Lagoas is located.

After meeting with the staff of Andre Luiz Creche (nursery) and fellow members of Partners in Sete Lagoas, I traveled to the state capitol of Belo Horizonte to purchase playground equipment to use. I had hoped to find equipment that we could simply install in the play area, based on my design, but I discovered none of the available equipment was safe. So I decided to construct our own equipment, using local materials and volunteer labor. For construction methods and community-based solutions, I relied on past experiences building playgrounds for childcare centers and Head Start programs. I also used the U.S. CPSC handbook as my guide for safety (Brazil does not have such a document).

We decided to build a swivel swing, a traditional swing with two seats, a platform with two ladders and a slide, and a tunnel made using a drainage culvert. Because of the limited space and configuration of the playground, we created a fall zone of sand under all the equipment. The walls of the playground kept dogs and cats away from the sand. The frame of both swings was made of eucalyptus posts, plentiful in this part of Brazil. Hardware for the swing came from hardware stores, chain from a local car shop, attachments for the swing were made by a welder, and the swing seats cut from car tires. The framework for the climbing structure was made from typical Brazilian construction lumber—ipe, a hardwood that splits when nailed!

➤ Building a safe playground in Sete Lagoas, Brazil, a project sponsored by the Partners of the Americas and Rotary International.

We used slate stones for the sand retainer. While not ideal, the slate was provided by Luiz Vierra, my host, a local Partner and the owner of a slate factory.

Building the playground was a tremendous challenge! First of all, the volunteers only spoke Portuguese, and I only speak English! Secondly, I am used to working with measurements of feet and inches, and construction units based on feet and inches (i.e., 2 × 4 lumber which is 2 inches × 4 inches thick), while the Brazilians use the metric system. In fact in Brazil you go to a lumberyard where you select the right-size lumber from a pile of assorted sizes and shapes. Also, when I build playgrounds in the U.S. I buy everything I need–wood, nails, screws, tools and hardware from one store. In Brazil, we wandered from shop to shop, buying chain here, nails there, and having a mechanic custom make the eyebolts and a carpenter the ladder rungs. And, finally, the Brazilians could never really understand some of my safety concerns.

But now the children at the Andre Luiz Creche are enjoying the playground and the Partner volunteers are very proud of our accomplishment.

*Source:* Wardle (1999b). Reprinted with permission from Child Care Information Exchange.

## PLAYGROUND DESIGN

Various approaches can be used to design playgrounds. One is to follow Richard Dattner's (1969) criteria for play. Another is to design the playground so that each kind of play discussed in Chapter 3—physical, social, constructive, and games with rules—is met.

### Criteria for Play

Richard Dattner (1969) developed the concept of criteria for play to determine what children need on the playground: experience, control of experience, graduated challenge, choice, exercise in fantasy, separation from adults, and expressive play.

For experience Dattner (1969) believes that "a playground should be like a small-scale replica of the world, with as many as possible of the sensory experiences to be found in the world included in it" (p. 44). Control of experience involves the need for children to change, adapt, influence, combine, and rearrange materials, textures, objects, and natural materials. Graduated challenge is the concept of continually matching the playground environment to each child's ever-changing zone of proximal development. Children need to be able to practice new concepts, challenge themselves when they have conquered old tasks, and progress as they become more adept and sophisticated. Thus a playground should provide challenges that range from simple to complex, from easy for the youngest child to challenging for the most advanced. As we pointed out in Chapter 10, the need for graduated challenge is particularly important for children with a variety of disabilities.

A playground should be a place where a child feels in control, and one of the best ways to feel in control is to have lots of choices—what to play with, when to play, how to play, where to play, and with whom to play: alone, with others, in private, for all to see, and so on. This is what Dattner calls choice. Dattner's concept of exercise of fantasy is the same as sociodramatic play (discussed below); his separation from adults is as follows: "children need the freedom to make mistakes, to be clumsy and fall, without an ever-present parent (or teacher) who, with a misguided desire to help the child avoid disappointment and pain, interferes with his natural process of trial and error by which we all learn" (Dattner, 1969, p. 51).

Finally, Dattner talks about the criterion of expressive play. For this criterion he suggests that playgrounds should be a place where children with "exceptional problems, whether emotional, physical, or mental (or, as is usually the case) a combination of all of these" (p. 57), can more easily express themselves. This criterion closely approximates our discussion of playgrounds as a place where children who struggle in conventional school-related activities and expected behaviors can excel and fully express themselves.

## Encouraging Different Kinds of Play

The first thing most people think of when outdoor playgrounds are mentioned is climbing equipment; many outdoor playgrounds for young children are dominated by expensive climbing structures. However, climbing is only one of the many kinds of play that should be encouraged outside. Good outdoor playgrounds for children, infants to age eight, should provide materials, equipment, and design elements for each of a variety of play and the developmental age of each child using it (Wardle, 1987).

**Physical Play.** In general, physical play should be encouraged by climbing equipment and swings (also in the toddler area), tricycle paths, and large areas of grass and hills on which preschoolers can run and crawl and infants and toddlers can lie, crawl, and roll. Tricycle paths are used for Big Toys, tricycles, scooters, balls, jogging, and wagons. Climbing equipment for infants and toddlers should be very basic, including a crawling tunnel, small steps, and a slide. Because toddlers are very insecure on their feet, special attention should be paid to barriers—the railings and sides of raised equipment. A variety of sloped areas help children to learn to adjust their balance to differing surfaces. Although encouraging specific motor skills, such as fine and gross motor development, is important, it is more important to support the development of the overall integrated physical aspect of the child—all the senses, muscle development, and brain and nerve functions and growth. Thus rolling, crawling, running and climbing, and swinging on swings are all absolutely critical activities for young children.

In the preschool area the climbing structures should be much larger and should include a variety of slides, bridges, crawling tubes, and ladders and steps. Although dramatic play panels such as steering wheels are a good idea, specific academic panels and tick-tack-toe panels are a waste of money (Wardle, 1994). Older preschool children also enjoy a swivel (tire) swing.

**Constructive Play.** Research continually shows that constructive play is preschoolers' favorite kind of play, probably because they can and do control it (Ihn, 1998). Constructive play is encouraged by using sand and water play, providing a place for art, woodwork and blocks, wheeled toys, and lots of loose parts throughout the playground. Constructive play occurs in sandboxes, in sand and water areas, on flat surfaces, even on grass (Wardle, 1994). However, constructive play occurs only is there is an ever-changing variety of loose parts—boards, blocks, cloth materials, sticks, boxes, pieces of clean wood, and the like—and a variety of tools: sand tools, gardening tools, tools to play in the water, painting tools, and so forth. Many programs have a concrete slab outside the classroom door, with a roof that provides shade and protection from rain that functions as an outdoor classroom for blocks, wheeled toys, art easels, and woodwork. Centers in Europe, Australia, and New Zealand often design these transitional areas into the building.

Adequate and convenient storage—storage sheds and containers (baskets or tubs) near favorite locations where children play with loose parts—is critically important (Wardle, 2000a). Dragging toys and materials to and from the classroom or inside storage is simply too much effort and usually does not happen. The challenge in providing adequate constructive play materials is that it makes the playground look messy and requires supervisors to make sure children place loose materials in storage bins and sheds when they leave the playground. Because many programs have inadequate storage and are concerned about how the playground looks to parents, the constructive play needs of children are often not met, which, as we said, is a shame because it is preschoolers' favorite form of play (Wardle, 2000a).

**Social Play.** Children need lots of opportunities outside to develop basic social skills and social competencies: pushing each other on the swing, pulling a wagon carrying another child, playing together in the sand, and so on. For school-age children a place to socialize and hang out is also needed, and swivel (tire) swings are a favorite of older (six- to eight-year-old) children. Clearly, physical play, constructive play, and sociodramatic play also involve social play, especially if the equipment encourages the engagement of more than one child. Projects such as gardening, observing the weather in a separate science area, and having a picnic can be—and should be—social activities.

**Sociodramatic Play.** A good playground must have playhouses, forts, and other structures that children can change, adapt, reconfigure, impose their own meaning on, and use to expand their imagination. These structures encourage rich sociodramatic play; further, they are an ideal place for the playground to reflect the cultures of the children who use it. A playground in the Indian Pueblo in Taos, New Mexico, has oven-shaped, adobe-looking structures for dramatic play; the Seminole Indian Head Start playground includes thatched shelters, which are common to Seminole Indian communities of the swamps of Southern Florida. These culturally relevant structures are much better than the universal plastic playhouse that is so prevalent in playgrounds across the country.

Because dramatic play requires children to impose their own details, information, and meaning onto their play, and is richer and more beneficial because they do so, dramatic play structures should be very simple and basic in design and construction. A basic structure of four walls, a roof, and a window can be the child's home, a classroom, a doctor's office, or a castle. On the other hand, a realistic replica of a 7-11 convenience store can only be a 7-11, and a rocket can only be a rocket (Wardle, 2003a).

**Games with Rules.** The well-known games Drop the Hanky, Red Light—Green Light, Simon Says, and Follow the Leader, are all simple games with rules, the highest level of cognitive play (Piaget, 1962). Children need places outside to play these games, and to "all fall down" is much more pleasant on grass than on concrete.

BOX 12.3

## *Remodeling a Head Start Playground on the Crow Reservation*

**by Francis Wardle**

Charles and I speed over the wide spaces of southern Montana toward our next Head Start site. We observe deer grazing in fallow cornfields, red-tailed hawks wheeling in the expansive sky, and wild pheasants scuttling across the road in front of the car. I'm to evaluate three playgrounds on the Crow Indian reservation, make drawings and recommendation for improvements, and then assist Charles in remodeling the playgrounds.

We pull up outside the modular Head Start building, check with the head teacher, and then measure the playground that extends directly out from the building. The existing playground includes an old swing (bent in the middle), a tricycle path created directly on the grass, an old merry-go-round, and a large storage shed. A ramp attaches the playground to the elevated classrooms. The entire area is protected by a six-foot-high chain-link fence.

We pull out the tape and record the playground measurements on the clipboard, and I take a variety of photographs from every possible angle. I then talk to teachers and the local maintenance man, all members of the Crow Nation, about ideas for remodeling the playground. Then, as we drive on to the next site, I query Charles about federal requirements for playgrounds (Head Start is a federally funded program) and other issues: safety, resources, labor, purchasing rules on the reservation, and health and safety issues.

After I return home, I use our drawings, my photographs, and the notes I took from the many conversations to design the new playground. I decided to include a central climbing structure, a new swing (in a different location), a tricycle/wagon path, a sandbox, a garden, and dramatic play structures. I kept the shed for loose parts for constructive play and for storing wagons, balls, and gardening tools.

Charles contacts local tradesmen to pour the tricycle paths and plant the trees and calls the local representative of a national playground equipment company to select the specific equipment and supervise its installation.

The result of all these efforts is a safe, accessible, and challenging playground for Crow Indian Head Start children that meets Head Start performance standards.

## The Playground in Relationship to the Main Building

In hot climates the main early childhood or school building should provide shade on the playground during the hottest part of the day; in colder climates the sun must be able to warm up the playground so that children enjoy playing. As concern about skin cancer increases, leaving some existing trees in the playground becomes critical. Streams, large boulders, drainage ditches, and old stumps should be creatively (and safely) included within the overall playground design. The playground should fit into the local environment beyond the playground and not look like some artificial environment that looks more like a new car salesroom (Wardle, 2000a). Children should see local shrubs, tress, grass, flowers, and bushes extended into their playground. Including a garden in the preschool and school-age playground is great because it provides a wonderful opportunity for children and teachers to grow, care for, harvest, and eat local vegetables and crops. Children can also learn about flowering plants that are a natural defense against pests. Parents who garden, work in fields as migrant workers, or are farmers can help with these gardens.

### Going Beyond the Playground

Although young children should enjoy outdoor play in well-designed and maintained playgrounds, opportunities beyond the playground fences are vast, unimaginable, and enrich the child's life (Rivkin, 1995; Wardle, 1995). These possibilities include farms, nature preserves, wetlands, old quarries, rock formations, streams, building sites, city gardens, beaver dams, road construction sites, sugar maple sap operations, sawmills, and the like. Many cities have urban walkways and greenways, outdoor museums (some historical), parks, redevelopment sites that include wildlife and conservation areas, outdoor botanical gardens, and converted railroad tracks and old irrigation canals. Also, many colleges have experimental farms, gardens, tree nurseries, and flower gardens that children can visit. These are especially fun when the children are caring for their own garden in the playground.

Select outdoor environments beyond the playground that allow children to explore, enjoy nature, and experience basic information about how the natural world works—textures, smells, colors, tastes, and sounds. Further, children need to be exposed to four seasons and how every part of the natural world—new and dead plants, dormant and growing trees, nesting birds, burrowing animals, migrating butterflies, and hibernating insects—reflect the seasonal time of the year (Greenman, 1993, 2003). Children should also learn from these forays that each geographic area is different, depending on weather, local soil conditions, rock formations, and indigenous trees and plants.

We have a responsibility to care for children during the day in our early childhood programs and schools, but we cannot make the mistake of assuming our little building and playground is the world. And children must learn that nature, with all its transcendent, powerful glory, open spaces, and environments that challenge the body and mind, exists beyond the comfortable school or early childhood facility (Greenman, 1993).

Finally, going out beyond the school and playground enables children to know about and care for their own community: the local duck pond with the nests around the edges, the new nature preserve with the bald eagle nest, the community gardens, and the city greenhouse that start the beautiful flowers that colorfully grace the city parks every year. Children learn about their community and people who care for their community, and they learn about places in their community they can enjoy alone and with their family, outside school, and after they graduate from school (Wardle, 1995).

## AGE-SPECIFIC PLAYGROUNDS

Most early childhood programs have two playground areas: one for infants and toddlers and one for preschoolers. Some programs also serve school-age children, who require a separate playground area (Wardle, 1998). Elementary schools, both public and private, have their own school playgrounds.

## Infant/Toddler Playgrounds

In infant/toddler playgrounds, close adult supervision is essential. Therefore seats and benches for adults need to be provided near the areas where children play, and shade needs to be included (Greenman, 1988, 1993). Because infants and toddlers are in Piaget's stage of sensorimotor development, they require lots of opportunities to move and lots of sensory activities: sound, light, texture, smells and tastes from water, hills, pathways, safe plants, and so on (see Figure 12.1). Of most importance for the infant playground is close proximity to the infant area in the center for diaper changing, phone calls, first aid, and a comfort zone. This proximity will encourage adults to take infants and toddlers outside, something that is not done enough in most programs.

## Preschool Playgrounds

A preschool playground requires four general areas: equipment areas (swings, climbers, balance beams); large grass areas for running, rolling, playing games, and having picnics; hard surfaces for wagons, Big Toys, and trikes and for ball games and an outdoor classroom (woodwork, art, blocks, etc.); and areas for dramatic play (playhouse, fort, store, etc.). The dramatic play area is often scattered on the grass, but it cannot be positioned in such a way that it interferes with large motor and car-

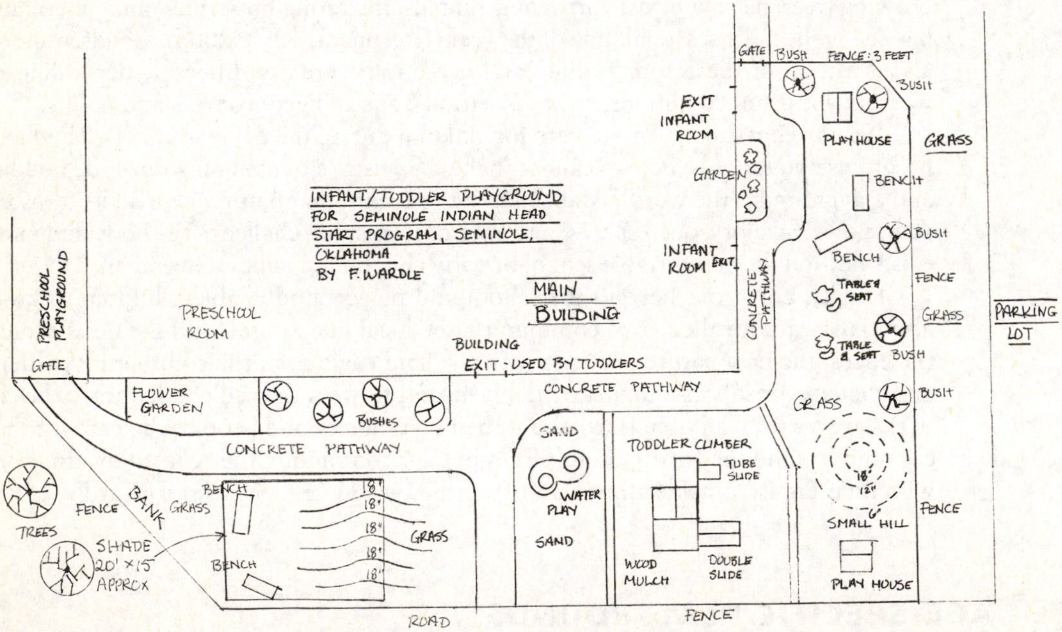


**FIGURE 12.1 Design by F. Wardle for an Infant/Toddler Playground for the Seminole Indian Head Start Program in Oklahoma.**

diovascular activities. Francis observed two beautiful new Migrant Head Start centers on the West Coast with new playgrounds. Unfortunately, both used grass simply to fill in the areas between the pathways and equipment fall-zone areas, more for aesthetics than to provide places for running, rolling, and having picnics.

As we have already discussed, it is recommended that preschool playgrounds have a garden. Gardens are wonderful ways for children to experience a vast variety and amount of leaning, from science, art, and culture to character development and math (Dunbar, 2001).

## School-Age Playgrounds

Programs for school-age children—parks, schools and before- and after-school programs—differ considerably from infant/toddler playgrounds and preschool playgrounds. Playgrounds designed for preschoolers (two to five years old) do not work for older children, partly because older children are tired of these playgrounds and partly because these playgrounds lack the physical challenges that bigger, stronger, and more coordinated children need (Wardle, 1998). Further, play needs of school-age children differ from those of preschoolers:

> They are moving from the physical play of climbing, running, crawling, and swinging to specific challenges like overhead rings and chin-up bars; they are progressing from cooperative play younger children enjoy to hanging out in groups and cliques; and they are now more interested in competitive athletic activities such as baseball, basketball, soccer, football, hockey and volleyball. (Wardle, 1998, p. 29)

These children are entering Piaget's concrete operational stage (age seven to eleven years) and Erickson's industry-versus-inferiority stage (five to twelve years). This means that school-age children can handle games with complex rules and are very motivated to master age-specific skills, including physical and social skills (Wardle, 2003a).

Unfortunately, many schools and public park playgrounds provide only for school-age children's motor play needs, ignoring their need for social play and games with rules. School-age children need a playground to call their own, not some part of a preschool playground. This area should include a variety of equipment, including the following:

- *Hangout area.* Areas where children can sit and socialize should be created. This may be as simple as picnic tables, benches, and shade in a secluded spot or equipment designed specifically for this purpose by several equipment companies (such as Kompan's 10 Plus Series of equipment).

- *Challenging physical activities.* There should be equipment that encourages isolated physical activities including chin-up bars, sit-up equipment, rope and rock climbing, overhead rings, and running challenges, including the kind of exercise areas found in parks and along public trails.

- *Games with rules and athletics.* Concrete operational children generally enjoy games with rules. They also enjoy honing their individual skills for cultural professional sports, such as basketball, baseball, soccer, hockey, cricket, and volleyball. Some playgrounds have single basketball hoops; others have basketball courts, four square hard-top areas, and even soccer fields, especially those next to a public park or a retention area pond. Volleyball, baseball, kickball, and other team games can be played on an unencumbered surface, preferably grass.

- *Adapted preschool equipment.* Preschool equipment can be made more appealing to school-age children by increasing the physical challenge and by including specific components: monkey bars, pulley or track runs, overhead rings, spiral slide, and swivel (tire) swings. The latter especially seems to meet the increasing social needs of school-age children.

## SAFETY

Accidents on playgrounds are caused by poorly designed equipment (e.g., teeter-totters, giant strides, swings); equipment that is too high; entrapments (any areas between 3½ and 9 inches high or wide), ropes and strings attached to clothing, which cause strangulation; protrusions, which cause cuts and eye injuries; and falling onto other equipment or hard surfaces, the number one cause of serious injury, which can lead to severe head injuries (Frost & Sweeney, 1996). Other accidents are caused by moving equipment, colliding with stationary equipment, hot surfaces (slides), sharp edges, playground debris, and equipment that tips over or collapses (Tinsworth & Kramer, 1990). According to the U.S. Consumer Product Safety Commission, more than 200,000 children are treated in U.S. hospital emergency rooms each year for injuries associated with playground equipment (1999). And according to Hudson et al. (2000), seventeen children die each year from playground-related injuries. One area of particular concern is the slide entrance, where clothes get entangled around a protrusion, and then the downward impact of the body on the slide causes the child's neck to break.

There are three primary areas that affect safety of young children, infants to eight years old, on playgrounds: equipment placement, supervision, and U.S. Consumer Product Safety Commission (1997) guidelines.

### Distribution and Placement of Equipment

Swings are an important piece of equipment in playgrounds, but they take up a very large area and therefore cannot be installed in small playgrounds. Swings are safe when they are adequately supervised, have safe rubber or belt seats, are situated away from traffic, preferably in a corner, and have the required amount of absorbent materials. Swings should never be attached to another piece of equipment.

Placement of other equipment can increase or decrease accidents. Active climbing equipment should be distanced from gardening and dramatic play; slide exits should be away from playing children, and climbing equipment must be a good distance away from classroom entrances and exits. Of most importance, children should not have to run through equipment to get to other equipment on the playground. Poor placement of equipment, play areas, and wagon and tricycle pathways can also cause children to collect and bottle up in certain areas, which is a formula for safety problems.

## Size of Playground

Both Head Start performance standards and state childcare licensing regulations set a minimum size for outdoor playgrounds that is based on a number of square feet per child using the playground at any one time. These standards do not provide enough space for a high-quality playground and often result in a playground that is too small and dominated by a climbing structure and a few scattered pieces of plastic dramatic play items Additionally, the new CPSC guidelines and the access regulations require considerable more space for certain equipment, such the swings and the pathway (see Figure 12.2). For example, the minimum pathway width is now five feet, to enable two wheelchairs to pass each other.

However, big is not always better. A playground that is too large poses its own problems. In a large playground children are very difficult to supervise, often resulting in teachers either doing lots of shouting or not allowing children to use the whole playground. Also, in large playgrounds equipment is often so scattered that social play is discouraged.

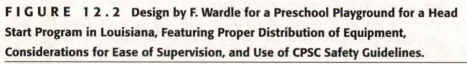

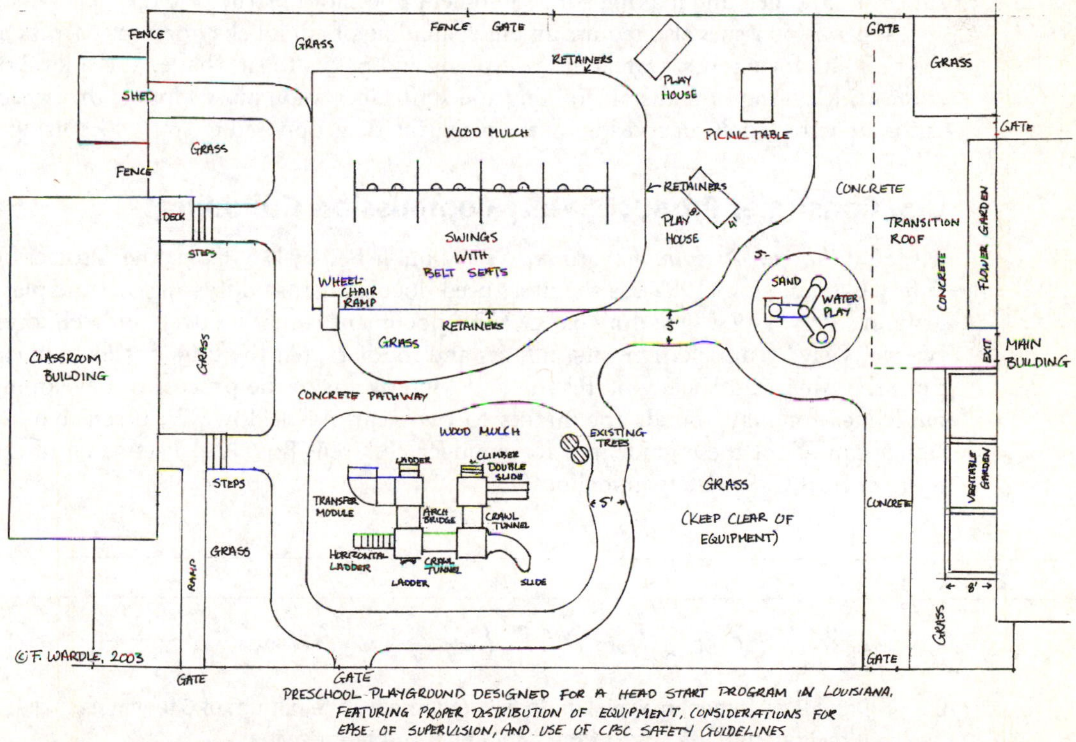


**FIGURE 12.2 Design by F. Wardle for a Preschool Playground for a Head Start Program in Louisiana, Featuring Proper Distribution of Equipment, Considerations for Ease of Supervision, and Use of CPSC Safety Guidelines.**

The ideal size of a playground depends on many factors, including the available space, supervision, equipment, and other factors. There are other ways to maximize space: scheduling children at different times, using one playground for several ages (licensing permitted), and being creative. Francis recently inspected two playgrounds in a Head Start program for three- to five-year-olds. Unfortunately, the program had divided the children into a group of younger students and older students and had built two small playgrounds. Creating one playground would have been a much better solution.

## Ease of Supervision

Active supervision of playgrounds will always be a hallmark of outdoor play safety (Wardle, 2003a). Because one of the central tasks of play is pushing physical and cognitive boundaries, children will always engage in unsafe play behaviors. Even children playing on a flat piece of grass with no equipment will find some way to endanger themselves and others. Actions that can improve supervision include eliminating blind areas (behind buildings or equipment and even under buildings), placing equipment close enough that teachers can stand at one piece of equipment and supervise another, and making sure equipment does not obstruct the teachers' view.

Supervision issues also require an understanding of adult behaviors: easy access to the building for phones, water, and restrooms and places to sit, shade, and a level of comfort. Most important, staff training and staff supervision must support the expectation of active adult supervision on the playground, as opposed to static socializing.

## U.S. Consumer Product Safety Commission Guidelines

The *Handbook for Public Playground Safety,* published by U.S. Consumer Protection Safety Commission (1997), is the most used document for addressing specific playground safety issues. One drawback of this document is that it covers only children two to twelve years old, ignoring infants and toddlers. (At the time of this publication, the American Society of Testing and Materials is in the process of developing guidelines for playgrounds for infants to two-year-olds.) However, a sensible designer can adapt these guidelines for younger children. Box 12.4 lists some of the more critical CPSC safety guidelines.

**BOX 12.4**

### *Important U.S. CPSC Safety Guidelines*

Provide absorbent material under all equipment—a minimum of 6 feet in each direction from the edge of the equipment (more for swings).

Avoid any parts that can pinch or crush fingers.

No exposed screws, nails, bolts, pieces of mental, metal pipes, etc., that protrude beyond the surface of the materials. This is a particular concern on slide entrances.

No metal slide surfaces.

All concrete footings must be below ground level.

Avoid openings–ladders, nets, windows, monkey bars, steps, etc.–between 3½ inches and 9 inches.

Avoid strings, cables, wires, rope suspended between equipment, including ropes/wires holding up new trees.

Fence in the entire area, and have secure gates.

Swings cannot be attached to other equipment; no more than 2 swings in any bay.

No metal, wood, or other heavy swing seats.

Avoid sharp edges and angles less than 55 degrees. These cause an entrapment.

Slides should have sides a minimum of 4 inches high and exits that are parallel to the ground.

Provide barriers around all equipment over 2 feet off the ground, except for entrances and exists. This includes bridges and steps.

Provide regular maintenance and repair, and keep wood splinter-free and check cracked wood for weakness.

*Source:* U.S. Consumer Product Safety Commission (1997).

## International Safety Guidelines

Canada, the United Kingdom, Australia, and the United States all have their own playground safety standards, and the European Community is developing its own. International playground equipment companies would like an international safety standard so that they can design equipment to meet just one standard rather than a variety of standards. A single standard would also help companies to sell their equipment globally.

Although everyone is obviously interested in playground safety, a variety of issues should be carefully addressed before international standards are adopted: local materials and available resources, the cultural role of play and play environments, public art in playgrounds (which obviously might not meet safety standards), supervision patterns in different cultures, geography, weather patterns, and the anthropometric properties—average size of children's bodies at specific ages—of each population for which the standard is used (Wardle, 1999a, 2000b). For example, in Brazil there are huge city parks, the weather includes severe rainstorms and extreme heat, cultural traditions include public art in public places, children in public playgrounds are carefully supervised by individual maids (nannies), and because of a lack of naturally available petroleum, plastics are expensive (Wardle 2000b). Surely, playgrounds in Brazil would require different standards from those used in the United States, the United Kingdom, or Iceland.

Yet in the absence of international playground guidelines and national standards, U.S. playground companies operating in Brazil are placing climbing structures directly onto concrete, and slides are placed less than twelve inches from walls—both extreme violations of the U.S. CPSC and the cause of many injuries in the United States. (Wardle, 2000b).

Playground safety is becoming a global issue: advisory on a playground in Abu Dhabi, the United Arab Emirates. Children wearing safety helmets cause entrapment hazards.

## Maintenance

Regular, thorough care and maintenance of playgrounds are critical for safety. Maintenance includes everything from picking up broken bottles and sweeping sand and gravel off the sidewalk to repairing broken equipment, removing dangerous equipment, and continually anticipating potential problems. Many programs assign a person to regularly check the playground using a predeveloped checklist to make sure important areas are monitored. What is included on the checklist depends on the kind of playground and equipment but might include wood splinters; loose nails or screws; protruding bolts; open S-hooks; not enough sand, gravel, or wood chips under equipment, especially swings; broken bottles and other sharp objects; entrapments; broken concrete or exposed footings; trip hazards; frayed rope; broken plastic or wood; holes in the fence; a gate without a lock; standing water; and enticing places for insects or snakes (Wardle, 1996–2003).

All early childhood programs and schools must have a budget to maintain and repair the playground. Just as classroom materials and equipment need to be repaired and replaced, playground equipment and surfaces, fences, and toys need similar care. To assume that a playground can somehow be maintenance-free is simply unrealistic. Further, for playgrounds to be rich, complex, challenging places for children to grow and play, they need to be continually changed, upgraded, and enhanced. Students and staff, depending on their interests, curricular themes, and family involvement, can initiate enrichment and change. A garden is a good example of this ever-changing nature of the playground; programs that capitalize on the natural changes of the seasons also build in this need for change.

But care must be taken when changes and additions to the playground are made. Something as simple as using a rope to dry artwork or tie-dye projects on the playground can cause a safety threat. Planting a beautiful but poisonous flower in the garden is likewise a potential danger. One approach to this dilemma is to have a knowledgeable person in charge of the playground. This person should be consulted when teachers, parents, and others improve, enhance, or simply use the playground to extend lessons, concepts, and overall program goals.

## ADA ACCESSIBILITY

The accessibility guidelines of the American Disabilities Act (ADA) are now being implemented for playgrounds. Unfortunately, they are often applied inappropriately. For example, one of the authors observed a playground in which the entire surface was covered with wood chips, thus making all equipment accessible but, in so doing, totally eliminating grass and hard surfaces and creating some additional safety problems.

The ADA recommendations require new or remodeled playgrounds to be accessible for children with disabilities, particularly children in wheelchairs. To a large extent, the requirements can be achieved by connecting all equipment with pathways (a minimum of five feet wide) and using wood mulch (what CPSC calls engineered wood fibers) or other absorbent materials that can hold a wheelchair under all equipment, including swings. For most programs a ramp to equipment is not needed (a transition module meets the requirements). Other general guidelines for making playgrounds accessible are as follows (U.S. Access Board, n.d.):

- One of each ground-level play activity must be accessible (say, one slide and one swing), not each one.
- Fifty percent of elevated activities must be accessible.
- Some activities, such as learning and play panels (steering wheels, etc.), can be made accessible by simply moving them to ground level of the equipment.
- Playgrounds that use something other than wood mulch (engineered wood fibers), such as rubber tiles, need use them only for the accessible parts of the equipment.
- Dramatic play equipment—playhouses, seats, and tables, etc.—do not need fall zones and therefore can be made accessible by simply connecting them with the pathways.
- Gardens, sand and water play areas, and the like, are made accessible by placing them on pathways and at a height to allow a wheelchair to park underneath or next to them.
- Pathways need to be a minimum of five feet wide, and have no steps or trips.
- Gates and doors need to be a minimum of 32 inches wide.

## THE ROLE OF THE TEACHER ON THE PLAYGROUND

Throughout this book we have discussed the specific role of teachers and parents in children's play. There are, of course, conflicting views on the role of adults in children's play, from total noninvolvement and allowing children to engage in free play to direct adult intervention that disrupts the vary nature of play, which we have discussed at length throughout this book. Clearly, adults have a critical role in children's play, depending on the purpose of play and the ability of the children to engage in complex social and cognitive play. There are also culture issues, such as the already mentioned Brazilian practice of constant, close supervision of young children on outdoor play equipment.

### Infant/Toddler Playground

In the infant/toddler playground, the role of the caregiver involves holding, rocking, and reading to the child and supporting children's investigation of the environment. It also involves diaper changing, protecting children from the sun, and comforting them when they fall or hurt themselves. As the toddlers begin to crawl and then walk, care must be taken to support their exploration and development while protecting their safety.

Because infants and toddlers put everything into their mouths, providers must be very diligent. However, programs must also understand the important value of having infants and toddlers enjoy the outdoors on a regular basis, weather permitting.

### Preschool Playground

Teachers in the preschool area have at least four different roles: supervision, observation, indirect strategies, and direct involvement.

**Supervision.** The first and most important role of the teacher in the preschool playground is direct supervision (Hudson et al., 2000). Direct supervision involves establishing safety rules, positioning oneself in the places of potential danger (swings, slides), anticipating possible problems, and continuously evaluating the playground for potential problems. A caution, however, must be made about overly restrictive playground rules (Greenman, 2003). We are aware of a playground where one of the rules is "no running"; another forbids back flips; a third, as we mentioned in our discussion of rough-and-tumble play, prohibits physical contact between children.

**Observation.** A great deal has been written about the role of the teacher as observer. We discussed this issue at length in Chapter 10. On the playground observation provides a rich collection of data for the teacher: How well is the playground functioning? Do new and more challenging materials need to be added? How well are children playing together? Do children who struggle indoors also have problems outdoors, or does the change in environment affect their behaviors positively? Are there activities that children enjoy outside that we can elaborate on inside? As we also discussed in Chapter 10, there are a variety of formal and less formal methods that can be used to collect information through observation.

**Indirect Strategies.** A variety of indirect teacher and caregiver strategies are discussed throughout this book that are also used in playgrounds, from arranging and monitoring the environment and scaffolding and modeling to directly participating in the activity and helping clean up at the end of the playtime. These direct behaviors have the same powerful effect on playground activities as they do on play indoors: helping children to develop within their zone of proximal development in all domains, assisting children in learning appropriate social skills and conflict resolution skills, and teaching children positive dispositions to outdoor activities. Because of the basic characteristics of play, which include the child's self-selection and direction of the activity, indirect strategies are one of the best ways for teacher to assist children playing on the playground.

**Direct Strategies.** Direct teacher strategies on the playground include intervention to prevent harm, reinforcement of safety rules, and teaching a variety of outdoor activities. The latter include teaching games such as Red Rover, Simon Says, and Red Light–Green Light; showing children how to prepare and sow the garden; and introducing art activities, science projects, and math problem-solving games. In most cases these direct interventions require the teacher to retreat from direct instruction to more of a role of scaffolder and modeler (following the normal progression within the zone of proximal development). Again, because play involves free choice and child control, teachers must avoid the temptation to control activities on the preschool playground.

### School-Age Playground

Older children are less open to direct adult intervention in play. Further, they often see play as a time to get way from adults and all that implies. This is particularly true in traditional elementary school settings. In before- and after-school programs and nontraditional school settings, there are many opportunities for teachers and children to play together: a pickup game of basketball, a formal game of soccer, working together building a fort, or caring for a garden together. At Da Nahazli School, an alternative school in Taos, New Mexico, at every recess throughout one entire school year teachers and students would engage in a roaring game of Captain Hook (a sophisticated form of tag) (Wardle, 1973). Unfortunately, in many public school playgrounds teacher are reluctant supervisors whose sole role is to keep the peace and maintain the often overly stringent playground rules.

## OUTDOOR PLAY ADVOCACY

According to Sutterby and Frost (2002), too many educators, politicians, and parents believe outdoor play takes time away from academic activities. As a result recess and physical education in many schools is limited or totally eliminated. Further, programs that do advocate outdoor play often focus on learning cognitive and academic skills, rather than encouraging needed physical pursuits and social interactions. Major reasons for this problem is the adoption of academic standards by many state departments of education, the move to accountability, and the Bush administration's No Child Left Behind initiative.

However, there is a growing number of people and organizations that are attempting to reverse this trend. They include IPA and IPA USA, People C.A.R.E, and countless individual teachers, professors, writers, and ordinary parents.

## International Association for the Child's Right to Play

The International Association for the Child's Right to Play (IPA) was founded in Denmark in 1961 as a nongovernment organization (NGO) that, among other things, "recognizes the right of the child to rest and leisure, to engage in play and recreational activities appropriate to the age of the child and to participate freely in cultural life and the arts" (IPA, 2003, p. 1). This quote is taken from the Declaration of the Rights of the Child (see Box 12.5). IPA publishes a journal, *Play Rights,* and organizes regular international conferences. There is also a variety of national IPA associations, including the American Association for the Child's Right to Play (IPA USA).

**BOX 12.5**

### U.N. Declaration of the Rights of the Child

**Proclaimed by General Assembly resolution 1386(XIV) of 20 November 1959**

*Now therefore,*

*The General Assembly*

Proclaims this Declaration of the Rights of the Child to the end that he may have a happy childhood and enjoy for his own good and for the good of society the rights and freedoms herein set forth, and calls upon parents, upon men and women as individuals, and upon voluntary organizations, local authorities and national Governments to recognize these rights and strive for their observance by legislative and other measures progressively taken in accordance with the following principles:

**Principle 1**
The child shall enjoy all the rights set forth in this Declaration. Every child, without any exception whatsoever, shall be entitled to these rights, without distinction or discrimination on account of race, colour, sex, language, religion, political or other opinion, national or social origin, property, birth or other status, whether of himself or of his family.

**Principle 2**
The child shall enjoy special protection, and shall be given opportunities and facilities, by law and by other means, to enable him to develop physically, mentally, morally, spiritually and socially in a healthy and normal manner and in conditions of freedom and dignity. In the enactment of laws for this purpose, the best interests of the child shall be the paramount consideration.

**Principle 3**
The child shall be entitled from his birth to a name and a nationality.

**Principle 4**
The child shall enjoy the benefits of social security. He shall be entitled to grow and develop in health; to this end, special care and protection shall be provided both to

him and to his mother, including adequate pre-natal and post-natal care. The child shall have the right to adequate nutrition, housing, recreation and medical services.

**Principle 5**

The child who is physically, mentally or socially handicapped shall be given the special treatment, education and care required by his particular condition.

**Principle 6**

The child, for the full and harmonious development of his personality, needs love and understanding. He shall, wherever possible, grow up in the care and under the responsibility of his parents, and, in any case, in an atmosphere of affection and of moral and material security; a child of tender years shall not, save in exceptional circumstances, be separated from his mother. Society and the public authorities shall have the duty to extend particular care to children without a family and to those without adequate means of support. Payment of State and other assistance towards the maintenance of children of large families is desirable.

**Principle 7**

The child is entitled to receive education, which shall be free and compulsory, at least in the elementary stages. He shall be given an education which will promote his general culture and enable him, on a basis of equal opportunity, to develop his abilities, his individual judgment, and his sense of moral and social responsibility, and to become a useful member of society.

The best interests of the child shall be the guiding principle of those responsible for his education and guidance; that responsibility lies in the first place with his parents.

The child shall have full opportunity for play and recreation, which should be directed to the same purposes as education; society and the public authorities shall endeavour to promote the enjoyment of this right.

**Principle 8**

The child shall in all circumstances be among the first to receive protection and relief.

**Principle 9**

The child shall be protected against all forms of neglect, cruelty and exploitation. He shall not be the subject of traffic, in any form.

The child shall not be admitted to employment before an appropriate minimum age; he shall in no case be caused or permitted to engage in any occupation or employment which would prejudice his health or education, or interfere with his physical, mental or moral development.

**Principle 10**

The child shall be protected from practices which may foster racial, religious and any other form of discrimination. He shall be brought up in a spirit of understanding, tolerance, friendship among peoples, peace and universal brotherhood, and in full consciousness that his energy and talents should be devoted to the service of his fellow men.

There is a wonderful children's book, *A Life Like Mine,* published by DK and the United Nations Children's Fund, that illustrates this declaration. This book includes beautiful photographs of children from around the world.

## People C.A.R.E.

Rebecca Lamphere is a dedicated advocate who has spearheaded a national effort to restore recess in our schools. Box 12.6 describes the valuable work that Rebecca and her group are doing to make sure that children have an opportunity to engage in free, recreational forms of play while at school.

**BOX 12.6**

### *Recess Advocate: Rebecca Lamphere*

When Rebecca Lamphere bought a new house next to an elementary school, she expected to hear the excited and joyful cries of children enjoying the age-old ritual of school recess. Instead, she heard dead silence. On investigating the situation, she was informed that school district school officials had encouraged teachers to "find something more productive to do with your children at recess."

Rebecca thought long and hard about what was going on. She discovered that other elementary schools around the nation were eliminating recess. For example, the entire Atlanta school district has an anti-recess position, and Florida has many school districts that officially discourage recess in their elementary schools.

At the same time Rebecca started taking classes in psychology, child development, and education to discover whether children really need to play. And she started an organization called People C.A.R.E. (Concerned About Recess and Education) in November 2000 to advocate for recess in elementary schools. "Children need recess to provide balance to their day . . . research shows that children who are physically active during the day do better in their academic subjects," she states with passion. And, Rebecca believes that our childhood obesity dilemma is a wakeup call for schools to provide a variety of physical activities for children, both during recess and in organized physical education programs.

People C.A.R.E. provides kits to help parents and other advocates at local schools address this issue. These kits provide summaries of research, networking hints, and proven approaches to produce change.

The results? "I get gifts from people I have never met," says Rebecca, "thanking me for what I am doing. Most people are very positive. Teachers are relieved they don't have to sneak in play and recess anymore." A Texas advocate wrote, "Thank you, thank you . . . this is a victory for you!" after Texas changed some of its policies.

Clearly, there is still work to do. Some school officials still believe that recess takes time away from important academic activities and preparing students for standardized tests; and some teachers do not see the value of play. According to the website www.ipausa.org, 40 percent of all elementary schools have either eliminated or are in the process of eliminating recess.

But according to Rhonda Clements (n.d.):

- The states of Virginia and Michigan are now mandating daily recess in elementary schools.
- Many Texas school districts are enforcing daily recess.

- The Centers for Disease Control are creating specific recommendations for school physical activities.
- The president's Healthy Kids Initiative is encouraging more physical activities in schools.

I guess one person can make a difference!

Find information about People C.A.R.E. at www.ipausa.org.

## Jim Greenman

Jim Greenman (2003) believes that contemporary playgrounds for young children deny children exposure to nature, the freedom to explore open spaces, and the opportunity to experiment, hide, and risk that all children must have to develop into mature, well-balanced citizens of a free world. "Our development as human beings is stunted without wide experience in the natural world. How can we become wise or spiritual without understanding our ecosystem and our place in it? How can we become sensual without an outdoor life and an appreciation for hot, fragrant, silky, resilient, oozing, hard and soft, and rough and smooth states of matter? How do we become physical and develop a sense of freedom without exposure to wide-open places to run and leap and climb?" (Greenman, 2003, p. 40).

Greenman believes that most childcare and elementary playgrounds are a very controlled space where children are allowed to release some physical and emotional energy for one or two short periods every day. This state of affairs is because regulators, licensing boards, teachers, and designers are interested only in supervision, order, minimal maintenance, and safety—all adult concerns. The solution, according to Greeman, is to refocus on what it is that children should be able to do outside: be able to jump, run, tumble, hide, escape, feel free, throw, crash, build, tear down, climb, make a mess, splash and pour water, rest, retreat, dig, throw, race, and destroy (Greenman, 2003). Programs need to decide how to make these things happen on the playground, and then they need to engage in a dialogue with all parties involved—teachers, parents, designers, regulators, insurance representatives, and others—to determine the extent to which they can make these things happen. In other words, Greenman believes that the design should start with what children should do outside, not with safety regulations, ease of supervision, limiting maintenance, and avoiding mess (Greenman, 2003).

## SUMMARY

Providing for the outdoor play needs of young children is a complex and challenging task. A variety of factors must be considered, including the various play needs of young children, supervision, safety, and ADA access. However, because our children experience fewer and fewer opportunities to explore nature, run, roll, climb, and swing and because outdoor play is part of being a child, we must find a variety of ways to provide quality outdoor play experiences for children, infants through age eight years. This task is made even more important as our early childhood programs focus more and more on teaching basic skills and early academics.

## PROJECTS AND ACTIVITIES

1. Observe an early childhood program that serves children, infants through preschool. Observe their playgrounds, and evaluate them based on criteria discussed in this chapter.
2. Use the safety criteria in this chapter to evaluate a public playground in your neighborhood. To what extent are playgrounds for infants/toddlers, preschoolers, and school-age children (ages six to eight) the same? To what extent are they different?
3. Preschool playgrounds that just include a central climbing structure are not good playgrounds. Respond to this statement.
4. Discuss Richard Dattner's criteria for play.
5. What are the various roles of the teacher in the outdoor playground? How does the teacher determine which role she or he needs to take?
6. Children, especially those of preschool age, appear to spend more time in constructive play than any other form of play. Why is this? What are ways a program can encourage this form of play in the playground?
7. Take an eight- by eleven-inch piece of graph paper, and design a playground for infants and toddlers, preschoolers, or school-age children (ages six to eight years). Consider all the design aspects discussed in this chapter, and make sure all four kinds of play are represented.

### Resources

*Earthworm. The Newsletter of the Early Childhood Outdoor Institute.* 1313 N. Bellevue Blvd., Bellevue, NE. 68005-4012

*The National Program for Playground Safety.* The University of Northern Iowa. Cedar Falls, Iowa 50614–0618
800-554-7529
**www.uni.edu/playground**

IPAUSA and People C.A.R.E.
**www.ipausa.org**

Recess and the Importance of Play: A position statement on young children and recess, by the National Association of Early Childhood Specialists in State Departments of Education. (NAECS/SDE) 2002.
**http://ericps.crc.uinc.edu/naes/psotion/recessplay.html**

*Play Rights, an International Journal of the theory and practice of play.* Published by IPA, 3 Earnings Street, Godmanchester, Huntingdon, Cambridge, England.

*A Life Like Mine: How Children Live Around the World.* Published by DK, in association with UNICEF, 2003.
DK Publishing,
375 Hudson Street,
New York, NY 10014
Website:
**www.dk.com**

UNICEF website:
**www.unicef.org**

# References


Allan, J., & Brown, K. (1993). Jungian play therapy in elementary schools. *Elementary Schools Guidance and Counseling, 28,* 30–31.

Allen, M. (2002). *An initial investigation of tangible interfaces in smart toys.* Paper presented at the Toys, Games, and Media Conference, International Toy Research Association, London, August.

Almqvist, B. (1994). Educational toys, creative toys. In J. Goldstein (Ed.), *Toys, play and child development* (pp. 46–66). Cambridge, England: Cambridge University Press.

American Academy of Pediatrics Committee on Hospital Care. (1993). Child life programs. *Pediatrics, 91,* 671–673.

Anderson, C., & Bushman, B. (2001). Effects of violent videogames on aggressive behavior, aggressive cognition, aggressive affect, physiological arousal, and prosocial behavior: A meta-analytic review of the scientific literature. *Psychological Science, 12(5),* 353–359.

Ardley, J., & Ericson, L. (2002). " We don't play like that here!" Understanding aggressive expressions of play. In C. Brown & C. Marchant (Eds.), *Play in practice: Case studies in young children's play* (pp. 35–47). St. Paul, MN: Redleaf Press.

Arnett, J. (2002). The psychology of globalization. *American Psychologist, 57* (10), 774–783.

Arnheim, R. (1969). *Visual thinking.* Berkeley, CA: University of California Press.

Aronson, S. (Ed.). (2002). *Healthy young children.* Washington, DC: National Association for the Education of Young Children.

Astington, J., & Jenkins, J. (1995). Theory of mind development and social understanding. *Cognition and Emotion, 9*(2/3), 151–165.

Athey, I. (1988). The relation of play to cognitive, language, and moral development. In D. Bergen (Ed.), *Play as a medium for learning and development: A handbook of theory and practice* (pp. 81–102). Portsmouth, NH: Heinemann.

Axline, V. (1969). *Play therapy.* New York: Ballantine.

Baghban, M. (1984). *Our daughter learns to read and write: A case study from birth to three.* Newark, DE: International Reading Association.

Bagley, K. (2001). *Bank tellers.* Mankato, MN: Bridgestone Books.

Bailey, D., Burchinal, M., & McWilliam, R. (1993). Age of peers and early childhood development. *Child Development, 64,* 848–862.

Bakeman, R., & Brownlee, J. (1980). The strategic use of parallel play: A sequential analysis. *Child Development, 51,* 873–787.

Bandura, A. (1977). *Social learning theory.* Englewood Cliffs, NJ: Prentice Hall.

Banks, J., & Banks, C. (Eds). (1997). *Multicultural education: Issues and perspectives.* (3rd ed.). Boston, MA: Allyn and Bacon.

Barell, J. (1995). *Teaching for thoughtfulness.* White Plains, NY: Longman.

Barnett, L. (1991). Characterizing playfulness: Correlates with individual attributes and personal traits. *Play and Culture, 4*(4), 371–393.

Barnett, L., & Kleiber, D. (1984). Playfulness and the early play environment. *Generic Psychological Monographs, 144,* 153–164.

Baron-Cohen, S. (1987). Autism and symbolic play. *British Journal of Developmental Psychology, 5,* 139–148.

Bateson, G. (1971). The message, "This is play." In R. Herron & B. Sutton-Smith (Eds.), *Child's play* (pp. 26–269). New York: Wiley.

Bauckham, R., & Hart, T. (1999). *Hope against hope: Christian eschatology at the turn of the millennium.* Grand Rapids, MI: Eerdmans.

Beach, B. (2003). Rural children's play in the natural environment. In J. Roopnarine (Series Ed.) & D. Lytle (Ed.), *Play and educational theory and practice* (pp. 183–194). Westport, CT: Greenwood Publishers.

Becher, R., & Wolfgang, C. (1977). An exploration of the relationship between symbolic representation in dramatic play and art and the cognitive and reading readiness levels of kindergarten children. *Psychology in the Schools, 14,* 377–381.

Belsky, J., & Most, R. (1981). From exploration to play: A cross-sectional study of infant free play. *Developmental Psychology, 17,* 630–639.

Benham, N., Miller, T., & Kontos, S. (1988). Pinpointing staff training needs in child care centers. *Young Children, 43* (4), 9–16.

Bennet, N., Wood, L., & Rogers, S. (1997). *Teaching through play: Teacher's thinking and classroom practice.* Buckingham, UK: Open University Press.

Benson-Hale, J. (1986). *Black children: Their roots, culture, and learning styles.* Baltimore, MD: Johns Hopkins University Press.

Bergen, D. (2002a). Preschool children's play with "Talking" and "Non-talking" rescue heroes: Effects of technology-enhanced figures on the types and themes of play.

Bergen, D. (2002b). The role of pretend play in children's cognitive development. *Early Childhood Research & Practice, 4(1).* [Online], 4(1). Available: http://ecrp.uiuc.edu/v4n1/bergen.html [2003, May 23].

Bergen, D. (2004, February). *Communicative actions and language narratives in preschoolers' play with "talking" and"nontalking" rescue heroes.* Paper presented at The Association for the Study of Play Annual Meetings, Atlanta.

Bergen, D., & Coscia, J. (2001). *Brain research and childhood education: Implications for educators.* Olney, MD: Association for Childhood Education International.

Berger, K. (2003). *The developing person through childhood.* New York: Worth Publishers.

Bergman, A., & Lefcourt, I. (1994). Self-other action play: A window into the representational world of the infant. In A. Slade & D. Wolf (Eds.), *Children at play: Clinical and developmental approaches to meaning and representation* (pp. 133–147). New York: Oxford University Press.

Berlyne, D. (1960). *Conflict, arousal and curiosity.* New York: McGraw-Hill.

Bettelheim, B. (1975). *The uses of enchantment.* New York: Random House.

Beyer, L., & Bloch, M. (1996). Theory: An analysis (part 1). In J. Chafel & S. Reifel (Eds.), *Advances in early education and day care: Theory and practice in early childhood teaching* (Vol. 8, pp. 3–39). Greenwich, CT: JAI Press.

Bishop, D., & Chace, C. (1971). Parental conceptual systems, home play environment, and potential creativity in children. *Journal of Experimental Child Psychology, 12,* 318–338.

Bjorklund, D., & Pellegrini, A. (2000). Child development and evolutionary psychology. *Child Development, 71,* 1687–1708.

Black, B. (1989). Interactive pretense: Social and symbolic skills in preschool play groups. *Merrill-Palmer Quarterly, 35*(4), 379–395.

Bloch, M., & Walsh, D. (1983, April). *Young children's activities at home: Age and sex differences in activity, location, and social context.* Paper presented at the biennial meeting of the Society for Research in Child Development, Detroit, MI.

Bloom, B. (Ed.). (1956). *Taxonomy of educational objectives. Handbook I: Cognitive domain.* New York: David McKay.

Blurton-Jones, N. (1976). Rough-and-tumble play among nursery school children. In J. S. Bruner, A. Jolly, & K. Sylva (Eds.), *Play: Its role in development and evolution* (pp. 352–363). New York: Basic Books.

Bodrova, E., & Leong, D. (1996). *Tools of the mind: The Vygotskian approach to early childhood education.* Englewood Cliffs, NJ: Prentice-Hall.

Bodrova, E., & Leong, D. J. (2003). Chopsticks and counting chips. Do play and foundational skills need to compete for the teachers' attention in an early childhood classroom? *Young Children, 58*(3), 10–17.

Bondioli, A. (2001). The adult as tutor in fostering children's symbolic play. In A. Göncü & E. Klein (Eds.), *Children in play, story, and school* (pp. 107–131). New York: Guilford.

Bornstein, M., Vibbert, M., Tal, J., & O'Donnell, K. (1992). Toddler language and play in the second year: Stability, covariation, and influences of parenting. *First Language, 12,* 323–338.

Boulton, M., & Smith, P. (1989). Issues in the study of children's rough-and-tumble play. In M. Bloch & A. Pellegrini (Eds.), *The ecological context of children's play* (pp. 57–83). Norwood, NJ: Ablex.

Boutte, G., Van Scoy, I., & Hendley, S. (1996). Multicultural and nonsexist prop boxes. *Young Children, 52*(1), 34–39.

Bowman, B. (1990). Play in teacher education: The United States perspective. In E. Klugman & S. Smilansky (Eds.), *Children's play and learning: Perspectives and policy implications* (pp. 97–111). New York: Teachers College Press.

Bowman, B. (Ed.). (2002). *Love to read: Essays in developing and enhancing early literacy skills of African American children.* Washington, DC: National Black Child Development Institute.

Bradley, R. (1985). Social-cognitive development and toys. *Topics in Early Childhood Special Education, 5*(3), 11–30.

Bredekamp, S. (Ed.). (1987). *Developmentally appropriate practice in early childhood programs serving children from birth through age 8.* Washington, DC: National Association for the Education of Young Children.

Bredekamp, S., & Copple, C. (1997). *Developmentally appropriate practice in early childhood programs* (Rev. ed.). Washington, DC: National Association for the Education of Young Children.

Bronfenbrenner, U. (1979). *The ecology of human development.* Cambridge, MA: Harvard University Press.

Bronfenbrenner, U. (1995). Developmental ecology through space and time: A future perspective. In P. Moen, G. Elder, & K. Luscher (Eds.), *Examining lives in context:*

*Perspectives on the ecology of human development.* Washington, DC: American Psychological Association.

Bronfenbrenner, U., & Ceci, S. (1994). Nature-nurture reconceptualization in developmental perspective: A bioecological model. *Psychological Review, 101*(4), 568–586.

Bronson, M. (1995). *The right stuff for children birth to 8: Selecting play materials to support development.* Washington, DC: National Association for the Education of Young Children.

Bronson, M. (2000). *Self-regulation in early childhood education: Nature and nurture.* New York: Guilford.

Brooker, L., & Siraj-Blatchford, J. (2002). 'Click on Miaow!': How children three and four years experience the nursery computer. *Contemporary Issues in Early Childhood, 3*(2), 251–273.

Brown, C. (2003, March). *Play and learning: Concerns of low income families.* Paper presented at the Playing for Keeps meetings, Yale University, New Haven, CT.

Brown, M., & Freeman, N. (2001). "We don't play that way at preschool": The moral and ethical dimensions of controlling children's play. In S. Reifel & M. Brown (Eds.), *Early education and care, and reconceptualizing play* (pp. 259–274). New York: JAI.

Brown, N., Curry, N., & Tinnich, E. (1971). How groups of children deal with common stress through play. In N. Curry & S. Arnaud (Eds.), *Play: The child strives towards self-realization* (pp. 26–38). Washington, DC: National Association for the Education of Young Children.

Brown, N., & Douglass, R. (1996). Making the invisible visible: The growth of community network organizations. In M. Root (Ed.), *The multiracial experience: Racial borders as the new frontier* (pp. 323–340). Thousand Oaks, CA: Sage.

Brown, S. (1994, Dec.). Animals at play. *National Geographic, 186*(6), 56–36.

Brown, W., Ragland, E., & Fox, J. (1988). Effects of group socialization procedures on the social interactions of preschool children. *Research in Developmental Disabilities, 9,* 359–376.

Brown, S., & Kennard, D. (Executive Producers). (2000). *The promise of play* [video/VHS]. (Available from Direct Cinema Limited, Post Box Office 10003, Santa Monica, CA 90410).

Bruner, J. (1972). The nature and uses of immaturity. *American Psychologist, 27,* 687–708.

Bruner, J. (1983). Play, thought, and language. *Peabody Journal of Education, 60*(3), 60–69.

Bruner, J. (1990). *Acts of meaning.* Cambridge, MA: Harvard University Press.

Bruner, J. (1996). *The culture of education.* Cambridge, MA: Harvard University Press.

Bruya, L., & Langendorfer, S. (Eds.). (1988). *Where our children play: Elementary school playground equipment.* Washington, DC: American Academy of Physical Education, Health, Recreation and Dance.

Buchanan, A., Gentile, D., Nelson, D., Walsh, D., & Hensel, J. (2002). *What goes in must come out: Children's media violence consumption at home and aggressive behaviors at school.* Paper presented at the International Society for the Study of Behavioral Development Conference, Ottawa, Ontario, Canada.

Bundy, A. (1997). Play and playfulness: What to look for. In L. Parham & L. Fazio (Eds.), *Play in occupational therapy for children* (pp. 52–66). St. Louis, MO: Mosby.

Burghardt, G. (1984). On the origins of play. In P. Smith (Ed.), *Play in animals and humans* (pp. 5–41). Oxford, UK: Basil Blackwell.

Burns, S., & Brainerd, C. (1979). Effects of constructive and dramatic play on perspective-taking tasks in very young children. *Developmental Psychology, 15,* 512–521.

Burton, L., & Price-Spratlen, T. (1999). Through the eyes of children: An ethnographic perspective on neighborhoods and child development. In A. Masten (Ed.), *Cultural processes in child development. The Minnesota symposia on child psychology* (Vol. 29, pp. 77–96). Mahwah, NJ: Erlbaum.

Cadwell, L. (1997). *Bringing Reggio Emilia home: An innovative approach to early childhood education.* New York: Teachers College Press.

Caldera, Y., Huston, A., & O'Brien, M. (1989). Social interactions and play patterns of parents and toddlers with feminine, masculine, and neutral toys. *Child Development, 60,* 70–76.

Carlsson-Paige, N., & Levin, D. (1987). *The war play dilemma: Balancing the needs and values in the early childhood classroom.* New York: Teachers College Press.

Carlsson-Page, N., & Levin, D. (1990). *Who's calling the shots? How to respond effectively to children's fascination with war play and war toys.* Philadelphia: New Society.

Carpenter, C., Huston-Stein, A., & Baer, D. (1978). *The relation of children's activity preference to sex-type behavior.* Paper presented at the 12th Annual Convention of the Association for Advancement in Behavior Theories, Chicago.

Carta, J., Schwartz, I., Atwater, A., & McConell, S. (1991). Developmentally appropriate practice: Appraising its appropriateness for young children with disabilities. *Topics in Early Childhood Special Education, 11*(1), 1–20.

Carter, D., & Levy, D. (1988). Cognitive aspects of early sex-role development: The influence of gender schema on preschoolers' memories for sex-typed toys and activities. *Child Development, 59,* 782–792.

Casbergue, R., & Kieff, J. (1998). Marbles, anyone? Traditional games in the classroom. *Childhood Education, 74,* 143–147.

Cazden, C. (1976). Play with language and meta-linguistic awareness: One dimension of language experience. In J. Bruner, A. Jolly, & K. Sylva (Eds.), *Play and its role in development and evolution* (pp. 603–608). New York: Basic Books.

Chandler, P. (1994). *A place for me: Including children with special needs in early care and education settings.* Washington, DC: National Association for the Education of Young Children.

Chang, P. (2003). Contextual understanding of children's play in Taiwanese kindergartens. In J. Roopnarine (Series Ed.) & D. Lytle (Ed.), *Play and educational theory and practice* (pp. 277–297). Westport, CT: Greenwood Publishers.

Chen, J. (2005). Project Spectrum approach to early education. In J. Roopnarine & J. Johnson (Eds.), *Approaches to early childhood education* (4th ed.). Columbus, OH: Merrill.

Chen, Y. (2002). *Taiwanese kindergartners' social interaction behavior and its relationship to computer software.* Unpublished doctoral dissertation, Arizona State University.

Children Now. (2001). Available at www.childrennow.org/media/video-games/2001/.

Christie, J. (1983). The effects of play tutoring on young children's cognitive performance. *Journal of Educational Research, 76,* 326–330.

Christie, J., & Enz, B. (1992). The effects of literacy play interventions on preschoolers' play patterns and literacy development. *Early Education and Development, 3,* 205–220.

Christie, J., Enz, B., & Vukelich, C. (2003). *Teaching language and literacy: Preschool through the elementary grades.* New York: Longman.

Christie, J., & Johnsen, P. (1985). Questioning the results of play training research. *Educational Psychologist, 20,* 7–11.

Christie, J., & Johnsen, P. (1987). Reconceptualizing constructive play: A review of the empirical literature. *Merrill-Palmer Quarterly, 33,* 439–452.

Christie, J., Johnsen, P., & Peckover, R. (1988). The effects of play period duration on children's play patterns. *Journal of Research in Childhood Education, 3,* 123–131.

Christie, J., & Stone, S. (1999). Collaborative literacy activity in print-enriched play centers: Exploring the "zone" in same-age and multi-age groupings. *Journal of Literacy Research, 3,* 109–131.

Christie, J., & Wardle, F. (1992). How much time is needed for play? *Young Children, 47*(3), 28–32.

Chukovsky, K. (1976). The sense of nonsense verse. In J. Bruner, A. Jolly, & K. Sylva (Eds.), *Play: Its role in development and evolution* (pp. 603–608). New York: Basic Books.

Clark, B. (1997). *Growing up gifted* (5th ed.). Upper Saddle River, NJ: Merrill.

Clegg, A., Jr. (1991). Games and simulations in social studies education. In J. Shaver (Ed.), *Handbook of research on social studies teaching and learning* (pp. 523–529). New York: Macmillan.

Clements, R. (n.d.). (Ed.). *Elementary school recess: Selected readings, games and activities for teachers and parents.* Boston, MA: IPA/USA & American Press Boston.

Clements, D., & Nastasi, B. (1993). Electronic media and early childhood education. In B. Spodek (Ed.), *Handbook of research on the education of young children* (pp. 251–275). New York: Macmillan.

Coates, S., Lord, M., & Jakabovics, E. (1975). Field dependence-independence, social-nonsocial play and sex differences in preschool children. *Perceptual and Motor Skills, 40,* 195–202.

Cohen, L. (1997, November/December). Documenting play. *Child Care Information Exchange* (Issue No. 118), 61–64.

Cole, M. (1996). *Cultural psychology: A once and future discipline.* Cambridge, MA: Harvard University Press.

Collins, A., & Kimmel, M. (1996). *Mister Rogers' Neighborhood: Children, television, and Fred Rogers.* Pittsburgh, PA: University of Pittsburgh.

Colorado Department of Education. (1991). *Colorado 2000–First Year Action Plan.* Denver, CO: Au.

Colorado Department of Education. (2000). *Title 1, Part A (Formerly Chapter 1)—Improving basic programs operated by local education agencies.* Denver, CO: Author.

Connolly, J., & Doyle, A. (1984). Relation of social fantasy play to social competence in preschoolers. *Developmental Psychology, 20,* 797–806.

Connolly, J., Doyle, A., & Reznick, E. (1988). Social pretend play and social interaction in preschoolers. *Journal of Applied Developmental Psychology, 9,* 301–313.

Cooney, T., and Radina, M. (2000). Adjustment problems in adolescence: Are multiracial children at risk? *Journal of Orthopsychiatry, 70*(4), 433–444.

Coplan, R. (2000). Assessing nonsocial play in early childhood: Conceptual and methodological approaches. In K. Gitlin-Weiner, A. Sandgrund, & C. Schaefer (Eds.), *Play diagnosis and assessment* (2nd ed., pp. 563–598). New York: Wiley.

Coplan, R. & Rubin, K. (1998). Exploring and assessing nonsocial play in the preschool: The development and validation of the preschool play behavior scale. *Social Development, 7*(1), 71–91.

Coplan, R., Wichmann, C., & Lagace-Seguin (2001). Solitary-active play behavior: A marker variable for maladjustment in the preschool? *Journal of Research in Childhood Education, 15,* 164–172.

Cordes, C., & Miller, E. (2000). *Fool's gold: A critical look at computers in childhood.* Available at www.allianceforchildhood.net/projects/computers/computers_reports_fools_gold_contents.htm.

Cornford, F. (Ed. & Trans.). (1951). *The republic of Plato.* Oxford, UK: Oxford University Press.

Corsaro, W. (1985). *Friendship and peer culture in early years.* Norwood, NJ: Ablex.

Creaser, B. (1990). *Pretend play: A natural path to learning. Australian Early Childhood Resource Booklet No. 5.* Canberra: Australian Early Childhood Association.

Creasey, G., Jarvis, P., & Berk, L. (1998). Play and social competence. In O. Saracho & B. Spodek (Eds.), *Multiple perspectives on play in early childhood education* (pp. 116–143). Albany, NY: State University of New York Press.

Crespo, C., Smit, E., Richard P., Bartlett, S., Macera, C., & Andersen, R. (2001). Television watching, energy intake, and obesity in US children. *Archives of Pediatric and Adolescent Medicine, 155*, 360–365.

Crosser, S. (1994). Making the most of water play. *Young Children, 49*(5), 28–32.

Csikszentmihalyi, M. (1990). *Flow: The psychology of optimal experience.* New York: Harper & Row.

Cuffaro, H., Nager, N., & Shapiro, E. (2005). The developmental-interaction approach at Bank Street College of Education. In J. Roopnarine & J. Johnson (Eds.), *Approaches to early childhood education* (4th ed., pp. 280–295). Columbus, OH: Merrill.

Cunningham (1998/1999). Men in child care. *Child Care Information Exchange.* Part 1, Sept/Oct, 1998, 20–22; Part 2, Jan/Feb, 1999, 66–69.

Cunningham, C., Jones, M., & Taylor, N. (1994). The child-friendly neighborhood: Some questions and tentative answers from Australian research. *International Play Journal, 2*(2), 79–95.

Curry, N. (1971). Consideration of current basic issues on play. In N. Curry & S. Arnaud (Eds.), *Play: The child strives towards self realization.* Washington, DC: National Association for the Education of Young Children.

Curry, N., & Bergen, D. (1988). The relationship of play to emotional, social, and gender/sex role development. In D. Bergen (Ed.), *Play as a medium for learning and development* (pp. 107–132). Portsmouth, NH: Heinemann.

Dahlberg, G., Moss, P., & Pence, A. (1999). *Beyond quality in early childhood education and care: Postmodern perspectives.* Philadelphia, PA: Falmer Press.

Dale, D., Corbin, C., & Dale, K. (2000). Restricting opportunities to be active during school time: Do children compensate by increasing physical activity levels after school? *Research Quarterly for Exercise and Sport, 71*(3), 240–248.

Damast, A., Tamis-LeMonda, S., & Bornstein, M. (1996). Mother-child play: Sequential interactions and the relation between maternal beliefs and behaviors. *Child Development, 67*, 1752–1766.

Damato, J., & Love, M. (2002). Explore! A child's nature. *Earthworm: The newsletter of the early childhood outdoors institute, 4*(1), 2–3.

Damon, G. (2003). Using everyday objects and materials to teach math. *Early Childhood News, 13*(1), 36–37.

Dansky, J. (1980a). Cognitive consequences of sociodramatic play and exploration training for economically disadvantaged preschoolers. *Journal of Child Psychology and Psychiatry, 20*, 47–58.

Dansky, J. (1980b). Make-believe: A mediator of the relationship between play and creativity. *Child Development, 51*, 576–579.

Dansky, J., & Silverman, I. (1973). Effects of play on associative fluency. *Developmental Psychology, 9*, 38–43.

Dansky, J., & Silverman, I. (1975). Play: A general facilitator of associative fluency. *Developmental Psychology, 11*, 104.

Dattner, R. (1969). *Design for play.* Cambridge, MA: MIT Press.

Dekylen, M., & Odom, S. (1989). Activity structure and social interaction with peers in developmentally integrated play groups. *Journal of Early Intervention, 13*, 342–352.

Davidson, J. (1998). Language and play. In D. Fromberg & D. Bergen (Eds.), *Play from birth to twelve: Contexts, perspectives, and meanings* (pp. 175–183). New York: Garland.

deMarrais, K., Nelson, P., & Baker, J. (1994). Meaning in mud: Yup'k Eskimo girls at play. In J. Roopnarine, J. Johnson, & F. Hooper (Eds.), *Children's play in diverse cultures.* Albany, NY: State University of New York Press.

Dennison, B., Erb, T., & Jenkins, P. (2002). Television viewing and television in bedroom associated with overweight risk among low-income preschool children. *Pediatrics, 109*(6), 1028–1035.

Derman Sparks (1997). *Teaching/learning anti-racism: A developmental approach.* NY: Teacher College Press.

DeVries, R. (1998). Games with rules. In D. Fromberg & D. Bergen (Eds.), *Play from birth to twelve: Contexts, perspectives, and meanings* (pp. 409–415). New York: Garland.

Dewey, J. (1934). *Art as experience.* New York: Capricorn.

Diamond, K., LeFurgy, W., & Blass, S. (1993). Attitudes of preschool children toward their peers with disabilities: A year-long investigation in integrated classrooms. *Journal of Genetic Psychology, 154*, 215–221.

Dierking, L., & Falk, J. (1994). Family behavior and learning in informal science settings: A review of the literature. *Science Education, 78*(1), 57–72.

Dockett, S. (1994). *Pretend play and young children's developing theories of mind.* Unpublished doctoral dissertation, University of Sydney, Australia.

Dorst, J. (1999).Which came first, the chicken device or the textual egg?: Documentary film and the limits of the hybrid metaphor. *Journal of American Folklore, 112*(445), 268–281.

Doyle, A., Connolly, J., & Rivest, L. (1980). The effect of playmate familiarity on the social interactions of young children. *Child Development, 51*, 217–223.

Drake, J. (2001). *Planning children's play and learning in the foundation stage.* London: David Fulton.

Dunbar, J. (2001). A Head Start garden: Nutrition education at its best. *Children and Families, 15*(3), 34–38.

Dunn, J. (1992). Sisters and brothers: Current issues in developmental research. In F. Boer & J. Dunn (Eds.), *Children's sibling relationship: Developmental and clinical issues* (pp. 1–17). Hillsdale, NJ: Erlbaum.

Dunn, L., & Herwig, J. (1992). Play behaviors and convergent and divergent thinking skills of young children attending full-day preschool. *Child Study Journal, 22*(1), 23–37.

Dunn L., & Kontos, S. (1997) Research in review: What have we learned about developmentally appropriate practice? *Young Children, 52*(5), 4–13.

Dunn, J., & Wooding, C. (1977). Play in the home and its implications for learning. In B. Tizard & D. Harvey (Eds.), *Biology of play.* London: Heinemann.

Durkin, K., & Barber, B. (2002). Not so doomed: Computer game play and positive adolescent development, *Applied Developmental Psychology, 23,* 373–392.

Dyer, K., Dunlap, G., & Winterling, V. (1990). Effects of choice making on the serious problem behaviors of students with severe handicaps. *Journal of Applied Behavior Analysis, 23,* 515–524.

Dyson, A. (2001). Donkey Kong in little bear country: A first grader's composing in the media spotlight. *The Elementary School Journal, 101*(4), 417–433.

Elias, C., & Berk, L. (2002). Self-regulation in young children: Is there a role for sociodramatic play? *Early Childhood Research Quarterly, 17,* 216–238.

Elkind, D. (1996). Young children and technology: A cautionary note. *Young Children, 51*(6), 22–23.

Elkind, D. (1999). The transformation of play. *Play, Policy, & Practice Connections,* 6(3), 1–3.

Elkind, D. (2001). The adaptive function of work and play. *Play, Policy, & Practice Connections,* 6(2), 6–7.

Elkind, D. (2003). Thanks for the memory: The lasting value of true play. *Young Children, 58*(3), 46–51.

Elkonin, D. (1978). *The psychology of play.* Moscow, Russia: Pedagogica.

Ellis, M. (1973). *Why people play.* Englewood Cliffs, NJ: Prentice-Hall.

Enz, B., & Christie, J. (1997). Teacher play interaction styles: Effects on play behavior and relationships with teacher training and experience. *International Journal of Early Childhood Education, 2,* 55–69.

Engel, B. (1995). *Considering children's art. Why and how to value their work.* Washington, DC: National Association for the Education of Young Children.

Erikson, E. (1950). *Childhood and society.* New York: Norton.

Erikson, E. (1972). Play and actuality. In M. Piers (Ed.), *Play and development* (pp. 127–167). New York: W. W. Norton.

Erwin, E., Carpenter, E., & Kontos, S. (1993, April). *What preschool teachers do when children play.* Paper presented at the meeting of the American Educational Research Association, Atlanta.

Etzioni, A. (2000). Creating good communities and good societies. *Contemporary Sociology, 29*(1), 188–190.

Fabes, R., Martin, C., & Hanish, L. (2003). Young children's play qualities in same-, other-, and mixed-sex peer groups. *Child Development, 74,* 921–932.

Fagot, B. (1981). Continuity and change in play styles as a function of sex of the child. *International Journal of Behavioral Development, 4,* 37–43.

Fagot, B., & O'Brien, M. (1994). Activity level in young children: Cross age stability, situational influences, correlates with temperament, and the perception of problem behavior. *Merrill Palmer Quarterly, 40*(3), 378–398.

Family Psychological Consultants. (1992). *Sandplay therapy.* Greeley, CO: Author.

Farran, D., Silveri, B., & Culp, A. (1991). Public school preschools and the disadvantaged. *New Directions for Child Development, 53,* 65–73.

Farver, J., Kim, Y., & Lee, Y. (1995). Cultural differences in Korean- and Anglo-American preschoolers' social interaction and play behaviors. *Child Development, 66,* 1088–1099.

Farver, J., Kim, Y., & Lee-Shin, Y. (2000). Within cultural differences: Examining individual differences in Korean American and European American preschoolers' social pretend play. *Journal of Cross-Cultural Psychology, 31,* 583–602.

Fasoli, L. (1996). Places for wandering and playing. *Play, Policy, & Practice Connections, 1*(5), 6.

Fein, G. (1987). Pretend play: Creativity and consciousness. In P. Gorlitz & J. Wohlwill (Eds.), *Curiosity imagination, and play* (pp. 281–304). Hillsdale, NJ: Erlbaum.

Fein, G. (1997, April). *Play and early childhood teacher education: Discussant remarks.* Symposium presented at the Association for the Study of Play Meetings, Washington, DC.

Fein, G., Ardila-Rey, A., & Groth, L. (2000). The narrative connection: Stories and literacy. In K. Roskos & J. Christie (Eds.), *Play and literacy in early childhood: Research from multiple perspectives* (pp. 27–43). Mahwah, NJ: Erlbaum.

Fein, G., Johnson, D., Kosson, N., Stork, L., & Wasserman, L. (1975). Stereotypes and preferences in the toy choices of 20-month boys and girls. *Developmental Psychology, 11,* 527–528.

Feitelson, W., & Ross, G. (1973). The neglected factor-play. *Human Development, 16,* 202–223.

Fenson, L., Kagan, J., Kearsley, R., & Zelazo, P. (1976). The developmental progression of manipulative play in the first two years. *Child Development 47,* 232–239.

Fenson, L., & Ramsay, D. (1980). Decentration and integration of the child's play in the second year. *Child Development, 51,* 171–178.

Fernie, D. (1988). Becoming a student: Messages from first settings. *Theory into Practice, 27,* 3–10.

Fewell, R., & Rich, J. (1987). Play assessment as a procedure for examining cognitive, communication, and social skills in multihandicapped children. *Journal of Psychoeducational Assessment, 2,* 107–118.

Field, T. (1980). Preschool play: Effects of teacher/child ratios and organization of classroom space. *Child Study Journal, 10,* 191–205.

File, N., & Kontos, S. (1993). The relationship of program quality to children's play in integrated early intervention settings. *Topics in Early Childhood Special Education, 13*(1), 1–18.

Fischer, M., & Gillespie, C. (2003). One Head Start classroom's experiences: Computers and young children's development. *Young Children, 58*(4), 85–91.

Fish, J. (Ed.). (2002). *Race and intelligence: Separating science from myth.* Mahwah, NJ: Erlbaum.

Fishbein, H., & Imai, S. (1993). Preschoolers select playmates on the basis of gender and race. *Journal of Applied Developmental Psychology, 14,* 303–316.

Fisher, E. (1992). The impact of play on development: A meta-analysis. *Play & Culture, 5,* 159–181.

Flynn, L., & Kieff, J. (2002). Including everyone in outdoor play. *Young Children, 57*(3), 20–26.

Forman, G. (1998). Constructive play. In D. Fromberg & D. Bergen (Eds.), *Play from birth to twelve and beyond: Contexts, perspectives, and meanings* (pp. 392–400). New York: Garland.

Forman, G., & Kuschner, D. (1984). *The child's construction of knowledge: Piaget for teaching children.* Washington, DC: National Association for the Education of Young Children.

Forman, G., & Landry, C. (2000). The constructivist perspective on early education: Applications to children's museums. In J. Roopnarine & J. Johnson (Eds.), *Approaches to early childhood education* (3rd ed., pp. 149–174). Upper Saddle River, NJ: Merrill/Prentice Hall.

Franklin, M. (1985, March). *Play and the early evolution of social life: Views of two-year-olds at school.* Paper presented at the Anthropological Association for the Study of Play, Washington, DC.

Freie, C. (1999). Rules in children's games and play. In S. Reifel (Ed.), *Play contexts revisited* (pp. 83–100). Stamford, CT: Ablex.

Freud, S. (1961). *Beyond the pleasure principle.* New York: Norton.

Friedrich, L., & Stein, A. (1975). Prosocial television and young children: The effects of verbal labelling and role playing on learning and behavior. *Child Development, 46,* 27–38.

Fromberg, D. (2002). *Play and meaning in early childhood education.* Boston: Allyn and Bacon.

Frost, J. (1992). *Play and playscapes.* Albany, NY: Delmar.

Frost, J., & Klein, B. (1979). *Children's play and playgrounds.* Boston: Allyn and Bacon.

Frost, J., Shin, D., & Jacobs, P. (1998). Physical environments and children's play. In O. Saracho & B. Spodek (Eds.). *Multiple perspectives on play in early childhood education.* Albany: State University of New York Press.

Frost, L., & Sweeney, T. (1996). *Causes and prevention of playground injuries and litigation: Case studies.* Wheaton, MD: Association for Childhood Education International.

Furstenberg, F., Jr. (1993). How families manage risk and opportunity in dangerous neighborhoods. In W. J. Wilson (Ed.), *Sociology and the public agenda* (pp. 231–258). Newbury Park, CA: Sage Publications.

Gabbard, C. (2000). Physical education: Should it be part of the core curriculum? *Principal, 79*(3), 29–31.

Gall, M. D., Borg, W. R., & Gall, J. P. (1996). *Educational research: An introduction* (6th ed). White Plains, NY: Longman.

Gallahue, D. (1993). Motor development and movement skill acquisition in early childhood education. In B. Spodek (Ed.), *Handbook of research on the education of Young Children.* New York: Mcmillan.

Gandini, L. (1998). Educational and caring spaces. In C. Edwards, L. Gandini, & G. Forman (Eds.), *The hundred languages of children: The Reggio Emilia approach—Advanced reflections* (2nd ed., pp. 161–178). Greenwich, CT: Ablex.

Garbarino, J. (1995). Affirmation and acceptance: Creating identity for children. In J. Garbarino (Ed.), *Raising children in a socially toxic environment* (pp. 89–100). San Francisco: Jossey-Bass.

Gardner, H. (1980). *Artful scribbles: The significance of children's drawings.* New York: Basic Books.

Gardner, H. (1983). *Frames of mind: The theory of multiple intelligences.* New York: Basic Books.

Gardner, H. (1989). The key in the slot: Creativity in a Chinese key. *Journal of Aesthetic Education, 23*(1), 141–155.

Gardner, H. (1999). *Intelligence reframed: Multiple intelligence for the 21st century.* New York: Basic Books.

Garvey, C. (1974). Some properties of social play. *Merrill-Palmer Quarterly, 20,* 163–180.

Garvey, C. (1977). *Play.* Cambridge, MA: Harvard University Press.

Garvey, C. (1979). An approach to the study of children's role play. *The Quarterly Newsletter of the laboratory of Comparative Human Cognition, 1*(4), 69–73.

Garvey, C., & Berndt, R. (1977, September). *The organization of pretend play.* Paper presented at the Annual Meeting of the American Psychological Association, Chicago.

Gaskin, S. (1999). Children's daily lives in a Mayan village: A case study of culturally constructed roles and activities. In A. Goncu (Ed.), *Children's engagement in the world: Sociocultural perspectives* (pp. 25–61). New York: Cambridge University Press.

Gentile, S., & Walsh, D. (2002). A normative study of family media habits. *Applied Developmental Psychology, 23,* 157–178.

Gesell, A. (1940). *The first five years of life: A guide to the study of the preschool child.* New York: Harper & Brothers.

Gilligan, C. (1982). *In a different voice: Psychological theory and women's development.* Cambridge, MA: Harvard University Press.

Gleason, T., Sebanc, A., McGinley, J., & Hartup, W. (1997, April). *Invisible friends and personified objects: Qualitative differences in relationships with imaginary companions.* Annual meeting of the Society for Research in Child Development, Washington, DC.

Glickman, C. (1984). Play in public school settings: A philosophical question. In T. Yawkey & A. Pellegrini (Eds.), *Child's play: Developmental and applied* (pp. 255–271). Hillsdale, NJ: Erlbaum.

Goerner, S. (1994). Chaos and the evolving ecological universe. Langhorne, PA: Gordon & Breach.

Goldhaber, J. (1994). If we call it science, then can we let the children play? *Childhood Education, 71,* 24–27.

Goldstein, J. (1992). Sex differences in aggressive play and toy preference. In K. Bjorkqvist & P. Niemela (Eds.), *Of mice and women: Aspects of female aggression.* New York: Academic Press.

Goldstein, J. (1995). Aggressive toy play. In A. Pellegrini (Ed.), *The future of play theory* (pp. 127–150). Albany, NY: State University of New York Press.

Goldstein, J., Buckingham, D., & Brougere, G. (2004). *Toys, games, and media.* Mahwah, NJ: Erlbaum.

Golomb, C., & Cornelius, C. (1977). Symbolic play and its cognitive significance. *Developmental Psychology, 13,* 246–252.

Goncu, A., & Kessel, F. (1984). Children's play: A contextual-functional perspective. In F. Kessel & A. Goncu (Eds.), *Analyzing children play dialogues* (pp. 5–22). San Francisco: Jossey-Bass.

Goncu, A., Tuermer, U., Jain, J., & Johnson, D. (1999). Children's play as cultural activity. In A. Goncu (Ed.), *Children's engagement in the world: Sociocultural perspectives* (pp. 148–170). New York: Cambridge University Press.

Gonzalez-Mena, J. (1993). *The child in the family and the community.* New York: Merrill.

Gonzalez-Mena, J. (1997). *Multicultural issues in childcare.* Mountain View, CA: Mayfield.

Gonzalaz-Mena, J. (2001). *Foundations: Early childhood education in a diverse society* (2nd ed.). Mountain View, CA: Mayfield.

Goodman, J. (1992). *When slow is fast enough: Educating the delayed preschool child.* New York: The Guilford Press.

Goodson, B., & Bronson, M. (1985). *Guidelines for relating children's ages to toy characteristics.* Contract No. CPSC-85-1089. Washington DC: U.S. Consumer Product Safety Commission.

Gore, A., & Gore, T. (2002). *Joined at the heart: The transformation of the American family.* New York: Holt.

Götz, I. (1977). Play in the classroom: Blessing or curse? *Educational Forum, 41,* 329–334.

Gould, S. (1995). *Full house: The spread of excellence from Plato to Darwin.* New York: Harmony Books.

Gowen, J. (March, 1995). The early development of symbolic play. *Young Children,* 75–81.

Greenberg, R., & Field, T. (1982). Temperament ratings of handicapped infants during classroom, mother and teacher interactions. *Journal of Pediatric Psychology, 7,* 387–405.

Greenfield, P. (1994). Video games as cultural artifacts. *Journal of Applied Developmental Psychology, 15,* 3–12.

Greenman, J. (1987). Thinking about the aesthetics of children's environments. *Child Care Information Exchange, 58,* 9–12.

Greenman, J. (1988). *Caring spaces, learning places: Children's environments that work.* Redmond, WA: Exchange Press.

Greenman, J. (1993). It ain't easy being green: Beginnings workshops. *Child Care Information Exchange, 91* (May/June), 36–37.

Greenman, J. (2003). Are we losing ground? *Child Care Information Exchange, 150,* 40–42.

Grieshaber, S., & Cannella, G. S. (Eds.). (2001). *Embracing identities in early childhood programs.* New York: Teachers College Press.

Grinder, B., & Johnson, J. (1994, April). *Gender-related teacher behavior and interventions and their consequences for preschool children at free play in day care settings: Preliminary results.* Paper presented at the meeting of the American Educational Research Association, New Orleans.

Gross, D. (2003). An introduction to research in psychology: Learning to observe children at play. In J. Roopnarine (Series Ed.) & D. Lytle (Ed.), *Play & Cultural Studies, Vol. 5: Play and educational theory and practice* (pp. 33–41). Westport, CT: Greenwood.

Guralnick, M. J. (1981). The efficacy of integrating handicapped children in early childhood settings: Research implications. *Topics in Early Childhood Special Education, 1*(1), 57–71.

Haight, W. (1998). Adult direct and indirect influences on play. In D. Fromberg & D. Bergen (Eds.), *Play from birth to twelve, and beyond: Contexts, perspectives, and meanings* (pp. 259–264). New York: Garland.

Haight, W. (1999). The pragmatics of caregiver-child pretending at home: Understanding culturally specific socialization practices. In A. Goncu (Ed.), *Children's engagement in the world: Sociocultural perspectives.* Cambridge, UK: Cambridge University Press.

Haight, W., & Black, J. (2001). A comparative approach to play: Cross-species and cross-cultural perspectives of play in development. Essay review of *Play and exploration in children and animals* by Thomas G. Power. *Human Development, 44,* 228–234.

Haight, W., & Miller, P. (1993). *Pretending at home: Early development in a sociocultural context.* Albany, NY: State University of New York Press.

Hale, J. (1994). *Unbank the fire: Visions for the education of African American Children.* Baltimore, MD: Johns Hopkins University Press.

Hale-Benson, J. E. (1986). *Black children: Their roots, culture and learning styles.* Baltimore, MD: Johns Hopkins Press.

Hall, E. (1969). *The hidden dimension.* Garden City, NY: Doubleday.

Hall, E. (1977). *Beyond culture.* Garden City, NJ: Anchor Press/Doubleday.

Hall, G. (1897). *The story of a sand-pile.* New York: E. L. Kellogg.

Hall, N. (1987). *The emergence of literacy.* Portsmouth, NH: Heinemann.

Han, M. (2002, February). *A bioecological view of play-literacy research.* Paper presented at the meeting of The Association for the Study of Play, Santa Fe, NM.

Han, M., & Christie, J. (2001). Environmental factors in play: Space, materials, and time. *International Journal of Early Childhood Education, 7,* 149–162.

Harper, L., & Sanders, K. (1975). Preschool children's use of space: Sex differences in outdoor play. *Developmental Psychology, 11,* 119.

Harrist, T., Zaia, A., Bates, J., Dodge, K., & Pettit, G. (1997). Subtypes of social withdrawal in early childhood: Sociometric status and social-cognitive differences across four years. *Child Development, 68,* 278–294.

Hartle, L. (1996). Effects of additional materials on preschool children's outdoor play behaviors. *Journal of Research in Childhood Education, 11,* 68–81.

Hartley, M. (2002). Helping parents take the lead: Preparing children for health care procedures. In C. Brown & C. Marchant (Eds.), *Play in practice: Case studies in young children's play* (pp. 107–113). St. Paul, MN: Redleaf Press.

Hartup, W. (1983). The peer system. In E. Hetherington (Ed.) & P. Mussen (Series Ed.), *Handbook of child psychology: Vol. 4. Socialization, personality, and social development.* New York: Wiley.

Haugland, S. (1997). What role should technology play in young children's learning? *Young Children, 54*(6), 26–31.

Haugland, S. (1999). The newest software that meets the developmental needs of young children. *Early Childhood Education Journal, 26*(4), 245–254.

Haugland, S., & Wright, J. (1997). *Young children and technology: A world of discovery.* Boston: Allyn and Bacon.

Hay-Cook, M. (1996). What I learned in school one day. *Teaching preK–8, 26*(7), 60–61.

Haywood, K. (1986). *Life span motor development.* Champaign, IL: Human Kinetic Publishers.

Heft, T., & Swaminathan, S. (2002). The effects of computers on the social behavior of preschoolers. *Journal of Research in Childhood Education, 16,* 162–174.

Heintz-Knowles, K., & Henderson, J. (2001). *Fair play? Violence, gender and race in video games.* Available at www.childrennow.org/media/video-games/2001.

Helm, J., & Beneke, S. (Eds.). (2003). *The power of projects.* Washington, DC: National Association for the Education of Young Children.

Helm, J., & Katz, L. (2001). *Young investigators. The project approach in the early years.* New York, Washington, DC: Teacher College Press and NAEYC.

Henniger, M. (1985). Preschool children's play behaviors in an indoor and outdoor environment. In J. Frost & S. Sunderlin (Eds.), *When children play.* Wheaton, MD: Association for Childhood Education International.

Hewit, J. S. (2001). Can play-based curriculum survive the standards storm? A teacher educator's perspective. *Play, Policy, & Practice Connections, 6*(2), 3–5.

Hill, D. (1977). *Mud, sand and water.* Washington, DC: National Association for the Education of Young Children.

Hills, T. (1993). Assessment in context: Teachers and children at work. *Young Children, 48*(5), 20–28.

Hirsch, E. (1996). *The block book* (3rd ed.). Washington DC: National Association for the Education of Young Children.

Hoijer, H. (1954). The Sapir-Whorf hypotheses. In H. Hoija, (Ed.), *Language and culture.* Chicago, IL: University of Chicago Press.

Holmes, R. (1992). Play during snacktime. *Play and Culture, 5,* 295–304.

Howard, S., & Roberts, S. (2002). Winning hearts and minds: Television and the very young audience. *Contemporary Issues in Early Childhood, 3*(3), 315–337.

Howes, C., & Matheson, C.(1992). Sequences in the development of competent play with peers: Social and social pretend play. *Developmental Psychology, 28,* 961–974.

Howes, C., & Smith, E. (1995). Relations among child care quality, teacher behavior, children's play activities, emotional security, and cognitive activity in child care. *Early Childhood Research Quarterly, 10,* 381–404.

Howes, C., Unger, O., & Seidner, L. (1989). Social pretend play in toddlers: Parallels with social play and solitary pretend. *Child Development 60,* 77–84.

Hsiung, P. (2000). *Conceptions of childhood in traditional China.* Unpublished manuscript. Taipei, Taiwan: Institute of Modern History, Academia Sinica.

Hudson, D., Mack, M., & Thompson, D. (2000). *How safe are America's playgrounds. A national profile of childcare, school and park playgrounds.* Cedar Falls, IA: The National Program for Playground Safety.

Hughes, M., & Hutt, C. (1979). Heart-rate correlates of childhood activities: Play, exploration, problem-solving and day dreaming. *Biological Psychology, 8,* 253–263.

Humphreys, A., & Smith, P. (1984). Rough-and-tumble play in preschool and playground. In P. Smith (Ed.), *Play in animals and humans* (pp. 241–270). London: Blackwell.

Hutt, C. (1966). Exploration and play in children. In *Play, Exploration and Territory in Mammals. Symposia of the Zoological Society of London, 18,* 61–81.

Hutt, C. (1971). Explorational play in children. In *Play, exploration and territory in mammals. Symposia of the zoological society of London, 18,* 61–81.

Hutt, S., Tyler, S., Hutt, C., & Christopherson, H. (1989), *Play, exploration, and learning: A natural history of the pre-school.* New York: Routledge.

Hyun, E., & Marshall, D. (1997). Theory of multiple/multiethnic perspective-taking ability for teachers' developmentally and culturally appropriate practice (DCAP). *Journal of Research in Childhood Education, 11,* 188–198.

IRA/NAEYC. (1998). Learning to read and write: Developmentally appropriate practices for young children. *Young Children, 53*(4), 30–46.

Ihn, H. (1998). Analysis of preschool children's equipment choices and play behaviors in out-door play. *Early Childhood News, 10*(4), 20–25.

International Association for the Child's Right to Play. (2003). Web site: http://www.ipausa.org page 1 of website.

Isaacs, S. (1930). *Intellectual growth in young children.* London: Routledge & Kegan Paul.

Jacob (1984). Learning literacy through play: Puerto Rican kindergarten children. In H. Goelman, A. Oberg, & F. Smith (Eds.), *Awakening to literacy* (pp. 73–86). Portsmouth, NH: Heinemann.

Jacobson, J. (1981). The role of inanimate objects in early peer interaction. *Child Development, 52,* 618–626.

Jago, L. (1971). *Learning through experience.* London: London Adventure Playground Association.

Janson, U. (2001). Togetherness and diversity in pre-school play. *International Journal of Early Years Education, 9*(2), 135–143.

Jarrett, O. (1997). Science and math through role-play centers in the elementary classroom. *Science Activities, 34*(2), 13–19.

Jarrett, O., Farokhi, B., Young, C., & Davies, G. (2001). Boys and girls at play: recess at a southern urban elementary school. In S. Reifel (Ed.), *Theory in context and out* (pp. 147–170). Westport, CT: Ablex.

Jeffree, D., & McConkey, R. (1976). An observation scheme for recording children's imaginative doll play. *Journal of Child Psychology and Psychiatry, 17,* 189–197.

Jenkins, M., & Astington, J. (2000). Theory of mind and social behavior: Causal models tested in a longitudinal study. *Merrill-Palmer Quarterly, 46*(2), 203–220.

Jennings, K. (1975). People versus object orientation, social behavior, and intellectual abilities in preschool children. *Developmental Psychology, 11,* 511–519.

Jenvey, V., & Jenvey, H. (2002). Criteria used to categorize children's play: Preliminary findings. *Social Behavior and Personality, 30*(8), 733–740.

Johnson, J. (1983). Context effects on preschool children's symbolic behavior. *Journal of Genetic Psychology, 143,* 259–268.

Johnson, J. (1994). The challenge of incorporating research on play into the practice of preschool education. *Journal of Applied Developmental Psychology, 15,* 603–618.

Johnson, J., Christie, J., & Yawkey, T. (1999). *Play and early childhood development* (2nd ed.). New York: Longman.

Johnson, J., Ershler, J., & Bell, C. (1980). Play behavior in a discovery-based and a formal education preschool program. *Child Development, 51,* 271–274.

Johnson, J., & Roopnarine, J. (1983). The preschool classroom and sex differences in children's play. In M. Liss (Ed.), *Social and cognitive skills: Sex roles and children's play.* New York: Academic Press.

Jones, E. (2003) Viewpoint: Playing to get smart. *Young Children, 58*(3), 32–36.

Jones, E., & Reynolds, G. (1992). *The play's the thing: Teachers' roles in children's play.* New York: Teachers' College Press.

Kagan, S., & Cohen, N. (2000). *Not by chance: Creating an early care and education system for America's children.* New Haven, CT: Bush Center in Child Development and Social Policy at Yale University.

Kaiser, B., & Rasminsky, J. (2003). Opening the culture door. *Young Children, 58*(4), 53–56.

Kalff, M. (1993). Twenty points to be considered in the interpretation of a sandplay. *On Sandplay Therapy, 2*(2), 17–33.

Kamii, C. (1985). *Young children reinvent arithmetic.* New York: Teachers College Press.

Kamii, C. (1989). *Young children continue to reinvent arithmetic, 2nd grade: Implications of Piaget's theory.* New York Teachers College Press.

Kamii, C., & Lewis, B. (1992). Primary arithmetic: The superiority of games over worksheets. In V. Dimidjian (Ed.). *Play in place in public education for young children* (pp. 85–103). Washington, DC: National Education Association.

Karnes, M. (1979). Young handicapped children can be gifted and talented. *Journal for the Education of Gifted, 2*(3), 157–172.

Katz, L. (1985). *Dispositions in early childhood education.* ERIC/EECE Bulletin, 18(2), 1–3.

Katz, L., & Chard, S. (2005). The project approach: An overview. In J. Roopnarine & J. Johnson (Eds.), *Approaches to early childhood education* (4th ed., pp. 296–310). Columbus, OH: Merrill.

Katz, L., & McClellan, D. (1997). *Fostering social competence: The teacher's role.* Washington, DC: National Association for the Education of Young Children.

Kieff, J., & Casbergue, R. (2000). *Playful learning and teaching: Integrating play into preschool and primary programs.* Boston: Allyn and Bacon.

King, N. (1979). Play: The kindergartners' perspective. *Elementary School Journal, 80,* 81–87.

King, N. (1982). Work and play in the classroom. *Social Education, 46,* 110–113.

King, N. (1987). Elementary school play: Theory and research. In J. Block & N. King (Eds.), *School play* (pp. 143–165). New York: Garland.

Kinsman, C., & Berk, L. (1979). Joining the block and housekeeping areas: Changes in play and social behavior. *Young Children, 35*(1), 66–75.

Kishimoto, T. (2002). Toys and the public policy for child education in Brazil. Paper presented at the World Congress–Toys, Games, and Media, London.

Kitson, N. (1994). "Please Miss Alexander: Will you be the robber?" Fantasy play: A case for adult intervention. In J. Moyla (Ed.), *The excellence of plays* (pp. 88–98). Buckingham, UK: Open University Press.

Klugman, E. (1990). Early childhood moves into public schools: Mix or meld. In E. Klugman & S. Smilansky (Eds.), *Children's play and learning: Perspectives and policy implications* (pp. 188–209). New York: Teachers College Press.

Kohlberg, L. (1976). Moral stages and moralization: The cognitive-developmental approach. In T. Lickona (Ed.), *Moral development and behavior.* New York: Holt, Rinehart and Winston.

Kontos, S. (1999). Preschool teachers' talk, roles, and activity settings during free play. *Early Childhood Research Quarterly, 14,* 363–382.

Kritchevsky, S., Prescott, E., & Walling, L. (1977). *Planning environments for young children: Physical space.* Washington DC: National Association for the Education of Young Children.

Kritchevsky, S., Prescott, E., & Walling, L. (1999). Planning environments for young children: Physical space. In K. Paciorek & J. Munro (Eds.), *Sources: Notable selections in early childhood* (2nd ed., pp 152–157). Guilford, CT: Dushkin/McGraw Hill.

LaFreniere, P., Strayer, F., & Gauthier, R. (1984). The emergence of same-sex affiative preferences among preschool peers: A developmental ethnological perspective. *Child Development, 55,* 1958–1965.

Lamb, M. (1977). The development of parental preferences in the first two years of life. *Sex Roles, 3,* 495–497.

Lamb, M., Easterbrooks, A., & Holden, G. (1980). Reinforcement and punishment among preschoolers: Characteristics, effects, and correlates. *Child Development, 51,* 1230–1236.

Lander, T. (1993). *Transdisciplinary play-based assessment: A functional approach to working with young children. Revised Edition.* Baltimore, MD: Paul H. Brookes.

Landreth, G. (2002). *Play therapy: The art of the relationship* (2nd ed.). New York: Brunner-Routledge.

Lee, D. (2002). *Sylvia's garage.* Bothell, WA: Wright Group.

Lee, E., Hong, Y., Cho, K., & Eum, J. (2001). A study of children's traditional play in Korea. *The Journal for the Study of Early Childhood Education, 21*(1), 117–140.

Leslie, A. (1987). Pretense and representation: The origins of "theory of mind." *Psychological Review, 94,* 412–426.

Levin, D. (2003). Teaching young children in violent times: Building a peaceable classroom (2nd ed.). Washington, DC: National Association for the Education of Young Children.

Levin, D., & Carlsson-Paige, N. (1994). Developmentally appropriate television: Putting children first. *Young Children, 49,* 38–44.

Levin, D., & Rosenquest, B. (2001). The increasing role of electronic toys in the lives of infants and toddlers: Should we be concerned? *Contemporary Issues in Early Childhood, 2*(2), 242–247.

Li, A. (1981). Play and the mentally retarded. *Mental Retardation, 19,* 121–126.

Liang, P., & Johnson, J. (1999). Using technology to enhance early literacy through play. *Computers in the School, 15*(1), 55–64.

Lickona, T. (1983). *Raising good children.* New York: Basic Books.

Lieberman, J. N. (1977). *Playfulness: Its relationship to imagination and creativity.* New York: Academic Press.

Lillard, A. (1998). Playing with a theory of mind. In O. Saracho & B. Spodek (Eds.), *Multiple perspectives on play in early childhood education* (pp. 11–33). Albany, NY: State University of New York Press.

Lillard, A. (2002). Pretend play and cognitive development. In U. Goswami (Ed.), *Blackwell handbook of childhood cognitive development* (pp. 188–205). Oxford, UK: Blackwell Publishing.

Linder, T. (1993). *Transdisciplinary play-based assessment* (Rev. ed.). Baltimore, MD: Paul H. Brookes.

Lindsey, E., & Mize, J. (2001). Contextual differences in parent-child play: Implications for childrens gender role development, *Sex Roles, 44*(3/4), 155–176.

Liss, M. (1981). Patterns of toy play: An analysis of sex differences. *Sex Roles, 7,* 1143–1150.

Lloyd, B., & Howe, N. (2003). Solitary play and convergent and divergent thinking skills in preschool children. *Early Childhood Research Quarterly, 18,* 22–41.

Loughlin, C., & Suina, J. (1982). *The learning environment: An instructional strategy.* New York: Teacher's College Press.

Lous, A., deWit, C., Bruyn, E., Riksen-Walraven, J., & Rost, H. (2000). Depression and play in early childhood: Play behavior of depressed and nondepressed 3- to 6-year-olds in various play situations. *Journal of Emotional and Behavioral Disorders, 8*(4), 249–260.

Lowell, C. (2000). *Christopher Lowell's seven layers of design: Fearless, fabulous decorating.* New York: Discovery Communications.

Lynch, E. (1998). Developing cross-cultural competence. In E. Lynch & M. Hansen. (Eds.), *Developing cross cultural competence: A guide for working with children and their families* (pp. 47–86). Baltimore, MD: Paul H. Brookes.

Maccoby, E. (1990). Gender and relationship: A developmental account. *American Psychologist, 45*(4), 513–520.

Maccoby, E. (1998). *The two sexes: Growing up apart, coming together.* Cambridge, MA: Belknap.

Maccoby, E., & Jacklin, C. (1987). Sex segregation in childhood. In H. Reese (Ed.), *Advances in child development and behavior* (pp. 239–287). Orlando, FL: Academic Press.

Maccoby, E., & Jacklin, C. (1974). *The psychology of sex differences.* Stanford, CA: Stanford University Press.

MacDonald, K. (Ed.). (1993). *Parent-child play: Descriptions and implications.* Albany, NY: State University of New York Press.

Mahoney, J. (2000). School extracurricular activity participation as a moderator in the development of antisocial patterns. *Child Development, 71,* 502–516.

Maltz, D., & Borker, R. (1982). A cultural approach to male-female miscommunication. In J. Gumperz (Ed.), *Language and social identity* (pp. 196–216). New York: Cambridge University Press.

Manning, K., & Sharp, A. (1977). *Structuring play in the early years at school.* London: Ward Lock Educational.

Marsh, J. (1999). Batman and Batwoman go to school: Popular cultural in the literacy curriculum. *International Journal of Early Years Education, 7,* 117–131.

Marsh, J. (2000). 'But I want to fly too!': Girls and superhero play in the infant classroom. *Gender and Education, 12,* 209–220.

Marsh, J. (2002). Electronic toys: Why should we be concerned? A response to Levin & Rosenquest (2001). *Contemporary Issues in Early Childhood, 3,* 132–138.

Martin, C., & Fabes, R. (2001). The stability and consequences of young children's same-sex peer interactions. *Developmental Psychology, 37,* 431–446.

Maslow, A. (1959). *New knowledge in human values.* New York: Harper and Row.

Masten, A., & Coatsworth, J. (1998). The development of competence in favorable and unfavorable environments. *American Psychologist, 53,* 205–220.

Matthews, W. (1977). Modes of transformation in the initiation of fantasy play. *Developmental Psychology, 12,* 211–236.

Mayer, R. (1996). Learning strategies for making sense out of expository texts: The SOI model for guiding three cognitive processes in knowledge construction. *Educational Psychology Review, 8,* 357–371.

McCormick, L., & Feeney, S. (1995) Modifying and expanding activities for children with disabilities. *Young Children, 50*(4), 10–17.

McCullough, D. (2001). *John Adams.* New York: Simon and Schuster.

McDevitt, T., & Ormrod, J. (2004). *Child development: Educating and working with children and adolescence* (2nd ed.). Columbus, OH: Pearson/Merrill Prentice Hall.

McGuffy, C., & Rich, B. (1999). Playing in the gender transgression zone: Race, class, and hegemonic masculinity in middle childhood. *Gender & Society, 13(5),* 608–627.

McLane, J. (1984). *Lekotek evaluation.* Chicago: Erikson Institute, Loyola University.

McLoyd, V. (1980). Verbally expressed modes of transformation in the fantasy play of black preschool children. *Child Development, 51,* 1133–1139.

McLoyd, V. (1983). The effects of the structure of play objects on the pretend play of low-income preschool children. *Child Development, 54,* 626–635.

McNaughton (2001). Even pink tents have glass ceilings: Crossing gender boundries in pretend play. In E. Dau & E. Jones (Eds.), *Child's play: Revisiting play in early childhood settings* (pp. 81–96). Baltimore: Paul H. Brookes.

McNeil, J. (1990). *Curriculum: A comprehensive introduction.* New York: Harper Collins.

McNeilly-Choque, M., Hart, C., Robinson, C., Nelson, L., & Olsen, S. (1996). Overt and relational aggression on the playground: Correspondence among different informants. *Journal of Research in Childhood Education, 11,* 47–67.

Millar, S. (1968). *Psychology of play.* Baltimore, MD: Penguin Books.

Moller, L., & Serbin, L. (1996). Antecedents of toddler gender segregation: Cognitive consonance, gender-typed toy preferences and behavioral compatibility. *Sex Roles, 35*(7/8), 445–460.

Monighan-Nourot, P. (1995). Play across curriculum and culture: Strengthening early primary education in California. In E. Klugman (Ed.), *Play, policy, and practice.* St. Paul, MN: Redleaf Press.

Montagner, H. (1984, December). Children's winning ways. *Psychology Today, 59–65.*

Montessori, M. (1964). *Dr. Montessori's own handbook.* Cambridge, MA: Robert Bentley.

Moore, G. (1987). The physical environment and cognitive development in child-care centers. In C. Weinstein & T. David (Eds.), *Spaces for children: The built environment and child development* (pp. 41–72). New York: Plenum.

Moore, N., Evertson, C., & Brophy, J. (1974). Solitary play: Some functional reconsiderations. *Developmental Psychology, 10,* 830–834.

Morrison, C., Bundy, A., & Fisher, A. The contribution of motor skills and playfulness to the play performance of preschoolers. *American Journal of Occupational Therapy, 45,* 687–694.

Morrison, G. (2001). Play and state standards: Are they compatible? *Play, Policy, & Practice Connections, 6*(2), 1–3.

Morrow, L. (1990). Preparing the classroom environment to promote literacy during play. *Early Childhood Research Quarterly, 5,* 537–544.

Morrow, L., & Rand, M. (1991). Preparing the classroom environment to promote literacy during play. In J. Christie (Ed.), *Play and early literacy development* (pp. 141–165). Albany, NY: State University of New York Press.

Moyles, J. (1989). *Just playing? The role and status of play in early childhood education.* Milton Keynes, UK: Open University Press.

Mueller, E., & Lucas, T. (1975). A developmental analysis of peer interaction among toddlers. In M. Lewis & L. Rosenblum (Eds.), *Friendship and peer relations.* New York: Wiley.

National Association for the Education of Young Children. (1996a). *Guidelines for preparation of early childhood professionals.* Washington, DC: Author.

National Association of the Education of Young Children. (1996b). Position statement: Technology and young children—Ages three through eight. *Young Children, 51*(6), 11–16.

National Association for the Education of Young Children. (1998). *Accreditation criteria and procedures.* Washington, DC: Author.

National Council of Teachers of Mathematics. (2000). *Principles and standards of school mathematics.* Reston, VA: Author.

National Toy Council. (1997). *Toys and children: Games.* London: Author.

Neuman, S., & Roskos, K. (1990). The influence of literacy-enriched play settings on preschoolers' engagement with written language. In S. McCormick & J. Zutell (Eds.), *Literacy theory and research: Analyses from multiple perspectives* (pp. 179–187). Chicago: National Reading Conference.

Neuman, S., & Roskos, K. (1992). Literacy objects as cultural tools: Effects on children's literacy behaviors during play. *Reading Research Quarterly, 27,* 203–223.

Neuman, S., & Roskos, K. (1993). Access to print for children of poverty: Differential effects of adult mediation and literacy-enriched play settings on environmental and functional print tasks. *American Educational Research Journal, 30,* 95–122.

Neuman, S., & Roskos, K. (1997). Literacy knowledge in practice: Contexts of participation for young writers and readers. *Reading Research Quarterly, 32,* 10–32.

Newburger, E. C. (2001). *Home computers and Internet use: August 2000.* Current Population Reports. Washington DC: U.S. Census Bureau.

Oden, S., & Hall, J. (1998). Peer and sibling influences on play. In D. Fromberg & D. Bergen (Eds.), *Play from birth to twelve, and beyond: Contexts, perspectives, and meanings* (pp. 266–276) New York: Garland.

Odom, S., & McEvoy, M. (1988). Integration of young children with handicaps and normally developing children. In S. Odom and M. Karnes (Eds.), *Early childhood intervention for infants and children with handicaps: An empirical base* (pp. 241–267). Baltimore: Paul H. Brookes.

Odom, S., & McEvoy, M. (1990). Mainstreaming at the preschool level: Potential barriers and tasks for the field. *Topics in Early Childhood Special Education, 4,* 97–116.

Ogbu, J. (1991). Immigrant and involuntary minorities in comparative perspective. In M. Gibson & J. Ogbu (Eds.), *Minority status and schools: A comparative study of immigrant and involuntary minorities* (pp. 3–33). New York: Garland.

Olszewski, P., & Fuson, K. C. (1982). Verbally expressed fantasy play of preschoolers as a function of toy structure. *Developmental Psychology, 18,* 57–61.

Ormrod, J. (1999). Human learning (3rd ed.). Columbus, OH: Merrill.

Packer, M., & Tappan, M. (Eds.). (2001). *Cultural critical perspective on human development.* Albany, NY: SUNY.

Pan, H. (1994). Children's play in Taiwan. In J. Roopnarine, J. Johnson, & F. Hooper (Eds.), *Children's play in diverse cultures.* Albany, NY: State University of New York Press.

Papert, S. (1996). *The connected family: Bridging the digital generation gap.* Atlanta, GA: Longstreet.

Parten, M. (1932). Social participation among preschool children. *Journal of Abnormal and Social Psychology, 27,* 243–269.

Parten, M. (1933). Social play among preschool children. *Journal of Abnormal and Social Psychology, 28,* 136–147.

Partington, J., & Grant, C. (1984). Imaginary companions. In P. Smith (Ed.), *Play in animals and humans* (pp. 217–240). New York: Harper & Row.

Paley, V. (1981). *Wally's stories.* Cambridge, MA: Harvard University Press.

Paley, V. (1984). *Boys and girls: Superheroes in the doll corner.* Chicago: University of Chicago Press.

Parminder, P., Harkness, S., Super, C., & Johnson, J. (2000, July). *American and Asian parents' ethnotheories of play and learning.* XVIth Biennial Meetings of the International Society for the Study of Behavioral Development, Bejing, China.

Pellegrini, A. (1980). The relationship between kindergartners' play and achievement in prereading, language, and writing. *Psychology in the Schools, 17, 530–535.*

Pellegrini, A. (1984). Identifying causal elements in the thematic-fantasy play paradigm. *American Educational Research Journal, 21,* 691–701.

Pellegrini, A. (1991). A longitudinal study of popular and rejected children's rough and tumble play. *Early Education and Development, 2*(3), 205–213.

Pellegrini, A. (1995a). A longitudinal study of boys' rough-and-tumble play and dominance during early adolescence. *Journal of Applied Developmental Psychology, 16,* 77–93.

Pellegrini, A. (1995b). Boys' rough-and-tumble play and social competence: Contemporaneous and longitudinal relations. In A. Pellegrini (Ed.), *The future of play research* (pp. 107–126). Albany, NY: State University of New York Press.

Pellegrini, A., & Davis, P. (1993). Relations between children's playgrounds and classroom behaviour. *British Journal of Educational Psychology, 63,* 88–95.

Pellegrini, A., & Jones, I. (1994). Play, toys, and language. In J. Goldstein (Ed.), *Play, toys and child development* (pp. 27–45). New York: Cambridge University Press.

Pellegrini, A., & Smith, P. (1998). Physical activity play: The nature and function of a neglected aspect of play. *Child Development, 69,* 577–598.

Pendleton, M. (2001). Becoming a child's advocate for toys—Instead of TV, video games, or computers! *Montessori LIFE,* Winter, 10–11.

Perez-Granados, D. (2002). Normative scripts for object labeling during a play activity: Mother-child and sibling conversations in Mexican-descent families. *Hispanic Journal of Behavioral Sciences, 24,* 164–190.

Perlmutter, J., & Burrell, L. (1995). Learning through 'play' as well as 'work' in the primary grades. *Young Children, 50*(5), 14–21.

Perry, P. (2001). Sick kids. *American Way, 4,* 64–65.

Petrakos, H., & Howe, N. (1996). The influence of physical design of the dramatic play center on children's play. *Early Childhood Research Quarterly, 11,* 63–77.

Peters, K. M., & Blumberg, F. C. (2002). Cartoon violence: Is it as detrimental to preschoolers as we think? *Early Childhood Education Journal, 29*(3), 143–148.

Peterson, N. (1987). *Early intervention for handicapped and at-risk children.* Denver, CO: Love.

Peterson, J. (2001, Nov. 18). As quoted in M. Whaley, Moving beyond drugs to fix attention woes. *The Denver Post,* pp. 29A–30A.

Phipps, P. (1999). Is your program brain compatible? *Child Care Information Exchange,* 126, 53–55.

Piaget, J. (1962). *Play, dreams and imitation in childhood.* New York: Norton.

Piaget, J. (1963). *The origins of intelligence in children.* New York: Norton.

Playground Association of America. (1909/1910). *Proceedings of the Third Annual Congress of the Playgrounds Association, 3*(3).

Polito, P. (1994). How play and work are organized in a kindergarten classroom. *Journal of Research in Childhood Education, 9,* 47–57.

Popper, K., & Eccles, J. (1977) *The self and its brain.* New York: Springer International.

Powell, M. (2001). Children's play and television. *Montessori LIFE,* Winter, 36–39.

Power, T. G. (2000). *Play and exploration in children and animals.* Mahwah, NJ: Erlbaum.

Powlishta, K., Serbin, L., & Moller, L. (1993). The stability of individual differences in gender typing: Implications for understanding gender segregation. *Sex Roles, 28*(11–12), 723–737.

Prescott, E. (1994, November/December). The physical environment: A powerful regulator of experience. *Child Care Information Exchange, 100,* 9–15.

Pulaski, M. (1973). Toys and imaginative play. In J. Singer (Ed.), *The child's world of make-believe: Experimental studies of imaginative play* (pp. 74–103). New York: Academic Press.

Ramsey, P. (1995). Changing social dynamics in early childhood classrooms. *Child Development, 66*(3), 764–773.

Ramsey, P. (1998). Diversity and play. Influences of race, culture, class and gender. In D. Fromberg & D. Bergen (Eds.), *Play from infants to 12 and beyond: Contexts, perspectives, and meanings.* New York: Garland.

Read, H. (1956). *Education through art* (3rd ed.). New York: Pantheon.

Reed, T., & Brown, M. (2000). The expression of care in the rough and tumble play of boys. *Journal of Research in Childhood Education, 15,* 104–116.

Reguero de Atiles, J., Stegelin, D., & Long, J. (1997). Biting behaviors among preschoolers: A review of the literature and survey of practitioners. *Early Childhood Educational Journal, 25,* 101–105.

Reifel, S. (1984). Block construction: Children's developmental landmarks in representation of space. *Young Children, 40,* 61–67.

Reifel, S., & Greenfield, P. (1982). Structural development in symbolic medium: The representational use of block constructions. In G. Forman (Ed.), *Action and thought: From sensorimotor schemes to symbolic operations.* New York: Academic Press.

Rheingold, H., & Cook, K. (1975). The contents of boy's and girl's rooms as an index of parents' behavior. *Child Development, 46,* 920–927.

Rifkin, J. (2000). *The age of access: The new culture of hypercapitalism, where all of life is a paid-for experience.* New York: J. P. Tarcher/Putnam.

Rivkin, M. (1995). *The great outdoors: Restoring children's right to play outside.* Washington, DC: NAEYC.

Robinson, C., Anderson, G., Porter, C., Hart, C., & Wouden-Miller, M. (2003). Sequential transition patterns of preschooler' social interactions during child-initiated play: Is parallel-aware play a bidirectional bridge to other play states? *Early Childhood Research Quarterly, 18,* 3–21.

Rogers, C., Impara, J., Frary, R., Harris, T., Meeks, A., Seamnic-Lauth, S., & Reynolds, M. (1998). Measuring playfulness: Development of the child behaviors inventory of playfulness. *Play & Culture Studies, 1,* 151–168.

Rogers, T., Kuiper, N., & Kirker, W. (1977). Self reliance and encoding of personal information. *Journal of Personality and Social Psychology, 35,* 677–688.

Rogoff, B. (1995). Observing sociocultural activity on three planes: Participatory appropriation, guided participation, and apprenticeship. In J. Wertsch, P. del Rio, & A. Alvarez (Eds.), *Sociocultural studies of mind* (pp. 139–164). Cambridge, UK: Cambridge University Press.

Rogoff, B. (2003). *The cultural nature of human development.* New York: Oxford University Press.

Rogoff, B., & Mosier, C. (1993). Guided participation in San Pedro and Salt Lake. In B. Rogoff, J. Mistry, A. Goncu, & C. Mosier (Eds.), *Guided participation in cultural activity by toddlers and caregiver. Monographs of the Society for Research in Child Development, 58*(7, Serial No. 236).

Roopnarine, J., Johnson, J., & Hooper, F. (Eds.). (1994). *Children's play in diverse cultures.* Albany, NY: State University of New York Press.

Roopnarine, J., Lasker, J., Sacks, M., & Stores, M. (1998). The cultural contexts of children's play. In O. Saracho & B. Spodek (Eds.), *Multiple perspectives on play in early childhood education* (pp. 144–170). Albany: SUNY Press.

Roopnarine, J., Shin, M., Donovan, B., & Suppal, P. (2000). Sociocultural contexts of dramatic play: Implications for early education. In K. Roskos & J. Christie (Eds.), *Play and literacy in early childhood: Research from multiple perspectives* (pp. 205–230). Mahwah, NJ: Erlbaum.

Roper, R., & Hinde, R. (1978). Social behavior in a play group: Consistency and complexity. *Child Development, 49,* 570–579.

Rosen, C. (1974). The effects of sociodramatic play on problem-solving behavior among culturally disadvantaged preschool children. *Child Development, 45,* 920–927.

Roskos, K. (1994). *Connecting academic work and play at school: Preliminary observations of young children's content-oriented interaction and talk under conditions of play in kindergarten.* Paper presented at the meeting of the American Educational Research Association, New Orleans.

Roskos, K. (2000). Through the bioecological lens: Some observations of literacy in play as a proximal process. In K. Roskos & J. Christie (Eds.), *Literacy and play in the early years: Cognitive, ecological, and sociocultural perspectives.* Mahwah, NJ: Erlbaum.

Roskos, K. (2001). Three easy steps to a print-rich house corner. *Children and Families, 15*(2), 21–22.

Roskos, K., Christie, J., & Richgels, D. (2003). The essentials of early literacy instruction. *Young Children, 58*(2), 52–60.

Roskos, K., & Neuman, S. (1993). Descriptive observations of adults' facilitation of literacy in play. *Early Childhood Research Quarterly, 8,* 77–97.

Rowe, D. (1998). The literate potentials of book-related dramatic play. *Reading Research Quarterly, 33,* 10–35.

Rubin, K. (1977). Play behaviors of young children. *Young Children, 32*(6), 16–24.

Rubin, K. (1982). Non-social play in preschoolers: Necessary evil? *Child Development, 53,* 651–657.

Rubin, K., Bukowski, W., & Parker, J. (1998). Peer interactions, relationships, groups. In W. Damon (Series Ed.) & N. Eisenberg (Vol. Ed.), *Handbook of child psychology: Vol. 3. Social, emotional, and personality development* (pp. 621–632). New York: Wiley.

Rubin, K., Fein, G., Vandenberg, B. (1983). Play. In E. Hetherington (Ed.) & P. Mussen (Series Ed.), *Handbook of child psychology: Vol. 4. Socialization, personality, and social development* (pp. 693–774). New York: Wiley.

Rubin, K., & Hayvren, M. (1981). The social and cognitive play of preschool-aged children differing with regard to sociometric status. *Journal of Research and Development in Education, 14,* 116–122.

Rubin, K., Maioni, T., & Homung, M. (1976). Free play behaviors in middle- and lower-class preschoolers: Parten and Piaget revisited. *Child Development, 4*(7), 414–419.

Rubin, I., Provenzano, F., & Luria, Z. (1974). The eyes of the beholder: Parents' views of sex of newborns. *American Journal of Orthopsychiatry, 44,* 512–519.

Rubin, K., Watson, K., & Jambor, T. (1978). Free-play behaviors in preschool and kindergarten children. *Child Development, 49,* 534–536.

Russ, S. (1998). Play, creativity, and adaptive functioning: Implications for play interventions. *Journal of Clinical Child Psychology, 27*(4), 469–480.

Russ, S. (Ed.). (1999). *Affect, creative experience, and psychological adjustment.* Philadelphia: Brunner/Mazel.

Russ, S., Robins, A., & Christiano, B. (1999). Pretend play: Longitudinal prediction of creativity and affect in fantasy in children. *Creativity Research Journal, 12*(2), 129–139.

Sachs, J. (1987). Preschool boys' and girls' language use in pretend play. In S. Philips, S. Steele, & C. Tanz (Eds.), *Language, gender, and sex in comparative perspective* (pp. 178–188). New York: Cambridge University Press.

Sackett, G., Sameroff, A., Cairns, R. & Suomi, S. (1981). Continuity in behavioral development: Theoretical and empirical issues. In K. Immelmann, G. Barrow, L. Petrinovich, & M. Main (Eds.), *Behavioral development* (pp. 23–57). New York: Cambridge University Press.

Saltz, E., Dixon, D., & Johnson, J. (1977). Training disadvantaged preschoolers on various fantasy activities: Effects on cognitive functioning and impulse control. *Child Development, 48,* 367–380.

Saltz, E., & Johnson, J. (1974). Training for thematic-fantasy play in culturally disadvantaged children: Preliminary results. *Journal of Educational Psychology, 66,* 623–630.

Saracho, O. (1998). What is stylish about play? In O. Saracho & B. Spodek (Eds.), *Multiple perspectives on play in early childhood education.* Albany, NY: State University of New York Press.

Saracho, O. (1999). A factor analysis of pre-school children's play strategies and cognitive style. *Educational Psychology, 19,* 165–180.

Sawyer, K. (1997). *Pretend play as improvisation: Conversation in the preschool classroom.* Mahwah, NJ: Erlbaum.

Sawyer, K. (2003). Levels of analysis in pretend play discourse: Metacommunication in conversational routines. In J. Roopnarine (Series Ed.) & D. Lytle (Vol. Ed.), *Play & Cultural Studies: Vol. 5. Play and educational theory and practice* (pp. 137–157). Westport, CT: Greenwood Publishers.

Sayer, G. (1988). *Jack: C. S. Lewis and his times.* San Francisco: Harper and Row.

Schiller, P. (1998). The thinking brain. *Child Care Information Exchange, 121,* 49–51.

Schrader, C. (1990). Symbolic play as a curricular tool for early literacy development. *Early Childhood Research Quarterly, 5,* 79–103.

Schrader, C. (1991). Symbolic play: A source of meaningful engagements with writing and reading. In J. Christie (Ed.), *Play and early literacy development* (pp. 189–231). Albany, NY: State University of New York Press.

Schwartzman, H. (1978). *Transformations: The anthropology of children's play.* New York: Plenum.

Serbin, L., Connor, J., Burchardt, C., & Citron, C. (1979). Effects of peer presence on sex-typing of children's play behavior. *Journal of Experimental Child Psychology, 27,* 303–309.

Serbin, L., Tonick, I., & Sternglanz, S. (1977). Shaping cooperative cross-sex play. *Child Development, 48,* 924–929.

Shade, D., & Davis, B. (1997). The role of computer technology in early childhood education. In J. Isenberg & M. Jalongo (Eds.), *Major trends and issues in early childhood education: Challenges, controversies, and insights* (pp. 90–103). New York: Teachers College Press.

Shapiro, L. (2003, March). *Raising children in the 21st century.* Chicago, IL: Leo J. Shapiro and Associates.

Sheehan, R., & Day, D. (1975). Is open space just empty space? *Day Care and Early Education, 3,* 10–13, 47.

Shell, R., & Eisenberg, N. (1990). The role of peers' gender in children's naturally occurring interest in toys. *International Journal of Behavioral Development, 13,* 373–388.

Sheets-Johnstone, M. (2002, October). *Child's play: A multidisciplinary perspective.* Keynote address for The Philosophic Society for the Study of Sport, The Pennsylvania State University, University Park.

Shin, D. (1994). *Preschool children's symbolic play indoors and outdoors.* Unpublished doctoral dissertation, University of Texas at Austin.

Shin, E., & Spodek, B. (1991, April). *The relationship between children's play patterns and types of teacher interactions.* Paper presented at the Annual Meeting of the American Educational Research Association, Chicago.

Shine, S., & Acosta, T. (1999). The effect of the physical and social environment on parent-child interactions. In S. Reifel (Ed.), *Play and Culture Studies: Vol. 2. Play contexts revisited* (pp. 123–139). Westport, CT: Greenwood Publishers.

Shine, S., & Acosta, T. (2000). Parent-child social play in a children's museum. *Family Relations, 49,* 45–52.

Shore, R. (1997). *Rethinking the brain: New insights into early development.* New York: Families and Work Institute.

Shweder, R. (1991). Cultural psychology: What is it? In R. Shweder (Ed.), *Thinking through cultures: Expeditions in cultural psychology* (pp. 73–110). Cambridge, MA: Harvard University Press.

Shweder, R. (2003). *Why do men barbecue: Recipes for cultural psychology.* Cambridge, MA: Harvard University Press.

Sigelman, C., Miller, T., & Whitworth, L (1986). The early development of stigmatizing reactions to physical differences. *Journal of Educational Psychology, 69,* 330–336.

Silva, D., & Johnson, J. (1999). Principals' preference for N-3 certificate. *Pennsylvania Educational Leadership, 18*(2), 71–81.

Silverman, L. (1989). Invisible gifts, invisible handicaps. *Roeper Review, 12*(1), 37–42.

Silvern, S. (1998). Educational implications of play with computers. In D. Fromberg & D. Bergen (Eds.), *Play from birth to twelve and beyond: Contexts, perspectives, and meanings* (pp. 530–536). New York: Garland.

Silverns, S., Taylor, J., Williamson, P., Surbeck, E., & Kelley, M. (1986). Young children and story recall as a product of play, story familiarity, and adult intervention. *Merrill-Palmer Quarterly, 32,* 73–86.

Simons, J. (2003). Games people should play. *Rocky Mountain News,* May 12, 3D, 16D.

Singer, D., & Bellin, H. (2003). *Training parents and child care providers how constructive play increases school readiness.* Paper presented at The Promise of Play: Cornerstone of Literacy and Learning. Playing for Keeps Conference, New Haven, CT.

Singer, D., & Singer, J. (1990). *The house of make-believe: Children's play and developing imagination.* Cambridge, MA: Harvard University Press.

Singer, J. (1961). Imagination and waiting ability in young children. *Journal of Personality, 29,* 396–413.

Singer, J. (Ed.). (1973). *The child's world of make-believe: Experimental studies of imaginative play.* New York: Academic Press.

Singer, J. (1995). Imaginative play in childhood: Precursors of subjunctive thoughts, daydreaming, and adult pretending games. In A. Pellegrini (Ed.), *The future of play theory: Multidisciplinary inquiry into the contributions of Brian Sutton-Smith* (pp. 187–220.). Albany, NY: State University of New York Press.

Singer, J. (2003). *Beyond daydreams and make-believe: The magic of children's play.* Paper presented at The Promise of Play: Cornerstone of Literacy and Learning. Playing for Keeps Conference, New Haven, CT.

Singer, J., & Singer, D. (1976). Can TV stimulate imaginative play? *Journal of Communication, 26,* 74–80.

Singer, J., & Singer, D. (1980). A factor analytic study of preschoolers' play behavior. *Academic Psychology Bulletin, 2,* 143–156.

Singer, J., & Singer, D. (1981). *Television, imagination and aggression.* Cambridge, MA: Harvard University Press.

Singer, J., Singer, D., Desmond, R., Hirsch, B., & Nichols, A. (1988). Family mediation and children's cognition, aggression, and comprehension of telivision: A longitudinal study. *Journal of Applied Developmental Psychology, 9,* 329–347.

Sinker, M. (1985). More than play: Lekotek. *Topics in Early Childhood Special Education, 5*(3), Fall, 93–100.

Skinner, B. F. (1974). *About behaviorism.* New York: Knopf.

Slade, A., & Wolf, D. (1994). *Children at play.* New York: Oxford University Press.

Sluss, D. (2002). Block play complexity in same-sex dyads of preschool children. *Play & Culture Studies, 4,* 77–91.

Smilansky, S. (1968). *The effects of sociodramatic play on disadvantaged preschool children.* New York: Wiley.

Smith, A., & Inder, P. (1993). Social interaction in same- and cross-gender pre-school peer groups: A participant observation study. *Educational Psychology, 13,* 29–42.

Smith, M., & Dickinson, D. (1994). Describing oral language opportunities and environments in Head Start and other preschool classrooms. *Early Childhood Research Quarterly, 9,* 345–366.

Smith, P. (1978). A longitudinal study of social participation in preschool children: Solitary and parallel play reexamined. *Developmental Psychology, 14,* 517–523.

Smith, P. (1997, October). *Play fighting and fighting: How do they relate?* Paper presented at the meeting of the International Council for Children's Play, Lisbon, Portugal.

Smith, P. (1999, February). *Pretend play and theory of mind: What is the relationship?* Paper presented at the annual meeting of The Association for the Study of Play, Santa Fe, NM.

Smith, P., & Connolly, K. (1980). *The ecology of preschool behavior.* Cambridge, England: Cambridge University Press.

Smith, P., Dalgleish, M., & Herzmark, G. (1981). A comparison of the effects of fantasy play tutoring and skills tutoring in nursery classes. *International Journal of Behavioral Development, 4,* 421–441.

Smith, P., & Dutton, S. (1979). Play and training in direct and innovative problem solving. *Child Development, 50,* 830–836.

Smith, P., & Syddall, S. (1978). Play and non-play tutoring in preschool children: Is it play or tutoring which matters? *British Journal of Educational Psychology, 48,* 315–325.

Smith, P., & Vollstedt, R. (1985). On defining play: An empirical study of the relationship between play and various play criteria. *Child Development, 56,* 1042–1050.

Smith, P., & Whitney, S. (1987). Play and associative fluency: Experimenter effects may be responsible for previous positive findings. *Developmental Psychology, 23,* 49–53.

Snow, C. E. (2002). Ensuring reading success for African American children. In B. Bowman, (Ed.), *Love to read: Essays in developing and enhancing early literacy skills of African American children* (pp. 17–30). Washington, DC: National Black Child Institute.

Sonnenschein, S., Baker, L., Serpell, R., & Schmidt, D. (2000). Reading is a source of entertainment: The importance of the home perspective for children's literacy development. In K. Roskos & J. Christie (Eds.), *Play and literacy in early childhood: Research from multiple perspectives* (pp. 107–124). Mahwah, NJ: Erlbaum.

Spielberger, J., & McLane, J. (2002). Can too many cooks spoil the broth? Beliefs about teacher's role in children's play. In C. Brown & C. Marchant (Eds.), *Play in practice: Case studies in young children's play* (pp. 3–12). St. Paul, MN: Redleaf Press.

Stone, S. (1995). Wanted: Advocates for play in the primary grades. *Young Children, 50*(6), 45–54.

Stoneham, L. (2001) Diabetes on a rampage. *Texas Medicine, 97*(11), 42–48.

Stoneman, Z. (1993). The effects of attitude on preschool integration. In C. Peck, S. Odom, & D. Bricker (Eds.), *Integrating young children with disabilities into community programs: ecological perspectives on research and implementation* (pp. 223–248). Baltimore: Paul H. Brookes.

Stoneman, Z., Brody, G., & MacKinnon, C. (1986). Same-sex and cross-sex siblings: Activity choices, roles, behaviors, and gender stereotypes. *Sex Roles, 15,* 495–511.

Strain, P., & Smith, B. (1993). Comprehensive education, social, and policy forces that affect preschool integration. In C. Peck, S. Odom, & D. Bricker (Eds.), *Integrating young children with disabilities into community programs: Ecological perspectives on research and implementation* (pp. 209–222). Baltimore, MD: Paul H. Brookes.

Stremmel, A. (1997). Diversity and the multicultural perspective. In G. Hart, D. Burts, & R. Charlesworth (Eds.), *Integrated curriculum and developmentally appropriate practices: Birth to age eight.* Albany, NY: State University of New York Press.

Sutterby, J., & Frost, J. (2002). Making playgrounds fit for children and children fit for playgrounds. *Young Children, 57*(3), 36–41.

Sutton-Smith, B. (1967). The role of play in cognitive development. *Young Children, 22,* 361–370.

Sutton-Smith, B. (1972), *The folkgames of children.* Austin, TX: The University of Texas Press.

Sutton-Smith, B. (1979a). Play as metaperformance. In B. Sutton-Smith (Ed.), *Play and learning.* New York: Gardner Press.

Sutton-Smith, B. (1979b). The play of girls. In C. Kopp & M. Kirkpatrick (Eds.), *Becoming female: Perspectives on development.* New York: Plenum.

Sutton-Smith, B. (1980a). Children's play: Some sources of theorizing. In K. Rubin (Ed.), *Children's play* (pp. 1–16). San Francisco: Jossey-Bass.

Sutton-Smith, B. (1980b). Piaget, play and cognition revisited. In W. Overton (Ed.), *The relationship between social and cognitive development.* New York: Erlbaum.

Sutton-Smith, B. (1985). Play research: State of the art. In J. Frost & S. Sunderlin (Eds.), *When children play* (pp. 9–16). Wheaton, MD: Association for Childhood Education International.

Sutton-Smith, B. (1986). *Toys as culture.* New York: Gardner Press.

Sutton-Smith, B. (1987). School play: A commentary. In J. Block & N. King (Eds.), *School play* (pp. 277–289). New York: Garland.

Sutton-Smith, B. (1990). Playfully yours. *TASP Newsletter, 16*(2), 2–5.

Sutton-Smith, B. (1995). Conclusion: The persuasive rhetorics of play. In A. Pellegrini (Ed.), *The future of play theory: A multidisciplinary inquiry into the contributions of Brian Sutton-Smith* (pp. 275–305). Albany, NY: State University of New York Press.

Sutton-Smith, B. (1997). *The ambiguity of play.* Cambridge, MA: Harvard University Press.

Sutton-Smith, B. (1998). *The ambiguity of play.* Cambridge, MA: Harvard University Press.

Sutton-Smith, B. (2001). Reframing the variability of players and play. In S. Reifel (Ed.), *Theory in context and out* (pp. 27–49). Westport, CT: Ablex.

Sutton-Smith, B. (2004). Preface. In J. Goldstein, D. Buddingham, & G. Brougere (Eds.), *Toys, games, and media.* Mahwah, NJ: Erlbaum.

Sutton-Smith, B., Gerstmyer, J., and Meckley, A. (1988). Play fighting as folk play amongst preschool children. *Western Folklore, 47,* 161–176.

Sutton-Smith, B., & Heath, S. (1981). Paradigms of pretense. *Quarterly Newsletter of the Laboratory of Comparative Human Cognition, 3,* 41–45.

Sylva, K., Bruner, J., & Genova, P. (1976). The role of play in the problem-solving of children 3–5 years old. In J. Bruner, A. Jolly, & K. Sylva (Eds.), *Play and its role in development and evolution* (pp. 244–257). New York: Basic Books.

Sylva, K., Roy, C., & Painter, M. (1980). *Childwatching a playgroup & nursery school.* Ypsilanti, MI: High/Scope Press.

Tamis-LeMonda, C. S., & Bornstein, M. (1993). Individual variation, correspondence, stability, and change in mother and toddler play. *Infant Behavior and Development, 14,* 143–162.

Tarr, P. (2001, May). What art educators can learn from Reggio Emilia. In *Art Education.* Available at www .designshare.com/Research/Tarr/Aesthetic_codes_3.htm.

Tarullo, L. (1994). Windows on the social worlds: Gender differences in children's play narratives. In A. Slade & D. Wolf (Eds.), *Children at play: Clinical and developmental approaches to meaning and representation* (pp. 169–187). New York: Oxford University Press.

Taylor, M., Carlson, S., & Gerow, L. (2001). Imaginary companions: Characteristics and correlates. *Play & Culture Studies, 3,*179–198.

Taylor, M., Cartwright, B., & Carlson, S. (1993). A developmental investigation of children's imaginary companions. *Developmental Psychology, 29,* 276–293.

Taylor, A., Kuo, F., & Sullivan, W. (2001). Coping with ADD: The surprising connection to green play settings *Environment and Behavior, 33,* 1, 54–77.

Tegano, D., & Burdette, M. (1991). Length of activity period and play behaviors of preschool children. *Journal of Research in Childhood Education, 5,* 93–98.

Tegano, D., Lookabaugh, S., May, G., & Burdette M. (1991). Construction play and problem-solving: The role of structure and time in the classroom. *Early Childhood Developmental Care, 68,* 27–35.

Terr, L. (1999). *Beyond love and work.* New York: Scribner.

Thompson, H., & Stanford, G. (1981). *Child life in hospitals.* Springfield, IL: Charles C. Thomas.

Tinsworth, D., & Kramer, J. (1990). *Playground equipment-related injuries and deaths.* Washington, DC: U.S. Consumer Product Safety Commission.

Tizard, B., Philps, J., & Plewis, L. (1976a). Play in preschool centres. I: Play measures and their relation to age, sex and IQ. *Journal of Child Psychology and Psychiatry, 17,* 251–264.

Tizard, B., Philps, J., & Plewis, I. (1976b). Play in pre-school centres. II: Effects on play of the child's social class and of the educational orientation of the centre. *Journal of Child Psychology and Psychiatry, 17,* 265–274.

Tobin, J. (Ed.). (1997). *Making a place for pleasure in early childhood education.* New Haven, CT: Yale University Press.

Tobin, J., Wu, D., & Davidson, D. (1989). *Preschool in three cultures.* New Haven, CT: Yale University Press.

Trageton, A. (1997, October). *Play in lower primary school in Norway.* Paper presented at the meeting of the International Council for Children's Play, Lisbon, Portugal.

Trageton, A. (2002a, February). *Creative writing on computers and playful learning: Grade 1.* Paper presented at The Association for the Study of Play annual meetings, Santa Fe.

Trageton, A. (2002b, February). *Creative writing on computers and playful learning: Grade 2.* Paper presented at The Association for the Study of Play annual meetings, Santa Fe.

Trawick-Smith, J. (1990). The effects of realistic versus non-realistic play materials on young children's symbolic transformation of objects. *Journal of Research in Childhood Education, 5,* 27–35.

Trawick-Smith, J. (1994). *Interactions in the classroom: Facilitating play in the early years.* New York: Merrill.

Trawick-Smith, J. (1998). Why play training works: An integrated model for play intervention. *Journal of Research in Childhood Education, 12,* 117–129.

Trawick-Smith, J. (2002, November). *An ethnographic study of the play of children from Puerto Rico: Working hypotheses.* Play, Policy, and Practices Interest Forum's Play Research Colloquium, NAEYC Pre-Conference, New York.

Truhon, S. (1982). Playfulness, play and creativity: A path-analytic model. *Journal of Genetic Psychology, 143*(1), 19–28.

Udwin, O. (1983). Imaginative play as an intervention method with institutionalized preschool children. *British Journal of Educational Psychology, 53,* 32–39.

Urberg, K., & Kaplan, M. (1989). An observational study of race-, age- and sex-heterogeneous interaction in preschoolers. *Journal of Applied Developmental Psychology, 10,* 299–312.

U.S. Access Board. (n.d.) *Guide to ADA Accessibility Guidelines for Play Areas.* Washington, DC: Author.

U.S. Consumer Product Safety Commission. (1993). *Which toys for which child? A consumer guide for selecting suitable toys: Ages birth through five.* Washington, DC: Author.

U.S. Consumer Product Safety Commission. (1994). *Which toys for which child? A consumer guide for selecting suitable toys: Ages 6 to 12.* Washington, DC: Author.

U.S. Consumer Product Safety Commission. (1997). *Handbook for public playground safety.* Washington, DC: Author.

U.S. Consumer Product Safety Commission. (1999). *Public playground handbook for safety.* Washington DC: Author.

U.S. Department of Health and Human Services, Administration for Children, Youth and Families, Head Start Bureau. (2003). Fiscal year 2003 fact sheet. Washington, DC: Author.

Valkenburg, P. (2001). Television and the child's developing imagination. In D. Singer & J. Singer (Eds.), *Handbook of children and the media* (pp. 121–134). Thousand Oaks, CA: Sage.

van der Kooij, R. (1989). Research on children's play. *Play and Culture, 2,* 20–34.

Vander Ven, K. (1998). Play, Proteus, and paradox: Education for a chaotic and supersymmetric world. In D. Fromberg & D. Bergen (Eds.), *Play from birth to twelve and beyond: Contexts, perspectives, and meanings* (pp. 119–132). New York: Garland.

Van Hoorn, J., & Hesse, P. (2003). Young American children's responses to September 11, terrorism, & war: The play, art, & stories of children 2–8 years. *Play, Policy, & Practice Connections, 7*(2), 2–4.

Van Hoorn, J., Nourot, P., Scales, B., & Alward, K. (1993). *Play at the center of the curriculum.* New York: Macmillan.

Van Hoorn, J., Scales, B., Nourot, P., & Alward, K. (1999). *Play at the center of the curriculum* (2nd ed.). Upper Saddle River, NJ: Merrill.

Varga, D. (1991). The historical origins of children's play as a developmental task. *Play and Culture, 4,* 322–333.

Vukelich, C. (1991, December). *Learning about the functions of writing: The effects of three play interventions on children's development and knowledge about writing.* Paper presented at the meeting of the National Reading Conference, Palm Springs.

Vukelich, C. (1993). Play: A context for exploring the functions, features, and meaning of writing with peers. *Language Arts, 70,* 386–392.

Vukelich, C. (1995). Watch me! Watch me! Understanding children's literacy knowledge. In J. Christie, K. Roskos, B. Enz, C. Vukelich, & S. Neuman (Eds.), *Readings for linking literacy and play.* Newark, DE: International Reading Association.

Vukelich, C., Christie, J., & Enz, B. (2002). *Helping young children learn language and literacy.* Boston: Allyn and Bacon.

Vygotsky, L. (1976). Play and its role in the mental development of the child. In J. Bruner, A. Jolly, & K. Sylva (Eds.), *Play: Its role in development and evolution* (pp. 537–554). New York: Basic Books.

Vygotsky, L.(1978). *Mind in society: The development of higher mental processes.* Cambridge, MA: Harvard University Press.

Wardle, F. (1973). *My first ½.* Denver, CO: Unpublished manuscript.

Wardle, F. (1973). Put a little play into a playground. *Early Years for Teachers of Preschool through Grade 3,* 32–36.

Wardle, F. (1976, Nov). A first look at education of Guatemalan Indians in post-earthquake Guatemala. *New School Exchange Newsletter, 136,* 12–15.

Wardle, F. (1987). Getting back to the basics of children's play. *Child Care Information Exchange,* September, 27–30.

Wardle, F. (1991). Are we shortchanging boys? *Child Care Information Exchange* (May/June), 48–51.

Wardle, F. (1994). Viewpoint: Playgrounds. *Day Care and Early Education, 22*(2), 39–40.

Wardle, F. (1996–2003). Playground safety. Series of lectures presented at the School of Public Health, University of N. Colorado. Greely, Colorado.

Wardle, F. (1995). Alternative . . . Bruderhof education: Outdoor school. *Young Children, 50(3),* 68–73.

Wardle, F. (1996a). Proposal: An anti-bias and ecological model for multicultural education: *Childhood Education, 72,* 152–156.

Wardle, F. (1996b). *Of labels, skills, and concepts.* Urbana, Ill. ERIC clearinghouse for early childhood education, # 402 022.

Wardle, F. (1997). Outdoor play. Designing, building and remodeling playgrounds for young children. *Early Childhood News, 9*(2), 36–42.

Wardle, F. (1998). Playgrounds for school-age after-school programs. *Child Care Information Exchange, 121,* 28–30

Wardle, F. (1999a). Educational toys. *Early Childhood News, 11*(1), 38.

Wardle, F. (1999b). The story of a playground. *Child Care Information Exchange, 128*(July/August), 28–30

Wardle, F. (1999c). In praise of developmentally appropriate practice. *Young Children, 54*(6), 4–12.

Wardle, F. (2000a). Supporting constructive play in the wild. *Child Care Information Exchange, 128* (July/August), 26–28.

Wardle, F. (2000b). Building a safe playground in Brazil. In Christiansen, M. (Ed.), *Playground Safety 1999 Conference Proceedings.* University Park, PA: The Pennsylvania State University.

Wardle, F. (2003a). *Introduction to early childhood education: A multi-dimensional approach to child-centered care and learning.* Boston: Allyn and Bacon.

Wardle, F. (2003b). Full immersion foreign language programs. *Child Care Information Exchange,* (September/October), pp. 54–57.

Wardle, F., & Cruz-Janzen M. (2004). *Multiethnic and multiracial children in schools.* Boston: Allyn and Bacon.

Wasserman, S. (2000). *Serious players in the primary classroom: Empowering children through active learning experiences* (2nd ed.). New York: Teachers College Press.

Wasserman, S., & Ivany, J. (1988). *The new teaching elementary service: Who's afraid of spiders?* (2nd ed.). New York: Teacher College Press.

Weikert, D., & Schweinhart, L. (2005). The High/Scope curriculum for early childhood care and education. In J. Roopnarine & J. Johnson (Eds.), *Approaches to early childhood education* (4th ed., pp. 235–250). Columbus, OH: Merrill.

Weinberger, L., & Starkey, P. (1994). Pretend play by African American children in Head Start. *Early Childhood Research Quarterly, 9,* 327–344.

Weisler, A., & McCall, R. (1976). Exploration and play: Resume and reflections. *American Psychologist, 31,* 492–508.

Weir, R. (1976). Playing with language. In J. Bruner, A. Jolly, & K. Sylva (Eds.), *Play and its role in development and evolution* (pp. 609–618). New York: Basic Books.

Wells, N. (2000). At home with nature: Effects of "greenness" on children's cognitive functioning. *Environment and Behavior, 32*(6), 775–795.

West, M. (2001). Teaching the third culture child. *Young Children, 56*(6), 27–32.

Whiting, B. (1980). Culture and social behavior: A model for the development of social behavior. *Ethos, 8,* 95–116.

Whiting, B., & Whiting, J. (1975). *Children in six cultures: A psycho-cultural analysis.* Cambridge, MA: Harvard University Press.

Whitmore, J. (1981). Gifted children with handicapping conditions: A new frontier. *Exceptional Children, 48*(2) 106–111.

Wien, C. (1996). Time, work, and developmentally appropriate practice. *Early Childhood Research Quarterly, 11,* 377–404.

Wiles, J., & Bondi, J. (1998). *Curriculum development: A guide to practice* (5th ed.). Upper Saddle River, NJ: Merrill.

Williams, K. (2002). "But are they learning anything?": African American mothers, their children, and play. In C. Brown & C. Marchant (Eds.), *Play in practice: Case studies in young children's play* (pp. 73–85). St. Paul, MN: Redleaf Press.

Winniscott, D. (1971). *Playing and reality.* Harmondsworth, England: Penguin.

Winter, R., Surr, J., & Leaf, J. (2003). Meeting child care needs in disasters. *Young Children,* July, 82–84.

Wisk Active Play Survey. (2003). Playing around. *Discovery Years Ages 4–7* (August/September 2003, p. 1). Colorado Springs, CO: Focus on Your Child.

Witkin, H., Lewis, H., Hertzman, M., Machover, K., Meissner, P., & Wapner, S. (1954). *Personality through perception.* New York: Harper and Row.

Wolery, M., Holcombe, A., Venn, M., Brookfield, J., Huffman, K., Schroeder, C., Martin, G., & Fleming, L. (1993). Early childhood programs: Current status and relevant issues. *Young Children, 49*(1), 78–84.

Wolery, M., & Wilbers, J. S. (1994). *Including children with special needs in early childhood programs.* Washington, DC: NAEYC.

Wolf, D., & Gardner, H. (1979). Style and sequence in early symbolic play. In M. Franklin & N. Smith (Eds.), *Symbolic functioning in childhood.* Hillsdale, NJ: Erlbaum.

Wolf, D., & Grollman, S. (1982). Ways of playing: Individual differences in imaginative style. In D. Pepler & K. Rubin (Eds.), *The play of children: Current theory and research* (pp. 46–63). Basel, Switzerland: Karger.

Wolfgang, C., Stannard, L., & Jones, I. (2001). Block play performance among preschoolers as a predictor of later school achievement in mathematics. *Journla of Research in Childhood Education, 15*(2), 173–180.

Wood, E., & Attfield, J. (1996). *Play, learning and the early childhood curriculum.* London: Paul Chapman.

Wood, D., McMahon, L., & Cranstoun, Y. (1980). *Working with under fives.* Ypsilanti, MI: High/Scope.

Wright, J., Shade, D., Thouvenelle, S., & Davidson, J. (1989). New directions in software development for young children. *Journal of Computing in Childhood Education, 1*(1), 45–57.

Wyver, S. & Spence, S. (1999). Play and divergent problem-solving: Evidence supporting a reciprical relationship. *Early Education and Development, 10*(4), 419–444.

Yang, C. (2002, February). *The commonality and difference of Taiwanese parents' and teachers' perception of play.* Paper presented at The Association for the Study of Play, Santa Fe, NM.

Yoffe, E. (2003, July 13). Play it again, mom, again and again. . . . *The New York Times.* AR 9, 11.

Youngblade, L., & Dunn, J. (1995). Individual differences in young children's pretend play with mother and sibling: Links to relationships and understandings of other people's feelings and beliefs. *Child Development, 66,* 1472–1492.

York, S. (2003). *Roots and wings: Affirming culture in early childhood programs* (2nd ed.). St. Paul, MN: Redleaf Press.

Zigler, E., & Jones, S. (2002). Reflections—where do we go from here? In B. Bowman (Ed.), *Love to read: Essays in developing and enhancing early literacy skills of African American children* (pp. 83–90). Washington, DC: National Black Child Institute.

# Name Index

# Subject Index